THE ETERNAL CITY

THE

ETERNAL

CITY

A HISTORY OF ROME

FERDINAND ADDIS

PEGASUS BOOKS
NEW YORK LONDON

THE ETERNAL CITY

Pegasus Books, Ltd.
148 West 37th Street, 13th Floor
New York, NY 10018

First Pegasus Books hardcover edition November 2018

ISBN: 978-1-68177-542-5

10 9 8 7 6 5 4 3 2 1

Printed in the United States of America
Distributed by W. W. Norton & Company, Inc.

To my mother, Noonie, whose Rome led to mine

CONTENTS

A NOTE ON DATES

Common practice now in academic history books is to designate years before and after the year – not as years BC and AD but rather BCE and CE, standing for Before the Common Era and After the Common Era.

The reasons for this are broadly commendable: historians don't want to impose a Christian-centric dating system on readers who may belong to any religion or none. They are uncomfortable with the religious claim implied by Anno Domini.

In another context I might very well have followed this convention. However, for this book, various considerations urged me towards the traditional AD and BC. This book is, above all, about the ways humans have located themselves within history. It is not an academic book, nor is it concerned with history as a quasi-scientific discipline. It makes no claim to abstraction, or impersonal authority. It might question the idea that any era could be 'common' to all. This is a book about people, and their experiences and prejudices and beliefs, the myths to which people have clung.

No solution is perfect, therefore. But AD and BC, as well as being familiar, is the system that most of the subjects of this book would have recognized. The claims implied in those abbreviations are claims to which most of the subjects of this book would have assented, however they might strike us today. I have located my subjects in history using, so far as possible, the landmarks they might have used themselves.

(Another candidate dating system would have been AUC – *Ab Urbe Condita* – years elapsed since the notional foundation of Rome in 753 BC. However, even the ancient Romans very rarely used this system. They usually dated years by the names of the men who served as consuls, or by the regnal years of emperors, and I thought even for the most committed reader that might be asking a bit much.)

ROME
IN THE AGE
OF THE
EMPERORS

MILVIAN
BRIDGE

VIA FLAMINIA

MAUSOLEUM
OF HADRIAN

NERO'S CIRCUS

CAMPUS MARTIUS

PANTHEON

QUIRI

THEATRE AND CURIA
OF POMPEY

CAPITOL
(ARX)

TEMPLE
CONCO

J
A
N
I
C
U
L
U
M

CAPITOLINE
HILL

ROMAN F

TIBER
ISLAND

TEMPLE OF
JUPITER
OPTIMUS
MAXIMUS

CLOACA MAXIMA

PALA
HILL

TRANSTIBERIM

LUPERCAL
CAVE

TE
OF AP

CIRCUS MA

AVENTINE HILL

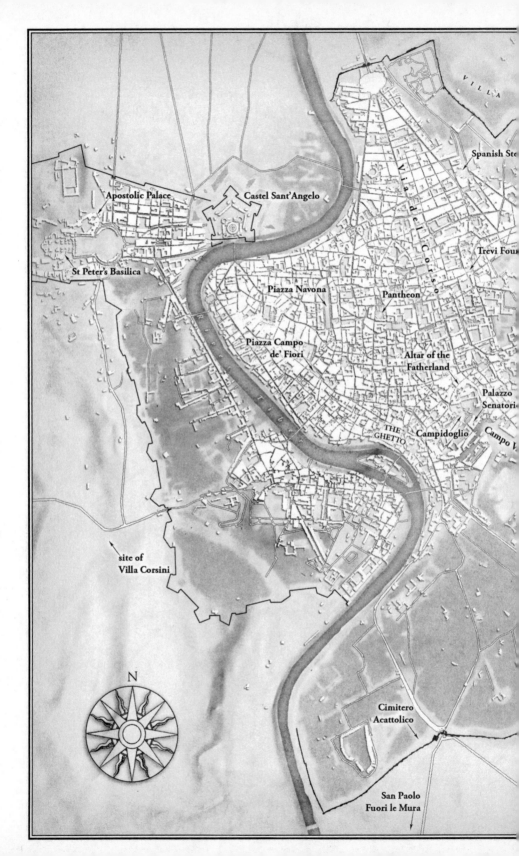

Apostolic Palace

Castel Sant'Angelo

Spanish Ste

St Peter's Basilica

Piazza Navona

Pantheon

Trevi Foun

Piazza Campo
de' Fiori

Altar of the
Fatherland

Palazzo
Senatori

THE
GHETTO

Campidoglio

Campo V

site of
Villa Corsini

N

Cimitero
Acattolico

San Paolo
Fuori le Mura

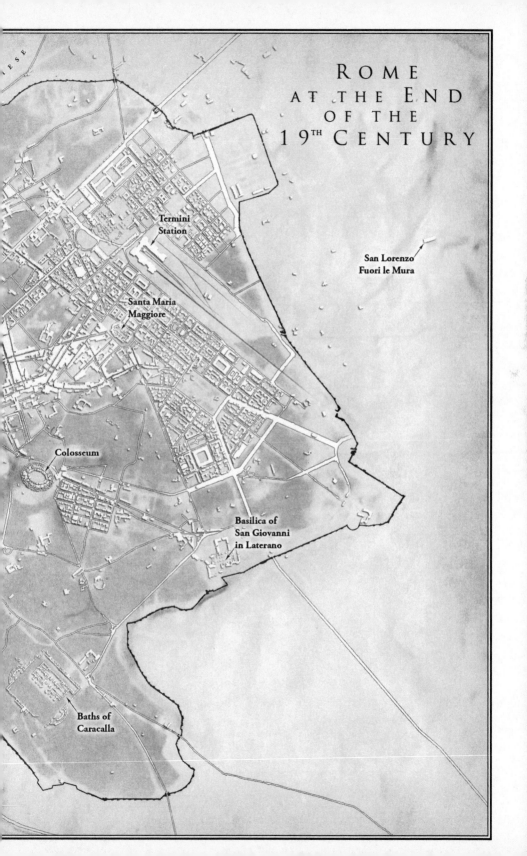

ROME
AT THE END
OF THE
19TH CENTURY

Termini
Station

San Lorenzo
Fuori le Mura

Santa Maria
Maggiore

Colosseum

Basilica of
San Giovanni
in Laterano

Baths of
Caracalla

1

THE WOLF CHILDREN

Romulus and the foundation of Rome

———

753 BC

I N THE MIDDLE of a fertile plain, halfway between the mountains and the sea, a river flows between a cluster of low hills. Seven? It depends on how you count them.

Three hills stand along the river: the Palatine, whose broad back will one day groan under the weight of imperial palaces. The great hump of the Aventine, a hill for rebellious plebs and foreign gods. Last, the Capitoline, craggy and steep, the hill that will be the sacred citadel of a city called Rome.

From the high ground away to the north, three ridges extend southward like long fingers: Quirinal, Viminal and Esquiline, their bare tops not yet disturbed by the rush of motorcars and movie stars and government ministers, of trains being made – or not – to run on time.

The Caelian hill makes seven, rising above a waterlogged hollow where, many centuries from now, the air will tremble with the roars of the Colosseum crowd.

But why stop at seven? What of the minor summits, the Oppian, the Cispian, the Velian ridge? What of the Janiculum on the far side of the river, the invader's hill, where Garibaldi's redshirts will shed their blood for Rome? What of the Pincian, with its Napoleonic gardens? What of the ground that will one day be Testaccio, a carnival hill, heaped from the shards of broken oil jars? What of the pilgrims' landmark, Monte Mario? What of the Vatican hill, where Christians will drive out pagan soothsayers to build, on their own tombs, the foundations of an all-conquering church?

On every side, the future presses in upon the empty landscape. There is no ridge, no valley, no wrinkle in the earth that will not one day witness great events. Each hill, each hummock, each pool, each patch of grass waits, silent, to assume its name, to take its place in history.

* * *

The River Tiber flowed down from the mountains, carving its way through the land, reed beds and water meadows and banks shaded with oak and pine, strawberry trees, the shivering leaves of tall poplars. These were the gifts of the river god, shaking out his watery locks over the plains of Latium.

This was a country peopled by gods and spirits only: nymphs in forest pools; satyrs with sunburned skin; two-faced Janus; almighty Saturn; Picus, the prophetic woodpecker; wild-eyed Faunus, tangling his horns in dark thickets.

And then, one day, Father Tiber in his foaming flood carried downstream a pair of human boys. And Roman history began.

They came ashore in winter, at the foot of the Palatine hill. The flood waters of the Tiber bore the boys up gently, washing them towards land until their makeshift cradle tangled with the roots of a spreading fig tree. There, in the ordinary way of things, they should have died.

But a she-wolf, living nearby in a cave under the Palatine, smelled their human scent on the breeze. Soft-footed through the mud, she sought them out. And though she was hungry, and the winter hard, she recognized in the children something of the divine. Curling around the twins, to offer them her teats, the wild she-wolf suckled them.

The image of the twins and the wolf became a symbol of Rome. It was a moment outside history, an image that needed no before or after to give it power. The wolf was as eternal as the gods, a fierce and paradoxical archetype, savage but protective; likewise the twins, naked and vulnerable, but fat with infant strength and infant appetite.

The twins and the wolf were timeless and divine. But the twins were also human. And to be human is to have history, to be burdened with it, weighed down with chains of cause and consequence. The storytellers who passed down the tale of the two miraculous boys could never resist the urge to add context, to give them a past and a future, to ask and answer those worldly mortal questions: where had they come from? Where were they going to? The twins, like the seven primaeval hills, were given names: Remus and Romulus, the founders of Rome.

The culture of ancient Italy was shaped, above all, by Greeks. Greek stories were well known in Rome, especially those stories that had been told in Greece's great epic poems, the *Odyssey* and the *Iliad*. The mythical chronology provided by those poems was the context into which Romulus and Remus would be made to fit.

The pivotal event of the Greek mythological timeline was the terrible ten-year conflict known as the Trojan war. The greatest heroes of Greece – Ajax, Diomedes, Odysseus, Agamemnon, the invincible Achilles – had laid siege to the rich city of Troy. The war dragged on. The defenders were indomitable. Even the immortal gods had taken sides, and appeared on the battlefield, to the terror of mortal men. At last, after much bloodshed, a party of Greeks was smuggled inside the walls concealed in a giant wooden horse. They sacked the city and put the inhabitants to the sword.

The heroes who fought at Troy won eternal glory. And in the diminished days that followed, towns and cities across the Mediterranean made much of their links, however tenuous, to the men who had fought there. Diomedes was credited with the foundation of cities across southern Italy. The wily Odysseus was said to have overcome the witch-queen Circe just off the Italian coast. An Arcadian hero, Evander – not a veteran of Troy but, at least, a Greek – was supposed to have founded a settlement on the Palatine hill itself, on the spot where a fire-breathing giant was killed by the mighty Hercules.

Quite early on in Roman history, it became established that Romulus and Remus too were part of this Greek mythological world. In fact, as later storytellers told it, the wolf-twins were distant descendants of a Trojan refugee.

The hero Aeneas, Romans proudly claimed, had been one of the very few men to escape the burning wreck of Troy. His subsequent wanderings were worthy of Odysseus himself: he fought off harpies, escaped the cyclops Polyphemus, circled the dread whirlpool Charybdis; he was driven by storms to Africa, where he broke the proud heart of Dido, Queen of Carthage. Compelled by destiny, he sailed away pursued by her dying curse. At last, after many adventures, Aeneas arrived in Italy, where he established a city in the Alban hills, overlooking the Latin plain. His descendants were kings among the Latins, ruling wisely and well for hundreds of years.

The last Alban king of Aeneas's line was Numitor, who was overthrown by a jealous younger brother. The usurper murdered Numitor's sons. To guarantee the extinction of Numitor's family, he forced the king's surviving daughter to become a Vestal Virgin, sworn to chastity, one of the keepers of Vesta's sacred flame.

When this daughter was found to be pregnant despite her vows, she insisted that the father was no mortal but one of the gods. She had been violated by Mars himself, she pleaded, the irresistible lord of war and spring, god of thrusting vegetation.

It was not enough to save her. She was entombed in a dungeon. Her baby twins, when they were born, were thrown into the Tiber to drown.

Thus the twins were accounted for, fitted into the broader structure of Greco-Roman legend. Their miraculous appearance under that fig tree was a twist in a mythological family drama, the sort of story to which ancient audiences were well-accustomed. The subsequent events of their childhood and youth followed the conventions of the genre: feats of boyish prowess against bandits and wild beasts; a joyous reunion with their lost grandfather Numitor; the overthrow of the usurper and the restoration of Numitor to his throne.

Only after all this backstory had been taken care of were the twins able to return to the river that had brought them forth, the land of the wolf and the fig tree, to complete their true purpose: the foundation of Rome.

At least, Rome was the name the new city ended up with. Things could have turned out otherwise. For the twins were not content to be equal partners in the foundation of the new city. While Romulus proposed to found Rome, his brother Remus intended that the city should be Remoria.

There was no settling the question by seniority. The brothers were twins, equals in strength and stubbornness. There was only one solution: the quarrel between Romulus and Remus should be settled according to the will of the gods. The right of one twin to rule over the seven hills would be made manifest in the sky overhead – for the immortals, it was known, sometimes communicated their wishes by directing the flight of birds.

Accordingly, each twin set himself up to watch the skies. Romulus stationed himself on the Palatine. Remus climbed the Aventine and settled down to wait. And it was Remus, the story goes, who saw the first sign: six great vultures soaring eastward, a very favourable omen.

But, even in the eyes of the gods, the fortunes of the twins were too deeply entwined to permit any clear distinction between them. Just at the moment when Remus was claiming victory, Romulus saw a sign of his own. And though his birds came later, they were more numerous. Where Remus saw six vultures, Romulus saw twelve.

There are several versions of what happened next. Most agree that there was a quarrel, and that it was Romulus who came out victorious. Remus went off furiously down the hill to nurse his resentment; Romulus started work on his new city alone.

There is no sign of Remus in the stories as Romulus performs the necessary founding rites. It was no small thing to create a city, the Romans understood – to summon a city, a living community, out of the untouched soil. With great solemnity, Romulus offered up the first fruits of the harvest in sacrifice to the gods. Then, with a bronze ploughshare hitched to a bull and a pure white cow, and praying all the while to Mars and Vesta and almighty Jupiter, he cut a furrow in the earth to mark out the perimeter of his city.

This furrow, called the pomoerium, was a sacred boundary, a boundary between two worlds. On the outside of the furrow was the open countryside, the land of wild beasts and ageless spirits, where time hardly ran. But within the furrow the air had changed. Something had been set in motion. Romulus, with his mortal eyes, could hardly see it, but perhaps with his divine parentage he could feel it: the thundering imminence of a thousand branching possibilities, of all the things that Rome would one day be.

Here, in the stories, at this moment of creation, Remus reappears. He sees the rampart rising along the city's sacred boundary, laughs a scornful laugh and vaults casually over Rome's half-built defences.

And in the next instant, Remus is struck down. Some say one of Romulus's men struck the blow; others say it was Romulus himself who dashed out his brother's brains with a builder's shovel. Twin killed twin. And Romulus, now alone, sternly justified the murder: 'Such, henceforth, will be the fate of any enemy who crosses my walls.'

* * *

This was the tale the Romans told about their origins. It was a story that changed over time. The fullest tellings of it that have survived from antiquity date from the first century AD, and even these highly crafted literary narratives cannot agree on the details of the myth. Only the core of the story remains consistent: the twins, the wolf, the birds and Remus's violent death.

The origins of the story are as obscure as its meaning. Did Romulus come first? His name is surely derived from the name of Rome itself, not the other way round. But when, then, did Remus appear, and why? Where does the tradition come from that makes Remus, not Romulus, the firstborn? And what can explain the fratricide? There are traces of an old tradition that has Romulus and Remus happily ruling Rome together. So why introduce murder into the story? Why stain with blood the moment of Rome's foundation?

There are some historians willing to argue that the myth has some basis in truth. That there really was a Romulus, or someone like him. That the story preserves, in mythological form, a lost history of settlement and conflict. Others have interpreted the story in purely symbolic or religious terms: the foundation of the city mirrors the creation of the universe; Romulus and Remus are primal twins, Man and Other. Man begins his ascent towards the heavens by dispatching his shadow-self to the underworld.

There were other stories that might have served for Rome's foundation myth. The founder could have been Aeneas, or Evander, or even Hercules. Romulus might once have been a son of Odysseus and Circe. He might once have been the son of a slave-girl, Ocrisia, who fell pregnant by a phallus that sprouted from the ashes of her hearth.

But for whatever reason, it was the story of the twins that was passed down through the generations and which came, in time, to be regarded as history. The story was embedded in the fabric of the city. Children in ancient Rome could point out the very fig tree where the twins came ashore. There was a crude wooden hut on the Palatine that people still called the House of Romulus when Rome's population was nearly a million strong.

Roman antiquarians even claimed to have worked out the date on which Romulus founded the city – 21 April 753 BC, in modern reckoning. Romans looking back over their own history sometimes named the years by the amount of time that had elapsed since the foundation of the city – *ab urbe condita.*

As to whether the story was strictly accurate, no one worried much. The myth of Romulus and Remus served, like the spurious foundation date, as a point of origin, a point from which Romans, looking back, might measure their progress. The story was a fiction, but it was part of the city's memory.

The story of the twins was a difficult myth for Rome. Its meanings were sometimes awkward: the wolf could be a symbol of Roman savagery; the fratricide a precursor to the violence of Rome's civil wars. Romulus appears in ancient literature variously as a warning or a paragon, a hero or a tyrant, a vessel for all the anxieties and hopes of the city of Rome. The story was always being contested, reused and reimagined, ancient events turned to new purposes.

And the same has been true of Roman stories ever since. Each generation provides new stories to be told and retold, new heroes and villains to be valued and re-evaluated, an ever-changing cast of priests, courtesans, peasants, soldiers, emperors, artists, princesses, vagrants and visionaries, parading through history.

The chapters that follow deal, so far as is possible, with historical facts – with real lives, lived in the Eternal City. But no retelling of Roman history can ever quite be neutral or objective. The facts, in Rome, always take on a mythic dimension.

2

BARBARIANS

The Gallic sack of Rome

———

*c.*387 BC

T HE YEAR IS 387 or maybe 386 BC. Spring has given way to summer, which lies hot and herb-scented on the valley of the Tiber. The river is narrow here, flowing green and silent between its banks. On each side, low hills rise in long, forested ribs towards the distant vertebrae of the Apennines.

This is Etruscan territory. West from here, in the rolling country between the Tiber and the sea, their cities perch on rocky heights and river bluffs. It is a country of wheat and vines, carefully tended. The fields here are furrowed with careful little drainage channels called *cuniculi*, whose traces will still be visible after millennia – a monument to the labour of forgotten peasant generations, coaxing each year's harvest from the land.

There is always work to be done. And yet, today, the fields are deserted. No brown-backed farmers stoop among the olives. The shepherds have vanished with their flocks. And then the sound of voices breaks the summer silence to reveal the reason why. There are armed men coming into view: armed men in the Tiber valley, hundreds of them, sleek and fierce like prize hounds.

No wonder the Etruscans are hiding behind their walls. This is a Gallic warband on the march. An awful sight. At each step the glint of sun on metal flashes a new warning – reflected off bronze helmets and long swords of beaten iron; off the blades of cruel notched spears; off torques of twisted gold at arm and throat. These are men who live for battle, and everything about them shouts the fact: their lime-bleached hair and bristling moustaches; the withered heads that decorate their chariot poles.

But, to the relief of the Etruscan peasants, the men of this formidable band appear to have no interest in raiding. They are not slowed down by kidnapped girls or stolen cattle, and they have not sent men to burn out the surrounding farms. Instead, they are heading steadily southwards in a purposeful column. They have a higher goal in mind: they are going to Rome.

* * *

Rome in the twenty-first century is a city where the dead outnumber the living. There are tombs everywhere: some full, some empty, some whole, some broken, recycled for use as flower-pots or fountains, lining the walls of churches, paving basilica floors, sprouting romantic weeds in old cemeteries or buried in the endless galleries of catacombs – tombs piled upon tombs like polyp skeletons in a coral reef.

It seems fitting then, somehow, that most of what we know about the earliest days of Rome is how the first Romans treated their dead.

We know, for example, that around 1000 BC, centuries before the supposed time of Romulus and Remus, there were late-Bronze Age settlers living on some of Rome's hills. Their remains are buried underneath the Roman Forum – the remains of people whose lives are otherwise completely lost to us: mothers and fathers, sisters and brothers, tiny briefly cherished children. Their ashes were gathered in burial urns, which in turn were sealed inside larger earthenware jars and sunk into the valley's marshy ground. Sometimes the burial urns are shaped to resemble the primitive huts in which the first Romans lived, with reed roofs and walls of wattle and daub. Sometimes they are accompanied by a crude statuette of the deceased, with miniature pots and little bits of food, as if the dead might play at doll's houses.

We know that as the Iron Age began, around 900 BC, most of the people who lived on the hills switched from cremation to inhumation – that is, they buried their dead whole instead of burning them first. Perhaps fuel for funeral pyres had become harder to find as the population of the area grew. At any rate, customs changed. Only warriors still warranted the traditional fiery exit. They lie in their jars accompanied by little models of spears and swords, to fight their way into the afterlife.

But most of the early graves belong to farmers, laid out unburned to rest and rot. Their wives lie buried with their spindles; not even death interrupts their long domestic toil.

Around 800 BC, the hamlets scattered across the Roman hills started growing and clumping together. This 'proto-urban' phase of Roman settlement was matched by developments elsewhere. All over the great fertile plain to the south and east of Rome, around the ancient volcano of *Mons Albanus*, farmers and herders speaking an Italic language known as Latin were banding together to form the primitive communities that would grow to become the flourishing cities of Latium.*

As these communities grew more organized, trade routes emerged to link the not-yet cities of the Latin plain, both to each other and to peoples further afield. Two of these routes crossed under Rome's hills: the Tiber island marked the furthest point downstream at which the river could be forded, the easiest crossing point for anyone travelling up Italy's west coast. Just as important was the trail that led upriver from the salt flats at the Tiber mouth towards the Apennines. These were two of the busiest commercial arteries in central Italy, and the early Romans were perfectly placed to take maximum advantage of both of them.

---

* There were about forty distinct languages and dialects spoken in Iron Age Italy. Most, including Latin, belong to the so-called 'Italic' subfamily, or at least to the wider Indo-European family of languages. The bizarre exception, however, is Etruscan, a language with no known relatives at all. This mysterious language fell into disuse some time after the first century BC, and is now more or less incomprehensible to modern scholars. Where it came from, whether it was brought to Italy by invaders or survived from some ancient past, is impossible to say.

Trade brought wealth; and wealth, of course, brought conflict. Rome's neighbours, Etruscans to the north and fellow Latin-speakers to the south, could hardly fail to notice the advantages of the proto-city's strategic position. The Roman hills were prizes worth taking. Sometime around the middle of the eighth century BC, just around the supposed time of Romulus, someone living on the Palatine hill found it necessary to lay out Rome's first ever set of fortifications.

There were new forces abroad in Italy in those years. Around 770 BC traders from the Greek island of Euboea established the first permanent Greek settlement at Ischia on the Italian coast – just one good day's sailing from the Tiber mouth – as an entrepôt for the valuable trade in Italian metal ores. The enterprise was a success. Within two generations of that first colonization, tens of thousands of Greeks had come west across the sea in search of mineral riches, unclaimed land or a better life.

Later Roman myths would tell that it was a Greek, Evander the Arcadian, who established the first real settlement at Rome. And the myth contains something of the truth. It was indeed the Greeks who brought the first really developed urban culture to Italian shores, planting cities in a great arc across the heel and toe of Italy: Tarentum and Croton; Sybaris, famous for luxury; Syracuse in Sicily; Cumae and later Naples (the *nea polis*, or 'new city') just beyond the southern borders of the Latin plain. It would be centuries before Rome could rival these settlements for wealth or art or civilization, centuries during which the whole southern portion of Italy came to be known as *Magna Graecia* – Greater Greece.

It took a while for city living to catch on by the banks of the Tiber. 753 BC is the traditional date given for Rome's founding. That would fit perfectly with the wave of Greek colonization but, to judge by the archaeology, it looks at least 100 years too early. A more realistic date for the birth of Rome as anything like a proper city would be around the middle of the 600s BC. It was then that the swampy dip between the Palatine and Capitoline hills, the valley that the first settlers had used as a burial ground, was drained for the first time and given a rough-beaten floor. This was the earliest incarnation of the Roman Forum, an open meeting space that gave the ancient city a proper commercial centre and a symbolic heart.

These were years of rapid change in the newborn city. From around 625 BC we have the remains of Rome's first permanent houses, with stone walls and tiled roofs replacing the old mud and thatch. Not long after that, around 600 BC, we get Rome's first proper public buildings: at one end of the Forum was the *regia*, a mysterious monumental complex associated with Rome's kings; at the other end of the Forum are the remains of a building that was probably the *Curia Hostilia*, Rome's earliest Senate House.

Rome was becoming political. That is to say, it was becoming what the Greeks called a *polis* – a city state, with a coherent government, monumental buildings, official cult centres and a meaningful public life.

The details of Rome's early government are impossible to make out. Roman tradition later held that there were seven kings, starting with Romulus in 753 BC, but Romulus is certainly a fiction, and most of his supposed successors must be too. Even if their names were handed down correctly through the generations, the tales of their heroic deeds are mythology rather than history.

Certainly there were kings of some sort though, sacred rulers presiding over what was, by the sixth century BC, a very real city, with a population in the low tens of thousands. Serving and advising the king was a loose council, precursor to the senate, composed of aristocratic clan-leaders who had begun to raise themselves above the simple agricultural society from which they sprang. These early Roman nobles were part of a well-connected elite – familiar with the leading men among their Etruscan and Latin neighbours. Tombs of the period are full of international luxuries: gold and silver, Athenian pots, beads of amber or glass.

Rome's horizons were steadily broadening. At the busy market which flourished beside the Tiber, at the river crossing that joined Latium to Etruria, visitors sailing upriver arrived with new ideas and practices from far afield. In the Rome of the kings you could worship a 'many-breasted' version of the goddess Diana with origins in Ephesus, or the Phoenician trader-god Melqart in the guise of the Greek hero Hercules.

By the end of the sixth century BC, Rome had grown rich enough to merit its own treaty with Carthage, an old Phoenician colony on the north African coast that was now the most important trading city in the western Mediterranean. The Romans carved the terms of the treaty in bronze and set them on the Capitoline hill for all to see, and their pride was justifiable. Carthage had acknowledged Rome as a significant local power, with territory that stretched across the Latin plain.

It was at around the same time that work began on the city's grandest building yet: an enormous temple up on the Capitoline. The temple's foundations are all that is left today, but the great blocks of buried tufa prove the ambition of the old Roman builders. On a platform the size of half a football pitch, the Capitoline Temple reared its triple rows of timber columns, a behemoth of brick and painted wood. At its pinnacle, riding a four-horse chariot of Etruscan terracotta, was Jupiter Optimus Maximus, Best and Greatest, father and ruler of the gods.

During the construction, some workers on the hill unearthed a human head with features miraculously well preserved. Soothsayers were summoned to make clear the omen's meaning: this head, or *caput*, discovered on the *capitolinus mons*, signified that Rome would be the *caput mundi* – the head of the world.

* * *

The truest witnesses to Rome's beginnings are the dead. Now, however, they fall silent. Partway through the sixth century BC, the rich tombs start to disappear. The Romans, for whatever reason, stopped burying bodies with precious objects beside them – and without those dateable objects, the bodies are unmoored in time, lost even when they are found.

Rome's story is taken up by a louder but less reliable voice: the voice of Titus Livius, better known as Livy, whose monumental work,

Ab Urbe Condita, composed in the first century BC, is the fullest ancient account we have of Rome's early history.

As Livy tells it, it was in the year 509 BC that the rich Roman monarchy fell apart. The king at the time was a nobleman of Greco-Etruscan origin called Lucius Tarquinius, surnamed Superbus – Tarquin the Proud. It was he, by Livy's account, who built Jupiter's great temple on the Capitoline, the crown on Rome's brow. He also gets credit for the construction of the great sewer, the Cloaca Maxima, which gave centuries of loyal service at the city's other end.

But despite these good works, Tarquin was hated as a tyrant and his days were numbered. An evil omen foretold his doom: a snake which slithered out from a cavity in a wooden column. Alarmed by this, Tarquin sent two of his sons to Delphi, in Greece, to consult the famous oracle there. They brought a companion, Lucius Junius, surnamed Brutus ('Stupid') on account of his dull wits.

At Delphi, the princes asked about the snake, but they also asked a further question. Who will succeed the king when he dies? The oracle replied: 'Whoever of you shall be the first to kiss his mother will hold the highest power in Rome.'

Hearing this, they hurried to get home as fast as they could. But on the way, the idiot Brutus tripped and fell flat on his face. As he lay on the ground, he surreptitiously pressed his lips to the soil – to Mother Earth.

Not long afterwards, the Romans were besieging the Latin town of Ardea. The nights in camp were long, and officers passed them in drinking and boasting. One evening, the conversation turned to the subject of wives. Each man claimed that his wife was the best, and the argument grew so heated that the young men decided to ride back to Rome and see for themselves.

They found their wives all together, feasting and making merry with their idle friends – except for one. Lucretia, the wife of a man named Collatinus, was discovered at home, spinning by lamplight, surrounded by her hardworking maidservants.

Such a dazzling display of wifely virtue astonished the officers. But among them was one of the king's sons, Sextus Tarquinius. Inflamed with desire for the chaste Lucretia, he snuck back the following night with sword drawn and forced his way into Lucretia's bed.

The next day, Lucretia called her husband Collatinus and her uncle, Lucius Junius Brutus, to her side. 'What can be well,' she said, 'when a woman has lost her honour? The marks of another man are in your bed. But only my body has been violated; my mind is not guilty. Death will be my witness.' With these words she drew a dagger from the folds of her robe and plunged it into her heart.

Up stepped Brutus, casting off the pretence of foolishness he had worn for so long. Holding up the fatal blade, still dripping with Lucretia's blood, he swore: 'I will pursue Lucius Tarquinius Superbus, together with his wicked wife and all his children, with sword, fire and indeed with whatever violence I can. Nor will I allow them – *or anyone else* – to be king at Rome.'

Rome was done with Tarquin and his debauched sons; and done with kings altogether – these tyrants who ruled the city according to their whim. In future, Rome would be governed according to fixed laws, passed and approved by the Senate and People, acting together for the public good – the *res publica*.

In 509 BC, Brutus and Collatinus, having successfully expelled King Tarquin, were elected to serve as Rome's chief magistrates to safeguard the *res publica* against all danger. They were the first consuls of the new Roman 'republic'.

That, at any rate, was how later Romans thought their republic had come into being. The stories of Brutus and Lucretia were handed down in Rome from a very distant past, transmitted through the centuries, probably in the form of epic verse or through dramatic performance, until they reached the ears of Livy and his scholarly predecessors, to be set down in the historical record like fossils hardening in mud.

How much truth these stories contain is hard to know. The Etruscan King Tarquin is a plausible figure for a time when aristocrats moved easily between cities, even across linguistic and cultural borders. But the account of his monarchy's fall sounds like pure myth.

The violation of women was a stereotypical vice of tyrants in literature. And the specifics of the Rape of Lucretia are suspiciously similar to a story which accompanied the overthrow of a tyrant in Athens at around the same time.

We do have an ancient list of consuls, recording the names of Rome's chief magistrates all the way back to the late sixth century BC – and Brutus and Collatinus are indeed the first two names. But uncertainties abound: is the list accurate or were the earliest names added in at some later date? Is the list complete? That is, are there some even older names that went unrecorded? And, even if the list is right and Rome really did have a system of paired magistrates starting around 509 BC, can we be sure that these magistrates had just taken over the running of the city?

Two theories suggest otherwise: one possibility is that King Tarquin was expelled not by rebellious aristocrats but by a rival Etruscan warlord named Lars Porsenna, who captured Rome and installed Brutus and Collatinus as his lieutenants there. Another is that the monarchy faded gradually, with power shifting in favour of Roman aristocrats over years or decades. Later religious ceremonies in Rome sometimes involved a mysterious figure called the *rex sacrorum*, or 'king of sacred things', a priest who fulfilled some of the king's old sacred function. It may be that this priesthood was not in fact created to *replace* the role of king but rather was what the kingship eventually became – an empty title for a symbolic figure whose worldly power had slowly leached away.

At any rate, Rome in the fifth century BC had entered a period of turbulence. The signs are readable, as always, in Rome's muddy ground: carbon layers from the fiery destruction of certain Roman buildings around 500 BC; the absence of new temple foundations after 474 BC; the scarcity of imported work among buried shards of fifth-century pottery. Rome – and indeed most of central Italy – appears to have suffered a major recession.

Economic hardship was compounded by war. Lars Porsenna, the Etruscan warlord, fought against the Greeks of Cumae; an alliance of Latin towns under the leadership of the nearby city of Tusculum fought against Rome. Latium then suffered an invasion of tribes from the mountains, Aequi and Volsci, who occupied huge areas of the Latin plain for most of the century that followed.

Most dangerous of all, from Rome's point of view, was ongoing conflict with the Etruscan city of Veii, which lay less than a day's march to the north, on the far side of the river. This was far too close for either Roman or Veientine comfort. Both cities were too powerful and too ambitious to let the other survive unmolested, and both were competing for control of the same vital trade route – the old salt road that led up the Tiber valley. As the Romans tried to cut off the Veientine route on the river's right bank, so Veii kept pushing to cut off the Roman route on the river's left.

And at first, Veii had the best of it. At the Battle of the River Cremera, in 477 BC, the noble clan of the Fabii – a clan that would play a huge role in later Roman history – is supposed to have been almost wiped out. But over the course of the 430s and 420s BC the Romans managed to subdue and capture a key Veientine ally – the town of Fidenae, a little upriver. The way was now open for an assault on Veii itself.

At the end of the fifth century BC Roman troops finally managed to beat the Veientines back behind their own walls. And even then, victory seemed a distant prospect. The Etruscan city was nearly impregnable, founded on a plateau of volcanic rock. Well stocked with food and water, the defenders looked ready to hold out indefinitely.

The stage was set for an epic struggle, and later Roman historians were keen to do the moment justice. The siege lasted ten years in Livy's telling of it – just like the ten years the heroes of ancient Greece spent besieging Troy – with the Roman leaders quarrelling like Achilles and Agamemnon and ferocious battles raging back and forth beneath the walls.

Meanwhile the gods made themselves felt through signs and prodigies. The lake under *Mons Albanus*, the old volcano, rose mysteriously without any rain and poured down into the country below – an event which caused great alarm in the Roman camp.

The epic siege demanded an epic hero: Marcus Furius Camillus. He was, we are told, a veteran of the long wars against the Volsci and Aequi, a man whose calm moderation of character disguised a keen talent for military leadership.

The ancient writers give Camillus all the best Roman virtues: among them, a sort of businesslike directness of will. Confronted with Veii's impenetrable walls, Camillus, in the story, has his men dig a tunnel straight through the rock of the Veientine plateau and up into the defenders' citadel. When the tunnel is complete, the Romans assault the walls from all sides while a picked force bursts out of the tunnel into the city's heart, like Greeks from the Trojan Horse.

The doomed Etruscans fought as best they could. Even as their husbands were cut down in the streets, the women of Veii took to the roofs of their houses, hurling bricks and tiles down at the invaders. It was not enough. By the end of the day, the men were dead, the women were slaves and Rome's most dangerous rival was no more.

Camillus returned home in triumph, drawn by four white horses like Jupiter himself. The shackled Veientine women came stumbling behind him. There was even a goddess in his train: Juno Regina, Queen of Heaven, the guardian deity of Veii. Her cult statue, after due prayers and exhortations, was taken from her temple in the conquered city and escorted by a troupe of white-robed youths to a new sanctuary in Rome. Rome had swallowed Veii whole – land, women, gods and all.

Amid the rejoicing, did anyone wonder why the other Etruscan cities had done so little to help the Veientines in their hour of need? They were happy to see a competitor humbled, the Romans may have guessed. The city states of Etruria were hardly models of solidarity; they spent as much time fighting each other as fighting anyone else. But there was another reason too. While Veii was locked in its final struggle against the Romans, the other Etruscans were coming to grips with an even more dangerous enemy: the Gauls.

* * *

Greek traders, venturing northward from their colonies on the Mediterranean coast, had long ago established links with the tribes of the vast European hinterland – tribes belonging to a common linguistic and cultural family. The Greeks had learned to call them *keltoi*, Celts. In Latin, they were *galli*, or Gauls.

These Celts were good business. The chieftains of central Europe were rich in iron, copper and tin; amber and fur; timber, honey and salt; dogs and slaves – goods which they traded away happily for the luxuries the Greeks could provide.* Soon, no great lord's feast was complete without a display of fine Mediterranean tableware. One tomb unearthed at the great Celtic stronghold at Heuneburg had traces of silk fabric hidden inside it – the oldest silk ever discovered in Europe.

And the Celtic lords loved wine. They would trade a slave for a single amphora of the stuff, Greek merchants reported. A little before 500 BC, just when the Romans were throwing out the Tarquins, a Celtic noblewoman from Mont Lassois in northern Burgundy was interred with an enormous Spartan-style wine jar at her side. More than 1.6 metres tall, it is a thousand-litre miracle of gold and sculpted bronze, the biggest wine jar that has ever been found.

But a change was coming to Celtic society. By the middle of the fifth century, great hillforts like Mont Lassois and the Heuneburg were abandoned, and some show traces of having been burned. Graves from the 400s BC contain more weapons than wine jars: javelins, spears, shields, and sometimes the distinctively elongated Celtic sword.

During these decades of turmoil there was a major shift in the pattern of north–south trade. The old sea route to Italy via the Greek city of Massilia (modern Marseilles) was largely abandoned. The Celts now traded directly across the Alps, doing business with Etruscans who rushed to control the vital ports and trading posts at the head of the Adriatic.

There was good land below the mountains, the fertile flood-plain

* The Celts were also known to produce a famously good cured ham.

of the River Po, and here, enriched by Celtic trade, new Etruscan colonies grew and flourished. But the Etruscan settlers were like farmers on the slopes of a volcano: the source of their wealth would be the cause of their destruction. Where Celtic goods could pass, Celtic warriors could follow.

The archaeology of Celtic migration to Italy is ambiguous and hard to interpret; the presence of Celtic-style pots, for example, might be a sign of trade or imitation rather than of Celtic settlement. Anyway, peoples very closely related to Celts had lived in northern Italy for generations. Their traces are not easy to distinguish from signs of more recent Celtic migration.

Nonetheless, there is good evidence that, at the end of the fifth century BC, just when Rome was besieging Veii, the Etruscan colonies of the Po Valley were overwhelmed by a sudden and massive Celtic invasion. Gravestones from the vital trade hub at Felsina show mounted Etruscans in desperate combat with naked warriors of the Boii tribe. Today, the city of Bologna sits where Felsina used to be, its name an enduring proof of Celtic victory.*

The Boii were just one of several groups who poured down into the Po Valley around 400 BC. The old Celtic heartlands beyond the mountains, far away on the Danube and the Seine, were poor and overcrowded. Young Celtic men lived in a permanent state of martial competition. In the feast-halls of Celtic lords, ambitious war leaders made peacock displays of plundered finery, showing off past successes while touting their plans for new raids and expeditions.

Italy offered rich pickings for such leaders. First warbands, and then whole tribes, travelled hundreds of miles to carve out new livelihoods under the Mediterranean sun: Laevi and Lebecii, Insubres and Cenomani, Ananes and Lingones. Last were the Senones from the upper Seine, who spread themselves along the Adriatic coast. Here, says a Greek historian, 'they followed no pursuits but those of war and

---

* The Boii, of *Bo*-logna, also left their name to their territory of origin: Bohemia, on the Upper Danube.

agriculture. They lived simple lives without being acquainted with any science or art whatever.'

This is not quite fair on the Celts. Their chariots were some of the most advanced wheeled vehicles of the era. Their illiteracy was made up for by a rich tradition of oral poetry. Their swords were some of the finest in Europe, testament to the skill of Celtic – Gaulish – metalworkers, who combined the geometric patterns of ancient European art with the vegetable motifs of Greek or Etruscan work to create a distinctive curvilinear Celtic style. In the 390s BC, as the Gauls were taking possession of northern Italy, the wider Celtic culture was approaching its colourful, vigorous height.

There can be no doubt that the Gallic warband – Senones, to be precise – who came marching down the Tiber in 387 or 386 BC would have made a fine show. These were warriors, wolves among sheep, come to extract tribute from terrified Italians. Their philosophy? *'Omnia fortium virorum'* – 'all things belong to the brave' – a claim pressed home at the tip of a spear.

Their first target was the Etruscan city of Clusium, a city that had once, under its great warlord, Lars Porsena, been one of the foremost powers of central Italy. But times had changed. The Clusines, as Livy tells it, were so dismayed by the sudden appearance of the Gauls that they resorted to the humiliating expedient of begging help from Rome. Buoyed up by their recent success at Veii, the Romans agreed to send ambassadors to negotiate with the invaders: three young men of the Fabii – members of the same aristocratic clan that had been all but wiped out by the Veientines a century earlier.

The ancestral defeat had done little to mitigate the haughty Fabians' natural hotness of spirit. The negotiations at Clusium collapsed almost immediately and soon a bitter little skirmish had broken out, with the three Fabian ambassadors, contrary to all established rules of war, fighting in the front line.

And so, unexpectedly, Clusium was saved. The behaviour of the Fabii enraged the Gauls so much that they abandoned the attack on the Etruscans. The full weight of their fury would be saved for Rome.

'How true it is,' wrote Livy, 'that destiny blinds men's eyes, when she will not have her threatened blows parried.' The story, as he tells it, has the ingredients of a classical tragedy: the Romans, led by Camillus, capture Veii and are puffed up with pride. Their arrogant ambassadors then break the laws of diplomacy – the laws of the gods. And, foolishly, Rome even ignores one final warning: an inhuman voice that booms forth one night from the dark beside the Temple of Vesta, prophesying doom.

The Gauls are coming, hurrying south as if driven by Nemesis herself. But instead of trusting to their great general, Camillus, the Romans expel him from the city in a fit of self-destructive jealousy. Command of the Roman army is entrusted to the very same Fabii who have invited Rome's doom.

The Celtic force came within a day's march of Rome before encountering any resistance. Then, at last, where a little stream called the Allia winds out of the hills to join the River Tiber, the glint of sunlight on iron first betrayed the presence of the city's defenders, strung out across the line of the *via salaria* – the ancient salt road.

These were not the famous legions that would one day conquer half the world. The Roman army that lined up to fight that day was still an army of citizens rather than professionals. Armour and weapons were provided by the soldiers themselves, according to their social rank. Cavalry cover was provided by the *equites*, young aristocrats who could afford to keep a warhorse and all the attendant gear. The poorest citizens fought as light troops with javelins or stones, or whatever they could find.

But the backbone of the army was a corps of heavy infantrymen, similar to the Greek hoplite armies of the same period, armed with a large round shield and a thrusting spear. The dominant tactic was the phalanx formation – a densely packed shield wall several ranks deep. So long as the phalanx held, with each man guarding his neighbour and a great iron bristle of spear points facing the enemy, it was nearly impervious to any direct assault.

This military set-up neatly captured the spirit of the Roman republic: stiff, highly stratified, but bound together into a hedgehog prickle against a hostile world. It was a normal enough model for an emerging city state and, for the most part, in the local wars Rome was used to fighting, it worked well enough.

The Gauls, however, were a new class of enemy. Ancient writers were always struck by how tall and fair the Gauls were, and how strong. There were some among the Gauls who used to fight completely naked except for their torques, disdaining to use armour, a sort of ritual bravado that was deeply intimidating for any enemy who stood in their way. 'Very quarrelsome' the Gauls were, one Roman reported. 'Madly fond of war', a Greek confirmed.

And so they had to be. Their whole worth as men was won by the sword, whether in single combat with their fellow tribesmen or on raids against softer neighbours. Let Romans cower in their phalanx! These adventuring Celts were not farmers to stand tight-packed like cattle but dedicated warriors, men for whom fighting was both a profession and an art.

Now, as they faced the nervous Romans, the Gauls filled the air with whoops of scorn and the magic songs of battle. The chiefs in their chariots dashed back and forth, hurling challenges at the Roman line, the bright plumes of their helmets trailing behind them. Then, with a great bellow of war-trumpets, the beast-headed Celtic carnyxes, the advance began.

They came on in loose order, spears and long swords at the ready, howling as they ran. It was no easy thing to charge a wall of shields, to be more keen to kill than afraid to die.

The Romans watched from their thicket of massed spears as the Gauls closed in for blood. They would survive, so long as their formation held. But suddenly, fear flickered along the line; spear-points trembled as if blown by a sudden wind; Gallic swords flashed forward and, where the two sides met, the defending army crumbled, the phalanx disintegrating into a chaos of fleeing men and biting steel.

On their left flank the Romans found themselves trapped between the Gauls and the Tiber. Many plunged in wearing full armour and sank in the river mud. Those with lighter gear crossed to the far bank and made for Veii, having already given Rome up for lost. In the centre, there was great slaughter as the herd of terrified fugitives trampled each other in their haste. The Gauls cut them down from behind with the efficiency of practised killers. Only on the right, where the reserves were holding some higher ground, did the Romans manage a successful retreat, fleeing in terror back down the road to Rome.

* * *

Gallic scouts arrived shortly before sunset to find the city at their mercy. The gates were open; the defences abandoned. Only the late hour and fear of a possible trap prevented the Gauls from attacking at once. Instead, the main body of the army made camp for the night, celebrating their easy victory.

Meanwhile in the Forum, Rome's fighting men weighed their options. The situation was bleak. Too few soldiers had come back from the battle at the Allia to keep the Gauls from breaching Rome's outer ditch and palisade. But the city was too crowded with women, children and old men for everyone to fit into the one remaining refuge: the fortified citadel, or *Arx*, on the Capitoline hill.

So an exodus began. The people of Rome, those who were able, loaded their children and parents and few precious belongings into wagons, which rolled in mournful procession under the Capitoline towards the cattle market, then across the river and out into the summer night.

Nervous amid the throng of refugees were the six virgin priestesses of Vesta, staring from behind their distinctive white veils. Vesta was goddess of the hearth and the Vestal Virgins were guardians of her flame, which they kept forever burning in their little round temple in the Forum. But now Rome's hearth grew cold. Gathering up the city's most sacred treasures from the temple's hidden store, the Vestals had buried what they could not carry and now were escaping with the rest, six frightened women with the fragments of Rome's soul held in their arms.

Meanwhile, any soldiers left in the city, their families, and those senators not too decrepit to fight made their way up the sloping street called the *clivus capitolinus*, towards the Capitoline hill. Here, in the shadow of Jupiter's temple, they prepared to make their stand.

The Gauls entered the city the next morning, down the salt road and through the Colline gate.* Nothing stirred. The village-dwelling Celts, so ferocious in battle, were silent as they passed through the streets, hushed by the blank faces of the shuttered houses.

The mood, as Livy describes it, was something like religious awe. This was not least because, sitting very still in the porticos of their houses, the old men of Rome – too proud to flee and too weak to fight – were calmly waiting to die. Wearing their finest robes and their badges of office and distinction, these elders appeared to the Gauls like strange silent gods, until, at last, one of the invaders dared to reach out and tug curiously at a snowy patrician beard. Such an assault on dignity could not be borne. Marcus Papirius, the prickly noble to whom the beard in question was attached, delivered the offending Gaul a sharp whack on the head with his walking stick. The spell was broken, and the massacre began.

For days the Romans watched the Gauls ransack the city. From the citadel they could see everything: the houses gutted, treasures ferreted out, prized possessions heaped up in the Forum. They heard the cries of the occasional stragglers – those not quick enough or fit enough to get away.

But on the Capitoline the Romans held. When the Gauls, shields locked, tried to rush the hill's defences, they were beaten back with heavy losses.

And when the Gauls attempted a night attack up one of the hill's precipitous but unguarded flanks, they were foiled by the quacking of

* By the Colline gate, unknown to the invading Gauls, was the underground chamber where Vestals were buried alive in the event that they ceased to be virgins. This was meant to be an ordeal from which their goddess could rescue them, if they had been falsely accused. Whatever the goddess may have done, impure Vestals were never released by the hand of any man.

Juno's sacred geese. The besieged Romans, with that rigid piety that Livy so admires, had refused, even in these desperate times, to eat the goddess's animals. Now, hearing the Gauls clambering up the rocks below, the frightened birds flapped and squawked loudly enough to wake the sleeping defenders just in time. Juno, so recently abducted from Veii, had saved Rome.

By this time even the Gauls were running short of food. Roman forces outside the city were gathering strength, having once again enlisted the exiled hero of Veii, Marcus Furius Camillus, as their leader.

But the defenders of the citadel were reaching the last stages of starvation, and eventually it was decided that the Gauls must be paid off. For 1,000 Roman *librae* of gold (around 327 kg – an enormous sum) the Celtic chieftain, Brennus, agreed to take his men and go, no doubt well pleased with the success of his expedition.*

The story is that as the gold was being measured out, a Roman tribune noticed that the Gauls were using unfair weights. Brennus, laughing, threw his sword on to the scales on the Gaulish side. '*Vae victis*,' he exclaimed. 'To the conquered, woe!'

* * *

It is at this moment, as Livy tells it, that Marcus Furius Camillus bursts back on to the scene. At the head of a newly raised Roman army, Camillus scatters the Gauls and recovers the shameful ransom, driving the few survivors back across the mountains to their territory on the Adriatic coast.

In Rome, all is swiftly set to rights. The people return. The Vestal Virgins dig up their trove of sacred things. Camillus makes a particular point of placating any gods who may be offended: all the holy places touched by Gauls are carefully reconsecrated; special games are held in honour of Capitoline Jupiter; and that mysterious god whose warning was ignored that night beside Vesta's temple is honoured

---

* This chief is traditionally named Brennus by ancient historians. In fact, Brennus is probably just a Latinization of the Celtic word for chief. The man's real name is unknown.

with his own brand new shrine, dedicated, in the absence of better information, simply to *Aius Locutius* – the Voice that Announces.

By this point, Livy's story has become a sort of moralistic fable. For neglecting the immortals and breaking the law of nations, he tells the Romans, 'we received such punishment at the hands of gods and men that we were a lesson to the whole world'. But with the pious Camillus back in charge, and the gods given due honour, Rome's fortunes rose again, and would rise further still.

A nice fable indeed – and beautifully pitched to resonate with Livy's own Augustan audience. But almost certainly a false one. In fact, the most likely truth is that Marcus Furius Camillus never existed at all.

So what really happened that summer of 387 – or 386 – BC? The Romans suffered a major setback. A Gaulish warband, perhaps not even that large, routed the Roman army, seized the city, extracted a fat bribe and left in triumph – altogether a very successful piece of work.

The defeat was enough of an embarrassment to be talked about by traders on the Mediterranean circuit. Young men in Athens were dimly aware that a city in the west had been sacked by an army of 'hyperboreans' – wild men from the land of the north wind.

The sack was news in Sicily too, where one man above all stood to gain from Gallic pressure on the cities of central Italy. Dionysius I, lord of the Greek city of Syracuse on the Sicilian coast, was, at that time, carving out a successful little empire for himself, with outposts all along the Italian peninsula. His new colony at Ancona on the Adriatic, right next to the territory of the Senones, was perfectly positioned to tap into the great north–south trade route over the Alps, especially if the Etruscans could be kept out of the picture. It is perfectly likely, though it cannot be proved, that the warband that sacked Rome was in Dionysius's service. That would explain – better than the story of the negotiation at Clusium – why the Gauls came so far south: they were hired mercenaries on their way to Sicily.

And if the Gauls ever were defeated, it was not by any Camillus. The only people with a plausible claim to have beaten Brennus and his warband are not Romans but Etruscans, Roman allies from the nearby port town of Caere, who, according to one tradition, intercepted the Gauls and defeated them on their return from the south. Camillus's *deus ex machina* moment is, in the words of the great nineteenth-century classicist Theodor Mommsen, 'a legend of late and wretched invention', designed only to save Roman face.

The Romans had been humiliated. But they were not a people to let anything go to waste. From the raw material of defeat, they made a story – a story of Roman courage and resilience in the face of disaster; of piety; of faith in the gods rewarded; of steadfast endurance overcoming the assault of the wild and passionate Celts, the great barbarian Others whose depredations, though painful, allowed the Romans to show the strengths through which they understood, and enacted, their own selves. It was a story they would tell and retell for hundreds of years.

To Livy, four centuries later, the Gallic Sack was like a new beginning for the city. It was also a milestone in his history. All the most ancient records of Rome were burned by the Gauls, he explained. The whole city was put to the torch and, as a result, events from before that time are shrouded in obscurity. The details of things that happened after the Sack will, Livy promises, be laid out with certainty and clarity in their proper order.

In other words: before the Gallic disaster we have myths; after it, history.

But Livy is wrong. That most reliable witness, the Roman mud, reveals an awkward truth: there is no carbon layer in the soil laid down in the 380s BC. Rome did not burn. The line of ash, the line between history and myth, is not so clear as Livy, and his successors, have liked to think.

3

THE LITTLE CARTHAGINIAN

Titus Maccius Plautus and the Hannibalic war

———

218–187 BC

A WOODEN STAGE. The set is simple: three doors in a high wall, like one side of a city street. Enter Prologue, stage right. 'It pleases me,' says Prologue, 'to do tragedy...'

A pause, for Prologue to survey the audience – *his* audience if he does his job right, but not his yet. They are still milling around, still chattering neighbour to neighbour, shifting their bums on packed benches, adjusting their tunics, scratching itches, hooting at pretty girls.

'Silence!'

Prologue is in high dramatic mode – he is *doing* tragedy. 'Silence and be quiet and pay attention! Listen! Thus commands your Thespian-in-Chief!'

A sudden hush. Murmurs of consternation.

But now Prologue's voice turns comforting: 'Come,' he says. 'Take your seats in good spirits, those of you who came hungry and those who are well fed. You people who ate before the show – bravo! Cleverly done! You lot who haven't already eaten will just have to fill yourselves up on our *fabulae*.'

A sigh of relief runs through the audience. For here, amid the pompous clouds of tragic verbiage, is a joke – a joke pitched right down low. The crowd today is as rough as any in Rome, but no one can miss the pun. *Fabulae* means stories, but if you change the stress it also means little beans.

'Beanicles!' This *is* a comedy after all.

* * *

A Roman theatre crowd was a fickle thing. Wine flowed freely. A festive atmosphere reigned in the city, making even the poorest Romans bold and unruly. One comedian is supposed to have lost an audience completely: they were distracted by a nearby troupe of rope-dancers.

But this play, on this day, will not suffer any such humiliation. The playwright is Titus Maccius Plautus, the finest comedian of his generation, and he has sent his 'Prologue' out with fighting words. Now the man on stage begins to hit his stride. He blusters like a conquering general, the 'Thespian-in-Chief' shouting orders at the rebellious crowd before him, picking out sections of the crowd each in their turn: 'We'll have none of you over-ripe bum boys sitting in the stalls!', he shouts.

'Lictors are not to mutter or rustle their sacred rods during the performance, and the ushers must *not* keep showing people to their seats while the actors are on stage. Those who overslept at home will just have to stand at the back and make the best of it!'

Who else to bully? Slaves! 'If you can't afford to buy your freedom then get yourselves home or be beaten black and blue.'

Nursing women should leave their babies behind, and themselves too, for that matter. No one wants infants in the theatre 'wailing like little goats'.

And ladies! 'Please watch in silence, laugh in silence and try to keep the tinkling of your singsong voices under control!' Please – 'don't be a nuisance to your husbands at home *and* at the theatre too!'

Prologue pauses, thinks for a second, the generalissimo surveying the field.

'I had almost forgotten!' He puffs his chest another inch. 'Go, footmen, while the Games are on, and mount an invasion of the eateries! Now, while you have a window of opportunity and the pies are hot, advance and engage!'

An invasion of actors! Even the slaves hiding at the back are laughing now, and the women with their singsong voices, the men, freeborn or ex-slaves, citizens or foreigners, Greeks, Samnites, Etruscans, Latins. Prologue has conquered them. Now the day's performance can begin.

The comedies of Titus Maccius Plautus, composed around the beginning of the second century BC, are the oldest works of Latin literature in existence.

Latin drama had, of course, been around long before Plautus. In a society where few could read, the best way to tell stories to a mass audience was by performing them. The mythology of Rome was transmitted and reenacted through the public rituals of Roman religion: the leaping dance of the Salian priests; the goatskin costumes of the Luperci; the Fetiales, solemnly casting their blood-dipped spear. Each ritual carried the memory of a story, even if the passage of years left the Romans unable to see clearly what the story might be.

The idea of putting on plays as entertainment may have come to Rome from the Etruscans, who, in their heyday, back in the sixth century BC, had developed a rich culture of festivals and shows. The Latin words *histrio* and *scaena*, 'actor' and 'stage', are probably Etruscan in origin. The evidence for early Roman drama is extremely thin but, given how much else the Romans and Etruscans had in common, it would be a surprise if Rome's sixth-century kings did not share the Etruscan enthusiasm for the stage.

After the fall of the monarchy in around 500 BC, the competing families of the new republican oligarchy had every incentive to keep up the tradition of dramatic shows. Aristocratic funerals became frequent occasions for drama: actors would recreate glorious moments in the life of the dead man, or from the history of his wider family. Theatre was a vital tool by which the great patrician clans wrote themselves into the legendary epoch of Roman history.

After 387 BC and the Gallic Sack, the evidence becomes a little clearer. According to Livy, stage shows became a part of Rome's official festive calendar in 364 BC, introduced as part of a great festival of Jupiter Optimus Maximus, the *Ludi Romani*. Supposedly, the novelty was a religious measure. Plays were added to the original programme of races and boxing in order to placate the gods after an outbreak of disease.

But the stage shows kept their place in the *ludi* not because they were holy but because they were fun. A whole theatrical culture developed: there were dances, mimes, burlesques, rustic farces, displays of improvised banter, re-enactments of Roman history. And of all these myriad works, a whole Roman dramatic tradition, stretching back centuries, nothing has survived. The first dramatist to leave a permanent trace was Plautus, a foreign author using an alien technology: the script.

* * *

In the fifth century BC, while Rome was still struggling to reinvent itself as a republic, the flourishing Greek city of Athens was enjoying a theatrical golden age. At the festival of Dionysus, in the shadow of the Acropolis, the great classical tragedians Aeschylus, Sophocles and Euripides shocked and inspired the people of Athens with dramatic scenes from legend, set to music or rendered in sophisticated metrical verse.

More popular still was the comedian, Aristophanes, whose plays – laced with obscenity, ferociously rude, brilliantly inventive – delighted the crowd, even as they terrorized the leading men of the young Athenian *demokratia.**

The Peloponnesian War divided Greece. The messy democracy of Athens was defeated by Spartan oligarchs; Greek power dwindled. Until, in 334 BC, a young prince named Alexander led an army of pike-wielding Macedonians eastwards against Persia on a campaign of conquest that spread Greek culture from Libya to the mountains of Afghanistan.

---

* Aristophanes's depiction of Socrates is supposed to have been so wildly insulting that the philosopher, who was in the audience, stood up in the crowd so that people could see how he really looked and behaved. When a jury later convicted Socrates of corrupting Athenian youth, his followers were convinced that Aristophanes was partly to blame.

Greek culture, in the fourth century BC, meant theatre. But after Alexander's death his loyal generals, dividing the Macedonian empire between them, promoted themselves to kings, and then to gods. It was no longer safe for aspiring playwrights to attempt too many jokes on the subject of politics. Old Comedy, as perfected by Aristophanes, was dead.

'New Comedy', spreading in Alexander's wake, would restrict itself to domestic concerns. The great theatre at Athens was now dominated by harmless stock characters: the cunning slave; the lusty old man; the lover-boy; the boastful soldier. These, obedient to the conventions of their genre, would move, in a reassuring manner, towards a satisfying conclusion in which, generally, order would be restored, Boy would marry Girl, parents would find lost children and the enemies of Love, pimps, husbands and bankers, would be laid low.*

These stories were suitable for everyone and they were widely enjoyed, all over the vast area where Greek was now the established *lingua franca*. The old Greek cities of southern Italy were no exception. Ancient metropolises like Croton and Tarentum had lively theatres of their own, connected to the wider culture of what was, by now, a Hellenistic world.

By this time, Greek comedy was a highly developed dramatic form, and one that was, despite its popular roots, essentially literary. The god-kings of the Hellenistic world established libraries. There, plays born for the stage lived on as texts, copied out on papyrus by careful scribes. Living dramas were captured and preserved like pinned butterflies, dusty specimens to be studied by the scholars of Athens, Antioch or Alexandria.

With study came sophistication. There was now a proper corpus of Greek drama, of works to be commented on, imitated and refined.

---

* The works of Menander, the greatest exponent of New Comedy, were thought completely lost until the twentieth century when surviving papyrus manuscripts were found, mixed with the papier mache of an Egyptian mummy case.

New writers could now be participants in a centuries-old literary conversation.

The Greek mastery of the written word, with all its advantages, was slow to arrive at Rome. At the start of the third century BC, while the Ptolemies were building the great library of Alexandria, stage shows in Rome were still being performed by improvisation and memory, lost as soon as they faded from their audiences' minds.

But, as Rome's power grew, new ideas began to reach the conquering city. After the trauma of the Gallic Sack, Rome slowly re-established its dominion over the plain of Latium, pushing southwards towards the Greek colonies in Campania. In 326 BC the Romans captured Naples. In 295 BC they subdued the Etruscans and the Samnites. In 272 BC, they defeated the Greeks of Tarentum. Each victory brought a new wave of slaves and captives to swell the population of Rome.

Into this warlike zone, on the frontiers of the Hellenistic world, Rome's first great comedian was born. He was neither a Greek nor a Latin. Titus Maccius Plautus was born around 250 BC in the small town of Sarsina, in Umbria, and grew up speaking a dialect of Oscan. Almost nothing is known about his early life. He may have been trained as a professional comedian or actor. That would explain his knowledge of Greek and of Greek comedy. It would also make sense of his name, which looks like a pseudonym: Maccius perhaps from *Maccus* – a stock character in traditional Italian farce – and Plautus meaning 'flat-footed'.*

All we know is that at some point, like so many other impoverished Italians, Plautus was drawn to Rome. He was a foreigner, speaking ill-gotten Latin; just another refugee from Italy's wars, another mouth for the city to feed. There was work to be had in Rome, at least. Plautus is supposed to have written three of his plays while labouring in a mill, treading the drive-wheel beside slaves, the lines in his head drowned out by the ceaseless grinding of the millstone. It was cruel

---

* One scholar, Amy Richlin, has suggested that the effect would be something like a modern playwright called R. Harpoe Clownshoes.

labour. Slave characters in Plautus's plays are forever being threatened with the dreadful prospect of being sent to work *in pistrinum*, that flour-covered hell.

But if Plautus did work in a mill, he did not have to toil there for long. The clever young Umbrian had arrived in Rome at a moment rich with opportunity for an aspiring dramatist. In 240 BC, when Plautus was around ten years old, one of Rome's immigrant Greeks, an ex-slave called Livius Andronicus, had been commissioned by the city magistrates to adapt some Greek tragedies and comedies into Latin.

These adaptations had proved very popular. By the time Plautus arrived in Rome the new movement towards Greek-style drama was taking off. A literary treasure trove, three centuries' worth of Greek writing, had been opened up in Rome: an endless supply of plays, carefully copied down by Greek scribes and ready for adaptation by anyone who could read Greek and write Latin.

The opportunity was there, and Plautus, an immigrant nobody, born between two cultures, was the man to seize it. 'Better get up and stretch your bums while you can,' as he wrote in one of his prologues. 'Here comes one of Plautus's endless shows.'

* * *

Plautus's surviving plays make no secret of their Greek antecedents. Characters have Greek names, the settings are Greek, the costumes are Greek, the plots are conventional specimens of Hellenistic drama.

But Plautus did more than simply translate Greek drama into Latin. In one play, *Curculio*, the eponymous hero unleashes a burst of xenophobic invective that is unmistakably Roman in origin: 'What about those Greeks in their cloaks,' Curculio exclaims to the audience, 'who walk about with covered heads, who stalk around bunged up with books and gift bags, who gather and gossip, those runaway slaves who get in your way, who get right up in your face, marching along with their *opinions*!'

Curculio, of course, is meant to be a Greek himself. This play is set in Greece. Curculio complains about Greeks in cloaks, while he himself is wearing one.

But Curculio's opinionated Greeks are not to be found on the streets of some notional Hellenistic town. Curculio, to the delight of his Roman audience, is talking about the Greek immigrants you can see any day on the streets of Rome.

If he meets any, he promises, he'll 'knock the farts out of them'.

So much is lost of Plautus's Roman theatre. The wooden stages on which the plays were performed rotted centuries ago; the spectators vanished into history, leaving no trace of themselves behind. Only the texts remain to us, pallid records of events that in their time were alive with energy – the fleeting charge that can only exist in the heat of the theatrical moment, between actors and their audience.

This makes it hard to feel the full impact of the location-shifting trickery Plautus uses in *Curculio*. In a city shaped by centuries of war, where Greekness and Romanness were deeply felt, where Romans felt simultaneously scornful of and threatened by their Greek neighbours, Plautus blurs the boundaries between the two. Greek characters suddenly speak like Romans.

Things get even more complicated if you consider the origins of the actors: mainly slaves or ex-slaves and probably Greeks from the south of Italy. That means, in prickly, pompous, parvenu Rome, you have real Greeks playing pretend Greeks who are really Romans who then complain about Greeks; slaves and ex-slaves playing citizens.

This is a crucial part of the frisson Roman drama would have provoked: that Romans should let slaves and foreigners tease them and boss them about. One of Plautus's favourite jokes is to make his actors, in character as snobbish Greeks, refer to Romans as 'barbarians' or 'porridge-eaters' and so on. When Plautus claims to have translated a Greek original he says he has 'barbarized' it: '*Plautus vortit barbare*'.

Plautus's plays are full of this sort of game. Like a picture on an old TV, the dramatic illusion flickers: now we are in Greece, now in Rome, now in Greece again.

And sometimes, Plautus smashes the illusion entirely. At one point in *Curculio*, the show's (Roman) producer suddenly wanders out on

to the stage. He is worried, he tells the audience, that he isn't going
to get his props back.

This is no brief interruption. Once 'Producer' has the limelight
he embarks – in the middle of a play set in Greek Epidaurus – on a
detailed and completely unprompted sociological tour of the Roman
Forum.

It is not a flattering portrait. 'Whoever wants to meet a perjurer,'
he begins, 'should head to the Comitium' – the public meeting space
below the Curia Hostilia where the senate meets.

'If you want to find a liar or a braggart, try the temple of Venus
Cloacina' – by the opening of Rome's great sewer, the Cloaca Maxima.

By the basilica you can find 'married men with more cash than
sense' and there too, not surprisingly, 'the clapped-out rent boys' with
their pimps. Down at the bottom end of the Forum are the filthy rich;
by the drain in the middle, the real show-offs; up at the top, by the
Lacus Curtius, the gossips gather to trade malicious whispers.

The old shops under the Palatine are infested with moneylenders;
the alley behind the Temple of Castor is for real dodgy types; Tuscan
Street, running down to the docks and the cattle market, is full of
prostitutes; the Velabrum slum close by is for butchers, bakers and
Etruscan soothsayers, none of whom are to be trusted. The men of the
Velabrum – and here, we may imagine the Producer leering meaning-
fully – they like a bit of 'turn and turn about'.

Bad enough to have some foreign stagehand being rude about the
sacred monuments and landmarks of the Roman republic. Worse
still if, as is almost certain, the play was actually being performed in
the Forum itself.

This is not just an imaginary tour, in other words. The places
Producer mentions so unkindly are right there, arranged in a great
arc around the auditorium and the audience, looking up, can follow
his accusing arm as he gestures from one degenerate hangout to the
next. It is as if the stage has broken its bounds and started spreading
out into the city. The invisible border between theatre and reality vanishes, and now the ancient buildings of the Roman Forum, steeped

in memory, in symbolic meaning, are populated by the grotesques of Greek comedy: randy old men; pimps and prostitutes; braggart soldiers.

How must the real soldiers in the crowd have felt, the veterans, stiff with wounds, when a mere actor dared to tease them about boasting by the shrine of Cloacina? How did the Forum's habitual loafers, who did indeed like to hang about by the drainage canal, enjoy being told they were nothing but hot air? When Producer pointed at 'perjurers' in the *Comitium*, was it the case that, as happened at later shows, the grandest members of the audience were actually sitting there? This, in a stern and hierarchical society like Rome's, was daring comedy.

* * *

Enter Pseudolus, the Cunning Slave.

Plautine comedy loves inversions. In Plautus, it is the rich and the mighty who are played for fools, while the spoils go to scroungers, parasites and slaves. In Plautus's play *Pseudolus* it is the eponymous slave who is the hero of the show.

One scene finds Pseudolus in a particularly triumphant mood. He has formulated a plan of attack against a hated enemy, a pimp named Ballio. He anticipates swift and total victory. Now, puffed up with martial exuberance, he breaks out into a merry little song:

'By Jupiter! How very well and charmingly all my projects today are turning out!… I have disposed my forces, my double and triple crosses, in such a way that, wherever I encounter the enemy… I'll conquer him easily!

'How nicely I shall blast this Ballio!' Pseudolus promises. 'I'll lay siege to his walls and capture his citadel this very day, so I will! I'll lead all my legions against him! Me and my allies will load ourselves up with plunder!'

These brave words are accompanied by brave music. Off to one side stands the piper, the *tibicen*, whose job it is to play Pseudolus through his song. This is not at all easy. It takes the most virtuoso musicianship to follow the complex patterns of long and short syllables that make up lyric verse; to anticipate the measures and match harmony and mood. On playbills for Roman shows, the name of the *tibicen* takes second place only to the playwright himself.

Musical numbers like this are the piper's big moments. Nimble fingers grip the twin stems of the *tibia*, the twin pipe with its doubled reeds. Cheeks puff out with the effort of the circular breathing that allows the *tibicen* to drive his melody always onward, inspiring the boastful slave on stage to greater heights of bombast and vainglory. The *tibia* is the instrument of Bacchus, the instrument of freedom, of madness, of abandon. It is the instrument the satyr Marsyas played in his musical contest with Apollo – the instrument with which the satyr dared outplay the immortal god, an insult for which Apollo flayed him alive. The *tibicen*, the piper, red-cheeked and untameable, is the spirit of the show.

Pseudolus is one of only two Plautus plays for which we know the date of the first performance: April 191 BC.* We even know where the play was shown. The first stage on which Pseudolus ever swaggered was set up opposite a new temple of the Magna Mater, on the southwest corner of the Palatine hill, overlooking the Lupercal cave and the cattle market. The stage was a temporary structure, built for the occasion, but there was no need to construct any seating. The audience sat on the stone steps of the temple podium, looking out over the city. At the top of the crowd, watching from the pillared darkness of the temple's inner chamber, was the image of the goddess herself: the *Magna Mater*, the Great Mother Cybele, the dark queen of Mount Ida presiding over plays in Rome.

Plautus's comedies were performed under the eyes of the gods, and in their honour. The various *ludi* at which plays were performed were religious festivals, city-wide holidays. The moneylenders of the Forum closed their stalls; the lawyers abandoned their positions by the Comitium; the perjurers and vote-mongers were silent. Instead,

---

* It was April by Roman reckoning at least. However, the Roman calendar at that time was badly out of step with the actual seasons. What the Romans called April was really the December of the previous year.

the streets were loud with the sound of pipes and drums, sacred songs, the stamping of dancers. The air smelled of incense and the smoke of animal sacrifice: fat and entrails burning on the altars to please Rome's gods; flesh to break the quotidian monotony of the Romans' staple porridge.

It was easy, on these festival days, for a skilful *tibicen* to pipe his audience, like the children of Hamelin, off into the world of comedy. Here, in the carnival world of Plautus's plays, the rules and certainties of Roman life were suspended, turned upside-down. Greeks might become Romans; stagehands might tease senators; slaves like Pseudolus might talk as if they were like generals marching to war. Comedy was no place for the mighty. Soldiers, fathers, rich old men, the men who ran Roman society, all had to be on their guard. The world of comedy was a world of tricks and traps – a world in which pride might be laid low.

* * *

Even cunning slaves, if they got ahead of themselves, might slip on one of Plautus's comic banana skins. One character who learns this lesson is the slave, Milphio, in a play called *Poenulus*, 'The Little Carthaginian'.

The play is getting on. Just as the bossy Prologue promised at the start, those audience members who didn't eat their beanicles before the show are regretting it, beginning to fidget.

But here comes a new character on to the stage, an unexpected distraction: enter Hanno, in outlandish foreign garb, followed by a retinue of barbarous-looking attendants.

'*Yth alonim ualonuth sicorathi symacom syth*,' he begins, '*chy malachthi in ythmum ysthyalm ych-ibarcu mysehi.*'

This is not Latin. Indeed it is not clear that it is anything at all. But, even if the speech is nonsense, the general sound is unmistakeable to the Roman audience. Hanno is speaking Punic, the language of Rome's deadliest enemies. With the play three-quarters done, the 'Poenulus' promised in the show's title has finally arrived: the 'little Punic man'. The little Carthaginian.

*

Qart Hadasht, or 'New City', was founded on the Gulf of Tunis by Phoenician settlers some time during the second half of the eighth century BC, one of several such 'Punic' colonies that the trading cities of the Levant planted on the African coast. Well situated, with a strong citadel, a good harbour and a rich agricultural hinterland, the city of Carthage prospered, gradually extending its dominion through north Africa and over the western Mediterranean to Sicily and Sardinia, the Balearic islands and the coast of Spain.

In many ways Carthage was the African twin of Rome. It was a powerful and expansionist city state, richer and more ambitious even than Rome was, led by a hereditary oligarchy – two chief magistrates elected annually and a deliberative council of old men. At first, contacts between the two powers were friendly. There were treaties in 509 and 348 BC, and a brief alliance against the Greek warlord Pyrrhus of Epirus in the 270s. But in 264 BC, competition between Rome and Carthage broke out into open hostility. A twenty-year war followed, with terrible losses on both sides. At last, Rome came out victorious.

Carthage was defeated, but only for a time. A generation later, in the 220s, Carthaginian generals embarked on a major programme of expansion in Spain, a vital source of potential wealth and manpower. The Romans, who had their own ideas about Spain, were alarmed, and moved to block them. In 219 BC, the first blows were struck of what would be known as the Second Punic War.

The outbreak of hostilities in Spain was hardly unexpected. The Romans, confident in their power, sent off an expeditionary force under a bold general, one Publius Cornelius Scipio. The Roman plan was the same as always: to storm in with the legions, blast the enemy out of their strongholds, put their towns to siege and load up with plunder. They advanced as if urged on by the piping of an invisible *tibicen*.

But while the Roman army was sailing westward, a Punic army was marching overland in the opposite direction. That winter an unexpected foreigner made his entrance on to the Italian scene, with a barbarous retinue. Hannibal Barca had crossed the Alps: a Carthaginian, but not so little.

*

Plautus's Hanno is a Carthaginian traveller. He is looking for his long-lost daughters who, unknown to him, are in this very city – this city that is meant to be somewhere in Greece, but feels like Rome. He is close. Unluckily for him, the first person he meets is the cunning slave, Milphio, walking along with his lovesick master Agorastocles.

'By Pollux,' exclaims the young master. 'He looks like a Carthaginian!'

'The man's a *gugga*,' Milphio agrees. 'Want me to try talking to him Punic fashion?'

'You know how?'

Milphio does not, but he is all confidence. 'Today,' he tells his master, 'there is no Carthaginian more Carthaginian than me.'

Squaring up to the foreign '*gugga*', the cunning slave deploys his non-existent language skills:

'*Avo*,' he begins, a genuine Carthaginian greeting. But that's all he has. He is forced back into Latin. He can try, at least, to speak it loud and slow and in a funny accent.

'WHO ARE YOU? WHAT CITY ARE YOU FROM?'

'*Anno byn mytthymballe udradait annech.*'

'He says he's Hanno, from Carthage. Son of Mytthumbalis.'

'*Avo*,' says Hanno.

'He says, hello.' Milphio is sure of that one word at least. But he is flailing. '*Avo donni*,' he tries.

'*Mehar bocca!*' – Hanno, sharply.

'Better you than me…' Trying again: 'WHAT DID YOU COME TO THIS CITY FOR? WHAT ARE YOU AFTER?'

'*Muphursio!*'

'What did he say?' the young master chips in.

'*Miuulec hianna!*'

'Why has he come?'

'Don't you hear?' Milphio blusters. 'He says he wants to donate some African mice for the procession at the *ludi*.'

In December 218 BC, thirty-seven war elephants lined up for battle on the banks of the River Trebbia in northern Italy. It was Hannibal Barca, the finest general of his generation, who had brought them across rivers and over the mountains, his marching column struggling through bitter miles of rock and snow. Hannibal had dared the impossible to bring his thirty-seven monsters into Italy, and now the Romans would see what they could do.

Across the plain, the legionaries stamped their feet in the icy air. They were wet and cold from the river crossing, and had gone without breakfast. But the Romans were accustomed to victory. They advanced to the fight.

This was the first full-scale engagement between Hannibal and the Romans, and it was a disaster. Lying concealed to the rear of the Roman army was Hannibal's brother Mago with a picked force of cavalry and foot.* The Romans, beset by elephants in front and ambushers behind, crumbled and were massacred by the riverbank.

Hanno is still talking gibberish, and Milphio is running out of steam. For a while he thinks the Carthaginian may be a salesman of spades and pitchforks; or perhaps he has come to dig the young master's garden? Wait… another idea, he wants… to be put under crates and then crushed to death with stones, Carthaginian style?

'*Gunebbal samem lyryla!*' Hanno is growing frustrated.

'Tell me what's going on!' the young master demands. 'What is he saying?'

Milphio is defeated. 'Now, by Hercules,' he confesses, 'I really have no idea.'

It is time for Hanno to spring his surprise. 'So that you may *get* the idea,' he says, clear as you like, 'from here on out, I'll speak Latin. What a worthless and wicked slave you must be to play a far-travelled foreigner for a fool.'

'Well you, by Hercules,' Milphio replies, 'are a telltale and a fraud, who has come to entrap us, you double-tongued snake!'

* Mago, a brilliant commander in his own right, was always overshadowed by his brother Hannibal. He achieved a sort of immortality of his own, however: Mago was the founder, supposedly, of the Balearic port of Mahon – a town famous around the world as the birthplace of mayonnaise.

*

Milphio should have seen it coming. Carthaginians were famous for their command of languages – an ability that was part of a general tricksiness that the Romans had learned, painfully, to respect. Romans in Plautus's day would talk about *punica fides* – 'Punic faith' – meaning 'no faith at all'.

It was a comfort to Roman egos to talk up Carthaginian cunning. 'This was what passed for Punic fortitude', wrote one Latin historian: 'tricks and ambushes and pre-prepared stratagems. And these are the surest excuses for the overthrow of our strength, seeing as we were tricked rather than truly defeated.'

The Battle of the River Trebbia had been the first lesson, and a hard one too. But the Romans learned slowly. The following year, a Roman army was pursuing Hannibal along the shore of Lake Trasimene when, out of the morning mist, volleys of whirring javelins announced the presence of Hannibal's Gallic and Spanish light infantry on the high ground along the Roman flank. In the rout that followed, 15,000 Romans were cut down.

The military situation in Italy was now desperate. All the Romans could do was buy time. Rome's normal constitution was suspended. A *dictator*, Quintus Fabius Maximus, was appointed to take supreme command during the crisis. Whenever Hannibal offered battle, Fabius retreated. Fabius Maximus Cunctator, they called him in Rome. Fabius the Delayer.

As the months went by, the Romans became bored of Fabius's caution, and prepared to face Hannibal again. The army they raised in 216 BC was the largest that had ever been assembled on Italian soil: eight full legions, plus contingents from the allied Italian cities, making a total force of perhaps 80,000 men, supported by 6,000 Roman and allied cavalry.

Hannibal could muster around 50,000 troops of his own, a barbarous, polyglot bunch: Gauls, Spaniards, Balearic slingers, Moorish skirmishers, his veteran Libyan infantry and, best of all, the fearsome Numidian light cavalry from the fringes of the Sahara – 4,000 fighters born to the saddle, who could put a javelin through a man's eye at full gallop without breaking stride.

Still, the Carthaginians were badly outnumbered, and the legions lining up that midsummer morning near the little town of Cannae must have made a fine, confident sight – the best heavy infantry in the world, formed up neatly in deep blocks called maniples, disciplined and steady. With mail shirts and helmets they were far better equipped than most of the Gauls and Iberians in Hannibal's battle line. They fought with the deadly, workmanlike *gladius* in the right hand and in the left the heavy-bossed *scutum* – the long Roman infantry shield.

In front of the heavy infantry, the skirmishers taunted each other with javelins, scurrying forward to throw – a deadly risk – then dashing back to the relative safety of the lines. Slingstones and arrows whistled overhead, fired by mercenaries from Crete and the Balearics, to bounce off armour or bury themselves in flesh.

And then, with much blowing of trumpets and shouting of orders and last-minute dressing of lines, the general advance began. Eight legions' worth of feet kicked up a cloud of dust that hung in the parching air, and each man fixed his eyes on the man in front, while the skirmishers filtered back through the Roman columns. For the soldiers towards the rear of this deep formation, the only way to know when the lines met was the sudden sound of weapons crashing on shields and foreign war cries. Then men, wounded or exhausted, started dropping back from the front to be replaced by those behind them, but still the columns advanced. Hannibal's Celts were putting up a brave fight, but they were outnumbered and overmatched. The centre of the Carthaginian line was bending backwards like a rubber band under Roman pressure. It could not be long before it snapped.

Then, quite quickly, the battle turned upside-down. Hannibal, in true Carthaginian style, revealed his twist. The Romans were not pushing forward to victory; they were pushing themselves, yet again, into a trap.

The Carthaginian infantry line had started off as a sort of backwards crescent, with the horns pulled away from the Roman maniples. But as the Celts in the centre retreated, the horns stayed where they were. The line that had been convex was now concave, with the Romans in the middle.

Now the Romans on each flank saw movement in the wings. From behind each of Hannibal's two horns, new soldiers were coming, swords in hand. These were the Libyans, the veterans who had followed Hannibal from Africa, marching fast in column to take their places on the Roman flanks. Most unsettling of all, these men were wearing the plundered equipment of Roman troops: high-quality Roman shields and armour, taken from the bodies of those who had died in the previous battles of the war.

At the same moment came a new and dreadful music from the Roman rear. Hannibal's barbarian horsemen, Celts and Iberians and Numidians, had driven off the Roman cavalry and now a mad wailing of horns gave the signal for these wild riders to throw themselves into the back of the Roman line. The soldiers there at the rear were the wounded, the fearful, men exhausted from the front lines, light-armed skirmishers. Now, unable to resist Hannibal's cavalry, they were thrown into a desperate panic. Somehow, in the dust and chaos, the battle had been turned on its head: the victors were now the losers, the rear was now the front, the barbarians were dressed up as Romans. A heroic Roman assault had turned, spun by its own momentum, into a nightmare.

* * *

A few weeks after the battle at Cannae, says the historian Livy, a crowd gathered in the Comitium, by the Roman Forum. A sombre crowd, it must have been, women and children and a few old men, united in their common grief and now tormented by a tenuous filament of hope. They came to hear the fate of the survivors from Cannae – the fate of the captives, whose spokesman was now begging the senate to buy their freedom.

Several thousand Roman soldiers had been taken after the battle. Hannibal set their ransom at 300 silver pieces per man. Ten of the captives were sent to Rome to put his terms to the senate. Slavery and freedom hung on the decision of the Roman Fathers: should the state pay to redeem men who had disgraced themselves by surrender?

Speaking for the captives, as Livy tells it, was one of the few men to have come unscathed through the thick of the battle itself. Now, to defend against the charge of cowardice, he needed to make the senators understand the things that he had seen: how the Roman army, encircled on all sides, had been crushed together in their panic; the horror of being packed like cattle, too tight to move your sword arm, so tight that the arrows and javelins plunging out of the dust-choked sky could hardly miss. He had to convey, somehow, the memory of the earth all slippery with blood; of feet tripping on bodies and armour and hacked-off limbs; the faecal stench of freshly opened guts; the cries of the wounded starting out on their hard slow journey towards death. It was not cowardice that forced the captives to surrender, he tried to explain, but despair. They had only survived at all because the Carthaginians, after hours of butchery, were too exhausted to keep on cutting them down.

Around 48,000 Roman soldiers are thought to have died at Cannae, mortality on an astonishing scale, hardly to be repeated until the advent of industrialized warfare two thousand years later. And these losses were suffered by a state that had endured two calamitous battles already, and by a city whose total citizen population at that time cannot have been higher than around 150,000. Livy may hardly be exaggerating when he says that there was no married woman in Rome who had not lost either a husband or a son. The annual *ludi* of the corn goddess Ceres had to be cancelled, since the entire city was in mourning.

Somewhere in this weeping city, very probably, was Titus Maccius Plautus. His first play came out in Rome within a decade of Cannae. And although his works, following the traditions of New Comedy, are hardly political, the emotional landscape from which they sprang was a landscape scarred by the horrors of the Hannibalic War.

One play, *Captivi*, deals directly with the subject of war prisoners. Slumped on stage, in a state of deepest despondency, we find Ergasilus, a flatterer, occasional wit and full-time scrounger of free lunches. He sighs pathetically. The most generous of his usual hosts, Philopolemus, went off to the wars and has been taken captive by the enemy.

Now the scrounger unburdens his sorrows to the prisoner's father: 'I am bones and skin,' he wails, 'wretched from thinness...'

'Don't cry!' – the father attempts a comforting gesture.

But both men are weeping now. 'If you, a stranger, take his misfortune so hard, what should I make of it, when I have lost my only son!' The father is touched by Ergasilus's clear distress. 'You are noble, to treat your friend's calamity as if it were your own!'

He puts a friendly hand on Ergasilus's shoulder.

'*Eheu!*' Ergasilus cries, shaking his head and pointing at his stomach. 'It hurts *here!*'

We have no date for *Captivi*, but Plautus died around 184 BC. There might have been veterans of the Hannibalic Wars at his funeral, scars still visible after thirty years.

Whenever *Captivi* was first performed, therefore, the recovery of prisoners of war would have been a matter of recent and painful history. On stage, a father weeps for his captive son – and there will have been many in that first audience who shared that sadness, many who remembered the mournful gathering in the Comitium after Cannae, reaching out their arms towards the Senate House, begging the senators to pay the ransom, to restore their children to them.

At the end of Plautus's *Captivi*, the lost son returns. The captives are freed. Ergasilus, the starving scrounger, celebrates with the dinner of his dreams: pork and lamb and spring chicken; ham, lamprey, pickled fish, mackerel, sting-ray, nice soft cheese; bacon and sow's udder; sizzling pork rind.

But though Ergasilus on stage got his dinner, none of the prisoners from Cannae were in the audience to watch him eat it. The senators, following the stern tradition of their forefathers, refused to pay the ransom. The captured Romans were sold as slaves, sent off to quarries, mines or galley-benches. None of these was a place in which anyone lasted long.

*

Hannibal stayed in Italy for a decade after Cannae; a decade of fear and hardship for Rome, of cautious shadowing manoeuvres in southern Italy, of sieges and counter sieges.

In 211 BC, for the first time, he came within sight of Rome itself. Mounted on a black horse, he rode a slow circuit of the city, and the Romans gathered on the walls to watch him go by. Straight-backed and still, he passed before his silent audience, the terror of Italy, the undefeatable Carthaginian.

But the Romans, so the story goes, put on a show of their own. That day, by chance, the plot of land on which Hannibal's army was encamped came up for sale. All Rome's senators gathered for the auction, competing to buy the enemy-occupied land at an inflated price, noisily certain that Rome would win it back again.

And Rome's courage held. Hannibal was a brilliant general, but he could not summon men out of thin air. It must have felt to him as though the Romans could. However many men Hannibal killed, there were always more, gathering from the towns and cities of Italy. The Romans even, in a very Plautine inversion of social norms, recruited two legions of slaves, who marched to battle led by an impeccable aristocrat named Tiberius Sempronius Gracchus, winning their freedom at the point of a sword.

And while Hannibal prowled through Italy, the Romans were advancing on other fronts. In Spain, a young member of the Scipio family, a survivor of Cannae, known to history as Scipio Africanus, was conquering Carthaginian outposts one by one. In 204 BC he crossed over from Spain to Africa at the head of a Roman army.

After a decade and a half on campaign, Hannibal and his few surviving veterans were called back to Carthage to defend their homeland. At the Battle of Zama, Scipio Africanus and Hannibal met. Hannibal had war elephants and his own tactical brilliance to rely on, but Scipio, brilliant too, had bought the loyalty of the deadly Numidian cavalry. After a hard fight, Hannibal was defeated for the first time. Carthage, its coffers depleted, sued for peace. Rome was victorious.

* * *

Victory over Carthage marked the beginning of a new phase in the history of the Roman republic. Having crippled their only real rival in the west, the Romans enjoyed mastery over vast stretches of the Mediterranean, including the fertile fields of Sicily and the mines of Spain.

Now the attention of Rome's battle-hardened armies turned eastward, across the Adriatic. The Romans had imported Greek comedy. They exported legions. Within half a century of Zama, Greece, heartland of classical culture, had been absorbed into Rome's dominion. A new Roman era had begun.

As for Plautus, the one-time mill worker became a star. The stages of Italy echoed to his comedies and – sincerest flattery – to other comedies that had nothing to do with him at all but still optimistically bore his name.

He had arrived at the perfect moment in Roman history, a moment when a new and exciting art form, Greek-style comedy in Latin, was just being pioneered. Just as importantly, he arrived in a Rome where comedy was badly needed; a Rome that had suffered traumatic losses, that had triumphed, but only at an agonizing price. There were wounds in the collective Roman psyche that were too raw to touch on openly – but the upside-down world of comedy, perhaps, provided a space in which Rome could heal.

4

CONCORD

The Gracchus brothers

——

133–121 BC

U P ON THE Capitoline hill, the plebeian assembly has gathered. Brown-clad figures press between the vast old pillars
of Jupiter Optimus Maximus, whose temple looms above
the open space. In the shadow of this monument to Rome's power,
the people gathered here look nervous and uncomfortable. This city
is theirs, but it has not always been kind to them.

A brief hush. Heads turn to follow pointing fingers. From somewhere in the middle of the crowd, a young man appears, clambering
up on to a wooden platform. You can tell from the whiteness of his
toga that he is a nobleman – a man with money to pay the fullers who
rinse greasy wool in urinal vats; a man with slaves to drape the long
semicircle of cloth about him. And yet, for reasons the plebeians do
not fully understand, this aristocrat has made himself their champion.

He speaks, and his words are passed through the crowd. He is
Tiberius Gracchus. They know him. They know he has been a soldier. They know he will fight for them. He has promised them land,
dignity, a future beyond the damp city slums.

But now he needs their help: he will fight for them, but they must
vote for him.

There are cheers. The mood lifts. Certainly they will stand with
Tiberius Gracchus. This is what they have gathered here to do.

Then, signs of trouble. Something has changed at the back of the crowd. Everyone is still shouting, but the tone is somehow different. There are cries of protest, then alarm, as the assembled plebeians realize that not everyone here is on the same side. A new element has started pouring into the Capitoline enclosure, an infusion of hostile intent whose advancing presence, in this sea of heads, is manifest as a sort of angry, standing wave.

What is happening? Another toga-clad aristocrat has clambered up at the back of the crowd and is gesturing something at Tiberius Gracchus on the stage. The noise is deafening now. The word is passed back. The newcomer is ushered through the crowd, burrowing his way between plebeian elbows. He has been with the senate, he says, and the situation is bad. The plutocrats have armed their supporters to stop the people voting. They will surely soon be here.

Some among the plebeians look for weapons. But the warning has come too late. The hostile senators are here now, ready to fight, togas wrapped around their left arms to fend off blows. Hard years have taught Tiberius's peasants not to punch their betters. They hesitate, then break, stampeding like the cattle they are no longer rich enough to own. The voting urns are abandoned. The benches of the assembly place are smashed under trampling feet. The wooden fragments will make useful weapons. The senators stoop to arm themselves with these ruins of Roman democracy, then come striding on.

Tiberius watches the rich in their white wool parting the crowd. He sees a few men try to stop them, and sees those men fall. He turns, but he has waited too long. Already hostile hands tangle in his clothes. He shrugs off his toga, the garment of a citizen and magistrate. Bare in his tunic, he recoils from snarling faces; trips, falls, tries to get up again. A young man – a colleague, someone he knows quite well – clubs him down with a bench-leg, and then he is hit again, and again, until it is clear that he will not be getting up any more.

* * *

Once, long ago, Romulus and Remus went to build a city. They quarrelled. Remus was killed. The soil on which Rome was founded was stained with blood. And this, the Romans understood, was the natural state of things among lawless men.

In order to have a city, there had to be rules. There were tens, then hundreds of thousands of people within Rome's walls, each with their own hungers, their own ambitions. But they lived together in comparative harmony, most of the time. They respected the ancient rules that bound them. The rules, written and unwritten, that constituted and preserved the city of Rome.

To give the rules power, the Romans fortified them with stories. The rules were old, the Romans insisted. It suited them to believe, so far as was possible, that things had always been done in a similar way, to trace their traditions back to the earliest epoch of Roman legend.

The great lawgiver of Roman myth was Numa Pompilius, successor to Romulus, second of Rome's seven kings. In those first days of Rome, it was Numa, as the poet Ovid wrote, 'who softened the temper of hasty and warlike Romans by teaching them just laws, and the fear of the gods'.

King Numa's laws were backed by the gods themselves. Numa was the lover of a nymph, Egeria, a wise spirit of stream and forest and pool. At midnight trysts, under the boughs of sacred oaks, she whispered in the king's ear the secrets of the immortals.

Instructed by Egeria, Numa dared to trap two of Rome's gods, Picus and Faunus, as they were drinking on the Aventine hill. Picus, the prophetic woodpecker, struggled against Numa's shackles. Faunus shook his moss-covered horns in grave protest. But Numa refused to free them until they helped him summon the father of the immortals, Jupiter himself.

The summoned god demanded a great sacrifice: a severed head, a human, a life. A fresh-cut onion bulb, some human hair, and a newly killed fish, the wise king gave him. And Jupiter, laughing at Numa's bold deceit, gave his blessing to Numa's god-fearing Rome.

There was an understanding in early Rome between gods and kings. Kings were distinguished by the right to take 'auspices' – to peer into the future by interpreting the flight of birds as Romulus himself had done. Divine favour, in those days, was always confirmed by unmistakeable signs and auguries. A king was not just raised up by men; he was *inaugurated* by the gods.

This divine connection extended to the Roman aristocracy. The so-called 'patricians', the 'fathers' of the state, men of the richest and most distinguished families, were distinguished from their fellow citizens by religious authority as much as naked power. Priesthoods in Rome, vital links between the community and the gods, could only be held by men of patrician blood.

This religious authority allowed the patricians to serve as king-makers. When a king died, the privilege of taking auspices reverted to the patrician class. It was the patricians, therefore, who chose – or found by divination – the next man on whom the favour of the gods would fall.

The patricians maintained Roman religion. They also upheld Rome's monarchy. And these two roles amounted to much the same thing. The city's political order was inseparable from its sacred order, and the patricians were guardians of both.

The kings ruled by the favour of the gods. Until, in 509 BC, according to the traditional narrative, the line of kings came to an end. The last king, Tarquin the Proud, abandoned the lawful monarchy of his predecessors. He became a tyrant, and was overthrown in an aristocratic coup, led by Lucius Junius Brutus. Rome would have new laws: it would no longer be a monarchy, but a republic.

The aristocrats who established the republic did their best to ensure that the new order retained the aura of divine approval which the monarchy had enjoyed. The patricians kept their custodianship of Rome's priesthoods. Once kingmakers, they now served as consuls, the chief magistrates of the republic, two elected each year for a one-year term. Like kings, the consuls had the power to take auspices. They kept the old insignia of kings, the *fasces*, birch rods bundled round an axe, to symbolize the royal power of life and death.

And if the gods really needed Rome to have a king, well, there was one, in a sense: a priest known as the *rex sacrorum* – the king of sacred matters. This '*rex*' was not the real thing at all, a king only insofar as religious traditions demanded one. Still, as the story of Numa's onions proved, the gods could sometimes be fobbed off with a stand-in.

The rebellious patricians had gathered what legitimacy they could to fortify their new republic. Even so, the overthrow of the kings had shown that change was possible, that the rules could be bent. There were some in Rome who hoped they might bend further.

In 494 BC, the story goes, a crowd of poor Romans gathered up on the Aventine.* Here, where Numa had summoned Jupiter from the sky, a humble mob assembled to make its own compact with the gods. Wealthy Romans, the patricians and their dependents, dismissed this gathering of 'the masses', the lowly *plebs*. But the 'plebeian assembly', as the crowd learned to call itself, would be a transformative power in Roman politics.

What happened in 494 BC is supposed to have been something like a general strike. The plebs were oppressed by debt, and by the tyranny of the rich. So, they withdrew themselves from the city. By going to the Aventine, they put themselves outside Rome's sacred boundary, the *pomoerium*. Symbolically, they put themselves outside the community, beyond the city's rules.

This 'Aventine Secession' resulted in the creation of a sort of parallel Roman state. The plebeians created their own assembly, the *concilium plebis*, which could pass its own resolutions, or 'plebiscites'. Presiding over this assembly were plebeian magistrates called tribunes, initially two, to match the patrician consuls, although the number was soon increased to five and then ten. The plebs swore to obey their tribunes, and the tribunes swore to protect them from patrician injustice, from debt-slavery and arbitrary punishment.

To give these new institutions their proper force, the plebs, of course, invoked the gods. The assembly bound itself with a terrible

---

* Secessions of the plebs came, during the later republic, to be strongly associated with the Aventine hill, which had deep religious significance to the plebeian movement. Livy reports, however, a well-supported tradition that during this first secession the plebs withdrew not to the Aventine but to the Mons Sacer, a hill to the north of Rome.

oath, an act of collective resolution known as a *lex sacrata*. Anyone who harmed even a hair on a tribune's head, the plebs declared, was to be considered *sacer*. That is, the offender's spirit was forfeit to the gods; he was no longer welcome in the world of the living, and all parties to the oath should exert all their strength to ensure he did not linger there. By this oath, mob justice was given the force of divine command; violent retribution became a sacred duty. The tribunes of the plebs, in their persons, were to be inviolable.

The 'conflict of the orders', between the patricians and the plebeians, stretched over generations. Plebeian victories were hard won. After the secession and the foundation of the plebeian assembly in 494 BC, it still took years of agitation before the plebeians were able, in 451 BC, to force a major reform. The rules of the young republic were inadequate, the plebs insisted, unjust and opaque. They allowed patricians to act like tyrants. Under intense plebeian pressure, a decemvirate, or ten-man commission, was appointed to examine and improve the laws of the state.

The decemvirs' new, improved code ran, in its final version, to twelve chapters. These Twelve Tables, as they were known, were engraved in bronze and displayed in the Roman Forum. Rome's laws were there for patrician and plebeian alike to read and know – for all to invoke in their own protection. Four hundred years later, Roman schoolboys were still set the Twelve Tables to learn by heart, the antique code with its obscure provisions and primitive Latin: 'If he summons to law, he is to go. If he does not go, he is to go. If he does not go, he is to call to witness.' Or: 'They are to make a road. Unless they laid it with stones, he is to drive carts where he shall wish.' The rules were crude, incomplete, inelegant. But they represented something vital about the community that brought them forth, and were the prized public possessions of the citizens of Rome.

After the constitutional upheaval that accompanied the publication of the Twelve Tables, the plebeian assembly and the plebeian tribunes were recognized as a legitimate part of the republican state. But plebeians were excluded from priesthoods and from the traditional magistracies. The consuls, inheritors of the power of the kings, were patricians. And tables of law would not feed a family, nor help a farmer pay his debts.

So the conflict continued. The capture and sack of Rome by the Gauls in 387 BC was cause for unrest and recrimination. How bravely the patricians had behaved, plebeians were sternly reminded, when the old men of Rome's great families waited in the Forum to die by Gallic blades. How wrong the unruly plebs had been to expel the patrician Camillus before the disastrous battle at the Allia! The whole episode was a hard lesson in respecting one's betters, at least in one telling of it.

But the privations caused by the recent Gallic raid fell hardest on the poor. Land was short. Harvests had been ruined. Many poor farmers fell into debt-bondage, selling themselves to wealthy landowners, their condition little better than that of slaves. Resentment grew. In 384 BC there was a major outbreak of unrest. Marcus Manlius, one of the heroes of the Gallic Sack, was executed, thrown from the Tarpeian rock for stirring up the plebs in hope of achieving some kind of populist tyranny. There was trouble again in 380 BC, and in 378, when Rome's citizens were called upon to devote scarce resources to the construction of a new rampart, the so-called Servian Wall, that ringed the city with huge blocks of tufa stone.

At last, in 376 BC by Livy's chronology, the plebeian tribunes presented a set of urgent demands to the patrician establishment. First, patricians were to be prevented from occupying all the public land, the *ager publicus*, that Rome had acquired through its expansion and conquests. Second, there was to be some relief for poor Romans, buried beneath unpayable debts. Third, the patrician monopoly on the great offices of the state was to end. Plebeians – meaning, by now, anyone who was not a patrician – were to be admitted to the consulship.

For ten years the patricians held out against these demands. But the tribunes, plebeian though they were, had a powerful tool at their disposal. The personal inviolability they had gained through the plebeian *lex sacrata* – that special aura of sanctity which the great plebeian oath had conferred – had naturally developed into a more active power, the tribunician veto. If a tribune interposed himself as an obstacle to the business of the state, that tribune, being inviolable, was impossible to remove. The tribunes, with their vetoes, could paralyse the republic.

Camillus himself, the saviour of Rome, is supposed to have come out of retirement to broker a compromise. The plebeian demands were met. The conflict of the orders was settled, at least for the time being. Camillus vowed a temple dedicated to the personification of Roman civil harmony: to the goddess Concord, whose calm and beneficent spirit, it was hoped, would rule forever from her new sanctuary under the Capitoline hill, looking out over the Roman Forum.

In this way, over many decades of struggle and negotiation, the republic developed and refined its constitution, the web of interlocking laws, traditions and religious taboos that bound and fortified the Roman state.

It was no small thing, for a city in those days, to avoid the endless cycles of demagoguery and despotism, corruption, oligarchy, populism, anarchy, murder, civil war that characterized ancient politics. Again and again, the great cities of Greece had wasted their energies in such infighting, until their power was eclipsed, first by Macedon and then by Rome.

The Greek historian Polybius, taken as a captive to Rome in the second century BC, marvelled at the political stability of the all-conquering city, which seemed to him to combine the best features of monarchical, aristocratic and democratic government. The consuls wielded the power of wise kings. The people (those people, at least, who were adult, male and free) chose the consuls in yearly elections, while their liberties were defended by the tribunes. Meanwhile, the aristocrats wielded power through their assembly, the senate, whose wise counsel guided magistrates and people alike. Each part of the Roman state served as a check upon the power of the others. 'It is impossible,' Polybius declared, 'to find a better political system than this.'

The plebeians, in 367 BC, had secured themselves a place in this harmonious system. Plebeians were elected to consulships. They sat among the greybeards of the senate. And yet, the very victory that broke the patrician monopoly on power, proved, in the end, to be a defeat for the Roman poor. The leaders of the plebeians, bold and ambitious men, used popular discontent to thrust themselves into the aristocracy. But, having achieved the heights of power, they forgot the suffering of the ordinary people who put them there. Plebeians and patricians combined to form a new aristocracy. As the power of the Roman republic grew, surviving the traumas of Pyrrhus and Hannibal and the Punic wars, the richest Romans grew only richer. Over the course of the third century BC the senate, composed of patricians and the very wealthiest plebeians, came to dominate the republic. The tribunes of the plebs, plebeian in name only, vetoed whatever their senatorial friends and patrons told them to. At least, for the time being.

* * *

Some time around the year 163 BC, three and a half centuries after the formation of the Roman republic, Tiberius Sempronius Gracchus was born. He was followed, in 154 BC, by a brother, Gaius. Two boys, born into a family that, although it was in a technical sense plebeian, had become one of the grandest aristocratic families in Rome.

The boys' father, also named Tiberius, had been a credit to the plebeian but proud lineage of the Sempronii Gracchi, twice consul and once censor. He died when the boys were young, leaving behind a memory of stern rectitude and impeccable aristocratic virtue.

Their mother, Cornelia, was a patrician, a daughter of the famous Cornelian clan and a model of noble womanhood: intelligent, educated, able to discuss philosophy and poetry as easily in Greek as in Latin. So famous were her qualities that, after her husband's death, she is supposed to have received an offer of marriage from Ptolemy VIII of Egypt, the pharaoh himself. Cornelia preferred, however, to be a Roman widow than an Egyptian queen, remaining for the rest of her life what the Romans called an *univira* – a one-man woman. She had borne twelve children for her husband, and of those twelve only three survived past childhood. The other nine she loved and lost with a fortitude that would have made her ancestors proud.

These were no ordinary ancestors. Cornelia's father was Publius Cornelius Scipio, known as Scipio Africanus, the conqueror of Carthage, the only Roman ever to have won a battle against Hannibal. There was hardly a boy in Rome, in other words, who could boast a more illustrious ancestry than Tiberius and Gaius Gracchus. Their father had been one of the leading men of the republic. But their grandfather, on their mother's side, was the very saviour of Rome, the man who had brought a triumphant end to the terrors of the Second Punic War. With such forebears as these, great things were expected of the Gracchus brothers.

In those high years of the Roman republic, the ultimate measure of success, for an aristocrat, was success in politics. Let barbarian chieftains dream of blood, of battle exploits hymned by obedient bards. Young Romans were to dream, above all, of winning elections. The practice of politics, after all, was a game that had been sanctified by centuries of religion and tradition, a game that provided a safe outlet for natural aristocratic rivalry. In the game of politics, the excesses of aristocratic ambition could be circumscribed, hedged about by Rome's ancient thicket of rules and customs. It was natural that a young man should hunger for glory, but his behaviour should never stray beyond the limits of the what the Romans called the custom of the ancestors, the *mos maiorum*.

Law and tradition laid out a clear path for young aristocrats like Tiberius and Gaius Gracchus to follow. They called it the *cursus honorum*, a sequence of magistracies that led to the consulship. To be elected consul was among the highest honours a Roman could attain. Former consuls, men of 'consular rank', held the places of honour in the senate. The nobility of a man's birth was reckoned above all by the number of '*consulares*' he could count among his ancestors.

But the path was not easy. Each year, ten men might be elected to the quaestorship, the most junior magistracy of the *cursus honorum*.

But with increasing seniority came increasing competition. Only four men each year could become aediles. Only four could become praetors. And those four praetors would soon be vying for just two consulships.

And even the first step, becoming quaestor, was not easily taken. Though he might aspire to wear the toga and take his seat among the senators, a Roman aristocrat, before anything else, had to serve out his time as a soldier. It might take ten years spent with the army for a young man to prove himself ready for the rigours of politics in Rome.

It was with soldiering, therefore, that Tiberius Gracchus's short career began. He had the blood of Scipio Africanus in his veins, the great ancestor who destined him for glory. But the international scene was much changed since Africanus's day. Victory over Carthage had cleared the most daunting obstacle to Roman expansion. In the fifty years following Scipio's triumph over Hannibal at the Battle of Zama in 202 BC, Rome's nearest rivals had fallen fast. In 197 BC, at the Battle of Cynoscephalae, Roman legionaries proved their tactical superiority over the once all-conquering Macedonian phalanx. At the Battle of Magnesia, in 190 BC, Scipio Africanus and his brother broke the power of the mighty Seleucid empire, greatest of the Hellenistic successor states. In 168 BC, at the Battle of Pydna, a Roman consul, Lucius Aemilius Paullus, defeated Perseus, the last king of Macedonia, winning a fortune in gold, silver and slaves in the process.

These victories secured Rome's dominance over great swathes of the Mediterranean and opened up the riches of the Hellenistic world for Roman exploitation. At the same time, they created a difficulty for aspiring young Romans. As Alexander the Great complained at the height of his power: there were no more worlds to conquer – or at least, no more worlds that seemed much worth conquering. The only major war going in the middle of the second century BC was a colonial war against tribesmen living in the wild hinterlands of Spain, a war that had so far been fought with much blood but very little glory.

Romans in Tiberius Gracchus's day had to make do as best they could. And towards the end of the 150s BC, an opportunity for worthwhile military exploits began to make itself apparent in Africa, where the Carthaginians, twice defeated but still proud, were chafing under the conditions of the peace they had accepted after the Hannibalic war. Small displays of the old Carthaginian spirit attracted intense and hostile Roman scrutiny. Rome had not forgotten how hard the Punic wars had been, how close the republic had come to destruction.

A party favouring war began to form in the senate. The leader of these hawks was Marcus Porcius Cato, known as Cato the Elder, a man so devoted to displays of antique Roman austerity that he drank vinegar to quench his thirst, the better to pickle any lingering softness of spirit. He made a habit of adding a bitter little nonsequitur to his speeches during senatorial debates: 'furthermore, I believe, *Carthago delenda est* – Carthage must be destroyed.'

An ill-advised Carthaginian attack on the neighbouring kingdom of Numidia provided a pretext. In 149 BC, a Roman expeditionary force landed in Africa. Carthage, hopelessly outmatched, surrendered at once. But Rome, with the gadfly Cato biting at its flanks, was determined not to take yes for an answer. Roman demands grew progressively harsher: first hostages, then complete disarmament, then, finally, the abandonment of the city of Carthage itself. Facing deportation, the Carthaginians prepared instead to die where they stood.

Here, in the final extermination of Rome's deadliest enemy, was an accomplishment of which a young Roman might be proud. Every nobleman in Rome was trying to get himself assigned to the expeditionary force but Tiberius Gracchus had a decisive advantage. The consular election of 148 BC, as the siege of Carthage entered its critical phase, had been won by Scipio Aemilianus, Tiberius Gracchus's brother-in-law.

Scipio Aemilianus was in many ways a difficult relation to have. He was married to Sempronia, the sister of the Gracchus brothers, and he always threatened to overshadow them. By birth, he was the son of Aemilius Paulus, the man who had defeated the Macedonians at Pydna a generation earlier. By adoption, he was a grandson of Scipio Africanus, whose name he bore, and whose reputation he very much aspired to emulate. Tiberius's mother Cornelia always exhorted her sons not to allow her to be more famous as the mother-in-law of Scipio than as the mother of the Gracchi. She got her wish, though it was bitter in the getting.

But though Aemilianus was overbearing, he was now consul, in command of the Carthaginian campaign, and perfectly placed to assist in the advancement of junior relatives. Tiberius, young though he was, was appointed to the consul's staff. Soon, he was on a war galley, heading for Africa.

Scipio Aemilianus proved himself an efficient and methodical soldier. Over the course of 147 BC, the Roman siegeworks crept towards the great walls of Carthage. In the spring of 146 BC, Roman legionaries achieved a foothold on the wall, and though the Carthaginians threw themselves into the counter-attack with despairing courage, the Romans came on by the thousand, pushing forward behind their long shields, slow but unstoppable, through the city's bloody streets.

Tiberius Gracchus had distinguished himself during the campaign, winning praise for an especially bold attack on the enemy fortifications. Now he shared in a great Roman victory. Carthage was methodically pulled apart, stripped of its treasures, then burned, and the embers of the smouldering city cast a fine martial glow on the young men who had brought it down. Scipio Aemilianus, above all, had proved himself worthy of the Scipio name. From that day onward, he called himself Africanus, as his grandfather had done. Only Polybius, the Greek historian, one of Scipio's close friends, heard him murmuring some lines from Homer at the moment of his triumph: 'A day will come when sacred Troy will perish, and Priam and his people shall be slain.' What did he mean? Polybius enquired. 'A glorious moment, Polybius,' the general replied; 'but I have a dread foreboding that some day the same doom will be pronounced on my own country.'

The final destruction of so feared an enemy had a profound effect on Roman psyches. There was now no hiding from the fact that Rome had become a world power – perhaps *the* world power. It was uncomfortable, the Romans found, no longer to be able to play the underdog.

Rome had always taken pride in a sort of rugged frontier spirit. Let the soft old nations of Greece and Asia keep their god-kings and diadems, their gold and their silks. In Italy, at the western edge of civilization, they bred tough men – farmers and fighters. There was a republican legend that Cato the Elder was very fond of promoting: a Roman general, Manius Curius Dentatus, won so many famous victories that Rome's enemies attempted to seduce him with a bribe. Ambassadors laden with gold found the general in a simple farmhouse sitting down to a meal of boiled turnips. He liked conquering the rich, he told them, better than being rich himself.

Cato lived in the house of the turnip-eating general. He devoted his life to the defence of the stern values of old Rome, threatened as they were by foreign vices, softness, indolence, the myriad degeneracies of the modern age. Carthage, to Cato, was a moral threat as much as it was a political one.

Cato died just too soon to see Carthage destroyed. But later generations of Romans, looking back, often pointed to Cato's pet war as the beginning of the republic's undoing. It was only after the fear of Carthage was removed that licentiousness and pride took root in Roman hearts, wrote one historian. Then the first tremors of discord ran through the citizenry. Nobles and people were divided. Each man took for himself what he could get. 'And so the Republic, split into factions, was torn apart between them.'

* * *

Having acquired some military reputation in Africa, Tiberius Gracchus had no trouble, when the time came, in securing his election as one of the quaestors for the year 137 BC. His duties, however, proved more onerous than had been expected; it was his ill-fortune to be assigned as an assistant to a consul, Gaius Mancinus, who was leading an army in Spain.

The Spanish wars had dragged on for generations. Tiberius was being sent to fight in places where his father had campaigned some forty years before. Rome had far greater resources of wealth and manpower than the Iberian tribes, but had suffered serious reverses against the rebellious Celtiberians and Lusitanians. Only by resorting to the most brutal and unscrupulous tactics were Roman generals able to destroy the Spanish fighting spirit.

By the time the new quaestor Tiberius arrived in Spain, only the Celtiberian city of Numantia was holding out. But, as Gaius Mancinus soon discovered, the Numantines, though few, were exceptional soldiers. Mancinus suffered defeat after defeat. At last, he and his entire army were trapped and surrounded, facing certain death.

Here, Tiberius Gracchus intervened. The young quaestor had inherited Spanish connections from his father's campaigning days, and used them now. The Numantines were willing to come to terms. The Roman army would be spared, so long as Mancinus, consul of the Roman republic, swore, by the most solemn oaths, to leave Numantia in peace.

Tiberius had helped save a Roman army from destruction. But if he thought the affair would win him any credit back in Rome, he had badly misread the mood of the Roman aristocracy. There was no glory in a peace, and the senate, it soon became clear, would never ratify the treaty Mancinus had sworn to uphold. There was some concern over the religious consequences of breaking Mancinus's oaths, but this was not the first time Rome had faced this problem, and the histories outlined the proper ceremonial workaround: the unwilling oath-breaker Mancinus was delivered naked to the Numantines, to do with as they wished. Rome, having washed its hands of the defeated general, prepared for war.[*]

*

* The last similar case had taken place during the Samnite Wars, after the disaster at the Caudine Forks, in 321 BC. The humiliation of the Roman army there – forced to surrender, and to march symbolically under a yoke, like so many oxen – had been a major embarrassment for the republic, an embarrassment that could only be washed away by the spilling of a great deal of Samnite blood. The Samnites, like the Numantines, were offered the life of the general who had sworn the empty oaths. Both Samnites and Numantines let the offending generals go.

Tiberius Gracchus managed at least to avoid sharing his commander's fate. Nevertheless, he had staked his reputation on the treaty. It ought to have been considered a diplomatic triumph. Instead, it was a humiliation.

Loud among the opponents of Tiberius's treaty were the friends and allies of the man who was then the most powerful in Rome, Tiberius's own brother-in-law, Scipio Aemilianus.

Aemilianus helped protect Tiberius from being sent naked to Numantia. More than that, however, he would not do. For here, once again, was an opportunity. In 148 BC, Scipio Aemilianus had mobilized mass popular support in order to get himself elected to the consulship in time to seal the destruction of Carthage, even though he was below the legal minimum age. In 135 BC, as the renewed Numantine war approached its inevitable conclusion, Aemilianus stood for the consulship a second time. Repeat consulships, in this period, were forbidden by law, but the people of Rome, once suitably primed, would not be thwarted in their desire to see the hero of Carthage elected again. As before, so now: where Aemilianus pushed, the laws of Rome buckled and gave way.

The campaign proceeded grim and inexorable. Numantia's fields were ravaged. The outlying villages were burned. The harvests ruined. Winter came. Aemilianus refused all offers of open battle. Instead, he surrounded Numantia with an impenetrable siege wall, and waited for the defenders to starve. They ate up all the grass, then boiled all the leather, then, the story goes, turned to eating each other, maddened by hunger and despair. When those few Numantines who had not commited suicide finally surrendered, they looked more like beasts than men.

The year was 133 BC. Scipio Aemilianus stood among the ruins of another conquered city; he added another title, Numantinus, to his name. And then came news from Rome. Even as Aemilianus celebrated his victory, Tiberius Gracchus, made bold by anger and ambition, had made moves of his own.

*

Travelling through Etruria on the way to war, Tiberius had taken note of the poor condition of the Italian countryside, the empty farms, the fields choked with weeds. The growth of Roman power after the Hannibalic war had enriched the richest beyond dreaming, but the constant pushing out of the frontiers made life impossible for the rural poor.

In those days, Rome still had an old-fashioned sort of citizen army, with recruitment based on the ownership of property. The unemployed masses in the city did not qualify for military service; the legionaries who won famous victories for Roman noblemen were usually small-holder farmers, conscripted from the agricultural hinterland.

The system worked well enough so long as Rome's wars were fought on Italian soil. It had been possible to fight a campaign against Samnites or Etruscans, say, and still be free in time for harvest. Being sent to Spain, on the other hand, might mean years away from home. Sixteen years was the maximum length of service, and to spend that long being marched up and down Spanish hills with the heat and the beatings and the sickness and the wet feet and the threat of ambush always tugging at the mind – that could change a man, if he returned at all.

He might anyway find that he had nothing to come back to. Farms did not prosper with their men off at the wars. Crops rotted in the fields. Animals went hungry. And smallholders had to survive in the face of constant and aggressive competition, for while Roman peas-ants fought Rome's wars, their commanding officers were discovering the advantages of large-scale slave-powered agriculture.

Cato the Elder had been a great enthusiast for the new agriculture. His pamphlet on the subject is the oldest surviving work of Latin prose and is full of good advice for the gentleman farmer: what crops to grow; how many animals to buy; how many wine vats and olive presses. Above all, how to manage slaves, Carthaginians, Numantines, Greeks, Libyans, Lusitanians, the captive populations of a hundred tribes, a hundred conquered cities, now toiling in the fields of Italy, backs bent under the whip.

There was an art to slave-owning, Cato explained to his readers.

Did you know, for example, that when your slaves are ill you can feed them less bread? Use science to breed good shepherds in the same way you breed good sheep! When it rains, slaves can still work; just set them to mending the patchwork rags they wear as cloaks. And when a slave is old and worn out, no matter! Just cast him off – call it freedom if you like – and buy another.

Through such economies, Cato and his fellows made remarkable profits. Smallholders could hardly compete. One by one, Rome's farmer soldiers gave up their ancestral lands. Some managed to scrape a living as itinerant labourers; others drifted miserably into the city to join the mass of the urban poor.

They were desperate, without prospects or property. But they were, at least, still Roman citizens. They could no longer farm, but they could still vote. Tiberius Gracchus, eloquent and ambitious, had been disappointed in his quaestorship. So he found another path to renown. He became a tribune of the plebs.

A Greek biographer, Plutarch, records – or invents – some of the flights of rhetoric with which Tiberius Gracchus won the love of the Roman poor.

> The wild beasts that dwell in Italy have each their own den or lair to shelter in; but the men who fight and die for Italy own nothing but the light and the air above them. They wander, homeless vagrants with their children and their wives… They are called the rulers of the world, these men who have not even a clod of earth to call their own.

It was accepted, even by many senators, that the condition of these poor farmers was a disgrace to the republic, and a danger too. These ruined men were the men on whom Rome's power was built. It was, therefore, with the backing of some of the most eminent men in Rome that Tiberius Gracchus proposed a new law to the plebeian assembly. It was a modest reform, given the circumstances. Rich landowners had been cultivating huge tracts of land that technically still belonged to the state, ignoring old rules, established in the early days of patrician–plebeian conflict, that should have limited the size of their holdings. Tiberius now proposed merely to enforce the forgotten limits. Any land found to be held in excess of the legal limits would be distributed to the poor.

Of course, a great many Roman aristocrats stood to lose by this redistribution. Once again, senatorial opinion moved against Tiberius Gracchus. The senate had killed his treaty, and now they would kill his land reform. But this time was different. Tiberius was a tribune. His person was sacrosanct and inviolable. His veto could shut down the state. Worse, he was willing to defy established tradition by bringing his law directly before the people without seeking senatorial approval first. This was a hard-won, though seldom used, right of the plebeian assembly: that its resolutions, once passed, should have the force of law. If Tiberius could hold on to plebeian support – and if he was willing to defy the wisdom of his seniors, to defy a tradition of deference to the senate that had been established for a hundred years – there was no limit to the laws he could pass.

Tiberius's opponents attempted to block him by raising up a tribune of their own. There were ten tribunes each year, and it had always in the past been an easy matter for powerful senators to find one who was willing to co-operate. In this case, it was one Marcus Octavius, who used his tribunician veto to prevent Tiberius's redistribution of land to the poor. The office created by plebeians to defend plebeian interests was, not for the first time, used against them.

But Tiberius refused to give in. He put it to the plebeian assembly that a tribune who acted against their interests was no tribune at all. A vote was taken. The result was clear. Octavius was deposed as tribune, and driven out of the assembly with insults and blows.

This was a radical move. No tribune had ever been deposed before. No one knew whether such a thing was even legal. But legal niceties, Tiberius insisted, could not be allowed to stand in the face of such a clear expression of popular will. Octavius's veto was withdrawn. The land reform law was passed. The slow process of redistribution began.

The year 133 BC drew to an end. Tiberius had achieved a great deal. He had made a name for himself among the poor, the desperate, the dispossessed. And he had made many enemies. To maintain his position, it was essential that he continue to hold tribunician power. Defying convention yet again, he stood for the tribuneship a second time.

What could he have done, given another year? No one knew. But before the vote could take place, they killed him.

* * *

Gaius Gracchus was in Spain with Scipio Aemilianus's army when he heard the news of his brother's death. We do not know how he reacted. He was a young man, just into his twenties, and hot-tempered. His commander offered no comfort. When Scipio Aemilianus heard of Tiberius's death he quoted Homer: 'May all who do such deeds perish so.'

Tiberius was damned as a demagogue, a rabble-rouser, a potential tyrant. There was a brief but brutal purge of his associates. One unfortunate friend is supposed to have been executed by means of a cage full of poisonous snakes, an ostentatious measure indicative of the profound, almost superstitious, alarm that Tiberius's career and death had caused among the great men of the republic.

The senator who led the attack on Tiberius was never formally condemned for what he had done. Nevertheless, it was not thought prudent for a man who had violated the sacrosanctity of a tribune to be allowed to remain in Rome. He was dispatched to Pergamum, where he died, alone and unlamented.

Tiberius's body was thrown into the Tiber. There would be no funeral to serve as a focal point for popular discontent. Gaius and Cornelia were left to their own private griefs.

At the same time, however, it was grudgingly recognized that the plight of the poor would have to be addressed. Tiberius's redistributive land law was allowed to stand.

It fell then to Gaius Gracchus to preserve his brother's legacy. With two senatorial colleagues, Gaius was appointed to the arduous and complex task of putting the new land rules into effect. Landowners resisted at every turn. The work was slow. Years passed.

And the city was calm. Laws, customs, the quiet rules of normal life, began to reassert themselves – the torn sinews of the republic knitting themselves back together, a fragile healing. The violence that had attended the land law's passage began to be forgotten.

Until, in the year 123 BC, Gaius Gracchus stood for election as tribune of the plebs.

Gaius had spent most of his adult life away from Rome, either working with Tiberius's land commission or doing military service. He had recently been in Sardinia as a quaestor and had behaved with the exaggerated probity of the politically ambitious. No prostitutes or pretty boys attended his table, he later boasted. His colleagues had arrived with jars full of wine, he complained, and left with the same jars full of silver. He, on the other hand, had drained his own private resources in the service of the state.

Tiberius's old enemies were determined not to allow another Gracchus to become tribune. If Gaius was so useful in Sardinia, they argued, let him stay there! But Gaius defied the senate's instructions and returned to Rome. Summoned to explain himself, he argued his case so eloquently that the senators felt compelled to let him stay in the city.

Tiberius had been a thoughtful orator with a considered, 'decorous' tone. Gaius had his brother's intelligence, but added to it a fierce passion that dazzled audiences. In the Roman Forum was a platform for public speaking. They called it the *Rostra*, 'the Beaks', for its decorative row of bronze naval rams, plucked from the prows of Carthaginian ships. Above these trophies, Gaius Gracchus would range like a captive lion. He tugged at the folds of his toga as he spoke, until the loops slipped from his shoulder. The memory of his brother's murder seemed still to burn inside him, driving him on. He had to be careful with his emotions. Sometimes he employed a well-educated slave to stand behind him. Whenever his voice rose to too harsh a pitch, the slave piped a soft note on a flute, reminding the furious Gaius to draw himself back in.

His opponents tried everything they could to prevent him winning election to the tribuneship. They bought all the votes they could buy; they mobilized all their supporters and clients. It was no good. Word had spread that there was a new Gracchus in Rome. Peasants abandoned their fields. They left their huts and hovels, packed bundles of cheese and onions and flat round loaves of bread, and crowded the roads heading into the city. They came from all parts of Italy. Every room was taken. Every archway, every colonnade, seemed to shelter a weathered farmer. And when it came time for the assembly to vote for tribunes, there were so many people gathered that they packed the roofs and attics of the neighbouring houses, shouting Gaius's name. The voting urns were filled and emptied; the votes counted. Gaius Gracchus, following his brother's footsteps, was a tribune of the Roman people.

For a year, Gaius Gracchus was the most powerful man in Rome. He had learned well the lessons of his brother's fall. The rural poor might pack the assembly at voting times, but they were too much tied to the land to serve as a permanent power base in the city. Agrarian reform would not be enough on its own. Instead, Gaius used his position as tribune to introduce a sweeping legislative programme. Tiberius had tried to rebuild Rome's countryside. Gaius was attempting to reform the entire Roman state.

There was something in Gaius's laws for almost everyone. Poor farmers were assured of a new commitment to land redistribution, and the minimum age at which their sons could be hauled off to war was increased to seventeen. In the city, Gaius promised the unemployed masses new rations of corn from the state. Rome's Italian allies – who supplied half the manpower for Rome's armies without any proportional political power – were promised new voting rights and even, for some Latin towns, full citizenship.*

---

* One of the most important benefits of Roman citizenship was the legal immunity it offered from the arbitrary exercise of power by Roman magistrates. Gaius Gracchus used colourful examples of Roman abuses to drive home the necessity of reform. The chief magistrate of one town was flogged in the public square after the wife of a visiting Roman magistrate complained that the local bathhouse was dirty. A peasant from Venusia was

Gaius also made overtures to those just short of the top of Roman society – men of substantial means, but without the wealth or ambition to embark upon the *cursus honorum* and take their place among the senators. These men, known as *equites* or knights – were exempt from the old custom that forbade senators from bidding for state contracts. As a result, they were able to make fortunes running logistics for Roman armies, managing Spanish silver mines, building military roads or carrying out any other of the myriad tasks entailed by Rome's growing dominion.

Gaius Gracchus now offered the *equites* a rich new prize: the job of collecting Roman taxes in one of Rome's new provinces. In addition, *equites* would be given the right to serve as jurors in the court where cases of provincial maladministration were usually tried. This was a powerful combination of new perks. The provincial extortions perpetrated with near-immunity by Roman *equites* would become the stuff of legend.

The programme as a whole amounted to a broad-fronted attack on senatorial privilege. Power in the provinces was to be shared with *equites*. Power in Rome was to be shared with Italians. Peasants and the urban poor got land and bread and, with those things, a measure of independence from senatorial patrons whose charity often came at the cost of freedom. Under Gaius's new laws, bread for poor citizens would be provided directly by the state. The loyalty of the city mob would therefore accrue to the state – represented, for the moment, by Gaius Gracchus himself.

It was an ambitious programme, and it was a successful one. At the end of his first year in office, the plebeian assembly defied tradition by electing Gaius Gracchus tribune for a second term.

*

---

scourged to death after making a rude remark within earshot of a Roman military officer. These, said Gaius, were only the most recent cruelties inflicted on Italy.

The republic had been set up as an aristocracy. The people might vote, but the 'best men', the *aristoi* – the '*optimates*', as they called themselves – were meant to rule.

But the Gracchus brothers had perfected a new form of Roman politics. They rejected the traditional route to power, the senatorial magistracies of the *cursus honorum*. Bypassing the senate, they drew their power directly from the plebeian assembly, putting their laws directly to the popular vote. This, the *popularis* way of doing things, would not be forgotten in the decades to come.

To the *optimates*, Gaius Gracchus appeared even more dangerous than his brother had been. Following his election to a second term as tribune, Gaius became bolder and less restrained in his actions. There was some settling of old political scores: he had one enemy driven from public life and another banished from the city.

But Gaius had not come so far for the sake of mere revenge and, despite what his enemies claimed, he did not intend to make himself a tyrant. Like his brother, Gaius Gracchus could see that the old republican constitution was beginning to fail. Farmers were desperate. The armies were undermanned. The allies on whom Rome depended were resentful. The riches of conquest accrued to a wealthy few while, in the filthy streets of the city, the hopeless masses multiplied.

So, in the second year of his tribuneship, Gaius embarked on a scheme that might ameliorate several of those problems at the same time. Where Cato the Elder and Scipio Aemilianus had brought destruction, Gaius Gracchus would plant new life: a brand new Roman settlement built over the ruins of Carthage.

This was the first time a major colony had been established outside Italy – a historic moment: the devouring city belches forth its first international spore – but the senators raised no objection. Perhaps it had become impossible to oppose Gaius Gracchus. At any rate it worked out to their advantage, as the work of founding the colony took Gaius away from Rome. It dragged. The omens were poor. Wolves tore out the stakes marking the colony boundary. It was seventy days before Gaius Gracchus was able to return to Italy.

There, he discovered, events had been turning against him. His opponents in the senate had hit on a new strategy to undermine his popularity among the people, setting up a tame tribune who countered every crowd-pleasing measure of Gaius Gracchus's with an even more crowd-pleasing one.

Gaius's popularity was anyway on the wane because of his proposal to enfranchise the Latin allies and empower the Italians. Aristocrats feared the power Gaius would wield if newly enfranchised Latins swung behind him, while ordinary Romans feared that Italian interests might be preferred to their own. A speech still survives from one of the consuls of that year, warning the urban poor that new 'citizens' from the towns of Italy would crowd them out of their seats at the theatre. The allegiance of the *equites* too, tenuous at best, now swung firmly back behind the establishment.

Gaius Gracchus did what he could. He moved his lodgings from the expensive Palatine hill down to a spot near the Forum to be close to the people. He made grand gestures. When the rich built seats round the Forum for a display of gladiators, Gaius waited until night and then had his workmen tear the seating down so that the poor would have a free and unobstructed view.

But when his second term as tribune came to an end, Gaius Gracchus was too politically isolated to win a third. He had the votes to do it, but even his fellow tribunes were against him now, and they rigged the count to keep him out of office. Meanwhile, one Lucius Opimius, a man of 'extreme oligarchic views', was elected consul on the promise that he would immediately set about repealing Gaius Gracchus's laws.

* * *

Rome was a bonfire, and once again, a voting assembly provided the spark. Lucius Opimius and his supporters had gathered to undo some of Gaius Gracchus's reforms. Gaius and his supporters had gathered to oppose them. Harsh words flew. There was a rude gesture; some shoving; a brief scuffle. Then a sudden downpour of rain dispersed the crowd. Left on the ground was a leaking lump that had once been one of Opimius's followers, his body porcupined by the long metal styluses the Romans used as pens.

Opimius, we are told, exulted at the news of his man's death: now he had the cause he had been seeking for so long. As dawn broke the next day, the senate gathered to weep pious tears over the body of the murder victim. The safety of the state was in danger, they shouted to each other and to the watching crowd. Then, in a state of livid indignation, they hurried into the Senate House to do what had to be done. The decree the senate passed that day came to be called the *senatus consultum ultimum* – the Ultimate Decree. It recommended that the consul, Lucius Opimius, do whatever he thought necessary for the security of the republic.

That evening, Opimius gathered his strength. He had the senators and *equites* arm themselves and their servants and loyal freedmen. He also summoned a company of mercenaries who happened to be near the city: Cretan archers, trained for war, men with no sentimental attachment to the laws of Rome.

Gaius had one aristocratic supporter remaining: Marcus Fulvius Flaccus, a colleague from Tiberius's land commission. Fulvius has gone down in the histories as a man of modest gifts and unattractive temper, but he was a loyal friend all the same. It was he who had come from the senate to warn Tiberius Gracchus of the impending attack ten years before.

Now, seeing the way things were going, Fulvius called his own supporters and clients to his and Gaius's defence. Soon a rowdy throng had gathered at Fulvius's house, armed with the crude weapons of the street. They filled the empty night with the sound of their boasting and dissolved their fears in sticky unmixed wine, straight from the jar.

While Fulvius drank with his mob, Gaius was in more reflective mood. Passing through the Forum towards his house, he paused for a long time in front of the statue of his dimly remembered father. Some men of Fulvius's rabble saw Gaius stand and sigh, saw him walk away with tears rolling down his cheeks. Much moved, they followed him home and spent the night camped defensively on the cobbles around his front door. Within, Gaius comforted his wife and his little son. Perhaps, as night darkened towards dawn, they slept.

The story, as preserved in the account of the Greek biographer

Plutarch, has something of the stage about it. The night-time doings at the houses of Gaius and Fulvius would, one scholar has suggested, fit neatly on a traditional Roman set, symmetrical doors in a blank wall.

The next morning, at any rate, brought a fine dramatic scene: Fulvius came blinking into the sun at the head of an outlandishly costumed retinue. His men had armed themselves with the spoils of their leader's old victories: swords and armour captured from barbarians in Gaul. So, bearing savage weapons, they marched to defend their Roman liberties.

Gaius, on the other hand, dressed as if for his usual business – a speech before the assembly or an appearance in the law courts. Before he could leave the house, his wife threw herself on the ground before him, begging him not to leave, not to go unarmed to face his brother's killers. As he stepped over her, she clutched at the hem of his toga, then lay still.

The Gracchans gathered on the Aventine, the broad hill rising above the cattle market and the river docks below. Here, to the Aventine, the first plebeians had come, many years ago. Here they had sworn the oaths that made their tribunes inviolable. Here, in the most distant past, King Numa had won Jupiter's blessing for the laws of Rome. Surely some scruple would stay the senators now – some ancestral memory of compromise, of a city governed by rules, not blows.

Fulvius dispatched his youngest son to negotiate with the senators, who now had gathered in the Forum. The youth returned with bad news: although there were many there willing to negotiate, the consul Opimius was insisting that Gaius and Fulvius present themselves in the Forum to stand trial. Gaius, trusting in his skill as an orator, or at least hoping to avoid bloodshed, was willing. Fulvius and the others were not. Once again, the son was dispatched with placatory messages. This time he did not return at all.

Instead, Gaius and his supporters watched as Opimius's hired Cretans came round the Palatine and into the valley of the Circus Maximus, with a crowd of senators pressing behind them. Fulvius's men were street fighters at best – masters of the hurled brick or the dagger in the dark alley. They faced soldiers; men for whom killing was not a sport but a profession, carried out with nerveless efficiency. And now the first long-shafted arrows came quivering through the air, sailing over the Aventine rooftops to plunge into the tightly packed crowd. A club was useless against a bow. Arrows loosed at close range burst the ribs of the men in the front rank who fell, tangling the legs of those behind them as they turned to flee. Cries of fear turned to groans and shrieks of pain. The resistance of the mob, so loudly trumpeted the previous night, was broken in an instant.

Marcus Fulvius Flaccus and his eldest son were found in a disused bathhouse, trying to look invisible against the dirty tiles. They were killed where they cowered. The youngest son was already in captivity; he would be granted the privilege of being his own executioner. Gaius himself, as soon as the fighting began, had retreated to the temple of Diana, that dark goddess, worshipped on the Aventine since the time of the kings. There the young Roman gathered the courage to take his own life.

But Gaius's journey was not yet over. At the last moment, two faithful friends, Pomponius and Licinius, snatched the sword out of his hand. There was still time, they said, for Gaius to save himself. So, accompanied by a Greek slave, the three men came back out into the street. Here, a curious stillness had settled. An amnesty had been declared for Fulvius's supporters, and many of the people had abandoned their Gracchan allegiance in the hope of saving their lives. Now they watched their champion set off on his final race, with the Cretan archers close behind him. At the river, Pomponius and Licinius turned to make a stand, holding off the pursuers until they were cut down.

Gaius ran on with the loyal slave towards the Janiculum, his sandals pounding on worn stone. A crowd lined his route. At each turn, they called encouragement, shouting at him to go faster, faster, out of the city, but no hand was raised to help him, nor did anyone dare to block the Cretans' way. At last, Gaius reached a grove dedicated to the Furies, the spirits of vengeance. Romans would bury curses here, lead tablets scrawled with prayers to infernal gods. And here, under the sacred trees, Gaius stopped running. The slave, whose name was Philocrates, killed his master with a dagger to the heart and then killed himself, accompanying Gaius Gracchus to the afterlife.

* * *

Opimius had announced before the battle that whoever brought him Gaius Gracchus's head would receive its weight in gold. The man who secured this trophy is supposed to have scooped out Gaius's brain and poured lead into the cavity to increase the size of his reward. Gaius's body was dumped in the Tiber, to follow the corpse of his brother down the river and out to sea.

Two and a half centuries earlier, Marcus Furius Camillus had celebrated a compromise between patricians and plebeians by vowing a temple to Concord. After killing Gaius Gracchus and three thousand other plebeian citizens of Rome, Lucius Opimius had the crumbling old temple rebuilt. All was well, he declared to the city. Harmony was restored.

The truth was quite otherwise. Over the years that followed, those first troubling symptoms which the Gracchi had seen in the body of the state – those symptoms they had tried, with their reforms, to cure – flared up into bouts of bloody fever. The Italian allies revolted against Rome. The slaves in the fields rose against their masters and laid waste to the countryside.

Meanwhile in the city, the urban plebs remained uneasy. Something had changed in Rome. The old laws and traditions, the *mos maiorum*, the whole republican constitution, had been tested to breaking point by the ambition of the Gracchus brothers. And everyone had seen how, in the end, it was naked violence that brought them down.

It was a lesson that would not be unlearned. The generations that followed would become accustomed to blood on the city streets, to Romans killing Romans. Within a hundred years of Gaius Gracchus's death, the Roman republic, with all its customs, all its sacred traditions of government, was dead too.

5

THE IDES OF MARCH

The assassination of Julius Caesar

———

44 BC

FEBRUARY 44 BC. WITH a burst of happy noise, a capering band of young men comes tumbling out of Etruscan Street and into the bustle and brightness of the Roman Forum. Dressed in nothing but strips of goatskin, they blink in the light like startled fauns before leaping into the crowd. It is carnival time in the city – the festival of the Lupercalia – and these are the *Luperci*, priests of a cult that is older than the city itself.

Around them is a very new Rome. This is a burgeoning city, a city enjoying peace, renewing itself like a forest in spring. Workers move amid thickets of scaffolding; walls glow with the bloom of fresh-cut marble; on each side of the Forum, north and south, fat pillars sprout in towering colonnades along the flanks of two brand-new basilicas – public halls, teeming with urban life.

And in the midst of all this growth, throned in gold like the heavenly Sun, is the man who has made it possible: Julius Caesar.

He sits on the Rostra, the speaker's platform in the middle of the Forum. His toga is of rich reddish purple, stained by the crushed glands of murex shells. His boots are bright-red leather and are modelled after the footwear of the ancient Latin kings he claims among his ancestors.* He is, he will have you know, descended from a great

———

* The tradition that Rome's ruler should be shod in red has continued to the present day: red shoes, and red indoor slippers, are the traditional footwear of a reigning pope.

hero: Aeneas the Trojan, the son of Venus herself.

But his glory is not based on blood alone. The golden palmettes on his tunic mark him out as a triumphant general. Caesar has been hailed as such many times by his victorious troops. They call him their 'commander' – their *imperator*.

Now, unexpectedly, one of the half-naked priests is approaching the platform. The crowd parts respectfully, growing hushed, not fooled by the man's skimpy costume. This sweating brute is Marcus Antonius, one of Caesar's most trusted lieutenants, a soldier and a killer.

Antonius goes down on one knee. He is close enough to see what others forget: that Caesar is only a man. The master of Rome is in his mid-fifties, and has fought many battles. His dark eyes are piercing, but tired. He is bald, which he hates, and has vainly combed some few remaining wisps of hair across his forehead, where he scratches them with a distracted forefinger. He looks thin, pinched. Antonius has campaigned at Caesar's side. He knows the general's health is not good – malaria, epilepsy – and that it is getting worse.

But Antonius must not be distracted. He has a mission to perform. He raises his hand to Caesar, and suddenly all eyes are fixed on what he holds. A golden crown.

* * *

The Julian clan was one of the most ancient families in Rome, but hardly the most distinguished. Julii had served in high office since the birth of the republic but still, the clan's overall impact on the historical record had been patchy.* As a young man, Gaius Julius Caesar was better known for the flashy way he wore his tunics

---

* The 'Caesar' branch of the wider Julian clan could trace their particular surname back a little over a century, to a man dimly remembered for having commanded the disgraced survivors of the battle of Cannae. It was not an especially distinguished pedigree, although the men of Julius Caesar's father's generation did manage to win some prestigious magistracies in the late 90s and early 80s BC. The meaning of the name Caesar was obscure even to contemporaries, but probably comes from a root meaning 'hairy'. Caesar himself was famously bald.

(long fringed sleeves, girdle loosely tied) than for the glories of his family tree.

The foremost nobles of the republic liked to live off the southern side of the Forum, on the slope of the Palatine hill by the Via Sacra, the Sacred Way. Young Gaius Julius was born and raised in a modest house on the northern side – the wrong side – between the Esquiline and the Viminal hills, in a district called the Subura. Here the urban poor lived crowded together in great stacked tenement blocks, which the Romans called *insulae*, or 'islands'. These burned and collapsed with grim frequency, but buildings and their occupants were easily replaced. Rome, the devouring city, was now sucking in humans by the thousand, not just from Italy but from across the Mediterranean world.

These were the days of the dictator, Cornelius Sulla, the first man to march a Roman army against Rome. It was in 82 BC, just as Caesar was reaching adulthood, that Sulla's notorious proscription lists started going up in the Forum. Each morning men gathered to read the names of the condemned. A stroke of a pen could transform an aristocrat into an outlaw. Thousands were arrested and executed, some because they had crossed Sulla, others just as victims of his greed, or the greed of his associates. Huge fortunes were harvested from those who appeared on the proscription lists – and yet more money was spent by desperate men hoping to stay off them.

Sulla's supporters made themselves rich. Two men in particular began to cast long shadows: Gnaeus Pompeius and Marcus Licinius Crassus. Pompey was Sulla's most successful general; Crassus his best extortionist.

Caesar, not yet out of his teens, was forced into hiding. His family was not quite rich enough to be worth wiping out, but they had very much the wrong sort of politics. Caesar himself had married the daughter of one of Sulla's great enemies – a daughter whom he now, with startling impudence, refused to divorce. As a result, he was hunted through Italy, a dandy with a price on his head, hiding out in marsh-bound villages and remote towns still scarred by the recent civil war.

*

It should have been suicide, publicly opposing Sulla's will, but Caesar toughed it out, staying ahead of the pursuit long enough for his mother to beg a pardon from Sulla with the help of some friendly Vestal Virgins. Impoverished and out of favour, Caesar now set off for the East to begin a military career. Here, in the province of Asia (that is, western Anatolia), Caesar distinguished himself, earning the oak crown, the *corona civica*, for exceptional valour during the Siege of Mytilene.

His charm was as potent a weapon as his sword. On a diplomatic mission to Bithynia, on the Black Sea, Caesar attracted the attention of the local monarch, King Nicomedes. Nicomedes was a ruler in the Hellenistic mould – an inheritor of the hybrid Greco-Persian culture that had grown from the conquests of Alexander the Great. Not for King Nicomedes, the famous self-discipline of the Roman senatorial aristocracy. He was a man unbound by any constitution, and though he might rule a patch of Anatolia smaller than the least of Rome's provinces, he had the airs and graces of a god.

A group of Roman businessmen visiting Nicomedes' court were surprised at a feast one evening to see a handsome Roman youth acting as the elderly king's personal cupbearer. Dark stories crackled back to Rome: that young Julius was catamite to an Asiatic king; that he lay in robes of purple on a golden couch, waiting for the creaky old despot to take his pleasure.

Whispers of 'effeminacy' would dog Caesar for the rest of his life, compounded rather than allayed by his insatiable appetite for other people's wives. He was, as a much-repeated witticism had it, 'Every woman's man and every man's woman.'

But the youth had steel in his soul. A few years later, Caesar was kidnapped by pirates off the Ionian coast. Throughout this ordeal, we are told, the young man behaved with the confidence of a born aristocrat, smiling and joking and bossing the pirates around with threats of what he would do to them when they let him go.

Everybody laughed at this, Caesar included. The ransom was paid. And straightaway, Caesar raised an improvised naval force and hunted his kidnappers down. Always merciful, he cut their throats before he crucified them.

By the time of this adventure, Sulla was dead. The dictator had been a tyrant, but also a fearsome traditionalist and reactionary who had restored the senate to what he regarded as its ancient and proper place as the supreme authority in Rome; the rabble-rousing tribunes of the Popular Assembly were firmly silenced. Sulla himself, in the last two years of his life, gave up his dictatorship and retired to a country estate, leaving his reconstituted republic behind him.

But the system Sulla was trying to restore had evolved for a city state, not a dominion that spanned half a continent. Rome had nearly fractured under the Gracchus brothers, half a century before, and since then, as one reform after another was blocked, the forces tearing at the republic had only grown stronger. Corruption was rampant. The countryside had become a swamp of human misery. The legions, no longer manned by peasant farmers, had lost their connection to the land. The professional soldiers of Caesar's day, outfitted by the state, knew the army camps as their only home, the sword as their only livelihood.

Caesar returned to Rome in 73 BC to find Sulla's conservative order breaking down. That was the year of the great Slave War – Spartacus's revolt. The rebel gladiator ran wild in the Roman countryside until 71 BC, attracting thousands of bandits and runaways to his cause and beating a series of Roman armies until Sulla's old follower Marcus Licinius Crassus hunted him down. Crassus crucified the survivors of Spartacus's army along the Via Appia: six thousand slaves, their dreams of freedom tortured out of them at last, lining the highway from Capua to Rome. No throats cut that time.

Crassus had become enormously wealthy during the proscriptions, amassing a vast empire in loans and property.* Now, to strengthen his

---

* Crassus is said to have created his own personal fire brigade. Whenever there was a fire in Rome, Crassus would buy buildings in the path of the blaze for next to nothing, then send his squad of firemen to put the fire out.

position, he put some of his extorted cash to use, propelling favoured protégés up the ladder of Roman politics. Caesar was an obvious candidate for this sort of favour; still young, handsome, talented, capable on the battlefield and in the law courts. Most importantly, he was a man whose ambition far exceeded his purse. Crassus took Caesar under his wing.

While Crassus manoeuvred in Rome, Sulla's other rising star, the 'teenage butcher' Gnaeus Pompeius, was carving out an even greater name for himself with a string of brilliant victories abroad: in Spain he fought the legendary Roman rebel, Sertorius, a man guided by a miraculous white fawn from the goddess Diana; later, sweeping eastward, he drove the great Mediterranean pirate chieftains from the sea; most glorious of all, in the mid-60s BC, he campaigned against Mithridates of Pontus, the Lion of Asia, one of Rome's most dangerous and determined enemies. Pompeius's armies drove through Anatolia as far as the Caucasus and down through Syria and the Levant, capturing Jerusalem in 63 BC. Mithridates was crushed, and all his rich territories and more besides were made subject to Rome. In the city, the people delighted in his successes. His soldiers, it was said, called him *Pompeius Magnus* – Pompey the Great.

In the shadow of these two giants, Caesar's influence grew slowly. He flattered Pompey, supported the deep-pocketed Crassus where he could, and tried to raise his own profile as much as possible in the meantime. In 70 BC he was elected to his first Roman magistracy, the quaestorship, a low-ranking post but a vital first step. Five years later he was elected aedile, with responsibility for the big public shows at the *Ludi Romani* and the *ludi* of the Magna Mater. Caesar spent wildly – his own and Crassus's money – on these dramatic spectaculars. He even decorated the Forum with his personal art collection. Everyone agreed that Caesar's generous *ludi* were a roaring success.

His other big shows in this period were a pair of lavish funerals for his aunt Julia and his wife Cornelia, who both died at around the same time. It was unusual to put on such a performance for an aunt, and even more so for a young wife, but Caesar spared no effort or expense. With much wailing of pipes and horns and weeping of hired mourners, the body of each woman was carried in state to the Roman Forum where Caesar delivered their eulogies.

Julia and Cornelia were daughters of the Julian and Cornelian clans – names that resounded through Roman history. At each funeral, as was traditional, actors wore masks in the likenesses of great Julii or Cornelii of generations past. These mimic ancestors, wearing their robes of office, rode in chariots in the funeral procession. They sat at the Rostra as Caesar delivered his speeches, watching like a row of silent ghosts.

In 63 BC, Caesar made his boldest political move yet, standing for election as chief priest of Rome – *pontifex maximus*. This was a post with little real power, but enormous prestige, and one which was being actively fought over by two much older and much more senior politicians. At first, they laughed at him. Later, they tried to buy him off. Caesar was ruinously in debt and now he was offered a huge sum to withdraw his candidacy. Instead, he borrowed even more, pouring every resource he had into the campaign. On the morning of the election, he told his mother that he would return home as *pontifex maximus* or never return at all.

The Popular Assembly convened. The votes were counted. Caesar had won a stunning victory. Straightaway, Rome's new *pontifex maximus* moved from his old house in the Subura to a new official residence, the *domus publica*. He now lived right on the Roman Forum, just beside the Temple of Vesta and next door to the *regia* with its aura of ancient kings. Julius Caesar had very much arrived.

* * *

That year, 63 BC, was the year Catiline tried to take over the republic.

One of the consuls at the time was a *novus homo*, a 'new man' with no great ancestors: Marcus Tullius Cicero. A nobody from the nowhere town of Arpinum, Cicero was widely acknowledged to be the finest public speaker in the city, a man whose persuasive powers made him a priceless ally in the courts and a powerful voice in the senate. Over many years, and in the teeth of aristocratic prejudice, he had worked his way to the consulship, the supreme magistracy in Rome.

This was the proudest achievement of Cicero's life, and although his success did not endear him to the blue-blooded patricians, Cicero keenly felt the responsibilities of his new role and was determined to be a leader in the grand old Roman tradition of cautious conservatism.

The *popularis* tendency was on the rise again in Roman politics. Cicero was forced to deploy his full rhetorical arsenal against a threatened land redistribution bill. More troubling still was a row that broke out over the limits of the senate's emergency powers. The Ultimate Decree, the *senatus consultum ultimum*, had been used to justify the extrajudicial killings of both the Gracchus brothers. In 100 BC, the next generation of senators had used it again, to dispose of another populist tribune. Under cover of the Ultimate Decree, an aristocratic mob had stoned the tribune to death in the Senate House.

Now, however, in what was a clear challenge to the senate's authority, an elderly senator who had participated in that long-forgotten killing was hauled to the law courts and condemned for the tribune's murder. The man who brought the case, it was widely noted, was an associate of Julius Caesar.

The fight over emergency powers took on a new and urgent relevance when Cicero uncovered a dangerous conspiracy against the Roman state.

The ringleader was Lucius Sergius Catilina (known in English as Catiline), an aristocrat of impeccable breeding, great personal charm and rather loose morals – the antithesis, that is to say, of the somewhat stuffy Cicero. Catiline had run against Cicero in the elections for the consulships of 63 BC, spending huge sums of money to try to swing the vote. The gamble had proved disastrous. Humiliatingly defeated by a *novus homo*, Catiline was left deep in debt – debt which he had no easy means to repay.

In desperation, Catiline began gathering accomplices for a take-over of the Roman state. There were many young men in his position, men who had bankrupted themselves in the hope of a political career, and such men had everything to gain from revolution.

In October that year, a pile of anonymous letters was discovered outside the house of Crassus, warning some of the leading men of Rome to leave the city ahead of a planned massacre. At the same time, word started coming in of a peasant army gathering in the Etruscan countryside, led by one of Sulla's old centurions. The republic was under threat, Cicero told the senate. There was nothing for it but to pass the *senatus consultum ultimum* – the Ultimate Decree.

Cicero now had the authority to defend the state, if necessary, by violence. Still he needed more evidence to connect the conspiracy to Catiline. He was not in any doubt himself – he had his own mole in Catiline's organization – but the events of that year had made him cautious. He had no wish to be hauled up on murder charges in a few decades' time.

Even after a failed attempt on his life on 7 November Cicero was relatively restrained. His only response was to summon an emergency meeting of the senate. Here he delivered a speech of such rhetorical power that Catiline felt compelled to leave Rome.

The end was now in sight. Catiline had promised to take himself off into exile. Instead, he joined the rebel army in Etruria and prepared for war. In the meantime, his allies were to sow fear and chaos in the city.

But the conspirators were reliable only in their incompetence. At the end of November, Catiline's accomplices attempted to recruit some Italian Gauls to their cause. Word reached Cicero straightaway, and he persuaded the Gauls to play along. Here was the evidence he needed: letters from Roman nobles, plotting with Rome's deadliest enemies to ravage the city with fire and sword.

Catiline's supporters were rounded up and Rome's senators convened in the Temple of Concord to decide what to do with them. One after another, Rome's highest nobles stood up to declare that the penalty must be death. Each man had his say, in order of seniority, going down until it was the turn of Gaius Julius Caesar.

The conspiracy had put Caesar in an awkward position. He and Crassus had both been supporters of Catiline's political ambitions. And Catiline's flamboyant style – the toga worn fashionably long, the oiled hair, the absurd chinstrap beard which he and his followers affected – all these things were very reminiscent of Caesar with his long fringed sleeves and plucked armpits.

Caesar had not been directly implicated, however, in the conspiracy. And now he had a perfect opportunity to allay senatorial suspicion; to demonstrate his loyalty to Cicero and the state. But Caesar stood up, in front of all his peers, and declared that the conspirators should live. Ultimate Decree or no Ultimate Decree, the principle stood: no Roman citizen should be put to death without a trial.

Back came Cicero's careful response. Caesar was to be commended for his devotion to the republic, his gentleness and kindness, worthy of his illustrious ancestors. But let him remember the dreadful crime the conspirators had attempted! Let the senate imagine, as Cicero proceeded loudly to do, the horrors that would have attended upon the conspiracy's success: the weeping of Roman matrons; children fleeing for their lives; the sore abuse of the Vestal Virgins. 'I seem to see this city, the light of the world, the citadel of all the nations, suddenly toppled in a single blaze!'

Still the senate wavered; Cicero fumed. But help was at hand. Up stood the stoutest defender of Rome's antique severity: Marcus Porcius Cato, great-grandson of that Cato the Censor who had been the terror of the city a century before. Where Caesar was sleek, Cato was harsh and rough; where Caesar was merciful, Cato was unbending; Caesar wore his tunic long and his toga full; Cato sometimes forgot to wear a tunic at all, brandishing his hairy knees like twin badges of republican virtue. And Cato was determined: the conspirators must die.

The senators were convinced at last, and though Caesar continued to defend his case, the argument was won. And now the senators began to wonder, why was Caesar so eager to save these criminals' lives? Cato was especially keen to cast aspersions, and now, just as he pressed his attack, a messenger came and delivered Caesar a secret note. What was the message? Cato demanded to know, and with angry cries the senators rallied behind him.

Without saying anything, or so the story goes, Caesar handed over the letter. Cato read, and went silent. He had in his hands a pornographic missive to Caesar from a woman named Servilia, his own half-sister.

The conspirators were brought to the Tullianum prison and strangled. Catiline himself was killed in battle with his rebel army. His peasants fell where they stood, with wounds borne bravely in the front. All agreed that Catiline had at least died in the proper manner for a Roman aristocrat.

As for Caesar, all efforts to tie him to the conspiracy failed. Cato was implacably hostile, but Cicero vouched for his innocence, which probably was genuine. Caesar, after all, was already a success. He had no need for revolution.

In 62 BC, Caesar was praetor, one step below consul, and at the end of his praetorship, as was traditional, he set out to govern a Roman province. Hispania Ulterior, or Further Spain, was not much of a prize, but Caesar made the best of it by contriving to start a decent-sized war for himself to win. When he returned to Rome in 60 BC, he was voted his first *triumphus,* the ceremonial victory procession that was the pinnacle of a Roman military career.

There was only one problem – a triumphing general could not, for legal and religious reasons, enter the city before his triumphal procession had taken place. And if Caesar could not enter the city, he could not present himself as a candidate in that year's consular elections – not, at least, without special senatorial permission, which was blocked by a Catonian filibuster.

So Caesar gave up his triumph. It was the highest honour a Roman could win, and he turned it down to stand in a hotly contested election. Like Catiline, Caesar gambled everything on gaining the consulship. Unlike Catiline, he won.

Caesar was consul. He had been a marsh-bound fugitive, a pirate prisoner and a king's lover. Now he was chief magistrate of the Roman republic. The other consul for that year, Cato's son-in-law Bibulus, was so far outshone that he soon gave up on ruling altogether. Instead, he spent most of the time at home, 'discovering' unfavourable omens.

In theory, bad omens meant all business for the day should be abandoned. But Caesar, having come so far, was not to be diverted by arcane religious scruples. Ignoring the letter of the law, he pressed on with an ambitious programme of reform.

And Caesar had reason to be confident in facing down senatorial opposition. That year, he had entered into a secret agreement with the only other men in the republic who now could stand against him: Pompey and Crassus. Each had suffered long enough from the senate's relentless obstructionism. Now, Caesar persuaded the two titans to set aside their old rivalry. With Crassus's gold, Pompey's soldiers and Caesar's consulship, they had the power to divide the Roman world up as they pleased.

It was not obvious at first what had happened. Only gradually did Cato and the senators realize that the old order of things had been fatally undermined. The republican system was broken, not, as Cicero feared, by fire and the sword, but through the formation of this new triumvirate – the quiet collaboration of three powerful men.

* * *

The agreement between the triumvirs was that, after his consulship, Caesar would govern Gaul. Only the area close to the Mediterranean was under Roman rule at the time. The rest of Gaul was controlled by fierce Celtic tribes, and through these tribes lay Caesar's path to glory.

Over the course of the next decade, Caesar conquered all the territory between the Atlantic and the Rhine, and even mounted a large-scale raid into Britain. He endured hard campaigning winters and desperate sieges; when battles were in the balance, he fought in the front lines with his men. To those tribes that surrendered, he was merciful. Those tribes that did not surrender faced slavery or extermination. It is unknown how many Gauls died. Ancient writers variously claimed that somewhere between 500,000 and a million were killed and as many again enslaved. At any rate, the debt incurred at the Allia three centuries before was now repaid a thousand times over.

The war made Caesar rich. The gold of warrior torques and druid shrines was melted down and funnelled back to Rome to be converted into the precious but unstable currency of political influence. It was with Gallic gold that Caesar embarked on his monumental building projects around the Roman Forum.

The city was extremely volatile in those years. Mob violence was endemic, elections were won by force or fraud, magistrates were attacked in the streets by armed thugs, and senators fought pitched battles at the Rostra. But still, through all the chaos and despite their mutual suspicion, the alliance between Caesar, Pompey and Crassus endured.

Then, in 53 BC, came disastrous news. Crassus, hungry for his own measure of glory, had led an army into the great eastern empire of Parthia beyond the Syrian border. At Carrhae, in northern Mesopotamia, the Parthians surrounded Crassus's legions in the desert and slaughtered them. Crassus had spent his life sucking up other people's money. Now the great extortionist was dead. His killers, it was later said in Rome, stopped up the general's mouth with molten gold.

The triumvirate could stand on three legs but not on two. Pompey, turning conservative in his old age, was increasingly sympathetic to Caesar's senatorial enemies. Cato and his friends worked on the great man constantly, urging him to put an end to the ambitions of the upstart Caesar. In return, they offered Pompey the respectability he had always craved. Caesar would be destroyed, and Pompey would be recognized as what he truly was – the saviour of Rome.

So long as Caesar held a military command, he was legally immune from prosecution. The efforts of the senators, therefore, were directed above all at recalling Caesar to Rome. Once he was a private citizen again, all those old irregularities, the bad omens he had illegally ignored during his consulship ten years before, could be made to haunt him.

Caesar was in trouble. The battle in Gaul was won; his excuse for maintaining his army was gone. He offered the senate any possible concession if they would just give him a magistracy or a military posting. But Cato and his supporters, the so-called 'good men' or *boni*, smelled weakness. Caesar must be recalled to Rome to face prosecution. Nothing less would do. 'An obsessive mania for fighting has got into everyone,' wrote Cicero despairingly.

And if it did come to that, Cato felt confident in the outcome. He had the support of Pompey, the conqueror of Mithridates, a man who boasted that he could summon legions just by stamping his feet. Soon Caesar would be crushed at last.

For a few tense weeks, the situation hung unresolved. Messengers flew up and down between Cisalpine Gaul (the old Gallic territory on the near side of the Alps) and Rome, bearing proposals and counterproposals. Cicero, representing the senate's moderates, worked desperately to arrange some sort of compromise. But in January 49 BC, Cato and his *boni* got their way: Caesar's tame tribunes were expelled from Rome. Yet again, the *senatus consultum ultimum* was passed.

At dawn a day or two later, Caesar and his loyal officers stood on the banks of the stream that separated Cisalpine Gaul from Italy proper. He had a single legion at his back. Opposing him were most of Rome's senators and one of the most successful generals Rome had ever produced, with the resources of Spain and the East at his command. But Caesar had never been one to back down, and he would not now. With a gambler's words, 'the die is cast', he crossed the Rubicon.

This was the war that Cato and his friends had wanted. By leading his army out of his province, Caesar unambiguously revealed himself to be an enemy of the state. His friends were embarrassed and uncomfortable; his enemies confirmed in their hostility. Now all that remained was for the rebel and his single legion to be destroyed, just as Catiline had been.

But the *boni* had not counted on the speed and boldness of Caesar's advance. Caesar's one legion, the Thirteenth, was a legion he had raised and trained himself; a legion he had led through the forests of Gaul; a legion he had made rich with plunder, whose centurions and officers he knew by name – men who owed their whole careers to Caesar's favour. With this legion, he marched at full speed towards Rome.

None of the Italian towns showed any desire to hold out against him, nor did any of Pompey's hastily assembled levies make a stand. When one commander, Domitius 'Bronze-beard' Ahenobarbus, tried to defend Corfinium, his men simply handed him over to Caesar along with the town. Caesar, with the clemency that was to be his signature in the civil war, let Ahenobarbus go.

Pompey, experienced as he was, had realized by now the danger of the situation. His best troops were scattered. There was no force immediately at hand that could match Caesar's Thirteenth. The only two veteran legions Pompey had in Italy had been lent to him by Caesar himself, and if called upon to fight, it was very likely that they would switch sides. So, to the surprise and horror of Cato and the rest, the great man abandoned Rome, leading a miserable procession of Roman aristocrats southward along the Via Appia. As they left the city, the fleeing senators passed under the shadow of their own ancestral tombs, lined up grandly along the ancient road.

* * *

In the summer of the following year, 48 BC, after much cautious manoeuvring, Pompey and Caesar confronted one another at last at Pharsalus in Greece. Pompey had had months to build up his forces, and his army outnumbered Caesar's two to one, but still Pompey would have been happier not to fight. Caesar had advanced into hostile territory and was now struggling for reinforcements and supplies. While Pompey's army grew steadily stronger, Caesar's was worn down. His surrender might only have been a matter of time.

But Pompey's senatorial allies were impatient. Almost every distinguished Roman had rallied to Pompey's standards: Ahenobarbus was there, still smarting from the humiliation at Corfinium; so were the grand ex-consuls Claudius Marcellus and Lentulus Spinther; Caesar's trusted legate Labienus was there, having defected to the Pompeian side with three and a half thousand Gallic horse. The younger political generation was well represented too, by Faustus Cornelius Sulla, son of the great dictator, and by a promising nephew of Cato's named Marcus Junius Brutus – a man who traced his name back to the founding of the republic.

Even the battle-shy Cicero had eventually gone over to Pompey, despite Caesar's best attempts to court him. He was horrified, however, by the bellicose mood in Pompey's camp: young aristocrats were already squabbling about who would stand for magistracies after peace was restored; who would succeed Caesar as *pontifex maximus*; which names should appear on the new proscription lists they would put up in the recaptured Forum. There was nothing good about the *boni*, Cicero joked, except their cause.

Confident and eager, the senators chafed at Pompey's constant delay. Caesar was at their mercy. The time to strike was now. So, on 9 August, Pompey deployed his legions on the plain of Pharsalus. Pompeius Magnus, greatest general of his generation, would lead his men to battle one last time.

Two years after the Battle of Pharsalus, Julius Caesar returned to Rome to celebrate an extraordinary quadruple triumph, celebrating victories in Asia, Egypt, Africa and Gaul.

The city had never seen such a spectacle. There were chariot and foot races; dances and stage-plays in each neighbourhood; great shows of gladiators and wild beasts; a mock naval battle on an artificial lake. People came in from miles around, sleeping in the streets and in the porticos of the basilicas. Thousands of tables were laid out in the open, piled high with bread and meat to feed the hungry throng. There were gifts, too: grain and oil and a little money, plus a year's rent for poorer citizens. This was much needed, and generous, but nothing compared to the bounty Caesar paid his soldiers: 5,000 denarii each – more than an ordinary man could expect to earn in a lifetime.

Four times in that long month of celebration, Caesar and his men marched along the old triumphal route through the city, down through the Campus Martius, along the length of the Circus Maximus, then round the Palatine, along the Via Sacra into the Forum and up to the Temple of Jupiter on the Capitoline hill.

These occasions had their own elaborate ceremonial – as much religious procession as victory parade. Caesar, the triumphing general, appeared in a cloud of incense, wearing purple robes embroidered in gold. In his left hand he held an ivory sceptre, topped with an eagle; in his right, a laurel branch. His chariot was gold, drawn by white horses, and fitted with a magical phallus hanging between its wheels. Riding with him was a slave, holding a gold wreath, whose duty it was to lean forward occasionally and whisper in his ear, 'Remember you are only a man.'

His legions followed: the Tenth; the loyal Thirteenth; the ill-fated Ninth Hispana.* As they marched they chanted rude songs about their commander, in accordance with ancient tradition: 'Romans guard your wives!' they sang. 'Here we bring the hairless adulterer!' And: 'Caesar conquered the Gauls, but Nicomedes conquered him!'

Wagons piled with loot led the column: barbarous weapons and armour; vessels full of gold and silver; statues, paintings and precious stones. Other floats carried painted scenes from the campaigns or boastful placards numbering the enemies killed and the cities taken. Of the brief Asian war, against an ambitious son of the legendary Mithridates, Caesar had nothing to say but 'I came. I saw. I conquered' – 'Veni. Vidi. Vici.'

At each triumph, Caesar's chariot was followed by hostages and prisoners from the relevant campaign, living trophies from the nations he had conquered. He had princelings from Asia and Bithynia dancing in his honour; an Egyptian princess walking in his train; from Africa, the infant son of Numidia's conquered king. For the triumph to celebrate victory in Gaul, Caesar brought out the Celtic rebel Vercingetorix, who had been kept in captivity for years to await this moment. Now, as was traditional, the defeated Gaul was led through the streets to the Tullianum prison, where he was ritually strangled.†

---

* Some time during the second century BC, the Ninth Legion vanished without explanation from the archaeological record. What happened to the Ninth is an enduring mystery. The traditional theory has been that the legion was annihilated in northern Britain, but it is now believed more likely that the Ninth met its end in the East.

† The Egyptian princess Arsinoë and the Numidian prince were spared the traditional garrotting on account of their youth. Arsinoë was murdered a

*

The four triumphs covered the four corners of the Mediterranean. The prisoners were Anatolians and Hellenized Egyptians, Numidians and Gauls. Caesar was laying claim to a world-spanning victory over barbarian foes; an unprecedented achievement.

Almost, but not quite, obscured by all this pomp and noise were certain painful silences, ghosts flitting at the edge of public attention, the missing faces of unmentioned men.

Few remained of those boastful nobles who once had filled Pompey's camp. Bibulus had died at sea. Ahenobarbus had been killed at Pharsalus when the Pompeian legions crumbled. Labienus, whose cavalry had been the first to break, had disappeared to Spain where he would fall in battle a year later.

As for Pompey himself, the great man had fled the battlefield and escaped with his family to the great city of Alexandria on the Nile Delta. Caesar made much of his Egyptian captives, taken in a local civil war. He did not show off the most important prize of the campaign: the fugitive Pompey's head, which had been delivered to Caesar's galley – rather to his horror – by the terrified Alexandrians as soon as he made landfall.

In Africa, Caesar had fought not just Numidians but also a Roman army, led by no less a man than Quintus Metellus Scipio, a descendant of Scipio Africanus. The family that had conquered Hannibal was now all but extinguished, the last great Scipio defeated and driven to suicide in the very territory that his ancestors had won for Rome.

Here too died Cato the Younger, Caesar's most committed adversary. He had been left in charge of the old Carthaginian city of Utica. As Caesar's victorious legions approached, he read through one last time his well-thumbed copy of Plato's *Phaedo*, a dialogue on the immortality of the soul. Then he stabbed himself in the belly.

Unfortunately for Cato, his aim was a little off. The wound was deep but not fatal, and his son and slaves were able to fetch a doctor

few years later on the orders of her more famous half-sister Cleopatra, but young Juba of Numidia grew up to be a notable scholar and writer in Rome.

to stitch him up again. But the grim old Stoic was as stubborn as ever. As soon as he had the chance, Cato tore out the stitches and disembowelled himself with his own hands, before anyone could stop him.

This was Cato's final attack on Caesar, a last bitter blow against his most hated enemy. He knew that if he were taken alive, Caesar would spare him. Nothing could have been more intolerable to Cato than Caesar's mercy.

Caesar's strategic *clementia* had been demonstrated again and again during the civil wars, and there were many men watching his triumphs who owed their lives to it. Cicero had been especially well received when he returned to Italy after the battle of Pharsalus, and publicly declared himself impressed by Caesar's 'great humanity' and 'exceptional moderation'.

Another surviving ex-Pompeian was that nephew of Cato's, Marcus Junius Brutus, who was now one of the most distinguished men in Caesar's Rome. Descended from the highest aristocracy, Brutus was a serious type, a student of philosophy, known in the law courts for his thoughtful, laconic style. 'I don't know what this young man wants,' Caesar commented, watching him speak one day, 'but whatever he wants, he wants it very much.'

Brutus's mother was Cato's half-sister Servilia – that same sister whose letter to Caesar had caused such embarrassment all those years before. Caesar had always loved Servilia, and treated her son with such affection that many thought the boy must be his own.*

But when Caesar crossed the Rubicon, Brutus had chosen Pompey's side. Probably this truly was, as everyone believed, a decision made on principle. Brutus had a strong personal reason to join Caesar: Pompey had put Brutus's father to death after a failed rebellion three decades before. But it was Caesar who had broken the law, leading his army into Italy, so Brutus followed his uncle Cato and the rest of the *boni* to the Pompeian camp.

* This is unlikely, as Caesar was just fifteen when Brutus was born; although, given his notoriety as a seducer, nothing should be put past him.

The day before the battle of Pharsalus, while the other aristocrats were drinking and dividing the imaginary spoils, Brutus sat quietly in his tent working at his books. Caesar's men are supposed to have had special instructions not to harm him, and after the defeat he was welcomed by Caesar, given the governorship of Cisalpine Gaul, and later a prestigious post as urban praetor in Rome.

Now, as Caesar celebrated his four triumphs, Brutus stood as a living symbol of peace and reconciliation. The civil war was over. Unity was restored. All was forgiven. One by one, throwing themselves on Caesar's mercy, the exiled Pompeians started coming home.

* * *

Those were good years in the city. At last there was peace and, even better, something like a proper government.

The senate, of course, was still a mess. Caesar had enrolled hundreds of his supporters to fill the gaps in the senate's ranks, including, to the horror of conservatives, some of the chief men of recently conquered Gaul. But while this did nothing for senatorial harmony, it hardly interfered with the running of the state. In practical terms, the senate had been quietly superseded. While the senators bickered, it was Caesar and his two right-hand men, Oppius and Balbus, who were running the republic.

There was much to be done. The corn dole for the urban poor was badly in need of reorganization. The veterans of the civil war and the Gallic campaign needed to be settled. Mixed groups of soldiers and poor citizens were sent out to new colonies, including a major new town at Carthage.

In the countryside, meanwhile, Caesar planned to drain the malarial Pomptine Marsh, south of Rome, reclaiming the land for agriculture. Landowners were compelled by law to employ at least some free labourers alongside their usual armies of slaves.

Time itself was in a state of disrepair. The old Roman calendar counted just 355 days in each year which meant that Rome's priests, the *pontifices*, sometimes had to add extra intercalary months in order to keep the dates synchronized with the seasons. Over the long years of chaos, this procedure had been badly neglected, with the result that midwinter was now falling in late February. With the help of an Alexandrian astrologer, Caesar now brought the Roman system in line with the latest astrological principles. The traditional calendar was replaced with a new, 'Julian' calendar, featuring the modern 365-day year.*

In 46 BC Caesar had to deal with a final flare-up of civil war. The sons of Pompey, Gnaeus and Sextus, had managed to raise a large new army in Spain. At the battle of Munda, in March of 45 BC, Caesar came within an inch of defeat. For a moment, he stood alone, catching enemy javelins on his shield while his men wavered behind him. At last, seeing their general in danger, the Tenth Legion charged forward to break through the enemy line.

The senators back in Rome were relieved at Caesar's victory. Brutus's brother-in-law, Gaius Cassius Longinus, had written to Cicero: 'I would rather stick with the old clement master than try a new and cruel one.'

All the same, they were having trouble reconciling themselves to Caesar's pre-eminence. The aristocratic competition that had been the engine of republican politics was dead. There was nothing left to compete for. The old positions of power were now little more than empty honours, bestowed on Caesar's loyal allies. One man, Caninius, was allowed, as a perk, to hold the consulship for a single afternoon. Caninius was so indefatigable, joked Cicero, that during his consulship he never slept.

Brutus, meanwhile, was becoming more and more obsessed with his dead uncle Cato, a man whose stern example he perhaps felt he ought to have followed. In an admiring biography, Brutus presented Cato as a hero of old-fashioned virtue. Caesar, fighting in Spain, published his own *Anticato* in response, but his characterization of

---

* This Julian calendar remained in general use in Europe until it was replaced by the Gregorian calendar in 1582. It is in honour of Julius Caesar, of course, that the old Roman month of Quintilis is now known as July.

Cato as a miser and an alcoholic failed to stick.

Cato dead was a much more attractive figure than he had been alive, and Brutus and his fellows made him the symbol of the lost spirit of the republic. Brutus even divorced his wife in order to marry Cato's daughter Porcia, a woman who was to prove every bit as bloody-minded as her father had been.

From the point of view of conservative aristocrats, Caesar's regime was a standing insult to the traditions of Roman politics. His official position was *dictator*, as Sulla's had been. It was an ancient role designed for moments of national crisis in which it was necessary for one man to hold unfettered power. Camillus, for example, had been appointed dictator to drive out the invading Gauls.

But dictators were meant to resign as soon as the crisis had passed – a rule that even Sulla had eventually followed. Caesar showed no sign of any such intention. As the months rolled by, those who, like Cicero, had hoped for a return to constitutional government began to despair. In February 44 BC, the month of the Lupercalia, Caesar took the title *dictator perpetuus* – dictator for life.

The honours voted to him by his carefully packed senate had grown ever more extravagant. He was the first living Roman to have his head stamped on a coin. His statue was set up among the statues of the ancient kings on the Capitol. He was given the titles Father of his Country and *imperator*, and awarded the right to wear triumphal clothing on all formal occasions.

Each new honour raised Caesar above his fellow man. Just how far was an open – and highly charged – question. Many of the rulers Caesar had met in the East considered themselves at least semi-divine. And indeed, Romulus himself had set a Roman precedent for the transition from mortal to immortal. Now a statue of Caesar was set up suggestively in Romulus's temple.

Better with Romulus than with Salus, joked Cicero. Romulus, in some versions of the story at least, had ended his life not swept up to heaven by the gods but torn to pieces by disgruntled senators. Salus was the goddess of safety and long life.

But the Romulus–Caesar identification was worrying. Above all things, the senatorial aristocracy hated kings, and Romulus was the father of the ancient Roman monarchy. Could Caesar be plotting to do away with the republic altogether? 'Once he wanted to sleep with a king,' people muttered. 'Now he wants to be one.'

The flames of republican ardour were stoked by xenophobic alarm. In a grand villa on the right bank of the Tiber, the beautiful Queen Cleopatra of Egypt had installed herself in royal state – an unwelcome prize of the battles Caesar had fought in Alexandria after Pharsalus. She had smuggled herself through enemy lines and into Caesar's presence in a laundry bag, the story was, and once the fighting was done, had induced the general to mis-spend an entire summer with her on a pleasure-cruise up the Nile.

Now, Cleopatra and Caesar spent long hours walking together in her gardens while she whispered who knew what into his ear. Worse yet, there was a son who, although an infant and not legally acknowledged, bore a name, Caesarion, that was a clear statement of ambition. The republic, it appeared, was to be handed over to an oriental dynasty.

* * *

Romans hated kings. So, when a half-naked Marcus Antonius offered a golden crown to Caesar at the Lupercalia of 44 BC, there was horrified silence.

With a slow, deliberate gesture, Caesar reached out a hand and waved the crown away. Wild cheers. Once more, the pantomime was repeated, the crown was offered and refused. Again, the offer was greeted with alarm; the refusal with applause.

Caesar cannot have been ignorant of what was about to happen. Antonius was impulsive, but he would not have made such a spectacle of himself without instruction. The best guess is that Caesar was hoping, by refusing the crown so publicly, to put an end to the monarchical speculation that was stirring so much aristocratic discontent.

In fact, the display had the opposite effect. The whole performance had been a test, the Romans suspected. Caesar had rejected the crown for now, no doubt, but if the crowd had cheered at the possibility of a new monarchy, Caesar would have made himself king on the spot.

Wherever such things were whispered, men looked to Brutus. He was a man of proven ability and high rank, highly educated, a distinguished orator, the nephew and son-in-law of the great Cato. More than all that, the overthrow of tyrants ran in his blood, or so everyone thought. It was a Brutus, after all, who, deep in Rome's mythic past, had expelled the last Tarquin king, becoming the first consul of the newly instituted republic.

Now, Brutus's great ancestor became a stick with which the senators beat him. The old hero's statue was daubed with revolutionary slogans: 'If only Brutus were alive!'; 'If only we had you now, Brutus!' Meanwhile, the living Brutus found his praetorian chair in the Forum, where he sat to judge court cases, inscribed with mournful reproaches: 'Are you asleep?'; 'You are not really Brutus!' When Brutus's brother-in-law Cassius urged him to join a conspiracy against the dictator, he was able to argue that the planned tyrannicide was 'a debt you owe your ancestry'.

Brutus hesitated. Caesar had saved his life, forgiven his rebellion and even raised him to high honour, treating him with an almost fatherly affection. Roman politics was built on bonds of friendship, of *amicitia*, and those bonds were not lightly to be broken. But the old Brutus of ancient myth set a stern example. This was a man who, supposedly, had not hesitated to execute even his own sons when they conspired against the republic. Across a half-millennium gap, the myth reached a grim hand to steer the younger Brutus into the arms of the assassins.

With Brutus on board, finding other recruits was easy. Cicero was left out – it was felt he was too cautious, and perhaps too much swayed by Caesar's personal charm – but there were dozens of other influential men willing to spill the dictator's blood. A simple plan was put together. There was reason to hurry: Caesar was planning another expedition, this time to Parthia to avenge Crassus's defeat. The window for action was closing fast, and so a date was set: 15 March, the midpoint of the month, which the Romans called the *idus* – the ides.

Romans would later remember the evil omens that had foretold Caesar's doom. A herd of sacred horses dedicated to the River Rubicon stopped grazing and began to weep. Strange men ran about the streets all wrapped in flames. Mysterious lights and booming sounds troubled the night sky. A sacrificial victim offered by Caesar to the gods was found to have no heart. And if all this was not clear enough, a soothsayer was on hand to deliver an explicit warning: 'Beware the ides of March'.

'He must fear many, whom many fear,' said a Roman playwright once to Caesar from the stage. There was plenty of reason for Caesar to fear for his life. He knew, too, from what quarter danger might come. 'It is not sleek, long-haired fellows who frighten me,' he is said to have remarked, 'but the pale thin ones.' His well-fed military underlings like Marcus Antonius, that is to say, were no threat compared to those like Brutus and Cassius, made sour by a diet of envy and idealism.

But Caesar had never been a man to take account of omens, of whatever sort. When warned specifically about Brutus's intentions, he laughed it off: 'Do you imagine that Brutus cannot wait for this poor flesh to end its days?' He refused to take any thought for his personal safety and walked through the city with no bodyguard except for the constant press of admirers and friends. When 15 March came around at last, that same soothsayer who had warned him of the coming danger approached him as he walked through the Roman Forum. 'Well,' said Caesar teasingly, 'the ides of March have come.'

'Yes,' replied the prophet, 'but they are not yet gone.'

Brutus and his fellow conspirators had spent those days in a state of mounting nerves. By the time the ides came round, some sixty senators were in on the conspiracy, not to mention any number of slaves, wives, associates and hangers-on. They knew that they might be betrayed at any time, and indeed a slave with evidence of the plot had narrowly missed Caesar earlier, while a Greek scholar had managed to press a scroll into the dictator's hand on which the names of all the would-be assassins were written. It remained unread.

Even those with no knowledge of the plan could tell that something was up. Brutus's wife Porcia, daughter of Cato, had immediately sensed that her husband was guarding some terrible secret. One night, she took a knife and carved a hole in her own leg, this to demonstrate her ability to hold out under torture. Brutus, impressed, took her into his confidence.*

The conspirators assembled at the Curia of Pompey, part of a huge theatre complex built by Pompeius Magnus with the spoils of his eastern victories out on the Campus Martius under the Capitoline hill. The senate was due to meet here and Caesar, the *dictator perpetuus*, was bound to attend.

But the day dragged on, and Caesar did not appear. Vague reports spoke of inauspicious omens at Caesar's house; of bad dreams that might keep him at home. At last, word came that he was on the move, coming down the Via Sacra through the Forum. Still the minutes stretched, as Caesar and his attendant crowd crept round the bottom of the Capitol. Casca, one of the conspirators, found himself grasped by a friend as he paced back and forth: 'You hid the secret from us, Casca, but Brutus has told us everything.' A heart-stopped silence. Then the man continued: 'You must tell me, dear fellow, how you got so rich as to be able to stand for the aedileship.'

Yet it was impossible not to feel as though every man there already knew their murderous intentions. Each greeting, each nod or glance in Brutus or Cassius's direction, seemed freighted with fear or encouragement. One man, Popilius Laenas, went so far as to wish Brutus well in 'the accomplishment of what you have in mind' and warned him not to hesitate. 'The matter is on men's tongues.'

And then, at last, a thickening of the crowd announced the arrival of the great man himself. Here he was, stepping down from his litter, splendid in his purple toga and his golden laurel wreath. And now

---

* This same Porcia, so the story goes, killed herself after Brutus's final defeat at Philippi by swallowing red-hot coals.

Popilius Laenas, Brutus's wellwisher, had plucked at Caesar's sleeve and had him deep in conversation. Brutus and Cassius looked at each other anxiously, gripping the daggers hidden under their robes. They were resolved, if it came to it, to take their own lives rather than be captured. But then Caesar was coming up the steps with his usual untroubled air. He passed into the hall where the senate waited. At the door the loyal Marcus Antonius was delayed by one of the conspirators on some spurious pretext. Caesar went on alone.

Inside, the usual crowd of faces asking for favours. This time it was Tillius Cimber and his friends who pressed about him, begging, kissing his hand, pulling at his robe. Impatience turned to anger. With a gesture, Caesar dismissed the mob of supplicants, but they kept pressing and then the dictator felt Cimber grasp his toga with both hands and pull it away from his neck.

Now suddenly, as if he dreamed it, the familiar scene was twisted into nightmare. The first dagger sliced at his shoulder, and Caesar, fighter that he was, grasped the blade in one hand while stabbing his assassin through the arm with a sharpened pen. But now other blades gleamed among the bodies. Whichever way he turned, Caesar was hemmed in by biting steel. Then, through the thicket of arms and legs, he saw his friend Brutus approaching, dagger drawn. Caesar spoke, some men later recalled, not in Latin but rather in Greek, the language of friendship, of intimacy: '*Kai su teknon?*' – 'Even you my child?' With those words, he pulled a fold of his toga over his face and gave himself up to death.[*]

* * *

Brutus expected the Romans to rejoice at their liberation from the dictator's yoke. Instead, the mood of the city moved rapidly from shock to resentment. To those on the lower rungs of Roman society,

---

* The historian Suetonius was aware of some accounts in which Caesar addressed Brutus in Greek. His own version, however, has Caesar collapsing without a word, which is just as plausible, if not more so. The familiar '*Et tu, Brute*', meanwhile, owes its fame to Shakespeare and is not in the ancient sources.

a stable monarchy had been vastly preferable to the endless destructive competition of a narrow ruling class.

Three days after the murder, Caesar's body was displayed in the Roman Forum, pierced by the twenty-three wounds the conspirators had inflicted. So keen had the assassins been to dip their blades in Caesar's blood that some had even cut each other in the melee.

The plan had been to cremate Caesar on the Campus Martius, near the tomb of his daughter Julia, but when the crowd in the Forum saw the corpse and the purple robe all torn and bloodied, they went wild with emotion. Weeping plebeians burst into the neighbouring buildings, basilicas just lately built with Caesar's gold, smashing up seats and benches to make an improvised funeral pyre. The actors hired for the funeral procession tore off their robes and fed them to the flames; Women threw in their jewellery; veteran soldiers threw in their shields and weapons, their whole selves and livelihoods, heaped on the blaze that burned at the city's heart.

Brutus had offered Caesar up as a sacrifice to the spirit of the Roman republic. He thought that by killing his friend he could save the state. He was wrong. The republic had grown enormous, spread its dominion across half the world. Now, though it appeared magnificent, it was rotten, ready to crumble.

The wait would not be long. At that moment, on a fast ship headed for Rome, was the young man who would give the tottering state the final kick. The republic was over. The new Rome would be ruled by one man alone: an emperor.

6

THE ART OF LOVE

Ovid exiled from Rome

———

AD 8

EARLY EVENING, SOMETIME during the 20s BC. A figure passes under the shadows of a monumental colonnade. A young man. He pauses, presses his back against a sun-warmed pillar of yellow Numidian marble. He is carefully groomed: tanned forearms show beneath a clean white toga; his teeth are clean; his beard is trimmed; his nostrils are scrupulously plucked – and he sniffs the wind, let us imagine, like a hound on the scent. High up here on the Palatine hill, in the newly built sanctuary of Apollo, the air is fresh enough. From the city below, a fine haze of woodsmoke. A waft of burning incense from the shrine. The warm note of pines in the summer breeze.

Rising all around is a sort of enormous architectural stage set. On three sides, the colonnade of the temple portico frames the scene: its double row of yellow columns broken up by black stone statues of mythical murderesses – the Danaids – and by fierce Danaus himself, brandishing a savage-looking blade. Rising above, up a broad flight of steps, the temple itself gleams triumphantly: the climax of the political and religious drama that is encoded here. Terracotta plaques, just like those on the old Temple of Jupiter on the Capitoline, link this temple to the ancient Italic past. Ivory panels reveal the new reach of a world-spanning empire. Sculpted reliefs show Apollo conquering the brutish Hercules, and Romans remember – and are constantly reminded – that not so long ago the drunken brute Marcus Antonius with his barbarous queen Cleopatra were themselves conquered in a great battle off Cape Actium, where, on the crag, another temple of Apollo stands as tall as this one here.

This temple of Apollo is a masterpiece of architectural propaganda. But the man by the pillar (a poet, he calls himself) is oblivious to the messages being beamed across Rome from the summit of the Palatine. His keen nose has picked up the smell of expensive perfume: rosewater maybe, or extract of Egyptian nard and now, as he sidles round the column's smooth flank, he sees the source: a girl in a fine silk dress, richly dyed in saffron or amaryllis, sea green or Paphian myrtle. He admires her hair, carefully curled with a hot iron. With the eye of a veteran seducer, he takes the measure of the eunuch chaperone who lumbers beside her.

The poet's senses hum with the excitement of new love; his awakened lust is already condensing into pretty words – words which will be his weapons to pierce any defences that fear or chastity may erect in his path. As he sets himself for the chase, he forgets his monumental surroundings; the victory being re-enacted in the stone symbols of this sacred compound, and what that victory means. He has forgotten whose house it is that stands next to this temple; who it is that sits at the paper-strewn desk in the small tower that rises across the way. He has forgotten Apollo's chosen protégé: the man who now rules Rome.

* * *

Publius Ovidius Naso was born in 43 BC in the small Italian town of Sulmo, high on the well-watered eastern flank of the Apennine mountains. His father belonged to an old family of the local aristocracy; not drowning in sesterces, exactly, but rich enough to buy his sons a proper education.

Ovid will have been sent first to a *litterator* to learn his letters; then, at around ten years old, to a *grammaticus*, for training in poetry and literary appreciation. Pupils in those days were expected to be fluent in both Latin and Greek, and to master a literary canon that stretched back over seven hundred years, from the great early epics of Homer and Hesiod through the elegant verse of Hellenistic Alexandria to the new Roman masterpieces that were being produced in Ovid's own day.

At around fifteen, however, boys would receive the *toga virilis* which signified their entry into Roman adulthood, and a turn away from childish versification. The final, and most important phase of a Roman education was conducted by a *rhetor* – an instructor in the art of public speaking.

By this time, Ovid had probably been sent from Sulmo to continue his studies in the capital. There had been a time when young men of ambition would learn rhetoric by listening to the magistrates and lawyers speaking in the Forum, and although this sort of on-the-spot training had long since been replaced by highly specialized professional instruction, there was still no doubt that Rome was the only place to learn the skills for a successful public life. Schools of various sorts could be found all over the city. Sometimes pupils gathered in private houses; more often, they would meet in gardens or porticos, or just in the streets. The city itself was the schoolhouse for ambitious youths, just as it would become their arena for the political battles ahead.

But Ovid and his contemporaries were entering a radically different political scene from the one their fathers and instructors had known. Back in 43 BC, the year after Caesar's assasination and about a month after Ovid was born, there was a battle between Roman factions at Mutina in the Po Valley. The consuls of that year – good republicans both – defeated Caesar's old lieutenant Marcus Antonius but both lost their lives in the process. Command of the senatorial army passed unexpectedly to an untested nineteen-year-old called Gaius Octavianus – a youth who owed what little stature he had entirely to the fact that he was the great-nephew, legal heir and posthumously adopted son of Gaius Julius Caesar.

Julius Caesar's death in 44 BC had splintered the Roman elite. Traditionalists still dreamed of restoring the integrity of the old republican system. The assassins, led by Brutus and Cassius, were in the eastern provinces, gathering support. In Rome, the men of ambition quietly weighed their prospects. Italy was full of leaderless veterans waiting to be mobilized. For aspiring autocrats, this was a land rich in opportunity.

At the battle of Mutina, Octavianus showed himself willing and able to grasp it. He had money, having inherited most of Caesar's fortune, and could command at least the provisional loyalty of Caesar's veterans, especially now he had a military victory to his name. Now, with the shamelessness of a born winner, he smoothly switched sides, joining Antonius along with another old Caesarian called Marcus Lepidus to oppose the traditionalists in the senate. Meeting once again at Mutina, the three men divided the state between them just as Caesar, Pompey and Crassus had done all those years before. Rome once again found herself governed by a triumvirate.

Ovid was still an infant when the triumviral proscriptions began – too young to feel the shadow of fear spreading through Italy. It was a thorough purge of political enemies, but it also included men whose only sin was to have amassed a fortune large enough to catch a triumvir's eye. Antonius and Octavianus traded deaths: Antonius gave up his own uncle to the executioners. In return, Octavianus allowed Cicero's name to be added to the list of the condemned. In the year of Ovid's birth, the severed head and right hand of Rome's greatest orator were nailed, in cruel insult, to the speaker's platform in the Roman Forum.

In Ovid's second year of life, Antonius and Octavianus finally caught up with Caesar's assassins. In a close battle at Philippi, Brutus and Cassius were defeated and committed suicide. It was Antonius's legions who carried the day, the general leading his men like a latter-day Hercules. Octavianus, suffering the after-effects of an illness, saw his wing of the army thrown back in confusion and only narrowly escaped capture himself. Perhaps it was the fright that made him so harsh in victory. The flower of the old Roman aristocracy died that day. Brutus's head was sent back to Rome in a box, to be cast in the dust at the feet of Caesar's statue.

There was peace, then, for a while, but it could not last. Ovid was twelve when the final confrontation began, the two uneasy allies, Antonius and Octavianus, challenging each other for the right to rule supreme in Rome. At Actium, in Greece, where a temple of Apollo rose above the sea, Octavianus's navy defeated the combined fleets of Antonius and Cleopatra of Egypt. The poet Virgil imagined a stirring scene:

> Both sides at once surge forth. The seas froth white,
> Churned by the oars and triple-pointed prows.
> They head for open sea. You'd think the Cyclades,
> Torn from their roots, were breasting through the wave
> Or looming cliffs rammed up against each other.
> In such huge ships the sailors pressed pursuit
> On towering sterns.

In fact, it had not been much of a fight. Antonius and Cleopatra had already decided to retreat towards the East. They escaped, but the competent admiralship of Octavianus's friend Marcus Vipsanius Agrippa meant that their finest ships – their huge bronze-armoured quinqueremes – had to be given up for lost.

Militarily, it was a survivable defeat, but Antonius's prestige suffered a fatal blow. His Roman allies were already uneasy at his close association with an Egyptian queen. Octavianus had none of Antonius's glamour or personal charm, but he did have Rome, and the strong aura of legitimacy that only the capital could bestow. Now, seeing their general's sails disappearing eastwards, the officers and men of Antonius's land forces abandoned the fight.

Octavianus learned the lesson well. He understood the importance of appearances, understood that his supremacy, if it was to endure, must depend not only on the support of Marcus Agrippa, his invincible military commander, but also on the good works of another close friend, Gaius Cilnius Maecenas, a flamboyant Etruscan nobleman who had made himself Italy's foremost patron of the arts.

Agrippa won the battle at Actium, but it was Maecenas's poets who turned Actium into the world-shaking triumph it became – a triumph so dazzling that it could serve as the foundation for a whole new political regime.

All through the 30s BC, Maecenas had been mustering his forces: a brotherhood of artists bound together by his careful generosity, ready to deploy their storytelling skills in Octavianus's service. Shining brightest amid a constellation of lesser names were Quintus Horatius Flaccus and Publius Vergilius Maro – Horace and Virgil.

Horace, like many idealistic young Romans, had fought for Brutus and Cassius at Philippi but was quickly brought round to Octavianus's side and inducted into Maecenas's inner circle. It was an excellent piece of business. The young man was a much better poet than soldier, and soon mended what little hurt he had done in fighting against what he now understood to be the march of destiny. 'Hail O Triumph!' he wrote after Actium. 'Why delay the golden chariots!' The new Caesar, Horace declared, was a greater general than Scipio Africanus himself. 'Fill, boy, the jar with new Caecuban wine!'

Virgil, perhaps the greatest poet Rome ever produced, was similarly useful to Octavianus's new regime. His *Aeneid*, written over the decade following the battle of Actium, was a work of extraordinary ambition – a Roman answer to the great Homeric epics from which the whole body of later classical literature had essentially sprung. In it, he told the story of Aeneas, the Trojan refugee who was the ultimate ancestor of Romulus and of the Julian clan and hence of Octavianus himself. No reader, having followed Aeneas through twelve books of verse in epic hexameter, could be in any doubt that Rome's current ruler represented the culmination of a divine scheme that went back to the founding of the city and beyond. The young man who led at Actium, 'standing proud on the poop deck with twin flames shooting forth from his happy brows', who fought 'with the elders and the people and the household spirits and the great gods at his side' – '*cum patribus populoque, penatibus et magnis dis*' – was surely the equal of the heroes of legend, if not of the gods themselves.

This all fitted perfectly with the developing themes of Octavianus's own propaganda. He had already presided over the deification of his adopted father Julius Caesar, whose newly built temple now stood at the eastern end of the Roman Forum. Octavianus was now *divi filius* – Son of a God – and no one was brave enough to mention that the only plausible biological son of the god in question, Cleopatra's little son Caesarion, had been quietly murdered in Alexandria, while his mother, rather than be paraded in Octavianus's triumph, bared her breast to a smuggled viper.* So the pharaonic monarchy of Egypt was finally snuffed out, after a run of over three thousand years.

In Egypt and the other eastern provinces, Octavianus was content to be regarded, like the pharaohs, as a sort of god-king. Romans knew that decadent orientals were used to worshipping their overlords.

In Rome itself, however, a little more delicacy was required – Rome had not tolerated a king since the fall of the Tarquins half a millennium before. The mere suggestion of monarchy had turned Julius Caesar's friends into his assassins. Returning to the capital after finishing off the last of Antonius's forces, Octavianus carefully avoided carving out a new official position for himself at the head of the Roman state.

'I accepted no office for myself in violation of ancestral practice,' he boasted in his autobiography. In fact, he claimed, he had in 27 BC formally relinquished the extrajudicial power forced upon him by the civil wars and restored the proper constitution of the Roman republic. The senate and consuls resumed control of the state and Octavianus took his place among them as, simply, a sort of first citizen: a *princeps*.

In reality, of course, the great 'restoration of the republic' was no such thing. Octavianus had made sure that the administration of certain key provinces remained in his own hands – frontier provinces in which the vast majority of Rome's legions were stationed. For all his loud talk of law and constitution, the whole edifice of Octavianus's power was built on a foundation of armed men.

---

* Constantine Cavafy, two thousand years later, spun one of his most beautiful poems out of his image of Caesarion's pale ghost: 'I fancied that you entered my room, / it seemed that you stood before me; as you might have been in vanquished Alexandria, / pale and tired, idealistic in your sorrow, / still hoping that they would pity you, / the wicked – who whispered "Too many Caesars."'

But appearances were important. One of Octavianus's most important monuments survives today, having been dug out from under a Renaissance palazzo: his Altar of Peace, the *Ara Pacis*. Visitors to Rome can see there, carved on to the altar's marble flanks, the ruler as he wanted to be seen: dressed in the toga of a citizen, at the head of his obedient family, surrounded by priests and magistrates, leading Romans in a sacrifice to the ancestral gods.

Octavianus wanted to rule not through legal power (*imperium*, in the Latin jargon), nor through the naked application of force, but rather through his own personal prestige – his *auctoritas*. He wanted to be seen to give advice, not orders. It was vital, then, for him to associate himself with the sacred traditions of the Roman state. His architects, his sculptors and his poets all assisted in an act of political transfiguration: Octavianus the young chancer, the brutal triumvir, the fighter of civil wars – all these past selves were eclipsed by a new and more dignified character. The new character even had a new name, one that echoed faintly that inaugural flight of birds which had appeared to Romulus at the dawn of Roman history. Octavianus was forgotten, and the age of Augustus began.

* * *

Ovid was just fifteen when Augustus took his new name, still a schoolboy learning rhetoric. We cannot know whether he realized, at that moment, that the old republican system was gone forever. There is almost nothing about Ovid's life in the ancient sources: just a mention from Seneca the Elder, who saw him practising rhetorical exercises and judged him to have an elegant and amiable talent, despite his already apparent love of vice. The young Ovid, says Seneca, had a particularly fondness for a type of rhetorical performance called a *suasoria*, in which students would impersonate famous characters from history. It was a sign of things to come.

Ovid never truly committed to his rhetorical studies, despite his natural ability. His orations, says Seneca, 'could be seen to be nothing more than poems with the metre taken out'. Ovid's elder brother was a gifted orator, 'born to use the weapons of the wordy forum', but

Ovid could already feel the pull of the poetic muse. 'Why waste yourself on these useless efforts,' Ovid recalled being told by his father. Doubtless, a life of artistic indolence was not what the old man had had in mind when he sent his sons to Rome. Ovid tried to oblige him with some serious prose, but 'poetry appeared of its own accord, metre and all, and anything I wrote came out in verse.' The irrepressible poet managed to control himself sufficiently to land a minor magistracy. The path to the senate – riches and respectability – was open, but 'neither body nor my mind was fit for the task'. Instead, Ovid chose a life of *tuta otia* – 'safe leisure'.

Despite paternal misgivings, Ovid's efforts were hardly useless. On the contrary, his talent was clear. His patchy adolescent beard had only once or twice been cut, he later wrote, when his juvenile poetry was first read aloud to the Roman public.

'I cultivated and cherished the poets of those days,' Ovid writes. 'Those bards that were present, I counted them as gods.' Years later, he named them fondly: Macer the didact; Bassus the master of iambics; Ponticus the epicist. Ovid was there to see Horace himself performing his verse, although he only glimpsed Virgil, who died in 19 BC. He may even have found himself an aristocratic patron, Marcus Valerius Messalla Corvinus, who, uniquely, numbered a woman among his literary protégés, the poet Sulpicia.

The most important poetic influence on Ovid was a young man named Sextus Propertius, only a few years older than Ovid himself. Propertius was one of Maecenas's finds, but unlike Virgil and Ovid, had largely resisted his patron's efforts to bend his talent to the service of the Augustan regime. It was not Apollo (Augustus's patron god) who inspired him, he lamented. Propertius was not a man for epic verse. His inspiration was a pretty girl, Cynthia. 'When she grapples naked with me,' he says, '*then*, I tell you, we produce whole Iliads.'

Propertius's verse was witty, sexy, satirical. Ovid was captivated. This was a poetry born of youth. A poetry removed from the high seriousness of matters of state; undarkened by the long shadows of the civil war. Ovid would become, like Propertius, a love elegist.

*

Love elegy was a specifically Roman poetic genre, characterized most obviously by its use of the elegiac metre. Latin verse does not rhyme. Instead, it is given its form by the arrangement of long and short syllables within a line, grouped into metrical units called feet. Epic metre, the form considered most suitable for 'high' subject matter, had regular lines of six feet: dumdidi dumdidi dumdidi dumdidi dumdidi dumdi.* Elegiac metre ran in couplets: lines of six feet alternating with lines of five, giving it a lighter feel.

So Ovid, in Propertian spirit, at the beginning of his own book of love poems, the *Amores*:

> *I planned to sing of arms and violent war*
> *In stately measures fitted to the tale*
> *Each second line being equal to the first.*
> *But a laughing Cupid, so they say,*
> *Came and stole one foot away.*

Like almost every other ancient poetic form, elegiac metre was invented by the Greeks. The Roman elegists of the late republic were copying Greek models laid down by the great Callimachus, an Alexandrian poet from two centuries before.

But it was in Rome that love elegy found its distinctive tone and subject matter, in a burst of poetic creativity that lasted little more than half a century, with the writings of Catullus, Gallus, Tibullus, Propertius and Ovid himself. Love elegy was rhetorical and skillfully crafted; it was also playful – sometimes subversive. It undermined the traditional ideas of Roman masculinity, of the tough citizen-soldier, the conqueror in arms.† The archetype appears in Ovid's poetry but

---

* This is epic hexameter in its simplest form. The 'dumdidi' foot – a dactyl – could be replaced with a spondee of two long syllables: dumdum. And of course there were complicated rules to follow regarding elision, the placement of a pause called a caesura, and the truncated foot at the end of each line.

† Romans considered it unmanly to be too fond of women. There was no special stigma attached to homosexual activity, however, so long as one was not being penetrated. So it made perfect sense for Catullus, accused of being

warped like an image in Cupid's mirror: 'Lovers are soldiers,' says the poet. 'Cupid has his corps.' Lovers evade husbands as soldiers sneak past sentries. Long watches are spent as much under lovers' windows as in frontier forts. 'A brave night fighter,' Ovid calls himself. His chosen weapon he leaves to the imagination.

Love elegy was about love, certainly; about sex and the pursuit of sex. But above all it was about the poet himself: the poet pierced with Cupid's arrows; the poet burning up with passion, pouring his heart on to the page. Love was not something that happened between two people but something performed, and suffered, by a man and expressed in intimate-sounding first-person verse.

Intimate-*sounding*, only, because of course the 'I' of love elegy is not to be regarded as identical with the real-life love poet. In his *Amores*, Ovid plays the role of Lover – a role he has learned from reading the work of the other love elegists who came before him. Do his poetic adventures reflect his true existence, outside verse? Ovid isn't telling. Indeed he loves the ambiguity. 'Trust me,' he will one day write. 'My habits are far from what you read in my poetry.' Elsewhere: 'the praise I gave my girl was lies... poetic license'. But as the poem goes on, we realize that his praise was true after all. He is dissimulating now because his poetry was too successful, and everyone in Rome has started chasing his girlfriend.

And there is no way to check any details in Ovid's verse. Apart from that one mention in Seneca the Elder, the only source we have on Ovid's life is Ovid himself.

So who is the man who was lurking in the portico of Apollo's temple on the Palatine that summer evening? We will have to call him 'Ovid' – not the real poet, although probably the real Ovid did cruise for girls in Augustus's new colonnade, but the persona. 'Ovid' is a character half-fact and half-fiction, a notorious seducer, a soldier in Love's war.

---

feminine, to threaten to prove his manliness upon his critics by anally and orally raping them.

From the love poems, we can reconstruct other scenes from the seducer's life. We have him writing to the girl from the portico: a proposition. Comes back the reply, scribbled in wax on a wooden tablet: 'It's not allowed!' He will examine this tablet carefully. The wax is reused – scraped flat after being read – but an attentive eye can still sometimes detect traces of past messages imprinted there.

Now we find him in the Circus Maximus. The banks of stone seats are packed full; the noise is deafening; the charioteers with their teams make a slow parade. But Ovid – 'Ovid' – is not here for the horses. He has managed to snag the seat next to his pretty girl (The same? We can imagine so) and she is hemmed in by the narrow seat dividers, unable to escape his attentions. The amorous poet is a whirlwind of unasked-for solicitude: he defends the girl's delicate thigh from the encroaching knees of her neighbour on the other side; he swats away a prodding foot; he lifts her hem – it was trailing in the dust – and steals a glance at her shapely ankles. Inflamed with lust, he fans her with his programme as the charioteers follow a statue of Victory round the oval course, and, while the crowd hoots and claps, the girl gives him a look, not much. A nod? Now the race is begun:

> Oh man! He took the turn too wide,
> What are you doing! The next chariot
> Sheered round and comes up close.
> What are you playing at you fool!
> You've rendered null and void my girl's good prayers.
> Pull hard I beg, pull hard on that left rein!
> We put our money on a nincompoop.

But the greater victory is creeping closer:

> She smiled; those bright eyes surely promised something.
> Enough for here. Give me the rest elsewhere.

We can find the Lover again in his bedroom. It is midday. One shutter is closed against the sun. The other swings ajar. The light is soft and dappled, as if under a canopy of trees. This is light for love and secret business.

And now, suddenly, the girl is here with him. She wears a long gown, loose. Her hair flows over her white neck in delicate curls. She stands by the bed, and Ovid reaches up a hand to grasp the thin material of her dress. A tug parts the seams at the shoulders; she clasps the torn cloth to her chest – token resistance – and then lets it fall, standing naked in the half-light, in the air that smells of smoke and cypress trees. He takes her in: arms, shoulders, smooth belly long under high breasts, delicate thighs…

Nothing I saw that didn't earn my praise,
I squeezed her naked with enfolding arms
The rest who cannot guess? Both rested in a daze.
May every midday grant me such sweet balms!

* * *

It is in this poem that the girl finally gets a name: Corinna. Not that this reveals much about who she really is. Corinna is an obvious pseudonym, Greek-flavoured, sounding like a Latinized mutation of the Greek word for 'girl'.

This vagueness is fitting. Ovid's love poems are much more interested in the lover than in the beloved. Corinna appears, like so many Roman women, only in snatches, seen through male eyes and sung by male lips.

In fact, she probably is not real at all, at least strictly speaking. Just as all the Roman love elegists create an illusory 'I' – a persona who shares the poet's name but may well have a life very different from the poet's real existence – so they also create a 'she', a *puella* who is whipped up out of frothing verse to be the proper recipient of the poet's carefully performed 'love'.

And yet, behind the elegiac Greek pseudonyms, some real women must be concealed, however much or little they may resemble their poetic avatars. The literary game of unmask-the-mistress has been going on ever since. The Roman novelist Apuleius was confident, in the second century AD, that Catullus's famous 'Lesbia' was none other than the notorious noblewoman Clodia Pulchra, whose lewd antics on the Baiae party scene had scandalized the aristocracy of the late republic.*

This may be right. There had been a gradual relaxation of sexual and social mores during the later years of the republic. The years of proscription and civil war left Rome full of rich young widows, liberated by the deaths of husbands and fathers, with money of their own and, within limits, the freedom to spend it as they liked. If Clodia, blue-blooded and beautiful, had decided on an affair with a penniless love poet, it would have been well within her power.

Even married women had a degree of freedom. Women had gained the legal right to divorce their husbands by the first century BC and divorces were common, most prompted by the changing demands of the complex political scene but some, at least, by the urgings of lust or love.

The *princeps* himself was married to a divorcée. A few years after the battle of Philippi, Octavianus, or Augustus as he now was known, had become infatuated with Livia Drusilla, the wife of one of his republican opponents. She and her husband were divorced immediately and she married Augustus soon after, no matter that she was pregnant with her former husband's son at the time.

As for Ovid's Corinna, she is a woman of some means, we can say at least. She has fine clothes, rich perfumes, a slave to do her hair. This last is vital. Artfully arranged hair is a status symbol, an indispensable accessory for anyone who wants to impress. More than that, it is a marker of what Ovid calls *cultus* – being cultured, civilized.

The legendary Sabine women, writes Ovid, in a poem entirely dedicated to the subject of feminine beautification, may have been content to live as dowdy farmers' wives, with fingers calloused from

---

* Clodia was the victim of a savage Ciceronian character assassination in a court case in 56 BC, which has made her a byword for Roman vice. Cicero's speech, the *Pro Caelio*, is a masterpiece of invective, accusing Clodia of drunkenness and incest, among other crimes, but since her brother Clodius was Cicero's chief political enemy at the time, it is not to be taken altogether at face value.

the loom and the stink of livestock in their nostrils. Then 'oxen grazed on Palatine, / where glitter now the palace and the shrine.'

Now ladies have gold-hemmed gowns and scented hair, and hands that blaze with jewels. Huge carbuncles or Indian emeralds nestle gleaming between perfumed breasts. And, as far as Ovid is concerned, this is all fine and right. 'The good old days indeed!' he snorts. 'I am, thanks be, / This age's child; this is the age for me.'

There is a cost, though. The cosmetic ointments with which Corinna covers herself are expensive: concoctions of ground antler, Libyan barley, Egyptian nitre and narcissus bulbs; of Attic honey, fennel, rose petals, frankincense, myrrh and salt from the temple of Ammon at Siwa, deep in the Sahara Desert. Expensive and poisonous too, as often as not, with frequent use of toxic ingredients like dangerous white lead.

So, in another of Ovid's poems, we find Corinna miserable: her long sessions with curling irons and poisonous dyes have made all her hair fall out. Long strands, brittle as straw, sit in the lap of her gown where she waters them with helpless tears, too disconsolate even to do as she normally does when in a temper and jab her maid in the arm with her hairpin.

At least, Ovid consoles her, she won't be hairless for long. This, happily, is the new Rome, which 'holds the treasures of a world enslaved'. A trip to the Temple of Hercules and the Muses, down by the Portico of Octavia, will take her to the wig-makers' arcade, where she can buy a new blonde headful, fresh cut from the scalp of a conquered German girl.

There was something not quite respectable about all this peacock finery. The women who lived in Augustus's compound on the Palatine favoured a much more modest style. In surviving statues, Augustus's sister Octavia and his wife Livia – now held up as paragons of Roman womanhood – keep their hair pulled back into the distinctive topknot and braid called the *nodus* – a severe look with a strong whiff of the Sabine peasant about it. Augustus based his authority on constant appeals to Rome's ancient past. He required his women to do the same.

Corinna was everything an Augustan woman stood against: Livia embodied chastity and duty; Corinna was promiscuous and flighty. Livia lived modestly, despite her wealth; Corinna was gaudy, and flaunted what she had, however little. Livia was what Roman women were meant to be – a wife and a mother; what Corinna was remains a hotly contested question. Probably, the woman or women who inspired 'Corinna' were the kind who would one day be described as courtesans: women whose means and beauty raised them above the mass of common prostitutes, but for whom, ultimately, sex was as much a trade as a diversion.

The good Roman woman was a producer of offspring. When Corinna finds herself pregnant by Ovid, on the other hand, she does not hesitate to do what she must. In an unusual sort of love poem, we find Ovid praying to the dark gods of Egypt – to jackal-headed Anubis, bull-horned Apis, Osiris, king of the dead – to spare Corinna's life as she lies stricken after the procedure. He has, he says, seen too many funerals of girls killed by some self-administered poison, or by injuries inflicted on their own stubborn wombs.

In compensation for Corinna's suffering, Ovid could provide only pretty words – a deficiency which meant he found himself in constant competition with richer rivals for Corinna's affection. There is a whole subgenre of poem in love elegy, the *paraclausithyron*, devoted to the experience of poets outside the locked doors of beloveds who are playing, for the moment, hard to get. This was not mere caprice. Having more than one lover made sound economic sense.

Ovid's verse did have some value to a woman on the make. Over the years the poet's fame grew, and so did the reputation of the woman who inspired him. In one poem, Ovid complains of impostors:

> *Many a girl hopes I'll make her name for her;*
> *I heard of one who claims to be Corinna.*
> *There's nothing she wouldn't give to make it so.*

Even so, relationships in love elegy never run smooth. Now Corinna suspects him of sleeping with her maid: 'Heaven grant me better,'

Ovid protests, 'if my fancy strayed, / Than such a low class slut for company.' What free man would want to put arms round a slave's 'lash-scarred waist'?

But the next poem is addressed to the maid herself: 'What gossip whispered we were intimate? / How did Corinna hear of our amour?' He flatters her, reassures her, finally blackmails her: 'If you're stupid and refuse, I'll tell your mistress all, betray myself as well.'

Corinna is roving too. We find the couple at a dinner party. Guests sprawl across low couches. Ovid lies with his eyes half-shut, pretending to sleep but secretly squinting in the candlelight to make out the stealthy signals passing between his mistress and another man at the table. 'I saw you both speak volumes with your eyebrows,' he complains, Corinna and some rival layabout, writing secret messages on the table with spilled wine. Now only drunkards are left at the table, and Corinna and the man are exchanging whispered words and now hot kisses. Ovid is in agonies: 'No love is worth so much – away cruel Cupid!'

And finally – at the end of the *Amores* – Ovid does seem to abandon the battlefield of illicit love: 'Mother of tender Loves,' he prays to Venus, 'find a new poet!'

* * *

Ovid was married three times in his life. We know little about the first two wives: one he described as 'worthless', the next as 'blameless', but both those first relationships were short lived, and doubtless afforded the poet plenty of time for womanizing. The third marriage, though, was a long and happy one, and lasted until the end of Ovid's life.

She was well connected too, the third wife, related to the ancient Fabian clan, and Ovid's ability to make such a match showed that he was moving up in the world. The precocious young love poet seemed, through his elegant, indecent verse, to have won himself a comfortable, almost respectable, middle age.

Around him in Rome, the times were changing. A new city was rising from the filthy alleys and chaotic streets of the old one. The historian Suetonius records Augustus's boast: that he had 'found the city built of brick, and left it built of marble'. Horace had once bleakly prophesied that the sins of Rome's fratricidal father, Romulus, would continue to be visited upon the sons in the form of civil bloodshed until the day came when the city's crumbling shrines and temples should be restored. Under Augustus's leadership, that day seemed to have arrived at last.

And out on the Campus Martius, the swampy ear of land in the Tiber bend to the northwest of the Capitol, Augustus was constructing a monumental new quarter – a rendering of the Augustan world order in polished marble. At one end of the Campus, the *princeps*'s mausoleum loomed like an artificial mountain, adorned with a ring of graceful young pines. At the other, the loyal general Agrippa was building a new temple to all the gods – the famous Pantheon.*

This new Rome needed new Romans. In 18 BC, Augustus introduced tough new laws against sexual immorality, penalizing the childless and instituting harsh penalties not only for adultery but even for those suspected of being complicit in adultery – a crime that, understood in its broadest sense, might be discovered to stain the honour of half the young men in the city.†

Ovid fitted into Augustus's gleaming city like grit in an oyster. Following his abandonment of love elegy at the end of the *Amores*, the poet had found a new role for himself, with a long didactic poem called the *Ars Amatoria*, the Art of Love.

In the *Amores* he was Cupid's victim. In the *Ars Amatoria*, he is Cupid's instructor, teaching the young of Rome how to have affairs. Many of the fine new buildings erected by Augustus and his family appear in the poem, listed as excellent places in which to pick up girls.

---

* Only the façade remains from Agrippa's original building. The famous Pantheon dome was constructed by the Emperor Hadrian more than a century later.
† It is worth pointing out that laws regulating public morality were neither a new idea, nor terribly successful. Homosexual acts had been illegal for years, strictly speaking, but an Augustan calendar from the Latin town of Praeneste gives male prostitutes their own special holiday.

The *princeps* had built a world capital; Ovid transformed the gleaming Augustan city into a playground for sex-crazed dandies.

Did some murmur of disapproval reach Ovid's ears, some threatening rumble from the Palatine? It is impossible to know. Certainly, though, Ovid's next works were less provocative: the *Remedia Amoris*, in which he pronounced himself 'cured of love'; the *Heroides*, set safely in the world of mythical heroines; the *Medea,* a conventional tragedy. Last came a work on a grander scale entirely: Ovid's masterpiece, the *Metamorphoses*.

The *Metamorphoses* was Ovid's answer to Virgil's *Aeneid*. Virgil had created a work of epic poetry fit to stand alongside Homer's *Iliad* and *Odyssey*. Now Ovid set out to prove he could do the same. Indeed, with characteristic assurance, the former love elegist announced an epic even grander in scope than Virgil's had been. Virgil had told the story of just one man. Ovid, in his prologue, boasts that he will, in one poem, 'spin a thread from the world's beginning down to my own lifetime' – a mythic history of the world running all the way from primordial chaos up to the reign of Augustus himself.

Like the *Aeneid,* the *Metamorphoses* establishes Augustus as the climax and culmination of Rome's history. 'Of all the achievements of great Julius Caesar,' writes Ovid in full panegyric mode, 'not one is more ennobling to his fame / than being father of his glorious son.' Verily, not the invasion of Britain, the conquest of Egypt, the subjection of the Gauls and the proud Numidians – none of these was so mighty a deed as standing father to Augustus, 'with whom as ruler of the human race, / O gods, you bless us past all reckoning?' Indeed, so great is Augustus that Julius Caesar needs must be worshipped as a god, lest Rome's hallowed *princeps* suffer the indignity of being sprung of mortal seed. And let there be no doubt that although the deification of Augustus has not yet occurred – and, by the goodwill of the immortals, may be long delayed – neverless Augustus surpasses Julius Caesar no less than father Saturn is surpassed by his son Jupiter.

And yet, even amid such extravagant praise, Augustus's keen nose may have detected something a little off in Ovid's latest work. Virgil's

Aeneid had its share of explicit praise for the *princeps*, to be sure, but its real power as a propaganda piece (and its brilliance as a piece of art) lay in the way its deeper themes came together: family, destiny, duty, the triumph of piety over passion – these were at the heart of Virgil's epic, as well as being the cardinal values of the Augustan regime. The *Metamorphoses* has no such purposeful structure. It is a compendium of myths, as told by a variety of often rather dubious internal narrators, connected only by the fact that each involves, however tenuously, some instance of metamorphosis.

The fictional world Ovid creates is a world of illusion in which the main lessons to be learned are about the brutality of power, the untrustworthiness of external appearances and the unreliability of historical accounts. Ovid sets Augustus at the head of history, as Virgil did, but Ovid's history is a chimerical, cobbled-together thing, shifting and deceptive, consistent only insofar as it is constantly mutating. The gods to whom Ovid so flatteringly compares Augustus have spent most of the book chasing nymphs around Greek hillsides; they are a drunken, lecherous rabble, no more fit to be worshipped than the bawdy Roman youths with whom they have so much in common.*

By the time the *Metamorphoses* appeared, Augustus was an old man. His power was unchallenged. But ever since a serious illness in 23 BC he had been preoccupied with the troubling matter of his own death, and what would follow it. *Princeps* was not yet a formally recognized position within the Roman state, and there was no established mechanism for the succession. As the years went by, Augustus settled on one after another of his junior male relatives as potential heirs, elevating them early to priesthoods and magistracies, heaping honours upon their young heads and, as soon as possible, sending them off to

* Augustus's favourite god Apollo makes a famous appearance in *Metamorphoses* Book 1 (Met.1.452 ff.). Having attempted to confiscate Cupid's bow, the great god finds himself shot in the heart with a love arrow, and ends up rubbing himself frantically against the ungiving bark of a laurel tree. The very kind of tree, notes Ovid, happily, that grows outside Augustus's front door on the Palatine.

take charge of military campaigns in Germany or Syria, where a few unconquered peoples still offered some chance of glory.

And one after another Augustus's chosen successors died before him. His sister's son Marcellus, a golden boy who got a glowing future-tense hagiography in the *Aeneid*, died of a sudden illness in 23 BC at the age of nineteen. Marcus Agrippa, his loyal general and later son-in-law, died in 12 BC. Next in line were Agrippa's sons, who were Augustus's grandsons through their mother, Julia. They died in quick succession, in AD 2 and 4.

Was it lonely, in that carefully modest house up on the Palatine? Augustus still had the indomitable Livia for company, but his sister Octavia was dead, as was his nephew, and his favourite stepson, and his old friend Maecenas and the grandsons, the beloved boys. Their absences echoed through the empty palace halls.

And there was one absence even more bitter than the rest. His daughter Julia, tired, perhaps, of serving as nothing more than a transmission vector for the imperial blood, had embarked on a series of very public affairs with various members of the old aristocracy and been banished by her reluctant father to a remote island in 2 BC.

It might have been the scent of power that still clung to these lovers' names that forced Augustus to act; there was a Scipio and a Gracchus in Julia's set, as well as a son of Marcus Antonius. But, in the accounts left by Roman historians, it was the sheer extent of her debauchery that forced the *princeps*'s hand. Right there in the Forum where Augustus's laws against adultery had been read to the Roman people, Augustus's daughter gave herself up to night-time revels and orgies, selling her favours like a common whore. That, at least, is how the story was later told.

* * *

Augustus had tamed the turbulent republic and won decades of untroubled peace – an unparalleled feat of war, politics and propaganda. But in the end his family, on whom he had counted, had let him down. No wonder then, in those sad, late years, if dark clouds seemed to hunch over the Palatine.

And at last, in AD 8, came the day when Ovid, a man perhaps insufficiently serious in his appreciation of Augustus's power, drew upon himself the thunderbolt of imperial wrath. No one knows, to this day, what the final provocation was. Ovid, in one cryptic line, blames his fall on *carmen et error* – a poem and a mistake. The poem is usually thought to be the *Ars Amatoria*: Rome after the exile of Julia was no place to be giving love lessons. The mistake is a mystery. The only tantalizing clue is that Julia's daughter, another wild one, and her surviving son were both banished from Rome at around the same time as Ovid's downfall. He seems to have been punished for something he saw rather than something he did. It may be nothing more than having attended the wrong party.

His sentence was exile; the penalty that had been decreed for adulterers in Augustus's marriage laws. There was hardly time to set his affairs in order. His property remained his own, a small mercy, and his wife, it was decided, would stay in the city to plead her husband's case to whatever influential friends she might have left after his fall from favour. His daughter was in Libya. By the time she heard of her father's fate, he was already gone.

It was night when Ovid left Rome for the last time. Outside his house, he saw the moon rise over the looming bulk of the Capitol. He prayed then, like a man in a dream, he wrote later: 'You holy powers who are my neighbours; temples my eyes will never see again; gods I must leave behind, who hold Romulus' city; receive, once and forever, my salutation.' From within the house, half-heard, came the sound of his wife's sobs. He found her flat on her face, with ash on her lips, praying her own wordless prayers to a deserted hearth.

In the sky the nymph Callisto, transformed by Jupiter into a celestial bear, revolved implacably through the firmament with the approaching dawn. More than once, Ovid said his goodbyes and then turned back weeping towards those few friends who had gathered to see him go. 'Why hurry off? I'll embrace you for as long as I still can, I who may never be allowed to any more.'

His wife clung to him now, changing her mind. 'You can't be torn away from me! Together from here! We'll go together! I'll follow you an exile... I'll be but a slight burden to the fugitive boat!' And when the poet, as if dragged in chains, turned at last away from the front door, she collapsed 'half-dead', unbound hair trailing in the dust of the road.

As a young lover, Ovid had devoted himself in verse to the pursuit of the *puella* – the imagined girl, beautiful and cruel behind her locked door. Now, an old man far from home, he aimed his verses at a loftier target. From his lonely exile in the decaying Greek colony of Tomis, on the shores of the Black Sea, Rome must have shimmered like a vision of colour and life: the heart and capital of the civilized world, dreamed of from a backwater town in a Danube swamp.

He called his songs his *Tristia* – his 'sorrows'. Four books' worth of them, in the end: messages to loyal friends; to his wife; long arguments aimed at the *princeps* himself, although there was no sign of softening from the Palatine. The months became years. Ovid's delicate ear hardened itself to the barbarous speech of the native Tomitians. One day, a ship up from the south brought the news that Augustus had died in his bed at the age of seventy-five, leaving the state in the hands of his stepson Tiberius, a man he had never much liked, and whose best qualification for the job was that there was almost nobody else left in the family who could do it at all.

Tiberius inherited whatever grudge it was that kept Ovid in exile. The last poems that made it back to Rome, passed from hand to hand by friendly traders along the sea lanes, are the work of a man who knows he will never see his home again. At last, after ten long years of fruitless pleading and flattery, Ovid followed Augustus to a lonely grave.

Augustus had turned Rome into an empire, among the greatest the world had seen, or ever would see. But Ovid triumphed too. At the end of his *Metamorphoses*, his masterpiece, he wrote:

And now I've brought it to a close, a work
Which neither wrath of Jove nor fire nor sword
Nor all-devouring time can cancel out.

And when it will, let it roll on, that day
Which ties up my uncertain span of life
But nothing save my corpse holds in its sway.
Meanwhile, immortal, in my better part
I'll soar above the lofty stars, my name
Indelible. And where the power of Rome
Extends in conquered lands I will be read
Aloud, and live, if poets' prophesies
Are true – through all the centuries in fame.

How true that prophecy would turn out to be, not even Ovid can
have imagined.

7

THE EMPEROR'S SHOW

Nero and the Great Fire

———

AD 64

A SUMMER NIGHT. Down by the foot of the Caelian hill, the darkness hangs thick in the alleyways. Sounds of a city asleep: a muffled snore; the whine of a mosquito. High overhead, a narrow crack of pale sky, framed by the black outlines of looming apartment blocks.

No one you want to meet is out this late. Respectable Romans are sleeping, up there in the dark in their tiny rooms. The streets have been left to drunks and vagrants; sleepers under bridges; prowlers who'll stick you for your money and your shoes.

Best to hurry on. Ahead, a short stumble through the gloom, is the curved end of the great racetrack, the Circus Maximus. By day, the Circus arcades would be crammed with butchers, barbers, pastry sellers, fortune tellers, hawkers, witches and beggars of every sort. Now these streets are silent. The shops are all shuttered, and the riches of an empire, silk and pepper, ivory and glass, spikenard and frankincense, are piled neatly in dusty storerooms to await the day.

But this night something is different. There is a sudden wind blowing from the Circus, acrid and hot. And now, rounding a corner, comes sound, unexpected, of shouts, and a sick orange glow lights up the graffiti on the plaster walls even though it is long before dawn, and now there are men running out of an alley with leather buckets from the cistern and pointing and clutching absurd sponges although it is already becoming clear that the moment for sponges and buckets has passed. And somewhere, in an apartment high above, a baby has woken up and is crying, and so he should be, because Rome is burning.

* * *

As dawn broke over the city, the fire was still gathering pace. Overnight, it had spread the length of the Circus Maximus, and morning found it chewing its way through the surrounding districts in great, slow arcs of flame. The huge blocks, four or five storeys high, that housed Rome's poorer citizens, gave themselves easily to the blaze. Every few minutes, another cheap-built *insula* would collapse, sending up a great flurry of sparks to be carried off by the hot summer wind.

Across the river, in the crowded region of Transtiberim, men watched the fire from their rooftops, vigilant against the threat of flying embers. These were commercial types – traders, longshoremen, warehouse guards, riverboat pilots – used to the smells of the river and the local knacker's yards and tanneries. Now, from across the water came the stench of burning storehouses; whole livelihoods going up in flames. It would have looked as though the whole city was burning. Only when the wind lifted the smoke for a moment or two did Rome's hills become visible, still green with gardens and spacious villas, standing clear like islands in an angry sea.

Down at ground level, the streets were choked with refugees. Some families were fleeing for a second time, as the fire that had chased them out of their homes during the night caught them up again in the morning. Clutching dazed children and sad valuables – a cloak, an old sword, a cooking pot, crude clay statues of household gods – they pushed in their thousands across the Tiber bridge, heading nowhere.

Beating through in the opposite direction came gangs of men: *vigiles* – the Watch, with their grapples and crowbars; and slave gangs sent by the rich to help clear firebreaks. Also looters, of course. Nor was the distinction so clear as all that: houses had to be pulled down in order to starve the fire of fuel. What shame if some few trifles should be rescued along the way?

And nothing could stand against this inferno. The roar of the fire filled the streets, heat beating off the paving stones, cracking windows, melting waterpipes into little rivers of molten lead. And all the while, unheard above the noise, those who had been too weak or frightened to escape, the attic dwellers and old wives, slaves in chains, the sick and the lame, died their lonely deaths, bodies surrendering fattily to the flames.

The Transtiberim was an immigrant neighbourhood, lined with docks where Tiber barges coming up from Ostia dropped off their cargos, human and otherwise. Many foreigners settled where they landed: Africans and Spaniards, Greeks and Syrians, Egyptians and Jews.

They brought their gods with them. In the great temple that rose close by on the Janiculum, Easterners gathered to worship their unfamiliar deities: Simios, Hadad the Bull, Mistress Atargatis. In the innermost sanctuary were the snake-coiled limbs of Syrian Adonis, the beautiful youth whose death and subsequent resurrection was celebrated by Transtiberine women in secret rites that guaranteed eternal life. Cybele was nearby too, the Great Mother of Asia, cloistered with her self-castrating priests on the Vatican rise. Just beyond that was the temple of Egyptian Isis, throned in glory with the holy infant Horus on her knee.

Here too the Jews would meet to practise their unusual and exacting superstition, with its relentless insistence on the unique divinity of just one solitary and jealous God.

This diversity of religions was only rarely a source of friction. For one thing, Romans were quite used to the idea that a person might devote themselves to one god or goddess above all others, depending on their own particular circumstances or station. It was possible to have very different sorts of religious life while staying well within the mainstream of Roman tradition.

It was generally understood that many of the strange divinities whose temples dotted the corners of the empire were really just the same old Roman gods being worshipped under different names. It was long established, for example, that Venus, the Roman goddess of love, must be identical with the Greek Aphrodite. It was no great leap then to conclude that Syrian Atargatis was just another manifestation of the same divine principle.

And faced with genuinely novel gods, Roman polytheism had proved very willing, over the centuries, to take newcomers on. Juno from Veii; Ephesian Diana; Cybele by ship from the woods of Mount Ida – all were accepted easily into the Roman religious scene. For gods as for people, Rome could be boundless in its appetite.

There was no equivalent, in Rome, of the separation of church and state. Rather, the practice of religion was one of the state's primary functions. After all, dealing with gods had always been considered a matter of great practical importance, just as much as dealing with invading tribes or hostile nations.

Much of traditional Roman religion was nakedly transactional – not ineffable mystery but a matter of clear and simple quid pro quo. Gods could bend the universe in your favour, and would do so in exchange for certain very specific observances: prayers uttered according to a given formula, say, some particular sacrifice, some magical ritual, correctly performed. No enterprise could be successful if the gods missed their due, and this was as true for the meanest peasant as for the highest magistrates and generals of the Roman commonwealth.

Always the emphasis was on scrupulous accuracy of execution, rather than any specially held belief or spiritual condition. Whole elaborate rituals might be stopped and repeated for as little as a mis-spoken word, or a trip on an uneven paving stone. This attention to detail was a point of special pride among the Romans, held up as a cause and justification for their remarkable success. And though sophisticated and philosophical Greeks might snigger at Rome's rigid piety, it was the Romans, not the snooty Hellenes, who had been chosen by providence as the masters of the civilized world.

During the civil wars that ended the republic, Rome's carefully maintained religious structure had fallen into disrepair. For the great

Augustus, carving out a place for himself in the 20s BC as Rome's first real emperor, the restoration of Roman religion was a vital objective, and Augustus restored it in such a way as to set himself at its apex. Julius Caesar had been deified after his assassination, but Augustus took on certain trappings of the divine even during his lifetime. Over the years that followed, the posthumous deification of emperors became such a formality that one, Vespasian, devoted his last breath to a grim joke: 'Dear me, I think I am becoming a god.'

This elevation of emperors was justified by its apparent results. For nearly a century, Rome's vast territory enjoyed an unprecedented period of peace. The correct ordering of matters on earth was a corollary and consequence of Rome's perfect harmony with the heavens: the Peace of the Gods – the so-called *pax deorum*.

Religion, then, was political, and it was at the broad intersection of religion and politics that the limits of Roman tolerance had always been revealed. In 186 BC, for example, not long after the peaceful introduction of Cybele, the republican government had conducted an unprecedentedly severe purge against devotees of the god Bacchus, lord of wine and debauchery. Disreputable though he was, Bacchus's cult was really less alien and unfamiliar than Cybele's. What made his followers intolerable to the Roman state, in a way that Cybele's had not been, was not so much who they worshipped as how they worshipped: secret meetings; initiations; clandestine rites. Roman religion was a public business, and a pressing public concern. Prayer conducted in private smelled uncomfortably conspiratorial. Any form of worship that removed religion from the public to the private sphere might in principle be a threat to the Peace of the Gods, and hence to the continued prosperity of the city itself.

Some sense of this might have weighed on the minds of Rome's Jewish population, as the fire continued into a second blistering day. Judea, only recently converted into an official Roman province, had spent a thousand years being squeezed by the great empires of the Middle East. The Jews still carried the memory of Pharaoh and the Red Sea. They remembered exile, in Nebuchadnezzar's Babylon, when Daniel, the magus and prophet, had dazzled the Mesopotamians with his miracles. They remembered the long fight against the Macedonian dynasts who had come east with Alexander the Great: the revolt of the Maccabees against the god-king Antiochus. They remembered how the kingdoms of the Greeks had given way to the power of the Romans; remembered – and shuddered at the memory – how Pompey the Great, arriving with his legions, had casually profaned the secret sanctuary in the Temple at Jerusalem, marching his hobnailed boots into the Holy of Holies, for no other reason than that he wanted to have a look.

All these hardships the Jewish people remembered, and the memories united them, binding them together even as the vicissitudes of ancient politics scattered them into a new and more lasting exile around the Mediterranean world. Many – perhaps most – Jews now lived outside Judea, in urban enclaves from Ecbatana to Cadiz. They had long been established in Antioch and Alexandria, the two great cities of the eastern Roman empire. Now, increasingly, they were settled in Rome as well, clustering in the trading districts: along the Via Appia to the south, and by the river, in the Transtiberim.

There *were* other religions that did not sit comfortably amid the babble of Roman polytheism: the cult of Isis with its flutes and rattles – too histrionic and feminine; the cult of Mithras the bull-slayer – a little sinister perhaps with its secret marks and signs and its ranked degrees of initiation. Efforts were periodically made to suppress the practice of magic – to expel Rome's legions of sooth-sayers and hill-witches and Chaldean astrologers, and sometimes even Greek philosophers.

But Judaism was particularly difficult for Romans to tolerate. Jews held private ceremonies like the mystery cults but they also, crucially, refused to pay even lip service to the traditional religion of Rome or to the developing cult of the deified emperors. That refusal, combined with a deep strand of apocalypticism, made the Jews look politically very dubious indeed. Hard to be a good imperial subject if all the while you live in certain hope of the arrival of the Anointed One – the promised Messiah who will overthrow all worldly powers.

Now, with the fire raging and emotions running high in the city, Rome's Jewish families had reason to fear the worst. Even in the short time the Jews had lived in Rome, they had three times found hostile official attention directed against them. First in AD 19, the Emperor Tiberius had tried to expel the Jews from the city. Then in AD 41, the Emperor Claudius had banned Jews from meeting at their synagogues.

And then, around the year AD 49, there had been another, slightly mysterious, clash with the authorities. The historian Suetonius explains, in a brief aside: Claudius expelled the Jews from the city because they had been making 'continuous disturbances'. They were stirred up, he says, by a man named 'Chrestus'.

* * *

The Emperor Nero, successor to the Divine Claudius (and great-great-grandson of Augustus himself), was at the seaside town of Antium when news of the fire reached him. As Nero's birthplace, the usually sleepy resort was enjoying an unaccustomed moment of imperial attention: new villas being built; a new colony set up for legionary veterans; a grand new harbour dug into the sandy Latin coast.

But now, all such schemes were forgotten. Swift on the sweaty backs of panting litter slaves, the emperor rushed towards the capital, with his train of secretaries, slaves, mimes, catamites and senatorial flatterers bustling along behind him. Ahead, beckoned the Calamity, a pillar of smoke.

Nero was still young, more or less – running a little to fat, despite a regime of regular enemas and emetics, but energetic. And here was a crisis worthy of his talents. Three days in, and four, the fire still burned in Rome. It had spread to the hills by now, sweeping aside the lines of slaves who fought to stop it with their crowbars and buckets of water, crackling through old temples and frescoed palaces.

Generations' worth of art and literature went up in the blaze: carefully stored manuscripts, antique statues and paintings looted from the cities of the East, now reduced to ash and shattered marble. In the sanctuaries of the gods, the fire burned away the ancient roof beams, burying altars and icons in heaps of blackened rooftile.

Meanwhile, Rome's tens of thousands of homeless fugitives were in a state of desperation. Shifting winds drove great burning fronts in all directions, threatening each safe haven. At last the crowds poured out into the countryside to sleep in ditches and bare fields, exposed to bandits and wild animals, but safe at least from the shifting flames.

Nero did what he could: huge refugee camps were established on public land in the Campus Martius; in the emperor's personal gardens, a temporary shelter provided some protection from the elements; emergency food supplies were summoned in from Ostia and the other nearby towns, and the price of corn was strictly controlled to prevent the profiteering that otherwise was an inevitable feature of such crises.

And in the burning city, every man imperial power could muster was set to work, clearing enormous firebreaks to preserve those few parts of Rome the fire had not yet reached. By the sixth day, hemmed in on all sides by artificial bands of devastation, the fire at last ate itself to a standstill, burning itself out at the foot of the Esquiline hill. Of Rome's fourteen districts, only four remained untouched; seven were largely ruined, and the remaining three were scorched flat.

The fire was a catastrophe for Rome, indeed for the whole empire, since provincials were required to volunteer enormous sums of money for the Roman relief fund. It was also bad for Nero. The emperor was the supreme protector of the people. The people had suffered terribly, and now the emperor was given much of the blame.

This must have struck Nero as rather unfair. Any reasonable critic, after all, would have to grant that he had really handled the whole crisis with some style. His emergency measures had been vigorous and effective. And although the destruction had been terrible, the new city Nero was building on Rome's ruins was going to be so much better than the old one: a grand modern city of sturdy apartment blocks and broad avenues, with fire-fighting equipment ready on each corner. No longer would visitors from the East scoff quietly at the cramped and haphazard Roman architecture: Nero's Rome was to be built on the very latest principles.

At the centre of this new world capital, Nero imagined a palace fit for an emperor. His old residence on the Palatine had burned with the rest. Now, taking advantage of the acres of newly cleared space in the city, Nero planned something on a scale that had never been matched, even by the great Greek kings of the East. His *Domus Aurea* – the Golden House – was the symbol of a new golden age, dawning at last on a dark universe. With its grounds, it was an entire world in miniature. At the centre, an artificial lake stood in for the Mediterranean. Around it, shady parklands and model villages were laid out in a carefully manicured vista of empire, overlooked by the 365-metre façade of a gargantuan triple-colonnaded palace on the Oppian hill.

Inside, the whole place was radiant, gleaming with gold and precious stones and mother-of-pearl that bathed each room in celestial light. There was a spectacular banqueting hall in which a system of hidden gears gave the illusion that the stars and planets were revolving around diners as they ate. And, lest there should be any doubt as to who stood at the centre of this new cosmos, Nero commissioned a special statue to stand at the palace entrance: a 35-metre colossus of the immortal Sun, cast in bronze by the best Greek artists, and wearing the features of Nero himself.

Perhaps Nero was too quick to grasp the opportunity the fire's destruction had afforded him. There was something unseemly, maybe, in his haste to build a bright new palace over the still-warm ashes of his incinerated subjects and their little livelihoods. At any rate, the rumour soon got around that Nero had not just failed to prevent the fire – he had really been responsible for starting it. Dark stories circulated: gangs of armed men had been seen obstructing firefighters; thugs throwing torches into shops had claimed it was 'by order of the emperor'.

There was another story too, uncomfortably plausible: that at the height of the fire Nero had mounted a private stage in his gardens and sung some verses of his own composition about the Fall of Troy, accompanying himself on the lyre. It would be just like this emperor, people said, to turn the greatest disaster in Rome's history into a mere backdrop for one of his theatrical shows.

No doubt, Nero would have been alive to the drama of the occasion. Romans had long been darkly obsessed with Troy and its fiery destruction. Troy had been the greatest city of its time, as Rome was now. The first king of Rome was descended, according to legend, from Trojan refugees. It was natural to wonder whether fire was the ultimate destiny of all human endeavour; whether all great cities would die in flames, as Troy had done, and Carthage too, burned at Roman hands. It was portentous that Rome had gone up in flames on that same black day which had seen its armies defeated by the Gauls at the Allia, half a millennium before. To people living through it, the burning of Rome might well have seemed like another great termination point in the history of civilization. If Nero really did perform the Fall of Troy, he was expressing, in a roundabout sort of way, the feeling that Rome's burning might be, in some sense, the end of the world.

* * *

Over the years, Nero's fondness for the dramatic had become embarrassingly clear. Even his birth, in AD 37, had been a *coup de théâtre*, or so the imperial propagandists had it. He had been born, they said, into the first ray of the morning sun, as though heaven itself was reaching out a benedictory finger.

As a child, growing up with his aunt, Domitia Lepida, Nero's first tutors had been a dancer and a barber, and the taint of theatricality had subsequently proved impossible to wash off, however much the boy was doused in the astringent precepts of traditional Roman virtue. There was a headstrong and willful streak in Nero's nature, inherited, people said, from his father's side. Nero had his imperial blood from his mother Agrippina, a granddaughter of Augustus's unhappy daughter Julia. He was always proud, however, of the tawny hair he inherited from his dead father, Domitius 'Bronze-Beard' Ahenobarbus. Nero's forefathers had been among the great nobles of the republic from the Civil Wars all the way back to the expulsion of the Tarquins.

Nero lost his family name at the beginning of his teens. In AD 48 Nero's mother, Agrippina, managed to wile her way into the bed of her malformed but goatish uncle, the Emperor Claudius. Incest would be no obstacle to the imperial lust. In AD 49, the senate declared that the marriage of uncle to niece was perfectly legal. In AD 50, Agrippina's son was adopted as Claudius's son and heir. The boy, Lucius Domitius Ahenobarbus, was now Tiberius Claudius Nero Caesar.

Various imperial princelings had borne the weight of those names before: the names that marked the branches of the tangled Julio-Claudian family tree. Augustus alone had been through half a dozen young Caesars in his day – bright, energetic young men, who might have grown to lead the imperial house. They were raised to high office, trained in government, rhetoric and war. And when, as always seemed to happen, they died suddenly on campaign or fell victim to some mysterious ailment back at home, they were duly mourned as paragons of Roman youth.

Nero was different. The formidable Agrippina pushed him steadily towards the imperial throne: she disposed of Nero's beloved aunt, on charges of witchcraft; she engineered the marginalization of Claudius's son Britannicus, and was assumed to have provided the fatal dose of poison that finally did for Claudius himself, spread on the emperor's favourite mushrooms.

But all the while, Nero devoted himself to an obsessive interest in chariot racing and to the study of music and art. When, in AD 54, the sixteen-year-old Nero found himself emperor of Rome, one of his first acts was to summon a *cithara* maestro called Terpnus to sing and play for him after his lonely palace dinners. Slaves would occasionally catch sight of their imperial master, flat on his back with a slab of lead balanced on his belly, doing exercises to strengthen his vocal chords.

While Nero was distracted, others were quite happy to run the empire in his place. Agrippina, for one, enjoyed her moment at the summit of Roman politics. Nero hailed her as Augusta and showered her with honours. The first watchword he issued to the imperial guard was *optima mater* – best of mothers – and she was, for the moment, as powerful as anyone in Rome.

Nero's public appearances, meanwhile, were carefully managed by his latest tutor, Lucius Annaeus Seneca, a Stoic philosopher, rhetorician and all-round literary man who had used a period of exile under the previous regime to produce some very respectable tragic plays, as well as several philosophical essays and a good deal of assorted correspondence. His first duty under Nero was to compose a funeral speech that the young emperor could read over the body of poor murdered Claudius.

Seneca had high hopes for the coming reign. 'Like the gleaming Sun,' he wrote, 'as soon as rosy Dawn has dispelled the shadows and led in the day… such a Caesar is at hand, such a Nero shall Rome now gaze upon. His radiant face gazes with gentle brilliance and his shapely neck with flowing hair.'

Perfect virtue was attainable, the Stoics believed, to one who gave himself wholly to the pursuit of knowledge. Nero was not such a man – but Seneca himself might be. Under Seneca's guidance, Seneca hoped, Nero might become the philosopher emperor the empire needed. He set out his hopes for the new reign in a philosophical treatise that was also meant to be a political manifesto: *De Clementia* – On Mercy.

But the imperial mercy proved thinner than anticipated. In AD 59, five years after his accession, Nero's long-nurtured resentment of his domineering mother drove him to decisive action. Agrippina was invited to join her son at the festival of Minerva at the Campanian resort of Baiae. The emperor's farewell after the show was a little strange – much weeping and clinging and kissing of her breasts. Then midway through the homeward voyage across the Bay of Naples, the grand boat she had been given for the journey suddenly collapsed like a stage set.

Agrippina had played the game for long enough to recognize an assassination attempt when she saw one. Dodging murderous sailors, the indomitable empress-mother leaped from the sinking ship and swam back to shore, having escaped with nothing more serious than a light wound to one shoulder.

Nero's plot had become a farce. Now his mother's death would be disappointingly banal. When she was cornered at last by imperial assassins, she is supposed to have pointed to her womb and exclaimed: 'Strike here!'

In the five years between his mother's death and the Great Fire, Nero had devoted himself with new energy to the pursuit of art and extravagance.

One scene: an artificial boating lake on the outskirts of Rome. A backdrop of satyr-haunted trees all hung with lanterns, in front of which, chorus-lines of painted prostitutes thrust their hips in crude pantomime. The emperor and his intimates float in the foreground on a great raft of gold and ivory. Lapped by the illuminated waters of the lake, they feast like gods, waited on by swarms of pretty cherubim, who flit about with washbasins and wine-jugs and pots of scented ointment to smear on the diners' feet while dodging drunken kisses.

Another evening: Nero wears the dress and flame-coloured veil of a young Roman bride. A Greek ex-slave named Pythagoras is the groom. Heaped treasures represent the dowry; wedding torches illuminate the marriage bed. '*Everything* was public which, even in a natural union, is veiled by night.'*

Among the guests at Nero's parties was one Gaius Petronius, a famous wit regarded by the emperor – and therefore by everyone who mattered – as being Rome's final arbiter of style and good taste. Petronius's comic novel, the *Satyricon*, catalogues the excesses of the Roman rich at table: singing waiters and acrobats; boar stuffed with

---

* There was a medieval tradition that Nero had managed, by the help of his doctors, not only to 'play a woman's part' in bed, but actually to get pregnant. In the fullness of time, says one German poem, the *Kaiserchronik*, Nero was delivered of a frog, by way of his mouth. Hence the name of the cathedral of Rome, the Lateran, is derived from *lata rana* – 'born frog'.

sausages and black pudding; snails, chitterlings, roasted dormice, dishes of liver, turnips and mustard, pickled cumin seeds. Petronius's fictional feast – surely inspired by Nero's real one – is full of culinary surprises: sea urchins that turn out to be quinces; thrushes made out of pastry and stuffed with raisins; a statue of the god Priapus hiding in the fruitbowl which, when nudged by a greedy hand, sprays out a jet of saffron water from its oversized member.

As the wine flows, the very Nero-like host of Petronius's fictional feast grows expansive: 'He stuck his hands up over his forehead and gave us his best impression of the actor Syrus, while all the staff sang in chorus: "*Madeia, Perimadeia*". In fact, if his wife Fortunata had not whispered in his ear, he would have taken the floor.'*

Nothing scandalized Rome's aristocrats more than Nero's love of showing off on stage. The emperor had spent years training himself to play the *cithara*, a sort of seven-stringed lyre, with which he accompanied himself singing lyrics of his own invention. Professional *citharodes* were celebrities in the ancient world and might tour the Mediterranean to enormous acclaim – but they were always understood, somehow, to be essentially un-Roman. The mere introduction, by Nero, of an arts festival in the Greek style had already provoked a moral panic about alien influences 'turning our young men into shirkers, gymnasts and perverts'. It was unthinkable for a free Roman citizen – let alone a nobleman – to display himself in front of a theatre crowd.

But Nero was emperor. He wanted to perform, and he had the ultimate captive audience. There were stories of women giving birth in the theatre; of men climbing the walls to escape Nero's songs and his effortful, husky voice.† And yet each piece was greeted with rapturous applause, supplied by a claque of five thousand specialist clappers.

---

* Forbidden from dancing, the host of Petronius's banquet contents himself instead with a stream of miserable puns. 'We laughed,' says the narrator, 'for *ages*.'
† The future emperor Vespasian was caught nodding off during one of Nero's later performances, according to Tacitus, and only narrowly avoided being put to death as a result.

These, apparently, were trained in the latest Alexandrian clapping techniques, and divided into three groups: the bees, the brickbats and the rooftiles, according to their particular sound.

* * *

Nero's enthusiasms had been eating away at his popularity even before most of Rome burned to the ground. Now, with the city in ruins, and the people looking for someone to blame, the mood threatened to turn dangerous. Some distraction had to be found, some way to avert hostile attention from the emperor. And so, at some point during those dark weeks, Nero hit upon a solution: another big show.

The stars of the show did not yet know that they had been singled out for the imperial spotlight. It was not something they would have wanted. These were modest people: slaves and ex-slaves mostly; foreigners; poor traders and craftsmen; women both respectable and not. Yet they had been brought to someone's notice. Within the haphazard sprawl of the imperial household, someone had been interested enough in the unusual faith of the Jews to notice that it was, at that moment, suffering a major internal schism.

Jews had always worried Romans by talking about their promised king, their long-awaited Messiah. But recently, the emperor was informed, a faction among the Jews had taken to claiming that the Messiah had already come: that one of the East's many wandering prophets, a certain 'Nazarene' executed by the Roman authorities in Judea some thirty years previously, had actually been the Son of God – not 'Chrestos' but *Ho Christos*, the Anointed One.

The more the Romans learned about these 'Christians' in their midst, the more they will have found to dislike about them. The religion, so far as it could be made out, had all the worst features of a mystery cult: there were arcane symbols and holy books; unsettling promises of salvation and rebirth; secret meetings called 'love feasts', held after dark in private houses.

Like all Jews, Christians refused to participate in the worship of the imperial family, or indeed in any part of the state religion of Rome. They were known to speak hopefully of a mysterious 'kingdom' – some new political order in which proper social hier-archies might be overturned, an event which the Christians seemed to pray for.

And there was worse: the Christian cult, as it turned out, was not in fact restricted to Jews. On the contrary, the charismatic leaders of the cult were spreading it among non-Jews as well: among Syrians, Greeks, even native Romans, all across the great international sub-stratum of slaves and toilers on which the great imperial edifice was constructed.

Here, as if made for the purpose, was a new menace that might force the muttering Roman elite to unite behind Nero's regime, and whose extermination, carefully stage managed, might satisfy the anger of the Roman plebs.

The oppressive machinery of the Roman state swung into action. First, as many Christians as could easily be found were arrested. Con-fessions proved easy to extract. The Christians, under interrogation, did not deny their criminal association with quite the urgency that self-preservation might have been thought to demand.

The first round of torture soon resulted in a second wave of Christian prisoners to be put to the question in their turn. There was nothing extraordinary in this. Generally, slaves involved in any sort of criminal investigation would be tortured as a matter of course.

With the victims duly assembled, the grand spectacle could begin. On the flank of the Vatican rise, not far from the Transtiberim, Nero had built a new circus in which more people might watch him perform. For this show, however, he was prepared to cede the limelight. While Nero watched from his chariot, the hateful Christians were brought in to die. Some were crucified, in the traditional manner. Others were torn apart by dogs. To make them ridiculous, Nero dressed them in animal skins so that the arena seemed full of misshapen beasts, furred and antlered heads lolling awkwardly on their straps as the prisoners beneath tried vainly to avoid the teeth of the emperor's hounds.

And when night fell on Nero's Vatican gardens, the spectators walked home by the light of human torches: Christians, dipped in pitch and set ablaze on poles along the paths, howling away in a grisly *son et lumière*.

Nero's tutor, Seneca, was a Stoic philosopher, and therefore a believer in the power of suffering. 'Never is the proof of virtue mild,' he had written once. 'Fortune lays into us with the whip and tears our flesh.' For 'God [and Stoics recognized, at this point, that strictly speaking there was only one God, the *Logos*, the Eternal Flame] does not pamper a good man like a favourite slave; he puts him to the test, hardens him, and makes him ready for his service.'

The greatest test of all was to die a noble death. A favourite example was that old republican icon Cato the Younger, whose drawn out self-disembowelment among the ruins of Utica a century before was 'a distinguished and memorable' end. 'Death consecrates', Seneca concluded, 'those men whose death wins praise even from the fearful.'

Soon Seneca and many of his Stoic friends were afforded the opportunity for their own self-consecrations. A year after the fire, an aristocratic plot against Nero was uncovered. The purge that followed was wide ranging, and the best mercy anyone could expect was the right to die by their own hand. Thrasea Paetus, a Stoic senator, cut his wrists and sprinkled the blood on the ground as 'a libation to Jupiter the Liberator'. The poet Lucan, Seneca's nephew, died while reciting his own verses. The party animal Petronius, no philosopher he, had his freshly opened veins bandaged up again, then died slowly over dinner, making jokes all the while.

Seneca himself was dining with his wife and some friends when the message arrived commanding him to die. There was no time for his will to be altered. All he could leave to the assembled company was his example.

In the event, his suicide was every bit as hard and painful as he can have wished: the cuts he made at his wrists were too shallow to let out enough blood, so he cut the veins at his ankles too. When that failed, he drank hemlock in the manner of Socrates, but his reduced blood-flow prevented the poison from having any effect. At last, having dictated his final musings to his secretaries, he had himself carried to a boiling hot steam-room, where he suffocated at last.

Such sternness was only to be expected from an educated Roman. We cannot know whether Seneca and his kind had been impressed by the surprising courage with which the lowly Christians had faced their own much crueller executions the year before. Many of them had been slaves, of whom no great endurance was ever expected. But perhaps their lives of quiet suffering – the whippings and the beatings; the curses and humiliations; the nights spent on the hard ground, or squashed together in some stinking attic; the rapes; the mutilations and the brandings; the selling off of children – perhaps such lives had equipped these humblest among the Christians well for their performance on Nero's blood-soaked stage. Here, finally, was something they could do that might matter: powerless in life they became in death, *marturoi*, 'witnesses' to the overwhelming truth that they believed in. Here was a way to make their mark upon a world that, even as it tortured them, was moving closer to the promised day of salvation, near at hand.

At any rate, Nero's spectacle did not go as planned. The historian Tacitus records that, 'even for criminals who deserved extreme and exemplary punishment, there arose a feeling of compassion'. The Romans, seeing the Christians die, began to pity them.

* * *

Five years after the fire. The imperial treasury is empty. The provinces are in open rebellion. There is unrest in the streets of Rome. One morning, Nero wakes up to find that the palace is empty: the bodyguards are gone, as are the palace servants with as much as they can carry – even the bed linen, and the box of poison he had laid up in case of emergency.

It is time for the emperor's last act. With an ex-slave and a beloved eunuch boy for his companions, he heads out of the city in disguise to take refuge in a suburban villa, clambering over the back wall through a reed bed and a bramble patch. It is clear that there is little time left; that the moment has come for his dramatic exit. 'Dead!' he mutters to himself through his tears 'And so great an artist!'*

Still, he cannot bring himself to strike the fatal blow. On and on he dithers. He picks up and throws down a pair of knives. Sporus the eunuch is forced to put on a display of lamentation to egg him on. Perhaps, Nero suggests, one of his friends might commit suicide first, to show him how to do it? At last, with the hooves of cavalrymen sounding on the street outside, he manages, with the help of a trembling secretary, to wound himself in the throat. His last request to his companions: that they make sure he is buried with his tawny head still on.

In the end, Nero could not play the tragic hero, nor even the good Roman. But posterity had another part lined up, and one not lacking in drama.

The first thing was that Nero would not stay dead. In the years after his suicide, at least two false Neros emerged in the eastern provinces, ready to lead the empire to glory once again. Even half a century later, a 'vast majority' of people were said to be convinced that the fallen emperor was still alive.

The second thing was that in AD 66, Nero's general in Judea, the future emperor Vespasian, had initiated the so-called Jewish war. By the end of that war, the Temple at Jerusalem had been destroyed; thousands of Jews had been slaughtered, and Nero had become a monster in apocalyptic Judaism. Inspired by the Roman prophecies called the 'Sibylline Books', anonymous Jewish seers, in their own 'Sibyllines', foretold that *Nero Redivivus* – the revivified Nero – would reappear from the east as an agent of the wicked angel Beliar, even at the very ending of the world.

The third thing was that among the Christians supposed to have disappeared in Nero's Rome were two travellers: a former fisherman

---

* To be fair to Nero, he had recently gone on a very successful Greek tour, at which he won every single one of the great Greek drama festivals. The organizers had helpfully altered centuries of established practice to enable all six festivals to be held in the same year.

known as Peter, and a younger, more intellectual type called Paul, much given to letter writing. Their fates were lost to history, but early Christians, wanting to account for the deaths of their two most important saints, were not slow in inventing legends: Paul, beheaded by Nero in person, after a miracle contest with the heretic Simon Magus; Peter, crucified upside-down for teaching sexual abstinence to Roman concubines. There were many versions, but all agreed that Nero was to blame.

And so, as the years went by, Nero passed from history into legend, not as a sun-king nor as an artist, but as the Regent of the Dragon; the Beast with Ten Horns; the Second Head of the Beast, whose number is 666 – a number that can be unravelled to give the letters *qsr nrwn*: Nero Caesar. Poor Nero, who loved applause, turned out to be the Antichrist.

8

GLADIATORS

The inaugural games of the Colosseum

―――――

AD 80

I T IS AD 80. WITH a blare of horns and trumpets, Verus and Priscus have entered the arena. *Verus* and *Priscus* – True and Ancient – not their real names. There is nothing real, nothing ordinary, about this pair. Half-naked, they look like Titans compared to the scrawny Roman city-dwellers hooting from the upper circle: even from up there in the gods you can see the great slabs of meat moving over their bare ribs. 'Stuffing', they call it, the bodybuilder's diet of bean stew and barley that is one of the perks of life as a gladiator.

Verus and Priscus stand exposed. All around are peering eyes, fifty thousand avid faces, staring down at them. What armour the fighters wear just highlights their general nakedness: a segmented armguard, greaves, a studded belt.

Only their heads are fully covered. Their helmets are enormous, heavy, almost grotesque – gleaming, wide-brimmed with jutting crests and brightly coloured plumes. And where a soldier's helmet would open up in front, the gladiator helmets have visors that encase both men's heads entirely. Their bodies are exposed, their faces have been swallowed up in iron.

Inside the helmets, the sensation is of hot breath and the weight of metal; a world narrowed to fit through a pair of eyeholes. Survival, soon, will be won by focus; a prize for whoever is better at the curious, intimate dance that these two must perform: circling, matching each other move for move; attentive to the subtle language of hands and eyes and balance and muscle. Yet, even as they stare at one another, some part of each man will still hear – still thrill to – the lifting, omnidirectional roar of the crowd, the thousands who have come from across the empire to be here on this day, to fill the empire's newest monument: the Colosseum.

* * *

In the audience that day, squeezed on to one of the hard stone benches towards the back of the lower bank, was Marcus Valerius Martialis, a man in early middle age with the stubborn hair and bristles of a Spanish Celt, and old clothes that allowed him, just about, to pass for a respectable citizen. Not that Martial was some hick, fresh from the provinces. He was an educated man, and had been in Rome for a decade and a half – since the year of the Great Fire. He had enjoyed the patronage of his compatriot, Seneca, before the old Stoic's disgrace and fall. He was known to his friends as a man of quick intelligence and subtle wit, although he had not yet achieved his later fame as a lewd and brilliant comic poet.

Urbane as he was, even Martial was impressed by the spectacle before him. 'Memphis should shut up about the wonders of her Pyramids!' he wrote later. 'Assyrians can stop boasting about Babylon.' The mausoleum at Halicarnassus? Apollo's horned altar at Delos? The Temple of Ephesian Artemis? Nothing to shout about. 'All works of man fall short before Caesar's Amphitheatre!'

The 'New Amphitheatre', as it was called, was by far the largest in the known world, a vast oval bowl of travertine limestone – 100,000 cubic metres of rock, quarried out of the hills at Tivoli to be carted to Rome at unimaginable expense.

Rome had plundered more than just mountains for her new monument. Nearby, on the Via Sacra, a new triumphal arch announced to the city the latest victory that had been won in her name: General Titus Flavius – now the Emperor Titus Caesar – had subjugated rebellious Judea, stormed Jerusalem, slaughtered the inhabitants and marched into the Jewish Temple, his feet still wet with Zealot blood.*

Vast piles of loot had been ransacked from the Temple to be paraded through Rome's streets. The greatest treasure of all was the sacred Menorah of Jerusalem, the seven-branched candelabra whose design was revealed by God to Moses himself. Now it languished in a Roman treasury. Its image was carved in gold-painted relief on to Titus's arch, where it remains today, still being led with the enslaved Jews in an eternal triumph before Rome's mocking crowd.

This was a story everyone could appreciate: a nice straightforward tale of foreign conquest. Much better to focus on Titus's triumph than what Titus's father Vespasian had been doing at the same time: taking advantage of the death of Nero to lead the eastern legions against Rome, and seize the empire through civil war.†

Titus, as the son of a usurper, the late (and therefore now 'divine') Vespasian, lacked the legitimacy that had been conferred on previous emperors by their direct blood connection to the great Augustus. It was important, therefore, for the Roman people often to be reminded of just how badly the old 'Julio-Claudian' dynasty of emperors had turned out.

It was to make this point that Vespasian, and then Titus, pressed ahead with the idea of a new venue for popular entertainment, placed, for maximum effect, right on top of what had been Nero's private boating lake. Martial was quick to pick up and amplify the desired message. Here, he wrote, 'the hateful halls of a cruel king used to gleam, and in the whole city there was just one house left standing.'

---

* Later rabbinical legends claimed that Titus had defiled the Holy of Holies by having sex with a pair of prostitutes there. To punish him for his sacrilege, God sent a flea that burrowed through his skull to drum mercilessly against his brain, causing the tumor that eventually killed him.

† Vespasian was not the only general to have had this idea. In AD 69, following Nero's suicide in 68, four different men in turn occupied the imperial throne, each relying on the support of one of the major frontier armies. It was a sign of things to come. This 'Year of the Four Emperors' was superseded just over a century later by another year (AD 193) in which there were five.

But now, where Nero's pools used to be, 'the awesome bulk of the amazing amphitheatre rears itself up'.

'Rome is restored to herself, and Caesar, under your care, a master's pleasures now the people share.'

Building the world's biggest amphitheatre on top of a lake would be hard enough even today. But the imperial engineers were accustomed to grandiosity. Thousands of metres' worth of pipes and conduits began to spread like roots through the damp earth of the valley. The lake was drained, then bounded with a trench dug 6 metres deep into the clay of the lakebed, 50 metres wide and running in a great oval 200 metres across at the long axis. For months, Roman sleep was disturbed by the sound of the waste from the excavation being hauled down at night to the Tiber port.

Next, the lakebed was covered over with concrete: a Roman innovation that, in the two or three centuries since the technique had been perfected, had had a transformative effect on ancient architecture. Roman concrete – lime from superheated limestone or marble, mixed with *pozzolana*, the volcanic ash from the Bay of Naples – would set hard in damp conditions, or even underwater, and could give buildings a degree of structural integrity unthinkable with just brick or stone.

So while the architecture of the Greeks, for all its centuries of refinement, had been compelled by physics to stay within the straight lines of pillar and lintel, the Romans had begun to experiment with ever more daring arrangements of concrete curves. Concrete could stretch a simple arch, deepening it to form a 'barrel vault' (shaped like a barrel cut in half from end to end). Two barrel vaults – shaped like a barrel, cut in half lengthways – could be made to intersect at right angles, making a cross vault. Or, most spectacularly, you could cross a whole set of arches over each other through a single central point to make a hemispherical dome.

These techniques opened up thrilling new possibilities for Roman architects when it came to enclosing space. And the incredible strength of curved concrete meant that buildings could be bigger than ever, vault piled upon vault. The Greeks had relied on natural slopes when building the banked seats of their ancient theatres, carving the curved hollow of the auditorium directly into the side of some convenient hill or mountainside. The Romans could build theatres without the mountains; in a sense, they made their own mountains, moulding them in graceful arcs of poured cement.*

A project on the scale of the Colosseum demanded the very cutting edge of Roman engineering. The precision of the design is extraordinary: the way each bank of seats is carefully angled – one at 30 degrees from the horizontal, the one behind it at 35; the mathematical exactitude with which eighty wedge-shaped entrance corridors pierce the building's oval outline; the remarkable uniformity of the huge annular corridor that runs around the outside of the structure, which varies in its width, over its entire circumference, by less than 1 per cent.

It had taken centuries to reach a point where such a building was possible. It took ten years' labour, and a vast expenditure of plundered wealth, to turn the vision into a reality. And although the Colosseum was immediately and widely imitated, no amphitheatre was ever built that could be its rival.†

'What tribe is so remote, what people so barbarous, Caesar, that no spectator from it is in your city?'

* The first free-standing stone theatre of this sort was the Theatre of Pompey, built in 55 BC by the great general and opponent of Julius Caesar. Little of the structure remains, but the curved outline of the auditorium can still be traced in the streets just east of the Campo dei Fiori.

† For the first millennium or so of its existence, the Colosseum was known only as the Flavian Amphitheatre – just as its builders, Titus and Vespasian of the Flavian clan, had intended. A colossal statue stood nearby, representing the sun god Sol, with radiate crown. This was the very same colossus that Nero had commissioned for his vestibule, still standing amid the wreck of Nero's *Domus Aurea*. Though his Golden House was destroyed by the Flavians, the statue Nero had built in his own likeness would stand by their amphitheatre for a thousand years, eventually giving it its familiar modern name.

This is Martial again, writing on the occasion of the Colosseum's inaugural show in AD 80. 'Rhodopean farmers have come from Orphic Haemus. Horse-blood drinking Sarmatians have come; people who drink from the source of the Nile; Britons are here from the farthest ocean; Arabs have hurried here, and Sabaeans and Cilicians... Sygambri from Germany with their top-knotted hair.'

The Roman empire in that year was not far from reaching its peak, in both population and territorial extent. Titus Caesar could call himself the master of some fifty or sixty million people, of whom as many as one million may have lived in the city of Rome itself.

Middle-class poets like Martial trod gingerly through the dirty and overcrowded streets, where flagons dangled on chains from pillars in front of the wine shops; where barbers 'drew their razors blindly' in the midst of the pressing crowd; where 'grimy snack bars occupied the whole road', sending clouds of steam and stink into the smoky air, drawing queues of busy workers with the promise of hot bean stew or lentil soup with a flat round loaf of bread; perhaps a strip of salt fish, or a dish of fried onion.

Decimus Iunius Iuvenalis, the famous Roman satirist known as Juvenal, suffered the urban crush too. He was in his twenties when Titus opened the Colosseum, but already, we may imagine, exhausted by the noise and the crowd. 'The deadliest disease in these parts is insomnia,' he wrote. 'For what apartment here will let you sleep? It costs a fortune to get any rest in the city. Here's the cause: the wagons scraping by the neighbourhood's narrow bends, the swearing of the drovers caught in traffic jams, could snatch sleep from dead Claudius himself.'

Nor was daytime any better. Here comes the grandee in his litter, cutting through the crowd like a warship as he dozes, borne up on the necks of his panting slaves. Restful enough for him, but:

Even so he overtakes us. As we hurry, the surging crowd blocks our way ahead, while the people behind, a mighty herd, press at our hips. This guy jabs me with his elbow. Another pokes me with his pole. One man thwacks a beam into my head, the next hits me with a storage jar. My shins are smeared with mud; now from all sides I'm trampled by great fat feet, and a soldier treads his hobnail into my toe.

Carts loaded with building material presented a deadly threat. 'What if that axle gives way under its load of Luna marble, and spills its mountain of rock into the crowd? What will be left of the bodies? Who'd ever find the limbs? Who'd find the bones? Each poor man's crushed-up body – vanished away with his life's breath.'

Rome was a city that could chew a person up. It must have been a relief, at last, when the crowds spilled out of the narrow streets and on to the open plaza of the Colosseum.

Lining up to get past the perimeter barriers that ringed the open space, spectators had time to take in the wonders of the building that loomed ahead of them, four storeys climbing, arch-upon-arch, 48 metres into the Roman sky.

The great curved walls gleamed with limestone cladding; engaged pillars framed the arches in a different style for each layer, first with plain Doric capitals, then the scrolls of the Ionic order, then the ornate Corinthian, leading the eye skyward. Marble statues peered down from the upper arches; eagles in gilded bronze perched above them, while over the building's main entrances were sculpted chariots with four-horse teams, rearing wild-eyed above the impatient crowd.

It was a rare enough treat to be going to the games. The games were free – a gift from the emperor – but there were only so many seats. The Colosseum had a capacity of around 50,000 by most modern estimates; impressive, but not enough to go around all of Rome's million or so citizens and visitors. Securing a place at the show was easier if you had a powerful patron or were a member of one of the more successful tradesmen's guilds.

Precious tokens clutched in eager hands directed their holders to designated spots around the amphitheatre. First you had to find your entranceway from among the eighty numbered arches that led into the honeycombed interior. The walls inside were bright with colour, richly decorated with frescoes, where nymphs and satyrs peeped between curling fronds of stylized acanthus, ushering spectators to their seats.

Stairwells winding upwards echoed with discussion of that day's programme. Titus's games, the inaugural games of the New Amphitheatre, would go on for months. There were 100 days of celebration in that single year, Romans later boasted, with events held all over the city as well as in the Colosseum. There was no telling, each day, what gruesome novelty might be hauled out on to the sand – the *harena* – that covered the amphitheatre floor.

The further you climbed, the less distinguished the crowd became. Senators had their own entranceways, whisking them straight to their cushioned chairs right on the edge of the arena. The *equites*, representing the wealthiest stratum of Rome's middle class, occupied the eight or nine rows immediately behind them. Further up sat the great mass of Rome's ordinary population, each person jostling to claim their alloted 40 centimetres of limestone bench.

If you were a slave, however, or a lowly freedman, you had to haul yourself up the whole height of the building before emerging on the fourth storey. Here, with Rome spread out behind you, and a vast crowd of Rome's citizens below, you squeezed on to steeply stepped wooden benches perched at the top of the vast structure. Overhead, so close you could practically smell them, sailors drafted in from the imperial fleet at Misenum clambered about on ropes, rigging the enormous canvas awning that sheltered spectators from the hot summer sun. Below sounded the din of trumpets and water organs, of fifty thousand voices raised, of hawkers and hustlers winding between the seats. And then, suddenly, the hush that signalled that the day's games were about to begin.

* * *

There is no record of the programme on the day that Verus and Priscus fought. All we have are Martial's fragmentary impressions, but no way to know when he saw what he saw nor even whether his *Book of the Games*, his *Liber Spectaculorum*, describes the events of a single week, or of many weeks, or months, or perhaps even years. Nor did days at the arena follow a strict pattern. The Romans loved novelty. A day might be built around some special performance: a massed infantry battle; a dance troupe. The ring might be flooded for an aquatic display – anything from naval warfare to synchronized swimming.*

An ordinary day at the arena, to the extent that there was such a thing, probably started with a display of wild animals. Ever since 146 BC and the final destruction of Carthage, Romans had scoured the new province of Africa for animals to entertain the crowd back home. As the empire grew, so did Rome's assortment of unusual beasts. One Roman historian records the appearance of Rome's first 'camel-opard' – an extraordinary creature, camel-like but with a leopard's spotted skin, which, 'towering high aloft... supports the rest of its body on its front legs and lifts its neck in turn to an unusual height'.†

Extraordinary energy was devoted to the trade in exotic fauna. It took a lot of hired courage to trap a rhinoceros, say, or a dozen crocodiles. Even more, perhaps, to ship a cargo of predators, unsedated, across the Mediterranean in a wooden galley. But the animals were considered worth the trouble and more. The assassin Cassius is said to have been moved to murder Julius Caesar by, among other things, Caesar's high-handed appropriation of Cassius's lions, which he had been saving for a celebration in Rome.‡

---

* The question of whether or not the Colosseum was flooded for Titus's games – indeed, whether or not such a thing was even possible – has been controversial. Traces of waterproofing around the arena pit, and the fact that the brick substructure that remains now was built under Titus's successor, suggest that such flooding might have been possible, but there were other places in Rome that would have been easier venues for the aquatic shows that Martial describes.

† The description is from Cassius Dio, whose 'camelopard' is really a giraffe. Rome's hunger for novelty had a major impact on Mediterranean ecology; by the fourth century AD there had been several local extinctions, including elephants in North Africa, lions in Greece and hippopotamuses on the upper Nile.

‡ This was during the war against Pompey. In the event, no one got the lions, since the citizens of Megara, where they were being held, opened the

Caesar stole Cassius's lions in order to outdo Pompey, who had astonished the Romans with a display of elephants in the Circus Maximus. With their intelligence and their impressive size, elephants were popular performers: they could be made to dance, or lie on couches as if at a feast; they could be dressed in hilarious costumes.

Alternatively, the sponsor of the spectacle could just do as Pompey did and have them all slaughtered: long remembered was the sight of a bull elephant with maimed feet, still crawling around the Circus on his knees and tossing his tormentors around like skittles; likewise the hair-raising moment when the remaining elephants tried all together to break through the barrier that separated them from the audience, trumpeting mournfully as they succumbed to the hunters' spears.

These hunters, the *venatores*, were a daring bunch. There was a particularly famous one, says Martial, at Titus's games in the Colosseum – a man called Carpophorus, who wowed the audience by killing a boar, a polar bear, a lion and a leopard in a single fight. A good *venator* had to kill with style too: there are accounts of *venatores* pole-vaulting over charging animals; leaping from horseback on to the necks of bulls; taunting lions by dangling acrobatically from beams, or confusing bears by chasing them around revolving doors. Failure was common and the result, according to one eyewitness, 'horrible to an unimaginable degree'.

A successful beast show would drive home an important message for the audience: that nature herself had been forced to submit to Rome's imperial power. Titus's games featured an elephant that had been trained to genuflect before the imperial box. 'Even he,' says Martial, 'could feel the presence of our god.' The elephant then proved its devotion by winning a fight against a charging bull, one of several arranged combats between different species. To all those old childish

---

cages in the hope that they would eat the Caesarian soldiers who came to collect them. The plan went badly. The lions turned on the unfortunate Megarians, who found themselves trapped between dozens of hungry predators on one side and some confused but vengeful legionaries on the other.

questions – 'Who would win in a fight between two leopards and a hippopotamus?' and so on – the Romans applied themselves in true empirical spirit.

Animals often had to be forced to fight. Sometimes they were whipped out of their cages, or burned with torches. Sometimes individuls from two different species were chained together. On one occasion a bull and bear were hooked by chains to a central ring, from which a naked convict then tried to detach them.

The sheer scale of carnage was important. Games sponsors, showing off, would boast about the numbers of animals killed: 400 lions in a single day under Julius Caesar; 300 ostriches slaughtered for the emperor Gordian I, who, to brighten things up, had them dyed a gaudy vermillion first. Nero massacred a whole menagerie of different species including arctic hares, bulls, boars, bears and seals. And Titus, proud builder of the Colosseum, could boast an incredible score by the time his inaugural games drew to a close: over the hundred days of shows, fully 9,000 animals had died in the arena sand.

One emperor would take things even further. Not content simply with sponsoring games, the Emperor Commodus made it his habit to participate in them. At one spectacle, the (captive) audience were forced to watch as the youthful emperor speared a hundred bears from a specially constructed walkway. He liked to make the senators chant in their front row seats: 'You are lord, and you are first and most successful of all! You are a winner! You will be a winner! You are a perpetual winner!'

They went along with it, as they had to. The historian Cassius Dio was there one day when Commodus decided to hunt ostriches, decapitating them with special crescent-headed arrows. Picking up a severed ostrich head in one hand, the emperor then rode a circuit of the arena, waving his trophy at the desperately applauding nobles with a meaningful grin. Only by stuffing his laurel wreath into his own mouth was Dio able to save himself from what would have been a very terminal attack of nervous giggles.

*

Sometimes the animals were allowed to get their own back. *Damnatio ad bestias* – being condemned to the beasts – was a common enough punishment in the Roman world, used at first for military deserters, but later against all sorts of middle-ranking criminals: murderers, forgers, temple-robbers and so on.

Bears were the worst, it was widely believed. They seemed to have an instinct for mangling their victims thoroughly before landing the killing blow. Big cats were better, though erratic. Female criminals were often made to face wild cows. In any case, it was an awful, humiliating way to die. Seneca, that connoisseur of suicide, speaks admiringly of one man so desperate to avoid facing the beasts of the arena that he choked himself to death on one of the stinking sponges that were provided for users of Roman public latrines.

Sometimes, the condemned were forced to play opposite animals in amusing re-enactments of mythical scenes. Martial was very impressed at Titus's games by the sight of a doomed 'Daedalus' whose home-made wings, however hard he flapped, did nothing to protect him from the wild beasts before whose claws he had been dangled. Another criminal, playing the notorious bandit Lauroleus, was nailed to a cross before being hollowed out by a bear.

Worse yet was the fate of one woman who was chosen to re-enact the twisted coupling of Queen Pasiphaë and the Cretan bull. Through some awful combination of stagecraft and agricultural science, a bull was induced to penetrate the unfortunate criminal (whose 'crime', of course, need not have been anything worse than to have displeased her master). 'Whatever Mythology can sing about, O Caesar, the arena recreates for you,' says Martial, admiringly.

These spectacles were meant to pile further indignity upon their victims. One group of victims, however, would use the ordeal of *damnatio ad bestias* to perform a drama of their own – a drama that made heroes of condemned criminals, turned humiliation into victory. In this spirit, around AD 107, a certain Ignatius of Antioch wrote to forbid his fellow Christians from trying to save him from execution:

Let me be fodder for the wild beasts; that is how I can get to God. I am God's wheat and I am being ground by the teeth of wild beasts to make a pure loaf for Christ… What a thrill I shall have from the wild beasts which are ready for me… I shall coax them to eat me up at once.

The Roman public were only too happy for Ignatius to have his way and, over the generations that followed, more Christians must have followed him on to the great killing floor of the Colosseum: Christians strapped to poles and fed to leopards; Christians tied to wild boar, or trampled by elephants or torn apart by bears and lions.

Such horrors ought to have been off-putting. Yet, during the great persecutions of the later empire, there were Christians who actively demanded to be fed to the beasts; such was the hold these scenes had acquired on the Christian imagination.

* * *

Noon, at the games of Titus. Sun, beaming straight down onto the arena through the opening at the centre of the awning. Dyed canvas casting a coloured glow on the white stone benches beneath. The smell, of human excitement, and spilled guts cooking in the hot arena sand, masked, perhaps, by sprays of scented saffron water, squirted from hidden outlets over the appreciative spectators.

Titus, most beneficent emperor, sometimes added an extra dimension to these 'sprinklings' by having little wooden balls or discs thrown out into the crowd, each carved with a different prize. A lucky catch could be traded in after the show for a free snack, a silver plate, a slave or a horse.

Down in the arena, the attendants will have been clearing away the remains of the morning's victims, using long poles to hook scattered limbs out through stage doors, while the last sleepy lions were whipped back into their cages and lowered through hatches into the darkness under the arena floor.

The midday lull might be padded out with some more executions: one person dismembered by chariots; another impaled; a third cooked in a sort of giant frying pan. Slaves with rakes hurried to erase the greasy black smear that incinerated bodies would leave as they were dragged from the arena.

Sometimes criminals were offered a chance to escape death if they could perform some terrible act of self mutilation. Martial saw a man imitate the republican hero Mucius Scaevola: holding his hand in a fire until it burned clean off. Another, playing the part of the god Attis, saved the rest of his body by cutting off his own testicles.

Sometimes too there was a comic interlude. Women fighting dwarves, say, or cripples beating each other with clubs. Nero once entertained a crowd with a fight between a whole tribe of 'Ethiopians': men, women and children too. Commodus, much later, is supposed to have gathered all the men in Rome who had no legs and given them snake-like prosthetic tails. Then, in costume as Hercules, he bludgeoned them all to death as they lay helpless on the sand.

Up in the stands, the crowd would thin at midday as people wandered off in search of food and drink. This was a good moment to attempt a surreptitious seating upgrade, with plebeians creeping forward into the seats that were supposed to be reserved for *equites*. A certain Nanneius, Martial reports, was forever being chased from the front rows by furious ushers, whom he tried to dodge by hiding in the aisles, or squatting behind pairs of wealthy shoulders, peeping one-eyed at the show from beneath his hood.

This sort of thing was infuriating to the more orderly minded emperors. Augustus, for example, had enforced strict rules about who should sit where in theatres and amphitheatres. In principle, the Colosseum should have been a sort of perfect map of Roman society: senators at the front; knights behind; freedmen in one place; slaves in another; Vestal Virgins in their special chairs on the front row; a wedge of seats in the middle for aristocratic boys, with a second wedge for their tutors conveniently next door. Women were banished to the back.

In practice the boundary rules were always being forgotten or flouted. There was a constant traffic of insults hurled, punches thrown, kisses blown by cheap seducers, while pretty girls and boys shot saucy glances over the tops of their programmes.

Such violations were a sign of the times. Rome's traditional class structure had been steadily corroded by the realities of empire. Old families found themselves shouldered aside by up-and-comers, who made up in hard cash what they lacked in breeding. Juvenal laments for himself and the other respectable poor:

> 'Get gone,' they say, 'if you've any shame, you lot whose bank accounts don't make the cut. Get off the VIP cushions. These seats are for pimps' sons, spawned in some dank brothel. Here's where the son of a sleek auctioneer applauds the show, here between the mighty-fine brats of the ring-fighter and sword trainer.'

Each day of the games, the ceaseless churn of Roman society played itself out anew amid the banked seats of the Colosseum. Greek theatres, the traditional sort, were one-sided: seats at one end and stage at the other, forming a giant 'D'. Roman amphitheatres – literally 'double-theatres' – were essentially two theatres glued end to end. Where the stage should have been, the audience now just found more of itself: the great *Populus Romanus* in all its misshapen glory.

* * *

This is where Verus and Priscus make their appearance, striding out on to the sand and into the pages of Martial's poetry. They will probably have arrived in the afternoon, marching in parade with their fellow fighters, escorted by trumpet players and flautists. This was the climax of the day's entertainment, a magnificent spectacle: each man's armour spotless and gleaming, inlaid with silver; dyed feathers waving on the helmets of the horseback-fighters; helmets crested with fish or snarling griffins. These were not convicts being led out to be murdered; more like modern sports stars greeting the adoring crowd.*

---

* This would be the moment for the famous gladiator shout *'Morituri te salutant!'* – 'Those who are about to die salute you!' There is almost no evidence that this was ever really done, however. The only mention of these

Gladiators came from all sorts of backgrounds. The earliest gladiator fights, back in the third century BC, had been held to mark funerals, fights between captives from beyond the republic, divided along ethnic lines. There was something almost religious or magical about it: Thracians, Samnites and Gauls, Rome's deadliest enemies, forced to kill each other, to wet the graves of the Roman rich.*

But by the time of Titus's games, at the high noon of the Roman empire, the supply of prisoners of war was beginning to dry up. The Gauls, conquered by Julius Caesar, were now calling themselves citizens and sending their aristocrats to swell the ranks of the Roman senate. And although Rome would still send the occasional army across the Rhine or Euphrates, the Germans and Parthians beyond the frontiers were increasingly difficult to subdue.

There were other routes to the arena, however. To judge by their names, Verus and Priscus started off as ordinary slaves – perhaps captured by bandits or pirates, sold off by desperate parents, enslaved to pay a debt, or just born that way. Slave mothers passed their status on to their children, and since slave women's bodies were not, legally speaking, their own, such children were plentiful.

A slave might be sent to the arena as a punishment – whipped out on to the floor of some provincial amphitheatre to be dispatched by a more practised killer, when the crowd demanded blood. But a slave who was tall and handsome – a potential champion fighter – could be highly sought after. The later emperor Marcus Aurelius had to limit the maximum price for a trained gladiator to 15,000 sesterces, and even that sum would have been enough to keep a peasant family fed for about thirty years.

*

words in the ancient sources is from a rather unlikely sounding story about a naval show, held in a lake outside Rome under the emperor Claudius.

* The famous rebel gladiator Spartacus was a Thracian, although the designation may have referred more to fighting style than ethnicity in Spartacus's day. The funereal association remained strong, however. Spartacus shocked the Romans by forcing captive legionaries to fight as gladiators at the funeral of a female slave.

Verus and Priscus, two of only a handful of gladiators ever to have been named in Latin literature, are likely to have arrived this way: bought as promising new recruits by a *lanista*, a master of one of Italy's *ludi*, or gladiator schools. Life in a *ludus* was hard and subject to military-style discipline. The 'gladiator oath' quoted in Petronius's *Satyricon* may not be too far from the real thing: to be 'burned, flogged, beaten, killed with cold steel… whatever else [the master] ordered. Like real gladiators, we very solemnly handed ourselves over, body and soul.'

The training was constant and exhausting. The new recruit, or *tiro*, would spend whole days working at the *palus*, a man-sized wooden stake which served as a stand-in opponent, leaping back and forth, aiming quick cuts at face and legs from behind his wicker shield.

Training equipment was made specially heavy in order to build stamina. Juvenal, frothing with scorn, describes a lady who imitates gladiatorial training as a sort of transgressive workout routine:

> Who doesn't know about the fancy purple gym kit at the women's training ground? Who hasn't seen the wounds on the target post as she chips away with her wooden sword and bashes it with her shield? She nails all the moves.
>
> Hark at her snorting as she thrashes away on command! See how she bends under the helmet's weight; the big bark bandages swaddling her hams – then laugh when she has to put aside her panoply to mount her little chamber-pot.

Gladiator training was hard, but there must have been some satisfaction in it; some pleasing sense of skill beginning to grow. Early on in their careers, gladiators were assigned to one of the various gladiatorial fighting styles that had evolved through the generations: beefy types might become heavy-shielded *murmillones*, with their distinctive crested helmets, or *secutores* – 'pursuers' – with their narrow eyeholes. More lightly armed were *thraeces* and *hoplomachi*, 'thracians' with their curved swords, and 'shield-fighters' who carried the Greek hoplite spear. Lightest of all were the scorned but deadly *retiarii*, who fought like fishermen with tridents, tangling their heavily armoured opponents in lead-weighted nets.

These main gladiator types formed sorts of tribes within the schools, with their own hierarchies, their own traditions and techniques, their own instructors, and probably their own separate sleeping quarters too.* Collapsing on to their cots in the *ludus* at the end of a long day's training, Verus and Priscus may well have felt themselves part of a strange sort of brotherhood-in-arms.

And indeed, each group of gladiators assembled by the *lanista* of a gladiator school was called a *familia* – a family. They trained together, lived together, ate their steaming bowls of barley stew together. They spoke different languages, perhaps; some were born slaves and others had been free. But they lived the same lives now, and shared the same fears, and prayed the same prayers to grim Nemesis, the Avenging Queen, who held life and death in her hands and was the particular deity of Rome's arena fighters. It was to her that the gladiators prayed when, once or twice a year, they were called upon to kill each other.

According to a Latin proverb, a gladiator watched his opponent's face, his weight, and his hands. Gladiatorial fencing was cagey and athletic. The most important piece of equipment was the shield, both as the primary means of defence and as a weapon, thrust forward suddenly to unbalance an opponent. It was a mark of inexperienced gladiators if the fight finished quickly, or was ended by a clean kill. More frequent, and more dangerous, were quick thrusts over the top of the shield, or cuts sweeping low against the back of the knees. An injured opponent was often a beaten one. No need to expose oneself to danger finishing someone off when simple blood loss would get the job done in the end.

So, like the professionals they were, Verus and Priscus drew the battle out, circling in the sand, stepping with cautious feet, perfectly balanced for the sudden spring that might carry one past the other's

* Juvenal, doubtless exaggerating, says *retiarii* had to be kept separate from more heavily armed gladiators because they were notorious for sexual deviancy. They were the only gladiators who fought without helmets, and the emperor Claudius is supposed to have enjoyed having them killed in the arena so that he could look at their faces while they died.

guard. From the side of the arena, the orchestra picked up the tension, amplifying it through the pipes of their trumpets and water organs, only to be drowned out by the gasp of the crowd each time one of the fighters made an attack.

The spectators were well able to appreciate the artistry of the display. Romans took gladiatorial combat as seriously as people take less blood-soaked sports today. Real enthusiasts would have visited the gladiator schools to watch fighters train; they might have attended the *cena libera* – the lavish 'Free Feast' that was given for gladiators on the evening before a fight. And although we do not know the gladiatorial types to which Verus and Priscus belonged, the audience would have recognized at once from the variations in their armour what sort of gladiators these were and what sort of fight this was going to be.

Indeed, different types of gladiators had their own special fans. Some spectators, called *parmularii*, favoured the gladiator types – *thraeces* and *hoplomachi* – who carried the small shield known as a *parma*. Others, the *scutarii*, preferred gladiators like the *murmillones*, who carried the larger shield known as a *scutum*.

Titus, watching from the imperial box, was a keen *parmularius*, and it is quite likely that Verus and Priscus were *parma*-fighters. If so, the emperor will have watched with the sharp attention of the true enthusiast. Proper fans knew the fighting style and the various moves by number, as they were called out in the training schools; helpful audiences might shout suggestions to gladiators in the arena.

Did Titus hop up and down under his purple canopy, screaming with the rest? *'Hoc habet!'* – 'He's had it!'; *'Iugula!'* – 'Kill!'; *'Verbera!'* – 'Hit him!' It was a delicate line to tread, for an emperor. Too much enthusiasm for blood, in the manner of Claudius, say, or Commodus, would go down badly with the audience. On the other hand, it didn't do to be caught not taking an interest. Julius Caesar had been notorious for using amphitheatre shows to catch up on his paperwork.

The balance had to be got right. The amphitheatre was one of the few venues in which emperor and people came face-to-face; where the crowd might dare to make their voices heard, their wishes felt.

Games were the sustaining rituals of the new political order, spectacular demonstrations of imperial beneficence and approachability. In
Latin, these shows were known as *munera*, or 'gifts' – gifts generously
bestowed in exchange for those small concessions the Roman plebs
had learned to make with respect to some of their ancient rights and
freedoms. Juvenal wrote, famously: 'We cast off dull duty when we
sold off our votes for nothing. The People – once source of power,
office, legions, everything – have learned to restrain themselves; now
they care only for two things: *panem et circenses*, bread and the games.'

The Romans loved their gladiators. Children dressed up as gladiators
to play in the street. People had gladiators painted on their walls or
mosaiced on to the floors of their grand country houses. There were
gladiator tables, gladiator lamps, gladiator winecups and fruit bowls
and chamber pots. There was hardly a piece of household furniture
that could not be improved by the addition of a little carved gladiator
waving his sword.

Women loved gladiators too much, it was believed. In AD 79, the
year before Titus's games, Mount Vesuvius had erupted, killing thousands and covering half of Campania in thick volcanic ash. When
the prosperous resort town of Pompeii was finally excavated, many
centuries later, the walls were found to be covered in graffiti about
gladiators: Celadus, a *thraex* 'the one who girls sigh for'; Crescens the
retiarius, 'lord of the girls' who 'nets the girls at night'.

Back in Rome, Juvenal spun a famous satire about a senator's wife
called Eppia who elopes to Egypt with a swordsman:

> What sort of beauty set her heart ablaze? What youthful charm
> was it that undid Eppia? What did she see that was worth being
> called a fighter's whore? For her darling Sergius was long in the
> tooth, his battle-scarred arm long overdue a rest – not to men-
> tion his grossly malformed face, that enormous wart where the
> helmet used to rub, right between his nostrils, and the vile stink
> from his always weeping eye.
>   And yet – he was a gladiator.

A fantasy, surely. But the strange sexual charge that attached to gladiators in Roman culture was very real. They came from the lowest
orders of society, and yet, confusingly to the traditional Roman
mind, they were extremely well-endowed with the quality Romans
had learned to value most: *virtus*, which gives us our word 'virtue',
but which translates literally as 'manliness'. Gladiators, hyper-virile
with their muscles and thrusting swords, carried *virtus* to an extreme.

A lucky windchime from another buried town, Herculaneum,
captures well the ambivalence gladiators could provoke. It is bronze,
sculpted into the shape of a gladiator who raises his sword to cut off
his own penis, an enormously oversized organ which, halfway along
the shaft, transforms into a wolf, head snarling back at the descending
blade.

Romans loved gladiators but, even more, they loved to see gladiators
die. 'We'll be having a holiday with a three-day show that's the best
ever,' says a character in the *Satyricon*. The giver of the games, he
knows, is 'no way wishy-washy. He'll give us the cold steel, no quarter,
and the slaughterhouse right in the middle where all the stands can
see it.'

To put on a 'slaughter' at the *munera* was munificence indeed.
Generally, the *editor* – the person giving the show – hired gladiators
on the understanding that most of those gladiators would be coming
back to their *familia* more or less in one piece. The compensation
paid to trainers for each dead gladiator was fifty times the hire fee
for a live one.

Good gladiators would reduce the burden on the show's host by
winning without killing. Most fights ended in submission by one
or other of the fighters, rather than with a straight kill. And a good
gladiator – a professional – could usually count on being spared if he
surrendered. The beaten man would raise a finger to signal his defeat.
The referee would then step in to hold back the winner's sword. The
editor, doubtless much relieved, could then grant *missio*, 'release', to
the loser, and all parties would survive to fight another day.

The gladiator fights of modern imagination are always to the death. In practice, however, such fights were rare. The actual death rate for gladiators, per fight, is variously estimated at between one in six and one in ten. There are gladiator tombstones which boast of fifty or sixty fights survived. Gladiators might fight two or three times a year, on average, so a sixty-fight career might span the better part of a Roman's working life.

And yet, sometimes, death was what the crowd demanded. A beaten gladiator, on his knees, would hear the jeers of the audience, see the forest of hostile thumbs, raised in threatening phallic imitation.* The *editor* in his box might pause for a moment, torn between his desire for popular favour and the demands of his purse. Then, he would give the signal to the referee, and the winner would deliver the killing blow. It was a matter of pride among gladiators, and much admired by spectators, that the loser would bravely present his throat to the sword, not shrinking from death. 'Down and outs or barbarians they may be,' as Cicero wrote, but 'they'd rather take a hit than dodge away in cowardly fashion.'

The violence seems to have had an electrifying effect on spectators. St Augustine tells the story of one Alypius, a young man who was dragged by his friends to see a gladiator show. At first he kept his eyes shut, but 'when one of the gladiators fell in combat, and the huge shout of all the spectators had powerfully resounded in his ears, he was overcome with curiosity... As soon as he saw blood, he drank in the savagery... and was made drunk with bloody delight.'

The emphasis on blood, in particular, seems to have been characteristic of the Roman experience of the amphitheatre. Gladiator

---

* The thumb signals used to signify life and death in the arena have been the subject of long controversy and confusion. Roman sources tell us only that people signalled for death *pollice verso* – with 'turned thumb' – and though this has usually been taken to mean 'thumbs down', there is no reason why this should necessarily be so. The best modern guess takes the 'turned thumb' to be a gesture similar to the modern thumbs up, based on the common ancient use of the thumb as a symbol for an erect penis.

blood was treated with fetishistic awe: it was mixed with bread in love charms; epileptics used to drink it warm, we are told, for its curative properties; brides, before their weddings, would part their hair with a spear dipped in gladiator gore.

Bodies, too, were the subject of intense curiosity. We know that at the arena at Carthage audience members were allowed to visit the arena mortuary after the show, to finger fresh wounds and peer into dead eyes. It seems perfectly likely that such ghoulishness was permitted at the Colosseum too. For all the Roman public's nerdy expertise on the finer points of gladiatorial fencing style, the popularity of the combats was based, ultimately, on bodies and blood.

* * *

Verus and Priscus were good gladiators; professionals, not clumsy butchers or novices to be lightly slaughtered. Still they must have known that at some point their respective runs would come to a bad end. And what place more likely for that end than the new-built Colosseum. The emperor, more than any other *editor*, could afford to buy acclaim with gladiatorial lives.

Perhaps they lacked faith in the imperial mercy. Or perhaps it was the simple hunger for glory that kept them fighting. Gladiator epitaphs are full of boasts: 'I was the favourite of the stadium throng'; 'great shouts roared through the audience when I was victor'. At any rate, though the fight was long and fierce, neither Verus nor Priscus was willing to surrender.

And, after a while, an eternity of seconds drawn out tight, Verus and Priscus will have become aware that, beyond their world of aching arms and sweat-stung eyes, there was a new tone in the surrounding cacophony – a new word, condensing into the massed consciousness of the crowd. *Missio*, people were chanting. *Missio*. The spectators, won over by the gladiators' courage and skill, were asking the emperor to release both of them.

Here was a problem for Titus Caesar. His own rule, as *editor* of the games, had been that no fight should end until the surrender or death of one of the participants. Now, rather than break his own edict, he promised great prizes in silver plate to both fighters, but signalled that the bout should go on.

By the end, Verus and Priscus must have been half-dead with exhaustion, still circling, breathing heavily behind the faceplates of their helmets, feet dragging in the sand. Then, quite suddenly, the two gladiators both collapsed in surrender, each submitting to the other at the exact same time.

It was the perfect ending to an extraordinary fight. Martial, watching from the stands, knew he had witnessed something worth commemorating. It was a fine occasion for a flattering poem. Titus had handled the moment with total confidence: he had been obedient, technically, to his own rules, while managing to reward Verus and Priscus's brave display with the generosity that was expected of an emperor. Both men had won, he declared, and both would receive the palm of victory. Better yet, both would get the wooden staff, the *rudis*, that signified release from gladiatorial service. Verus and Priscus were free.

As Verus and Priscus leave the arena, they disappear from history. We can only guess at what became of them, but men with their skills, and the money earned from the sale of all that imperial plate, will not have found opportunities lacking. Perhaps it was their sons, rich 'ring-fighters' brats', who would one day enrage Juvenal and his like by elbowing them out of the front rows at the Colosseum.

Most gladiators died before they were free. Few lived longer than five years in the ring. But for some, the arena was a path to wealth and status that should have been impossible under the traditional Roman system. A foreign slave, by the strength of his arm, could make himself a champion at Rome, and free, and richer even than the lawyers and lyric poets of the old respectable classes.

Traditional Romans thought gladiators shameful. There was an *infamia*, a legal and social stigma, that attached to the profession, as there was for prostitutes or actors. But the lure of gladiatorial glory was strong enough to attract even freeborn citizens to the arena. Most will have been poor and desperate, but not all. Juvenal writes of a certain 'Gracchus' who, despite the antique pedigree of that illustrious name, 'took a trident, put on the net thrower's tunic, and dodged about the arena in a gladiatorial act'. And the emperor Commodus devoted himself to gladiatorial training. It wasn't enough to rule most of the known world; he wanted to be Rome's best *secutor* too and chase *retiarii* around the ring.

A century and a half before Titus's games the Thracian gladiator Spartacus had broken out of a training school in Capua and terrorized Rome with an army of slaves and bandits, destroying three Roman armies before Crassus and Pompey brought him down.

Now, in men like Verus and Priscus, Romans faced a more insidious threat than Spartacus's rebellion. The Colosseum reflected Roman society like a carnival mirror, flipping and distorting the proper relations of things. It was a place where slaves could become heroes, outmanning Roman men and undoing Roman women. It was a place that could reduce aristocrats and emperors to capering showmen, and where the lowest citizens could condemn a man to death with the turn of a thumb. Here the gladiators lived out their brief, transgressive moments of glory. Here, in their thousands, they paid for this impudence with their lives, leaving their broken bodies to be dragged, by masked attendants, into the dark under the stands.

9

A GOD DANCES

The reign of Elagabalus

—————

AD 218–222

I T IS AD 218. THE Senate House feels old. In ones and twos,
senators appear in the doorway, dark against the grey light of
this winter morning. They huddle in their heavy woollen togas,
stepping with weary purpose across the threshold, with their slaves
and silent secretaries following behind.

It was Julius Caesar who first planned this house, two dozen
generations ago. Augustus built it. Titus's paranoid younger brother
Domitian gave it its great bronze doors. Vanished tyrants from vanished dynasties, but their works still loom. No brazier can protect the
frigid old men of the senate from the chill of all this sparsely windowed
marble – a shrine to a vanished democracy, built by imperial writ.

Little thunderclouds of incense smoke gather under the flat, high
ceiling. There is a statue of Victory here, even older than the Senate
House itself, a trophy from the wars against Pyrrhus, back in the great
days of the republic. Senators still gather each morning to pour wine
at the statue's feet and burn offerings of Arabian incense in memory
of happier times.

On this particular morning, however, the men at the base of the
statue are in a state of muttering fury. Above old Victory's laurelled
head is hanging an unasked-for novelty: gaudy paint on varnished
wood. It is a portrait: a boy, perhaps fourteen, dressed in gold and

A silver didrachm from the 260s BC showing the Roman she-wolf suckling the twins – one of the earliest images we have of Romulus and Remus.

The Dying Gaul, a Roman copy of a famous Hellenistic statue, made long after the Gallic sack. The figure was long believed to be a dying gladiator, and inspired Lord Byron's famous raptures on the theme.

A typical central-Italian burial urn from around the traditional date
of Rome's foundation, in the shape of a simple wooden hut.

The Cloaca Maxima flows into the Tiber by the ancient cattle market. Nearby, the legendary
king Evander built the great altar of Hercules, whose temple overlooks the riverbank.

Masked comic actors on a fourth-century wine jar from southern Italy. The Greek comic tradition in southern Italy was a key influence on the development of Latin comedy in Rome.

left: A bust of Julius Caesar, discovered in Tusculum in 1825 by Lucien Bonaparte, younger brother of Napoleon. It is probably the only surviving portrait of Caesar made during his lifetime. *right:* Gnaeus Pompeius, later known as Pompeius Magnus – Pompey the Great. To raise legions, he boasted, he had only to stamp his feet.

Detail from a fantastical urban scene, from the villa of P. Fannius Synistor, near Pompeii. A goddess stands on a column near a grand door, whose lintel is protected by a series of apotropaic phalluses.

A love scene, frescoed on a bedroom wall in in Pompeii, which was buried by volcanic ash in AD 79. Several surviving buildings from Pompeii and Herculaneum contain erotic art, sometimes surprisingly explicit.

A gold coin from the reign of Nero, showing the emperor's
distinctive heavy profile and double chin.

A defeated gladiator awaits the verdict of the crowd, painted, with much artistic
licence, by Jean-Léon Gérôme in 1872. The downturned thumbs of popular
imagination are in fact more likely to have been turned the other way.

SER PENIVS

above: Detail from the fourth-century *Gladiator Mosaic* showing a successful beast hunter, a *venator*. Venators could become stars in the arena, but the price of failure was death.

right: Marble head of Elagabalus. His hair is short, in the military style favoured by Severan emperors. In an effort to look authoritative, he has grown a sparse teenager's moustache.

The Roses of Heliogabalus, 1888, by Sir Lawrence Alma-Tadema.
A stunning Victorian fantasy of Roman decadence and decline.

A preserved stretch of the ancient Via Appia,
where Romans built their monumental tombs.

purple silk. His eyes are dark with kohl. His pale throat is laden with necklaces and baubles. His head is crowned with a tiara, gleaming with jewels. His pose is delicate – priestly. And indeed, the painted boy has been frozen in the act of making a sacrifice, presenting some oriental offering to what looks, as far as the grumbling senators can make out, like a lump of black volcanic stone.

They already know better, however, than to speak their thoughts too loud. There have been letters from the East: news of upheavals on the Parthian frontier. The stone, they are given to understand, is the earthly embodiment of the sun god Elagabal. And the pretty boy is Rome's new emperor.

* * *

Caesar Marcus Aurelius Antoninus Augustus was the boy's name, officially speaking. Not his birth name, obviously. Rather, it had been carefully chosen for him by his propagandists. Each word was a bright, if unearned decoration; an attempt to crown the boy with stolen laurels from Rome's glorious past.

The Caesar and Augustus parts of the name now more or less came as standard. Julius Caesar and his adopted son, founders of Rome's post-republican monarchy two and a half centuries earlier, had been translated through various stages of abstraction: first they were men; then emperors; then gods; and finally just titles to decorate the imperial throne. The 'Augustus', by the third century AD, was whoever was in charge of the empire. 'Caesar', similarly, just meant 'emperor' or, increasingly, something like 'deputy-emperor', or heir apparent.

The middle words of the boy's new name, 'Marcus Aurelius Antoninus', were inspired by a more recent namesake – a man whose memory the boy-emperor's advisors desperately wanted to evoke. The so-called Antonine emperors had taken over after the assassination of Domitian (paranoid, but they *were* out to get him) in AD 96, with the accession of a respectable old senator called Nerva. He was followed by a string of particularly successful emperors: from AD 98–117 was the reign of Trajan, a Spanish general whose column with its hordes of conquered Dacians still stands in the ruins of his imperial forum.

After him came Hadrian, famous for his fashionable beard, his wall across northern Britain and his doomed love of the Bithynian youth Antinous, the beautiful boy whose marble features decorate so many of Rome's museums today. Antoninus Pius came next. His reign, from AD 138–161, was marked by one of Rome's longest ever periods of perfect peace.

Last – finishing off nearly a century of unprecedented political stability – was Marcus Aurelius himself. This philosopher emperor was a Stoic sage in the tradition of Seneca and Cato the Younger; he wrote twelve volumes of 'Meditations' while fighting the German Marcomanni. 'Whatever this is that I am, it is a little flesh and breath,' he told himself; 'blood and bones and a network, a contexture of nerves, veins, and arteries.' It must have been easy even for an emperor to feel small, out there on the Danube frontier, scribbling away by lamplight in his tent while, outside, the trees of Europe's primaeval forest loomed endlessly from the north and east.

There were real threats to Roman security in those days, out there beyond the border. The German tribes, once so easy to push around, had become organized and therefore dangerous. One year, the group presuming to call itself the Marcomannic Confederation had even dared to raid south across the Alps into Italy – the closest any barbarian force had come to the capital since the fall of the Roman republic. Rome was vulnerable, its citizens suddenly realized. The old Servian Walls, built after the trauma of the Gallic Sack back in the fourth century BC, were ancient and crumbled, and had anyway long since been outgrown by the swollen imperial city.

And while the Germans were confederating in the north, the old Iranian empire of the Parthians was stirring in the east. Initial Roman attempts to suppress this new menace led to disaster in AD 161 when an overambitious Roman governor, following the instructions of an oracular snake, led an entire legion to annihilation in the mountains of Armenia. It took four long years for the Roman generals in Syria to put together a successful punitive expedition, marching down the Euphrates to the Parthian capital, which they burned, along with the ancient city of Seleucia on the River Tigris, founded in the time of Alexander the Great.

The story is that, while ransacking the Temple of Apollo in Seleucia, the Roman commander found a mysterious gold casket which he opened up, inadvertently releasing a 'spiritus pestilens' that had been sealed inside.

And this will have sounded plausible enough to the citizens of Roman Syria, who saw the victorious legions come limping back over the frontier covered in bloody pustules, dying in their own faeces, stinking and black. The Antonine Plague, as it came to be known, would play back and forth across the empire for the next twenty-three years. In Rome, the sickness – probably a virulent outbreak of haemorrhagic smallpox – tore through the cramped apartment blocks and down the crowded streets. At its height, it is said to have killed 2,000 people in the city in a single day. Casualty figures across the whole empire will have been in the millions, with the cities and the legionary camps especially badly hit.

With his forces weakened by the plague, Marcus Aurelius found himself hard-pressed by the Germans. The soldiers on his triumphal column, which stands today in the Piazza Colonna, are carved with expressions of perfect calm. Things were always under control, they seem to say.

But the strange scene halfway up the column's spiral relief – a vague, half-formed figure, spreading dripping arms over a huddle of men below – tells a different story: the men are Marcus's soldiers, dying of thirst, surrounded by hostile Quadi warriors; the figure looming above is a mysterious deity, saving the day with an unexpected shower of life-giving rain and scattering the Germans with bolts of lightning. While the Romans drank, the barbarians burned. There was a time, though, a pessimistic observer might have pondered, when Roman soldiers could deal with Germans without having to resort to divine intervention.

There was some confusion in the empire over precisely which god had saved Marcus Aurelius that day. In Rome, people assumed it was Jupiter the Thunderer; in Carthage (now a fat Roman colony) the Christian author Tertullian assured the faithful that it had been the prayers of Christian legionaries that had summoned the rain. Those who had been closest to the action, however, gave credit to an Egyptian sorcerer called Arnuphis, who had invoked the power of Hermes Aërios, who in turn was nothing more than a Hellenized reinvention of ibis-headed Thoth, whose cult had been honoured in Egypt for thousands of years.

Marcus Aurelius presided over military near-misses and dubious foreign gods. And yet, in the reign of the boy-emperor fifty years later, he was held up as a model of benevolent imperial monarchy. Old men in the senate on that winter morning were still able dimly to recall the ideals that Marcus Aurelius had himself articulated: 'A polity in which there is the same law for all, a polity administered with regard to equal rights and equal freedom of speech... a kingly government which respects most of all the freedom of the governed.'

Only one great crime was laid against the Stoic emperor by later historians: that he allowed fatherly affection to blind him to the faults of his son. The Antonine emperors were so successful partly because each ruler adopted his successor from outside his immediate family, which meant that people with outstanding talents and suitable temperaments could be drafted from the ranks of the aristocracy into the imperial house. For a hundred years, the empire was passed from one set of capable hands to another, more or less without interruption.

But Marcus Aurelius died in AD 180 leaving the empire in the hands of his ostrich-killing, gladiator-loving, Hercules-impersonating son Commodus. The era of wise rulers and smooth imperial succession was drawing to an end. In AD 192, the increasingly unhinged young autocrat was strangled by a wrestling partner in his own bath.

In AD 193, the empire was sold at auction by the Praetorian Guard. The men of the elite imperial bodyguard, 5,000 strong, were meant to protect emperors; instead, they killed Commodus's successor Pertinax, then openly offered the imperial title to the highest bidder.

Inside the praetorian barracks, on the outskirts of the city, a Cretan official named Titus Sulpicianus was promising the guardsmen

20,000 sesterces for each man and more for the officers if they would raise him to the imperial purple: several years' wages for one night's work. But word spread that the empire was up for sale, and before long a wealthy senator called Didius Julianus came puffing out of the evening gloom to shout tempting offers over the praetorian ramparts, promising with desperate hand signals to match Sulpicianus's bid and then some.

The guardsmen were duly bought, but the mood in the streets was sufficiently threatening that they refused to open the barracks gate. Instead, Rome's new emperor was forced to scramble for the safety of the fortified camp by means of a hastily deployed ladder. And when poor Julianus went to the Senate House later that night, to inform the senators of his accession, he travelled through the streets in a *testudo* of fully armed praetorians, while angry citizens pelted him with rocks and chamber pots.

Five different men claimed the empire in that year of AD 193 – a height of political instability that had not been reached in generations; not since the fall of Nero back in AD 68. It took years for one of them to emerge victorious: Septimius Severus, a provincial aristocrat from Roman Libya, who spoke Latin, his whole life, with a slight North African accent.

His triumphal arch, which stands today outside the Senate House, in the Forum, offers no hint that his mastery of the empire was paid for in Roman blood. The enormous Battle of Lugdunum, a two-day affair in which more than 100,000 Roman soldiers fought each other to a standstill in central Gaul, is not commemorated. Severus took care to mask his grim civil war with a brief but satisfyingly successful Parthian campaign.

A very keen observer might detect something amiss on the triumphal arch, however. Just visible between the characters of the bronze inscription on the arch's attic are empty peg holes, where the letters have been wrenched out of the stone and rearranged. Reconstructing the vanished words from the arrangement of the empty holes gives a name, carefully erased: Geta – Severus's younger son.

When he died in AD 211, Severus left the empire to his two sons, Geta and Caracalla. They hated each other. For several unbearable months, they lived at opposite ends of the imperial palace on the Palatine Hill, surrounded by their respective sycophants and circled with mutually hostile armed guards. When Caracalla finally managed to have his brother murdered, he persuaded the senate to impose the penalty of *damnatio memoriae*: all traces of the dead man's existence were systematically erased from Rome and the empire. Soon, where Geta had been, there was nothing left but empty plinths and suspicious patches of blank marble.

Caracalla lasted six years before being murdered in his turn. On campaign against the Parthians in Syria, his praetorian prefect, a lawyer called Macrinus, dispatched a soldier to kill the emperor as he squatted in the bushes, afflicted with diarrhea. Caught with his breeches round his ankles, Caracalla was unable to defend himself. He left no sons. With no one else to turn to, the army in Syria declared that the scheming Macrinus would be Rome's next emperor.

* * *

That should have been the end for the unhappy Severan dynasty. But although Macrinus had disposed of the last of Severus's male descendants, he vastly underestimated the threat which was posed to him by the female members of the imperial clan.

Many years earlier, at the end of Marcus Aurelius's reign, Septimius Severus had met and been enchanted by an aristocratic teenager called Julia Domna while stationed in the town of Emesa – now the war-torn Syrian town of Homs – a rich trading city on the upper reaches of the River Orontes, south of Antioch.* He was an ambitious, middle-class legionary commander in early middle age. She was the

---

* Julia Domna had an attraction beyond just her personal charm. Severus, checking, as a matter of course, the horoscope of his prospective betrothed, is said to have learned that Domna was destined to be the wife of a king. Severus, like many of his contemporaries, was a firm believer in the prophetic power of astrologers.

daughter of an ancient family of priest-kings, as bright and strong-willed as she was beautiful.

They were divided by age, culture, class and language, but the marriage was a successful one.* While Severus fought his way to supremacy, his desert-princess-turned-Roman-empress presided over a new flourishing of art, culture and scholarship within the imperial court.

Whether shivering among the bogs of Scotland or baking on the Parthian frontier, Julia Domna was attended by an ever-changing circle of intellectuals. There were no great literary figures to compare with Ovid and Virgil, but the Severan age could boast some pioneering jurists, top-class rhetoricians and philosophers who were moving away from the stale Stoicism of Cato or Marcus Aurelius to develop new doctrines, new readings of the six-hundred-year-old ideas of Plato: ideas that were attaining a fresh relevance in what was an increasingly spiritual and mystical age.

Philosophy and law bled easily into religion. Julia Domna seems to have been particularly interested in one Apollonius of Tyana, a travelling Neo-Pythagorean sage and miracle worker of the first century AD, who enjoyed a wide following under the later Roman empire. She will have heard of Jesus too – but the stern insistence of Christians and Jews on the non-existence of other gods ran contrary to Julia Domna's instincts, and there is no evidence that she ever flirted with Christianity herself, however much she may have been in need of spiritual comfort.

As the Severan dynasty unravelled, her need for comfort will have become acute. When Caracalla murdered Geta in AD 211, it was Julia Domna, their mother, who was tricked into arranging the fatal meeting. She was there when the assassins burst into the room, and she held Geta in her arms as they delivered the fatal blow.

---

* It says a lot about the changing nature of the Roman empire in the late second century AD that the state came to be ruled by an emperor who had grown up speaking Punic and an empress whose first languages would have been Aramaic and Greek. Neither was a native speaker of Latin.

The next day, Caracalla forbade her from mourning her dead son, newly declared 'an enemy of the state'. She had to compose herself and carry on. She was, after all, vital to the Severan regime. While her fratricidal son stayed with his army, running border campaigns or putting down revolts, it was Julia Domna who handled the day-to-day administration of the state.

Only after Caracalla was murdered did the formidable empress relinquish her duties. With both sons dead, the empire in hostile hands, and her own body being eaten away by breast cancer, Julia Domna committed suicide at Antioch in AD 217. She was in her middle forties.

So far, so good for the usurper Macrinus. There were now only three adult survivors of the Severan clan, the sister and nieces of Julia Domna, all also called Julia. Julia Maesa was the matriarch – a little older than her sister Domna, but no less formidable. Now, she and her daughters, Julia Sohaemias and Julia Mamaea, each with one young son, were rounded up and sent back home to Emesa, the dusty, no-account town from which they had originally sprung. There, it was hoped, the three remaining Julias would vanish back into oriental obscurity.

It was a critical mistake. Julia Maesa had no intention of allowing herself and her daughters to be sidelined. More than that, in Emesa she was able to take full advantage of the one title that still remained to her family: the hereditary priesthood of the local sun god Elagabal, currently held by her pubescent grandson Bassianus.

He was a stripling, barely into his teens, but he was the only semi-plausible male relation the Julias could come up with, so he would have to do. Soon little notes and presents were flowing back and forth between Emesa and the nearest legionary camp, some 65 kilometres away. Maesa had the treasure of Elagabal's temple at her disposal, it was soon widely known. Her generosity might be counted upon. Macrinus, on the other hand, was a skinflint, and was anyway responsible for Caracalla's murder. And let no one be deceived! The boy, young Bassianus, was no mere cousin of the murdered emperor but rather his bastard son, born of a secret union between Caracalla and his beautiful cousin Julia Sohaemias.

Certainly there was something princely about the boy, thought those who saw him. Legionaries passing through Emesa watched sometimes as the young priest danced his ritual dance in honour of the god. The splendour of the ceremony was overwhelming: rich scents and colours competed with the sound of pipes and flutes to drown the senses of spectators. Panting like a satyr at the centre of this whirl of silk and gold, with the light of faith shining in his eyes, skinny, painted Bassianus did indeed look something more than human.

Back in Rome, the senators in their draughty hall were struggling to keep up with the pace of events. When the letter arrived, after two weeks' gallop across Europe by horse relay, telling the senators that Caracalla was dead, they at first refused to believe it. They suspected a trap laid for anyone who might be unwise enough to be caught celebrating.

Certainly Caracalla, the rude emperor of the army camps, had made himself little loved. Macrinus was a usurper and a nobody, but he was a lawyerish, semi-respectable nobody, who might be persuaded to treat the senate of Rome with something like the respect to which that institution was accustomed.

But the stream of exhausted messengers kept pouring in, with their time-lagged news: a Parthian invasion force was pouring into Syria; Macrinus had gone to defend the frontier; an inconclusive battle; a humiliating settlement.

At the same time, news of Maesa's scheming was arriving in the capital. A son of Caracalla, the senators heard, previously unknown, had been smuggled into a Syrian legionary camp, dressed in the costume of an emperor. The army sent to crush the revolt had joined it. Rebellion was spreading through the East. Macrinus was marching at top speed back to Antioch.

Battle was inevitable, and the senators prepared themselves for the final outcome. Even in this distant war, Rome's nervous aristocrats had much at stake. Loyalty to Macrinus would certainly be punished if the Julias were victorious, but then if Macrinus won, the penalties would flow in the opposite direction. Backing the right side, and to the right extent, was a matter of the most delicate political calculation.

So the mood in the Senate House will have been tense as reports of the final fight came in at last. The initial encounter, the senators heard, had gone in favour of Macrinus's praetorian cohorts. Then the Julias themselves had plunged into the scattered ranks, rallying their men with their own fierce courage; and little Bassianus, looking every inch the son of Caracalla, had charged the enemy head-on, scattering men before him like a thunderbolt.

Macrinus fled back to Antioch while the battle was still being fought. He had been growing a philosopher's beard in an attempt to look like Marcus Aurelius; now he shaved it off and galloped north in a borrowed cloak in a desperate attempt to get to Europe before the news of his defeat could overtake him. Just before the Bosphorus, he was caught by enemy agents and executed by the side of the road.

Macrinus earned one distinction during his short reign: he was the first Roman emperor never to set foot in Rome itself. Already, in those days, the centre of economic gravity in the Roman empire was shifting towards the provinces: rich old cities like Antioch and Alexandria were regaining their former self-confidence. The thousand-year-old Greek culture of the Aegean coast was enjoying a long renaissance, and young men of Athens or Ephesus were as likely to study Hellenic philosophy as Roman law.

Anyway, the armies demanded constant imperial attention if they were to be prevented from throwing up a steady stream of military pretenders. Rome, halfway down the peaceful Italian peninsula, felt increasingly far from the crucial action taking place on the Rhine and Danube frontiers.

So, for a year, the new emperor dawdled at Nicomedia on the coast of Turkey and the senators in Rome were left in suspense about what sort of man their teenaged monarch would turn out to be. The masters (and mistresses) of the new regime were not shy of killing – this had been anticipated – nor over-concerned with legal protocols:

'I will not send you the proofs of their plots,' read an imperial message about two accused senators. 'It would be useless to read them, since the men are already dead.'

But there was sparse information about the character of the emperor himself. Only the shining new portrait in the Senate House gave them any hint, and that little enough. He was young, handsome, and devoted to a foreign god. His birth name, they knew, was Bassianus; his regal name was Marcus Aurelius Antoninus; but now in Rome he began to be called after the mysterious deity with whom he was obviously so concerned. The priest of Elagabal came to be remembered as the Emperor Elagabalus.

* * *

If Elagabalus's god made the senators uncomfortable, it was not because of any sense that he was a false god, competing with 'true' Roman religion. The Romans both understood and expected that the thousands of different polities and tribes that made up their vast empire would each have their own sets of gods and goddesses, rituals, sacrifices and taboos, all collectively forming a body of practice that could be described as a *religio* – a word for which 'religion' is a misleading translation. For each political group within the empire, there was a unique *religio*: just as the Romans worshipped Jupiter, Venus and Mars, the Emesenes might worship Azizos, Monimos, Kypris Charinazaia and Elagabal. Indeed, the Romans welcomed foreigners to continue their religious practices: they liked to see gods being honoured, and didn't mind particularly which ones.

Nor was there anything too threatening about the arrival of a foreign god in Rome. When Elagabalus finally reached the capital, with the triumphant Julias close behind him, the senators soon learned that he had brought his Emesene sun god with him. This was literally true. The 'betyl' – the cone of black meteoritic rock from the great temple at Emesa that was the physical embodiment of the god Elagabal – had been carefully carried two thousand miles from its home in the East, and was now to be housed in an enormous new temple in Rome itself.

But this sort of thing had been happening ever since Juno's statue was stolen from conquered Veii back in the fifth century BC. Rome was a city of immigrants, each with their own shrines to this or that exotic deity. Plenty of respectable Romans even prayed to some of the more alluring imports, joined the cults of Isis or Dea Syria or Jupiter Dolichenus. Elagabal was just one more foreign god to add to the polyglot religious babble.

Still, as Elagabalus, his mother, grandmother and aunt installed themselves in the various wings of the imperial palace on the Palatine, it was becoming clear that the boy's religious feelings might be deeply held enough to cause a problem. While Elagabalus lingered in the East it had been possible to treat his religion as a mere eccentricity. In person, however, the boy revealed himself to be a true believer and, worse, a believer with missionary zeal. To please the emperor, the Romans would have to become believers too.

The new Temple of Elagabal, rising enormous from the northeast corner of the Palatine, loomed over the old sanctuaries of the Forum and the Via Sacra, the *regia* that had housed the ancient kings, the temple of Castor and Pollux, the temple of the deified Julius, the little round shrine of the Vestal Virgins, with its plume of carefully tended smoke.

Now, in the cold of each early morning, Rome's senators found themselves clambering up the Palatine hill, to gather respectfully around the new temple's richly decorated altars. Muttered conversation was concealed by the lowing of alarmed cows, wide-eyed and steaming in the bright air, by the bleating of sheep, plaintive and stupid. Soon the pipes would strike up their strange tunes and the drums would signal the start of the slaughter. The sacred butchers would get to work on the morning's herd of victims, piling fleecy bodies up on the altars, where streams of blood mingled with jars of old and expensive wine.

Sometimes the senators would recognize their friends and colleagues taking part in the day's performance. There, dressed in Phoenician robes and the linen shoes of an eastern prophet, would be some praetor or consul, trying not to spill his heaped golden dish of fresh spiced sheep entrails all over his fine costume.

And then the emperor himself would appear, smiling beneficently at those men who were lucky enough to be allowed to participate in Elagabal's rites. He was dressed just as he had been in the painting, in a floor-length purple tunic, long-sleeved and embroidered in gold. His cheeks were freshly rouged; his eyes flashed from under his black-painted lashes. A troupe of Syrian girls followed him, accompanying his movements with the deft sound of tambourines, and the stamping of delicate feet.

This was the boy-emperor's gift to the Senate and People of Rome: every morning, in honour of the god Elagabal, he would dance for them, just as he had danced under the sun of his ancestral home. He had found his calling – what he had to do, what he loved to do. Even when he had more mundane business to attend to, says the hostile historian Cassius Dio – giving speeches, receiving official salutations, or even just walking along – he seemed always to be quietly dancing.

Everyone, from rich to poor, was invited to join in Elagabalus's celebration. Once a year, just as he had back home, the emperor paraded the black stone of Elagabal through the streets on a chariot drawn by six white horses. No one was permitted to ride in the chariot with the sacred rock; only the emperor himself walked ahead holding the reins. To avoid insulting the god by turning his back, he walked the entire parade route backwards, with a burly man on either side ready to catch him if he fell.

The festive mood was to be enhanced by new proofs of imperial generosity. From specially constructed towers the emperor rained down bounty on the assembled crowd: all sorts of treasures in gold and silver, and even live animals – except for pigs, whose flesh was forbidden to followers of Elagabal. The scramble for prizes was unexpectedly desperate. Dozens were killed, some crushed to death by the mob; others impaled on the spears of the emperor's bodyguard.

Still the emperor kept trying to make a good impression. It was now announced that Elagabulus would be getting married, and in such a way as to demonstrate his profound respect for traditional Roman religion: his bride, Aquilia Severa, was a Vestal Virgin. What could be more appropriate? The high priest would marry Rome's chief priestess, and together they could produce infants that would be nearly divine!

At the same time, the god Elagabal would also acquire a heavenly consort. Initially, Elagabalus considered Athena for the role. The Palladium – a crude image of the goddess that had been rescued from the ruins of Troy by Aeneas himself, and stored in the Temple of Vesta for a thousand years – was introduced to the Elagabal stone.

Sparks failed to fly, however. A replacement bride was sent for. Fresh from the city of Carthage came the statue of the Phoenician moon goddess Urania, also known as Astroarche or Kypris Charinazaia. There was public feasting across Italy, games and celebrations, and the whole population competed in buying the god expensive wedding presents.

* * *

The god's marriage may have been a happy one. The emperor's cannot have been. The gossip picked up by Cassius Dio – hiding in Bithynia at the time – had it that Elagabalus's real interests lay elsewhere. There was a charioteer, in particular, Dio records, a rough type called Diocles, with whom the young emperor was besotted to the point of madness. Elagabalus would appear before the senate sometimes with two black eyes, picked up in furious arguments with his beloved the evening before.

There were other stories too: a special room tucked away in the palace that had been made up to look like a street brothel; the emperor standing in the doorway, naked except for his make-up, jingling a curtain of gold rings and soliciting passers-by 'with soft and melting voice'.

His agents around the empire were on the lookout for new pleasures. There was an athlete, Zoticus, who gained a reputation for the extraordinary size of his member. When word reached Rome, he was escorted to the city with all possible pomp and brought by torchlit procession to the imperial palace. He hailed the emperor 'Lord'. Elegabalus blushed at this. Bending his neck in an attitude of the most perfect modesty, he replied in soft tones: 'Call me not lord, for I am a lady.'

This may have really been what the emperor wanted – to be a lady, that is. He was circumcised, like many followers of ancient Eastern religions, but an (admittedly very dubious) passage in Dio claims that he wanted to amputate his genitals altogether, and that he had his doctors working on a way to cut an artificial vagina into the flesh of his perineum.

At any rate, the mightily endowed Zoticus was whisked off at once to the emperor's private bath, where Elagabalus pecked at some dinner while nestling happily in the athlete's broad bosom. When the time came for the night's performance, however, Zoticus found himself afflicted with a debilitating case of nerves – that or the jealous Diocles had slipped him a potion – and was shipped back home in flaccid disgrace.

While all this was going on, the Julias and their allies were busy with the smooth running of the empire. How much power was wielded by the women themselves is hard to know. There were men involved in their faction: a mysterious soldier called Comazon; a lover, Gannys, murdered by Elagabalus, apparently, in Nicomedia. One of their supporters succeeded in becoming so grey an eminence that we have lost the first half of his name; he is known to history simply as '…atus'.

Senatorial lists, meanwhile, show a remarkable consistency of personnel between the reigns of Severus, Caracalla and Elagabalus. Those senators who supported Julia Domna while she handled Caracalla's administration appear to have been content to support her sister Julia Maesa just as well in her new role as Augusta, Mother of the Senate and of the Army Camps.

Still, the behaviour of the emperor himself was becoming a problem that Maesa could no longer ignore. His foreign god might have been tolerated so long as his worship could be kept relatively private, but Elagabalus seemed determined to thrust his oriental cult to the centre of Roman public religious practice – a serious threat to the *pax deorum.* Debauching a Vestal Virgin was sacrilege enough, but there were reports of other horrors too: sacrifices of little boys; occult amulets and chants; a snake, a monkey and a lion, shut up in Elagabal's temple and fattened on human genitals.

Even Rome's other foreign gods were horrified by the newcomer's antics: the statue of Isis, riding a dog on the pediment of her temple, had been seen to turn her face away from the city in disgust. So, over the objections of Elagabalus's mother, Julia Sohaemias, a solution was found. To help him cope with the burdens of empire, Elagabalus would adopt his young cousin Alexander.

At first, the emperor was very pleased with this arrangement, tickled by the incongruity of himself, still a teenager, having acquired a twelve-year-old 'son'. Anyway, here was someone with whom he could share his sacred pleasures: Alexander was straightaway enrolled into the priesthood of Elagabal and preparations made for his instruction in the Syrian dance.

But Alexander's mother, Julia Mamaea, would not allow her son to follow in Elagabalus's footsteps, however gracefully they were turned. The emperor, to his mounting fury, soon found his adopted son was being trained in the traditional arts of rhetoric and law, and was better at wrestling than oriental ballet.

Too late, Elagabalus realized that he had adopted not a successor but a replacement. Alexander was strictly guarded by his mother and grandmother, and the emperor could not touch him. Any attempt even to remove young Alexander from the public eye was met with terrible outbursts of worried indignation from the Praetorian Guard, whose loyalty Maesa had quietly bought.

The last of these outbursts was sufficiently severe that Elagabalus felt compelled to visit the praetorian camp in person to restore order, with his mother Sohaemias at his side and his adopted son Alexander, stubbornly alive, following behind him.

Exactly what happened within the praetorian barracks is impossible to tell. Dio records only that at a certain point, Elagabalus realized that the ground had shifted beneath him: he had come as an emperor, issuing commands, but with the mood in camp what it was, he might never be allowed to leave again. And while Julia Sohaemias was urging his case to the troops, Alexander's mother, Julia Mamaea, was urging the opposite.

Elagabalus panicked and tried to have himself smuggled back to the comparative safety of the imperial palace. He did not get far. The Praetorians, now on the hunt, found their soft boy-emperor cowering at the bottom of a chest being hauled by a pack of nervous-looking imperial slaves. Desperate, his mother clung to him, but her body, soft with luxury, was no defence against praetorian swords. Son and mother were cut down in each others arms. He was eighteen years old, and had reigned for just four years.

The bodies, naked and headless, were dragged through the streets of Rome to satisfy the curiosity of the crowd: his mother ended up in a ditch somewhere, food for dogs. He, with his graceful dancer's limbs, was thrown into Rome's Great Sewer. The city chewed him up, the delicate boy, and then released him from its brick-ringed cloaca to go bobbing with the rest of the filth down to the sea. At birth they had called him Bassianus; at accession they called him Marcus Aurelius Antoninus; behind his back they called him Elagabalus. Now, in death, they called him Tiberinus, in honour of the river that carried him out of the city for the last time.

* * *

Elagabalus died in AD 222. It will not have felt, at the time, like a great historical turning point. The older senators, in that year, will still have been able to remember the reign of Marcus Aurelius, just half a century before. They had grown up with the dynastic stability of the Antonines, a legacy which the Severans had done their best to carry on. They will have seen no reason, in the death of Elagabalus, for that to change. There was, after all, a new Severus – Severus Alexander – to carry on the line. Meanwhile, the Syrian Julias might now number two rather than three, but they still remained at the centre of power: a strong, consistent core.

But although Severus Alexander would rule, successfully enough, for another dozen years, the glory years of Roman imperial power would end with him. The Praetorians had tasted blood too often now to be easily intimidated; over the next fifty years, more emperors than not would be installed at the point of a *gladius*, whether wielded by the Praetorians in Rome or, more often, by one of the great armies of the frontiers. It would not always be clear, over the coming decades of anarchy, whether Rome's legions were there to defend the city or to bleed it dry.

Soon enough, the centrifugal force that was driving power away from the capital and towards the imperial fringes would be strong enough to split the empire into three separate parts: in the West, a breakaway Gallic empire based on the strength of the Rhine armies was able to survive for a generation, defying Rome to do anything about it. In the East, another Syrian princess, Zenobia of Palmyra, was able to turn Rome's richest provinces into her own personal domain.

It took a great soldier to stitch the empire's pieces back together again. It would take more than soldiery, however, to keep the empire whole. Stability required that one of the endless military usurpers find a source of legitimacy beyond mere force of arms. At last, nearly a hundred years after Elagabalus's death, a brilliant soldier-emperor came to follow in his footsteps, bringing to Rome not just a fresh army, but another new god.

10

CONQUER BY THIS!

The Battle of the Milvian Bridge

———

AD 312

Autumn, 28 October, AD 312. Out on the Via Appia, where the city fades into the countryside, an unusual silence hangs in the spaces between the old tombs. The cypresses are frozen in the early morning sun as if trying to escape notice. In the cool columns of air overhead, a flock of starlings kaleidoscopes its way through a series of mute question marks.

No sign of the morning's usual traffic. The only faces here belong to the dead, who stare out across the highway, carved in stone with their humble professions and old-fashioned hair: 'Gaius Atilius Euhodus, freedman of Serranus, a pearl-dealer of the Via Sacra, is buried here'; 'Here lie the bones of a man, modest, honest and trusty – the crier Olus Granius.' Repeated now and then is a bleak little refrain, so familiar that it can be abbreviated to a string of letters: 'N. F. F. N. S. N. C.' *Non Fui* – I was not; *Fui* – I was; *Non Sum* – I am not; *Non Curo* – I care not.

Amid this funerary landscape, a recently-built wall rises somewhat incongruous beside the ancient road. This is the curved flank of Maxentius's Circus, stretching five hundred paces end to end.

It is a lavish building, a stadium fit for an emperor. Winged victories cavort along its central spine; walls gleam with expensive marble cladding; an Egyptian obelisk rises at one end, a crude and ancient symbol of imperial potency.

But here, the silence of the Via Appia gives way to a deeper desolation. No horses press at the gates of the starting cages; no spectators jostle for the 10,000 empty seats. By the far turning post, the dirt of the racetrack is untroubled by skidding chariot wheels. Down the return straight, past the imperial box, nothing breaks the long-lined symmetry of the stands.

And beyond the finish line, where victorious chariots should have rolled, rises the bulk of an enormous mausoleum. Here, the body of the emperor's son is quietly rotting, under a great round drum of brick and stone. His name was Romulus, after Rome's founder, and he was meant to offer a new start, but he died before he was out of his teens, and now sleeps in peace in his marble sarcophagus. So much the better for him, perhaps. Far away, on the other side of the city, his father Maxentius is preparing for battle.

* * *

A man born in the reign of the boy-emperor Elagabalus would have been more than ninety years old by the time Maxentius rode out to fight. And yet, the city in that year would have looked much the same as he remembered it from his childhood. There was only one major change: the tombs of the Via Appia were now cut off from the city by a formidable defensive wall. Four metres thick and about 13 metres high, with carefully spaced ballista towers, it loomed over the villas of the suburbs, a reminder to all who passed of the vastness and grandeur of imperial Rome.

But the wall was also a sign of the empire's insecurity. Elagabalus's cousin and successor Severus Alexander had been murdered in AD 235. Under the emperors that followed, the empire was struck by a series of crises that brought it to the point of disintegration. The army raised a series of rival claimants to the purple, debasing the imperial office to the point that it could be claimed by a grotesque-looking barbarian trooper called Maximinus Thrax. A fresh plague swept through the cities and the army camps.

Meanwhile, in the East, a renewed Persian empire seized the opportunity to threaten the rich towns of Roman Syria. The Emperor

Valerian, defending the frontiers, was captured by the Persian Shapur I. The great *shah*, it was said, forced his unfortunate captive to serve, while he lived, as a human mounting block. When he died, Valerian was stuffed and put on display like a prize boar.

Meanwhile, new tribes and confederations threatened the Roman peace, with names that would etch themselves into Europe's history: Goths and Vandals on the Danube; Franks and Burgundians on the Rhine. In AD 271, a Germanic group called the Iuthungi joined with the Confederation of the Alemanni to launch a massive invasion of Italy. The then emperor, Aurelian, raced back from the frontiers just in time, but Rome had been terrified by the reports of raiding armies marching down the Via Flaminia. Certainly the huge Aurelian walls sprang up over the following years with a speed that gave no hint of a capital in decline.

Aurelian managed to avert military disaster, for Rome and for the empire as a whole. Breakaway states based in Syria and Gaul were brought back under imperial command. Queen Zenobia of Palmyra, who had aspired to rule the Roman East, was led in chains behind Aurelian's triumphal chariot.

But in AD 275, Aurelian, like so many of his predecessors, was murdered by the Praetorian Guard. In the decade that followed, no fewer than six emperors managed to claim the purple, of whom only one died of natural causes.* One of the six, Numerian, enjoyed a brief period of posthumous rule, for as long as his advisors could conceal the fact that the imperial litter was carrying a rotting corpse.

Into this miasma stepped Diocletian, a veteran commander from Dalmatia, who, after Numerian's death was discovered, was raised to the purple by the universal acclamation of the soldiers under his command. Diocletian was determined to bring order back to the

---

* Tacitus, murdered by his own men in AD 276; Florian, killed by his men in the same year; Probus, killed by his own men in 282; Numerian, killed in mysterious circumstances in 284; Carinus, killed by his own men, 285. The exception is Carus, who was reported to have been struck by lightning in 283 – although this may just be cover for another assassination.

empire. Coins, which had long been debased with cheap metal, were restored to their old silver standard. With an edict on maximum prices he tried to control the empire's runaway inflation. The army was reorganized and new units dispatched to hold the frontiers. Provinces were divided into new units called 'dioceses'.

Above all, Diocletian changed what it meant to be an emperor. A strong arm was not enough to ward off the assassin's knife – this was the clear lesson of recent history. Diocletian, therefore, would augment brute strength with a carefully cultivated mystique. The ceremonial of the imperial court, on its perpetual journey from one trouble spot to another, was to be as elaborate as any religion. When the emperor (*basileus*, in Greek) appeared in one of his great audience halls, or *basilicas*, the choreography of bowing courtiers and grovelling sycophants was worthy of Elagabalus himself. No pretence now of being *princeps*, first among equals; Diocletian was a *dominus* – a master. His subjects, if they were lucky, might be permitted to prostrate themselves before him; to kiss the hem of his gem-encrusted robe. Even the senators of Rome knelt in his presence, to 'adore his sacred face'.

Emperors were lifting themselves higher: away from the sweat of the barracks and the streets and into closer communion with the gods. At the same time, they were multiplying. Diocletian, recognizing that the empire was too big for one man to hold alone, took the unusual step of electing a colleague to the imperial purple. The new co-Augustus was another old soldier, named Maximian – a man who could hold the Rhine while Diocletian took care of the Persians in the East.

Additionally, to ensure that the succession struggles of the turbulent third century would not be repeated in the fourth, Diocletian and Maximian nominated heirs to rule beneath them. Each 'Augustus' now had a 'Caesar' ready to step into his place: Galerius in the East, serving under Diocletian, and Constantius, a promising young officer from the Balkans, under Maximian in the West.

With this 'rule-of-four' system, the *tetrarchy*, firmly established, Diocletian felt ready to try his final innovation. In AD 305, after a remarkable twenty years in power, the emperor retired to a palace on the Dalmatian coast. Like a latter-day Cincinnatus, the master of the universe now busied himself with the farming of cabbages.

Diocletian's carefully built succession system lasted for just a year before coming unstuck. The Caesars, Constantius and Galerius, had duly promoted themselves to the status of Augusti and had taken on new Caesars of their own. But when Constantius died unexpectedly in York while campaigning against the Picts in AD 306, his soldiers refused to let his officially designated 'Caesar' take over. The official successor was far off in the south. And the legions at York had a much more attractive candidate ready at hand: Constantius's son, a soldierly and charismatic young man named Constantine.

Young Constantine was declared emperor by the British legions, in clear violation of the rules of succession. Diocletian's tetrarchy was meant to work through adoptions, not the crude ties of blood. And Constantine's accession set a dangerous precedent. Not long afterwards, inspired by Constantine's example, another neglected son claimed his own place in the limelight: Maximian's son Maxentius, supported by his prematurely retired father, established his own imperial domain, basing himself – quite unusually for an emperor in those days – in the city of Rome.

For a while, a tense peace was maintained. Constantine and Maxentius, the usurping sons, held the West, with the Alps serving as a dividing line between them. In the East, Diocletian's successor Galerius was now senior emperor, content, for the moment, to bide his time. Complicating the picture were the two retired Augusti: Maximian, plotting with his son, and Diocletian, lamenting the ruin of his constitution from his Balkan cabbage patch.

In AD 308, a peace summit was convened at Carnuntum on the Danube, with Diocletian himself in attendance. Grudging accommodations were reached between the chief players, new statuses confirmed. Constantine had seized power illegally but could at least, it was conceded, serve as a junior emperor – a Caesar. Maxentius's little sister Fausta was dispatched to his court to be his child-bride, a living token of his acceptance into the imperial family.

It was not enough to satisfy him. In AD 312, emboldened by victories against barbarians on the Rhine, Constantine punched his way south across the Alps with an outnumbered but veteran force, took the vital fortress town of Segusio at the mouth of the Mount Cenis pass, and defeated Maxentius's northern armies in battle outside Turin and again at Verona. With the mountains and the River Po secured, the young usurper gathered his strength for the final march on Rome.

* * *

Behind Aurelian's great walls, Maxentius had reason to feel secure. Twice already, in that chaotic period after Diocletian's retirement, Rome had stood firm against the armies of rival emperors. Galerius himself, at the height of his power, had marched an army all the way to Rome, thinking – like the crude provincial that he really was – that the city would fall easily like some petty eastern town. When he arrived and saw the true scale of the old capital and its defences, he realized straight away that an assault was impossible. There was nothing for it but to turn his army around and go back home again.

Now, as Constantine made his way south, Maxentius once again prepared his defences. On the Tiber, barges hauled their way upstream to the river docks with cargos of Spanish oil and African grain. Work crews were sent to bolster up the walls, where grunting slaves were stacking catapult stones. Brave-talking senators quietly moved their treasures to secure vaults. In his villa on the Appian Way, looking out over his empty circus and the tomb of his dead son, Maxentius waited for the invader to come to him.

But then, mysteriously, something changed. There may have been disturbances among the Roman populace: the mob at the games were reported to have called out Constantine's name. There are stories, too, of a misleading prophecy found by Maxentius among the ancient oracles of the Sibylline Books: that an enemy of Rome would perish on 28 October. That day was the anniversary of Maxentius's accession – an auspicious day indeed for Rome's last and greatest defender to crush the city's enemies.

Either way, whether in fear of popular treachery, buoyed up by superstition, or, as a later rhetorician has it, driven to madness by 'the divine spirit and eternal majesty of the City itself', Maxentius now committed himself to a desperate risk. On 28 October AD 312, he abandoned the safety of his carefully prepared fortifications and led his army to do battle with Constantine outside the walls of Rome.

The quickest way from northern Italy to Rome was by the Via Flaminia – a great old republican highway that ran northwards out of Rome across the Apennines towards the Po Valley and the Adriatic Sea. Over the centuries, many invaders had followed this old route south to test Rome's strength: Etruscans, Gauls and Carthaginians; Caesar marching against Pompey with his loyal Thirteenth. Now, as so many times before, the city prepared to fight, sending out what defenders she could to block the ancient road.

As they marched, Maxentius and his men will have made a reasonable show: there were fresh recruits from Italy and Africa; press-ganged farmers from Campania and Sicily, uncomfortable in their mail; Moorish cavalry from the empire's southern frontier; Berber hillmen from the Atlas mountains.

There too, far outshining these motley contingents, were the elite soldiers of the Praetorian Guard, splendid in scale coats of gilded steel and high-domed helmets, shields and standards flashing the scorpion crest that had been the badge and warning of the praetorian cohorts since the empire began. Armed with darts and thrusting spears and the long *spatha* swords that had replaced the old legionary *gladius*, these men were the equal of any soldiers Constantine could throw at them, at least so far as their training and equipment were concerned.

Rivalling the Praetorians for glamour were the picked horsemen of the *Equites Singulares Augusti* – the emperor's mounted bodyguard. These were formidable fighters, huge in their armour, the spreading silvered cheek-guards of their helmets robbing them of expression as they rode past the first milestone from the city, then the second. In their midst, on a horse caparisoned in purple, was Maxentius himself, glimpsed like some rare beast amid a thicket of shoulder-slung lances.

The road out of the city led past the suburban villas and pleasure gardens of Rome's rich. The Emperor Nero, in more peaceful times, had spent happy evenings of debauchery in the wine shops by the riverside. The satirist Juvenal had watched young men spin their chariot wheels here, tearing up and down to impress the girls on long summer evenings. But now Maxentius's columns rode past barred gates and empty homes, down towards the Tiber where it flowed under the leaping concrete span of the Milvian Bridge.

Accounts of what followed are confused and contradictory. It seems that the bridge – along with, we must assume, the other crossings further downstream – had already been cut, to slow the advance of Constantine's army. And yet, for some reason Maxentius appears to have thought it right not only to abandon Rome's walls but to take his army over to Constantine's side of the river by way of a hastily constructed pontoon.* At the dawn of the Roman republic, he will have remembered, the hero Horatius Cocles had held off an entire Etruscan army by making a stand on the Tiber's far bank. Perhaps, in some half-formed sort of way, Maxentius had the idea that he might do the same.

At any rate, with the river at their backs, the Romans arrayed themselves for battle; shuffled into their lines, cohort by cohort, under the standards, shield lined up by shield in the parade-ground lines that pleased old centurions. Ranged on each flank, cavalrymen passed their secret fears to their shifting horses, breathed quiet nothings into flicking ears. They would not have long to wait. Just down the road, not far distant, Constantine's troops had begun to move.

It was the cavalry that saw the first action. From their lines on the river bank, Maxentius's footsoldiers watched the *equites singulares*

* A few of the sources offer the intriguing suggestion that this pontoon bridge was in fact the centrepiece of Maxentius's plan. Zosimus, a Byzantine historian writing long after the event, claimed that the pontoon was rigged to collapse. It is just about within the limits of plausibility that Maxentius hoped to lure Constantine on to the bridge and then cut it loose while his enemy was in midstream.

throw themselves into the melee, driving long lances into mailed flesh or down over the breastbones of the onrushing horses. Then the swords came out, flashing from jewelled scabbards as the riders, knee to knee with their enemy, began the deadly wheeling dance of a close-quarter cavalry engagement.

Then the first missiles started falling on the infantry line and here or there a man cried out and another dropped to his knees, and the foot fight had begun. Roman soldiers in those days had largely swapped the old javelin, the *pilum*, for a sort of lead-weighted dart, flung high up in the air in a looping trajectory to plummet on to the heads and necks of the men below. Next came the throwing spears, thwacking into shield boards. A spear stuck in a shield would be a problem when the lines clashed – a lever for an enemy to grasp at, wrenching open your guard to a fatal thrust. You could try to take the spear out from your shield, but you had to move fast not to leave yourself exposed, as some of those found who tried: for among Constantine's Gaulish and British veterans were contingents of Franks, warriors from the lower Rhine, deadly with their eponymous *francisca*, the throwing axe.

Constantine had recruited men even from beyond the frontier. They were called the 'horned ones', the *cornuti*, for the curled horns they wore on the fronts of their helmets and the double-headed rams they painted on their shields, and they announced themselves in battle with a famous war cry, the *barritus*, raised above the din.

And quite soon, by all accounts, it was clear to Maxentius's Italians that the *equites singulares* had been overwhelmed, cut down in all their finery by Constantine's frontier fighters and his hired Germans, and that enemy horsemen, serpent standards spattered with Roman blood, were bearing down and coming round the flanks and that only those who moved soonest would make it back across the river over Maxentius's pontoon bridge. Men at the back started peeling off. The line was thinning. Soon, only the proud Praetorians were holding together. But a sword in experienced hands was a terrible thing. Ancient accounts speak of shoulders sheared off; heads split down the middle to flop left and right from the neck; hands and arms severed;

calves spitted to the ground. It took inhuman courage to stand and die on an ancient battlefield. Gradually, even the Praetorians were forced back towards the riverbank.

There, they found a scene of complete disaster. The pontoon bridge was packed with men, with others sliding down the bank to pack on to the blood-slicked boards or to miss their aim and go slipping into the river mud, sucked down by their golden scales. Somewhere in the crush was Maxentius himself, pushing through the crowd on his panicked horse, recognizable by his jewelled and ornamented war gear.

It was not until the emperor was nearly across that the pontoon finally broke. Men tipped left and right into the river. Others clung, desperate, to disintegrating beams. Maxentius himself was submerged just short of land, vanished, then reappeared, like Horatius of old, the legendary Roman borne miraculously to safety in the bosom of Father Tiber. Clinging to his horse's neck, Maxentius struck out towards land; hooves made brief contact with the steep clay bank, skidded, took; now the horse, mane plastered to its back, began to rise in heart-bursting lunges from the waves. But there was no escape for the doomed emperor. 'Sacred Tiber,' wrote one of Constantine's later flatterers, 'you allowed neither the false Romulus to live for long nor the City's murderer to swim away.' Like a watery hand, rising from the deep, a sudden eddy snatched Maxentius up and pulled him under.

As they watched their emperor die, and with the certainty of defeat upon them, it is impossible to know if Rome's surviving Praetorians, the last of the guard, noticed a new badge among the foreign blazons of their enemies: a vertical stripe with a looped head, like a narrow-bodied 'P', bisected horizontally to make a simple upright cross. The cross triumphant.

* * *

Two and a half centuries before the Battle of the Milvian Bridge, the soon-to-be emperor Titus had put down a revolt in Judea, sacking Jerusalem and putting the city's population to the sword. Just another provincial campaign, for the Romans. Another city looted. A new triumphal arch and monumental amphitheatre in the capital.

For the Jews, however, it was a world-shaking catastrophe. To punish the rebels, Titus destroyed their Temple, a building that had been the sacred centre of Judaism for six hundred years.

The indiscriminacy of Titus's bloodbath obscured a Gordian tangle of ethnic and religious rivalries that had long rendered the province of Judea almost ungovernable. Jews fought Samaritans; Temple priests squabbled with pro-Roman aristocrats; Pharisees, Sadducees and Essenes disputed the true meaning of God's Law, while ragged prophets wandered the desert with their fanatical followers. It was a time of fear and confusion. The rebels known as Zealots were just as willing to send their murderous *sicarii* against more moderate Jews as against the Romans themselves.*

What was a Jew anyway? The question was hotly contested. Did one have to be descended from the ancient Hebrews, or could foreigners be converted? Was it religious belief that defined the term? And belief in what? Jews shared the common inheritance of scripture. They remembered the prophecies of Isaiah – that there would come a child 'whose name will be Emmanuel'. They knew the dreams of Daniel, who, during the long exile in Babylon, had seen 'one like the Son of Man, coming with the clouds of heaven… He was given authority, glory and sovereign power; all nations and peoples of every language worshipped him'.

But interpretations of these scriptural prophecies varied widely. There were, for example, some Jews who believed that the events foreseen by Isaiah and Daniel had already come to pass: that the blessed child, Emmanuel, had already been born and died; that the End Times, long promised, had come.

---

* The *sicarii*, or 'dagger-men', waged a vicious assassination campaign against supporters of the Romans in Jerusalem. When the rebellion broke out into open war, a force of Zealot *sicarii* occupied the impregnable Herodian fortress of Masada, holding out there long after Jerusalem had fallen. In AD 73 or 74, Roman soldiers finally got over the walls, only to find that the defenders had committed suicide en masse, setting the fort on fire behind them.

There had been several rival candidates for the role of Messiah. Some Jews had followed a desert preacher called John, known for baptizing his followers in the river Jordan. He ended up, as the legend has it, murdered in the dungeons of Herod Antipas, his head served up on a silver plate. Others believed that the Zealot leader, Menahem, was the Messiah – as indeed he loudly claimed to be. Opposed to the Zealots were the pacifist and apocalyptic followers of a third preacher, a carpenter, who had caused a stir in Jerusalem and Galilee before being executed by the Roman authorities some forty years before the great revolt: Jesus of Nazareth.

'Truly I say to you,' Jesus had told his followers, 'that there be some of them that stand here, which shall not taste of death, till they have seen the kingdom of God come with power.' The arrival of the Messiah signalled that the end of the world was near at hand.

And when the Zealots raised their rebellion against the Romans, the followers of Jesus – who had not yet learned to call themselves Christians – will have found it hard not to see the ensuing catastrophe as a fulfilment of their teacher's prophecies: 'Do you see all these great buildings?' Jesus had said, in Jerusalem. 'Not one stone here will be left on another; every one will be thrown down.'

'Nation will rise against nation, and kingdom against kingdom. There will be earthquakes in various places, and famines. These are the beginning of birth pains.' There was great suffering to come, he had warned his followers. 'You will be handed over to the local councils and flogged in the synagogues. On account of me you will stand before governors and kings... Everyone will hate you because of me.'

There was plenty of hatred to go around. Even the small community of Jesus-followers in Jerusalem was divided, between Greek-speaking Jews and those who spoke Jesus' own language, Aramaic. Shortly after Jesus' death, the Greek-speakers were expelled from the city, and their leader, Stephen, sentenced to death by the judges of the Sanhedrin. He was executed by stoning, becoming Christianity's first martyr.

This expulsion of the Hellenizers was an important moment in the evolution of the early church. The conquests of Alexander the Great

in the fourth century BC had made Greek a sort of *lingua franca* for
the entire eastern Mediterranean. Now, the exiled Greek-speaking
Jesus-followers of Jerusalem were scattered among the Jewish communities of the East, where they found fertile ground in which to plant
their *euangelion* – their Good News. And while the Aramaic-speaking
Jesus-followers left behind in Jerusalem, led by Jesus' brother James,
still insisted on obedience to the traditional Jewish law of the Old
Testament (circumcision, dietary restrictions and so on), the Hellenizers, under the intelligent leadership of a Cilician Jew named Paul,
were willing to spread the Good News to Greek-speaking Jews and
even to non-Jews as well.

Paul was tireless in his evangelizing. All through the 40s and
50s AD he plodded the dusty roads of the eastern empire, founding
churches wherever he went. At Troas, people whispered, he raised
a young man from the dead. At Ephesus, famous for its temple of
Artemis, his preaching caused a riot among the disgruntled manufacturers of Artemis-statuettes and souvenirs. At Athens, he visited the
Areopagus, the rocky outcrop where murder trials had been held back
in the Athenian golden age, and where Socrates himself was thought
to have been condemned. There he argued the case for Jesus with the
best Greek philosophers:

> Ye men of Athens! I perceive that in all things ye are too super-
> stitious. For as I passed by, and beheld your devotions, I found
> an altar with this inscription, TO THE UNKNOWN GOD.
> Whom therefore ye ignorantly worship, him declare I unto you.
> God that made the world and all things therein, seeing that he
> is Lord of heaven and earth, dwelleth not in temples made with
> hands.

*

In AD 57, Paul returned to Jerusalem. He was quickly caught up in
the fractious politics of the city. Arrested as a troublemaker, he was
sent to Rome for trial, where, according to his legend, he helped the
Apostle Peter found the church in the capital, before Nero finally
beheaded him.

But the seeds Paul had planted in places like Athens took deep root. This was at the beginning of the era known as the Second Sophistic: a flowering of scholarship across the grand old cities of Greece and Asia Minor. At Athens, reports the Book of Acts, everyone 'spent their time doing nothing but talking about and listening to the latest ideas'.

Not since the days of Plato and Aristotle had Greece seen such rich discussions of science, ethics, metaphysics, religion – any subject except politics, since the arrival of the emperors had settled political questions for good. Athens was full of Stoics, Epicureans, Platonists, Neo-Pythagoreans, Cynics and everything in-between, men who were used to debating the world's complexities, both natural and divine. The Greek world was perfectly ready to find truth in Paul's new teaching.

In return, the Christians had much to learn from the debates of the philosophers. They absorbed modes of ascetic practice from the Cynics; ideas about the nature of the soul from the Platonists; from the Stoics, they took the idea of a divine 'rational principle' underlying the universe – the Logos. '*En archē ēn ho Logos*', begins the Gospel of John. 'In the beginning was the Word.'

There was great need for this sort of Greek philosophical vocabulary because, as the communities of Jesus-followers grew, the theological questions they faced became ever harder. Should Christians be circumcised? When would the Final Judgement come? What were angels? Were pagan gods to be understood as devils, or did they not exist at all? Was celibacy a virtue even for a married couple? Was the physical world evil or good? Did God give some of his faithful the gift of prophecy? Around the middle of the second century in Asia Minor, old heartland of the Goddess Cybele, a newly baptized Christian called Montanus embarked on a full-scale soothsaying spree with a pair of Phrygian prophetesses. Were they truly blessed by the Holy Spirit, or were they – to use a word the early churches were just learning to deploy – 'heretics'?

By the beginning of the second century AD, Christians had become sufficiently widespread to attract the notice of the Roman provincial

authorities.* The Roman writer Pliny the Younger, serving as governor of Bithynia in AD 112, found that his province was riddled with
followers of the new religion. 'The infection of this superstition has
spread', he reported to the Emperor Trajan, 'not only through the
towns, but also through the villages and the countryside', taking in
'many persons of every age, of every rank' and 'of both sexes'.

Uncertain what to do, but aware that Christianity was officially
illegal, Pliny had a few of the offenders executed. He did not know,
however, what exactly he was executing the Christians for – whether
for some crimes that Christians were supposed to have committed,
or just the mere fact of their being Christian at all.

To find out more, Pliny had a couple of slave women, 'who were
called deaconesses', tortured to see what secrets they might spill. The
results were unsatisfying. As far as Pliny could ascertain, Christianity
was nothing more harmful than 'a depraved and extravagant superstition'. The Christians gathered before dawn on a fixed day to sing
hymns to Christ. They bound themselves by an oath, or *sacramentum*,
to behave virtuously and to refrain from killing, stealing or breaking
faith. Later, he learned, they would gather for a simple meal. That
seemed to be as far as it went.†

To educated Romans like Pliny, Christianity was just another
vulgar enthusiasm, to be peddled by ragged preachers among market
traders and kitchen slaves. 'They would not dare to enter into conversation with intelligent men,' wrote one philosopher, 'or to voice
their fancy beliefs in the presence of the wise. On the other hand,
wherever one finds a crowd of adolescent boys, or a bunch of slaves,

---

* The total number of Christians in those days was probably still only in
the several thousands – but their concentration in the empire's rich eastern
provinces and major cities gave them a visibility that was disproportionate
to their numbers.
† More lurid stories began to circulate in later years. One hostile account
has Christians presenting new initiates with a large lump of dough. The initiate cuts the dough with a dagger, accidentally killing an infant, carefully
concealed inside. 'Thirstily – oh Horror! – they lick up its blood and eagerly
divide its limbs. By this victim they are bound together.'

or a company of fools, there will be the Christian teachers also – showing off their fine new philosophy.'

Pliny had no idea just how complicated Christian philosophy could be. The religion of the Jesus-followers, as it spread through the patchwork cultures of the Roman empire, had mutated into myriad local forms, each with its own distinctive practices and beliefs.

Ever since Titus's destruction of the Temple in AD 70, both Jews and Christians had been dispersed across the wider Roman world, deprived of a natural centre on which to focus their religious attention. Judaism was now led by rabbis, focused on the study of the Torah and the laws of Moses. Meanwhile, Christianity was accumulating sacred texts of its own: the letters of Paul; the Gospel accounts of Jesus' life; the Acts of the Apostles; the mysterious prophecies of the Book of Revelation.

There was little agreement on exactly which texts should be included in the Christian 'canon'.* In the 140s AD, in Rome, a Pontic Christian named Marcion attempted to separate Christianity from Judaism entirely, purging the canon of everything except an abridged version of Luke's Gospel and most of the letters of St Paul. Conversely, other Christians turned to texts that were ever more arcane: apocalyptic prophecies; spurious 'Acts'; apocryphal Gospels attributed to figures like Doubting Thomas, Mary Magdalene, or even Judas Iscariot himself. These Gnostic sects, as they came to be called, were united by one key idea: that only by way of deep mysteries and esoteric knowledge could a person attain any understanding of an unfathomably distant, ineffable and untouchable God.

The first Christian communities had been radically egalitarian. The Jesus-followers in Jerusalem, at the time of the Acts of the Apostles, appear to have held all property in common. Their leaders were the Apostles themselves – the men and women with first-hand experience of Jesus' teachings.

---

* The word 'canon' comes to Latin via Greek from the Hebrew *kaneh*, meaning 'measuring rod'. The religious sense – of an officially sanctioned collection of sacred texts – became widespread in the fourth century AD.

As the first generation of Christians passed away, the early churches produced leaders to safeguard apostolic teaching: *diakonoi* – deacons; *presbuteroi* – elders; *episkopoi* – overseers or, as the word came to be rendered in English, 'bishops'. Holders of these posts were all more or less equal. Any special authority was derived from personal qualities, some particular charisma or scholarship, for example, rather than from institutional rank itself. Some of these ministers were drawn from the lowest social orders. Some were women. Paul's letter to the church in Rome addresses, among others, a certain Junia – a woman described as 'outstanding among the apostles'.

But in later manuscripts 'Junia' has turned into the masculine: 'Junias'. As the church grew through the second and third centuries after Jesus, so did its hierarchy evolve and harden. The bishops, or *episkopoi*, emerged as single and senior figures within each local Christian community – a 'monarchical episcopate' that was increasingly the preserve of candidates who were male, free and rich.

In the 140s AD, Marcion had been able to promote his eccentric 'purified' canon in Rome quite happily, more or less unmolested by the capital's other Christian groups. By the time Elagabalus arrived with his sun cult in AD 219, however, there was a relatively well-defined Roman church which, under its leader Bishop Callistus, was both willing and able to exclude those whose beliefs strayed too far from the emerging orthodoxy.*

By the middle of the third century, the church in Rome, if not the equal of the cult of Isis, say, or Mithras, was nevertheless a substantial organization: one bishop, seven deacons, seven subdeacons, forty-two acolytes, forty-six presbyters and fifty-two assorted readers, doorkeepers and exorcists. It was wealthy enough to provide for 1,500 of Rome's Christian poor.

---

* The vital question of the time was this: If there was only one God – God the Father – what exactly was the nature of Jesus, the Son? To say that Jesus was a man was to deny his divinity. To say that Jesus was a god was to run the risk of polytheism. Callistus's solution was to suggest that Son and Father are both aspects of the same divine being, but the argument was still rumbling on, sometimes bloodily, hundreds of years after Callistus's day.

This was one of the crucial means through which the Christian message spread and strengthened itself. Church funds 'are not wasted on banquets and drink and eating houses', a Christian in Carthage boasted, 'but are used to feed and bury the poor, to care for boys and girls... for old servants and victims of shipwreck and those condemned to the mines'.

A decent burial was the most frequent claim on Christian charity. Christians had learned from Jews (who had learned from Persian Zoroastrians) to expect the resurrection of the body at the end of the world. In the meantime, Christian bodies were stored in the cheapest space available. Burial *kata kumbas*, Greek-speaking Christians called it – burial 'down by the hollows' – the disused quarries along the Appian Way.

Callistus, before he was bishop of Rome, had been in charge of one of the first of these new catacombs, as they came to be known. While, in the world above, the empire struggled, a new dominion was spreading underground: the pitch-dark territory of the Christian dead.

* * *

Bishop Callistus died in AD 222, the same year as Elagabalus, just early enough to miss the Roman empire's plunge into full-scale crisis. Over the years of chaos that followed, Rome's rulers made several attempts to find spiritual solutions to the empire's worldly problems: to find some new religious accommodation that would ward off angry gods, while bolstering the position of emperors whose claims to legitimacy were otherwise dagger-blade thin.

It was with this sort of thing in mind that, in AD 250, the Emperor Decius decreed that all Roman citizens should perform a special sacrifice to the gods for the safety of the empire. Aurelian, in the 270s, promoted the cult of *Sol Invictus*, the Unconquerable Sun. Diocletian, as he set up his delicate tetrarchy in the 290s AD, made a careful show of honouring Jupiter and Hercules.

There was a baffling array of possibilities to choose from. The Roman empire encompassed a vast diversity of religious practice, from the secret ceremonies of the mystery cults to the noisy processions and street parties of the old Olympians; in Rome, there were festivals so ancient that the language in which certain rituals were conducted was no longer understood, even by the officiants themselves. And there was plenty of cross-cultural fertilization: one of the notable features of religion in the late empire was the number of gods with hyphenated names, products of a melding of Greco-Roman religion with local cult. In Anatolia, men worshipped Zeus-Abozanos. In Egypt, Jupiter-Ammon. In Gaul, the warlike Mars-Caturix.

And yet, even amid this diversity, Christianity marked itself out as unusual. It was not monotheism that was the problem – philosophers had been talking about 'God' rather than 'gods' for centuries. Nor was it the cult's eastern origins. The problem with Christians was their refusal to take part in the small but significant civic rituals that the rest of the empire's believers had in common. Christians would not, for example, swear the traditional oaths associated with military or civil office. And they refused to perform the political theatre of emperor-worship.

Christian practices were different to those of most other cults. The various religions that would one day be grouped, misleadingly, under the term 'paganism' shared a tradition of offering sacrifices to the divine. Christians – and Jews after the destruction of their Temple – were conspicuous in their refusal to engage in this sort of spiritual quid pro quo.

So when Decius demanded his universal sacrifice in AD 250, the quietly growing Christian communities found themselves in an awkward position. Decius had not intended his edict to be an attack on Christians, but the refusal of many high-profile church leaders to perform the mandatory sacrifice represented an intolerable affront to the authority of the state. Torture and imprisonment persuaded some of the obstinate Christians to be more accommodating; others bribed local officials to falsify their records, or fled into temporary exile; a few, stubborn to the last, achieved martyrdom, including the bishops of Jerusalem, Antioch and Rome.

Decius died in AD 251, but the damage was done. Christians had revealed themselves as enemies of Rome's gods. The offensive was renewed in AD 257, by the Emperor Valerian, trying to secure divine favour for his ill-fated Persian campaign. The church in Rome suffered the loss of its bishop and several deacons including a certain Laurentius, popularly supposed to have been roasted to death on a gridiron.

A period of quiet followed. The emperors were too busy with enemies from outside Rome's borders to worry about enemies within. Then came Diocletian, the great reformer, whose plans for the renewal of the Roman empire extended far beyond the political domain. Around AD 302, he moved against not Christians but Manicheans, followers of a prophet called Mani who had been executed in Persia a generation before.

'No new belief should criticize the religion of old,' wrote Diocletian. 'We command that the authors and leaders of these sects... shall be burned in the flames with their detestable books.'

No group was more notoriously disrespectful of old religion than the Christians. One day, the legend goes, Diocletian was sacrificing to the gods when the attendant *haruspices* complained that Christian magic was preventing them from seeing the future in the sacrificial entrails. A church historian, Eusebius of Caesarea, witnessed what followed: 'The Lord hath darkened the daughter of Zion in his anger and hath cast down from heaven the glory of Israel.' Imperial agents were sent to churches to find and burn the holy scripture. Christians were imprisoned and tortured. In Palestine, where Eusebius was bishop, 'so many were killed that the murderous axe was blunted and, having been weakened, broke into pieces, while the very executioners grew weary.'

In Rome, more martyrs were 'baptized in blood' to join the growing ranks of the sanctified dead. Romans, with a characteristic mix of piety and prurience, liked telling the story of Agnes, an aristocratic Christian girl, taken by the city prefect. Dragged naked through the streets to a Roman brothel, she prayed to God, who covered her with a miraculous coat of fast-growing, rapist-repelling hair. She was condemned to burn at the stake, but the flames parted around her. At last, like a defeated gladiator, she presented her virgin throat for the executioner's sword.

Diocletian's 'Great Persecution' lasted ten years and was the most sustained effort any emperor had yet made to destroy the Christian church. The cult had spread widely through the empire. Nonetheless, Diocletian might reasonably have expected his decade-long purge to be enough to eradicate the superstition. Only perhaps around one in ten of the empire's sixty million inhabitants was a Christian when the Great Persecution began – and most of those were willing, in the end, to give up their faith rather than face torture.

Still, Diocletian found that plenty of Christians were willing to die. 'The poor fools,' wrote one late rhetorician, 'have persuaded themselves above all that they are immortal and will live forever, from which it follows that they despise death and many of them willingly undergo imprisonment.' Eusebius saw martyrs in Palestine who 'received the final sentence of death with joy, laughter and cheerfulness, so that they sang and offered up hymns and thanksgivings to the God of the Universe till their very last breath.'

The words of another Christian writer, Tertullian, echoed loud in those days: 'Nothing is accomplished by your cruelties, however exquisite... The more we are cut down by you, the more we grow in number. The blood of the martyrs is the seed of the Church.'

Christian stubbornness kept the church alive during the long years of oppression. So too did the fact that, despite severe violence against Christians in some areas, there were other places where the persecution was hardly pushed at all. There were four tetrarchs running the empire, and not all of them took much of an interest in Diocletian's religious campaign.

Notably, Constantine's father Constantius appears to have done almost nothing against the Christians beyond, perhaps, the demolition of a few churches. He had more pressing concerns, up on the northern frontiers among the Franks and the Picts. And anyway, he may not have regarded Christianity as quite so outlandish a cult as all that. Constantius's religious beliefs remain somewhat mysterious, but it seems likely that he practised a sort of solar monotheism. Like Aurelian before him, Constantius worshipped some version of the Unconquerable Sun. When he died at York in AD 306, it was the Sun himself, in an 'almost visible' chariot, who came to sweep the deceased tetrarch up to heaven.

Constantine, raised at Diocletian's court at Nicomedia, came late to his father's religion. Bishop Eusebius, in his account of the civil wars, has him wondering what deity will help him against Maxentius's 'wicked and magical enchantments': 'While engaged in this enquiry, the thought occurred to him that, of the many emperors who had preceded him, those who had rested their hopes in a multitude of gods... had met with an unhappy end.' On the other hand, his father Constantius had 'honoured the supreme God during his whole life' and 'had found him to be the Saviour and Protector of his Empire'. He resolved 'to honour his father's God alone'.

So far so good, but who exactly was his father's God? Constantine 'called on him with earnest prayer and supplications that he would reveal to him who He was'.

A god of the sun, certainly. But which one? In the years before the Battle of the Milvian Bridge, Constantine liked to claim that he had visions of Apollo, that ancient sun god who had guided the great Augustus to victory at the battle of Actium long ago. In those far-off days, the poet Virgil had written of a holy child, born when 'Apollo reigns'. 'Mankind shall be free from its age-long fear,' the poet had promised; 'all stains of our past wickedness being cleansed away'. Now, three centuries later, Constantine's propagandists were willing to suggest that Virgil's promised child had arrived – in the person of Constantine himself.

But old-fashioned Apollo was hardly the only option. In the 240s AD, in Rome, a philosopher called Plotinus had begun building the teachings of Socrates (as found in the writings of Plato) into a sort of quasi-religion called Neoplatonism. Constantine, if he had been feeling philosophically adventurous, could have decided that his sun god was a sort of emanation of the deep god of the Neoplatonists, a distant and ineffable divinity whom they called 'The Good' or 'The One'.

Had he wished to be even less specific, Constantine could have addressed his prayers to the god known in the East as Theos Hypsistos – a name that means nothing more than 'The Highest God'. It would have been a typically pragmatic piece of bet-hedging: 'Which is your god?' 'The highest one!'

In that same spirit, an early panegyrist of Constantine's addressed his prayers simply to the 'Supreme Creator of things, whose names you wished to be as many as the tongues of the nations (for what you yourself wished to be called we cannot know)'.

And yet, by the time Constantine fought the Battle of the Milvian Bridge, he appears to have discovered the true identity of his mysterious God. The story of this revelation grew in the telling. In his old age, Constantine described the crucial moment to Bishop Eusebius. 'He said that about noon,' – this on some unspecified day before the battle – 'when the day was already beginning to decline, he saw with his own eyes the trophy of a cross of light in the heavens, above the sun, and bearing the [Greek] inscription *toutōi nika* – CONQUER BY THIS!'

It is possible that Constantine really did see a cross in the sky. There is an atmospheric phenomenon, the solar halo, that might produce a cross such as Constantine described, although without the accompanying Greek text. If so, the whole course of European history was determined by a freak weather event.

Or perhaps he had a dream of some sort – something that pushed his ill-defined religious feelings in the direction of the Christians in his entourage. That is the account given by his son's tutor Lactantius, writing much sooner after the battle.

Or, just as likely, the stories of dreams and visions were concocted quite cynically, to impart a mythic lustre to a mundane change of heart. All that can be said with confidence is that there was *some* mark of Christian devotion on display at the battle. Lactantius, probably the better source, says Constantine had his men paint their shields with the sign of the *staurogram* – a loop-headed cross. Eusebius, capturing the spirit, at least, of Constantine's religiosity, says that the emperor had the Greek initials of Christ – Chi Rho, the *Christo-gram* – mounted on a military standard in gold and jewels.

Certainly Constantine followed such a standard in later campaigns. Jesus of Nazareth, the pacifist Jew, was transformed into *Christos Pantokrator* – Christ the Ruler of All. His initials, until recently a secret sign between persecuted believers, were now affixed to Constantine's sacred banner – the holy *labarum* which, for the rest of his long reign, would lead his legions into war.

* * *

After the battle, Constantine had Maxentius fished out of the Tiber. The dead man's head, fixed on a cavalry lance, was held aloft above the victorious crosses on the soldiers' shields, and with these competing totems, the conqueror marched his men the last few miles to the gates of Rome.

The city was then more than a thousand years old, by Roman reckoning, and for half of those years it had been the capital of the most powerful state in the known world. Now, as Constantine marched through the Eternal City, every building on his route boasted the achievements of Rome's glorious dead. There was the mausoleum of Augustus. Further away, on the river's right bank, the Mausoleum of Hadrian. Down the road was Aurelian's temple of Sol Invictus and the great concrete dome of the Pantheon with its proud, if inaccurate, inscription: M.AGRIPPA.L.F.COS.TERTIUM.FECIT.*

Here, as the procession headed south towards the river and the cattle market, was the Theatre of Marcellus. Close by, the Theatre of Pompey, whose portico Julius Caesar had stained with his own blood. A little further was the Altar of Hercules, set up by Evander before Rome was Rome. Marching down the length of the Circus Maximus, Constantine's troops could count the imperial palaces on the Palatine

---

* 'Marcus Agrippa, in his third consulship, built this,' says the inscription. In fact, although Agrippa did establish a temple on the site, the Pantheon as it stands today was built by Hadrian about a century and a half later. In an uncharacteristic display of imperial humility, Hadrian let the long-dead Agrippa claim the credit.

to their left, or look right to see the rich houses on the once-plebeian Aventine where Gaius Gracchus made his stand. At the end of the Circus, where the Great Fire started, the army turned left, past the stacked colonnades of the Septizonium of Septimius Severus and left again down the Via Sacra under the shadow of Nero's Colossus. Then past the Arch of Titus and the Temple of the Vestal Virgins and the new-built Basilica of Maxentius to enter the memorial thicket that was the Roman Forum.

All along the way, living Romans who had come to meet their new master were crowded by hundreds of statues, accumulated over the course of centuries. Gods and heroes, emperors and empresses, consuls, praetors, priests and tribunes; they haunted the city like silent ghosts, lurking on every building, arch or pillar. On horseback, standing or cut off at the shoulders; armoured, toga-clad or nude; marble, bronze or antique terracotta – they peered down from their plinths at Constantine with his legions of Gauls and Franks, this new invader, with the mud of the provinces still fresh on his boots.

Rome must have been oppressive to Constantine, who was accustomed to life in younger cities: the military outposts of the Rhine; the northern capital at Trier. Rome was thick with old gods and dangerous memories: memories of what the empire had been before it was a military despotism ruled from the frontiers; memories carefully cherished by a class of pagan and conservative senators, whose sense of their own importance had been fed to hypertrophy on the myths and legends of the vanished republic.

Through the November and December of AD 312, Constantine stayed in the city. Maxentius's ruling apparatus was carefully dismantled. Key players in the old regime were bribed or forced into compliance. Occasionally, there was a carefully targeted execution. Maxentius's head, still passably fresh in the late-autumnal cool, was dispatched to Africa for the instruction of the provincials there. With Egypt now administered by eastern Augusti, it was Africa that had to provide the grain dole that fed the hundreds of thousands of hungry, underemployed poor still living in Rome's tottering apartment blocks.

In those cold months, Constantine took steps to write his own story into the city's fabric, and to obliterate the memory of his predecessor. Maxentius's baths on the Quirinal hill, only half-built at the time of the battle, were completed and renamed the baths of Constantine.

Likewise, Maxentius's basilica in the Forum was renamed and remodelled. In the great half-domed apse of the north wall, an unfinished colossus was hastily adapted: its newly carved eyes looked up towards the heavens; its nose grew an aquiline point; its lips curled into a sneer of cold command. Henceforth, the huge hall would be the Basilica of Constantine, with the emperor himself, eight times the size of a living man, enthroned at one end. In his hand was a staff, probably shaped into the loop-headed cross – the *staurogram* – which his men had painted on their shields before the battle. At his feet was a stern inscription: 'By this saving sign, the true proof of courage, I saved your city from the yoke of the tyrant and set her free.'

In January, satisfied that he had made the Romans understand who was who and what was what, Constantine felt able to head back home to the northern frontier, where he stayed for two years. Only in AD 315 did he pay Rome another brief visit. The senators had by now finished work on his triumphal arch, a striking three-gated structure, clad in porphyry and marble, straddling the *via triumphalis* outside the Colosseum.

Certain happy economies had lessened the burden of construction on the people of Rome. The core of the arch had been built by Maxentius to celebrate his own victories; now the unfinished work was hastily repurposed. And most of the sculptural decoration was lifted from other imperial monuments. By choosing selected pieces from works dedicated to famously 'good' emperors like Hadrian, Marcus Aurelius and Trajan, the arch's builders were able to save effort and deliver a hopeful compliment at the same time. The final satisfaction was finding the right wording for the inscription to go at the top: 'To the emperor Constantine', they wrote, who delivered the state from the tyrant '*instinctu divinitatis*' – inspired by the divine.

The Romans knew that Constantine had a new sort of relationship with God. 'You do indeed,' a Roman flatterer conceded, 'have some secret understanding with that Divine Mind [which] reveals itself to you alone.' With the ambiguous phrase, *'instinctu divinitatis'*, Rome's pagans acknowledged that Constantine was favoured by a supreme God without having to say which one. And yet, the identity of Constantine's God was becoming increasingly clear. In the god-haunted centre of the city, Constantine's new monuments were tactfully conservative in spirit. Out in the suburbs, however, the emperor's building projects were unmistakably Christian.

In February AD 313, Constantine had met the reigning eastern emperor, Licinius, at Milan, where the two men agreed to divide the empire between them.* Six months later, once Licinius had dealt with his local rivals, the word went out: the Great Persecution, long cooled, was officially ended. Christians emerged, blinking, from the long, dark years of oppression and out into the bright light of imperial favour.

In Rome's hostile atmosphere, Christians had been accustomed to worshipping in private. The simple ceremonies and communal meals of the early church would take place in whatever space any of the brothers or sisters in Christ could provide: a meeting hall, a shuttered shop, a room in someone's home. But after the Battle of the Milvian Bridge, an extraordinary new edifice began to grow under the Aurelian walls. Constantine had ordered the dissolution of Maxentius's loyal cavalry, the defeated *equites singulares*. Now, where their grand barracks had been, near the old palace of the Laterani family, he ordered the construction of what looked like another royal reception hall – a *basilica*. The architectural plan – a long nave flanked by two

* Licinius had to fight for mastery of the East against a rival tetrarch, Maximinus Daia, a notable persecutor of Christians. Before the final battle between the two, Licinius, like Constantine, was blessed with a divine vision, after which he made his men recite a special prayer to 'God the Most High' before leading them to a decisive victory. Once he was secure in the East, however, Licinius turned out to be less in tune with Constantine's religion than had been supposed.

narrow aisles, lit by clerestory windows; a curved apse – was familiar from imperial capitals across the empire. This basilica, however, was not erected for the honour of an emperor but for the worship of the Christian God.*

The Lateran Basilica, as it came to be called, set Christian worship on a stage of imperial magnificence. The Eucharist – a re-enactment of a modest Passover meal – now acquired the spectacular trappings of court ceremonial. Sunlight, streaming through high windows, gleamed off golden chalices and silver plates, illuminated the rich vestments of bishop and acolytes, the pillars of coloured marble, the gilded apse, the gaudy tapestries; brightened the upturned faces of the crowd, three thousand strong, who, after so long in hiding, now came together to worship in one of the grandest religious buildings of the entire empire, the head church of a new Christendom: *omnium urbis et orbis ecclesiarum mater et caput.*

When Constantine, now master of the entire Roman empire, returned to Rome for the third time, in AD 326, a ring of lesser basilicas was springing up around the city. But while the Lateran Basilica celebrated the living power of the church, the new basilicas were all about the dead, and the blessed martyrs of the Roman persecutions. St Paul got a little church on the Via Ostiensis; St Peter would get a grand basilica built across a cemetery on the Vatican hill.† The grilled deacon, Laurence, got a church, as did poor little martyred Agnes, whose basilica was built over the graves of the now disbanded Praetorian Guard.

Out on the Via Labicana too, by the cypress-shaded graveyard of the *equites singulares*, a basilica was constructed to stand beside a new imperial mausoleum. The grave markers of Maxentius's cavalry were dug up, smashed and used for builders' rubble.

* No original Constantinian basilica has survived intact. The closest in Rome today, in terms of atmosphere, are the basilicas of Santa Sabina on the Aventine, and the reconstructed San Paolo fuori le mura.
† There is some debate over whether the old Basilica of St Peter was built during the reign of Constantine or under his son, Constans.

And out on the Via Appia, sounds of unexpected merriment disturbed the quiet of Maxentius's Circus on its long, slow slide into decay. The old departed Romans were as silent as ever, lining the road. But just across the way, near the old quarries where Bishop Callistus had once looked after his catacombs, yet another new basilica had sprouted.

This church, like so many others, was built on Christian graves. Old Roman law had pushed tombs beyond the city walls, to avoid polluting the living with the taint of death. But Christians knew that death had been defeated – that to die was to enter into new and better life, free from pain and suffering. So, they gathered among the tombs, above the soon-to-be-resurrected bones of their ancestors, and feasted with their families late into the evening, disturbing the sharp-eared bats in Maxentius's deserted halls.

* * *

Constantine's trip to Rome in AD 326 would be his last. He had come in order to celebrate twenty years since his accession, but horrors had followed him on his journey to the old city. First, on the way to Rome, Constantine had surprised everyone by having his eldest son, the loyal and capable Crispus, executed for treason. Then, in Rome itself, his wife Fausta (Maxentius's younger sister) was boiled to death in an overheated bath. Some said she had tricked Constantine into killing Crispus, and that he punished her by having her stewed. Others claimed she had loved her stepson all too well, and had steamed herself to death out of guilt – or perhaps in hope of burning out an incestuous child.

Either way, Constantine never married again, and never returned to Rome. The mausoleum he had prepared was left for the use of his old mother, Helena.* The emperor himself headed east, where

---

* Her sarcophagus, in carved porphyry, can still be seen in the Vatican Museums. The warlike and masculine decoration on the side panels has been taken as evidence that it was originally intended for Constantine himself.

he was building a new and more fitting capital. Far from Rome, on the Bosphorus, in the Christian city of Constantinople, Constantine was buried at last, in a magnificent mausoleum surrounded by twelve tombs which held, supposedly, the bones of all twelve of Jesus' original Apostles.

In the years that followed, it was cities like Constantinople, Antioch, Milan and Trier that would be the seats of imperial power. Rome was left to its gloomy old senators, stubbornly pagan, and to the Christians under their bishop. This man, Sylvester, newly installed in the great basilica at the Lateran, was now the undisputed leader of the Christians in the city. They called him their father – their *papa*: their pope.

11

UNDER SIEGE

Belisarius and the Goths

———

AD 537

A THIN LAYER of silt, soft in the dark, has settled in the Aqueduct of Trajan. There is no water, although the damp still clings to the walls. It chills the air of this buried conduit through which, for four hundred years, the stolen water of an Etruscan spring was drained into the stomach of Rome.

Up ahead, a glimmer of daylight has permitted a little lichen to bloom on the cement. The water channel is divided here, part of the stream diverted to run over the backs of a series of water wheels, cascading down the flank of the Janiculum under the shadow of the Aurelian walls.

But now, the stepped sheds of concrete and reused brick are silent, and the cogs of the mill mechanism stand idle on their axles. The wide millstones are still and the always-false measuring cups hold only the dust of yesterday's always-too-little flour.

Onwards the empty channel plunges, down under the streets and the garbage piles of the Transtiberim, where the potters and the glass blowers and mosaic makers pile their scraps against abandoned houses. Here, invisible in the subterranean blackness, gape the mouths of dozens of lead pipes, piercing the aqueduct like parasitic worms. Squeezed by carefully regulated bronze collars, these pipes once sucked precise volumes of water directly to the houses of those who could afford it – and of those who knew how to sweeten up the local water commissioner.

Now, each pipe chokes on air. The channels laid on for public benefit are empty too. The fountains at the street corners are dry; the fullers' tubs are dry; at night, the roads are dry, and the filth on the paving stones, flung from upper windows, crusts where it lies, with no overflow from the cisterns to wash it into the great municipal drains and down into the Tiber.

The river, at least, is reliable. Here, the women of the city can still gather to wash their clothes in the fast-flowing winter current. It is cold work, and the water is yellow and bad. Still, there is at least something new to talk about today. Out in mid-stream, on a straining wooden pontoon, new mill wheels have started to turn, driven by the river's flow. Even without the aqueducts, there will still be flour – the clever Greek general has seen to that. The city, even surrounded by enemies, will not starve.

But look upstream. There, rounding the river bend, dark shapes are bobbing in the water: crudely felled trees, launched like battering rams to smash their way down the Tiber itself. Trunks boom as they collide, spinning in foaming eddies under the piers of the Pons Aurelius. And as the churning mass approaches, smaller shapes are visible. Tangled in branches and roots are the bodies of Roman dead.

* * *

Rome was born among streams and marshes. Romulus himself was said to have arrived at the foot of the Palatine carried on the river flood. The earliest Romans trod carefully by the springs of the seven hills, wary of the nymphs who haunted the fern-draped pools and wooded streams.

But the city grew fast. The swamp under the Capitol was drained, then paved to become the Forum. The streams were culverted and buried beneath paving stones; the springs were buried under the foundations of grand houses and apartment blocks. Clean water became scarce.

So, in 312 BC, the censor Appius Claudius Caecus – Claudius the Blind – initiated the construction of Rome's first aqueduct, a 16-kilometre channel that brought a flow of cool clear water from the Alban hills, down its carefully calibrated gradient to a giant storage tank near the Forum Boarium. From here, it was piped to public fountains for the thirsty inhabitants of the Velabrum slum by the Palatine hill.

Underfoot, beneath the streets, the Cloaca Maxima – the Great Sewer dug by the Tarquin kings – followed its own dark course, carrying the waste of the city out into the river to be washed down to the sea.

It took a powerful city to build an aqueduct. The expense was vast, for one thing, driving a waterproof channel through thousands of metres of volcanic rock. And in times of war, aqueducts were impossible to defend and easy to destroy. A city with an aqueduct had also to dominate the land through which it ran.

Roman dominion grew fast. In 144 BC the young Gracchus brothers were alive to see Rome's first above-ground aqueduct raise itself from the Latin plain. Financed with the riches taken from the ruins of Carthage and Corinth, the Aqua Marcia ran for 81 kilometres underground before leaping the final ten on a run of graceful arches that brought it into the city near the Via Praenestina, over the shoulder of the Esquiline. It brought 300,000 cubic metres of water a day into the city, fresh and cold and at high enough elevation that it could be siphoned all the way up to the top of the Capitoline hill.*

Watered by these channels and fed by the wealth of defeated enemies, Rome swelled like a mushroom, and as it swelled it sank new aqueducts to suck more water out of the conquered land. The treasures of the world flowed to Rome, and so too did the peoples of every nation, and likewise even the very streams of Italy, diverted

---

* The water of the Aqua Marcia was prized in Rome for its especial purity and sweetness. Among the many scandalous doings of the Emperor Nero was an expedition to the countryside during which he was rumoured to have bathed his sweaty body in the waters of the Aqua Marcia's source.

from their ancient courses, gave themselves up to the city's endless thirst. The wealth of Rome could be counted not just in its slaves and statues and temples and great houses but also in the number and beauty of its fountains, proliferating on every corner. Marcus Agrippa, right-hand man to Augustus, built 700 public basins and 500 fountains in his own name, decorated with marble statues for young Ovid to chase girls around. An entire aqueduct, the Aqua Alsietina, was built on the right bank of the Tiber just to supply the emperor's mock sea battles.

As the Roman empire reached the zenith of its power, so water became the defining element in Roman social life. The baths – of which there were hundreds, from simple *balnea* on street corners to the vast imperial *thermae* – were the hubs around which all other activity revolved. Friends gathered each day after lunch for their ritual circuit of the *tepidarium*, the boiling *caldarium*, the dry heat of the *laconicum*, where the smell of sweat mingled with smoke seeping from the heating furnaces below. The slapping of masseurs' hands on plump backs beat out a rhythm to accompany the grunts of young men lifting weights, the shouts of people playing ball, the umpires keeping score, the cries of sausage sellers and cake bakers and prostitutes, the occasional hue and cry when some daring thief tried to make off with a bather's unattended toga.

Splashing around in the warm and greasy water, the healthy bathed with the sick, the old with the young. It was a bad idea, wrote the doctor, Celsus, to come to the baths with an open wound. Martial, the Spanish satirist, complained about men who sat in the communal plunge pool scrubbing their arses. Also to be avoided were the legions of penurious flatterers who haunted the fashionable *thermae*, plucking at the elbows of the rich in the hope of scoring a dinner invitation. Poets could be found stalking the colonnades, tormenting potential patrons with their verses, while Rome's lovers prowled in the steam, hoping to catch their girls away from the watchful eyes of chaperones.

Emperors could sometimes be seen bathing with their subjects. Titus made carefully staged appearances at the *thermae* that bore his name. Nero presided over the grand opening of his own *thermae* on the Campus Martius. Elagabalus, according to legend, loved bathing with hernia victims, whom he used to tease mercilessly. And even as the cracks in the imperial edifice began to show, rough frontier emperors who had never seen the capital still sent architects to Rome to impress the populace with new monumental baths. The enormous bathing complex of Diocletian on the Viminal hill, fed by the famously clear waters of the Aqua Marcia, represented an extraordinary display of imperial munificence: a building of almost unparalleled grandeur, covered in rich mosaics and marble panelling, full of statues in stone and bronze, with silver fittings and painted stucco walls. Thousands of Romans at a time could gather amid this watery profusion, disporting themselves like so many Scrooge McDucks.

Diocletian retired to his cabbage patch. Years passed. Rome became a Christian city and slowly lost what claim it had left to the status of imperial capital. As the Rhine and Danube defences crumbled, emperors moved north to Milan and Ravenna, better placed to respond to the incursions of Germanic tribes across the frontiers.

The empire had, in some ways, ceased to feel very Roman at all. In the East, though they called themselves Romans, it was Greeks and Thracians and Syrians who filled the streets of the new imperial city of Constantinople. In the West, true power came more and more to rest with the leaders of the army who were, like the men under their command, mostly of Germanic origin.

Assailed by plague, political instability, civil war and foreign raids, the economy of the Roman empire, especially in parts of the West, had entered a period of decline. The cities, so central to ancient culture and thought, were shrinking into themselves, huddled behind hastily built defensive walls. Meanwhile, a new set of rural aristocrats, landowners on a vast scale, had begun to extract themselves from the oppressive machinery of the imperial state. Secure in their fortified compounds, they presented a front of stubborn resistance to the emperor's recruiting sergeants and tax collectors, whose desperate demands therefore fell upon an increasingly immiserated peasantry. 'The tributes due from the rich are extracted from the poor,' wrote a

Christian poet of the fifth century, 'and the weaker bear the burdens of the stronger.' The Roman commonwealth 'is dying, strangled by the cords of taxation'.

In the frontier zones, barbarians, bandits and poverty depopulated huge tracts of countryside. The army, chronically underpaid, produced a steady stream of hungry and battle-trained deserters, who plundered from the civilians they were supposed to protect.

Under these bleak circumstances, an easy way of raising additional manpower for the latest campaign or civil war was to invite a friendly (or at least, recently cowed) Germanic tribe to settle within Rome's borders. Yesterday's raiders could become tomorrow's defenders of the frontier. German families, used to hard living, could plough the weed-choked fields of the borderlands, while their menfolk provided an emperor, real or aspirant, with a formidable fighting force. Provincials might complain, finding their land doled out among Franks or Sarmatians or worse, but their suffering weighed little in the great game of imperial survival.

The Germans had their own reasons for wanting to live on the Roman side of the border. Sometime during the 370s AD, a hitherto unknown tribe of pony-riding steppe archers had established a powerful nomadic confederacy on the grasslands north of the Black Sea and were now terrorizing the Germans of central Europe. Submission to the emperor was bitter, certainly, but preferable to the attentions of the Huns.

But the troubles of the frontier were easy enough to ignore in Rome. The economy of the city was not directly bound to its provinces in the manner of a modern capital. There was no rich nexus of imports and exports that an invader could disrupt. For the great majority of the empire's inhabitants, the circle of production and consumption was a very small one: you ate what you grew. In this world, where wealth was created through agriculture, cities seemed to exist almost as parasites; the surplus of the countryside was creamed off by urban elites who in turn sustained the urban poor with bread and circuses.

If cities were parasites, Rome was the arch-parasite, squatting vast and useless on its seven hills, with its roots sunk into the flesh of the decaying empire. So long as its nutrient channels continued to flow – water from the hills; grain from Africa; slaves from the north; oil from Spain – life in the capital could continue more or less as it had always done, albeit without the gloss of regular imperial patronage. The frescoes in the baths of Diocletian might have been allowed to moulder a little in the steamy air, but Romans still gathered there each day to splash around under the cavernously vaulted ceiling, idly picking the moss from between the tiles of the mosaics.

It was not until AD 410, nearly a century after Constantine's victory at the Milvian Bridge, that the city was made to feel some little share of what many provincials had already suffered. For years, a Germanic people now known as the Visigoths had been operating as a semi-independent military force within the empire, having crossed the Danube in the 370s AD to escape the Huns. Sometimes they fought for emperors, sometimes against them, but always with the aim of carving out a permanent position within the Roman imperial system: land for their men, and high military office for their king, Alaric.

In the first decade of the fifth century, frustrated ambition drove Alaric to a new strategy. Raiding deep into Italy, he bypassed the imperial court at Ravenna and headed straight to Rome, which he threatened to sack if his demands were not met. This was a hostage situation, not a barbarian raid. Once his price was paid – and it soon was – Alaric left. He had no great desire to be known as the destroyer of the empire's founding city.

Soon, however, a fit of ill-advised imperial stubbornness brought him back again. This time there was no ransom. Alaric's Visigoths broke through Rome's walls after a short siege and subjected the city to three days of rape and plunder. Rome, which had brought all Europe under her sway, was sacked for the first time since the invasion of the Gauls, eight centuries before.

The sack was a horror, no doubt, for Rome's inhabitants. But the city itself survived, minus whatever moveable valuables had not been safely stashed away. The Visigoths had come to steal, not burn, and anyway they wanted to preserve the possibility of finding some accommodation with the imperial regime. Indeed, just a few years after taking Rome, the Visigoths were officially settled as supposed imperial subjects in Aquitaine – much to the dismay of the provincial aristocracy.

Rome still stood, solid and magnificent. The poet Rutilius Namatianus, in AD 416, was still able to wax defiantly lyrical about the city: 'Queen of the World and brightest jewel in the vault of heaven', whose glories outnumbered 'the stars in the sky'. He was especially thrilled by the aqueducts: 'Those structures are like mountains in the streets; the Greeks would say giants had built those arches. Rivers are channeled within the walls, lakes vanish in the baths; rivers flow in the gardens, and the walls echo the sounds of water.'

'You have lived a millennium,' he addresses the city. 'You need not fear the Furies. The years that remain have no limit but the Earth's firmness and the strength of Heaven supporting the stars.'

Events of the next few decades would test Namatianus's optimism. Rome's Rhine frontier had been comprehensively breached by a wave of German invaders back in AD 406, who set about ravaging the peaceful land beyond. 'Through villages and villas,' lamented a Christian poet,

> *Through countryside and market-place,*
> *Through all regions, on all roads, in this place and that*
> *There was Death, Misery, Destruction, Burning and Mourning.*
> *The whole of Gaul smoked on a single funeral pyre.*

Spain, peaceful for centuries, suffered a similar fate. Then, in AD 429, one wandering tribe, the Vandals, penetrated all the way to north Africa, where they established an independent Germanic kingdom. All at once, the most significant flow of grain into Rome – from the fertile plains around Carthage – was cut off. Sicily, the next best source of food, was subjected to devastating pirate raids. The Mediterranean, *mare nostrum*, was now a Vandal sea.

In AD 451 the Huns, having long threatened from the fringes of the empire, at last invaded in force under their king Attila. A combined

Romano-Gothic army turned the terrifying nomads away from Gaul, but nothing could prevent a devastating raid into Italy in AD 452. Rome was spared only by the miraculous intervention of the pope, Leo I, who rode out with an escort of sword-wielding angels to persuade the Scourge of God to confine his aggression to the Po Valley.

Disaster was not averted for long. In AD 455 the Vandals of north Africa, emboldened by years of successful raiding, dared to sail against Rome itself. This second sack was far more devastating than the first. For two full weeks, the pirates systematically stripped the city of everything of value; by the time they returned to Carthage their ships were almost sinking under the weight of slaves and loot, including two imperial princesses, and even the sacred menorah of the Jews, stolen from Jerusalem by the Emperor Titus centuries before. In a final insult, the Temple of Jupiter on the Capitoline, monument to Roman glory since the days of the Tarquins, was stripped of its gilded roof tiles and left to stand bald beneath the sky.

Meanwhile, the power of the western imperial court at Ravenna continued to diminish. The Visigoths now ruled Spain more or less independently. Africa was entirely lost. Northern Gaul and the Rhine were the territory of the Franks, while the Rhône valley was divided between the tribal confederations of the Burgundians and the Alemanni.

Only Italy remained firmly under imperial rule, but even that had a strong Germanic flavour. Germans controlled the army, so Germans controlled the emperors. And, after a while, it was no longer clear that a strong German general needed even to pay lip service to an emperor at all. In AD 476 a soldier of the Scirian tribe named Odoacer deposed the reigning child-emperor in a coup, and appointed no replacement. The boy, Romulus Augustulus, was so insignificant a figure that Odoacer did not even bother to have him killed. Rome's last emperor in the West was sent to live out his life in a comfortable villa in the countryside, and was never heard from again. From that moment on, Italy would have not a Roman emperor, but a German king.

*

Four centuries earlier, Rome had killed Julius Caesar for merely having entertained the idea of kingship. The city's allergy to kings was legendary – a proud tradition stretching back to the expulsion of the Tarquins and the foundation of the republic in the sixth century BC.

Now, after a thousand years, Rome was subject to a king once more. Worse still, the new kingdom of Italy was, from the year AD 493, held by a dynasty of invading Goths: not city-sacking Visigoths, at least, but their long-lost cousins, the Ostrogoths, who had recently wrested themselves from the dominion of the Huns.

And yet the Romans, who must have expected the worst, found life under the barbarously named King Theoderic quite civilized. There was peace, at last. Peace for long enough that a child born in Rome in the first year of Theoderic's reign could grow to adulthood with the happy confidence of someone for whom peace was the natural state of affairs. The Vandal sack was fading from human memory, although the city still bore scars: empty plinths for vanished bronzes; grand houses looted and abandoned.

Where the damage was worst, Theoderic and his ministers did their best to patch things up again. The city may not have been worth much economically, but as a symbol of continuity, legitimacy, civilization, it was unparalleled. 'Care for the city of Rome keeps perpetual watch over my mind,' wrote Theoderic to his urban prefect. 'What is worthier than to maintain the repairs of that place which clearly preserves the glory of my state!'

Even in its dilapidated condition, the city had the power to impress. The vaults of the Theatre of Pompey, wrote the king, were magnificent as 'the caverns of a lofty mountain'; the endless empty rows of seats above stood witness to the unimaginable vastness of Rome's population in former times.

Special praise was reserved for the Roman sewers, which:

> Surpass the wonders of other cities. There you may see rivers enclosed, so to speak, in hollow hills... you may see men sailing the swift waters in the boats prepared – with great care, lest

they suffer a seafarer's shipwreck in the headlong torrent. Hence, Rome, we may grasp your outstanding greatness. For what city can dare to rival your towers, when even your foundations have no parallel.

* * *

In the spring of AD 537, in the fifth decade of the Ostrogothic kingdom, Rome's artificial rivers ran suddenly dry. War had come once again to Italy. Out in the neglected fields of the city's hinterland, bright curves of falling water spilled gracefully from broken arches – captive streams, liberated after centuries of confinement. The Goths had cut the aqueducts, and the precious liquid they held drained off into the soil like spilled blood.

This was not what the Romans had been expecting, at the close of the previous year, when they had exchanged their Gothic king for a new Roman emperor. For while the old Rome, the real Rome, had been subjected to the barbarian yoke, the 'new Rome' established by the Emperor Constantine two hundred years before was flourishing. The eastern court at Constantinople was fat with the wealth of Syria, Egypt and Asia Minor, lands that had survived the turbulent fifth century more or less intact.

Now, under the leadership of the Emperor Justinian and his beautiful, scandalous wife Theodora, the eastern empire was pushing back towards the lost provinces of the West. The Roman empire still survived, people had whispered in Rome's streets. Perhaps it was time for that empire to be reunited with its ancient capital; for Rome to reclaim its place as the ruling city of the civilized world.

The agent of Justinian's ambition in the West was a brilliant young general named Belisarius, still in his thirties but already a veteran of successful campaigns against the Persians in Mesopotamia and against the Vandals in north Africa, whose kingdom, after a successful run of more than a hundred years, was now ruthlessly dismantled and reincorporated into Justinian's renewed empire. Sicily fell next; then southern Italy; then Naples, which stayed loyal to the Goths and was mercilessly sacked by Belisarius's brigade of Isaurians, wild hillmen from the Taurus Mountains.

So, at the end of AD 536, when Belisarius marched up the Via Latina to the walls of Rome itself, he found the gates already open. The Goths had sensed the mood in the city. While Belisarius and his spearmen marched in through the Porta Asinaria, up from the south past the great basilica of St John Lateran, the Gothic garrison was marching north out through the Porta Flaminia. Only their commander was left, one Leuderis, refusing to abandon his post: a speck of courage in the vastness of the crumbling city.

But if the Romans cheered Belisarius's coming, the mood swiftly turned to alarm. For one thing, it soon became apparent that the few thousand men the general had with him – a detachment which, in the high days of the empire, would hardly have constituted a respectable advance guard – were in fact the whole of Belisarius's available army. For another, as soon as Belisarius entered the city he set his men to work on strengthening the Aurelian walls, rebuilding the ramparts where they had crumbled and digging a ditch around the entire 19-kilometre course to slow down siege engines.

This was all very well – 'the Romans applauded the forethought of the general,' records the historian Procopius drily – but the inhabitants of the city still very much doubted their ability to withstand a prolonged siege, and had very little inclination to try. Suddenly it was clear to the Romans that, dazzled by the glamour of imperial prestige, they might, in their enthusiasm, have allowed themselves to join the losing side.

All through that anxious winter, Belisarius was everywhere in the city, a purposeful vector in a brownian crowd, all magnitude and direction, striding the walls wrapped in his military cloak. All around him, people burst into activity: engineers setting up war machines on the bastions; diggers deepening the trench before the walls; reluctant civilians gathering what provisions they could from country holdings.

Two months or so passed this way: cold days and anxious evenings. Then, in February or March of AD 537, Belisarius's scouts reported the approach of a large Gothic force, led by King Vittigis, an experienced soldier and grandson-in-law to the great Theoderic, recently elevated to the throne of Italy in the hope that he might deal with the new Roman menace.

This was a challenge that the new Gothic king felt confident to undertake. Apart from anything else, word was getting out about just how small the imperial army was, and how doubtful the loyalty of the Roman populace. The only question, it seemed to Vittigis, was whether he would reach Rome with his vast army before Belisarius had time to run away.

It was a happy surprise, therefore, to learn that Justinian's general was staying put. When the Gothic advance guard crossed the Tiber, they encountered none other than Belisarius himself, scouting outside the city at the head of a thousand-strong cavalry division. The imperial forces charged in without hesitation, Belisarius at their head, fighting in the front line despite the danger – danger which became acute when he was recognized by deserters on the Gothic side. His warhorse, black with a distinctive white blaze, soon became a target for every javelin in the Gothic army. Young men pressed towards him through the throng, hoping to win glory by taking his head. They were thwarted, however, by the courage of the general's household cavalry. As had become the common practice in late imperial armies, Belisarius's force was built around a core of *bucellarii* – household guards – bound to him by bonds of personal loyalty and friendship. Now these picked soldiers clustered round Belisarius with shields raised, enclosing him in a protective sphere of bodies and splintering board, while he, at the centre, thrust left and right, killing all who came by him, his horse wheeling and stamping in the din.

Only the arrival of the main body of Gothic infantry forced Belisarius to retreat. Now the situation was truly desperate. The Romans, assuming the worst, had already given him up for dead, so when Belisarius came galloping back to the walls with his men, they refused to open the gates for fear that these were Gothic impostors, or that the Goths might pour into the city behind them. Bloodied and exhausted, the imperial cavalry huddled in the narrow space between the ditch and the walls, while more and more enemies arrived to gather in the twilight beyond the defences. It must have taken a great clenching up of courage, a hard setting of jaws, to draw swords again from scabbards and turn back out into the night – but the men trusted Belisarius, and they followed where he led, and their last despairing charge was so unexpectedly fierce that the Goths, who had thought themselves victorious, were gripped with sudden fear. For a moment, they recoiled, retreating into the darkening night, and the Romans, convinced at last that Belisarius was who he said he was, opened the gates and let Belisarius and his survivors in.

So the siege of Rome began. The Goths spread themselves slowly around the circuit of the walls, sending out raiders to reap the resources of the Latin countryside: pine groves were felled for Gothic palisades; fat-uddered cows were herded from abandoned farms to roast on the cookfires of the fortified camps; looters trod grime into the mosaics of old country villas, hunting for precious scraps, or stores of forgotten grain. And the Goths cut the aqueducts.

Inside the city, the rhythms of daily life went into a state of immediate arrest. The mill wheels stopped turning to feed the bread ovens; the streets choked up with filth; the corner fountains coughed out their last drips. Worst of all was the closing of the bath houses. Spaces that had crawled with activity, teeming in the hot, wet dark, now gaped dank and empty as if Rome had been disembowelled.

There were still wells, of course, and springs buried under the paved streets. Rome had been a marsh once, and no one would die of thirst, although you never knew how far each water-source was from the nearest cesspit. The shutting down of the mills, however, was a real problem. Without flour, the city would run out of bread, and without bread it would not hold.

Belisarius, alarmed, set his military engineers to work on a set of new mill wheels, strung out on rafts to be turned by the Tiber current. It was not long afterwards that the Goths launched their grisly countermeasure, sending trees and corpses downstream to jam the mechanisms and smash the pontoon. Entire mill wheels were broken off by the force of the floating trunks, and flour production ceased once again. At last, Belisarius managed to string a length of chain across the Tiber where it flowed into the circuit of the walls. Here the flotsam accumulated in a grim tangle. A detachment of unfortunate labourers was set to work hauling the branches and bodies into shore, to prevent Rome's last artery being choked by Roman corpses.

Enclosed in brick and iron, the city sulked behind its walls. The streets in certain districts were now crowded with foreign fighters, who terrified the Romans with their bright painted spears and well-used scale armour, scowling faces framed by long greasy hair. They spoke most often in Greek, which at least the educated citizens could understand, and sometimes in heavily accented Latin, but sometimes too in the harsh Libyan of the Berbers and Moors, the steppe languages of Avars and Massagetae, the Germanic dialects of Gepids and donkey-molesting Heruli. They returned at night, these children of forest and desert, to the old apartment blocks where they were quartered, cowering in superstitious fear of the vast dark city with its empty rooms.

On the eighteenth day of the siege, the Goths launched their first major assault. The morning sun, rising over the Alban hills, struck long shadows from the Gothic war machines, rolling now towards Rome's fortifications: towers to overtop the walls; enormous rams in their wooden housing, heavy enough to crush the bricks to powder. The sight was terrifying to the Romans, unfamiliar with battle. Belisarius's veterans were silent, crouched behind their merlons. Only the general himself was heard to make a sound. As the siege engines crept on, the Romans realized, horrified, that he was laughing.

It was only once the rams had almost reached the ditch that Belisarius opened fire. He shot the first arrow himself, and took a Gothic officer in the neck. A second arrow followed; another kill. And now the men around him began to draw and loose. They were few, certainly, but these were elite imperial troops, schooled through long warfare against the Persians to use a bow as easily as they used a lance: the composite bow of the steppe nomads, which could send an arrow

230 metres at a stretch, or put an armour-piercing bodkin through the centre of a man's mail coat at sixty. The Goths, close under the walls, were now exposed to withering fire more accurate and deadly than anything they had experienced before. So unprepared were they that – and this was the reason for Belisarius's laughter – they had thought to bring their siege engines to the wall drawn by teams of un-protected oxen. Exposed to the imperial arrowstorm, the poor beasts were felled in seconds, collapsing like sacks on to the gore-slicked mud. The towers and rams stood useless, half a bowshot short of their target, while the Goths milled around desperately, heaving at stuck wheels, unable to move the great machines either forward or back as steel death rained down around them.

Still the fight was hard. To the west, on the far side of the Tiber, Belisarius had stationed some men in the Mausoleum of Hadrian out-side the walls, to guard against Goths trying to attack across the river. The mausoleum, a great round drum of brick and marble cladding, was a solid strongpoint, but the men inside were taken unawares by Goths who approached in secret, hidden by a colonnade running from the Basilica of St Peter outside the fortifications. Suddenly, there were Goths with ladders inside minimum ballista range, numerous enough to overwhelm the few defenders. The assault was only foiled when some inventive soldiers thought to smash the statues that decorated the mausoleum's parapet and use the fragments as missiles to hurl at the Goths below. The attackers were thrown back in confusion, amid volleys of shattered marble arms and heads. The mausoleum, stripped of its carved inhabitants, began to look more like the grim fort it would later become: the Castel Sant'Angelo.

As the Goths fell back, the ballistas on the walls creaked into action. These were something like enormous crossbows: twin-armed launchers with torsion springs that could throw a short thick bolt further than the eye could see. These machines terrified the Goths. At the Porta Salaria, where the old salt road left the city, one Gothic noble who strayed too far from his lines was hit by a sharp-eyed ballista crew. The bolt, passing through his breastplate, pinned him to a tree where he dangled, squirming, while the Goths in that sector, too frightened to help him, tripped over each other in their haste to get out of range.

Elsewhere on the walls, the Goths managed to breach the defences only to find themselves encircled by sudden counterattacks which Belisarius made behind them. One attacking force broke through a section of wall to find themselves trapped in an old animal pen, once used for keeping wild beasts destined for the Colosseum. Surrounded, they were cut to pieces where they stood. By the afternoon, the Gothic assault was over. All around the circuit of the walls, the Goths were in retreat. Their siege engines, so painstakingly built, burned in the setting sun.

Direct assault had failed. Now the Goths and the Romans settled into the rhythms of an extended blockade, the Romans behind their walls and the Goths within their wooden palisades. The city was quieter than it had been in centuries. On Belisarius's orders many of the city's non-combatants had slipped away in the nights following the battle, heading south towards Naples, Calabria or Sicily with their possessions bundled on their backs. Scant shelter awaited them, but there was only famine behind.

On the walls, soldiers shared their watches with the remaining civilians, men mostly, who patrolled the defences in return for a small wage. All night, specially posted musicians filled the silence with defiant little tunes to keep the sentries lively and to let the Goths know that Rome had not yet died. Further out, Belisarius's Moorish auxiliaries stalked the darkness. Goths who wandered too far from their camps would be found in the morning with their throats slit.

The days passed in skirmishes outside the walls, and the squabbling of anxious men within. There was a row over Rome's then bishop, Silverius, suspected of colluding with the Goths. Some senators were implicated too, and precautions were redoubled at the gates to prevent any sentries being bought off by Gothic sympathizers.

On another morning it was discovered that someone had tried to pry the lock on the bronze gates of the Temple of Janus in the Forum, gates which, in pagan times, had traditionally been opened in time of war. After a thousand years and more, some Romans still placed their hopes in the ancient two-faced god.

Rome's situation worsened significantly when the Goths captured the town of Portus, the fortified harbour at the mouth of the Tiber near Ostia, through which the imperial fleet had been supplying the city with grain. A little after that, things looked up again: two veteran officers arrived from the East, bringing with them a formidable detachment of 1,600 Hunnic mercenaries. The Goths had no answer to these deadly skirmishers, who cantered about outside the walls shooting arrows into the Gothic camps. To sit and do nothing was unbearable. To pursue was worse. The Huns would wheel back towards the city, shooting arrows behind them as they went, until they drew the Goths within range of Roman ballista fire.

Across the river, Huns and Goths fought running battles in the alleys around St Peter's and the crumbling stadium of Nero, spilling new blood on the sand where, five centuries before, Rome's first Christians had burned. The city was rougher now, showing its old brick bones under the polished marble facings, but still it was a grand stage for a drama, and Belisarius's chosen warriors rose to the occasion. We may imagine Procopius, the historian who served as Belisarius's secretary, watching like Helen on the walls of Troy as the Hunnic horseman Chorsamantis raged like a swarthy Hector with sword and bow to the gates of a Gothic camp – one man scattering twenty. He rode back slowly towards Rome's walls, Procopius records, and as he rode, the Goths circled in again, a great throng, and cut him down.

Other names flash briefly bright against the dwindling city: Tarmoutos, the Isaurian, cut off with his infantry by the Pincian gate, still standing with a javelin in each hand, blood flowing from a dozen wounds; Koutilas, a Thracian, seen charging towards the enemy with a throwing spear embedded in his skull; Bochas, who took a cut to the thigh rescuing an outnumbered detachment and died of it three days after; Arzes, who miraculously survived an arrow that passed through his right eye and all the way to the back of his neck behind, where the point could be felt just under the skin.

Then there was the nameless soldier who spent a night stuck with a Goth in an underground grain store into which both men had fallen. Cut off from the world, down in the dark under the battlefield, the two swore friendship with each other. When they were finally rescued by Gothic forces, the Goth, honouring his word, sent the Roman on his way unharmed.

As spring turned to summer, famine and disease arrived in the city at the same time. The Goths, having seized the port of Rome, had also set up an improvised fortress where the Aqua Claudia intersected with the Aqua Anio Novus on the southern side of the city by the Appian Way. It was too dangerous now to venture into the country-side to scavenge food. The soldiers had their reserves, but ordinary citizens were reduced to eating the herbs and nettles that grew in the abandoned gardens within the walls. Even in those days, there was enough deserted land within the walls to pasture a good-sized cavalry force. Not that any animal was safe behind Rome's defences. There was a secret trade, Procopius reports, in the flesh of worn-out old pack mules, worked by the ingenious Romans into dubious sausages, along with who knew what else.

At last, the Romans could bear no more. 'General, we were not expecting the fortune that has overtaken us at the present time...' Procopius has them complain.

> These fields and the whole country have fallen under the hand of the enemy. This city has been shut off from all good things for we know not how long a time. As for the Romans, some already lie dead, although it has not been their lot to be buried in the earth.

Nor were the survivors to be envied. 'For those suffering of starvation learn that all other evils can be endured.'

* * *

Way back in the earliest days of Rome's imperial existence, Augustan writers like Ovid, Livy and Virgil got into the habit of describing Rome as eternal – an *urbs aeterna*, ruling an *imperium sine fine*, as Virgil famously put it. An empire without end.

As the years passed, and the empire grew, the idea of Eternal Rome became a commonplace of imperial propaganda, stamped on coins and repeated piously in official dispatches. In the 120s AD, the Emperor Hadrian built a whole temple dedicated to *Roma Aeterna*. The Eternal City was *Roma Dea*, an undying goddess, who held the sun and the moon in her hands and who had brought all peoples and all nations under her sway.

When the Eternal City was first taken, in AD 410, by Alaric and his Visigoths, the whole Roman world trembled. In far-off Britain, soon to be abandoned to Saxon pirates, 'everyone was mingled together and shaken with fear'. In Palestine, St Jerome 'was so stupefied and dismayed that day and night I could think of nothing but the welfare of the Roman community'. It seemed, in those days, as if 'the bright light of all the world was quenched... that the whole universe had perished in one city'.

In Carthage, St Augustine was thrown into a theological torment. How could the God in whom the Romans had so recently placed their trust have allowed such a calamity? Over the twenty-two volumes of his monumental work, the *City of God*, Augustine explained that the 'universal catastrophe' was a spur to moral improvement when viewed with the 'eyes of faith'; that the ravages of the Goths were a just punishment for sin and corruption; that if Rome's Christians had suffered along with the unbelievers it was because they had been insufficiently stern in condemning the sins of their godless fellow citizens. Anyway, no loss of limb or life or property counted as a real misfortune for true Christians, 'who are strangers in this world and who fix their hope on a heavenly country'.

So the story of Eternal Rome's fall was set in perpetual motion, to ripple down the stream of history in wave and counterwave. Often Rome has been the City of Men, the earthly city brought low by some vice which each generation reimagines as it sees fit: the worship of false idols; sexual libertinism; love of luxury; the embrace of tyranny; inequality of wealth; political corruption. Conversely, Rome has been a sort of lost paradise – the great burning sun of civilization, extinguished by the forces of darkness and ignorance: barbarian invaders;

dangerous immigrants; even, in some versions of the story, too many Christians, who, as Gibbon put it, 'refused to take any active part in the civil administration or the military defence of the empire'.

It was Gibbon above all who set the tone for later histories with his 1.5 million-word account of Rome's *Decline and Fall*. Ever since, historians have tried to unravel the obscure threads of causation that led Europe's mightiest and most durable political entity to ruin. Each subsequent nation that has risen to great power has anxiously scanned Rome's history to try to avoid meeting the same end.

Were they aware, Belisarius and his men, as they shivered through their second winter in the starving city, of the scale of the historical drama in which they were taking part? Rome's fall was slow – stretching across generations – and if each year the city was a little thinner, a little quieter than it had been before, still the daily business of life continued. The necessities of survival in war left little time for grand historical contemplation. And Rome had proved, in the past, surprisingly resilient. After AD 410, she had sprung back to life, a little pale perhaps but still vigorous. After AD 455, the recovery had been slower, but the tender attentions of Theoderic at the end of the fifth century had restored some of her old beauty, though her the empire was lost.

Now Justinian had sent Belisarius to shake life into her inert body, so that *Roma Dea*, the Eternal City, might once again stand colossal over vanquished Europe. And, by luck, courage and exceptional generalship, Belisarius was victorious. Reinforcements had been trickling into Italy from the East. While the general himself stayed in Rome, harassing the Gothic army which was still too large to be faced in open battle, his lieutenants spread out across Tuscany and towards the north, capturing strategic fortresses and securing vital supply routes until their advance forces were within reach of the Gothic capital at Ravenna. Now, after two years of frustration, hunger and sickness outside the walls, and facing a threat far to their rear, the Gothic army finally withdrew towards the north.

They were halfway across the river when Belisarius launched his final attack. The whole imperial army, let off the leash at last, fell on the Gothic rearguard, slaughtering hundreds and putting the whole besieging force to flight. Rome was saved. Over the coming months, Belisarius, aided by the eunuch general Narses and his force of Lombard mercenaries from beyond the Danube, would recapture the whole of Italy. The empire had reclaimed its ancient heart.

Rome was saved, but Rome was also dying. Depopulated by the siege, the city lay decaying on its seven hills. The aqueducts, severed by the Goths, poured out their water uselessly into the dust. The great bathhouses crumbled.

There was still more violence to be endured. The Goths, pushed to the brink of extermination, suddenly rebounded under a new king, Totila. Rome was besieged again, and this time captured and Totila, not unreasonably, considered levelling the place. It had been a sheep pasture once, and to pasture it could return. Only a desperate letter from Belisarius, we are told, persuaded him to leave the city standing, a 'memorial to the virtue of former generations'.

A memorial, however, was all Totila would allow it to be. At the beginning of AD 547 the last of Rome's population, the few brave souls still clinging on after ten years of war, were driven out into the cold and barren countryside of a ravaged Italy. The city lay bare and silent, its ancient monuments sticking up like ribs on an old corpse.

Belisarius had grown old fighting for the Eternal City. But the project was hopeless from the beginning. No amount of human voltage, of shock and violence, would bring *Roma Dea* back to life. The imperial city, the world-dominating city of marble and gold, of Caesar and Augustus, that city was gone.

But life in Rome was not completely extinguished. Weeds sprouted in the mud that covered the streets; ivy climbed the pillars of old temples, where pigeons nested under the eaves and wild flowers pushed through cracks in the roof tiles.

And gradually a few of the Romans started to return, creeping back into the city to see what fragments of past selves they could salvage among the ruins. Like worms in a corpse, they busied themselves in the wreck of the great city, scavenging stone and bricks from the old buildings, grazing their herds in the gardens of the emperors. There was no time to mourn the past. There were new lives to feed, and a new city waiting to be born.

12

THE CLAN

The rise of the house of Theophylact

———

I T IS FEBRUARY, or maybe March, AD 897. These are the first
hungry weeks of spring, but the chill spreading through the
Lateran Basilica is more than just a consequence of the weather.
Here, in the mother church of Christendom, are assembled all the
notables of the city, lay and clerical: deacons and subdeacons, priests,
arch priests and abbots, monks, exorcists, bishops of suburbicarian
sees. Here, shifting uncomfortably on hard benches, are the lay nobility: counts from the surrounding countryside; gastalds from the
south; even one or two of the great margraves, the marcher lords who
divide Italy between them. Here are the high officials of Rome, an-
ciently titled, the *primicerius*, the *arcarius*, the *nomenclator*, the palatine
judges. And here, tiny figures in the cavernous space of the basilica,
are two popes. One of the popes is spitting rage; the other is dead.

Formosus is the name of the dead one – Latin for 'handsome' –
an unfortunate name for an eleven-month-old corpse. He has been
stuffed into a set of papal vestments for the occasion: silk stockings
and red leather sandals; the cope and pallium; the long dalmatic
whose stripes imitate the senatorial tunic of long ago; the simple white
cap – the *camelaucum*. No vestment can disguise, however, the horror
of his peeled-back lips and vanished gums, his empty eyes, the smell
of putrefaction.

Stephen is the living pope, and the impresario behind the grisly

Your receipt
Brentwood Library

Contra Costa County Library

104 Oak Street

Brentwood, CA. 94513

(925) 516-5290

Customer ID: **************

Items that you checked out

Title: The eternal city : a history of Rome /
ID: 31901063822540
Due: Saturday, September 07, 2019
Messages:
Item checked out.

Total items: 1
Account balance: $0.00
8/17/2019 11:19 AM
Ready for pickup: 0

_____

Items may be renewed online at ccclib.org

or by calling 1-800-984-4636, menu option 1.

Have a nice day!

show. He has dug Formosus up to charge him with abandoning his old bishopric in contravention of canon law and usurping the papacy in a spirit of deplorable ambition. All the forms and protocols of a trial have been observed. The corpse even has its own counsel, a trembling deacon, to mount a token defence.

But the outcome is not in doubt. Now Pope Stephen pronounces sentence on his recent predecessor. The corpse is stripped. The thumb and first two fingers of Formosus's right hand – the fingers used in papal benedictions – are torn off. The rest of him will go where so many have gone before, into the River Tiber.

In the basilica, a brief but heavy silence. The faces of the nobles and bishops are carefully blank, eyes as glassy as the mosaic saints on the lamplit walls. These are dangerous times. Somewhere in the crowd, however, not in the first rank, not among the greatest of the magnates, a man allows himself a cautious inward smile. Where others see horror, he sees opportunity. Cracks are appearing in the established edifices of power. In these cracks, there may be space for a new family, a new dynasty, to put down roots.

* * *

At the cadaver synod, as it came to be known, the dignity and standing of the papacy in Rome approached its nadir. And yet the nightmare, pantomime trial of Formosus's corpse was, in a way, a logical, perhaps inevitable consequence of a golden dream that had been born in Rome a century earlier: the imperial dream of Charles the Great, king of the Franks, known to history as Charlemagne.

Of all the Germanic states that had emerged from the ruin of the Roman empire in the west, it was the kingdom of the Franks in northern Gaul that had, over the succeeding centuries, proved the most successful. Their first king, Clovis – Louis, the name would be in modern French – had converted to Christianity back in AD 496. His Franks, absorbing the old Gallo-Roman aristocracy, established a dominion that had prospered ever since, even as other barbarian confederacies failed. The Franks held on while the Vandals in Africa and the Ostrogoths in Italy were destroyed in turn by Belisarius's armies. They watched as most of Italy, so painfully won by Belisarius, was lost again to new masters, the Lombards. They saw the Visigothic kingdom in Spain destroyed by the Arab and Berber followers of a new religion, Islam. At the Battle of Tours, in AD 732, it was Franks who finally halted the Muslim advance into Europe – Franks led by Charlemagne's grandfather, Charles 'the Hammer' Martel.

Rome, up until those years, had remained under the precarious authority of the eastern emperors in Constantinople – 'Roman emperors', as they called themselves, although historians have tended to refer to them less flatteringly as 'Byzantine'.* The Byzantine government in Rome was led by a local general, the *dux*, reporting to a provincial governor, the exarch of Italy, based at Ravenna. The *dux* shared authority with Rome's bishop, the pope, who was himself usually an appointee of the Byzantine emperor.

But if Muslim expansion shook the West, in the old Roman East it turned the political landscape upside-down. Arab mercenaries had spent generations selling their swords to Persia and Byzantium, as the two old superpowers fought each other to death over centuries of war. Suddenly, united and inspired by Muhammad and his successors, the Arabs swept out of the desert to claim both empires for Allah. The richest territories of the old Roman and Persian empires fell easily into the invaders' hands. By the year AD 717, after decades in retreat, an exhausted Byzantine army was defending the the walls of Constantinople itself.

As the Byzantine empire crumbled before the Caliphate, it was less and less able to keep control of Rome. The imperial treasury had been emptied by war. Byzantine military leaders in Italy were now paid in land, rather than gold, and possession of land – an endlessly renewable source of wealth – tended to foster a certain independence of spirit among ambitious aristocrats.

* Constantine's new city at Constantinople was founded on the site of an old Greek colony called Byzantium, hence the name. Traditional Western historiography, seeing in the Eastern empire a model of decadence and bureaucratic corruption, allowed the term 'byzantine' to acquire its unflattering – and unfair – modern connotations.

To make things worse, the catastrophic campaigns in the East and the near loss of the capital itself provoked a major religious crisis in Constantinople. It was well established – St Augustine had made this clear after the Visigothic sack of Rome in AD 410 – that worldly disasters were a consequence of religious misdeeds. A good emperor was responsible not only for armies and taxes but also for churches and prayers. He had to keep his subjects safely in the favour of God.

Clearly something had gone wrong in that department. The problem, in this case, was determined to be the veneration of holy images, a centuries-old practice among Christians but one which seemed closer, somehow, to ancient paganism than was quite proper and which anyway was against God's explicit command to Moses in the Old Testament. When the Israelites had been caught worshipping a golden calf, imperial theologians recalled, the Lord had sent a plague upon them, killing thousands. Surely the same divine wrath must be behind the Arab invasion.

Imperial agents were duly sent across what remained of the eastern Roman empire to chip murals off church walls and dig up mosaic floors and smash the ancient paintings, worn thin by the kisses of the faithful. This was painful and difficult in Greece and Asia Minor – and it was impossible in Rome. The populace and clergy were furious; the aristocrats felt the same, and anyway the chief men of Rome were ready to seize any opportunity to escape from the Byzantine emperor's increasingly desperate tax demands. In AD 729, not long before the great Frankish triumph at Tours, Rome was cutting the last political ties that bound it to the eastern empire. The imperial city prised itself out of the emperor's grasp.

Out of the frying pan, in other words. The newly independent Rome, with the pope at its head, controlled a little patch of territory squeezed between two rising and hungry powers: the duchy of Benevento to the south and the kingdom of Italy to the north. Very soon, the Lombard rulers of kingdom and duchy were pressing in to claim the old imperial possessions for themselves.

In AD 751, a particularly aggressive Lombard king even managed what so many kings had failed to do in the past, and captured the marsh-girt fortress-city of Ravenna, seat of the Byzantine exarch. If Ravenna's defences had not been able to keep out the Lombards, there was no question of defending Rome's 19 kilometres of crumbling wall. Another solution had to be found before the Lombard army turned its attention southwards. So, in AD 753, Pope Stephen II, to save his Roman flock, embarked on a dangerous winter journey, heading north across the frozen passes of the Alps. His destination: the royal court of the Franks who, following the victory at Tours, had established themselves as the foremost power of the Christian West.

Frankia, at that moment, was in the middle of an awkward political transition from the old royal clan of Clovis to the new 'Carolingian' dynasty. Charles Martel, who had led the Franks to victory over the Saracens at Tours, had never officially made himself king. By AD 753, his son Pepin was moving to fix this oversight, and all the Frankish lords were busy forgetting as hard as they could that the previous crowned king, ceremonially dethroned, was still alive somewhere in a monastery on the North Sea coast. Now, with perfect timing, Pope Stephen II came hurrying across the mountains to dignify Pepin's usurpation of the Frankish throne with the special blessing of St Peter. In January of AD 754, in the great cathedral of St Denis in Paris, the pope anointed Pepin king of the Franks.

Two years later, Pepin was in Italy to repay the favour. The Lombards were kicked out of Ravenna and sternly warned off Rome. The keys to the cities they had conquered in the old imperial terri- tory – a diagonal strip running across Italy from Rome and Lazio to Ravenna and the so-called Pentapolis on the Adriatic coast – were placed symbolically in St Peter's Basilica. Pepin established the pope as a major territorial lord – a princely power – in Italy, with the Frankish army acting as his guarantor.

Pepin was a formidable king. His son, Charles, was determined to be even greater. And so indeed he proved. By the time of his death in AD 814, Charles – Charlemagne – had established the largest dom- inion western Europe had seen since the fall of the Roman empire, a territory that encompassed most of modern France, Germany and Italy, stretching from the Elbe to the Pyrenees.

With vast territory came vast ambition: Charlemagne had a vision, a dream of power that was not just the power of the mailed fist and the lance. He was not content merely to be a warlord. Frankia, in Charlemagne's dream, was a new Israel. Charlemagne himself was David or Josiah, a holy monarch, set on high by the Lord to lead his people to a new state of religious and political perfection.

These perfections, religious and political, were by no means separate, nor even separable. Ecclesiastical institutions, from the grandest cathedral to the most humble rustic church, were the sites of real power in that early medieval world, and the bishops and abbots of Frankia ranked among the foremost magnates of the kingdom, not just through spiritual authority but by virtue of vast landed wealth and the men at their command.

At the same time, the correct political ordering of Frankia had a strong religious dimension. A good Christian kingdom was an imitation not only of Old Testament models but also of heaven itself. The plebs and potentates of Frankia arranged themselves under their monarch in their divinely appointed stations as the choirs of angels and saints in paradise took their places before God.

A perfect kingdom should practise a perfect Christianity. 'Exert yourselves,' Charlemagne commanded his clerics in AD 789, 'to bear the erring sheep back within the walls of the ecclesiastical fortress... lest the wolf who lies in wait should find someone transgressing the sanctions of the canons... and devour him.'

But what constituted perfect Christianity was not always easy to discern. With the fragmentation of the western Roman empire, the church – which had, under Constantine, been practically an arm of the Roman state – suffered a similar fragmentation. Christianity in Ireland, for example, isolated even before the empire fell, developed in a quite different way to Christianity in Frankia or Visigothic Spain.*

---

* Harmonizing Christian practice within a dominion was often a priority for the stronger kings of the Early Middle Ages. The conflict between Irish

Charlemagne, conqueror of many nations, found many incompatible Christianities practised by his subjects. To bring these into order – to build his perfect kingdom, in other words – even the formidable scholarship of the Frankish bishops was inadequate. For a realm that extended from Germany to Spain, some religious authority had to be found that would transcend the merely national. There was only one answer. Charlemagne turned to Rome.

In AD 774, Charlemagne's armies wrapped up the conquest of the Lombard kingdom of Italy. It was surprisingly straightforward; no army could stand against the assembled might of the Frankish warrior aristocracy. Soon, the chief among those warrior aristocrats found themselves installed as territorial lords. The Lombard kingdom was divided into border regions or marches, each with its own margrave, appointed by the king.

With the Lombards pacified, an intense two-way traffic began between Charlemagne's court at Aachen and the city of Rome. Heading north were clerics and scholars, even choirmasters to teach the Franks the latest Roman modes. They brought with them texts from Rome's ancient libraries: teachings of the Church Fathers; the best Latin Bibles; prayer books and liturgies. Secular works were of interest too. The five hundred years since the reign of Constantine had seen a marked decline in the quality of people's Latin, even among the learned. An edition of Ovid or Virgil might be profane in subject matter, but could at least be used as a model for correct Latin grammar.

Heading in the other direction came an endless procession of princely gifts: silver candelabras and golden chalices for the churches; great timber beams for the repair of the old basilicas; tapestries, carpets, cloaks, gems and amber – all the luxuries of an early medieval

---

and European forms of Christianity in England, for example, was famously settled at the Synod of Whitby by King Oswiu of Northumbria in AD 664. He settled for the Roman-style traditions of the missionary Augustine, with consequences that have been felt ever since.

court. More importantly, the popes were confirmed in their possession of most of the rich estates that Pepin had promised, and more
besides – lands freed from the Lombards were now put firmly into
papal possession. The pope could now count himself among the
wealthiest magnates in Charlemagne's kingdom.

These gifts did not mean, however, that Charlemagne in any way
acknowledged the pope as his superior, or even as an equal. Popes had
been trying to establish themselves as supreme, in spiritual matters at
least, for centuries. Way back in AD 494, Pope Gelasius I had laid out
the position. *'Duo sunt'*, he told an emperor – 'there are two powers'
by which this world is ruled: 'the sacred authority of the priests and
the royal power. Of these that of the priests is the more weighty.'

But Charlemagne was no believer in the separation of church and
state, and far less would he have accepted the idea that the pope might
be in any sense his superior. Church and state, after all, were welded
firmly together. Bishops might have special spiritual responsibilities,
but they had the same temporal powers and duties as other great lords,
and like the other great lords they owed obedience above all to their
king – the king who, in most cases, had appointed them in the first
place, just as he appointed dukes and counts and margraves.

The pope, to be sure, was no ordinary bishop. The breadth and
richness of his possessions marked him out, although the Frankish
world was full of rich and powerful bishops ruling great areas of land.
More importantly, the pope could trace his bishopric back to the first
bishop of Rome, St Peter himself. 'Thou art Peter,' Jesus had told his
disciple, long ago. 'Thou art Peter, and upon this rock' – *petros*, in
Greek – 'I will build my church.' Popes had long understood this verse
of Matthew's Gospel to mean that the Christian church was founded
not just on St Peter personally, but on his bishopric, the Apostolic See
that he had founded in Rome.

Very well then, the pope was no ordinary bishop. Yet still he
was *some* kind of bishop, and from the point of view of the king
of the Franks and the Italians, conqueror of Saxons and Saracens,
it made no odds at all if the pope was, as he claimed, the senior

bishop of all Christendom and the very rock and foundation of God's church – he was still at best, as one historian has put it, no more than Charlemagne's 'senior vice president for prayer'. Supreme authority, both temporal and spiritual, would always rest with Charlemagne himself.

This was not a novel conception. On the contrary, Charlemagne had only to look east across the Adriatic Sea to find a model: the Byzantine emperor. And indeed, if you thought about it – as Charlemagne doubtless did – there was something absurd about the contrast between that emperor, with his tiny rump state on the Bosphorus, and the king of the Franks whose lands extended beyond the dreams of the ancient Caesars.

This was easily put right. On Christmas Day, AD 800, in the Basilica of St Peter, Charlemagne announced to the world, as if there were any possibility of confusion, what sort of place he really regarded himself as having in God's holy scheme. There, before the assembled magnates of Frankia, Lombardy and Rome, the deacons and subdeacons, the bishops of suburbicarian sees arranged by rank, Charlemagne was crowned with gold and precious gems and the pope bowed down and prostrated himself before him, and all the grandees and the people together hailed him 'Charles Augustus, crowned by God, great and pacific emperor of the Romans'. After a gap of four hundred years, the West had an emperor once again.

* * *

It was far from obvious, at the time, that the triumphant Christmas of AD 800 would lead to the trial of a rotting pope in the Lateran ninety-seven years later. Nonetheless, the currents of history flowed towards that grim spring day like water to a plughole, as Charlemagne's dream of empire rushed to its own undoing.

The problem was that in those days of the Early Middle Ages, it was hard, if not impossible, for any central authority to hold power for long. A great leader could do it, by the force of his personality and the dread of his reputation. But that leader would not live forever. For three generations from Charles Martel the Carolingians had enjoyed smooth successions from a strong king to a dominant son who was able quickly and effectively to eliminate any rivals. After Charlemagne, the pattern held for one generation more. Louis the Pious was crowned by his father as co-emperor at Aachen in AD 813, and succeeded Charlemagne as sole ruler of the Frankish empire the year after. By the 830s AD, however, the empire was being pulled apart by Louis's sons. When Louis died in AD 840, Charlemagne's great empire was divided between them, in shares corresponding very roughly to Germany, Italy and France.

The grandsons and great-grandsons of Charlemagne were soon locked in an endless struggle for supremacy. To win the support of important magnates in their bids for power, they traded away the land and titles, both lay and clerical, that had been in the gift of the old Frankish kings. The result was that the higher-ranking aristocrats, by selling themselves to imperial and royal pretenders, soon became extraordinarily rich. The great dukes and margraves of the old Frankish empire were now as powerful, if not more so, than some who called themselves kings.

With the decay of Carolingian authority, the popes in Rome were once again abandoned. Worse than abandoned. In a pool of post-imperial sharks, the papacy, fattened with estates and revenues by Charlemagne's generosity, now found itself the plumpest fish. By the end of the ninth century, half the great magnates in Italy, descendants of Charlemagne's Frankish lords, were queuing up to bite off chunks of papal territory for themselves.

Pope Formosus, before he became a horror story, had been a proficient player of this deadly game. As bishop of Portus, at the Tiber mouth, one of the influential 'suburbicarian sees' that surrounded the city, Formosus had been in a position to be of valuable service to his faction – service which was eventually rewarded with possession of the papal throne itself.

As pope, he could distribute a bountiful haul of papal land to his aristocratic patrons, and profitable deaconries and bishoprics to those clerics who had helped him rise. That was why, in AD 897, his enemy Pope Stephen VI put on his grisly show trial – and why he was so determined to cut off Formosus' benedictory fingers. The many rich blessings Formosus had bestowed upon his followers were thus legally and symbolically revoked.

The consequences of the cadaver synod rippled through Europe. In Germany, Duke Arnulf of Carinthia, once crowned Augustus by Pope Formosus's hand, now shivered his displeasure. His ally Berengar, the wily old margrave of Friuli, lurked in his northern stronghold. In Rome, meanwhile, the ambitious local margraves, Adalbert of Tuscany and Lambert of Spoleto, scented new and thrilling opportunities.

But Formosus's faction had not died with him. The balance of power in ninth-century Italy was always shifting with the loyalties and ambitions of the leading players and soon the fragile order established at the cadaver synod was overturned: Lambert was dead in a mysterious hunting accident, Berengar was king of Italy and Stephen VI was strangled in Rome, after a papacy of just over a year. Formosus was rehabilitated. His body, miraculously, was discovered still bobbing around in the Tiber and buried in St Peter's. As the pope's supposed corpse was carried to its final resting place, the images of the saints on the walls are said to have bowed their heads in sorrow.

Charlemagne's empire was a shattered ruin. The papacy, which was meant to raise that empire up to God, had been debased by the ambitions of the Italian lords. Formosus, successor to St Peter, was a disintegrating lump of Tiber gristle.

So began what came to be known as the *saeculum obscurum*, the dark century. Papal turnover was extremely rapid, and often contested, with more than one pope in office at the same time. Violence was frequent. Fully a third of the popes who ruled between AD 872 and 1012 died in shady circumstances, and yet more were exiled, deposed or imprisoned.

As if to mirror the dark circumstances of the papacy, the official papal biographies that had been written in previous years now vanish too, as if the doings of tenth-century popes were too grim for history to record. Peering back into the murk, the historians of later years could see Rome only as reflected through the warped and black-ened glass of non-Roman church chroniclers: Benedict of Soracte, Flodoard of Rheims, the annalists of Fulda. Most influential of all were the bitterly hostile writings of Liudprand, bishop of Cremona. It is in Liudprand's work, especially in the volumes called *Antapodosis* – Retribution – that a curious outline emerges from the fog of murder and ambition: a family, four generations, men and women, scram-bling in the shadows of Rome's dark century, emerging to claim and hold the dangerous honour of being the most powerful clan in Rome.

Theophylact was the name of the dynasty's founder. A Byzantine name, ostentatiously unlike the Germanic names borne by the Franks and Lombards, but not unusual among the higher Roman aristocracy. The city might have broken free from Constantinople politically, but Romans still felt the pull of Byzantine imperial glamour and they still ran the city along Byzantine lines.

It is in this context that Theophylact first comes into view – as a member of Rome's civilian bureaucracy. At the cadaver synod he is invisible: just one in the crowd of ambitious Romans on the make. Four years later, in AD 901, he has become a somebody: a palatine judge, a name on a list. In AD 904, he appears again. He is *vestararius* now, master of the papal wardrobe, which in practice means master of finances for Rome. Soon he will be *magister militum* too.

By AD 905, Theophylact has made a bold play for power: somehow, with the help of the local margraves, he has arranged for one of his friends to take the papal throne. The new pope, Sergius III, belongs to the anti-Formosan faction; Formosus, already condemned and rehabilitated once over, is condemned again. His gifts and appoint-ments are yet again declared invalid.

A little later, we find that Theophylact has revived an ancient title to add to his collection. He is Rome's most powerful citizen, and now, harking back to the glorious oligarchy of the Roman republic, he will be its senator. Never mind that a *senator* should, by tradition, be one of a few hundred *senatores*; this title has the proper air of antique respectability to fit Theophylact's new pre-eminence.

We can trace his rise, but still we know almost nothing about him. He lives with his family in a grand house on the Via Lata (the modern Corso), the ancient road that runs down vertically through the Campus Martius. He has at least five children – or has had five. Two die in infancy. Another, a son who bears his name, is an invalid and does not last long. Theophylact buries his children in the Basilica of Santa Maria Maggiore. He and his wife are devoted to the Virgin Mary in particular; she cures one of their sons of paralysis after they build a shrine in her honour near their home.

Theophylact's wife is Theodora, and she is as important as she is mysterious. We assume she was born into Roman aristocracy, but she may be even grander, perhaps even related to the margraves of Tuscany. Theophylact calls her *vestararissa*, an extraordinary position for a woman to hold, and certainly she plays a vital role in Theophylact's new regime. 'The scent of your piety spreads everywhere,' a Neapolitan churchman tells her, albeit under some duress. 'Everywhere you diffuse the sweet smell of Christ.'

Then, on the other hand, comes bishop Liudprand, thundering away. A 'shameless harlot', he calls Theodora, who 'was holding the monarchy of the city of Rome, and not in an un-manly fashion'. The only people worse than Theodora, in Liudprand's telling of it, are her surviving daughters. These, Marozia and Theodora the Younger, 'were not just her equals but if anything even faster in the exercise of Venus'.

It was precisely through this 'exercise of Venus', if Liudprand is to be believed, that the clan of Theophylact cemented its hold on early tenth-century Rome. Sergius III, Theophylact's tame pope, was supposed to be a lover of the probably still teenage Marozia.*

When Pope Sergius died in AD 911, the family reconfigured itself to maintain its grip on the papal throne. After a few years of manoeuvring, a certain archbishop, John of Ravenna, was summoned

---

* This is according to Liudprand of Cremona, of course. In fact, the relationship, if it existed at all, may have had more the character of a marriage or at least official concubinage than a scandalous affair.

to Rome. Theodora, 'inflamed with the heat of Venus', had 'forni-cated' repeatedly with this man in the past. Now, Liudprand claims, the lustful *vestararissa* elevated her former lover to the Apostolic See.

Young Marozia, now free to form a new marriage bond, was handed off to Alberic, margrave of Spoleto. It was an astute polit-ical match. Spoleto, Tuscany, Ravenna and Rome were united into a formidable power bloc, and one in which women played a vital role. Men provided the faction's land and steel, to be sure, but it was the women of the clan of Theophylact who held the whole unstable structure together.

In AD 915 Theophylact's project reached its apogee. There were Saracen raiders at the mouth of the River Garigliano. They had been there for years, ravaging the country around Rome from their forti-fied camp. Now, Theophylact and his allies assembled a multinational force to end the threat forever: King Berengar I sent men from the north; Marozia's husband led the Spoletans; the princes of Salerno and Benevento brought their men, and the nearby dukes of Gaeta too, forgetting, conveniently, that they had until just recently been used to enjoying a friendly cut of Saracen profits. Most importantly, the emperor in Byzantium was persuaded to send the imperial navy to cut off the Saracen retreat by sea. Pope John X, former archbishop of Ravenna, fought in the front rank, with Theophylact at his side. Surrounded by Italian swords, with Greek fire waiting out at sea, the Saracens were cut down to a man, bringing an end to decades of plundering.

This was Theophylact's great triumph, and also his last. By the late 920s AD Theophylact, Theodora and Alberic of Spoleto were all dead. Their ends are as mysterious as their origins. A brief flash of fame, in a forgotten corner of history, and then they fade away into the dark.

* * *

Left behind to mourn was Theophylact's daughter Marozia, the margrave of Spoleto's widow. Without parents, without husband, she cut a lonely figure in the city. She will have felt, in those years, not just the absences of family but also the thinning of the crowd of notables who had been regulars at her father's *domus* on the Via Lata and at her own grand house up on the Aventine. The poles of the city had shifted. It was the papal residence, the Lateran Palace, that drew the grandees now, to scheme like mischievous bees, buzzing conspiratorially behind those inscrutable walls of antique brick.

In AD 926 John X of Ravenna, Theodora's tame pope, made his move at last, throwing off his allegiance to Theophylact's clan. As had become usual in Italian politics, the plot involved summoning a foreign power from across the Alps; in this case it was Hugh, duke of Provence, who was invited to become king of Italy. John would provide his papal blessing to the usurper. In return, Hugh would install John's brother Peter as margrave of Spoleto, the title that had belonged to Marozia's husband. With his brother ruling as margrave of Spoleto, Pope John X would hold supreme power in Rome.

Marozia was at bay, but not defeated. As a woman she was at a severe political disadvantage, but the situation was not completely hopeless. Women could not fight, nor expect equality in law, nor count easily on the obedience of men around them. They could, however, own property. Crucially, the rule of strict male primogeniture – of rights and property passed exclusively through the line of eldest sons – had not yet become established European custom. The deaths of her husband and of her father left Marozia rich. Moreover, and just as importantly, Marozia was the main inheritor of Theophylact's accumulated prestige, his networks of friends and allies, the web of mutual obligations and symbolic bonds that had formed and sustained the wider Theophylact clan.

The last tool Marozia had at her disposal was her own person. She was in her mid-thirties by now – older than most people ever got to be in those days, but not too old to be an attractive match for an aristocrat with ambition. Sometime in AD 926 or 927 she found the right man, Guy of Tuscany, who was willing to buy her Roman connections with his military might. In AD 927 or 928 there was a brief and bloody encounter at the pope's stronghold at the Lateran. Peter, the pope's brother, was cut down on the spot. John X, after fourteen years on the papal throne, was deposed and cast into prison where, depending on who you believe, he either died of neglect or was quietly strangled.

When Guy died in turn at the beginning of the following year, Marozia found herself the unchallenged mistress of Rome. Husbandless again, she now made use of her various sons. Alberic II, named after his father, was given the crucial margravate of Spoleto. Another son was made bishop of Nepi. Best of all, she was able to find the perfect role for her eldest child, a boy who was whispered to be the product of her first teenage affair with Pope Sergius III. Here was a perfect scandal for Bishop Liudprand's gleeful pen: the wicked mother elevating a papal bastard to the papal throne.

For four years, Marozia was Rome's ruling matriarch. The pope was hers. Spoleto was hers. Rome was hers, bound to her by the memory of her father and by her own force of will. The city called her 'patrician', like the old Byzantine governors, and *senatrix romanorum*. Bishop Liudprand called her 'the Roman Harlot', an insult that acknowledged her supremacy all the same. Centuries later Protestant historians, taking their cue from Liudprand, called this period of Roman history the Pornocracy: the government of whores.

In AD 932 we find Marozia at the end of her run. 'Why, Marozia, do you rage, urged on by Venus' stings?' cries Liudprand, in impeccable Latin verse.

> *What does it profit you, O wicked woman, to ruin such a holy man?*
> *While you hope, through such a great crime, to seem a queen,*
> *Actually you shall lose great Rome, with God judging you.*

The 'crime' Marozia has committed, in Liudprand's poem, is to get married for what may have been the fourth, and certainly was the final, time. The 'holy man' she has 'ruined' is her new husband, in fact an aristocratic adventurer of notable cruelty, her old enemy Hugh of Provence, who had taken over the Lombard kingdom of Italy.

Why she allowed him to share her bed is a mystery. Perhaps his growing power left her no choice. Or perhaps she was ambitious. To marry Hugh was to become queen of Italy as well as mistress of Rome. Moreover, with Rome at her command, Marozia could have her son, Pope John XI, crown Hugh emperor. Hugh was, on his mother's side, a very distant descendant of Charlemagne; perhaps Marozia hoped that Charlemagne's imperial dream could be resurrected, with Marozia herself triumphant at the new emperor's side.

Things turned out quite otherwise: 'At the entrance of the Roman city,' Liudprand writes, 'there is a certain fortification, built with wondrous craft.' It is the Castel Sant'Angelo that Liudprand means, the old Mausoleum of Hadrian, marble cladding stripped away to reveal walls of bare Roman brick. The season is winter. The scene, perhaps a feast. Outside the window, far beneath, the Tiber runs slow through the mist, and the fields lie bare.

In the fort, we must imagine a gathering of aristocrats in their finery, and wealthy clerics, distinguishable from the laymen only by their shaved chins and their neglected tonsures. They will be sitting down to eat, probably on one long table, each arranged in his place according to a strict and delicately calculated order of precedence. Likewise the costumes, produced over toilsome hours by legions of poor women with needle and loom, spell out a hierarchy of jealously maintained degrees. Status, in this world, is inseparable from display, and can be read on each guest's person, in the gold thread sewn through their cloaks, the dye of their tunics and undertunics.

No portrait has survived of Marozia. We can only guess at her splendour: a long robe, fashionably tight around the belly, studded with precious stones; surely a head covering, the modest veil of a married woman; perhaps she would have been rich enough for eastern silk, woven into the bold symmetrical patterns that only the artisans of Byzantium had the technology to produce. These silks were impossible to buy; rare gifts from the Byzantine court, worth much more than their weight in gold and circulated around the highest ranks of Europe's aristocracy.

This context – elaborately hierarchical; symbolically charged – is important for making sense of what happens next. As Liudprand tells it, Marozia asks one of her sons, young Alberic II, to pour out water for his new stepfather, King Hugh, to wash his hands. Alberic, sensitive to the loss of status this implies, telegraphs his own message to the assembled grandees by pouring the water in a sloppy fashion. Hugh, no less aware of what is at stake, cannot let the insult stand. In proper tenth-century fashion, he decides to escalate, striking Alberic a blow across the face.

It is a mistake. Alberic now storms out into the city to rouse the Roman people. They remember his father, the hero of Garigliano, and resent the foreign king who squats among them. Now Alberic – Liudprand's Alberic at least – reproaches them: 'What is more debased than that the city of Rome should perish by the impurity of one woman?' What more shameful than that 'the one-time slaves of the Romans' – by which he means Hugh's Provençal troops – should now come to be their masters!

Puffed by this appeal to historical vanity, Alberic's Romans now storm back towards the Castel Sant'Angelo. The defenders are few and easily overwhelmed. Hugh escapes into the night, lowering himself off the ramparts on a rope.

Marozia, overthrown by her own son, vanishes from history. The best guess is that she ended her days in a nunnery in Rome where, one June – we know the day but not the year – she passed quietly away. She was buried with honour at the Convent of Saints Cyriacus and Nicholas on the Via Lata, not far from the house where she was born.

* * *

Old Theophylact fought for his family's ascendency; Marozia held it, against the odds. Now Alberic, Theophylact's grandson, Marozia's son and her downfall, took his turn as *senator omnium romanorum*.

The Emperor Augustus, having seized power by violence, had used the vague title *princeps* to mask the naked realities of his rule. Alberic, a millennium later, did the same. Rome had a prince again, and for twenty years, under the prince's guidance, the city prospered.

It prospered by the standards of its day, that is. Augustus's city had been home to between half a million and a million people, spreading in teeming multitudes across Rome's hills. The city of Alberic had a population of twenty or thirty thousand, scattered in clusters over what was now a vast and mostly empty expanse enclosed by the Aurelian walls. Augustus's Romans, even the poorest, had lived in great apartment blocks of brick and mortar. The poor under Alberic huddled in huts made of mud and thatch, huts that were built over the paving of old palaces and whose mud walls were stiffened with the shattered fragments of marble gods.

The remains of the ancient city were everywhere, sometimes tumbled and ruined, sometimes still standing monumental; so intact, in places, that Augustus himself, summoned back to life after a thousand years, might have had to blink a second or two before he realized the interval. Where the ancient architecture still stood, it was enthusiastically made use of. Families squatted the lower floors of abandoned blocks, patched up over the years with timber and recycled brick. Concrete vaults – *cryptae* – made excellent dwellings, as did old porticos, once haunts of poets, now roughly partitioned into peasant hovels. At night the Colosseum, looming over the ruins of the Forum, glowed with the little lights of people sheltering under the arches.

All in all, the city could make a bleak impression. The English scholar Alcuin, visiting with Charlemagne, had been moved to verse: '*Roma caput mundi, mundi decus, aurea Roma / nunc remanet tantum saeva ruina tibi*' – 'Rome, the world's capital, world's glory, golden Rome / now, wild ruins are all that is left of you.'

The Tiber, eating away at its decaying embankment, now presented an almost pastoral scene: fishing jetties and eel traps; cattle flicking their tails in the wallows; floating mills, as in the days of Belisarius, still turning gently in the woodsmoke-scented air by the Tiber island. In the spring and autumn, if there was heavy rain up in the Apennines, the river would flood, inundating the low-lying areas of the city up to the height of two men. When the water came, the Romans would perch together on the taller of the ruins, clinging for survival, literally for once, to the fragments of their glorious past.

When the river retreated, it would leave behind a coating of thick fertile mud. The impression, in the worst-hit areas, was of a city being dissolved: mosaics, marble pavements, pediments, potshards, broken toys, stashes of coin, all the human traces of Rome's vanished multitudes were gradually covered by the black earth, as if engulfed by a slow-motion natural disaster. The seven hills, icons of Rome's sacred topography, seemed to shrink into the ever-rising sediment of the valley floors.

But for the medieval inhabitants of the city, with mouths to feed, the mud was a living. Everywhere, between the standing ruins, strips of land were given over to agriculture: vegetables, vines and fruit trees flourished in the rich soil, and each house had its garden and its little yard for chickens to scratch. Alberic's Rome could seem, sometimes, more like a giant farmyard than a city.

Amid this rustic scene were areas of fertile spiritual activity. Up on the Aventine, for example, near the house where Prince Alberic was born, a new monastery of Santa Maria was growing under the oversight of the famous Abbot Odo of Cluny, brought in specially from Burgundy. All over the city monks and nuns were rousted out of their complacency by the reformer's zeal, so that the churches of Rome echoed to the sound of their *kyries*.

Likewise the aristocratic compounds were always busy. The *domus* of a rich family was a sprawling thing, a hybrid architecture of converted ancient buildings and reused fragments known as *spolia*, a complex large enough to house not only sons and daughters but also servants, retainers, relatives, chaplains – the crowd of people essential to the dignity of a medieval VIP. And the number of men who might merit such a house was growing. Sometime around the middle of the century an associate of Alberic's, one Caloleo, thought it worthwhile to build a whole new luxury development in the remains of Caesar's Forum: earth carted in for gardens; gravel roads; new stone buildings propping up the ancient walls.

Around the great houses, poorer dwellings buzzed with industry. Already – early in comparison to other medieval cities – there was a developing class of artisans. Rome's potters, in the tenth century, produced the finest ceramics of western Europe. There was wealth here, real wealth by the standards of the time, drawn not just from city gardens but from a broad and efficiently exploited agricultural territory beyond the walls – a vast hinterland of wheat that fed a population larger than in any city west of Constantinople.

Rome, like all cities in those days, saw many more deaths than births. Nonetheless, a steady stream of poor young immigrants from the countryside kept the population always swelling, and the new arrivals soon learned to partake in the Romans' civic pride. There was a sense of unique history, of a glorious past that had to be lived up to, that fed a fierce resistance to foreign domination. The Romans had fought in AD 932 for the native-born Alberic against the northerner, Hugh, and they would fight again, the militia of the twelve *regiones*, whenever Hugh returned over the years that followed. In AD 942, the militia even triumphed over a force of Magyar raiders who threatened the Lateran Basilica – the men of Rome driving off a warrior people who had been the terror of Europe for a hundred years.

* * *

No triumph lasts forever. Outside the Lateran Basilica, in those days, was a bronze statue of Marcus Aurelius on horseback – the same statue that can now be found in the Capitoline Museum.* The Stoic emperor was eight centuries old, but Romans passing by one morning in the year AD 965 found that he had grown a grotesque new dangling appendage: no less a person than Rome's city prefect, suspended underneath the statue by his own hair.

There was a new power in town. Alberic had died peacefully in AD 954, leaving the city to his son Octavian. The choice of name was unusual, and significant. In giving the boy the birth name of Augustus, Alberic was invoking, as he had done before, the spirits of Rome's

---

* The statue that stands in the Piazza del Campidoglio is a copy of the original, one of very few bronze statues to have survived from antiquity. That the Marcus Aurelius statue lasted so long is partly thanks to a case of mistaken identity: in the Middle Ages, when so many other ancient bronzes were melted for scrap, the equestrian emperor at the Lateran was believed to be not the pagan Marcus Aurelius but the Christian Constantine.

glorious history. But Octavian, the great-grandson of Theophylact, was to rule Rome in a very new way, as *princeps* and pope.*

Octavian was a very young man when he took the papal throne in AD 955 – perhaps still in his teens. Certainly, he was more a man for fighting than for prayers, launching a series of campaigns to assert papal control over disputed lands in the old exarchate of Ravenna and in central Italy. His timing, however, was unfortunate. Far to the north, after generations of political disorder, the lords of East Frankia and Germany had finally produced a leader fit to inherit the ambitions of Charlemagne.

In AD 962 King Otto I 'the Great' of Germany arrived in Rome to be anointed emperor. At his side was his formidable wife Adelheid, now empress. At his back, several thousand armoured German knights. Octavian, in his ecclesiastical guise as Pope John XII, had to bite down his pride and place the imperial crown on the German's head.

Like Charlemagne, Otto was building a holy empire, and he needed a co-operative bishop in Rome to help him do it. Octavian – a mere boy, and one with far too much dynastic baggage – was not the man for the job.

In AD 963 therefore, the notables of Rome, lay and clerical, gathered for a synod to condemn another pope. The venue was the Basilica of St Peter this time. There, by the tomb of the Apostle, the high nobility of Rome heard and spoke about the wickedness of Alberic's son: they complained about the nightly orgies at the Lateran; a deacon killed by castration; incest committed by the pope with his own aunt. They spoke of the neglect of the church, of terrifying Masses celebrated by shivering priests with rain flooding through gaps in the rafters. 'How the sodden roof beams do terrify us!' they complained. 'When we request holy services there, death reigns in the roofing.'

The pope 'set fires'. He wore a sword and a helmet. 'He drank wine

---

* Octavian may also have been a distant descendant of Charlemagne through his mother Alda, daughter of Alberic's old enemy, Hugh of Provence.

for love of the devil.' He even 'invoked the help of Jupiter, Venus and other demons while playing dice'. There was no question, Octavian must be deposed. Marozia's grandson was cast from the papal throne *in absentia*, and the man who read the sentence, covering for Otto's embarrassing inability to speak Latin, was none other than Bishop Liudprand of Cremona. It must have been the highlight of his career.

Roman resistance to the new order of things was crushed with unhesitating firmness. The twelve *decarcones* of the militia were hanged. An opportunistic antipope was removed from the throne. Marcus Aurelius acquired his unlucky hanger-on. The Roman people, for all their independence, were forced to bend the knee. 'Woe, Rome, oppressed and downtrodden by so many,' wrote Benedict of Soracte. 'At the height of thy might thou didst triumph over peoples... thou didst conquer the earth from South to North... now the Gauls have taken thee, thou wert too fair.'

As for Octavian himself, more fortunate than most, he died in bed with another man's wife, either because a devil struck him on the temple or from a sex-related aneurysm.

There were three Ottos, in the end; father, son and grandson, three ruling emperors. Their heartland was the duchy of Saxony, the flat land where the Weser and the Elbe meet the North Sea. Charlemagne long ago had brought Christianity to the Saxons with spear and sword, and over the centuries that followed the dukes of Saxony transmitted the Good News by the same method to the unlucky Slavs on the far side of the Elbe, becoming rich and powerful enough in the process to establish a new monarchy in the eastern half of the old and fragmented Carolingian empire.

In AD 955 Otto I, then king of Germany, rode to battle against a Magyar horde that threatened Europe. He carried no less a relic than the Holy Lance, which had pierced Jesus' side as he hung on the cross and, by God's favour, he routed the invading Hungarians and became the saviour of Christendom. Otto came to Rome, therefore, to claim the honour that was rightly his. An emperor was the defender of the church, the shield of the faithful. Otto had more than proved himself in that capacity, and his coronation in St Peter's set a ceremonial seal on what was already established fact.

Otto II was still a teenager when his father died in AD 973, and had rather more to prove. He had inherited a great deal of prestige, to be sure. He also had a brilliant accessory: a clever, spirited wife, Theophanu, who was an actual Byzantine princess – a living link to a millennium-old tradition of unbroken empire. But these advantages helped him little when he was beaten by Saracens in southern Italy in AD 982, and less against the Roman malaria that killed him the following year.

That left the third Otto. A toddler when his father died, he grew up in an empire ruled by women: his mother, the Byzantine princess Theophanu, and his grandmother, the dowager empress Adelheid. Mistresses of a vast territory, the Ottonian women had no time to assert themselves much in Rome. Once again the papacy became a prize for Roman aristocrats. A certain Crescentius had filled the vacuum left by the family of Alberic – Crescentius of the Marble Horse, people called him, referring to the antique statues of Castor and Pollux that stood by the family palace amid the ruins of the baths of Constantine – and with his son, who succeeded him in AD 984, he dominated the political scene for a generation, although the other half-dozen great families of medieval Rome were never far behind.

The empire, as Otto III inherited it, was a fragile creation. Under Charlemagne, the great territorial ranks – duke, count, margrave and so on – were positions handed out by the monarch himself to his loyal followers; by the time Otto III came to power, they had become hereditary titles, handed down from father to son. These entrenched aristocratic dynasties served the emperor only grudgingly. Without the support of the great dukes of Germany, Otto's military strength would vanish fast.

But being emperor was not a matter of mere military strength, and the empire was more than just marches and duchies. Parallel to the lay aristocracy ran the hierarchy of the church, of abbots, bishops and archbishops, as powerful and wealthy as any dukes or counts. The grand cathedrals of medieval cities provided careers for the brothers and younger sons of the aristocracy. The nunneries of Germany were bases from which women of the imperial family, as abbesses, could draw formidable power. Most importantly, the church, with its literate and well-travelled clerics, its rich infrastructure, provided crucial channels through which the emperor's influence could run, swinging territorial disputes in the right person's favour, getting chosen followers elected to important sees and handing out to preferred bishops the special permissions – to hold markets, coin money, collect taxes and so on – that allowed the empire's fledgling economy to function.

No surprise, then, that a young emperor like Otto, reaching manhood towards the end of the tenth century, should take an interest in the most important bishopric of all – the Apostolic See. In AD 996, having settled matters in Germany, he set off south from Marcus Aurelius's old legionary fortress at Regensburg – by Otto's day, the leading town of the duchy of Bavaria – across the Brenner Pass and down into Italy, with the Holy Lance, that harbinger of divine justice, carried before him.

His father, mother and grandfather had all been this way before, trying to bend Rome's bishops to their will. But Otto had a new approach. When, as he approached the city, the old pope conveniently died of fever, Otto rejected all the local candidates to replace him. Instead, he elevated his own chaplain, his cousin Bruno, to the papal throne. Bruno, in turn, solemnly placed the imperial crown on Otto's head in the Basilica of St Peter. He was *Otto tercius Romanus Saxonicus et Italicus, apostolorum servus, dono dei Romani orbis imperator Augustus.**

All very well for Otto, but poor Bruno – only in his mid-twenties – was now left behind, a German, friendless and alone, to survive the Roman snakepit. It was an impossible task. As soon as Otto's back was turned, the Roman nobles were in revolt again, with Crescentius II at their head and a rival antipope to set on the papal throne.

---

* Otto III of Rome, Saxony and Italy, servant of the Apostles, by God's gift emperor augustus of the Roman world.

So, in AD 998, Otto was back at the head of an army, besieging young Crescentius in the Castel Sant'Angelo. Appeals for mercy were in vain. Crescentius – taken, perhaps by treachery, although accounts are confused – was beheaded and thrown from the battlements of the fortress. The antipope, an otherwise harmless Greek called John Philagathos, was deprived of his eyes, nose, lips and tongue, stripped of his papal robes and led through the streets of Rome sitting backwards on a donkey. Once the chief priest of Christendom, now a naked and disfigured old man, he gripped the donkey's tail like a bridle and the Romans laughed at him.

It was around this time that a new motto appeared on Otto's imperial seal. The message stamped on his documents and charters was *renovatio imperii romanorum* – 'renewal of the Roman empire'.

To the dismay of Rome's aristocracy, the emperor now appeared to have taken permanent root in the city. The Palatine hill was still littered with the dwelling of Augustus; the grander ruins left by Titus's brother Domitian; the vast Sun Temple where Elagabalus had used to dance. Now, rather than knocking heads and then running back to Germany, as Ottos One and Two had done, Otto III earned his modest spot in the Roman archaeological record by building a Palatine Palace of his own.

'We declare Rome to be the *caput mundi*,' he wrote, in an imperial charter. 'The head of the world. We avow that the Roman church is the mother of all churches.' Fine sentiments indeed, but unwelcome to Rome's grandees, who guessed that Otto's enthusiasm for Rome meant his stay would be a long one. Nor did all of Rome's clerics appreciate the young emperor's circle of rather severe northern churchmen, his friendships with withered Italian hermits, nor his latest 'barbarian' pope, the brilliant Frankish intellectual and former imperial chaplain Gerbert of Aurillac, now called Pope Sylvester II.

It was a richly significant name for a pope to choose. Sylvester I was the pope who baptised the Emperor Constantine.

*

This was the most wholehearted effort anyone had made in centuries to re-establish Rome as a real imperial capital. It must have been miserable, therefore, for the serious young emperor to find himself resisted at every turn by the Romans themselves. For three years, as Otto struggled to build his holy empire, the city seethed underneath him. At last, in 1001, things came to the boil.

We have, recorded in the *Vita* of a German bishop, the words that Otto is supposed to have said – may indeed really have said – to a Roman crowd:

> Are you not my Romans? For your sake I left my homeland and my kinsmen. For love of you I have rejected my Saxons and all Germans, my own blood… I have preferred you to all others. For your sake I have made myself loathed and hated by all … and in return now you have cast off your father [himself, he means] and have cruelly murdered my friends.

'You have closed me out,' Otto continues, 'although you in truth cannot exclude me, for I will never permit that you, whom I love with a fatherly love, should be exiled from my heart.'

But the Romans could close him out. They could and they did, his stalkerish protestations notwithstanding. Otto, his power slipping, was forced to leave the city. For the next few months he haunted the marshes of Ravenna, consorting with the mystics and holy men who lived in the swamp. Then, quite unexpectedly, early in 1002, he died. After him, there were no more Ottos.

* * *

Back in Rome, the aristocrats celebrated. Chief among them was a man who had been a trusted associate of Otto in the city, a man close enough to the emperor to have been given the grand and ancient post of Master of the (non-existent) Fleet but who later led the uprising against him. This was Count Gregory of Tusculum, whose great-grandfather, on his mother's side, was none other than old Theophylact himself.

The family had survived. By cunning and determination, by luck, through the wars of Theophylact, the wiles of Marozia, the princely government of Alberic; through the adaptability, let's call it, of Gregory of Tusculum; somehow, the clan of Theophylact emerged at the end of the *saeculum obscurum* with its power more or less intact, having outlasted emperors, Saracens, Magyars, Germans and their own aristocratic rivals.

Now, as the new millennium began, the family prepared for an uncertain but not unpromising future. Emperors would always be a threat, appearing from the north to claim the old imperial capital, full of grand dreams of a restored and renewed Rome.

Meanwhile, the Roman clergy had their own growing ambitions. Perhaps, where emperors had failed, priests and bishops might succeed, uniting the fractious territories of Europe under the authority not of an emperor but of a pope.

Between these opposing forces were Rome's ordinary citizens. The farmyard days of the city were coming to an end. New industries were flourishing. A new mercantile and urban aristocracy was beginning to assert itself, pushing back against the demands of pope and emperor.

This three-way contest would shape Rome's history for generations. And, through it all, the descendants of Theophylact, aligning themselves this way and that, adapting to the changing times, would survive and prosper. The line of the counts of Tusculum, and their successors, the famous Colonna barons, would endure for a thousand years – and counting.

13

ROME-SEEKERS

The pilgrimage of Nikulás of Munkathverá

———

*c.*1154

THE YEAR IS 1154. Early summer. Not far from the city, a small party of travellers turns south off the old Via Cassia, following a well-trodden path that leads up through neat rows of vines to a pine-covered height in the middle distance.

They have come a long way, these travellers with staff and scrip. It was weeks ago that their ship set off from Iceland, a speck upon the face of the waters, keel and strakes and stem, held together through seven long Atlantic days by rivets and prayer.

Norway, at last, sea-washed skerries like black teeth under the sky. South across the Skagerrak to Jutland. Landfall at Aalborg. Then down the great war road of the Danes to the *Aegisdyrr*, the River Eider, the border of the Holy Roman Empire.

They remember, the Icelanders, how impressed they were by German manners, by the richness of the land, the splendour of the churches. They walked in the footsteps of Christian emperors, the successors to Charlemagne. In the forest south of Paderborn, they passed the place where Sigurd killed the dragon Fafnir with his magic sword, Gram. They remember the hardships of the journey, cold nights and sore feet, the constant fear of bandits on the road. They remember the sweat of the long climb up through the mountains to the Great St Bernard pass, still spotted with snow even on St Olaf's day in June.

Down into Italy, and across the the Apennines. At Luni, the Icelanders walked for miles along the beach, feeling the warm sand. Here, they were told, was the snakepit into which Gunnar of Burgundy was thrown by Atilla the Hun. Not far away, at Lucca, they saw a crucifix made by the pharisee Nicodemus in the image of the Lord. Once, they heard, the carved figure came alive and gave a poor man a shoe.

At Pisa they marvelled at the polyglot babble of traders in the marketplace: Greeks and Sicilians, Syrians and Berbers. At Siena, they stared at handsome women with dark eyes and olive skin. At Viterbo, they saw the ancient baths of 'Thithrek' – Theoderic the Goth.

They have gathered many memories, these pilgrims, seen many wonders. They are weary and far from home. But here, by the Via Cassia, their pace has quickened. Some new energy drives them on. Fingers point to the horizon.

And, yes, their leader confirms it. This hill that rises before them is the *Fegins-brecka*, the *mons gaudii*, the 'Hill of Joy'. From its crest – from the heights of Monte Mario – they will get their first sight of Rome.

* * *

Years later, safe at home by the waters of the Eyjafjord, a humble churchman, Abbot Nikulás of Munkathverá set down some fragmentary recollections of his great journey to Rome. His account, of a city he had travelled more than two thousand miles to see, is straightforward to the point of simplicity. He was not moved to verse, as more sophisticated travellers were. If he was stirred by the sight of the great metropolis spread out before him, he does not tell us so. He just lists the things he saw, in more or less the order he saw them. 'Rome is four miles in length and two in breadth', he begins, sizing up the Eternal City as a farmer might measure a prize cow.

But though it is short and matter-of-fact, the pilgrim itinerary of Nikulás of Munkathverá is a rare and precious document. Hundreds of Icelanders made the long journey south to Rome in the Middle Ages. They followed in the footsteps of Norwegians and Danes,

Angles, Saxons, Poles, Magyars, thousands of pilgrims who set out from cold northern villages, leaving behind family and farm and hearth, their whole earthly lives, to get closer to God.

But of all those pilgrim journeys, almost no record survives. Nikulás of Munkathverá, for all his limitations, left one of the fullest medieval pilgrim itineraries we have. Those thousands of faithful travellers, their voices lost, have no better spokesman than him.

Rome, Nikulás says, has 'five bishop's thrones'. Five patriarchal basilicas, he means. The first of them is *Jóns kirkiu* – the Basilica of St John Lateran.

The Lateran Basilica was a natural starting point for a medieval pilgrim. The vast and crumbling old hall, much repaired, had been the first great basilica in Rome after the Christianization of the Roman empire, eight centuries before. It took precedence, in theory at least, over any cathedral in Christendom.*

The Lateran Palace, which stood nearby, was the official residence of the popes in Rome. In the angle formed by the palace and the old basilica was an area of open ground, the *campus lateranensis*. Here, a humble pilgrim might get his first glimpse of the successor to St Peter.

Appearances were everything on such occasions: the pope, resplendent in precious silks, crowned in gold, shaded by the imperial umbrella his predecessors had received from Constantine; the people gathered below, humble, joyful and obedient. 'You see who comes!' little boys would shout when the pope appeared during Lent. 'Comes the Sun! Comes the Moon! Come the clouds of Heaven with manna!'

Arranged behind him, like saints around Christ's throne, Roman clerics made a kingly retinue: bishops, priests, presbyters and deacons row by row. A person's dignity, in those days, was measured by the quantity and quality of their followers. A pope, of course, could

---

* The Lateran Basilica or, strictly speaking, Archbasilica, is the cathedral seat of the popes, as bishops of Rome, and remains, as the inscription on the façade puts it, the head and mother church of all the churches in the city and in the world – *omnium urbis et orbis ecclesiarum mater et caput.*

boast a matchless assortment of ecclesiastics in his train.

And if ecclesiastics were not enough, popes had, over the years, gathered an assortment of more ancient personages in the *campus lateranensis*, to lend their authority to the papal retinue: there, with teeth bared and swollen teats, was the bronze figure of Rome's totem she-wolf, mother and mistress of the Roman people. Nearby, a naked boy, one thousand years old, bent to pluck a thorn from his foot. The thorn was a reminder of the crucifixion, to pilgrim minds. The wolf represented a different aspect of papal power: the popes were masters of a city that had once ruled half the world.

Reinforcing this message was a man on horseback, his gilded skin giving way to verdigris, who stretched out his hand over the square in a gesture somewhere between blessing and admonition. This, it was believed, was the Emperor Constantine, the righteous emperor who, long ago, had given Rome to the popes.

The whole story was laid out in a famous document, supposedly written by Constantine himself. Before his conversion to Christianity, Constantine was afflicted with leprosy. His pagan priests suggested that he bathe in the warm blood of infants to cure the disease. Instead, guided by a vision of the Apostles, Constantine had himself baptized.

Pope Sylvester I washed away the emperor's leprosy with holy water. In return, Constantine gave Sylvester and his successors the Lateran Palace. In the basilica, a pope might sit in authority over God's church. From the palace, he was to govern Rome and the whole western empire.

The document in question was, of course, a total fraud, probably cooked up in northern Frankia sometime in the ninth century. But the popes enjoyed the fantasy of imperial power. The so-called Donation of Constantine fed their ambitions, and the popes whose cause the forgery served felt no great compulsion to enquire too deeply into its origins.

From the Lateran Palace, each year, on the first Monday after Easter, the pope and all his retinue set off on a grand ceremonial circuit of the city of Rome.

Some thirty or forty thousand people lived Rome in those days; the city was bigger and busier than it had been under Marozia or Alberic two centuries before. The population was still far too small, however, to fill the space enclosed by the Aurelian walls. The landscape through which the Easter procession began to move was green with vines and fruit trees. In the outskirts, by the Lateran, only scattered peasant hamlets stood where the apartment blocks of the ancient city had been.

As the great papal procession approached the Colosseum, the density of settlement began to increase. Medieval Rome was built around a series of close-knit neighbourhoods called *regiones*, each with its major church, its own set of dominant families, its own militia and its own distinct character. One such neighbourhood had grown up around the church of Santa Maria Nova, built a hundred years earlier at the edge of the ancient Forum, among the ruins of what had been the Temple of Venus and Rome.

The Easter procession passed through as many of these *regiones* as it could. Turning north from the Forum past Trajan's Column, it went up towards the crowded districts along the Via Lata, the modern Corso. Turning west again, the procession passed through the Campus Martius, where little islands of bourgeois respectability held themselves aloof, as best they could, from the Ripetta, the hurly burly Tiber port nearby, with its workshops and warehouses, loud with the cries of the river boatmen who plied the stream.

On the far side of the river, by the Vatican hill, was the Borgo Leonino, a district that was both legally and spiritually distinct from Rome proper. Since the Saracen raids of the ninth century, the Borgo had had its own circuit of defensive walls. The Castel Sant'Angelo loomed above, dominating the bridge that linked the Borgo to the city.

At St Peter's, the pope would stop to celebrate Mass, before setting off back towards the Lateran. The return journey took a more southerly route. Passing the busy *regio* of Pigna and the less reputable Scorteclari (named either for its tanneries or its brothels but, either way, for traders in skin) the procession made for the ruins of the Theatre of Pompey, then back to the Forum, the Colosseum and, at last, the Lateran again.

*

Though the procession was held at Easter, its significance was as much political as religious. The processional route, and much of the accompanying ceremony, was copied from the *adventus* – the procession by which a newly elevated pope took possession of the Eternal City. This *adventus*, in turn, was part of a tradition of formal entries into the city that stretched back to the pagan emperors.

Constantine, when he 'donated' Rome to the church, was understood to have given Pope Sylvester the right to use all the *imperialia* of the Roman state. Each Easter, Sylvester's successors put on an imperial show. They glittered with gold and jewels, went mounted on proud white horses just as the emperors had done. Behind the pope came the city prefect with his judges, wearing his ceremonial robe and his traditional stockings, one red and one gold. By the pope's side was a subdeacon, holding a special towel in case the pope should want to wipe his mouth or spit. Ahead, riding in pairs, came the priests, deacons and bishops of the most ancient churches of Latium, a group of senior clerics who had come to be known as the 'hinges' of the church – in Latin, the *cardinales*. Lesser clergy lined the route, clutching crosses and thuribles, burning clouds of incense to purify the path the pope had to tread and to protect his blessed nostrils from the earthly odours of the streets.

Rome's poorer citizens gathered in crowds to watch the pope pass by. At points along the route, there would be distributions of money from the pope to his loyal subjects. 'I take no delight in silver and gold,' a cryer would proclaim, on the pope's behalf. 'What I have I give to you.' Or: 'He dispenses to the poor; his justice remains forever and ever.'

All along the way, the Roman *populus* showed its appreciation by constructing a series of temporary arches: flimsy scaffolds stretching across the road, decorated with whatever bits of fabric and bright metal the people of the *regio* could lay their hands on. Sometimes a garland of laurel or palm would add its particular symbolism: palm for Jesus entering Jerusalem; laurel for the triumphant generals of ancient Rome.

This was the message that the popes wished to send to their subjects, and to the world. And yet, Nikulás of Munkathverá, following the processional route towards the Lateran in the year 1150, might, if his eye was very acute, have been able to detect certain troubling countermessages, legible in the fabric of the city itself. Why, he might have asked himself, did so many of the houses along the way have the air of fortresses? What trauma had ruined the church of the Santi Quattro Coronati, and why, newly rebuilt, did it present so high and formidable a front towards the city? What was the meaning of the newly erected obelisk that jutted towards the Lateran from the brow of the defiantly un-papal Capitoline hill?

There were other forces at work in the pope's city. In Germany, new emperors were always reaching southwards to the old imperial capital; in the *regiones* of the city and the baronial castles of Latium, new families were always rising, with ambitions of their own. And then, often overlooked, there were the ordinary people in the streets, the crowd, cheering now, but always fickle when hunger made them so. In this city no pope could ever hope to rule in peace for long.

* * *

'A second bishop's throne,' says Abbot Nikulás, 'is in the church of Santa Maria Maggiore, where the pope must sing Mass on Christmas Day.'

That is all. The great basilica on the Esquiline hill provokes no further comment. The Icelander makes no mention of the seven-hundred-year-old mosaics that glittered at him from the walls, the shining assembly of toga-clad saints watching him from the the transept arch overhead. He was unperturbed, certainly, by any pagan emanations wafting up from the old Temple of Cybele buried beneath his feet, the pagan Great Mother superseded by a greater one.

Nikulás arrived in Italy in the summer, crossing the mountain passes while the weather was kind. He may, therefore, have been lucky enough to be in Rome on 15 August, for the festival of the Assumption of the Virgin Mary.

This was a highlight of the liturgical calendar; every pilgrim in

Rome would have been there, joining the crowd that gathered in the evening in front of the Lateran, more people gathered in one spot than most Icelanders had ever seen. Those who could afford it brought candles, and as they set off in procession towards Santa Maria Maggiore, they began to sing, the human mass flowing through the night like a bright river.

At the head of the procession went Christ himself, or at least, Christ's image: a miraculous icon created by St Luke, with the help of heavenly angels. At the church of Santa Maria Nova, and at Sant'Adriano a little further on, the feet of the image were tenderly washed. Now, borne aloft again, Christ turned north to meet his mother at her basilica on the hill; his mother, who, taken up and enthroned among the angels of heaven, would also be his symbolic bride.

At Mass at Santa Maria Maggiore, on Assumption Eve, there would have been readings from the Song of Songs, a book that was, it was believed, a sort of prophetic love song to Mary: 'Behold, thou art fair, my love; behold, thou art fair; thou hast doves' eyes within thy locks: thy hair is as a flock of goats, that appear from mount Gilead.'

Mary was the image of perfect womanhood – a perfect womanhood that was, in the twelfth century, being given new imaginative force by the chivalric romances spreading through Frankish Europe. But the veneration of Mary was not just a concern for Roman women. Mary, as bride of Christ, was understood to represent God's holy church. As Mary was to Christ, so the church should be to God. As Mary might intercede with God, so the church should be a shining bridge from earth to heaven. And, just as Mary was pure and immaculate, so should the church be. If the church was corrupted, what hope was there for the common herd of humankind?

But the church often did fall short of its proper perfection.

By the ruins of the Forum, close to Santa Maria Nova, the pilgrim guides in those days would turn aside to show their pious charges two pairs of shallow depressions, sunk into a slab of ancient stone.

It was recorded in the Book of Acts that once a certain magician named Simon tried to buy the favour of the Apostles by offering them gold. He had seen the power of their miracles. 'Give me also this power,' he asked them, 'that on whomsoever I lay hands, he may receive the Holy Ghost.' Peter was not impressed: 'Thy money perish with thee.' The gifts of God were not to be purchased for a handful of coins.

So far, the story would have been familiar to northern pilgrims. Less well known, however, was what happened afterwards. The tradition, handed down in certain late-antique apocrypha, was that this Simon Magus travelled to Rome and deceived the people there with his conjuring. He even tricked them into worshipping him as the son of God.

Right there by the church of Santa Maria Nova was the site of the final confrontation between Simon and the Apostles. The Emperor Nero judged the contest. Simon Magus summoned demons to lift him high into the air above the Forum. But as Simon flapped triumphantly about, Saints Peter and Paul knelt down and prayed to the Lord so vehemently that their knees left marks in the solid stone. Simon's devils were banished. The magician fell to earth and broke into four pieces, and although Nero watched his body carefully for three days and more, he did not, despite his messianic promises, rise again.

Simon was smashed, and yet Simon's sin – the buying and selling of holy offices – was alive and well in the medieval church. In 1045, a hundred years before Nikulás of Munkathverá's pilgrimage, a most spectacular example of 'simony', as it was called, had shamed the Holy See: Pope Benedict IX, grandson of Count Gregory I of Tusculum (and great-great-great-grandson of old Theophylact himself) had sold his own papacy.

After the death of the Holy Roman Emperor, Otto III, in 1002, Count Gregory of Tusculum held the papacy in his hands, just as Marozia and Theophylact had done. Two of Gregory's sons, one after the other, occupied the throne of St Peter. Benedict IX, Gregory's grandson, followed close behind. The Tuscolani prospered. No longer content to be city administrators in Rome, they left urban squalor behind, to start building strongholds in the Alban hills, like proper Frankish lords.

But while the Tuscolani played at castles, the city was changing under them. By the middle of the 1040s, Pope Benedict had become so unpopular with his flock that his position had become untenable. In May of 1045, he sold the See of St Peter and retired to the countryside.

The buyer, a man named John Gratian, was perfectly respectable, but his timing was poor. In the north, a new king had managed to assert his right to rule over the feudal magnates of Germany. This king, Henry III, was now ready to come to Rome to have the pope crown him Holy Roman Emperor.

Henry III was a devout young man. Accordingly, he was horrified by the mess he found waiting for him south of the Alps, where three different men were all claiming to be pope. Of the three, Gratian was the only one with any virtues, and he was disqualified from the papacy by the fact that he had bought it. At a special synod at Sutri, Henry declared all three papal contenders equally unfit. The Romans had proved themselves irredeemably corrupt; Henry trusted only loyal German churchmen to clean up the See of St Peter.

With German popes ruling in Rome, the whole make-up of the cardinalate and the papal court began to shift. Out went the old Roman aristocrats, and in came new men, devout and serious: respected bishops from the heartlands of the empire; a radical monk, Humbert of Moyenmoutier; the famous hermit Peter Damian. Most important of all, a reformer known as Hildebrand, so fierce in his zeal that Peter Damian nicknamed him the 'holy Satan'.

The 'barbarian popes', as the Romans called them, were determined to reform and purify the church in Rome and across the world. They intended 'to reform this iron age to one of gold, with the hammer of just government'. Just as the Apostles Peter and Paul had smashed Simon Magus into pieces, so the reforming popes would smash simony, turning back 'to the innocence of the primitive church'.

This was no easy task they had set themselves. Simony was everywhere, as was another deplorable practice: priests keeping wives or concubines. This was widespread but, as the reformers explained, it was an affront against God. The blessed sacraments should never be profaned by the hands of a priest fresh from some woman's bed.

It was hard enough persuading the Roman clergy to give up their bribes and their women. But the German reformers also had to contend with the dangerous political environment in which they found themselves. Ambitious aristocrats like the Tuscolani were always ready to make trouble when the opportunity arose, and other dangers lurked further afield. One reformist pope felt compelled to lead an army against bands of Norman mercenaries who had taken over much of southern Italy. Humiliatingly defeated, he spent most of his last year of life in Norman captivity.

But though the task was hard, the reformers were determined. In 1059 they achieved a major victory by fixing the rules of papal succession. There would be no more buying and selling of papacies. Popes, thenceforth, would be elected by the senior clerics of the church, the priests and bishops known as cardinals.

The priority, above all, was to free the church from the worldly entanglements that always threatened to corrupt it. Money and women and the politicking of ambitious aristocrats were all distractions that turned the church away from its proper purpose: the praise and glorification of God.

On Christmas night of the year 1075 the 'holy Satan', Hildebrand, celebrated mass in Santa Maria Maggiore. Hildebrand, recently enthroned as Pope Gregory VII, was a true believer, a man so pious that he only ate herbs and beans and would weep openly while administering the sacraments. He and his reformist friends had held sway in Rome now for some thirty years. And that Christmas, in Mary's great basilica, as the singing of the choirs lifted his spirit up towards the mosaic angels shining above, he must have felt optimistic about the state of the church.

God had a challenge in store for him that evening: a raid on the basilica by the armed followers of a disgruntled aristocrat. For one long night, Gregory was held captive in a tower in the district of Parione, his fate uncertain.

But the following morning, a miracle: the people of the city had rallied, coming together as one to demand the release of their pious pope. Rome was his. The earthly city really could be what the reformers dreamed it could be: the seat of a supreme and irreproachable papacy, the glorious capital of a purified and exalted church. Rome could be renewed, to glitter in glory like the golden city shown in the mosaics of Santa Maria Maggiore, a city that looked like Rome but was really Jerusalem.*

The kings of Germany – those kings who were accustomed, when possible, to have themselves crowned Holy Roman Emperors – had brought the reform movement to Rome and given it the backing it needed to flourish there. In doing so, they had thought to emulate the founder of the renewed empire, the great Charlemagne. They, as much as anyone, wanted a church that was powerful, dignified and respectable. Such a church would reflect its glory on to the emperors themselves.

But over time the ambitions of the reformers grew. For Hildebrand – Pope Gregory – and his allies, it was not enough to rescue the church from the petty politics of Rome. They came to feel that the church should also be free from the politics of the empire. Emperors often awarded powerful bishoprics to their followers. They used their loyal bishops as instruments of imperial control. But if a man was made a bishop for some service he had done a king, was this not, the Roman reformers started asking themselves, a subtle form of simony?

The dispute came to a head in 1075, the year of the Christmas kidnapping. Trouble had flared up in Milan where a pious mob, known scornfully as the 'rag-pickers', or *patarini*, had rioted against the corrupt and venal clergy there. A new young emperor, Henry IV, was

---

* The top right-hand corner of the transept arch of Santa Maria Maggiore shows Jesus being presented at the temple in Jerusalem. The people in front of the temple, however, wear Roman tunics. And the temple itself is decorated with gorgon heads, just as was the Temple of Venus and Rome.

ruling in Germany at the time. Dismayed by the unrest in Milan, he appointed a new archbishop. But Pope Gregory, a quiet supporter of the patarine cause, responded furiously. Bishops were not to be appointed at the whim of emperors, but according to the will of God. The quarrel escalated quickly. In 1076, the emperor formally deposed the pope. Shortly afterwards, the pope excommunicated the emperor.

It was a battle of two equally stubborn wills, but the exigencies of imperial politics forced the emperor to back down first. In 1077, in a piece of well-choreographed political theatre, Gregory and Henry met at the fortress of Canossa in the Appenines. There, while Gregory sat warm in the great hall, the king of Germany and Italy, rightful emperor of Rome, fasted at the gates for three days, a hair-shirted penitent, humbly begging for the pope's pardon.

But Gregory's triumph was emptier than it looked. Henry had sacrificed some measure of his imperial dignity, but he had made few real concessions, and had gained precious time in which to consolidate his position back at home. When the emperor returned to Italy, he brought the full might of Germany with him. In 1084 the imperial army entered Rome, warmly received by the Roman people.

Gregory had overreached. Now, abandoned by his friends, the pope was trapped in the Castel Sant'Angelo. Only one potential ally remained to him. The Norman warlords who had humiliated Gregory's reformist predecessor had proved themselves ruthless and cunning, holding their own in southern Italy against Byzantines and Saracens alike. Now, with the emperor against him, it was to the Normans that Gregory turned. Led by the notorious Robert Guiscard – Robert the Fox – the Normans broke Gregory out of the city.

However, true to their Viking heritage, the Normans sacked large areas of Rome on their way through. The Basilica of the Santi Quattro Coronati, one of the oldest churches in Rome, was left blazing behind them on the Caelian hill, a baleful beacon signalling the ruin of Gregory's exalted vision for Rome.

* * *

The third bishop's throne, Nikulás records, 'is in the *kirkiu Stephani et Laurenti*' – the Basilica of St Laurence, outside the walls.

At the end of the fourth century AD, back when a few stubborn pagans still clung to their old philosophies, a certain Eunapius of Sardis complained of Christian barbarism: 'They collected the bones and skulls of criminals who had been put to death for various crimes… made them out to be gods, haunted their sepulchres and thought that they became better by defiling themselves at their graves.

This was true, more or less. Christians venerated martyrs and worshipped at their tombs. It was for this reason that, in Nikulás's day, pilgrims doing the circuit of the great basilicas would turn east from Santa Maria Maggiore, away from the city, heading out beyond the old Aurelian walls. There, along the Via Tiburtina, was a vast and ancient cemetery called the *ager Veranus*, where the bones of St Laurence lay.

Laurence was a popular saint – one of Rome's first deacons, toasted to death on a gridiron during one of the persecutions of the third century AD. It was Laurence who was meant to have joked to his executioner: 'Turn me over, I think I'm done on this side.'

Admirable sangfroid. All the same, there was something remarkable – perverse, it would have seemed, to pagan eyes – about the pilgrim willingness to trek around outside the city walls among the bones, making the long walk out in winter rain or summer heat to reach Laurence's basilica. There were other martyrs even further afield who claimed their share of faithful traffic: poor little martyred Agnes by the Via Nomentana; St Sebastian, pincushioned with arrows, on the Via Appia; St Valentine on the Via Flaminia; St Pancras across the river; St Anastasius, a strangled Persian soldier, furthest out of all.

What was it, unsentimental Romans must have wondered, that impelled the pilgrims to plod their endless extramural circuits? Indeed, what brought them to Rome at all? It was no small undertaking to travel across half of Europe, across mountains, forests and the war-troubled plains of northern Italy. Many who set off on pilgrimage never came home again.

For lords and knights with money to spend, the path was easier.

On horseback you could get to Rome from the English Channel in six weeks, if all went well. But poorer pilgrims might easily take a year to get to Rome and back again, assuming they weren't murdered by robbers on the way, or frozen to death in the Alps. There were some pilgrim hospices to be found along the route, but most of the time the pilgrims were left to choose between a cold night in a hedge and the doubtful mercies of a roadside inn.

And yet each year thousands still came, as they had been coming for centuries, armed only with the traditional pilgrim equipage: a staff for walking and a scrip to hold a little food and coin. This last was always kept symbolically unfastened, to signify both generosity to others and faith that the Lord would provide for the needs of the self.

Some pilgrims came for healing. It was well known that the physical remains of saints had magical powers. Miracle cures were common even at the tombs of very minor saints in those days – but if the local shrine could not cure your palsy or your kidney stones, or fill a barren womb, the pilgrim road beckoned.

Rome was able to boast the remains of some of Christianity's most potent martyrs and Apostles. On the Tiber island, where the Temple of Asclepius had stood, the flayed Apostle Bartholomew – or some of his skin at least – had taken up the old healer-god's vacant position. At the Forum, pilgrims could venerate the relics of the doctor saints, Cosmas and Damian, whose church now occupied the Temple of Romulus, built by the Emperor Maxentius in honour of his drowned son. Or you could aim even higher: the Lateran Basilica had the heads of Saints Peter and Paul themselves, and each September, just at the time of year when ancient Romans had celebrated the *Ludi Romani*, the heads were paraded through the streets for all to see.

The physical presence of the holy relics was crucial. The souls of the saints, the holy multitude of the Church Triumphant, were held already in the hand of the Lord. At the same time, saints, like everyone else, would ultimately enjoy the full and literal resurrection of the body. The bodies of the saints were not mere discarded vessels, in other words. The bones and skulls that propped up Rome's old churches had an ongoing and meaningful link to heaven; to be close to these relics was to draw close to the divine.

Of course, as any properly educated priest could have told the pilgrims, there was no need to travel to get close to a God who was, by his very nature, everywhere. But ordinary people with any experience of kings and counts and dukes and so on knew perfectly well that approaching any ruler directly was futile. One had to have friends in high places. Accordingly, they preferred to beg their petty favours from martyrs and Apostles, or even from the Virgin Mary, than dare to trouble the Father himself.

Anyway, though an educated priest might have discouraged pilgrimage, poor pilgrims might not have had much contact with a priest at all, let alone an educated one. The church, in those days, was above all concerned with its own purity, the clergy more focused on the glorification of God than the salvation of their fellow man. Clerics were encouraged to withdraw from the world, to raise themselves above it. The job of a priest, just as in ancient Rome, was, above all, to ensure that rituals were carried out at the right time and in the proper manner. Pastoral care was a much lower priority. Both baptisms and marriage could be – and regularly were – performed by lay people. Many of Rome's pilgrims would hardly have heard a sermon in their lives, lives which offered them little opportunity to express religious feeling.

Pilgrimage, despite all its dangers, was attractive partly because it was something to do: a way to express deeply held religious feelings that found no outlet in the church; to go out into the world like the Apostles, leaving behind the sins and cares of daily life. Rome, when and if the pilgrims reached it, was a grand stage on which a person's piety could be performed and enacted. Everywhere in the city were reminders of great religious drama: here was the crib in which the newborn Jesus was first laid; here was the spot where they grilled St Lawrence; here were the chains that bound St Peter in his prison; here they boiled the Evangelist, John.

The relics of the saints were props, bringing the familiar stories thrillingly to life. Rome had the Seamless Robe and Crown of Thorns that Jesus had worn before his crucifixion. It had Mary's veil, the coat of John the Baptist, a piece of bread from the Last Supper. There was even a scrap of circumcised foreskin, the Holy Prepuce, the only bodily part that Jesus left behind.

Best of all Rome's relics was the sacred veil of St Veronica, with which Jesus had wiped his brow on the way to be crucified. When he gave it back to the pious woman, she found that it was imprinted with a *vera icona*, a true image, still preserved in St Peter's Basilica after a thousand years: the true, authentic face of the Saviour Himself.

In the evenings, the pilgrims would come tramping back within the walls. Few lingered in the city proper. It was safer to pass the evenings on the other side of the river, in the Borgo Leonino. It was here that most pilgrims had arrived in Rome in the first place, coming down the slope of Monte Mario and through the new Leonine Walls. Here, below St Peter's, was the frothing deep end of Rome's pilgrim trade, where hungry and well-practised Romans circled the floundering newcomers, drawn by the scent of pilgrim coin.

Innkeepers were a particular menace. Surviving laws from Rome and elsewhere provide a record of attempts by city administrators to protect pilgrims from the touts who clustered at the gates, plucking at travellers' cloaks or grabbing the bridles of their horses, baffling them with patter, hollow promises of soft beds and unwatered wine. Sickly pilgrims were in particular demand – Rome's malarial climate killed visitors by the hundred each year, and a dead pilgrim might leave a nice windfall for the keeper of their final hostelry, so long as the church didn't get wind of it first.

The best strategy for pilgrims in the face of this onslaught was to stick close to their own countrymen. In previous centuries there had been well-established pilgrim colonies in the city, the so-called *scholae*, where Franks, Frisians, Saxons and Lombards could cluster together for safety, comforted by the sound of familiar accents, so far from home.

But by Nikulás of Munkathverá's day the *scholae* appear to have been in decline. There were fewer northern Europeans in Rome in the twelfth century than there had once been. There were so many other towns competing for pilgrim business: Compostella, Cologne, Walsingham, even Jerusalem. Increasingly it was more recent converts who came to see Christendom's founding city: Icelanders like Nikulás; Poles and Wends from beyond the Oder; Magyars from Hungary, whose grandfathers had been the terrors of Europe.

These newcomers found what accommodation they could: the richer pilgrims might take rooms in the various degrees of lodging house; the poor, as often as not, just lay down to sleep in the porticos of churches, even in the atrium of St Peter's Basilica itself.

Nikulás, characteristically, has nothing to say about where he stayed and in what company. Pilgrims were meant to be sober and ascetic, hearts lifted up to God – and Nikulás was not just a pilgrim but also a monk, soon to be an abbot. Perhaps he passed his Roman nights in unremarkable prayer and contemplation.

But not all pilgrims were so virtuous, nor all churchmen. This was the age of the Goliards, rambunctious young clerics, happier in a tavern than in a cloister, who scandalized the university towns of Europe with their antics, their appetites, their bouts of irreverent verse. Even in Rome, among the martyrs, there may have been some opportunity for medieval boisterousness after dark. The Goliardic drinking songs collected in the famous *Carmina Burana* give a sense of the spirit of such occasions: *In taberna quando sumus, non curamus quid sit humus* – 'When we are in the tavern, we don't trouble ourselves about the meaning of life.'

Outside in the dark, in castles and palaces, the grandees of Rome worried about politics, alliances, the endless struggle of faction against faction. But in the tavern, people made no fine distinctions. *Tam pro papa quam pro rege, bibunt omnes sine lege* – 'As for the pope, so for the king, we drink to both without counting.'

* * *

The fourth of Nikulás's 'bishop's thrones' was at *Páls kirkia*, the Basilica of St Paul, out beyond the walls on the old road to Ostia. To get there, Nikulás had to skirt the city, heading southwards towards a landscape of ruin.

The way may have run by the Porta Latina, the only one of Rome's gates that Nikulás mentions by name. Not far away were the tombs of the Via Appia, the villa and Circus of Maxentius, silent and overgrown. Just inside the walls, the mausoleum of the Scipios lay buried beside the road, not to be discovered for another five hundred years.

Rising ahead were the great green arches of the baths of Caracalla, the ancient brickwork now covered over by layers of vegetation. Even after a millennium of decay, the scale of the ruin was sufficient to attract Nikulás's attention. It was unthinkable that so vast a building had served as a mere bathhouse for the city plebs. Whoever was guiding Nikulás told him it was a palace of the Emperor Diocletian.

The inhabitants of medieval Rome were proud of the city's ancient remains, though they were often foggy about details. The ancient buildings were familiar and well-known features of the urban landscape, useful as shelters, quarries or strongholds. You could navigate by them. A manuscript from Nikulás's time describes certain papal processions in the city. But the author, a canon of St Peter's, plots out the routes with reference not to churches, as one might expect, but to ruins: go left at such and such a temple, right at these baths, straight on at this old palace. The ruins were landmarks that reached across history, mapping the medieval city on to the ancient one, so that as you went through the streets you moved as if through both cities at the same time.

Nikulás of Mukathverá arrived in Rome at a time when interest in the ancient buildings was higher than ever. About ten years earlier, a Roman cleric had written what was, in a sense, the city's first guidebook. The *Mirabilia Urbis Romae* – the *Wonders of the City of Rome* – is an extraordinary compendium of medieval myths and half-remembered history. It is a record of a Rome in which each shattered arch or broken pillar attracted its own legend, in which each half-buried vault became the palace of an emperor or a temple to some infernal god.

In the Rome of the *Mirabilia*, Christian and pagan stories are intermingled. Just as the ancient Romans invented the story of Aeneas in order to tie their city to Homer's *Iliad*, so in the Middle Ages the Romans found ways to trace their origins to the Old Testament. It was Noah and his sons who founded Rome, readers learned, arriving after the Great Flood.

Ancient myth was woven neatly into the new Christianizing framework. The palace of Romulus had stood in the Forum, the *Mirabilia* claimed. Inside, there was an image set up in gold that was destined never to fall until a virgin bore a son. Nearby, on the Capitol, the Emperor Augustus saw a vision of the Christ and worshipped him, following the advice of a prophetic sibyl. On the Campus Martius, the great general Marcus Agrippa spoke to the goddess Cybele and built the enormous Pantheon in her honour. Only many years later, we are told, did Pope Boniface IV finally re-dedicate the temple to the Virgin Mary, in order to prevent Romans from being seized by devils as they passed by the door.

There were other dangerous vestiges of paganism in the city. A gateway to hell had once opened in the Forum, it was believed, on the spot that the ancient Romans called the Lacus Curtius. There was still, it was feared, a dragon hiding underneath the ruins of the Temple of Vesta.

More often, though, the emphasis is on the scale and grandeur of ancient Rome: the richness of the precious metals that covered the arcades of the Circus Maximus; the great height of the monumental columns; the splendour of the arches; the baths full of 'fresh waters so the court could dwell in the upper chambers in much delight'. The ruined Colosseum had once been a miracle of engineering: 'A heaven of gilded brass, where thunder and lightning and glittering fire were made, and where rain was shed through slender tubes.'

There was a touch of melancholy to Rome's awestruck rehearsal of past glories. By the Vatican was an obelisk, familiar to pilgrims who used to crawl through the gap under its metal base in the hope of absolution. At the obelisk's point was a gilded orb believed to hold the ashes of Julius Caesar. 'Caesar who once was great as is the world,' says the *Mirabilia*, 'now in how small a cavern thou art closed.'

*

The Rome that Nikulás found in 1154 had, for centuries now, been a city strung out between two poles, the great papal basilicas of the Lateran and the Vatican. Over those centuries, the stretched fabric of the city had worn thin. The pilgrim traffic that kept the city alive was largely restricted to the churches of the periphery, avoiding the old urban core.

Nikulás appears to have followed this usual pattern on his way to the Basilica of St Paul. But though the pilgrims mostly kept to the outskirts, there had been, in the years leading up to Nikulás's pilgrimage, new stirrings of political life at the city's heart: on the sacred heights of the Capitoline hill.

The Capitoline had dominated Rome since the days of the first kings, when Tarquin the Elder built the Temple of Jupiter Optimus Maxima on its crown. The Capitoline was the *caput mundi*, the *Mirabilia* tells us: 'the head of the world... adorned with marvellous works in gold, silver, brass and costly stones'. Among these, supposedly, had been carved figurines representing all the countries in the world that were subject to Rome. Each statue had a bell around its neck that would ring to tell the senators when that country was in rebellion.

How far Rome's horizons had shrunk! During the crisis years after the papacy of Gregory VII, the city had at times come close to total anarchy. The emperor far off in Germany was distracted by civil war. In Rome, the senior clergy spent their energies on factional infighting. Many of the older noble clans had abandoned the city, moving out to grand castles and estates in the surrounding countryside – the same process by which the descendants of Theophylact had become counts of Tusculum.

New families sprang up to fill the power vacuum. These were not landowners, in the traditional aristocratic fashion, but bankers and merchants, men whose wealth was drawn from the economic life of the city itself.

From the Capitoline hill, you could pick out their various strongholds, rising above the rooftops: simple square towers in recycled brick, combining military strength with a crude phallic symbolism that anyone could understand. Trastevere was dominated by the Normanni and the Tebaldi. On the near side of the river, a man calling himself Crescentius had built a tower lavishly adorned with ancient *spolia* – one of the few such towers still standing today. The Pierleoni held the river bank to the north, controlling the Tiber bridges from their fortress in the old Theatre of Marcellus. There were the Corsi, the Boboni, the Papareschi, the Sant'Eustachio. Strongest of all, were the mighty Frangipani, who had fortified part of the Colosseum itself, controlling the main road towards the Lateran.

Once, boasts the *Mirabilia*, senators had gathered on the Capitol to send Roman armies to the very edges of the earth. Now, the city was divided against itself, fragmented into semi-fortified enclaves whose petty-aristocratic masters could hardly project power into the next street.

There was a strong sense, in medieval Rome, of the city's historic greatness. The Romans were very much aware of the lofty position which their distant ancestors had held – and the uncomfortable difference between Rome's power then and its power now was one of the things that prompted the creation of the *Mirabilia* in the first place.

The *Mirabilia* has often been described as an aid to tourists – a sort of medieval Baedeker. But, as Nikolás's account shows, pilgrims were surprisingly oblivious to the history of the ancient city. Anyway, a book was too cumbersome and too precious a thing to carry around in a pilgrim pouch. In fact, the *Mirabilia* was probably created for the benefit of Romans themselves.

The papacy of the radical reformer Hildebrand – Pope Gregory VII – contributed to a broader destabilization of the Holy Roman Empire. Imperial weakness allowed the cities of northern Italy to gain a measure of independence, and with independence came increasing prosperity. Around the year 1100, the city of Milan overtook Rome in population for the first time.

As the twelfth century advanced, the newly independent cities evolved new forms of government. By the time of Nikolás's pilgrimage, many Italian cities had come to be ruled by so-called 'communes' – sworn associations of leading citizens and nobility. This was a form of government that recalled, more than anything else, the classical city states of the ancient world. Once again, after an interval of centuries, individual cities were meaningful political actors in their own right. But the new system required new sources of legitimacy, new mythologies.

A new literary genre began to flourish: descriptions of cities. Self-description was a form of self-definition. It had become a matter of vital importance for cities to mark out their own sacred limits, to boast of their fine buildings and great accomplishments.

Rome could not allow itself to be left behind. The *Mirabilia* is much more than just a catalogue of curiosities. It is an attempt – by quarrelsome, divided Rome – to mark out a place among the rising cities of Italy. The *Mirabilia* reasserts Rome's place as the Eternal City, a city above all others, a city of which Milan and Pisa and the rest are the merest and slightest imitations.

* * *

The greatest of Rome's five patriarchal basilicas, Nikolás saves for last: *Pétr's kirkia*, 'the noble church of St Peter, very large and splendid. There is to be had full absolution from the perplexities of men.'

By now, St Peter's was extremely ancient. Eight centuries had passed since the first Christian emperors had cut the basilica's foundations into an old cemetery on the flanks of the Vatican hill. The years had not been kind. Even so, the building was impressive: huge, by medieval standards, and rich with history, with its venerable murals and mosaics, its antique pillars, its foundation of millennium-old graves. Outside stood the golden-orbed obelisk that had once been the turning post for chariots in Nero's Circus – where Rome's first Christians were torn apart by hounds. Inside, by the high altar, was the spot where St Peter himself was crucified upside-down. So, at least, Nikulás believed, and certainly no Roman was going to disabuse him.

Amid the jutting keeps of the urban aristocracy, the church had to assert its proper station. From around the year 1100, as if in answer to the aristocratic fortresses, churches in Rome began growing bell towers, pushing up rows of plain round arches into the Roman sky.

These were a rare architectural novelty in a city whose church-building was otherwise extremely conservative. Even so untutored a traveller as Nikulás of Munkathverá must have noticed the contrast between the solid brick basilicas of Rome and the cathedrals he had passed by in the north, heralds of the new Gothic style. The best Gothic cathedrals were stretching themselves ever taller and narrower, leaping through curves and countercurves, vaults soaring towards spires. Roman churches, by contrast, were stubbornly earth-bound.

Rome remained aloof from showy architectural experimentation. Roman church-builders had an architectural vocabulary of their own, a vocabulary handed down from the golden age of Constantine. Nave and apse and transept followed the pattern of the old imperial basil-icas. Round arches sat heavy on antique pillars. Brick walls enclosed perfect static volumes, stately hemispheres.

The church of Santa Maria in Trastevere, for example, completely rebuilt around ten years before Nikulás arrived in Rome, is a perfect mixture of reused Constantinian archetypes: the high transept was a copy of the transept at the Basilica of San Paulo; the flat-beamed colonnade lining the nave was copied from St Peter's and the columns have the same ionic capitals as Santa Maria Maggiore.*

Let barbarous nations innovate, the building seemed to say. Rome's glorious past provided a foundation that could not be improved upon. 'On this rock I build my Church.'

Behind the Frangipane stronghold at the Colosseum was another im-portant twelfth-century church, the Basilica of San Clemente. Here, as at Maria in Trastevere, every brick and tile delivered a message of ecclesiastical unity and strength. The vine that sprouts in glittering

---

* Amid this chorus of pious architectural quotations, the deeper memory of Rome's pre-Christian past clings discordant and faint. It would have taken a much more learned visitor than Nikulás to recognize that the columns of the nave had once sheltered bathers at the baths of Caracalla or to spy the little heads of the gods Isis and Serapis that peep from the scrolls at their tops.

mosaic across the apse represents the church itself, reformed and restored to its ancient vigour – a visitor like Nikulás would have been deaf to the Dionysian echoes. The magnificent marble patterns that curl along the floor in what was then the very latest style are traced for a truly regal pope, 'the father of kings, the priest of the most high'. His processional route up the nave is marked out in slices of porphyry from ancient pillars, a stone that was strongly associated with the ancient emperors.

These bold assertions of strength and continuity were made against a background of constant crisis. The fortunes of various emperors waxed and waned. In Rome, Pierleoni schemed against Frangipani, and vice versa. The calm geometries of the new churches obscured a reality of conflict and turmoil.

At San Clemente, the erasing of uncomfortable realities had taken especially literal form. The gleaming twelfth-century basilica was built on top of a much older basilica from late antiquity, which itself was built on top of an ancient shrine to the Persian god Mithras, which remains, to this day, buried under the two church floors.

The older basilica at San Clemente had been redecorated a little before the twelfth-century remodelling, with murals commissioned specially by a pair of local lay people: Beno de Rapiza and his wife, Maria Macellaria – Maria the Butcher. 'I, Maria the Butcher, had this painted for fear of God and the remedy of my soul', reads an inscription above a blocked and buried door. The family portraits are on a wall not far away: Beno, Maria, a daughter called Altilia and a little son called Clemente, after the saint. The church was probably meant to be their final resting place.

But this sort of lay involvement with the church was exactly the type of thing that generations of papal reformers had been fighting against. The church was supposed to be removing itself from the secular world, renewing itself in majesty. Rome's basilicas were not there to be daubed by nobodies. The new basilica at San Clemente, built by a proper cardinal, a prince of God's holy church, came splatting down on top of the old one like a reproving hand, to obliterate Beno and Maria from the record.

'No one is so wise', writes Nikulás, 'as to know all the churches in the city of Rome.' Historians have devoted a great deal of attention to decoding the subtle differences between the grand new churches of the twelfth century, between Santa Maria in Trastevere and Santa Maria in Cosmedin; San Crisogono, San Clemente and Santi Quattro Coronati.

But these grand medieval churches rose in common against a background that has long since disappeared – a city littered with the little shrines of popular, rather than papal, piety: churches dedicated to St Benedict of the Kettle Makers or St Nicholas of the Scissor Manufacturers; St Nicholas of the Lime Burners; Mary of the Blacksmiths. Such churches were everywhere in medieval Rome, often tiny, sometimes just a single room with an altar, buried deep in the vaults of some ancient ruin.

None of these churches was noticed by Nikulás of Munkathverá, and none of them survives today. The religious life that they sustained was very different from the religion of popes and cardinals – and the more exalted the dreams of popes and cardinals became, the less worthy these messy proletarian churches seemed of a place in St Peter's city. The papal reformers wanted a Rome of porphyry and gold, a glittering mosaic Rome at the head of a united, purified and all-powerful church.

The grand new churches of the twelfth century rose solid and imposing over the ruins of the old. Likewise, the church itself had begun to construct itself anew as an institution. Around the year 1140, less than fifteen years before Nikulás's arrival in Rome, a Bolognese cleric by the name of Gratian compiled a monumental text known as the *Concordia Discordantium Canonum*, the *Concordance of Discordant Canons*, a landmark in the development of ecclesiastical law.

Church rights and property were, by this period, extensive and dauntingly complicated. Legal conflicts between or involving churchmen were frequent: which church ought to collect such and such a toll; who should sit where at the archbishop's feast; had this abbot or that bishop been correctly ordained?

To find answers to such questions, diligent church lawyers had to dig back through centuries' worth of accumulated manuscripts: the records of provincial synods; stray letters from this or that pope; the writings of the church fathers. Gratian's *Concordance* was an attempt at simplifying matters. At last, the main sources of legal authority were assembled in one text and, as far as possible, harmonized.

At the same time, inspired by the bold claims of the old papal reform movement, a new pope, Innocent II, started experimenting with a new sort of legal instrument: the papal decretal, an official letter in which the pope would respond to a legal query directly, citing no authority but his own.

Something was taking shape here. The church's newly harmonized legal apparatus came closer than ever before to binding it into a single, coherent organization, one set of laws transcending the petty boundaries of fiefs and kingdoms. The pope and his secretaries could dispense legal judgements across the continent. During the reign of Innocent II, the papal court, or 'Curia', began to be not just a monarch's entourage but also something like an international court of appeal.

Naturally, the influx of legal appellants to the papal Curia provided another precious stream of income to Rome. Educated churchmen mingled uneasily with the common pilgrims, disdainful of their crude piety and half-baked ideas. Still, they had to sleep and they had to eat, and Rome could provide, for a fee.

Papal coffers swelled too. It would not be long before bitter little jokes started circulating in Europe: how the Romans only worship Saints Albinus and Rufinus – Saints Silver and Gold. '*Roma capit singulos et res singulorum*', goes one Goliardic rhyme. '*Romanorum Curia non est nisi forum.*' 'Rome hoovers up everyone and everyone's business. The Roman Curia is nothing but a marketplace.'

By the mid-twelfth century, the papacy was in a strong enough position that it could start re-asserting control over the lands of the old papal principality – the central Italian territories granted to the pope by Charlemagne. City families, the Frangipani especially, started chipping away at the once impregnable holdings of the counts of Tusculum. Meanwhile, the pope led a Roman militia against the neighbouring town of Tivoli to bring it back under direct papal rule. The See of St Peter was in the ascendant once again.

* * *

Until, quite suddenly, the papal project was halted by opposition from an unexpected quarter. The pope had forgotten – an easy enough mistake to make – about Rome's little people, the ones erased and left behind: Beno, Maria the Butcher; the kettle makers and lime burners and scissor manufacturers who now emerged from their humble houses and primitive churches to make a bid for a Rome of their own.

Ordinary Romans had participated enthusiastically in Pope Innocent II's successful campaign against Tivoli in 1143. But, when Tivoli surrendered, it swore allegiance to the pope alone.

The Romans were furious. Cheated of their share of the spoils of Tivoli, the Roman militia now occupied the Capitoline hill. There they declared the reinstitution of a body which had not held governing authority for more than a thousand years: the senate of Rome.

Not that the ancient and the medieval senates had anything much in common. The ancient senate, apart from anything else, had been a fiercely aristocratic body, while the medieval version was a creation of the middle class, an assembly of tradesmen and working professionals that would have horrified a Brutus or a Cato. Also, though the senate had long vanished, the title 'senator' had never really gone away. It had been used extensively by Theophylact and his clan, for example.

Still, Rome's newest crop of 'senators' were unusually assertive in their attempt to dress their bid for power in the toga of ancient precedent. The anti-papal uprising was billed as a proper *renovatio sacri senatus*, a restoration of the sacred senate. In letters to the emperor up in Germany, the senators boldly reclaimed the old Roman acronym: SPQR, *Senatus Populusque Romani*, the Senate and People of Rome.

There was no doubting the senators' ambition. Leaning up against the eastern flank of the Capitoline above the Forum were the remains of the ancient Roman administrative centre called the *Tabularium*, from which the government of the city had once been run. Now, the senators started construction on a new palace, the *palazzo senatorio*, perched directly on top of the ruins. As a final touch, the senators also managed to procure their own obelisk. Set up on the Capitoline height, it was visible across the city, answering the papal obelisks at the Vatican and Lateran with all the silent eloquence of a raised middle finger.

Pope Innocent II died shortly after the uprising in 1143. His successor, Lucius II, was determined to reassert papal supremacy. In 1145, he marched on the Capitol leading a mob of heavies provided for the occasion by his allies, the Frangipani. The assault was a disaster. The pope's men were routed by the senators, and in the chaos, the pope himself was struck on the head by a flying brick. A few days later, he died of his wounds, the first and last pope to die in battle, and at the hand of his own flock.

Not long after the dramatic events of 1145, a radical cleric named Arnold of Brescia made his way to the city. This Arnold, a charismatic monk with radical views on church reform, provided the senatorial movement with new theological impetus. The bold monarchical claims of the medieval papacy were condemned. The pope should renounce his earthly powers, chorused the suddenly very pious senators. He should devote himself to prayer.

This battle between senate and pope was raging even as Nikulás of Munkathverá arrived in the city. The pope had the backing of Europe, but Arnold and his senators held the heart of Rome. Meanwhile, in St Peter's Basilica, Nikulás and his Icelanders offered their prayers, and what little money they could, up to God.

Not long after Nikulás left the city, the quarrel was brought to a bloody, if impermanent, conclusion. In 1152, power in Germany had fallen to the formidable Frederick Barbarossa who, for the next twenty years, would terrorize the upstart communes of northern Italy, until the Lombard cities won their decisive and unexpected victory against him at Legnano in 1176.

In 1155, with all that still to come, Barbarossa arrived in Rome. On the way, he met and captured Arnold of Brescia, who had been driven out of the city at last. As a gift to the new pope, on the occasion of his imperial coronation, Barbarossa delivered the heretic Arnold into his hands, to be hanged and then burned. It was traditional, in Rome, to pay executioners from the coins left by pilgrims on the altar of St Peter.

Despite this imperial intervention, the senate managed to hold on, and, taking advantage of yet another papal schism over the following decades, enjoyed the peak of its political power in the city. In the 1170s and '80s, senatorial armies finally destroyed the power of Tusculum. Only a minor branch of the old Tusculan clan remained, a family that would become known as Colonna, perhaps the greatest aristocratic family in Roman history. In the city, Frangipani and Pierleoni sat quiet in their fortress-houses.

Meanwhile, in Rome's churches and libraries, the legal experts multiplied. A unified church, with a unified body of law, needed an arbiter in case of disputes. Rome fulfilled that need, and the more the papal court issued judgements, the bolder were its claims to ultimate authority. At the end of the twelfth century the seeds planted by Gregory VII and nurtured by Innocent II would flower at last into a truly international and imperial church, directed by the most forceful pope of the entire Middle Ages: Pope Innocent III. The senate was dissolved. The churches of kettle makers and scissor manufacturers were forgotten.

But by the time any of this happened, Nikulás of Munkathverá was far away. Had he found in Rome what he was looking for? There was a tradition in Rome that favoured pilgrims might approach the tomb of St Peter, which was buried under the centre of the basilica in his name. There they would dangle a little strip of cloth called a *brandea* down through a special hatch in the floor, lowering it on a string until it almost touched the very bones of the saint. And here the miracle: when you raised the cloth, it was always found to have been imbued with some weighty and mysterious nothing. Loaded with ghosts, the cloth was heavier coming out than going in.

14

THE LAUREATE

Petrarch and Rome

———

1341–1354

SOMEWHERE IN THE narrow streets just off the Via Lata, where the Colonna barons have their urban strongholds, the ruins of an ancient portico lie buried under the haphazard houses of medieval Rome. People have no time for ruins now, in these troubled early years of the 1330s. The city is at war with itself. Colonna fighters patrol the alleys; crossbowmen scan the roads from their high towers. None of them know, or care, that here, thirteen centuries ago, there used to be a map of the world.

The map was made in the time of Augustus: a monument to peace, to the broad untroubled stretch of Rome's dominion. And as Rome's empire crumbled, the map crumbled too, vanishing away like so much else into the Tiber mud. But though its fragments would never be found, the memory of the map never quite passed away. Among those who saw it was a young geographer from Spain, Pomponius Mela, who was inspired to sketch out in writing a description of earth's regions and continents.

Pomponius lived and died, and soon every detail of his life was forgotten. But his picture of the world survived the decades and then the centuries. During the fifth century AD, as successive waves of barbarians crashed through the Italian peninsula, an imperial scribe at the court at Ravenna copied the old scroll, adding his signature.

Three hundred years after that, the Frankish emperor Charlemagne set his cathedral schools to work preserving ancient documents. At the monastery of St Germanus, in Burgundy, a Benedictine scholar, Heiric of Auxerre, added his annotations to a fresh Carolingian copy.

From the tenth century to the twelfth the manuscript was held at Orleans, gathering dust in a neglected corner of some royal library. But sometime in the twelfth century, someone thought it worthwhile to make another copy.

And now, at last, in the 1330s, that copy of a copy of a copy has made its way into the hands of someone who understands its true significance. Augustus's map disappeared a thousand years ago, but his idea lives on: a world of peace, order and unity; a world ruled by Rome.

* * *

Francesco, son of Petracco, was born in the old Etruscan city of Arezzo in the year 1304. His father – Petracollo, people called him – was a notary, a man of humble enough origin but careful education, trained in the art of letter writing, the sealing of contracts and the niceties of official Latin.

These were disputatious times in Italy. A century and a half had passed since the overthrow of the Roman commune at the hands of Frederick Barbarossa. But while Rome's commune had failed, many other Italian cities were still clinging on to the idea of collective government; still maintaining some degree of independence, even under the noses of the great competing powers: popes, emperors and kings.

Politics in these free city states could be ruthless – Petracollo, a Florentine by birth, had been condemned in his native republic on trumped-up corruption charges, a victim of conflict between the 'white' and 'black' Guelphs – factions within a faction. But though his accusers kept his property, he escaped before they could cut off his right hand – and, even for a notary in exile, there was a good living to be made from Italy's litigious and increasingly prosperous middle classes.

The old feudal order was beginning to crumble. But the papal territory around Rome was still dominated by great baronial families, ruling from their castles and fortified towns. Greatest of all were the

Colonna, distant successors to Alberic and the counts of Tusculum, the oldest and strongest of the dynasties of Rome.

Of course the Colonna were deeply involved in papal politics. At the end of the 1290s, Pope Boniface VIII, a member of the rival Caetani clan, had excommunicated the whole extended Colonna family, driving them into exile in France. It was a mistake. In 1303, the year before little Francesco was born, the Colonna were back in Lazio, supported by a French army. Boniface was captured and roughly handled, struck in the face by a steel-gauntletted Colonna hand. He never recovered from the shock and died in October that year, leaving Rome and its hinterland firmly under baronial control.

The city, clearly, was no longer a fit base for papal rule. In 1309 a new pope, Clement V, moved the papal court to the Provençal city of Avignon. It was a pleasant spot, a possession of the Angevin king of Naples, a papal vassal, close to the centres of European power in France and Germany and blessedly free of both rebellious barons and malarial mosquitos, the twin scourges of Roman life. And although the pope always planned, in principle, to return to his Roman flock, the passing months and years found pontiff and cardinals installed ever more comfortably on the banks of the Rhône.

The sleepy old town was now a bustling centre of papal bureaucracy – just the sort of place for an ambitious notary to get ahead. In 1312, Petracollo the Florentine took ship from Genoa to Marseilles, then headed up-river to Avignon with his son Francesco beside him.

For four happy years, the boy Francesco breathed the quiet air of Provence. The family had settled at Carpentras, a short day's ride from the papal court, at the head of the wild valley of Vaucluse, and Francesco and his younger brother Gherardo spent long hours splashing in the pools of the Sorgue or ranging across the slopes of Mont Ventoux. At the same time, Francesco made his first expeditions into the fields of history, his tutor having introduced him to the joys of Cicero.

In 1316, Francesco was sent off to study law at the university of Montpellier. But the boy's enthusiasm for ancient authors continued to tempt him from the strait and narrow: Cicero above all, but also Virgil and other Latin poets. Law was the path to a respectable future, but Francesco's eyes were fixed firmly on the long-vanished past. Petracollo, a stern and ambitious father, is supposed, on one visit, to have burned Francesco's stash of frivolous Latin books, despite the boy's howls of lamentation.

The best legal education in Europe was to be had in Bologna, and there Francesco was duly sent, arriving pimply and precocious in the autumn of 1320. He had a good aptitude for legal studies, but still lacked enthusiasm. More fun to run wild with his student friends, admiring the city's famous courtesans or rampaging around the country to sneak back past the closed gates after dark, climbing over the city's crumbling palisade.

But although Francesco later described his student years as seven years wasted, the time he spent in Bologna was not spent in vain. Francesco, charming, intelligent and urbane, was making friends: highly educated, intelligent young men, and women too, friends to whom he would remain close for the rest of his long career.

The notary's son returned to Avignon something of a dandy, fond of fine perfumed gowns and crippling tight shoes. 'What pirate could have tortured us more cruelly than we did ourselves?' Francesco wrote to his brother, remembering the burns they had suffered together through inexpert use of the curling iron.

It was as a dandy, in the year 1327, that Francesco encountered a young woman named Laura, one April in Avignon outside the church of St Clare. His love verses, composed in the Tuscan dialect of his youth, would make her famous, and win him an undying place in the poetic canon.

Vidi fra mille donne una già tale
Ch' amorosa paura il cor m'assalse
Mirandola in imagini non false
A li spirti celeste in vista eguale

Among a thousand women one I saw
Who filled my heart with trembling love and fear

I gazed at her – true vision without flaw,
With angels she an equal did appear.

But for all his noisy adoration of the incomparable Laura, the most
important relationship Francesco forged in those days was of quite a
different sort. Francesco had come to the attention of a lively young
churchman: Giacomo Colonna.

Giacomo Colonna was the youngest son of Stefano il Vecchio, the
current Colonna patriarch, and therefore a nephew to that Colonna
whose mailed fist had stunned Pope Boniface some twenty years
before. This ancestral violation had done nothing to keep the younger
generation of Colonnas out of the church. Giacomo's older brother
Giovanni was a cardinal, and Giacomo himself had risen rapidly to
become bishop of Lombez, at the foot of the Pyrenees.

There, in 1330, Francesco spent the happiest summer of his life.
Lombez was poor and dirty; the bishopric humble. But Francesco was
captivated by the company. There was Giacomo, the generous host;
Lodewyck, a Belgian lutenist, and Lello, a dashing Roman nobleman,
and along with Francesco they made a merry band, swapping poems
and songs, and whiling away the long summer evenings with talk of
love and other matters: the wisdom of the ancients; the mysteries
of religion; the merits of the church fathers, Jerome versus Augustine.
As a mark of admiration, Francesco gave his companions new names:
Lodewyk the Belgian was rechristened Socrates, while Lello became
Laelius, the famous friend and companion of Scipio Africanus.

Francesco was conjuring a new name for himself too. At university
he had been distinguished by a simple patronymic, Petracchi. Now,
he stretched those staccato syllables into something languid and Lat-
inate: he would be, from then on, Francesco Petrarca – in English,
Petrarch.

On his return to Avignon, Petrarch was invited into the service of
another Colonna, Giacomo's brother, Cardinal Giovanni. This was
a much appreciated generosity. His duties were few; his income ade-
quate and secure and, more valuable still, he now had access through

his patron to the highest reaches of society, both at court in Avignon and across Europe.

It was a splendid position for a man with Petrarch's particular enthusiasms. Soon, amiable man that he was, he had a network of friends stretching across Europe, bound together, above all, by a shared enthusiasm for the ancient past. Always Petrarch badgered his new friends with the same request: to send him books.

Petrarch had been collecting books all his life, of course. Cicero had been a particular favourite, and Seneca too, but he read whatever he could get his hands on with the attention of a true scholar. At the end of the 1320s he had compiled an edition of Livy more complete and accurate than any that had existed to that date – an academic achievement that would set an example for centuries of painstaking classical philology to come. On a journey to Paris and the north on Colonna business in 1333 he was forever turning aside to ransack some mouldy monastic library or cathedral school, rescuing valuable ancient manuscripts in the process. He found a rare speech of Cicero's and a book of Propertius's. And it was during this period, too, that he discovered the faded two-hundred-year-old parchment on which was copied the geographical work of Pomponius Mela, descended from the long-lost map that had vanished from the Colonna quarter of Rome so long before.

Petrarch's love of books was more than merely academic. Books, he claimed, were his 'secret friends'. 'Sometimes they sing for me; Some tell the mysteries of nature; Some give me counsel for my life and death.'

Through his books, Petrarch was able to engage with the ancients, 'conversing with them more willingly than those who think they are alive because they see traces of their stale breath in the frosty air.' Later, indeed, he would write letters directly to the ancient authors, adding them, in a sense, to his network of friends – Cicero, then Virgil, Horace and Seneca: 'I daily listen to your words with more attention than one would believe.'

These trans-temporal encounters were sources of both pleasure and moral value, a value that seemed painfully absent from the more immediate reality that surrounded him every day. Petrarch, growing older, was increasingly disgusted by the venal buzz of Avignon: the palaces; the intrigues; the crowded streets; the noise; the prostitutes, whose services Petrarch could not quite bring himself to forgo despite the resulting agonies of shame. But walking with the ancient poets, he felt himself lifted from the filth of the papal Babylon. New vistas opened up before him, a bright new virtual geography that stretched both outwards in space through his web of scholarly friends and correspondents and also back through time, back to the imagined days of the vanished empire where Petrarch could discern, hazily unfolding, the bright contours of a vanished golden age.

At the centre of Petrarch's mental landscape was the city of Rome, the pole around which his various worlds all spun. It was the focus of his historical interest; he knew almost by heart the stories told by Livy, of the city's foundation, the Gauls, of Brutus and the fall of the Tarquin kings. 'What else then is all history,' he asked, 'if not the praise of Rome?'

But Rome was a concern for the present too. In 1335 Petrarch wrote an extraordinary verse letter on behalf of the Eternal City, begging the pope to end the church's 'Babylonian Captivity' in Avignon and return to St Peter's See. Through Petrarch's pen, the city speaks; Roma Dea, the city-goddess of ancient days, now reduced to the condition of a ragged widow, with 'filthy aspect and untended hair'. 'Rome I am called,' she pleads. 'Do you not, Father, recognize my aged countenance, the sound from my trembling throat...?'

The tone is an echo of Ovid – the poet banished to the desolate Pontic shore. Like Ovid, Petrarch longed to be in Rome, but while Ovid's exile was a mere matter of physical distance, Petrarch's was an exile of time; an exile of the spirit. He longed for a city that had fallen; a Rome that no longer existed – and perhaps never had.

Nevertheless, when his old friend Giacomo Colonna invited him to visit the Eternal City, Petrarch leaped at the chance. Friends had warned him that he might find Rome's condition disappointing. And the journey was hard: the countryside through which he had to travel was at that time held by the Orsini clan, deadly rivals of his Colonna hosts. Only when Bishop Giacomo arrived in person with an escort of a hundred knights was Petrarch able to reach the city itself.

He found it poor, filthy and violent, deserted by its pope and scarred by years of street fighting and baronial civil war. The population had fallen to perhaps as low as 17,000, the smallest it had been since the Gothic Wars. The area of settlement had shrunk, too, retreating towards the river. The ancient heart of the city was now more or less completely abandoned: it was in this era that the Forum came to be known as the 'field of cows', the *campo vaccino*; the Capitoline was the *monte caprese*, or 'goat hill'.

But even in its dilapidated condition the city still made a mighty impact. Wherever he went, Petrarch populated the ruined streets with antique ghosts plucked out of Livy: unchaste Vestals; Lucretia falling on her dagger; Curtius, throwing himself down the abyss in the Roman Forum. In the evenings he would climb the fragile brick of the baths of Diocletian to sit on the ancient vaulted roof and watch the city spread out below. 'I know not where to start,' he reported to his patron Cardinal Giovanni. 'Overwhelmed as I am by the wonder of so many things… In truth, Rome was greater, and greater are its ruins, than I imagined.'

Back in Avignon, Petrarch threw himself into the project of Roman revival with renewed vigour. He continued to urge the pope to return to his seat in Rome. At the same time, he embarked on a pair of literary endeavours on an unprecedently grand scale – works that would herald a rebirth of classical literary culture: in prose, Petrarch would attempt a series of biographies, *De Viris Illustribus*, retelling the stories of Rome's great men from Romulus to the Emperor Titus. This was to be written, not in the degenerate Latin of the Middle Ages, but in the most exact antique style, using the language of Livy and Cicero.

In verse, Petrarch imagined something even more dramatic. He had always been a particular admirer of Scipio Africanus, the saviour of Rome during the Hannibalic Wars. Now, just as Virgil, long ago, had given the Emperor Augustus a poetic vision of Rome's founding myths, so Petrarch set out to deliver a poetic vision of real Roman history: the *Africa*, twelve books of perfect Virgilian hexameter, recording the defeat of Carthage by the armies of the Roman republic.

These projects were wildly ambitious, but Petrarch was sure that such works – unlike the vulgar Italian sonnets he kept firing off at his beloved Laura – would secure him a place among the great poets.

As word spread of his new endeavours, the learned men of Europe started to take notice. Petrarch's friends and correspondents led a swelling international chorus of praise. By 1340 the promised masterwork had become the object of heated anticipation in the two leading cultural centres of the age: the University of Paris and the royal court of the king of Naples, the Angevin Robert the Wise. In September that year two letters arrived from opposite directions – twin fruits from seeds that Petrarch himself had planted. Each letter invited Petrarch to come and be crowned a poet laureate. He just had to choose where. Would he accept the laurels from the learned masters of Paris or from the citizens of Rome?

Paris, in 1340, was a far greater city than Rome, richer, safer and grander. But Rome, with its antique ghosts, exerted an irresistible pull. In February 1341 he took ship for Naples, where King Robert would pronounce him fit to be crowned in Rome.

Naples was one of the most civilized cities of the age: a place of piety and poetry and boating trips; a place where kissing in churches was so popular that it had to be specifically banned. Petrarch spent a happy month here, taking part in archery competitions in the palace gardens and talking literature with the king. Here, he underwent his royal examination, which he passed *summa cum laude*. But although the king would happily have crowned him on the spot, Petrarch insisted that the ceremony must take place in Rome as planned.

How could it be otherwise? The ceremony of laureation had very little precedent in recent history. This was an honour that Petrarch had largely dreamed up for himself, an amalgam of medieval university practice with an ancient Roman tradition that awarded a leafy crown to the winner of a certain poetry contest on the Capitoline (this crown was meant to be of oak, but Petrarch, perhaps with his Laura in mind, wrongly presumed that the crown must be of laurel). Petrarch, keen antiquarian that he was, had found references to the ancient prize in Statius and Suetonius. Now he was determined to re-enact the ceremony with himself in the starring role.

It was an extravagant occasion. Young noblemen in scarlet robes led him in procession, chanting his verses. In the footsteps of Pompey and Caesar, he marched in triumph over the wrecks of ancient buildings, past the new Franciscan church of Maria in Aracoeli to the summit of the Capitoline. With a blare of trumpets, he entered the *Palazzo Senatorio*, the old headquarters of the Roman commune. His path was cleared by an escort of Rome's foremost citizens, flower crowned and clad in festive green.

Silence fell. The poet delivered his oration – a discourse on some lines from Virgil: *sed me Parnasi deserta per ardua dulcis raptat amor*; 'I, across the wild slopes of Parnassus, the Muses' home, am drawn by sweet desire.' Desire for Laura; desire for the laurels of victory; desire for a restored and shining Rome.

The Romans wept, Petrarch remembered later, when the speech was done. The laurel crown was placed upon his head. Petrarch recited a victory sonnet, blushing gracefully as the crowd raised a clamour of love and praise. He was pronounced a true poet, a learned teacher and an honorary Roman citizen.

After the ceremony, Stefano Colonna, formidable head of that most formidable clan, gave a banquet in Petrarch's honour. He had cause to be satisfied. His sons, Giovanni and Giacomo, had of course been instrumental in arranging the whole coronation, and Petrarch's glory reflected well on the family that fed him.

Petrarch too was happy. He had spoken to the Romans of the value of poetry. Reaching across the great gulf of centuries, the ages that men were just learning to think of as 'dark', he had touched the living light that had been kindled by the ancients; a light whose modern representative he himself aspired to be.

Petrarch enrolled himself among the ancients, partly in the hope of inspiring a new flourishing of literature, learning and poetry. And inspiring he may well have been. In Rome, at that moment – very likely in Petrarch's coronation crowd – was a young man for whom Petrarch's vision rang as loud and clear as the trumpets that had played him up the Capitoline; a man with an answering vision of his own.

* * *

The young man's name was Niccolo, son of Lorenzo. The Romans clipped the names, in their usual way: Cola di Rienzo, they called him on the streets where he lived. The effect would be something like Nick, Larry's son.

Here, in the riverside district of Regola, Cola's parents kept a tavern, supplying food and lodging to riverboat pilots and fishermen and pilgrims travelling along the Tiber bank. A fugitive emperor had stayed there once, Cola later claimed, hiding from Orsini patrols during a Guelph-Ghibelline war in 1312 – and nine months later, Cola himself had been born, destined for greatness. So he added a specious imperial lustre to his humble origins.

Cola's myth did his real father a great injustice. Old Rienzo may have been a mere tavernkeeper, but he did not stint on his son's behalf. At the first chance, the boy was sent off to live with an uncle in Lazio, safely away from the violence of Rome and the city's malarial summers. He was provided with a first-class education: 'from his youth he was nourished on the milk of eloquence', as his anonymous biographer later put it. By the time he returned, a young man, around 1333, he was well on the way to becoming a member of the professional classes – a licensed notary.

A new world opened up before Cola, the tavernkeeper's son. Notaries were everywhere in late medieval Rome: they were socially fluid, highly trained in the learned culture of the day, able to converse as well with counts as with costermongers, and indispensable to both. Notaries were witnesses to truth, guardians of authentic record. In Rome, where the higher levels of government were so anarchic, the city's notaries retained a precious aura of civic authority. The Roman administration, such as it was, depended on notaries to serve as its judges, ambassadors and bureaucrats.

Notaries were defenders of law. And law, in those days, needed defending. There was, in Rome as in other Italian cities, a growing middle class: lesser landowners, merchants, bankers, guildsmen, ranchers, canons, shoemakers, millers and so on. But the enterprises upon which their budding prosperities depended were threatened by the lawlessness and violence of the great baronial clans – those dozen or so great old families whose towers loomed over the city.

Cola's early career was constantly overshadowed by baronial conflict. In 1333 Stefanuccio Colonna killed Bertoldo Orsini with his own hands in a roadside skirmish in the Campagna. In 1335 fighting between the Colonna and the Orsini led to the destruction of the old Milvian Bridge, blocking off a main route into the city. In 1338 the Orsini allied with the Savelli to continue their assault. The fighting was right on Cola's doorstep. Cola's local church, Sant'Angelo in Pescheria, happened to be the titular church of Cardinal Giovanni Colonna. Beside it, a looming curve of reinforced antique brick showed the outline of the ancient Theatre of Marcellus, a fortified strongpoint of the Savelli clan (who had inherited it from the Pierleoni).

At some point in those chaotic years, a brother of Cola's appears to have been caught up in a melee and killed. 'Cola could do nothing to help him,' says the anonymous *Life*. 'He thought for a long time of avenging his brother's death; he thought for a long time of rescuing the ill-governed city of Rome.'

By 1343 the Roman bourgeoisie, the *popolo grasso*, had had enough. Gathering in their thirteen districts, the old *rioni*, they rose up to install a popular government of thirteen Good Men to put an end to baronial squabbling. Ambassadors were dispatched to Avignon to beg papal support. Among them was Rome's most promising rhetorician: a handsome young notary from the Regola district, known for his quick mind and his strange fleeting smile.

There, before the court of Pope Clement VI at Avignon, Cola di

Rienzo, in his new official role as Rome's 'Consul for Widows and Orphans', poured out the full measure of his persuasive powers. He begged the pope's pardon for the coup of the Thirteen and affirmed the pope's overlordship of the Roman government; he hoped that a jubilee pilgrimage year might be declared for 1350; and he asked, above all, that the pope heed the suffering of his abandoned flock and return in person to Rome.

His speech was so excellent, says the *Life*, 'that Pope Clement loved him at once'. The Roman ambassadors were hopeful. 'Let the City of Rome rise again from its fall and long decline,' Cola reported home. 'Let her take off her mourning widow's weeds… For behold! the heavens have opened, and from the Glory of God the Father, the rising day of Christ, pouring out the light of the Holy Spirit, has prepared for you… a grace of unexpected and wondrous clarity.'

Cola's celebration was premature. Impressive as his speech might have been, the pope had no intention of leaving Avignon while Roman politics remained so unstable. Nor did he intend to support the government of the Thirteen. That May the pope named two baronial senators to run the city, terminating the popular regime.

Cola was now the ambassador of a dissolved government. Worse yet, his constant invectives against the barons had attracted the hostile attention of Petrarch's patron, Giovanni Colonna. Cola, stranded in Avignon, fell into deep disfavour. He was left stranded and penniless, the anonymous biographer records: 'With his little coat on his back, he stood in the sun like a snake.'

On the other hand, Cola had also come to the notice of Petrarch himself, Rome's newly minted poet laureate.

'No one is more ignorant of Rome', Petrarch had once complained, 'than the Romans themselves.' But Cola stood ready to prove him wrong. Like Petrarch, Cola was an avid reader of Livy, Seneca and Cicero; he knew by heart the legends of Romulus and Caesar. As a young man, striding the streets, he had gazed at the marble fragments of the ancient city, reading the inscriptions on old tombstones (*non fui, fui, non sum, non curo*) and shattered arches: 'Where are those good Romans?' he used to exclaim. 'Where is their high justice? If only I could live in such times!'

Here was a height of feeling to match Petrarch's own – and Petrarch delighted in it. 'As I recall that most inspired and earnest conversation we had two days ago,' he wrote to Cola, 'I glow with such zeal that I consider your words those of an oracle... I seem to have been listening to a god, not a man... Whenever I recall [your words], tears leap to my eyes and grief again grips my soul.'

It was a meeting of two kindred spirits. And by the sound of Petrarch's letter, they had allowed themselves to dream – to dream something too great to be trusted to writing. 'Oh! If it would only happen in my day,' was all that Petrarch could commit to the page. 'Oh! If I could only share in so noble, so glorious an enterprise.'

Petrarch's support was enough to earn Cola the grudging acceptance of Cardinal Giovanni Colonna, and that, in turn, was enough to restore him to the good graces of the pope. Clement had anyway perceived that the clever and ambitious young notary might have his uses. In 1344, the pope sent Cola back to Rome to serve under the senators as Notary of the Civic Chamber.

The manner of Cola's return to Rome was a clear signal of papal favour. And the post to which he had been appointed gave him intimate access to the financial workings of the Roman government. He was perfectly placed to undermine baronial control of the city.

Hostilities were opened at a meeting of the Roman Assembly in the Franciscan church of Santa Maria in Aracoeli on the Capitoline: in a blast of silver-tongued invective, Cola accused the councillors of 'sucking the blood of the poor.' A Colonna ally slapped him in the face. Another made a filthy gesture at him. But Cola bore the insults patiently. He had, at least, managed to get under the barons' skin.

His second assault was an ambush: a surprise salvo of hostile propaganda that appeared one day, painted on the wall of the Palazzo Senatorio, the seat of the city administration. From the top of the Capitoline hill Cola's painting shouted its message: here was Rome, once again a widow in torn clothes, foundering in a stormy sea, praying for salvation. In the waves beneath, four women lay drowned in four shattered ships: Babylon, Carthage, Troy, Jerusalem – the mighty fallen. 'Once you held dominion over all,' the ruined cities whisper. 'Now, here we await your fall!'

Overhead, in the threatening sky, bestial forms crowded in ranks, blowing barbarous horns to stir the raging sea: lions, wolves and bears; dogs, pigs and roebucks; lambs, dragons, foxes, cats, goats, monkeys. Lest the meaning of the allegory be mistaken, each row of beasts was labelled: here are the robbers, murderers and adulterers; here the false officials and notaries; here the barons and their followers. Above them all, a shining figure stood, a figure from Apocalypse, with two swords issuing from his mouth: the Divine Majesty.

For his third demonstration, Cola invoked the authority of the ancients. In the great Constantinian basilica at the Lateran, he mounted a pulpit to address the congregation, speaking in the local dialect, Romanesco, for everyone to understand. Old Stefano Colonna and his son, Cardinal Giovanni, sat in silence while Cola expatiated on the meaning of the antique bronze tablet which hung behind him: Rome's ancient and treasured copy of the *lex de imperio Vespasiani*. The Senate and People of Rome, he explained, had once bestowed power even upon emperors – a great power that they might, if they chose, reclaim.

This was an extremely bold interpretation of the text – Vespasian's law was not at all intended to support such populist claims – but the long-dead emperor was not there to protest his enlistment in Cola's cause. Cola had managed a powerful and clever display of classical erudition.

And while his lips spoke the language of humanistic scholarship, his costume was blaring its own quite separate and equally powerful message to the crowd: he wore a cape, white-hooded with a white hat, circled with gold crowns; protruding from the hat was a silver sword.

* * *

Long before this, at the beginning of the thirteenth century, a young merchant from Assisi had made a pilgrimage to Rome. Outside

St Peter's Basilica, the usual crowds of beggars held out desperate hands. Much moved, the young man took off his fine clothes and exchanged them for a beggar's rags. From that day forward, he would devote his life to God.

Francis of Assisi's spiritual seeds found fertile ground. He preached a simple message of love, poverty and brotherhood. He was a layman himself, with a religious vision accessible to the lay multitudes, the humble everyday Christians excluded from the high theology of universities and cathedral schools. Before long, his followers had multiplied to become an entirely new religious order: the Franciscans.

Franciscans, like their spiritual cousins the Dominicans, were a so-called 'mendicant order' – they lived in the everyday world, rather than in monastic seclusion, surviving on alms or by their own labours. Holding property was strictly forbidden.

But as the years went by, this rule was found to be irritatingly impractical. Gradually, the majority of Franciscans found ways to get round the restriction. Only a hard core clung to the truly mendicant life: the Spirituals, or Fraticelli, radical friars who kept themselves pure through a diet of poor food and rich apocalyptic prophecy.

Christians had, of course, been worrying about the End Times for some thirteen hundred years. But the Franciscan Fraticelli had their own particular spin on the events promised by the Book of Revelation. Inspired by another thirteenth-century holy man, Joachim of Fiore, they believed that the world was destined to pass through three distinct ages, corresponding to the Holy Trinity: the Age of the Father was the age of laws, of the Temple, of the Old Testament; the Age of the Son was the age of grace, the age of the New Testament and Christ's holy church.

Most glorious of all would be the third and final age, the age that would precede the Final Judgement, the Age of the Holy Spirit.

'I, John, saw the holy city', says the prophet:

New Jerusalem, coming down from God out of heaven, prepared as a bride adorned for her husband… And I saw no temple therein: for the Lord God Almighty and the Lamb are the temple of it. And the city had no need of the sun, neither of the moon, to shine in it: for the glory of God did lighten it, and the Lamb *is* the light thereof.

Now, a century and a half after Francis's pilgrimage, the influence of the Franciscan Spirituals and their Joachite prophecies could still be felt in Cola di Rienzo's propaganda. The notary had decided to follow his lecture at the Lateran with another public painting, shown on the wall of his home church, Sant'Angelo in Pescheria. Here, where the arches of the *campanile* rose above the plebeian bustle of the fish market, Cola displayed his final scene.

On the left was a great fire in which many people and kings were burning. At the edge of the fire an old woman, Rome again, writhed in pain, her body already two-thirds blackened. But on the right-hand side of the picture there stood a church with a high bell tower, recognizably the church of Sant'Angelo itself. Indeed, the eponymous angel was there too, emerging from the church all dressed in white, with a scarlet cloak and a naked sword in one hand. With the other, he reached out to draw the old woman from the flames. Salvation. And all around, proud falcons were dropping dead from the sky, falling before the wings of a pure white dove – the dove of the Holy Spirit.

Below the picture, Cola had set these words: 'The time of great justice is coming.'

'It will take more than pictures to reform the government of Rome,' bystanders are reported to have said.

But Cola was not relying on pictures alone. By the spring of 1347 he had gathered the support of a powerful coalition drawn from the ambitious middle classes: landowning 'ranchers' or *bovattieri*; bankers and *mercanti* growing rich off trade; minor nobles or *cavallerotti*; notaries, doctors and lawyers; the canons of the basilicas; deacons and subdeacons. These were the *bona iente* of Rome, members of guilds and syndicates and confraternities – sober, businesslike men who had every reason to resent the mayhem of baronial rule.

On the Friday before Pentecost, Cola and his closest supporters gathered in the great fourth-century basilica of Santa Sabina on the Aventine hill. Cola was a scholar of the classics. He will have recalled the fate of Gaius Gracchus – how quickly the plebeian crowd, gathered on that same hill a millennium and a half before, had withered in the face of mercenary arrows and aristocrats' swords. But Cola had gone too far to back out now. Weeping, he addressed his co-conspirators, spoke to them of the misery of Rome's condition compared to the glories the city had once enjoyed; he lamented the servitude of Roman citizens, who once had been accustomed to the faithful obedience of their neighbours near and far.

Most of all, he reassured the practical burghers on the matter of the city finances. His years in the city administration had given him a perfect command of the possibilities of Rome's tax revenues, how much might be raised in hearth tax and salt tax and taxes on cattle and castles. And in the short term, he promised them, he had access to a very encouraging 4,000 florins in papal funding.

It was agreed. All present swore an oath that the people of Rome would rise once again in revolution. And the perfect opportunity soon presented itself, when old Stefano Colonna and his followers left the city to fight the town of Corneto, which was interfering with Rome's grain supply.

On the evening of Pentecost, that night when, long ago, the Spirit of the Lord came down upon the Apostles, Cola and his supporters met at Sant'Angelo in Pescheria. All night solemn Masses to the Holy Spirit were sung, repeated thirty times until the sun had risen. Then, splendid in full armour, Cola emerged like an angel from the angel's church. With his sacred banners flapping ahead of him and a knightly escort behind, he rode the short distance past the deserted fish market and the ruins of the Theatre of Marcellus, past the spot where Caesar was murdered. Then, gathering his courage, he climbed towards the summit of the Capitoline.

All across the city, the bells sounded, in warning or celebration. But his way was not blocked by barons or their retainers. Instead, the people gathered to witness the triumphant coming of a new age – the salvation of Rome and her rebirth as the new Jerusalem. In front of a vast crowd, Cola di Rienzo laid out the laws of his new regime, the *buono stato*, or Good Estate, and with one voice, the joyful people chose him as their lord.

Cola had pulled off a spectacular and bloodless coup under the noses of Rome's baronial overlords. Stefano Colonna galloped back to Rome as soon as he heard the news, but it was too late. As soon as he dared to threaten Cola di Rienzo, the bells began ringing out again across the city and a vast mob gathered to the former notary's defence. When Cola ordered all barons to leave the city, Stefano found himself with no choice but to obey. With a single footman, he slunk out of the city by the Tiburtine Gate, heading for the Colonna stronghold at Palestrina, leaving a triumphant Cola behind him.

His title, he had decreed, would be 'tribune of Rome'. It was a title rich in ancient resonances: it recalled the old Roman tribunes of the plebs and the tragic Gracchus brothers; it recalled the military tribunes who had once led Roman legions; it had a suggestion of law – of the judicial tribunal. Most of all, it recalled Rome's first emperor. It was by using his legal powers as a tribune that the great Augustus had made himself master of the Roman world.

Now, thirteen and a half centuries after Augustus, Cola di Rienzo tried to secure his own hold on the city. And with the *bona iente* at his side, his efforts were stunningly successful. There was peace, at last, on the streets. Law was administered in the courts. Wrongdoers were brought to swift and severe justice. Around the city, the fortifications and palisades of the barons began to be pulled down. Cola's anonymous biographer has left us the image of a young aristocrat, Martino del Porto, who suffered so much from dropsy that when Cola hanged him on the Capitoline, his body looked like an overripe pear, visible, dangling over the city, for miles around.

The warning was salutary. One by one, the barons, those agents of anarchy, came back to Cola's seat on the Capitoline to swear allegiance to the *buono stato*. Truly the Good Estate – and the new Age of the Spirit that Cola's sacred imagery had promised – appeared to have come to pass, when Rome's old lions might consent to lie down so meekly with the lamb.

Petrarch, when news of the coup reached Avignon, immediately fired off a delighted missive to the tribune. 'What terms shall I use in the midst of such sudden and and unhoped-for joy?... Liberty stands in your midst... Give thanks to God, the dispenser of such gifts, who has not yet forgotten his holy city.'

The poet's faith in the enduring Roman spirit had been amply justified: 'There will be no one who will not prefer to die a freeman rather than to live a slave, provided a drop of Roman blood flows in his veins... Hail,' now he addresses Cola directly, 'our Camillus, our Brutus, our Romulus!... Hail author of Roman liberty, of Roman peace, of Roman tranquillity.' And as for 'you citizens, be fully convinced that this man has been sent to you from heaven'.

In the particulars of its day-to-day operation, Cola's *buono stato* followed in what was, by that time, a well-established tradition of Italian communal government. Rome had had varying degrees of popular participation in politics since at least the establishment of the senate in 1143. The city's merchants and guildsmen knew how to run things, and Cola, with his notarial training, was himself a most capable administrator. Soon, business in Rome was thriving: traders used fair weights; deliverymen were no longer ambushed for their goods; the fishermen in the market stopped selling dogfish as mullet. And between the taxes Cola was efficiently raising and his reorganization of Rome's old regional militia, the *buono stato* was developing into a substantial new player on the Italian scene.

But Cola's *stato* was not meant to be just another city state, and he himself was more than a mere temporal lord, a *signore* such as other parts of Italy had seen. The very name of *stato* was a declaration of difference, the word meaning, not state exactly, but something more like 'status' or 'condition'. Indeed, the term had been used by Joachim of Fiore and his followers in describing the advancing condition of humanity – part of the technical vocabulary with which they discussed the three ages of the world: of Father, Son and Holy Spirit.

That summer, the summer of 1347, as the city basked in its grand renewal, the full scope of Cola's vision was made apparent. For too long, Cola wrote to Petrarch that July, Rome had endured 'the irreverent lot of a handmaid'. Now, all Italy was invited to witness her rebirth as 'the very head and fountain of liberty'.

Cola and Petrarch both believed, passionately, in Rome's rightful claim to be the *caput mundi*. It seemed obvious to Petrarch that Rome and Italy should, if possible, be united. He was, he told Cola in another letter, both astonished and dismayed to find that there were some who disagreed.

Cola certainly entertained no doubts on the matter. Messengers from Rome kept up a constant epistolary assault on the great cities of Italy, as Cola attempted to subdue the communes of Tuscany and Lombardy with fusillades of carefully turned Latin prose. That August, representatives of twenty-four lands, cities and provinces were treated to a Mass of the Holy Spirit, celebrated at Santa Maria in Aracoeli on the Capitoline. Ambassadors from Perugia, Florence, Todi and Siena were singled out for special honour, each given a beautifully made banner bearing Roman symbols: Romulus and Remus; the eagle and palm; the old letters, SPQR. These banners were gifts of friendship, but also carried a strong suggestion of political overlordship. The ambassadors of Florence – representing a city that was, after all, then several times bigger and richer than Cola's *caput mundi* – perceived the significance perfectly clearly, and left their banner untouched.

Cola now treated his foreign visitors and all the worthies of Rome to a magnificent feast in his own honour. Cola was resplendent in scarlet; dancers and musicians delighted the crowd, dressed in motley or animal skins. There was fine food, pheasant and sturgeon, and leftovers for the poor. Best of all, Cola had arranged some device that caused wine to spurt out of the mouth of one of Rome's most prized classical relics: the ancient bronze horse that had stood for so long with its imperial rider in the piazza outside the Lateran.

As ever, at such feasts, it was important to recognize the source from which all good things flowed. As the old emperor's horse poured forth wine, so Cola di Rienzo, the tavernkeeper's son, tribune of Rome, the Severe and Clement, Liberator of the City and Zealot of Italy, poured forth his blessings upon an ungrateful world.

The extravagant peformance culminated on the festival of the Assumption of the Virgin Mary on 15 August. Enthroned in the Basilica of Santa Maria Maggiore, Cola was crowned with a wreath as Petrarch had been those seven years before. As with Petrarch, the ceremony was intended to evoke the classical past: there were readings from Virgil and the ancient poets; and Cola had found some wretched pauper to stand by him, in imitation of the custom of triumphing generals: 'Remember, you are only a man.' But where Petrarch had been content with just one crown, Cola di Rienzo was crowned with six wreaths, and he held in his hand an apple and a sceptre, to match the orb and sceptre of an emperor. Cola, thenceforth, would be not just tribune but Tribune Augustus.

Cola's imperial borrowings had both a political and a religious dimension to them. Two weeks before his classical coronation in Santa Maria Maggiore, Cola had had himself dubbed a White Knight of the Holy Spirit. This earlier ceremony had been rather more medieval in flavour: following established chivalric tradition, Cola spent the night in solitary vigil at the Lateran, having heard Mass and taken a ritual bath. But one innovation shocked the crowd: the ancient marble basin in which the tribune washed away his sins was widely supposed to have been the baptismal font of Constantine.

Given the religious rhetoric that had accompanied Cola's rise to power, this sacral association with Constantine was very highly charged. Constantine, after all, had combined in his person both the full temporal might of the Roman empire and the spiritual leadership of the church. His memory was a challenge to the dual powers of the medieval status quo. With the pope far away in Avignon and the Holy Roman Emperor even further in Germany, here was a man encroaching on both imperial and papal prerogatives, supporting his claim with every drop of symbolic power that could be squeezed from the city of Rome.

Newly knighted, Cola addressed his Romans. 'With the authority and grace of God and the Holy Spirit', he declared that Rome was the capital of the world, that all the people of Italy were now Roman citizens, and that Rome and Italy were now free. Then, drawing his sword, he 'divided the air into the three parts of the world and said: "This is mine, this is mine, this is mine."'

'I saw heaven opened,' says the Book of Revelation:

And behold a white horse; and he that sat upon him was called Faithful and True, and in righteousness he doth judge and make war. His eyes were as a flame of fire, and on his head were many crowns... And out of his mouth goeth a sharp sword, that with it he should smite the nations: and he shall rule them with a rod of iron. And he hath on his vesture and on his thigh a name written, KING OF KINGS, AND LORD OF LORDS.

The Age of the Holy Spirit – the final age – had come at last. And Cola was its herald, the White Knight of Revelation. Greater than pope and emperor, the tavernkeeper's son was now a figure of the Apocalypse.

* * *

The seven stars of the Apocalypse decorated his banner. The dove of the Holy Spirit was his badge. The blessing of the Holy Spirit was carved into his mace of authority. He held in his hand the rod of iron foretold by the ancient prophecy. And yet, despite the successes of the *buono stato*, the world refused to conform as closely to Cola's vision as he would have liked.

For one thing, the pope, who had backed Cola's revolt, and to whom Cola had never stopped declaring his allegiance, was increasingly alarmed by the reports of his agents in Rome. Popular government was one thing, but Cola's apocalyptic displays had come dangerously close to heresy. The Joachites and Spiritual Franciscans had already been declared enemies of the church, and Cola now seemed to have joined them.

In Avignon, Petrarch now found himself one of Cola's few faithful defenders. 'I call God to witness that I seem somehow to partake in your dangers, your labours and your glory,' he complained to Cola that August:

> As often as Fortune brings me among those who are discussing your affairs with stubborn insolence, I take up arms in your defence... Nor have I cared whom I might sting or offend with my words. Thanks to my unrestrained speech, I have estranged many whose favour I had gained through long intimacy.

This was quite true. Petrarch's defence of Cola di Rienzo had alienated his patrons the Colonna – men to whom he owed his whole livelihood. For Petrarch, whose friendships were everything, this estrangement was a bitter burden.

Meanwhile, the Italian cities were politely declining to submit to Roman rule. Some were friendly to Cola's enterprise – the merchants of Florence were no supporters of baronial rule – but they certainly were not prepared to accept the authority of crumbling, impoverished Rome.

And of course the Holy Roman Emperor – or rather, the two men who were competing to be Holy Roman Emperor at the time – conceded not an inch to Cola's grand claims. Emperors were to be elected, as always, by German princes, not Roman fishmongers.

Finally, there was the matter of the barons. Most had sworn allegiance to Cola's *buono stato* – most, but never quite all. Through most of July 1347, Cola's Roman militia had been facing down the feudal forces of one Janni de Vico, an ambitious – people said fratricidal – baron who was building himself a little princedom to the north of the city. When Janni's resistance was crushed, with the help of his local rivals, the Orsini, it was the turn of another baron to revolt against Rome. Nicola Caetani, a grand-nephew of Pope Benedict VIII, was a formidable opponent. Once again, Cola's militia combined with local aristocratic rivals – the Colonna this time – to defeat the Caetani army. Nicola Caetani was killed in battle on 28 August, less than two weeks after Cola's multiple coronation.

But as soon as Nicola Caetani fell, his stepbrother Giovanni took over the Caetani rebellion and renewed the war, which dragged bitterly into the autumn, a cruel campaign of scorched earth, siege and countersiege.

The other barons could no doubt see the way things were going – and Cola was bristlingly aware of their ill-intent. The tribune's biographer recalls a feast given in Rome on 14 September, at which old Stefano Colonna dared to criticize Cola's extravagant wardrobe. 'For you, Tribune, it would be more appropriate to wear the honest clothes of a poor old man than these pompous things.'

Whether it was this insult that provoked him, or evidence of some graver injury being planned, Cola reacted with unexpected force. Several barons, both Orsini and Colonna, including Stefano himself, were hauled off to prison in Cola's fortress on the Capitoline to await execution. Friars were sent into the dungeon to hear the prisoners confess their sins and make their peace with the Lord. Only old Stefano refused to speak or take a final communion.

For two long days, the barons were left to sweat. Then, on 17 September, Cola had them hauled down to his audience chamber. There, with a grand and beautiful speech, the tribune pardoned them. They swore reconciliation, made their confessions, and were subjected to one of Cola's Masses of the Holy Spirit. Then, Cola wrote, they were joined to him and to the Roman people 'in a love that is not false'. It was a miracle of peace, inspired by the Spirit's holy flame.

The barons, of course, could not forgive the tribune's clemency. Over the weeks that followed, fortifications were quietly strengthened, supplies laid in. At the end of October a branch of the Orsini clan rose in open revolt. Once again the Roman militia was raised, to sit wearily outside the Orsini stronghold at Marino, in the Alban hills. It was a miserable time of year for a siege, and the Romans spent their fury on whatever came in reach, but they could not penetrate Marino's walls.

A papal legate, Cardinal Bertrand de Deaulx, now entered the game, sent by the pope to end Cola's run as best he could. The tribune was forced to return to Rome to secure his position, leaving the Orsini defiant in the field. As a parting gesture, he named a pair of hounds after the Orsini leaders, then drowned them in a nearby millstream.

Cola was able to face down the cardinal for the moment, but it was clear that the pope was now working actively against him. So hostile was the climate in Avignon that even Petrarch's faith began to waver. The poet laureate was at Genoa, heading south into Italy at the invitation of some friends, and also, perhaps, to be close to Cola in his hour of need. But, he wrote to the tribune, 'letters from my friends have followed me since I left the Curia'. Was it true, he asked, that Cola was now associating only with the 'worst element' of the mob? 'Shall the world behold you, who have been the leader of patriots, become the accomplice of criminals?'

'Recollect,' Petrarch implored, 'the role you are playing in your city's history, the title you have assumed, the hopes you have aroused… You are not the master of the Republic, but its servant.' Perhaps the stories were false? Petrarch dared to hope. 'Never shall I be more gladly proven wrong.'

'A long farewell to you, Rome, if these rumours are true. I shall visit the regions of Garamant and of India instead.'

Now the Colonna, greatest of the barons of Rome, joined the rebellion. At the family stronghold at Palestrina, old Stefano raised his banner, gathered his knights and vassals, seven hundred plate-armoured cavalry along with four thousand foot. This army, summoned into being by a single clan, now set off towards Cola's holy city.

Towards the end of November, the Colonna force arrived at the walls of Rome. The Orsini had come out from Marino to join the army – the army of their former enemy – along with an assortment of lesser baronial malcontents. Now the combined rebel force was camped on the plain by the old pilgrim basilica of San Lorenzo Fuori le Mure, and Cola's defeat seemed certain.

The Colonna were not just relying on force of arms. They had made contact with traitors inside the wall. When the Colonna knights attacked, the Porta San Lorenzo was to be opened from within.

But Cola had learned of the barons' plan. The guard on the gate had been changed, and when, on the morning of 20 November, old Stefano's son Stefanuccio approached the gate, he was met only with warnings. No one would open the gate to him, the Romans declared, and to prove it, the guard threw the key into the mud at Stefanuccio's feet – a key that would open the gate only from the inside.

With no siege train and their allies in the city missing, the Colonna army was at an impasse. It was decided to make one last show of force, at least, before withdrawing. In their companies, with banners flapping in the autumn rain, the Colonna chivalry paraded past the wall, calling insults at the city's defenders.

And then, with much commotion, and to the astonishment of the watching knights, the San Lorenzo gate began to open. The man nearest the gate at the time was a young Colonna named Janni, the son of Stefanuccio and grandson of Stefano himself. Now, seeing the opportunity that presented itself, he raised his shield and lance and spurred his war horse straight towards the widening gap. Romans scattered in terror as he pounded across the mud, the young paladin, beard downy on his cheeks and the light of battle in his eyes. He crossed the field at a gallop, burst through the gate, and stood like Mars, daring any Roman with the courage to face him.

Only then, it appears, did he realize that he was alone.

Somehow, in the speed of the moment, Janni's companions had failed to follow him. And there were no friendly faces waiting within the walls. The sudden clamour, the hammering at the lock, these had not been signs of traitors letting the Colonna in, but of the furious Roman militia, mad for war, trying to get out through the keyless gate.

Janni's courage deserted him like air from a balloon. He turned this way and that, begged the people, in God's name, not to take his armour. But there was no escape. The Romans knocked him down, stripped off his plate and killed him, one blade in the chest, another in the groin.

Outside the walls, Janni's father Stefanuccio had realized that his son was missing and made his own way to the open gate. There he saw the boy, naked on the ground amid the daggers, hair trailing in the mud. He recoiled in horror, turned instinctively towards the safety of his own lines. Then he stopped, turned again, back through the gate to try to rescue his son.

No hope of that. The Romans turned from son to father, closing the way back. Someone hurled a rock from the walls, struck Stefanuccio on the shoulders, then lances pushed into his horse and he was thrown, hard on his heavy armoured back, into the mud. They opened his visor and stabbed him below the eyes, a terrible wound, 'like the cleft of a wolf's jaws'.

Now the Romans, having tasted blood, poured out of the gate to fall upon the baronial host. Confusion turned to panic. Horses slipped on churned-up soil. Crossbows and ballistae hurled bolts from the battlements. Each man tried to save himself as best he could. A third Colonna, Pietro, was found grovelling in a vineyard. Fat and bald, it was the first time he had carried arms. 'He did not look like a man of war.' First they took his money. Then they took his weapons. Last, his life.

Old Stefano Colonna paid a terrible price for his rebellion. He had told Petrarch, years before, that he would rather die fighting than become a subservient old man. But he had missed the massacre at the San Lorenzo gate. Now he lived on at Palestrina, having presided over the wreck of his family, while his son and precious grandson lay cold on the winter ground.

This was a most unexpected triumph for the citizens of Rome. Cola had the trumpets sounded, led his holy knights triumphant to the Capitoline. But there was something odd about his reaction to the victory that day. At Santa Maria in Aracoeli, before the ancient icon of the Black Madonna, he took off his olive crown and laid it before her; put down too his rod of iron. After that day, reports his biographer, 'he never carried the sceptre, nor the crown, nor the banner over his head'. He wanted, he told the people, to return his sword to its sheath.

The bodies of the three dead Colonna were carried into the same church, covered over with cloth of gold. There, at the Colonna chapel, the women of the family came to mourn, with torn clothes and dishevelled hair.

On the morning after the battle, Cola once again assembled his victorious knights. 'I want to give you double pay,' he told them. 'Come with me.' Again, the trumpets sounded, and Cola led them, in procession, back to the Porta San Lorenzo. He must, they all assumed, have some reward for them in mind.

But when they reached the gate, the tribune dismounted to pick his way across the torn-up ground until he reached the filthy puddle that marked the spot where Janni and Stefanuccio Colonna had been slain. Calling his own son, Lorienzo, to his side, Cola reached his hand into the water, red with Colonna gore, then sprinkled the bloody mixture over his son's forehead. 'You will be a Knight of the Victory,' he declared. Then he had the constables of the cavalry dub the boy with the flats of their swords.

It was a bizarre and macabre display. Worse yet, it had not been accompanied by any of the rewards that the knights of Rome expected for their valiant service. The full militia would never fight for Cola again.

The weather continued to darken. The price of grain was high, and so were taxes. The pope's legate, Cardinal Bernard, was agitating against the *buono stato* and had proclaimed Cola a heretic. The Orsini were still raiding the countryside from Marino, raping and robbing pilgrims and passers-by. There was chaos too in the kingdom of Naples – Angevin princes squabbling with the king of Hungary after the death of King Robert the Wise – and that chaos was spilling over into Rome. Cola had come out in support of the Hungarian, much to Petrarch's dismay, in exchange for a battalion of Magyar mercenaries.

This was not the government that the *bona iente* had wanted, the *mercanti*, the *bovattieri*, the *cavallerotti*. More radical elements among the populace still loved their tribune, were pleased that the barons had been laid low. Still, without the support of the wealthier citizens, Cola's coalition was coming apart. On 14 December a baron, Luca Savelli, publicly summoned his followers to arms.

Soon warning bells were ringing out in every district of the city, from the territory of the Savelli and the Colonna, from the church of the Aracoeli on the Capitoline. At the church of Sant'Angelo in Pescheria, from which Cola's *buono stato* had first sprung, the bell rang all night and day.

This time no great mob rallied to the tribune's defence. He had some loyal fighters, to be sure, and his Hungarians. Enough, perhaps, to break down the baronial barricades, to take back the city, street by street. But Cola had no appetite for further fighting. 'He breathed quickly and trembled,' says the biographer. 'He wept; he did not know what to do. With his heart jolted and stricken he didn't have the strength of a little boy.'

The traditional narrative is that Cola was driven mad. He went from ambition to megalomania to cowardly despair, the time-honoured trajectory of the Roman tyrant. But perhaps his despair sprung from a true understanding of the hopelessness of his position, the full magnitude of his failure. He had dreamed of a new age, a new Rome, a new Italy. A dawn of peace and reconciliation, a *buono stato* in which all might live together in the light of the Lord. But here he was, just another lordling in a fortress, defended by mercenary swords, squabbling over a few filthy streets. A great chasm had opened up between glorious vision and squalid reality, a yawning blackness into which Cola's courage fled. On 15 December 1347, the tribune of Rome, the Clement and Severe, disappeared into voluntary exile, leaving Rome to its barons and its pope.

* * *

Towards the end of Cola's tribunate, in the October of 1347, a Genoese galley had come limping into the port of Messina with a cargo from the Black Sea. In the hold were rats. On the rats, fleas. In the fleas, plague.

By the end of 1348, perhaps half the population of Europe had perished. Whole cities were deserted, villages wiped out. It must have seemed indeed like the end of the world. In Avignon, Petrarch suffered two terrible losses: the deaths of his beloved Laura and his dear, if recently estranged, patron, Cardinal Giovanni Colonna. Petrarch wrote a letter to Stefano Colonna to express his sorrow – sorrow for an old man who had now outlived all seven of his sons. Stefano shed so many tears at this, reported Petrarch's messenger, that when he dried his eyes, he declared that he would never weep again.

In 1349, Rome was struck by a great earthquake, worse than any in memory. Buildings that had stood for a thousand years and more came tumbling down; the Basilica of St Paul was ruined; the *torre dei conti* lost its head. When Petrarch visited Rome in 1350, for the pilgrim jubilee, it was a sad and ruined city that welcomed him. 'The world has been destroyed,' he wrote to his old friend Socrates, 'brought to an end by the madness of men and by the avenging heart of God.'

Cola, meanwhile, was hiding out in the mountains with the renegade Spiritual Franciscans, the Fraticelli who haunted the wild places of the Abruzzi. In 1350, following the prophetic guidance of a certain Fra Angelo – Brother Angel – he travelled to Prague to the court of Emperor Charles IV. 'I am a worm,' he told the emperor:

> A frail man, a weed like all the others. I used to carry in my hand the rod of iron, which in my humility I have converted into a rod of wood, because God wished to castigate me... I believe that you will defend me. You will not let me die at the hands of tyrants; you will not let me drown in the lake of injustice.

Cola was, he claimed, of imperial lineage. Alone in Prague, a penniless fugitive, he dared to tell the court his tall old tale about Henry VII's fateful stay at a certain Tiberside inn.

Cola's hopes were entirely misplaced. At first the emperor had a use for his classical expertise, his silver tongue and instinct for the theatrics of power. But certainly he had no intention of restoring this former rival, however petty, to his place in Rome. The pope, meanwhile, was eager to get his hands on the notorious heretic. Beware, he told the bishops of Bohemia, lest the healthy flock be infected by a single diseased sheep.

On 1 August 1352 Cola arrived at Avignon, sent in chains by the emperor, there to languish in a papal dungeon with nothing but a

right: Colossal head of the Emperor Constantine, part of a huge statue that was placed in the apse of the Basilica of Maxentius, after Maxentius was defeated at the Milvian Bridge.

below: Mosaic from San Vitale in Ravenna, dedicated after the recapture of the city from the Ostrogoths. The Emperor Justinian is resplendent in imperial purple. The man to the left of him may be Belisarius himself.

left: The Casa dei Crescenzi is a remarkable medieval tower-house dating to the eleventh or twelfth century. The stronghold, which dominated the nearby Ponte Emilio, is decorated with reused architectural fragments of antique marble.

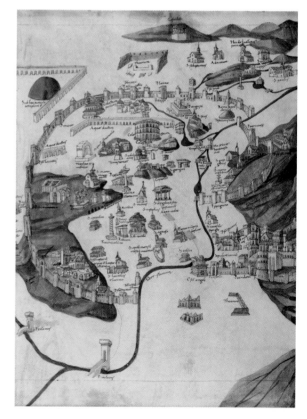

right: A fifteenth-century map of Rome, oriented as though the viewer was standing on the Monte Mario. Highlighted are Rome's ancient ruins and pilgrim basilicas.

A sixteenth-century portrait of Petrarch, wearing
the Roman laurels of which he was so proud.

It is believed that this portrait, long thought to be of a young man, may
in fact be a likeness of a severely dressed Lucrezia Borgia. The dagger
in her hand recalls the suicide of her Roman namesake.

The Creation of Adam, from the Sistine ceiling. Here, the full power of Michelangelo's 'muscular rhetoric' is displayed.

Raphael's *School of Athens*. The seated figure in the foreground is the philosopher Heraclitus, believed to have been painted in the likeness of Michelangelo.

Michelangelo was present for the unearthing of the *Laocoön*
in 1506. It is one of the greatest surviving masterpieces of
ancient art, and a major influence on the Sistine ceiling.

A group of German landsknechts, recognizable by their extravagantly slashed sleeves, and by the easy swagger with which they brandish their weapons.

The Castel Sant'Angelo, looming over the Tiber. The former mausoleum of Hadrian was the key to medieval and renaissance Rome.

A self-portrait from 1623 shows
Gian Lorenzo Bernini as a young man.

St Peter's Basilica, by Piranesi, showing off Bernini's curving
colonnade: the enfolding arms of the Catholic Church.

Light streams into St Peter's through a gilded window designed by
Bernini, and framed by the twisted pillars of his baldacchino.

Bible and an edition of Livy for company. 'He is extremely miserable,' wrote Petrarch to a friend, lamenting Cola's failure to die a glorious death on the Capitol in the proper antique style. It was an awkward situation altogether. 'The constant praise and exhortations that so busily engaged my pen are, perhaps, better known than I should like at present.'

But though tempted, like Peter, to deny his friend, Petrarch was moved once again to come to Cola's defence, writing a passionate letter to Rome in which he begged the Romans to help their fellow citizen, at least by demanding that he receive a fair trial. 'Do not treat lightly the safety of one who, on your behalf, has exposed himself to a thousand dangers.' Remember, he wrote, 'how everything beneath the vault of heaven assumed a different look. So marvellously and rapidly was the world changed!'

Cola, Petrarch argued, had 'revived an important question, a question of great interest to the world but that has been forgotten and buried in the sleep of many centuries, the question that alone can lead to the reformation of the state and can usher in the golden age'.

And, to the surprise of all, Cola did get a second chance. In 1352 the pope who had hounded him, Clement VI, died, to be replaced by the rather milder Innocent VI. Rome was in a terrible condition – an embarrassment to the papacy, violent and ungovernable. So, in 1353, a new expedition was dispatched to Lazio, led by Gil de Albornoz, a warrior cardinal, veteran of the wars of the Reconquista in Spain. In the cardinal's train, restored to papal favour, was Cola di Rienzo, ready to take up arms against the Colonna once again. In August 1354 the former tribune arrived at the Monte Mario on the pilgrim route to Rome, where the people 'welcomed him joyfully, as if he were Scipio Africanus'.

But this new tribunate did not last. Rome had been ruined by plague and civil war. Mercenary bands fought over the deserted fields of Lazio, and their demands for pay forced taxes ever higher. Cola's support rapidly ebbed away. In October, a mob rose against him, stirred energetically by the Colonna, and advanced on Cola's fortified compound on the Capitoline. Men poured pitch on the gate of his stronghold, set it ablaze. Soon the whole palace was in flames. Cola, taking off his fine robes, shaved off his beard and tried to escape by mingling with the crowd. But he was recognized, given away by the gold bracelets at his wrists, and stabbed to death, there on the Capitoline hill. They dragged his body through the streets up the Via Lata to the Colonna district, hacking at him as he passed. When they strung him, pale and fat, upside-down outside the church of San Marcello, his head had come clean off and the guts were slipping out of his torn belly. At last, they took his body to the old mausoleum of Augustus, little more than a tree-covered mound. There, in ceremonial mockery, they cremated him, on a fire of thistles, tended by the city's Jews. They threw his ashes in the river.

Cola had dreamed of a Rome that would be the capital of a new age, a new Jerusalem. But he had not been able even to take control of Lazio, let alone Italy, and certainly not the world. His failure was catastrophic and complete.

Petrarch had dreamed of a Rome restored to ancient glory, illuminated forever by his glorious Latin verse. But his hopes in Cola's revolution turned to ash, and his poem, the epic *Africa*, was never finished. Today it is hardly read except by specialist scholars.

But though both men were disappointed, both had mistaken what their role in history was to be. As a herald of the Apocalypse, Cola had failed, to be sure, but in his short reign he had served as a mostly admirable exemplar for popular rule, and had done fatal damage to the baronial cause. Cola's reorganized militia survived his downfall; never again would the Orsini or the Colonna be able to dominate the city as they had before. For the rest of the fourteenth century, and much of the fifteenth, the old three-way struggle for Rome would swing decisively in favour of the people until, a century after Cola's death, Rome was finally brought, once and for all, under the firm authority of the pope.

And though such mundane politics might not have given Cola much satisfaction, he would have been pleased to know that at least one of his grand ideas would survive him. Centuries later, Cola di Rienzo was remembered as a martyr, not for Rome, but for a unified Italy.

Petrarch, meanwhile, remains one of Italy's most important and widely read poets. But it was not Latin epic that secured his reputation. Petrarch's immortal fame is based on the little sonnets in Italian that he wrote for his beloved Laura, back in Avignon. He thought he would be a new Virgil for a new Rome. Instead, he became a new Ovid, for a future Italy.

In Rome, thirteen centuries before Petrarch, there had been a map – a map that showed Rome as the centre, the head of nations, the *caput mundi*. Petrarch had thought this Rome could live again. Cola's failure showed him he was wrong. Rome would never again be mistress of the world.

But Petrarch's passion for antiquity, his devoted reading of ancient texts, his promotion of antique values – all these had a profound influence upon fourteenth-century Italy. His enthusiasm spread through his network of like-minded souls – spread until it had become a movement, a learned culture of Humanism that came to dominate the courts and universities of Europe. A new world was emerging – a world of learning and letters whose defining point, the co-ordinate from which all angles were taken, all distances measured, was Rome. Not a physical Rome, of blood and bricks, but a Rome of ink and parchment, scrolls and codices – a Rome that Petrarch had discovered in his libraries, and which he nurtured in his heart. Rome the city would not be renewed, but Rome as an ideal could be – and this renewal would set the course of Western civilization for hundreds of years.

The Age of the Spirit had not come. But later generations, looking back, would one day come to see the years of Cola and Petrarch as the beginning of a new human era. A rebirth, they called it, a *rinascita*. A renaissance.

15

MY DEBT TO NATURE

The marriages of Lucrezia Borgia

———

1493–1501

A PARTY AT the palace of the Vatican. The food has been eaten. The plates are cleared. Tables pushed aside. There has been dancing. Fifty of Rome's finest courtesans are here, summoned by the duke of Valence, Il Valentino, the pope's own son.

Courtesans are famous for their finery. They count their admirers in pearls and precious stones; their romantic successes are visible in the fineness of their silks.

But as the courtesans danced, they lost their clothes. Candelabras, placed around the floor, shine on discarded dresses – dresses that are fortunes, whole livelihoods – cast aside amid the party debris. Moving back and forth between the candle flames are the courtesans themselves. Naked now, they are bent down on hands and knees, playing a game. Someone has scattered chestnuts around the room, chestnuts for autumn, and the courtesans, pale and bare, are rooting around in the darkness, collecting them.

Everyone is laughing. What else can they do? The courtesans are laughing, on their hands and knees. Later, the men in the room will strip off too, and join them. It will be like a performance. There will be prizes.

The duke of Valence is delighted with the show. His father the pope sits nearby, an old man, but fleshy and full of appetite. And next to him, unreadable through the murk of history, is the Pope's daughter, Lucrezia Borgia, twenty-one years old. She is about to be married for the third time.

* * *

'Rome always has been, and ever will be… the city of whores.' So wrote the scurrilous poet Pietro Aretino, but he was hardly exaggerating. The city of St Peter was also Italy's most notorious centre of prostitution.

Prostitutes started young – coached in the game, often enough, by their mothers. Choreographed well, the appearance of a fresh new face on the scene could cause a profitable stir. It was important not to be too brazen. At first the girl would show herself only for a moment at her mother's window, a shy child peeping down from a seedy room.

Word would go around. Soon the local bravos would be haunting the street outside, editions of Petrarch peeping from their pockets – not his Latin poetry, but the love sonnets in Italian which had, since his death, become wildly popular. Kisses would be thrown at the window. Gifts promised. Dainty words exchanged.

And then, at last, after the proper maternal negotiations, the girl's virginity could be sold for a handsome sum, and, if you knew the trick, sold again and again – the sheets stained each time with gum arabic and betel nut.

So the life of a prostitute began – a life of standing in open windows, lighted windows whose night-time glow shone like a promise on to muddy streets. Rome's thousands of lonely men longed to be in those well-decorated rooms, to be warm, to be loved. A prostitute's life was a life of 'friendships', based on the exchange of gifts: the men gave valuables and coin, the women gave their bodies, carefully rationed.

And though it was disgraceful to be a prostitute, the neighbours rarely raised much objection. Prostitution was too common a thing to retain much power to shock. Of Rome's 30,000 inhabitants, some 6,800 were prostitutes, according to one contemporary estimate – an exaggeration, but remarkable just the same. Prostitutes filled the city's streets and the city's churches. They were incorporated into Rome's rituals. At carnival time, prostitutes ran in their own special foot race, delighting the city crowds.

The living was precarious, of course. A prostitute's 'friends' could be insistent – violent. It was dangerous to refuse to grant what a man thought he had bought. Sodomy was a frequent request, dangerous because illegal, and all the more sought after for that. A woman who resisted might get a midnight visit from the young man's friends, come to disgrace her house, to hurl rocks and filth at her all-important windows. She might open her door one morning to get a faceful of shit, carefully parcelled in green-and-white paper.

These insults at least could be wiped away. Much harder to survive was the punitive thirty-one-man gang-rape known as the *trentuno*, or the *sfregia*, which ended a woman's career by cutting up her face.

And yet despite the horrors, young women for whom marriage was difficult – no dowry; no family – turned in huge numbers to the only profession that was open to them. While it lasted, it was a good living. And for some, a few hundred women among the thousands, prostitution offered a path to a different sort of life. If a prostitute could acquire certain graces, fine clothes, some skill at dancing, a few love sonnets ready at hand, she might be counted among Rome's *meretrices honestae*, or courtesans, women who could boast of 'friends' in the highest positions at the papal court.

The popes were back in Rome, and trade in bodies was booming. The city was full of womanless men: pilgrims, diplomats, canon lawyers, and priests most of all – priests who were forbidden from marrying, but were perfectly willing to keep concubines.

It had been a struggle, bringing the papacy back from Avignon. Pope Urban V, encouraged by the ever-optimistic Petrarch, had tried to return in 1367, but had found Rome profoundly inhospitable. Its inhabitants, stirred up both by and against the barons, were impossible to subdue. And the Patrimony of St Peter, that slice of central Italy supposedly donated to the popes by Constantine, had been carved up between a hundred little lords and their hired mercenaries. Soon the notorious White Company, under Sir John Hawkwood, a veteran of Crécy, was threatening the papal town of Viterbo. In 1370, Urban and all his cardinals packed up and set off back to Avignon again – to their comfortable palaces on the banks of the Rhône.

Nevertheless, the pull of Rome remained strong. Urged on this time by a fiery young nun, the future St Catherine of Siena, Pope Gregory IX came in 1377 to reclaim his Holy See. This time he stayed, but the limbs of the papal bureaucracy left behind in Avignon rebelled against their head, so to speak – or, at least, they sprouted a new one. Before long, a new pope had been elected in Avignon to rival the one in Rome, causing a schism that would split the church in half for the next thirty years.

In 1409, a council of senior clerics assembled in Pisa to end the schism, but they only succeeded in electing a third pope to rival the existing two. The church was split three ways until 1415, when a new council met at Constance to settle things once and for all. There was urgent need for some kind of solution. The papacy was now being contested between two quarrelsome geriatrics and a former pirate; radical reformers like John Wycliffe and Jan Hus were spreading heresy in northern Europe; the lands of the church were ravaged and lost, and the city of St Peter was a depopulated wreck of toppling antiques, sinking slowly into the Tiber.

Fortunately, the man elected at Constance to save the church was the perfect person for the job. Oddone Colonna, who became Pope Martin V, was a formidable character, backed by the resources of Rome's oldest and greatest noble clan. Supported by the conflict-weary cardinals and by Colonna men-at-arms, Martin V brought the papacy back to the city for good.

In the years since Petrarch's coronation on the Capitoline in 1341, his humanist enthusiasm for ancient culture had taken deep root in the great courts of Italy, the papal Curia included. There were cardinals who spent more time with Cicero and Virgil than with Eusebius and Augustine.

Now, under the great popes of the fifteenth century, Rome began to regain some of its ancient colour. Martin V brought the artists Donatello and Masaccio to beautify the city. Nicholas V, known as the first humanist pope, spent thousands of ducats restoring a vital aqueduct, the Aqua Virgo, and collecting ancient texts to fill his Vatican library. Pius II – who took his papal name from Virgil's *pius Aeneas* – was an acute reader of Petrarch's poetry, both vernacular and Latin, and had himself been the author of a slim volume of pornographic verse.

Under such men, worldly and ambitious, money and people flowed back into Rome, much to the benefit of the city's prostitutes and courtesans. And during these long years of growth, the reign of a rather lesser pope passed by without much stir. He was a man chosen solely on the basis that he was favoured by none of the Curia's main factions, and was considered certain to die before he could do any harm: a gouty, sober, septuagenarian Catalan, Alfons de Borja.

Alfonso Borgia, as the Italians called him, spent much of his pontificate wrapped up in international politics. In the mid-fifteenth century Italy was dominated by four major powers: the republic of Venice, controlling the Adriatic; the Sforza dukedom of Milan; Florence, now run by the Medici banking family, and the kingdom of Naples, recently taken over from the Angevins by the royal family of Aragon. Maintaining the balance between these competing powers was a constant preoccupation for the Renaissance popes.

Meanwhile, events overseas demanded attention. In 1453, two years before Alfonso's accession, the Ottoman Turks under Mehmet II had finally breached the formidable landward defences of Constantinople. The Byzantine emperor, Constantine XI Paleologos, died under the Theodosian Walls, finally ending a line of political succession that stretched, with a few interruptions, all the way back to Julius Caesar, a millennium and a half before.

Alfonso was determined to organize a new crusade against the ever-advancing Turks – but other than a brave Hungarian victory outside Belgrade and a successful naval skirmish in the Aegean, his efforts bore little fruit. Cajoling the princes and kings of western

Europe into any sort of collective endeavour was an impossible task, exhausting for a man approaching his eightieth year.

But if his international efforts were in vain, at least Alfonso was able to do something for his own family. It was common for Renaissance popes to bring young relations into the management of the vast ecclesiastical bureaucracy. Nepotism – the advancement of papal nephews, or *nipoti* – was an accepted practice in Rome. Nonetheless, the cardinals of the Sacred College were dismayed when Alfonso enrolled two nephews among their number who were still only in their twenties. Nor was their discomfort lessened when one of the two young men began to show signs of real talent. By 1458, when Alfonso Borgia died, his nephew Roderigo had risen to become vice-chancellor of the church, second in importance only to the pope himself.

Strong-willed and eloquent, with a 'versatile intellect' and a brilliant grasp of papal politics, Roderigo Borgia managed to hold on to his high office even after his uncle's death, by changing sides at the critical moment of the conclave that chose Alfonso's successor. Roderigo was anyway a very capable administrator, who served the church well, even as he flaunted his own ambitions. His palace overlooking the Via dei Banchi Vecchi drew comparisons to Nero's *Domus Aurea*.

Nor was Roderigo shy about his baser desires. 'His attraction for beautiful women and the manner in which he excites them – and they fall in love with him – is quite remarkable,' wrote a tutor of his. 'He attracts them more powerfully than a magnet does iron.'

In 1460 the young cardinal attracted a furious letter from Pope Pius II: 'Our displeasure is beyond words!' he wrote. Roderigo had spent an evening in a Sienese garden with several women 'wholly given over to worldly vanities… We heard that the dance was indulged in, in all wantonness; none of the allurements of love was lacking.'

But during the 1470s, Roderigo Borgia appears to have settled down, entering into a long relationship with a woman of obscure family named Vannozza Catanei. Vannozza was not, as Pius had it, 'wholly given over to worldly vanities' – she was around thirty years old, and married, though she may well have earned her dowry as some kind of courtesan. Certainly, she did not allow her marriage to get in the way of her relationship with the papal vice-chancellor.

In 1475, Vannozza bore the cardinal the first of four children they would have together, a boy, Cesare. A second son, Juan, followed soon after in around 1477, and a third, Jofré, in 1481. Between the sons, in 1480, Vannozza gave Roderigo a daughter, Lucrezia.

It was not unusual for cardinals, and even popes, to have illegitimate children. Innocent VIII, who became pope in 1484, had several himself, though he at least pretended they were nieces and nephews. Lucrezia grew up in a city that was perfectly accustomed to the sight of papal bastards strutting around the Vatican. And, as she learned more about the world beyond her mother's modest house, the world beyond Ponte and the Piazza Pizzo di Merlo, Lucrezia may have become aware that she too might yet become a pope's child – that the too-big man Roderigo, who visited, bent-nosed and heavy-jowled in his robes, was, first of all, her father, and second, one of the most powerful cardinals in Rome.

Lucrezia had a fine Renaissance education: Latin and a little Greek, poetry and letters, music and dance; she will have had some religious training too, probably from the Dominican nuns at the convent of San Sisto by the baths of Caracalla, which later became her favourite Roman retreat.

Not that Lucrezia – named after the chaste Lucretia of Roman legend – was to be allowed to join a nunnery. At the age of ten the girl found herself betrothed to a Spanish nobleman. When she was eleven, her first engagement was broken off in favour of a second more prestigious one. Her father's power was growing, his influence spreading, and Lucrezia had her own part to play in that. Not even a teenager, she prepared herself for the voyage to Valencia, to marry a man she had never known.

But then, just in time, in July 1492, Pope Innocent died. Roderigo's carefully husbanded resources, his reserves of wealth, his friendships, the rich church benefices that were his to assign, all were now deployed to the fullest. Borgia was a Catalan, which counted against him, since all Romans assumed that Catalans were secret Jews, but his pockets were deep and his bribes generous. The promise of the vice-chancellorship bought off a rival, Ascanio Sforza, brother of the duke of Milan. Now the Sforza faction among the cardinals came over to the Borgia side.

It was a decisive swing. On the fifth morning of the conclave, the waiting crowd was duly informed that the next bishop of Rome would be Roderigo Borgia, taking the papal name Alexander VI. Lucrezia was now the daughter of a reigning pope; her marriages, her body, might decide the fate of nations.

* * *

Roderigo Borgia, Pope Alexander VI, paraded through the streets to the great Lateran Basilica to take possession of the papacy, and of Rome. Cannons sounded from the Castel Sant'Angelo. The figure of Rome herself, *Roma Dea*, divine spirit of the city, held in her hands the triple-crowned papal tiara. Beside her stood the Borgia emblem, a bull.

Alexander was sixty-one years old, energetic, with an amazing capacity for both pleasure and work. His likeness, frescoed by Pinturicchio on to the walls of the Borgia apartments in the Vatican Palace, shows the new pope in profile: fleshy; neatly tonsured; large hands with gold rings; a faint smile.

Nearby, another painted scene has lasted to this day: the centrepiece of Pope Alexander's magnificent *sala dei santi*. It is Rome – the Arch of Constantine stands in the background, although Pinturicchio has crowned it with a great golden bull. On a dais sits the Emperor Maxentius, surrounded by his wise men, who are dressed in the robes and turbans of Ottoman Turks. They have been stunned into silence by the wisdom of St Catherine of Alexandria, who will pay for her impudence when her body is broken on the wheel. But there she is, still upright and untouched in her blue embroidered dress, blonde hair streaming freely down her back, down to her waist. And her features, delicate and pale, are the features of the thirteen-year-old Lucrezia Borgia.

At some point during her childhood, Lucrezia had been taken away from her mother Vannozza. She appears to have relinquished her children without much complaint. A more fitting guardian had been found for the Borgia cardinal's daughter – his cousin, Adriana Mila, who had married into Rome's great Orsini clan.

Now, on Roderigo's accession to the papacy, Adriana and Lucrezia moved out of the Orsini Palazzo Montegiordano and into a new magnificent residence, the Palazzo Santa Maria in Portico, right next to the Vatican Palace. They were joined there by a third woman, Giulia Farnese, an eighteen-year-old of exceptional beauty, who was married to Adriana's son, Orsino 'Monoculus' Orsini, but who was, more importantly, the lover of Pope Alexander himself.

It was soon widely known in Rome that although the pope lived in the Vatican, the quickest path to papal favour led not through St Peter's but through the Palazzo Santa Maria. There, one Christmas Eve, a Florentine, Lorenzo Pucci, arrived to pay his court and record the scene. Three women together by a fire: Adriana, the gatekeeper; Lucrezia, bright, girlish smile, white teeth; and then Giulia Farnese, la Bella Farnesina, sitting by the hearth to dry her hair. Pucci was stunned by this 'most beautiful creature. She let her hair down before me and had it dressed; it reached down to her feet; never have I seen anything like it … she wore a headdress of fine linen, and over it a sort of net, light as air.'

Lucrezia, meanwhile, was showing off, changing out of her robes to put on a violet velvet gown. Her father doted on her – and all of Italy's aristocrats knew that what she asked on behalf of her favourites, the pope would surely grant.

By the time Pucci visited the Palazzo Santa Maria, Lucrezia, aged thirteen, was a married woman. Shortly after the papal election, her Spanish fiancé, Don Gaspar de Procida, had turned up in Rome to claim his now extremely valuable bride.

Procida, however, was no fit match for a pope's daughter. Alexander had debts to pay and grand alliances to forge, and Procida's replacement had already been found. The Spaniard was paid off and sent home. The way was now clear for a better-connected husband. He was a man of twenty-six, with a respectable income of 12,000 ducats a year, one of the papal governors, or 'vicars', who held much of the old Patrimony of St Peter under their de facto control. The principal attraction, however, lay in his name: Giovanni Sforza.

The Sforza marriage, celebrated, after much negotiation, in June 1493, rewarded Cardinal Ascanio Sforza, the new papal vice-chancellor, for his vital support during the recent conclave. It also created an alliance with Ascanio's brother Ludovico Sforza, nick-named Il Moro, the duke of Milan – an alliance that might help the pope push back the kingdom of Naples which was, with the help of the Orsini, encroaching on the Papal States.

Ascanio was delighted. The pope was 'a very carnal man', wrote the cardinal to his brother the duke, 'and very loving of his flesh and blood'. The marriage of young Giovanni Sforza to Lucrezia, therefore, would 'so establish the love of His Beatitude towards our House that no one will have the opportunity to divert him from us'.

From Naples, meanwhile, King Ferrante wrote disconsolately to King Ferdinand of Spain: 'The Pope desires war and rapine, and his cousins the Sforza drive him on, seeking to tyrannize over the papacy and make Rome a Milanese camp.'

But the game was not over. Pope Alexander's sons remained un-married, and the two kings quickly scrambled two minor princesses to win back the pope's favour for Naples and Spain. Juan Borgia, the pope's favourite son, went off to his Spanish duchy at Gandia to marry King Ferdinand's cousin, Doña Maria Enriques, while Jofré, the youngest, got Princess Sancia of Aragon, who brought with her the valuable south Italian principality of Squillace. In January 1494, the marriage was celebrated in grand style, and consummated, to the approval of all. Jofré 'performed very well', wrote the pope, 'notwith-standing he is not more than thirteen years old'.

Lucrezia's marriage to Giovanni Sforza, the year before, had been celebrated with great pomp. The groom had glittered in his bor-rowed jewels; Lucrezia had arrived escorted by all the young ladies of

Rome – who infuriated the papal master of ceremonies by forgetting to genuflect before the pope – and she herself looked 'very beautiful', though rather outshone by la Bella Farnesina, who was at the pope's side throughout. All the nobles of Rome and the great princes of the church had been present to witness the ceremony. However, in view of the bride's youth, there had been no formal consummation.

Only in November of 1493 was Giovanni Sforza permitted to visit his young wife to *accompagnare in tutto*. And even then, the pope was reluctant to let her leave Rome. At last, an outbreak of plague in May 1494 persuaded Alexander to let her travel to her husband's fief at Pesaro, with Giulia Farnese and Adriana Mila for company.

The political situation was becoming increasingly dangerous. In January 1494, King Ferrante of Naples had died, leaving the throne to his son Alfonso. But Alfonso had a powerful rival. The house of Aragon had originally taken Naples from the Angevin descendants of Charles of Anjou. A claim to the throne of Naples still flowed along with the Angevin bloodline, passed down through the generations to be taken up by no less a power than Charles de Valois – King Charles VIII of France.

The pope, since the marriages of his sons Jofré and Juan, had backed the Aragonese claim, giving Naples to King Alfonso. The Sforzas of Milan, however, feared Naples and backed France. The pope's great rival, Cardinal Giuliano della Rovere, had joined the French cause too, and was organizing a general council of the church to depose Alexander for simony.

Giovanni Sforza was caught in the middle, trapped between Il Moro of Milan on the one hand, and his Borgia father-in-law on the other. It was a situation of immense delicacy, and Lucrezia was little help. She and Giulia Farnese were too busy with society to pay much attention to politics. A celebrated beauty, Caterina Gonzaga, had arrived in Pesaro, and Lucrezia was determined not to be impressed: her skin and hands were beautiful indeed, confessed Lucrezia, and her figure fine, 'but her mouth is ugly and her teeth very ugly indeed… I wanted to see her dance, and it was not a very satisfactory performance'.

Nor was the pope much concerned with his son-in-law's fate. The only thing that mattered to him was getting Giulia Farnese back to his side as soon as possible – a matter complicated by the fact that her husband, Orsino Orsini, had for some reason chosen this moment to start making a fuss about his wife's ongoing infidelity. Orsino had forbidden Giulia from returning to Rome, and she could hardly defy her husband's explicit commands however much Alexander might rage, however much he threatened her with excommunication and hellfire.

In September 1494 a huge French army crossed the Alps into Italy. There was little resistance; none of the Italian states was a match for the national might of France. King Charles VIII, his horse face and watery eyes fixed on Naples, marched south with no one to stop him.

Lucrezia, at Pesaro, was out of the way of the French advance, but Giulia Farnese and Adriana Mila were not so lucky. Giulia had rushed to the bedside of a dying brother at the Farnese family home on Lake Bolsena. Now, on the way back, she and Adriana were captured by a French captain, Yves D'Allegre. The pope had to pay 3,000 ducats to get them back – and Ludovico, Il Moro, was furious when he heard the sum had been so little. Alexander would have paid 50,000, he declared, since Giulia and Adriana were his 'heart and eyes'.

Either way, the pope's prospects looked grim. Charles, supported by Swiss pikemen and a state-of-the-art artillery train, was smashing his way south through Italy. The Colonna and then the Orsini abandoned the pope's cause, turning their castles over to French garrisons. The Neapolitan army was in full retreat. It was clear that the French advance could not be halted. Pope Alexander threw open the gates of the city and retreated to the Castel Sant'Angelo, while French soldiers poured into the streets of Rome.

But the Borgia pope was not beaten yet. Now that the young King Charles was in Rome, Alexander was finally able to gain his ear, dazzling him, as many monarchs had been dazzled before, with the antique lustre of St Peter's See. A general council of the church, as proposed by Giuliano della Rovere, was a challenge to the authority of

God's vicar on earth, and pope argued, and could only lead to further destructive schism.

A schism would have complicated Charles's military ambitions. Naples, technically speaking, was a papal fief, and only an unchallenged pope could truly confirm the French king in his possession of it. Better to head south with a firm new friend in the Vatican than to leave the Holy Mother Church broken and divided. As a token of good faith, the pope's own son, Cesare, would join the French army as a papal legate, accompanied by trunks full of papal gold.

Cesare Borgia, the pope's eldest son by Vannozza Catanei, had been committed to holy orders as a child and propelled by his father to high rank within the church. He was bishop of Pamplona at the age of fifteen. Two years later, on Pope Alexander's election, he was given the old Borgia bishopric of Valencia, with an income of 16,000 ducats a year; the year after that, he was created cardinal, over the objections of the Sacred College. He was far too young for such a dignity, and anyway had no inclination at all towards the spiritual life, as Charles soon discovered. As soon as the French army passed the Alban hills, Cesare swapped his cardinal's robes for the costume of a groom and galloped off into the night. His heavy trunks turned out to hold nothing but rocks.

'All Italians are dogs, and the Holy Father is the worst of them,' raged the king, but it was too late to turn back now. King Alfonso had fled and Naples waited, the richest city in Italy, ripe for the taking. Charles and his men entered in triumph, hardly having struck a blow.

But though taking Naples had been easy, holding it was another matter. For two months the French army enjoyed the pleasures of the city, but they quickly made themselves very unwelcome there. The French were 'clownish, dirty and dissolute', wrote an observer, 'always to be found in sin and venereal acts'. The king was the worst of all, 'one of the most lascivious men in France', who never deigned to have the same woman twice.

Meanwhile, the powers of Italy were mobilizing at last. Urged on by the faithless Pope Alexander, along with Ferdinand of Spain and the Holy Roman Emperor Maximilian, Milan changed sides and joined with Venice to block the French retreat. At Fornovo, near Parma, in July 1495, an Italian army under the experienced condottiere Francesco Gonzaga drove the French from the field and seized their baggage train. Among the looted treasure of Naples was discovered a book containing intimate details of the many sexual conquests the king of France had made during his stay.

Charles returned to France without his trophies. Three years later, he died after hitting his head on the lintel of a door. But though his Italian expedition had failed, it was not soon forgotten. In 1492, the year of Pope Alexander's election, the rich Italian cities were the envy of Europe. With the invasion of 1494, France proved that Italy's splendour was fragile, showed how easily its squabbling duchies and republics could be brushed aside by the army of a strong centralized state. It was a sign of things to come. The golden age of Italian independence was nearly over.

* * *

That winter, December 1495, there were terrible floods in Rome. Tavern gossips spoke of a monster washed up on the Tiber bank, some infernal beast of ill omen.

Around that time Rome's prostitutes started getting ill. Nothing much at first – a painless sore or 'chancre' that appeared on the genitals, then vanished after a few weeks. But soon the disease would return, and with new virulence. There was a rash, purple pinpricks on the hands or face; warts around the anus and genitals; fever; fatigue; hair loss; crippling pain around the joints.

These symptoms might recur over months or even years. Or they might vanish entirely. But in many cases there was a third and final stage. As the 1490s advanced, Romans began to understand the full horror of the pestilence that had come upon them. They saw women with their flesh eaten away; faces warped beyond recognition by gummas swelling beneath the skin. They heard the crying of the sufferers as the disease dug into bones and eyes and nerves, as it nourished pus-filled abscesses among the soft folds of the brain. The wretched *incurabili*, stinking and demented, filled the streets and the hospitals, haunted the churches and the shrines of plaster saints.

Morbus Gallicus, physicians called it – the French disease. Where the French army had passed, on its return from Naples, the disease had followed, and the papal doctors had their suspicions about the cause. They blamed the alignment of stars, the action of Saturn in the constellation of Scorpio. They blamed the poor lifestyles of the afflicted, too much indulgence in anger or melancholy, too few baths, too much bitter food or sweetened wine. They blamed a 'peccant humour', traces of menstrual blood lingering in the body from its creation in the womb, blooming years later as a murderous pox.

But most agreed with Cesare Borgia's personal doctor, Gaspar Torrella, that the most important cause was direct contagion by corrupt vapours that wafted from the uterus of an infected woman during coitus to sink into the pores of the male member.

Above all else, men should avoid contact with infected women, argued Torrella. If all the diseased prostitutes in Rome could only be rounded up and isolated, the disease might yet be eradicated from the city.

It was a vain hope. There were too many infected prostitutes in Rome, and nowhere to put them, and anyway the *Morbus Gallicus* was too strong and had already spread too far to contain.

The bacterium responsible is believed to have been a new arrival in Europe, the spirochete *treponema pallidum*. It came as a stowaway, coiled microscopically in the blood of Columbus's sailors as they returned with their captives and plunder from that 'virgin' territory they had discovered for Spain in their pioneering voyage of 1492. And though kidnapped Taino women did not survive long in Europe, the spirochete flourished among a fresh population with no resistance to the disease, no built-up immunity. From the ports of Spain, it was a short hop to the dockside brothels of Spanish-dominated Naples and the camp of the conquering French, who duly spread it along the length of Italy. By time anyone recognized the threat, this pox had become a Europe-wide pandemic. Syphilis, as it came to be known, would kill millions.

Gripped by the new plague, Rome wavered between fear and anger. There was a new and dangerous mood on the streets. Johann Burchard, the papal master of ceremonies, recorded the fate of a courtesan named Cursetta, who was led in shame through the city for having harboured a certain Moor in her household, who 'dressed as a woman' and 'called himself Barbara the Spaniard' and who 'knew [Cursetta] carnally in I know not what manner'. Cursetta, at least, was released after her circuit of the city. The unfortunate Moor was led to the Campo de' Fiori by a constable brandishing a pair of 'testicles cut from a Jew who had copulated with a Christian woman'. There he was garrotted and burned at the stake.

Jews and Moors were often blamed, along with the French, for having brought and spread the *Morbus Gallicus*. In 1492, the year of Pope Alexander's election, Their Most Catholic Majesties King Ferdinand of Aragon and Queen Isabella of Castile had completed the Reconquista of the Iberian peninsula with the defeat of the Moorish emirate of Granada, and had celebrated their triumph by expelling all the Jews of Spain from their dominion. Pope Alexander had welcomed these refugees into Rome – for a fee – which came as no surprise to the Romans. Moors, Catalans, Jews – to the Romans it came to much the same thing.

None of this touched the fifteen-year-old Lucrezia Borgia, however, safe behind the walls of the Palazzo Santa Maria in Portico. As the French army withdrew, she had returned to Rome while the hapless Giovanni Sforza remained in Pesaro, organizing his troops for the campaign against remaining French garrisons. Through much of 1495 and 1496 he was kept busy with military duties. Like many minor lords, finding the income from his lands inadequate, he supported himself by working as a captain for hire, a condottiere.

He spent little time with his teenage bride. Not that he was insensible of her value. In 1495 he was still boasting that she could get him anything he and his family wanted: a bishopric, a benefice, a cardinal's hat. But a visit to Rome in April 1496 was brief and strained. 'Perhaps he has something at home,' wrote a Mantuan diplomat, darkly. 'Something which others would not suspect.'

Spanish and Neapolitan influence was growing in the papal city, and Lucrezia's husband, with his Milanese connections, was now more of an encumbrance than an asset. Lucrezia herself leaned towards Naples. In the summer of 1496, Jofré Borgia and his wife Sancia of Aragon had returned to Rome from southern Italy, and Lucrezia soon became good friends with the Neapolitan princess.

Sancia was twenty-two, dark, with aquiline features. She was not exactly a beauty – Lucrezia, who had deployed all her finery for their first meeting, had 'surpassed her' in looks – but Sancia's 'glancing eyes' carried an unmistakeable charge. Young Jofré was no match for such a woman. On arriving in Rome, she soon struck up a relationship with his eldest brother, the handsome and ambitious Cesare. 'By her gestures and aspect,' wrote the Mantuan diplomat, 'the sheep will put herself easily at the disposal of the wolf.'

The other brother, Juan Borgia, duke of Gandia, was in Rome that summer too. The pope was overjoyed to have his favourite son back at his side and appointed him *gonfaloniere* of the church. He was sent off into the *campagna* to punish the Orsini for their treachery during the French invasion two years before, and though the campaign began with a series of embarrassing disasters, he did eventually manage, with Spanish backing, to reassert papal authority in the Roman hinterland.

By the spring of 1497, Giovanni Sforza had become seriously alarmed about his position. He had been living with Lucrezia in the Palazzo Santa Maria in Portico since January, but his presence had very clearly become unwelcome to the Borgias. Cesare had probably been threatening him. At any rate, in March 1497 he fled Rome, fearing for his life.

He sent back word that Lucrezia should follow him, but there was little chance of that. The pope was now openly demanding that the marriage be dissolved, and by June it was clear to Giovanni, and to his uncle Il Moro, that the situation was irretrievable. The best that could be hoped for now was some sort of financial compensation and to escape with his dignity intact.

He would get neither. Cardinal Ascanio Sforza negotiated hard on his nephew's behalf, but was unable to change the terms of the deal. Lucrezia's dowry of 30,000 ducats would be returned to her. There would be no pay-off. And worst of all, the official grounds for the dissolution of the marriage would be Giovanni's inability to have intercourse with his bride. His claim on Lucrezia had to have been enacted upon her body, otherwise it was no claim at all. There had been no official consummation on the wedding night, and though Giovanni claimed that he 'had known her an infinite number of times' since, he could produce no witnesses. At last, towards the end of the year, he was forced to accept the pope's terms and declare that he was indeed impotent. In December 1497, Lucrezia was declared *virgo intacta* – a virgin and an unmarried woman. She is reported to have given a speech in Latin 'worthy of Cicero' to express her gratitude.

Giovanni Sforza retreated to Pesaro, muttering blackly about the villainy of the Borgia clan. Lucrezia might have kept her dowry, but he saw to it that she would not retain her reputation. The lustful pope had wanted his daughter all to himself, was the story the Sforzas put about. It was an easy enough thing to believe, given the pope's immoderate love for his daughter and his known weakness for beautiful young women.

And Lucrezia had hardly been a model of chastity and discretion. Indeed, at the very ceremony that affirmed her virginity, she was probably some months pregnant, and not by her husband. It was 'common knowledge', wrote a hostile Perugian chronicler, 'that she had been and still was the greatest whore there had ever been in Rome'.

In June 1497, when the wrangling over the Sforza divorce was at its height, Lucrezia had withdrawn to the convent of San Sisto on the Via Appia. There was something rebellious in this; she had quarrelled with her father, it was whispered. He had sent a constable to fetch her out, but she had refused to come, clinging to her refuge among the nuns. For once in her life, she was beyond the reach of any man.

Seven months later, on 14 February 1498, the body of a Spaniard was found floating in the river. His name was Pedro Calderon, a young man in the pope's service, who 'fell, not of his own will, into the Tiber', as Burchard put it. A maid of Lucrezia's was found with him, one diarist recorded, and Rome was perfectly able to imagine how that combination of corpses had come about: Calderon had 'got His Holiness's daughter, Lucrezia, with child', reported a Bolognese spy. And the murderous Cesare, clearly, had had him killed to shut him up. As for the maid, Pentesilea – she, perhaps, had facilitated the affair.

What became of the supposed child? It is impossible to be sure. There was a Borgia child, named Giovanni, born around this time. Pope Alexander claimed to be the father, by an unknown Roman woman – a claim that is perfectly plausible given his character. Much later, however, it was Lucrezia who would take her young 'half brother' into her care.

It was an awkward time for Lucrezia to be caught up in a scandal. Now that she was free of the unfortunate Sforza, Lucrezia had once again become a valuable asset in the papal arsenal, and indeed, negotiations for her second marriage were already ongoing.

The target this time was a Neapolitan: Alfonso of Aragon, duke of Bisceglie, the younger brother of Lucrezia's new friend and sister-in-law Sancia. He was seventeen and good looking, and whatever Lucrezia had felt about the murder of Pedro Calderon, she raised no objection to the marriage now.

The wedding was celebrated with a nuptial Mass at the Palazzo Santa Maria in Portico on Sunday 5 August 1498. This time it was consummated to everyone's satisfaction – Lucrezia's notional virginity sold for the second time.

There was feasting in the Palazzo Santa Maria and merrymaking in the Vatican. Lucrezia, with golden hair flowing about her shoulders, danced at the pope's command. Sancia served him wine. In the Borgia apartments, Cesare and his gentlemen put on a show, appearing in costume as animals amid an enchanted wood – a sea goose, an elephant, a fox, a stag, a lion, a giraffe. Cesare himself came as a unicorn, splendid in satin, to claim his sister for the dance. Then all were dancing, and the saints frescoed brightly on the walls of the Borgia apartments were outshone by the revellers prancing around the floor below, until at last the party broke up with the dawn.

Cesare, who had taken the lead in arranging these celebrations, was an increasingly dominant figure within the Vatican. Pope Alexander, vigorous though he still was, had suffered a terrible blow to his spirits. The previous summer, Cesare and his younger brother Juan, duke of Gandia, had visited their mother Vannozza at her villa outside Rome. On the way back, the party had paused at the Ponte Sant'Angelo. Juan had something he had to do, he had told them, somewhere he had to go alone. Then he rode off towards the Jewish ghetto by the Theatre of Marcellus.

He did not reappear that night, to nobody's great surprise. It was perfectly reasonable to assume that Juan Gandia was with one of Rome's many courtesans. But as the following day dragged on, the pope became more and more alarmed. Armed men were sent out to search the city. Any possible witnesses were questioned. On the second day, they found a timber dealer, who had been sleeping in his boat that evening, close to the Ospedale degli Schiavone. He had seen five men that night, disposing of a body in the river. It had floated at first, he remembered, so they threw rocks at the man's cloak until it sank.

Why had he not reported the incident? 'In the course of my life,' he replied, 'on various nights, I have seen more than a hundred bodies thrown into the river right at this spot, and never heard of anyone troubling himself about them.'

Rome's Tiber fishermen soon found Juan Gandia. He was fully clothed, nine stab wounds on his body, and with thirty ducats untouched in his purse. 'Had we seven papacies,' the pope lamented, 'we would have given them all to have the Duke alive again. God has done this perhaps for some sin of ours.'

Not that there was any need to invoke God in explanation. The Borgias had plenty of earthly enemies: the Sforzas, the Orsini, Giuliano della Rovere and many more. But the man whose prospects changed the most following the murder had also been among the last to see him. Cesare Borgia, restless with ambition, was ready to put off his cardinal's robes and inherit his brother's position as *gonfaloniere*, the military representative of the Holy Mother Church.

* * *

On 1 October 1498, Cesare Borgia, newly released from the Sacred College, set off for France. His retinue was fit to dazzle a king, so richly equipped that even his horses' shoes were made of silver, and his travelling privy covered in gold and scarlet brocade. 'The ruin of Italy is confirmed,' wrote one observer, 'given the plans which father and son have made, but many believe the Holy Spirit has no part in them.'

The new French king, Louis XII, had made Cesare an irresistible offer. To replace his old archbishopric of Valencia the king offered Cesare the dukedom of Valence and the chivalric order of St Michael. He would also help facilitate Cesare's marriage to Carlotta of Aragon, the king of Naples's legitimate daughter, who was staying at the French court. Last, and best of all, Cesare would be given command of a large company of French lancers, to serve the new duke of Valence wherever he saw fit. In exchange, the king asked only that the pope support the dissolution of his current unwanted marriage, and his upcoming conquest of the Sforza duchy of Milan.

Cesare made an awkward progress up the Rhône from Marseilles with his great train of richly dressed gentlemen, his dozens of grooms and lackeys in Borgia gold and red. He was haughty and cold, French nobles found, and rather pompous in his black velvet mantle and pearl-encrusted boots. And Cesare himself was in a foul mood. On an official visit to Naples in 1497, Cesare had contracted the *Morbus Gallicus*, and the purple 'flowers' of the pox were spreading across his once handsome face. It was an unfortunate condition in which to meet his prospective bride, but his arrival at the French court could only be delayed for so long.

When he met the king at last, at Chinon in December 1498, his worst fears were realized. The French courtiers were amused by his Italian airs, and his intended, Carlotta of Aragon, flatly refused to marry him, her own natural disinclination being compounded by the unease of her wider family at this new rapprochement between Rome and France.

But Cesare was charismatic and, to his great good fortune, managed to win over the king himself. Carlotta had put Cesare in an extremely awkward situation, and though the king put her under great pressure, he could not force her to marry against her will. He was able, however, to find Cesare a new match, one that would bind him even closer to the cause of France.

The chosen bride was Charlotte D'Albret, a pious girl of sixteen, a quiet beauty of impeccable lineage, sister to the king of Navarre. The marriage was celebrated in May 1499 at the chateau of Blois, and Charlotte's ladies-in-waiting spied through the keyhole as the marriage was consummated. Cesare had mistakenly taken some laxative pills in place of aphrodisiacs, but his constant trips to the privy did not prevent him from 'breaking the lance' with Charlotte eight times that evening. The pope was delighted at this, and had all the letters from France read aloud in the Vatican – eight marital bouts, two before supper and six after, eight doses of pox for poor Charlotte D'Albret.

In Rome, while Cesare was in France, Lucrezia was pregnant by Alfonso of Aragon. In February 1499, however, she tripped while running through a vineyard and subsequently miscarried. Still, she was happy enough with her young husband. She, Alfonso and Sancia – his sister, the wife of Jofré Borgia – made a merry trio within the walls of the Palazzo Santa Maria.

It could not last. As the news of Cesare's progress trickled in from France, it became clear that the house of Aragon, like the house of Sforza before it, was falling rapidly from papal favour.

Cardinal Ascanio Sforza had courted Lucrezia assiduously throughout the spring, but by July he recognized that the game was up, and fled to join friends among the Colonna. In August, Alfonso followed, leaving Lucrezia alone in Rome. Once again, she was pregnant, and she wept bitterly at the separation.

She was not one to mope, however. At the age of nineteen, the quick-witted Lucrezia was becoming an impressive woman. Her father trusted her much more than her useless brother Jofré, who had been locked up in the Castel Sant'Angelo for brawling with the city police. Sancia, who dared to defend him, was expelled from the city, sent off to Naples to join Alfonso.

When Pope Alexander needed a governor for the papal stronghold of Spoleto, it was to Lucrezia that he turned. 'Having perfect confidence in the intelligence, fidelity and probity of the Duchess,' he instructed his priors there, 'we trust that you will receive the Duchess Lucretia as is your duty, with all due honour as your regent, and show her submission in all things.'

Lucrezia now had an independent power base of her own, and as her belly grew, so did her territory. In September, the pope entrusted her with the strategic fortress of Nepi, near the Via Flaminia. Here she was reunited with Alfonso, who had finally dared to return to his wife's side. That November, Lucrezia gave birth to a healthy son, named Roderigo, after her father.

That October, as Lucrezia was preparing for her confinement, King Louis XII with his whole court had marched in triumph into Milan. With him, at the head of his lancers, was the former cardinal of Valencia, now duke of Valence – Il Valentino, Cesare Borgia. The main French objective was now complete. The pope had supported France in Milan. Now it was time for King Louis to hold up his end of the bargain, and lend his troops to the pope's beloved son.

Soon after the capture of Milan, the pope formally deposed his 'vicars' in Rimini, Imola, Forlì, Camerino, Faenza and Pesaro (Giovanni Sforza's seat), for failing to pay their annual dues to the Apostolic Chamber. The independence of these vicars, these minor papal feudatories, was coming to an end. Pope Alexander was determined to reassert central control over the Papal States, and Cesare, backed by France, would be his sword.

One man who was impressed by the conquering Cesare was the famous Florentine diplomat Niccolo Machiavelli. Cesare 'is very proud', the Florentine wrote:

And, as a soldier, he is so enterprising that nothing is so great that it does not seem trivial to him. And, for the sake of glory, he does not rest, and acknowledges no fatigue or danger. He arrives at one place before he is known to have left the other; he endears himself to his soldiers; he has got hold of the best men in Italy, and these factors, together with continual good fortune, make him victorious, and dangerous.

His first targets were the towns of Imola and Forli, strongholds of the Riario family, on the Via Emilia in the valley of the Po. Imola fell quickly – but Forli was another matter. The defenders were led by the famous Caterina Sforza (a niece of Il Moro) thirty-six years old and a widow, but utterly undaunted by the straits in which she found herself. Every day she could be seen moving around in front of Cesare's borrowed French guns, picking her way across the rubble of her keep in her shining cuirass. Sometimes she brandished a sword, or carried a falcon perched on one arm. She was a poisoner, men knew, and probably a witch too – but still a famous beauty. When Cesare's men finally broke through the walls he had her dragged to his private quarters. 'O good Madonna,' wrote one blunt condottiere, 'now you will not lack for fucking.'

In February 1500, the conqueror returned to Rome, where the pope was beside himself with fatherly pride. All the cardinals were sent out on mules to meet Il Valentino outside the Porta del Popolo, while the papal master of ceremonies, Burchard, did his best to corral Cesare's unruly Swiss and Gascon mercenaries along their processional route towards the Campo dei Fiori. Cesare was received with tears of joy at the Vatican, and even the captive Caterina Sforza – a woman who, the year before, was supposed to have sent the pope a letter that had been rubbed with plague sores – was swept up in the general benevolence, consigned to comfortable lodgings within the papal palace.

February was carnival time in the city, and the pope's artists and scholars had carefully arranged an appropriate festive programme. The theme of that year's decorated cavalcade was the triumphs of Julius

Caesar, and the Romans thrilled to the sight of the great carnival floats trundling through the streets with tableaux of Caesar's ancient victories – subdued Egyptians, vanquished Gauls. Cesare was not too shy to embrace the parallels with his famous namesake. *Aut Caesar aut nihil*, was the motto he adopted: 'Caesar or nothing.'

The pope had now formally invested Cesare with the titles of *gonfaloniere* and captain general of the church. Cesare 'has the pope in his fist', the diplomats reported. 'The pope loves and fears his son', wrote another spy. 'Physically most beautiful, he is tall and well-made... he will be, if he lives, one of the first captains of Italy.'

Lucrezia was fading in her brother's shadow. She was known to be 'wise and generous' but although she had been the pope's favourite, 'now he does not love her so much'. There were rumours of incest between her and Cesare, who had ended his affair with Sancia to take up with an Ovid-quoting courtesan named Fiametta. Lucrezia and her brother loved each other, certainly, but not in such a way as to impede his summary appropriation of the richest part of her territory around Rome. 'She is a woman. She could not keep it,' was Cesare's only comment. With the pope's help, he was forging the Papal States into a personal principality, and his sister would not be permitted to stand in his way.

On the evening of 15 June 1500, Alfonso of Aragon was attacked on the steps of St Peter's Basilica by three armed men who wounded him severely on the head and shoulder before being chased off into the night. The pope had him carried to the Borgia apartments, where he lay unconscious, close to death.

Rumour and suspicion ran wild in the city. It was assumed that such a bold attack must have been ordered by someone very powerful. 'Who may have wounded him, no one says,' wrote a Florentine diplomat, 'and it is not obvious that diligent inquiries are being made as they should be... in that palace there are so many hatreds, both old and new, and so much envy and jealousy.'

Lucrezia and Sancia had rushed to Alfonso's bedside, and now kept up a constant vigil over the stricken duke. A guard was posted at his door. A trustworthy doctor was summoned from Naples. Lucrezia, fearing poison, prepared all Alfonso's food herself. And, as the days and weeks passed, he stubbornly refused to die. By August, he was able to sit up in bed and receive visitors, and there was every reason to think he might soon be back on his feet.

On 18 August Alfonso was joined by an Aragonese uncle and an envoy from the Neapolitan court, as well as his loyal guardians, Sancia and Lucrezia. As they were talking, they were interrupted by Don Miguel da Corella, Cesare's most feared enforcer, who bound the two Neapolitans and made as if to take them off to prison. Lucrezia and Sancia protested. Corella excused himself. 'He was obeying the will of others,' he said. 'He had to live by the orders of another.' They might, he suggested, make appeal to the pope himself.

Off they went, Lucrezia and Sancia, to remonstrate with Pope Alexander. But when they returned, they found Alfonso's chamber guarded by armed men. They had left Alfonso alone, and in that moment, Miguel da Corella had strangled him.

* * *

Pope Alexander had not wished for Alfonso's death. He was still little more than a boy, just nineteen when he was killed, and there was no need to open up so irreparable a rift with the house of Aragon.

But Cesare had done the deed, and the pope took it in his stride. He was seventy years old, but 'younger every day', a Venetian envoy reported. 'Worries never last him a night.' He had the College of Cardinals under his complete control. Ascanio Sforza was a prisoner in France. Only Cardinal Giuliano della Rovere remained to oppose him, and he was far away. Nothing remained to impede his true ambition: to set up Cesare as the greatest prince in Italy.

Lucrezia, meanwhile, was heartbroken. Her marriage had been a happy one. Alfonso had been a handsome and charming youth and Lucrezia had loved him well enough. Now, bereft and alone, she so troubled her father's peace with her constant tears that he felt compelled to banish her to the Borgia fortress at Nepi until such time as she should manage to cheer up again.

La Infelicissima, as she signed herself in letters, might anyway have been pleased to escape the poisonous atmosphere of the city. 'Every day in Rome one finds men murdered,' wrote the Venetian envoy, 'four or five a night, bishops, prelates and others.' The Borgias 'are men to be watched', agreed another spy, reporting in cipher to his masters in Florence. 'They have done a thousand villainies, and have spies in every place.'

Cesare was hated by many, and feared by all. On the day after the murder of Alfonso, he had visited Lucrezia with an escort of a hundred fully armoured halberdiers. Even within Rome, even with his own sister, he would not hesitate to make a show of force, and all the minor lords of Italy felt the threat. The marquis of Mantua, Federico Gonzaga, the man whose victory at Fornovo had driven Charles VIII back to France, was so alarmed that he tried to marry his son to Cesare's daughter, an infant Cesare had left behind with the forgotten Charlotte D'Albret.

And Gonzaga's sense of urgency was justified. In October 1500, at the head of a formidable army of 10,000 men, Cesare marched out to resume the conquest of Italy.

By February 1501, less than a year after Alfonso's murder, Lucrezia was being lined up for another marriage. The intended groom this time was another Alfonso – Alfonso d'Este, heir to the duchy of Ferrara, and scion of one of the most ancient and distinguished noble houses in Italy, a family that had arrived with the invasion of the Lombards, seven centuries before.

Into this impeccable lineage, the Borgias proposed to insert themselves, a prospect that was mortifying for the Este family in general and, for Alfonso himself, a profound humiliation. The deeds of the Este clan had been a subject for epic poets; the duchy of Ferrara, under the redoubtable Duke Ercole, was the richest and most sophisticated minor state in Italy. Lucrezia Borgia, meanwhile, was illegitimate, tainted by scandal and had no ancestors to speak of beyond the most venal pope in living memory and an unknown Roman whore.

On the other hand, Cesare and his 10,000 men did command

attention. And the most important ally of the Este family, King Louis XII, clearly supported the Borgia ambitions, at least until the planned French takeover of Naples was complete. Duke Ercole, despite his reluctance, was compelled to begin the matrimonial negotiations and, by July, sustained pressure from both France and Rome had worn down his stubborn opposition. Besides, like many a lord before, he found his pride to be soluble in gold. Pope Alexander was promising an extraordinary dowry with his daughter: 100,000 ducats in cash, plus lands, benefices and exemptions that Ercole reckoned worth 300,000 ducats more.

The marriage contract was signed that August, and Ercole began planning ways to spend the vast bounty his son's marriage had won. At the same time, he discovered an unexpected upside to the match: the character of Lucrezia Borgia.

The contract had been agreed, and a proxy marriage, *ad verba presente*, had been conducted. But Lucrezia's position remained fragile. As she knew well, the marriage agreement was worth little until it had been consummated – and the Este family were in no hurry to let her meet her reluctant groom.

Lucrezia was as determined as anyone to secure the Este marriage. Now, as the pope and Duke Ercole continued to wrangle over details, Lucrezia set herself to winning over her new father-in-law, throwing herself into the negotiations on Ercole's side. The Ferrarese envoys in Rome reported that she had been pressing the pope hard – that indeed, his holiness was dismayed by her zeal in the interests of the house of Este. She had also proved willing to make a hard but important sacrifice: she would let go of her infant son. Young Roderigo, the son of Alfonso of Aragon, would stay behind in Rome.

Best of all, Lucrezia was able to help Duke Ercole with a particular passion of his: collecting nuns. He was deeply impressed by holy women who had been blessed with the marks of Christ's wounds, the stigmata, appearing on their hands and feet. He had managed to secure one such nun, a Dominican known as Sister Lucia, from her convent, smuggling her into Ferrara in 1499, where he established her in great state with a convent of her own. But the pious Lucia was lonely, and Ercole's attempts to fill the new convent with Lucia's old friends were being stubbornly opposed by the Dominican Order.

Lucrezia sprang into action. The Dominicans were browbeaten into compliance. The nuns were dispatched to Ercole's court. 'We have received singular pleasure from this,' gushed the duke. 'We could not thank your Ladyship more.'

At the end of October 1501, Lucrezia is supposed to have attended the notorious chestnut ball, with the fifty naked courtesans. It seems an extraordinary risk for her to have taken, to attend a scandalous party at that moment when she was under such particular scrutiny, but the story comes straight from the stolid pen of the master of ceremonies, Johann Burchard, a man whose love of gossip was always moderated by a certain orderliness of spirit.

At any rate, as autumn faded into winter, spirits were high in the Borgia camp. Burchard relates another gossipy scene: the pope and Lucrezia, on a balcony of the Vatican Palace, provoked to helpless mirth by the energetic coupling of a pair of peasant donkeys.

At the beginning of December, there was even more cause for cheer: after months of delay, the bridal escort party that was to bring Lucrezia to Ferrara had set off at last towards Rome. On 23 December the Ferrarese dignitaries were trumpeted across the Tiber, and they immediately set to work analysing the nature of the new Este bride. The groom's sister, the famous Isabella d'Este, had sent her own dedicated spy, El Prete, along with the cavalcade, who dispatched a string of letters to his mistress in Mantua. 'She is an enchanting and exceedingly gracious lady', he conceded, though he judged one of her dresses to be 'in the fashion of ten years ago', and one of her rubies 'not very big and not a fine colour'. Meanwhile Duke Ercole had been getting new reports as well. His ambassador, Johannes Lucas, had heard dark rumours but, face-to-face with Lucrezia, he found it 'impossible to suspect anything "sinister" of her'. He was dazzled by her beauty – 'but her charm of manner is still more striking'.

Christmas brought more festivities. On the streets, wrote El Prete, 'one sees nothing but courtesans wearing masks'. There were bullfights, in which Cesare demonstrated his prowess. There were foot races and horse races and dances, at which El Prete amused himself by picking out his favourite of Lucrezia's ladies-in-waiting. In the Piazza of St Peter, there was held a mock battle between eight noblemen, who fought with such gusto that five of them were carried wounded from the field. On 30 December the bride was given a matrimonial ring, along with other jewels of great value, which gave the pope enormous pleasure. To celebrate the New Year there was another parade organized by the thirteen *rioni* of Rome, with floats showing the deeds of Caesar and Scipio and Hercules. In the evenings, the pope and his guests passed the time with jugglers and jesters, or watching girls in moorish costume dance the *moresca* pantomime. There was a performance of Plautus's *Menaechmi* in the pope's chamber, into which some clever scholar had stitched flattering cameo appearances for the personifications of Ferrara and Rome, who competed in their praises for the fair Lucrezia.

And then, very soon, it was 6 January, the Feast of the Epiphany, the date set for Lucrezia to depart. All was prepared. Lucrezia's vast retinue assembled: Roman and Ferrarese grandees, ladies-in-waiting and the chambermaids, squires, grooms, muleteers, trumpeters, jesters, two chaplains, a major domo, a reader, a secretary, men to take care of her knives, her cup, her plate. Her trunks were full of priceless clothes and jewels. And books; she treasured an edition of Petrarch's sonnets bound in red leather.

In the Sala del Pappagallo, in the Vatican Palace, she said her last goodbye to her father. She stayed with him for some time. She should be cheerful, he called after her, and should be sure to write if she wanted anything at all. And then she left, and rode away, the hooves of her jennet silenced by soft-falling snow. The pope, it is recorded, watched her from his empty palace, moving from window to window to follow her until she vanished out of sight.

* * *

When Lucrezia left Rome, Borgia power was approaching its zenith. Cesare was a bold and ruthless commander, every bit as dangerous as his rivals had feared. All through 1502 his territory expanded, so much so that even the republic of Florence was under threat. Given time, he might have made himself master of the whole of central Italy.

But his time was running out. In August 1503, Cesare and Pope Alexander were both taken ill at the same time. Cesare survived, though seriously weakened. Alexander, however, did not, and with his death the whole basis of Cesare's power began to crumble. Perhaps if he had been healthy at the time, he might have held on, forced the election of a compliant new pontiff in his father's place. But as things were, his enemies were too strong for him, and too numerous. Ascanio Sforza and Giuliano della Rovere had returned to the city, and were determined that the conclave should not go Cesare's way.

By October 1503 della Rovere had forced himself on to the papal throne, and Cesare's prospects were grim. He cast this way and that for support, as his fortresses and towns deserted him, until in 1504 he was arrested by the Spanish general Gonsalvo de Cordoba and shipped off to prison in Castile. In 1506 he managed to escape to join his brother-in-law (through Charlotte D'Albret), the king of Navarre. Fighting for that king, in 1507, he was caught in a melee outside the Castle of Viana, under the Pyrenees, and killed at the age of thirty-one. He had been one of the most feared men in Europe.

Lucrezia mourned her brother deeply, but her life away from him had turned out to be a happy one. Her husband, Alfonso, was a stiff character, obsessed with metalworking and the science of artillery, but they got on well enough. She was also able to have two romantic affairs, one with the Venetian poet Pietro Bembo – the greatest Petrarchist of his time – and one with the marquis of Mantua, Francesco Gonzaga, who had been the victor at the battle of Fornovo all those years before.

Gonzaga and Alfonso were both syphilitic. If Lucrezia was not already carrying the spirochete, she got it soon enough – a cruel burden because, apart from anything else, it is likely to have made it harder for her to produce children. Her position in Ferrara, especially after the fall of her father, was desperately insecure, so long as she kept failing to give Alfonso d'Este a healthy heir. There were several failed pregnancies and deaths in infancy, but in 1508, the year after her brother's death, Lucrezia gave birth to a baby boy, named Ercole after his grandfather. Alfonso d'Este had succeeded to the duchy of Ferrara in 1505, and Lucrezia ruled beside him as duchess, loved and respected by her citizens. As she grew older, she continued her late father-in-law's interest in nuns, even becoming a lay Franciscan herself.

The constant pregnancies, however, took their toll. On 14 June 1519 she gave birth to a child who would not feed and did not live long. After the birth came a fever, with fits and paroxysms. Weaker every day, she wrote a letter to the then pope, Leo X: 'Having suffered for more than two months... as it pleased God, I gave birth to a daughter, and hoped then to find relief from my sufferings, but I did not, and shall be compelled to pay my debt to nature.'

For two hard days after that she lingered. Then, on 24 June, with Alfonso at her side, she died at last. During the final crisis, in the hope that it might ease her, the doctors had cut off all her golden hair.

16

THE VAULT OF HEAVEN

Michelangelo and the Sistine Chapel Ceiling

1508–1512

JUNE 1508. IN the Sistine Chapel, an august and solemn congregation has gathered to hear vespers. It is the vigil of Pentecost, the day when, long ago, the Holy Spirit descended upon the Apostles, breathing into them the vision of an all-conquering church.

Now, a millennium and a half later, the church that was born in spirit has taken on a more worldly substance. Its physical members are built of wood and stone and brick, grand cathedrals and humble churches, limbs of an organization whose body sprawls across most of the known world. Just as impressive, although less visible, are the Church's bureaucratic ligaments: parchment and ink, laws, ledgers and inventories. The footsore evangelists of the early church have been replaced by papal courtiers, who do God's work across whole continents without ever having to leave the safety of the Vatican.

Whenever the religious calendar demands it, the greatest of these high officials gather to hear mass in the *capella magna*, the Sistine Chapel. This is a building fit to house princes of the church. Its masonry is thick and imposing, its proportions copied from the ancient temple of Solomon. Its walls are richly decorated and hung with precious tapestries and, if ever any of the papal functionaries have felt moved to lift their eyes to God, they have been accustomed to the sight of glittering stars, painted in gold on a field of ultramarine.

The Sistine chapel stands for the church, and the church for the whole world, bounded only by the heavens above.

But today, on this Pentecost, the bureaucrats of the papal curia are unable to enjoy their exalted surroundings with the usual serenity. The air in the chapel that should be rich with incense is thick with dust. Scaffolding obscures the starry ceiling, and the sacred music of the chapel choir is interrupted by the beating of hammers and the tread of heavy feet up above. Occasional lumps of plaster, dislodged from on high, plummet like rebel angels to land among the congregation. In the Sistine Chapel the sky is falling.

* * *

Paride de' Grassi, papal master of ceremonies, confided to his diary his fruitless indignation: 'On the upper cornices of the chapel, there was building work going on, with the greatest amount of dust, and the workmen did not stop even when ordered to do so.' The cardinals were most displeased. Was there a foreman on the ground, or was the furious master of ceremonies forced to mount the ladder to the wooden working-platform twenty metres above? If he did, his effort was wasted. 'I myself,' he says, 'argued with several workmen, and they did not cease.'

De' Grassi stormed off to report the insolence of the labourers directly to the pope himself. But if he hoped that a blast of pontifical wrath might clear the hammerers from the Sistine ceiling, he was disappointed. On the contrary, it was he who found himself fixed in the papal glare. His holiness 'almost seemed annoyed with *me*', the incredulous master of ceremonies reported.

Things could have been worse. From *this* pope, so mild a display of anger was remarkable restraint. Pope Julius II, formerly known as Giuliano della Rovere, was a ferocious character. As a cardinal, Giuliano della Rovere had been bitterly hostile to Rodrigo Borgia, Pope Alexander VI. He had triumphed over the Borgias in the end, ascending to the papacy himself in 1503, but years in the wilderness had done nothing for the new pope's temper. When crossed, the newly crowned Julius would fly into violent rages, screaming and shouting and thrashing about with his stick. 'In the hospital in Valencia,' wrote a Spanish ambassador, 'there are a hundred people chained up who are less mad than his holiness.' People called him the 'Fearsome Pope' – *Il Papa Terribile.*

Julius made determined efforts to regain control of the papal territories lost in the collapse of the Borgia dominion. In 1506, he led an army against Bologna and Perugia, the pope in martial majesty, with an escort of twenty-six red-hatted cardinals puffing and wheezing in his baggage train. Four years later, in 1510, Julius took personal command of a second campaign – the geriatric pontiff defying syphilis, malaria and inflamed hemorrhoids to go cantering round the walls of the fortress of Mirandola, dodging cannonballs. When *Il Papa Terribile* died at last, in 1514, the Dutch humanist Desiderius Erasmus famously imagined him leading his mercenaries against the very gates of heaven.

Julius saw himself less a pope than as a caesar, as his regnal name showed. He knew, though, as any Italian prince in those days had to know, how fleeting and ephemeral temporal power could be. He had seen how fast Cesare Borgia's little empire had crumbled. Julius's most lasting legacy would be won, therefore, not on the battlefields of Italy but in the workshops and building sites of Rome.

Rome at the beginning of the sixteenth century presented a somewhat gloomy aspect to the well-travelled visitor. Naples, not far to the south, was a richer and more splendid city, a royal seat for generations of Aragonese and Angevin kings. And with 200,000 inhabitants, Naples was four times Rome's size. Other Italian cities were similarly impressive. Venice had 160,000 citizens, and the treasures of a whole maritime empire to adorn its streets. Milan, Palermo, Florence and even Bologna and Genoa were all comfortably larger than the papal capital. Among the great Italian cities, Rome could claim only the melancholy distinction of having the most ruins.

These ancient ruins, however, had begun to take on a new significance. The pilgrim guides of the Middle Ages had liked to boast of Rome's vanished glories, to be sure. But the medieval view of the past had had a certain shallowness to it. The past was glorious but unreal, gilded and flat like the background of a gothic altarpiece.

Around 1415, the goldsmith and architect Filippo Brunelleschi sketched out the rules of linear perspective. Through diligent study, fifteenth-century painters were able to perform a miracle, giving two-dimensional surfaces the appearance of perfect three-dimensional space. Artists, by skilful use of converging lines, began to deepen the flat medieval backgrounds, stretching them out towards a distant vanishing point.

Similarly, over the century and a half before Julius II ascended to the papal throne, the past had been brought into a new sort of perspective. At the great Italian universities, the traditional *quadrivium* – a curriculum of music, arithmetic, geometry and astronomy – was being squeezed by a new programme, the *studia humanitatis*. Humanists, following the example of the great Francesco Petrarca, among others, devoted themselves to the study of the rhetoric, ethics, poetry and history of the ancient world.

Humanists learned the subtleties of classical Latin, learned to recognize the ways in which the language had evolved over time. They prided themselves on being able to imitate the perfection of Cicero, rather than what they saw as the degenerate Latin of later antiquity. With greater precision came an understanding of anachronism: one humanist scholar, Lorenzo Valla, was able to prove by close examination of language that the Donation of Constantine, the foundational document of the Papal States, was a forgery, several centuries less ancient than it was supposed to be.

In other words: with diligent study came depth. For the well-read humanists, the flat and mythic past deepened into three dimensions, diachronous lines of cause and consequence reaching back towards a vanishing point. There was a new awareness, among humanists, of the great stretches of time that separated past events from each other, and from the present day.

And with that awareness new questions presented themselves, especially to humanists who lived among the wreckage of ancient Rome. What terrible events had transformed the city, over so many centuries, from the glittering metropolis of Cicero and Ovid into the ruin that remained? The story was there to be read in the city itself, legible in crumbling basilicas, medieval tower-houses, broken aqueducts, in defensive walls and narrow streets.

Of course, the city – as a text – was confused and ambiguous. But the humanists understood a clear narrative to be encoded there: there had been a golden age, classical antiquity. Then had followed many centuries of darkness, a dark age. And now, with the rediscovery of classical learning, there was a rebirth: a renaissance.

Such was the narrative, as scholars understood it in Pope Julius's day. The achievements of late antiquity and the great works of the middle ages were dismissed as mere steps on a journey of decline – a decline that was only just now being reversed. And this history, though it did Julius's predecessors a grave injustice, was perfectly acceptable to Julius himself. The time was right to sweep away the rubbish of dark centuries past and create a new Rome that would be a fit inheritor of the vanished golden age.

And so it was, in that June of 1508, that papal workmen took their hammers to the outmoded gothic ceiling of the Sistine Chapel. The great Julius required something new, something spectacular. And he had just the man for the job.

* * *

Michelangelo Buonarroti was born in Tuscany in 1475. His family called themselves nobility, but the fortunes of the Buonarroti had long been in decline. Michelangelo was born into an awkward social position: it was beneath his dignity to practise a trade, but he was not quite rich enough to live as a gentleman.

As a child Michelangelo was put out to nurse with a family of stonecutters near the Buonarroti family farm at Settignano. Many years later he would wax sentimental to his obedient friend and biographer, Giorgio Vasari: 'Giorgio, if my brains are any good at all it is because I was born in the pure air of your Arezzo countryside, just as with my mother's milk I sucked in the hammer and chisels I use for my statues.'

Like many stories told by Vasari, and by the other contemporary biographer, Ascanio Condivi, this is part of the myth of Michelangelo – a myth expertly sculpted by the great man himself. He liked to present his talent as essentially homegrown. Michelangelo, as he appears in Vasari, is a man born 'under a fateful and lucky star', an artist springing, as it were, fully formed from the Tuscan soil, chisel in hand, a solitary genius inspired by the divine.

In fact, Michelangelo was fortunate to have been born into a republic which, by the end of the fifteenth century, had established itself as perhaps the greatest artistic centre in Italy. The Florentine tradition went back to the great Giotto at the beginning of the fourteenth century, and deepened from there, new skills and new techniques passed from master to student, often from father to son. Brunelleschi, the pioneer of perspective, was a Florentine. So was the great Lorenzo Ghiberti, whose bronze doors for the Baptistry of St John by Florence cathedral would one day be praised by Michelangelo as equal to the very gates of heaven. Ghiberti helped train several Florentine masters, including Paolo Uccello and the sculptor Donatello, who brought his figures to life with a technical confidence born of the long study of ancient art. Donatello was friends with the painter Masaccio, whose work, reaching new heights of realism and expressiveness, inspired a young friar named Filippo Lippi, a wonderful talent and a notorious seducer of nuns. Filippo Lippi's influence is clearly visible in the delicate lines of his pupil Sandro Botticelli, who in turn was a frequent collaborator and competitor of Domenico Ghirlandaio, neglected by later critics but held in his day to be one of the finest painters in Florence.

Ghirlandaio had inherited a grand tradition. And, as was usual, he took apprentices to pass his skills along. Among them, in the year 1488, was a thirteen-year-old boy, young, but very gifted: Michelangelo Buonarroti.

Florence in those days was ruled, in fact if not in name, by Lorenzo de' Medici. Lorenzo was a leader in the spirit of the great Augustus, loudly proclaiming his adherence to Florence's republican constitution while keeping a firm grip on power behind the scenes.

As with Augustus, Lorenzo's authority was bolstered by his prestige as a patron of learning and the arts. Lorenzo the Magnificent, admirers called him, and his generosity attracted some of the brightest talents in Italy: Botticelli, Verrocchio, even the young Leonardo da Vinci before he went off to join the Sforza court at Milan.

As well as artists and architects, Lorenzo cultivated scholars. The Medici had a longstanding association with the philosopher Marsilio Ficino, who had set up a 'Platonic Academy' in the family villa outside Florence. Just as Renaissance artists drew upon ancient statues for inspiration, so Ficino and his friends hunted for wisdom in the ideas of the vanished past. This was not a matter of mere scholarly curiosity. The philosophy of Plato, it was believed, contained vital metaphysical truths, truths that predated the birth of Jesus by four hundred years.

Plato's ideas had been further developed by the so-called neoplatonists – most famously Plotinus and Porphyry – who, during the years of imperial crisis following the reign of Elagabalus in the third century AD, had spun them out into an elaborate philosophical and cosmological system. The neoplatonists went questing after the divine, tracing the hierarchy of existence up and out from the base material world, through whole taxonomies of consciousness and spirit until, by great mental discipline and imaginative effort, they were able to touch upon the indivisible 'One', from which all being was derived.

This was strong stuff, even after an interval of over a thousand years. And this highly developed platonism was not altogether easy to harmonize with theological orthodoxy, however much Ficino tried. Porphyry, one of the forefathers of the neoplatonist tradition, had written a whole polemic against the dangerous ideas of early Christians.

But Renaissance scholars were increasingly willing to dabble in antique esoterica. Ficino had his platonists. Another prominent member of the Medici circle, Pico della Mirandola, explored the mysteries of Kabbalah and Zoroastrianism, the alchemical secrets of the Hermetic Corpus. After a thousand years of neglect, even the pagan gods of the classical pantheon were making a comeback: not as deities exactly, but still as potent magical and astrological symbols, connected to the motion of the planets and the turning of the spheres.

The Christian God was supreme, to be sure, but under him in the scheme of things were whole layers of being in which lesser spirits might cling on to some sort of metaphorical existence.

Pagan mythology offered useful symbols. But more than that: the stories were good. Educated humanists had rediscovered the pleasure of reading Ovid. From them it spread to the sculptors and painters. Ancient myths, especially those that featured in Ovid's *Metamorphoses*, began showing up with ever greater frequency in Renaissance art.

Among these pagan scenes is a striking example from the year 1492, an early work from the teenage Michelangelo. The boy had left the Ghirlandaio workshop behind him. His status-conscious father, Ludovico Buonarroti, had been alarmed by the move: he understood his son to be embarking upon a career as a lowly stonemason. In fact, Michelangelo had joined the household of Lorenzo de' Medici as a sculptor. Lorenzo had established what the biographer Vasari describes as a sort of school for young artists: choice works of ancient art from the Medici collection were displayed in a special sculpture garden off the Piazza San Marco in Florence. Here, Michelangelo and a few others were permitted to live and work. Proximity to the antique masterpieces, it was hoped, might nurture a new generation of talent worthy of the reborn golden age.

Certainly, the young Michelangelo quickly learned to imitate the techniques and sensibility of ancient art. Michelangelo had little academic schooling, and was no Latinist, but one of Lorenzo's scholars, the poet and polymath Angelo Poliziano, helped him find a passage from Ovid that would work as an artistic scene. The resulting sculpture, an ambitious Battle of the Centaurs in marble relief, was stunningly accomplished for one so young. Michelangelo, clearly, was capable of great things.

The road would not be altogether easy. These were troubled times. Indeed, trouble was brewing just a stone's throw from Lorenzo's sculpture garden, at the Dominican convent on the other side of the Piazza San Marco where, in 1482, a new friar named Girolamo Savonarola had moved in.

Passionate and eloquent, Savonarola was a gifted preacher who had won the admiration of, among others, Lorenzo de' Medici's kabbalist philosopher, Pico della Mirandola. He made a deep impression on the young Michelangelo. But the indulgent attitude of the Medici circle towards the fiery Dominican was not reciprocated. Savonarola was a preacher of the apocalypse. A time of tribulation was at hand, he believed. Florentines should cast off the shackles of worldly sin, wealth, vanity, the pleasures of the flesh, and prepare themselves for the great judgement to come.

In 1492, while Michelangelo was still working on his centaurs, Lorenzo de' Medici died. He summoned Savonarola to his deathbed, the story goes, but it was not a comforting encounter: the Dominican refused to grant the dying tyrant final absolution.

Lorenzo de' Medici was succeeded by his son Piero, but the young man could not match his father as a politician. And the balance of power in Italy, which Lorenzo had so carefully maintained, was about to be shattered by the French invasion of the peninsula in 1494. With hostile French forces in Tuscany, and Savonarola stirring trouble in the streets, Piero de' Medici fled Florence, never to return.

Michelangelo took religion seriously, and had admired and respected Savonarola, but revolutionary Florence was no place for a young artist, especially not one who had been so close to the Medici. Savonarola's followers, the so-called 'weepers', or *piagnoni*, controlled the city. In the new purified republic there was to be no room for frivolous aestheticism and pagan dalliances. Savonarola held ceremonial 'bonfires of the vanities', on which were incinerated great piles of profane literature and art. In 1496, after two unsettled years spent between Florence, Venice and Bologna, the twenty-one-year-old Michelangelo set off for a city where artists were in ever greater demand: Rome.

Michelangelo first attracted the attention of Roman connoisseurs by his mastery of the techniques of ancient art. A statue of cupid he produced in Florence was such a perfect imitation of ancient style that it passed as an antique and was sold to a cardinal for a suitably inflated price. When the fraud was eventually discovered, the cardinal was furious and demanded his money back. He also, recognizing the sculptor's skill, became Michelangelo's first Roman patron.

It took two more statues for Michelangelo to establish himself in Rome. The first was a drunken Bacchus sculpted with such tender eroticism that the cold marble seemed to breathe. Next came the famous *Pietà* that can still be seen in St Peter's today. A Madonna – of superhuman size and beauty – cradles the dead Christ in her lap. His head is flung back across her knee. His tortured body, framed by the drapery of Mary's robe, is rendered with a lover's care and an anatomist's skill, learnt through long nights dissecting corpses in a Florentine hospital.

Savonarola fell from power in 1498. He was hanged, and his corpse burned, to purge Florence of his heresy. Three years later, Michelangelo returned at last to his home city, where he found the new *gonfaloniere*, Piero Soderini, to be an enthusiastic commissioner of monumental art. Michelangelo's marble David, completed in 1504, was immediately adopted as a heroic emblem of the renewed Florentine state, the biblical shepherd boy reimagined as a muscular republican Adonis.

It was during this period, too, that Michelangelo produced his first design for a fresco, to decorate the Palazzo della Signoria. Michelangelo's *Battle of Cascina* was commissioned to match a mural by the great Leonardo da Vinci. Michelangelo's stock had risen far indeed.

But the fresco was never completed. Working for the Florentine *signoria* was all very well, but, in 1505, Michelangelo was summoned back to Rome by an offer he could hardly refuse: he was invited to deploy his talents in the service of the recently crowned Julius II, *Il Papa Terribile* himself.

* * *

Rome had not, during the fifteenth century, been a great producer of artists. Of the great painters and sculptors of the Renaissance, disproportionately few were native to Rome. There was no artistic tradition in the papal capital to compare with the extraordinary flowerings of talent that had been seen in, for example, Florence or Venice.

But what Rome could not provide, the forceful Pope Julius II would acquire, one way or another. Michelangelo was one of several artists who were drawn into the pope's service. Giuliano da Sangallo, formerly the favourite architect of Lorenzo de' Medici, had been working for the pope since the fall of the Medici government in 1494. Another Florentine, the sculptor Andrea Sansovino, arrived in Rome not long after Michelangelo. He was put to work with the Umbrian painter Pinturicchio, beautifying the interior of the basilica of Santa Maria del Popolo, the della Rovere family church.

The most important of the pope's artists, however, was Donato Bramante, a painter and architect from Urbino who had come to Rome at the end of the 1490s. Bramante's masterpiece, the *Tempietto* at San Pietro in Montorio, is a small but perfect specimen of high Renaissance classicism, a circular shrine modelled after, among other things, the ancient temple of Vesta, and admired by contemporaries as the most harmonious building in Rome.

It was to Bramante that Julius turned with his most ambitious architectural commission: the rebuilding of St Peter's basilica. The existing structure had stood since the reign of Constantine, and was by now on the verge of collapse. And if its walls should crumble, so much the better. The basilica's simple structure and late antique brickwork offended the Renaissance eye, trained in the subtleties of classical pagan proportion.

The new basilica, when it rose, all soaring domes and polished marble, would be more appropriate to the papal dignity. And inside, Julius planned to erect his own personal monument: a tomb, on the grandest scale, whose sculpture and design would be the work of his promising new Florentine, Michelangelo.

This was the perfect project for an ambitious young sculptor. Michelangelo threw himself into it. The pope advanced him the considerable sum of a thousand ducats for raw materials, and Michelangelo travelled in person to the great quarries at Carrara to choose the right blocks of stone, 34 tons of perfect white marble that arrived in Rome by river barge one stormy January day in 1506. The Tiber was running high. Not long after the blocks were unloaded, a sudden flood swamped the docks under the Aventine. For hours, the precious marble sat soaking underwater.

It was a sign of things to come. Even as work on the monumental tomb was getting under way, the restless pope was brewing a new scheme that threatened to divert Michelangelo's energies disastrously from the matter in hand. Julius had decided to renovate the Sistine Chapel ceiling.

By April 1506 Michelangelo was in Florence again. He had left Rome in anger, and in fear. The pope had cut off funds for the tomb project. Michelangelo, applying for money to buy the next batch of marble, had been rudely shut out by a papal functionary.

And that was not all. 'There was also something which I do not wish to write about,' he told a friend. 'It is enough that it led me to think that, if I remained in Rome, my own tomb would have been made sooner than that of the pope.'

Had Michelangelo caught wind of some mysterious threat against his life? It is hard to think who might have profited by his assassination. In fact, his alarm may have been caused by the mere prospect of being forced to paint the Sistine ceiling – a task for which he had neither time nor inclination.

And if Michelangelo dreaded the Sistine Chapel, he had reason to do so. To fresco the vaulted ceiling of the chapel was an enormous technical challenge, as well as an artistic one. Julius's architect Donato Bramante, Michelangelo learned, had told the pope as much: 'Holy father, I don't believe Michelangelo has the spirit for the job; he hasn't done many painted figures, and what's more these figures are to be high up, and in foreshortening, which is quite a different thing from painting at ground level.'

Worse yet, any fresco on the chapel ceiling would have to compete with the frescoes that already existed on the chapel walls. Back in 1480, Lorenzo de' Medici had sent a team of Florentine artists to Rome as a peace offering to the then pope, Sixtus IV. The frescoes on the Sistine Chapel had been done by some of the greatest painters of the previous generation: Sandro Botticelli, Luca Signorelli, Michelangelo's old master Domenico Ghirlandaio and – perhaps most intimidatingly of all – the great Pietro Perugino, an immigrant to Florence, whose *Delivery of the Keys to St Peter* is one of the finest existing examples of high Renaissance art.

However reluctant Michelangelo may have been, Pope Julius was not a man to be crossed lightly. In November 1506, the papal army seized Bologna. One week later, Michelangelo received a new summons from the all-conquering pope. It was clear by now that continued obstinacy might endanger not just Michelangelo but the entire Florentine state. With great reluctance – 'with a rope around my neck', as he later put it – Michelangelo was forced to go and seek the pope's gracious pardon. Piero Soderini sent him off regretfully but firmly. Michelangelo was 'an artist without equal in Italy, perhaps even in the world,' Soderini told the pope by letter. 'With kind words and tender treatment, he can achieve anything.'

In March 1508 the errant Michelangelo arrived back in Rome at last to begin work on the Sistine ceiling. From the first moment, the project was beset with difficulties. Michelangelo liked to recall a furious argument he claimed to have had with Bramante over the correct way to install the necessary scaffolding.

By June, Michelangelo's workmen had set up their precarious scaffold and were busy infuriating Paride de' Grassi by chipping the old painted stars off the Sistine vaults. This was hard work, and it had to be done quickly: before any painting could take place, a plaster undercoat, the *arriccio*, had to be applied, and this undercoat might take months to dry, even in the heat of the summer. Once winter set in, and the chilly *tramontana* wind started blowing in from the Apennines, working on the fresco would become a damp, miserable ordeal.

While the undercoat dried, Michelangelo began sketching out his preliminary designs. The initial idea had been that he would paint twelve Apostles in the lunettes around the chapel's upper windows, then cover the rest of the ceiling in the standard decorative manner of the day: a pattern of geometric frames with enclosed scenes, inspired by ceilings that had survived from classical antiquity.

But Michelangelo, who had been so eager to avoid the difficulties of the Sistine ceiling, now complained that the proposed scheme was too modest in its scope. 'Having begun that work,' he wrote to a friend, 'it seemed to me that it would prove *una cosa povera* – a poor thing.' Michelangelo said as much to Pope Julius who was, above all else, determined that he should never appear poor. 'So, he gave me a new commission: that I should do what I pleased.'

This cannot be quite true. Even an artist as much in demand as Michelangelo could not expect to be allowed to paint a papal chapel according to his whim. But however much guidance he may have had from papal theologians, the concept that was settled upon at last could not be faulted for lack of ambition: down the centre of the vaulted Sistine ceiling, Michelangelo would fresco a series of scenes from the book of Genesis, going back from Noah's flood to the creation of the universe.

This Genesis story told across the ceiling would, in a sense, complete the work that had been done by the Florentine team – Perugino, Botticelli and the rest – on the chapel walls a generation before. The frescoes on the walls showed scenes from the life of Moses and from the life of Jesus. At window level were figures of past popes. Now, on the ceiling, Michelangelo would, as it were, fill in the gaps: as well as the Genesis scenes there were to be Old Testament prophets, ancestors of Christ and even pagan sibyls, honoured for their foreknowledge of the divine truth that was to redeem them. Taken in its entirety, the finished Sistine Chapel would amount to a full sacred history of the world.

* * *

Of all artistic techniques, wrote Giorgio Vasari, fresco 'is the most masterly and beautiful... being truly the most manly, most certain, most resolute and durable of all other methods.'

Painters in tempera or oil depended on fixatives to keep their pigment on their canvases. In fresco, the unadulterated pigment soaked directly into wet plaster. The plaster used was a paste of slaked lime – calcium hydroxide made from limestone or marble burned to powder in a kiln. When this lime plaster was wet, it could be worked and spread and painted upon. When it dried, however, it was not much different in its chemical and physical properties from the hard unyielding stone it had once been. Pigment locked in dried plaster might retain its colour for a thousand years.

Fresco had unique advantages. At the same time, as Vasari noted, it was 'supremely difficult to bring fresco work to perfection.' Success required 'a hand that is dextrous, resolute and rapid' and, above all, 'a sound and perfect judgement' based on 'the very greatest experience'.

In the Autumn of 1508 'the sculptor Michelangelo', as he signed himself in his letters – a man who had hardly touched a fresco since his brief apprenticeship with Domenico Ghirlandaio twenty years before – began work on one of the most ambitious frescoes Rome had ever seen. The stars were gone from the ceiling. The plaster undercoat was dry. Lime for the fresh top coat had been hoisted up the 20 metres to the scaffold, ready for mixing. The artist's assistants stood ready with trowels, buckets of water, brushes and precious pigments. Rolled up on the boards were the full-scale sketches, or cartoons, from which Michelangelo would copy the design for each day's painting on to the surface of the vault.

The day's first task was that of the *muratore*, the plasterer, who mixed sand and lime in precise quantities with the volcanic ash known as *pozzolana*. The addition of water completed the plasterer's alchemy: the powdery corrosive lime transformed into calcium hydroxide, fresh wet plaster that swelled and grew during the reaction, giving off noxious fumes and heat like a living thing.

Each morning, the *muratore* would make and spread only enough plaster to cover a few square feet of ceiling, an area known as a *giornata*, as much as a painter could finish in a single day. This final layer of plaster, the *intonaco*, was buffed and polished until it was perfectly smooth. The cartoon for that day's work was laid against the ceiling so that the design could be transferred. For rough work, an assistant could simply trace the outlines on the cartoon with a knife, leaving an impression on the soft plaster beneath. For details like faces, the more laborious *spolvero* method would be used, pricking holes in the cartoon and then dusting it with charcoal from a cloth bag, like a sort of stencil.

At last the pigment could be applied, brushed on to the plaster overhead. The gap between scaffold and ceiling was a little over the height of a man, and Michelangelo and his assistants worked standing, bent backwards uncomfortably with one arm raised. Fresco painters worked hard and fast, sometimes with bags of pigment strung around their waists for ease of access, like climber's chalk. These pigments were hard to come by and often very expensive: rich ochres from the Italian earth; *smaltino* made from ground glass and cobalt by an order of Florentine friars; powdered lapis lazuli, imported from the East by Venetian galley. Many pigments were highly temperamental, changing shade as the plaster dried. It took care and expert knowledge to keep colours consistent from one day's work to the next. At the same time, speed was vital. Once the plaster dried, at the end of the day, it would no longer take pigment. If that day's plaster was for any reason unfinished or unsatisfactory, the only remedy was to smash it off the ceiling and start again.

It is still possible, from up close, to make out the *giornate*, the work-days by which Michelangelo's fresco advanced across the vaults of the Sistine ceiling. He began with Noah's Flood, a cluster of refugees climbing hopelessly away from the rising waters, as the Ark floats off into the distance behind them. The *giornate* here are cautious; Michelangelo was not covering much ground each day. And yet, despite this caution, the painting did not go well. At some point, for an unknown reason, Michelangelo took a hammer to the fresco, destroying nearly half the scene.

Michelangelo had hired four unspectacular but well established Florentine fresco painters to help him. He may even have hoped, by letting them do most of the brushwork, to keep working on his own favourite project, the monumental della Rovere tomb that had been his first papal commission. No chance of that now, however. Weeks of work had somehow been ruined. No doubt it was a grim day up on that gloomy scaffold when the offending plaster was finally chipped off the ceiling.

The whole professional arrangement could have been calculated to cause unpleasantness. The assistants and Michelangelo lived together in the artist's cramped workshop not far from the Vatican, working in the chapel all day before retiring to their spartan shared quarters at night. Conditions were poor. 'His nature was so rough and uncouth,' wrote one contemporary, 'that his domestic habits were incredibly squalid.' Michelangelo had been instructed by his father never to wash himself; he slept in his clothes, and was in the habit of wearing his boots for so long at a time that when he removed them a layer of skin would peel off too.

Even at the best of times, Michelangelo was not an easy man to get on with. In his teens, his nose had been broken by a rival young artist whom he had offended – 'I felt the bone and cartilage crush like a biscuit,' his assailant later recalled. But that violent encounter served to bring Michelangelo's face in line with his character: craggy and unforgiving. He was suspicious of others and jealous of his own prestige. Even the ever-loyal Condivi acknowledged that the great man was *bizzarro e fantastico* and 'withdrew from the company of men'.

And Michelangelo knew how to hold a grudge. Years later, Biagio da Cesena, successor to Paride de' Grassi, dared criticize Michelangelo's Sistine frescoes. Such a carnival of nudes, he suggested, was more suitable for a bathhouse or a tavern than for the Pope's own chapel. Michelangelo did not forget the insult. He painted the hated Biagio into his Last Judgement above the altar wall, giving the Papal Master of Ceremonies the donkey ears of Minos – a king of hell. *His* nudity at least was covered by a snake, which sank its teeth into Biaggio's painted penis.

Vasari and Condivi will have had no trouble, therefore, believing the slightly far-fetched story Michelangelo told about the breakdown of his relationship with his assistants in the Sistine Chapel. One day, the artist claimed, when the assistants turned up for work, they found that he had had the doors of the chapel locked against them. For a while, they thought he was playing a joke at their expense. At last, worn out by unsuccessful entreaties, they had no choice but to head back in disgrace to Florence. After that, says Condivi, Michelangelo worked 'with no help whatsoever, not even someone to grind his colours for him'.

This picture of the solitary artist labouring at his masterpiece has become fixed in popular imagination. This is Michelangelo as played by Charlton Heston in *The Agony and the Ecstasy* – but surely not as he was in real life. His Florentine fresco painters may have left simply because their contracts had expired. Michelangelo's bank records show he was careful with money to the point of avarice; he probably let the Florentine assistants go in order to replace them with cheaper hands. He certainly did not finish the Sistine ceiling entirely alone.

And yet, Michelangelo might reasonably have felt that while he did have helpers, they were not much help. They had, above all else, been meant to help him get to grips with the technicalities of fresco. Then, in January 1509, Noah's Flood was suddenly attacked by damp and mildew – the deadliest enemies of the fresco painter's art, and exactly what the assistants were meant to guard against. Michelangelo was miserable. 'It's been a year,' he wrote to his father, 'since I have had a *grosso* from this Pope; and I don't bother him, because my work is not going along well enough to merit anything. This is the trouble with this work: it's still not my true profession and I waste my time. Lord help me!'

Things were about to get even worse. Not far from Michelangelo's mouldy Noah, a new artistic endeavour was getting underway – one that threatened to eclipse the Sistine ceiling. Since 1507, Julius had been forming a new team of artists to decorate his apartments in the Vatican Palace. Some of the finest artists then alive had answered the pope's call: Pinturicchio, Luca Signorelli, Lorenzo Lotto and, worst of all, Perugino, whose wonderful fresco of St Peter so effectively dominated the Sistine Chapel wall. Among these artistic giants was a slight young man from Urbino, not well known but with a rapidly growing reputation: Raphael Santi.

The young Raphael was set to work with Giovanni Antonio Bazzi, an eccentric Sienese painter better known as *Il Sodoma*, famous for his flamboyant dress and for the small menagerie of monkeys, badgers and birds he kept in his home. While Sodoma was tending to his zoo, Raphael busied himself with stealing the show in the Vatican. His initial frescoes in the room now known as the *Stanza della Segnatura* were far more accomplished than those of his eminent peers. Julius, decisive as always, dismissed the lot of them. The decoration of the pope's apartments was entrusted entirely to the young Raphael.

Suddenly, Michelangelo found himself facing a rival who could compete with him in genius and who was far better at managing the politics of the papal court. Raphael had all the charm and delicacy of character Michelangelo lacked. He painted his own likeness into one of the frescoed scenes on the walls of the *Stanza della Segnatura*: he stands in the foreground of *The School of Athens*, second from right. His features are fine and a little girlish, his gaze thoughtful but confident. His contemporaries thought him a very handsome man.

Michelangelo also put himself into his paintings, but in a very different manner. In the Sistine Chapel he is thought to be visible in two places: on the ceiling his likeness appears on the severed head of Holofernes; in the *Last Judgement*, frescoed above the high altar twenty years later, his face is attached to St Bartholomew's flayed skin.

While Michelangelo sulked and fought with his assistants, Raphael gathered friends and apprentices. He lived 'like a prince', wrote the poet Pietro Aretino, 'bestowing his virtues and his money liberally on all those students of the arts who might have need of them'. His paintings in the Vatican Stanzas demonstrate his sociable instincts. Many of the characters who populate his historical scenes have the features of respected contemporaries: Bramante, Il Sodoma, Giuliano da Sangallo, Leonardo da Vinci and Pietro Bembo, among others, have all been recognized by keen observers at one time or another, painted into *The School of Athens*, Renaissance artists impersonating ancient philosophers, ancient wisdom taking modern form.

Of course, wherever any pope appears in Raphael's *Stanza della Segnatura*, that pope looks like Julius II. Michelangelo's relationship with his patron was famously stormy. Vasari tells the tall story that on one occasion, when Julius tried to climb up to get a better look at the paintings, Michelangelo fended him off by pelting him with planks of wood. Condivi claims, more plausibly, that Julius got so angry over Michelangelo's slow progress that he thrashed him with a stick and threatened to have him thrown off the scaffolding. Raphael, on the other hand, was a perfect courtier, charming and deferential. He rapidly became the most favoured artist in Rome.

* * *

Late in 1509, Michelangelo addressed a melancholy little poem to his friend Giovanni da Pistoia:

> *This toil is pushing my stomach up into my chin;*
> *It has already done my neck in, swelling*
> *Like the necks of those cats who've been drinking*
> *The fetid water in Lombardy, or wherever it is.*
> *My beard to the sky, I feel my brain shoving*
> *Into the hump of my back, my chest bulging*
> *Like a harpy's, while under my dripping brush, my face*
> *Is a patterned floor, ever more ornate.*
>
> *My lower back has pushed its way into my chest,*
> *Which makes sense, because my arse is now my back,*
> *While my feet move as they like, well out of sight.*
> *[...]*
> *Come save my dead painting now, Giovanni,*
> *Save both that and my honour: I'm really*
> *Not in a good place here, and I am no painter.*

Michelangelo was tired, lonely and miserable, and he hated Rome – and yet things were not quite so hopeless as he was making out. His damp problem had been solved with the help of the artist Giuliano da Sangallo, who instructed him on the correct way to mix the unfamiliar Roman plaster to make it properly waterproof. Michelangelo's confidence as a painter was growing. His first of the central panels,

Noah's Flood, had taken him thirty *giornate* to complete, and had needed extensive retouching. The fourth panel, *The Fall of Man*, took just thirteen.

It is also a far superior design. The figures in *Noah's Flood* had been too small and the image too cluttered to make a powerful impression when seen from ground level. In *The Fall of Man* the busy background landscape has disappeared. The slightly stilted composition of the Noah panels has given way to a bolder and more perfect vision, in which space is dominated by the monumental human form.

In 1506, two years before work on the Sistine ceiling began, Michelangelo had witnessed one of the most exciting artistic discoveries in history. Workers digging in a vineyard on the outskirts of the city hit upon a marble statue buried underground. Michelangelo and Giuliano da Sangallo were summoned to the scene, and watched as the statue emerged from the soil. This, it soon became clear, was no ordinary find. The buried statue was none other than the famous Laocoön, a work named by Pliny the Elder as one of the greatest masterpieces of ancient art.

It is a scene of extraordinary dramatic power. The Trojan priest Laocoön wrestles against the coils of a monstrous serpent that will devour him and his two sons. Laocoön's body is idealized, as is usual in Hellenistic art, but through his posture, his straining muscles, the angle of his neck, the arch of his back, the still marble manages to express desperate extremes of human struggle and despair.

This bodily drama made a profound impression on Renaissance artists who saw it. So, in Michelangelo's *Fall of Man*, it is human bodies that deliver the scene's narrative thrust. The figures of Adam and Eve are repeated on both sides of the scene, which is divided in two by the tree that bears the forbidden fruit. On the left-hand side of the painting, they tell a story of sexual desire. The fingers of Eve's right hand are pointed in obscene suggestion. Adam reaches a thick arm into the foliage for the fruit (a fig, more suggestive than the usual apple) and in doing so turns his genitals towards Eve's face. That face, so beautiful in its prelapsarian condition on the left, is disfigured by grief when she reappears with Adam on the right. Here, on the wrong side of the tree, we see Adam and Eve after the fall. Their two bent bodies are contorted in shame, cowering before the angelic sword that drives them from Eden.

The influence of the Laocoön can also be seen in the so-called *ignudi*, nude youths who perch on a series of painted pediments running the length of the Sistine ceiling. Through their various poses, Michelangelo displays a perfect mastery of the possibilities of the human form. The *ignudi* surround the central panels with a symphony of bodily perfection.

Raphael, as he proved with *The School of Athens*, had a gift for the eloquent placement of figures within an architectural space. His Greek philosophers with the faces of modern artists are set within a harmonious and well-proportioned volume, laid out in perfect perspective so that each figure occupies gracefully his allotted position in the painted room.

Michelangelo, likewise, creates a sort of painted architecture for his figures to inhabit, an illusionistic structure of cornices and pediments designed to give the sense that the Sistine Chapel opens up towards the heavens. But whereas in Raphael's work it is the architecture that defines the space, the great nude figures on the Sistine ceiling, bending this way and that, overwhelm the architecture with the sheer force of their arched backs and bunched muscle. Michelangelo's nude colossi are not content to sit meekly within their painted framework. Rather, they bend it to themselves, distorting perspective so that they are always at the centre of the action. Michelangelo's bodies are eloquent, full of meaning. They come together to form a sort of 'muscular rhetoric', to steal Leonardo da Vinci's phrase – a rhetoric of extraordinary power.

In the summer of 1511 Michelangelo moved on to the second half of the Sistine ceiling, and the scaffolding over the first half was removed. At last the true grandeur of Michelangelo's vision began to be revealed. His symphony of naked bodies was really about the triumphant ascent of the human spirit.

The neoplatonist philosophers at the court of the Medici had dedicated themselves to understanding the sacred hierarchy of existence. Beyond the base material plane of the everyday, they believed, lay worlds of pure mind and spirit, the realm of the divine.

Something of this can be seen in the Sistine Chapel ceiling. At the edges of Michelangelo's design, in the lunettes around the windows, the ancestors of Jesus are portrayed. These figures are strikingly ordinary: they argue and work and read and comfort babies; they are entirely occupied with the mundane.

Above them, at the edges of the vault proper, are the prophets and the sibyls. These giant seers are beginning to feel the stirrings of divine vision. They hear angelic voices; they look up from their books; they stare off into the distance, as if they had caught a glimpse of another world.

Next come the *ignudi*, like wingless angels. Here, near the middle of the design, they have no need for clothes. In their physical perfection, they embody the perfection of the divine spirit.

Running along the apex of the ceiling are the central panels with scenes from the Book of Genesis. In chronological terms, the narrative runs from the creation of the universe to Noah's Flood. In a sense, though, the scenes are best understood in the opposite direction, in the order Michelangelo painted them. This metaphysical story starts with the drenched and scattered humans fleeing the flood. Moving eastward, the figures grow: Noah and his sons; Adam and Eve leaving the garden; Eve created by God.

Here Michelangelo pauses to move the scaffolding – and to wring more money out of the Pope, who is off on one of his endless campaigns. When work begins again, Michelangelo produces an image that will become one of the defining masterpieces of high Renaissance art: *The Creation of Adam*.

Adam, languid and beautiful, lies on the grass. As if still half asleep, he extends a finger towards his creator. God, on the other side, has been transformed since his last appearance. In *The Creation of Eve*, God stands, in traditional fifteenth-century style, firmly rooted to the ground. In *The Creation of Adam*, by contrast, God has taken flight. He now floats at the centre of a whirlwind of heavenly energy, supported by a team of hovering cherubim. His arm, stretched out to meet Adam's, forms a bridge that takes the viewer from the human to the divine.

By this time 'the sculptor' Michelangelo is working with complete confidence, often freehand – without the use of preliminary cartoons. He is moving so fast that he leaves hogs' hair bristles stuck in the plaster. They are still there today. In the last three central panels, God is the only character, magnificent in his odd pink gown. He glides through the aether in perfect *di sotto in su* foreshortening, as if he is about to smash straight through the ceiling and burst into the chapel below. Then, he turns away again. In the final panel – which Michelangelo painted in a single day – he is at the beginning of time, separating light and darkness. He gazes upward, into the great beyond.

* * *

Even before it was finally unveiled, Michelangelo's ceiling had become a sight any visitor to Rome had to see. In 1512, Lucrezia Borgia's husband, Alfonso d'Este, spent most of a hot summer's day on the scaffold in conversation with Michelangelo. Lodovico Buonarroti would have been amazed and gratified to hear that his son, a mere craftsman, was now being visited by great lords. The social status of artists was beginning to change.

When the scaffolding at last was taken down, Julius rushed to the chapel to see the full fresco for the first time, arriving before the dust had even settled. He had commissioned an astonishing masterpiece of religious art. For centuries since, visitors have been left speechless and undone by the Sistine ceiling, struck down like the figure of Jonah who lies at the altar end of the fresco, flattened by the majesty of Michelangelo's painted God.

The Sistine Chapel ceiling made Michelangelo a star. No other artist could ignore his triumph. Prints of the frescoes circulated around Europe, bringing proof of Michelangelo's fleshy brilliance to an astonished world. By the time Vasari wrote his biography, fifty years later, he was regarded as nearly divine – an artist sent of God.

Raphael certainly was deeply moved and affected by the frescoes. With typical generosity of spirit, he is supposed to have knocked a hole in his *School of Athens* and added a figure of the Greek philosopher Heraclitus to the scene. It had the face of Michelangelo.

17

JUDGEMENT

The sack of Rome

———

1527

MAUNDY THURSDAY IN Rome, the fifth day of Holy Week, the day of the Last Supper. On this day, by long tradition, the pope issues a bull, *In Coena Domini*: an edict against the ills of a corrupt and dangerous world. *In Coena Domini* – at the table of the Lord. But the bull's purpose is to mark out those who will *not* be welcome at the Lord's table, to renew each year the sentence of excommunication against heretics and pirates and obstinate bishops and quarrelling kings and anyone who should dare to oppose the authority of God's holy church and her supreme pontiff.

This year, as every year, the bull is read. And this year, as every year, the pope takes a lighted torch and hurls it to the ground among the people, like Jupiter with his thunderbolt, to prove the burning heat of this anathema. There is a good crowd, it being Holy Week: Romans gathered for a papal blessing, along with those pilgrims who have dared to stay in the city, even in these times of war.

But this year, as the pope gives his blessing, the pious hush is disturbed by a displeasing and unexpected commotion. Thousands of eyes that should be bowed in prayer now swivel about in impertinent curiosity; thousands of faces turn all together, in shocked amusement. Because there, by the very steps of St Peter's, a half-naked man is clambering up on to a statue of St Paul.

The scrawny figure perches awkwardly on the Apostle's shoulders. His red hair hangs to his shoulders. A ragged apron covers his thighs. His cheeks are gaunt. In his right hand he carries a crucifix; in his left, what looks like a human skull.

And now, even during the solemn blessing, the wild-eyed creature speaks, cries out, his gaze fixed firmly on the pontiff, 'O Bastard of Sodom!' Stunned silence now. 'For your sins, Rome will be destroyed. Confess and repent. And though you may not wish to believe me, yet, on the fifteenth day from now, you shall see it come to pass.'

* * *

Sixteen years before this grim prophecy was delivered, an Augustinian friar named Martin Luther had arrived in Rome. He came on business, probably in early 1511, as a legal representative of the Augustinian monastery at Erfurt. Nevertheless, he approached the city with the enthusiasm of a pilgrim: he thrilled, as so many had done before, to his first sight of the Eternal City from the Via Cassia; when he reached the Augustinian church of Santa Maria del Popolo, garlanded with della Rovere oaks, he fell to his knees. 'Hail, holy Rome!' Luther exclaimed, 'made holy by the holy martyrs, and by the blood which has been spilt here'.

Over the four weeks that followed, his opinion soured markedly – or so he later told it. The basilicas were splendid, certainly, but the priests who lurked within them were cynical unbelievers, who vied with each other in the perfunctory shortness of their Masses. 'Get on! Get on!' they prodded him, when he took his place at the altar to chant a lengthy rite. 'Free-thinking' Italians, half-pagan to Luther's eyes, had no time for such Germanic solemnities.

The ordinary Romans were even worse, he recalled. Most of the women seemed to be prostitutes, and the men were mere animals, who shocked the Germans by relieving themselves wherever they pleased. Only by painting up images of Saints Sebastian and Anthony on their walls were householders able to avert the urinal torrents.

'If there is a hell,' Luther would write, 'Rome is built upon it.' Rome was a whore of a city – he realized, 'a filthy stinking puddle' – and this realization had been granted him by divine grace. He would not have missed his trip to Rome for 100,000 guilders. Without seeing the city with his own eyes, he declared, he would always have feared that by his invectives he was doing the pope an injustice. But he had seen it for himself: the cardinals were inverts and degenerates; the pope as villainous as the Grand Turk; the monks and priests who haunted Rome's streets were, beneath their habits, little better than beggars and thieves.

The artistic treasures of the great papal city had little appeal for the pious peasant's son. How vain it all seemed to him, Rome's worldly glory. How clear the message of the giant ruins scattered all around: that all cities of men, in the end, come to nothing but ashes and dust.

Only the shrines and relics of the pilgrim trail drew his attention. And even here he was assailed by doubt. He joined the throng climbing the Holy Stairs of Pontius Pilate on his knees, hoping that the indulgence won thereby might spare his deceased grandfather the torments of purgatory. 'But did it work?' he wondered. Even as he climbed those sacred steps, he heard a voice echoing in his mind, a voice that seemed to speak with the authority of heaven: 'The just shall live by Faith.'

At that moment in the church's history, the popes were interested less in faith and more in works: specifically, the great work of rebuilding the Basilica of St Peter. The plans, developed over the years by Alberti, Bramante, Giuliano da Sangallo and even Raphael, now called for the complete destruction of the original Constantinian building in favour of a structure that would be the largest and grandest church of the entire Christian world, with a price to match: a fit monument to the princely papacy of the Italian Renaissance.

This was a great work, a noble work, dedicated to the glory of God and his church. It was almost generous of the popes, therefore, that they should offer their flock the chance to share in it.

Pope Leo X, who claimed the papal throne when old Julius II finally relinquished his grip on life in 1513, was a Medici, a son of Michelangelo's old patron, Lorenzo the Magnificent. As a scion of Italy's greatest banking family he was perfectly comfortable with the imaginative financing solutions his predecessors had pioneered. As was by now established practice, preachers around Europe were sent out among the faithful to solicit contributions to the grand project in Rome.

One of the most successful of these preacher-salesmen was a Dominican monk named Johannes Tetzel. His ecclesiastical master, Albrecht of Brandenburg, had spent a borrowed fortune in bribes to add the archiepiscopal see of Mainz to his existing bishoprics of Magdeburg and Halberstadt. Now Tetzel was unleashed on the combined dioceses, to win that fortune back. The profits of his preaching would be split between Mainz and Rome.

Urged on by the insatiable archbishop, Tetzel's patter became ever more extravagant. No one should doubt, he assured his congregations, that those who donated an earthly coin to the Holy Mother Church would receive their spiritual reward. They need only give him a few coppers. In exchange, the pope with his divine keys would unlock the treasury of merit.

'Lay up for yourselves treasures in heaven,' Jesus said, 'where neither moth nor rust doth corrupt.' Over fifteen Christian centuries, legions of saints and martyrs had laid up such treasure to the point of surplus – a surplus that the pope might disburse if he chose. And though such treasure might be intangible, it was precious currency in the economy of salvation. 'As soon as the penny in the coffer rings,' ran the notorious jingle, 'the soul from purgatory springs.'

The doctrine of indulgences, as these gifts of spiritual treasure were called, was no novelty. A Christian might, under certain special conditions and having fully confessed their sins, be spared the punishment that ordinarily should be associated with those sins – penances due in life and even after death when the impure soul might be detained in purgatory before ascending to its final rest.

And when such indulgences were reserved for pilgrims and crusading knights, the system provoked few complaints. But Tetzel and his colleagues offered much softer terms. God's grace, it appeared, was being hawked about for earthly coin.

*

Luther, by the time of Tetzel's commission, was teaching at the University of Wittenberg, not far from Archbishop Albrecht's diocese of Magdeburg. He was horrified by reports from the province. As a doctor of theology, the doctrinal crudity of Tetzel's simoniacal indulgence-trading appalled him. As a priest, he was infuriated by the impact of these fraudulent peddlers on the Christians in his care, who flocked to Magdeburg to feed their modest savings to the bottomless stomach that was Rome. The rebuilding of St Peter's seemed a thin pretext to Luther, who had seen the wealth of the papal city first hand. 'Why,' he asked, 'does not the pope, whose wealth is today greater than the wealth of the richest Crassus, build this one Basilica of St Peter with his own money rather than with the money of poor believers?'

'The Kingdom of Heaven,' Jesus said, 'is like a man who sowed good seed in his field; but while men slept, his enemy came and sowed tares among the wheat.' Likewise, it seemed to Luther, had tares been sown among the true doctrines of scripture, worthless weeds, planted in God's church while the bishops slept. The very idea of purgatory, unsupported in scripture, was such an error; so was the false notion that the pope had any jurisdiction over the penalties due after death.*

Man, wrote Luther, is 'a corrupt tree', capable of nothing but evil. No pilgrimage, no crusade, no gift to the church, nor any other work of man is capable of redeeming the fallen human soul. Only through faith – faith in the freely given and unearned grace of God – do sinful humans reach salvation.

Luther marshalled his arguments. He was an excellent writer and thinker. More importantly, he had access to a powerful new weapon in the struggle against error: the recently invented printing

---

* Even if the pope *could* grant remission of the penalties of sin, Luther argued, the doctrine of indulgences was self-refuting. Everyone agreed that only a truly penitent person could be spared divine punishment. But a truly penitent person would not seek to avoid such punishment; on the contrary, such a person would seek punishment out. The buyers of indulgences, by that very purchase, revealed their unfitness to recieve them.

press. In October 1517, Luther finished work on his great polemic, the *Disputation on the Power of Indulgences*, and posted it off to the offending archbishop, Albrecht of Brandenburg. But if Albrecht hoped the matter would go no further, he was disappointed. The *Disputation* was the talk of the theological colleges. University presses across Germany sprang into life. Before long, dozens and then hundreds of of copies of Luther's work were in circulation, enough for every serious theologian in Europe.

Amplified a thousandfold by the clattering of the presses, Luther's text began to resonate even beyond the halls and cloisters of the universities. Luther is supposed to have nailed a copy of his *Disputation* to a church door in Wittenburg. There, for everyone to see, were his ninety-five theses against indulgences – ninety-five numbered points, clear and concise, that together constituted a great hammer blow, driven against the millennium-old edifice that was the Roman Catholic Church.

It was not immediately obvious, however, quite how devastating to the church Luther's work would be. The writer of the theses presents himself as a loyal Catholic theologian. The preaching of indulgences was surely contrary to the pope's will. The pope would forbid it if he only knew the abuses being carried out in his name. Luther was arguing for the pope's own benefit. For as things stood it was 'difficult even for learned men to rescue the reverence which is due the pope from slander, or from the shrewd questions of the laity'.

Luther's local opponents – Archbishop Albrecht, Tetzel and his fellow Dominicans, the papal legate Cardinal Cajetan – reacted furiously to this attack. But Pope Leo's response was constrained first by distance and then by politics. At the beginning of 1519, just over a year after the publication of the ninety-five theses, the Holy Roman Emperor, Maximilian I, died in Austria after a long decline. The succession was contested, and would be decided by seven hereditary electors who, at that moment, held the future of central Europe in their hands.

On the one hand stood King François I of France, desperate to add the imperial crown to his existing dignities; on the other, Charles of the house of Habsburg, a teenager whose slight and unprepossessing frame ran blue with the blood of half the great dynasties of Europe. As duke of Burgundy, he held the rich cities of Flanders and the Netherlands; from his mother, Joanna the Mad of Castile, he claimed the Spanish dominions of Ferdinand and Isabella. Now he had a chance to inherit the title of his grandfather Maximilian. As Holy Roman Emperor he might unite, in his person, a monarchy whose territory stretched from the borders of Poland to the mountains of Peru.

For Pope Leo, this was a nightmare prospect. The papal principality, forged at such great cost by the houses of Borgia and della Rovere over the preceding decades, would find itself caught between Habsburg jaws: to the north, the old imperial claims in northern Italy, backed by German swords; to the south, the Aragonese kingdom of Naples and the limitless New World wealth of Spain.

It was not, therefore, a good time to be antagonizing the German elector princes. And one of those elector princes was a supporter and protector of Luther's. Friedrich the Wise of Saxony was Leo's best hope of preventing young Charles Habsburg from claiming the imperial throne. Luther might well be the worst kind of rebel and heretic, as Tetzel and the Dominicans were urging, but Leo was not about to let his geostrategic aims be compromised by mere theology.

As it turned out, Leo's restraint was all for nothing. In June 1519, the electors installed Charles as Holy Roman Emperor, to the alarm of the pope and the fury of France.

Luther, meanwhile, was hardening his position. In 1520, he read the treatise of the Italian humanist Lorenzo Valla, who proved, by rigorous scholarly analysis, that the Donation of Constantine, the foundational document of the papal principality, was nothing more than a medieval forgery.

The Emperor Constantine, whatever his qualities, had not been the sort of man to give away bits of his empire, Valla argued. More importantly, a pope as wise as the legendary Pope Sylvester would have spotted the moral danger in such a 'donation' of worldly *imperium*. No pope, Valla argued, could retain his 'honour and purity' while also playing the role of 'Caesar'. It was a moral lesson whose truth had recently become all too clear.

Luther had not intended, with his ninety-five theses, to set himself up against the whole might of the Catholic Church. But reading Valla he came to see the true nature of the papal beast. What God gave freely, the imperial church tried to sell. The bishops in their cathedrals were hoarders of divine grace. The pope, playing at Caesar with his armies and his palaces, was in fact none other than the Antichrist. 'Your see,' he wrote to the pope in 1520, is 'more corrupt than Babylon and Sodom'.

At last, in December 1520, Pope Leo issued a bull excommunicating the renegade theologian. The papacy had faced such threats before: Wycliffe in England, Jan Hus in Bohemia, Savonarola in Florence. Even in Rome itself there was a tradition of dissent going as far back as Arnold of Brescia or Cola di Rienzo and the Fraticelli. The careers of Luther's antecedents had ended at the stake, more often than not.

And the pope, to his surprise, found an ally in the young emperor, Charles V. Charles had to rule a larger empire than had existed in Europe since the days of Constantine. He could hardly afford to add religious schism to the forces tugging at his vast dominion. When the imperial *Diet* met at Worms in 1521, Luther was summoned to defend himself.

In the face of every possible argument, Luther held his ground. 'I am bound to the scriptures,' he said. 'My conscience is captive to the Word of God.' It was a turning point in the history of Europe, and the tale has grown in the telling. 'Here I stand,' Luther tells the emperor. 'I can do no other.'

In May 1521, Luther was condemned by pope, *reichstag* and emperor. It was too little, too late. In the four years between the posting of the ninety-five theses and the Diet of Worms, Lutheran ideas had gripped Germany with a speed no one could have anticipated. The burghers of the trading towns longed for a purer piety, a church free from the venal influence of Italy, from corrupt bishops and greedy lords. The poor dreamed of a world in which salvation would be available to all, not just to those who could afford to pay.

Meanwhile, some of the great princes of Germany detected an opportunity. The electors had been well bribed to make Charles their emperor but they had no intention of allowing him any more power than was strictly necessary. Just as Charles recognized the need for religious unity, the princes saw the possibilities in dissent, especially as it had formed around the charismatic figure of Martin Luther. Against the international regimes of pope and emperor, the princes might raise a Christianity that was proudly German in origin and local in its scope – a Christianity that might, not incidentally, allow for the confiscation of some of the rich assets of the church.

Charles tried to have Luther arrested, but without success. On leaving the Diet of Worms, Luther had been spirited away by agents of Friedrich of Saxony. Safe in Friedrich's stronghold at Wartburg, perched impregnably on a Thuringian crag, Luther was hidden while the movement he had initiated swept through Germany like a flood tide, bringing war and revolution in its wake. Bishops and theologians, nobles and emperors, no one could hold back the great wave of Reformation.

* * *

Charles had bigger things to worry about than one German heretic. His mother, Joanna the Mad, remained stubbornly alive. Strictly speaking, Charles ruled Castile only as her regent, and in the early 1520s he faced a major revolt among his Spanish citizens, some of whom had begun to suspect that poor confined Joanna might not be quite so mad as her son liked to pretend.

More alarming still were the ambitions of François I of France, who had revived the old French claim to Milan. Whoever held Milan, Charles understood, held Lombardy. Whoever held Lombardy might, if they so chose, split Charles's empire, cutting Germany off from Spain, while threatening the rich kingdom of Naples.

In 1513, the duchy of Milan had been taken over by the Swiss Confederacy, who held it through their puppet duke, Massimiliano

Sforza, a young son of the great Ludovico Il Moro. The Swiss were the most feared soldiers in Europe. Through two centuries of war, they had wrenched their mountain cantons from the grip of Europe's dynasts. Now they had turned their pikes towards the Italian plains.

But the young King François was undaunted. In 1515, accompanied by the flower of French chivalry, and a state-of-the-art artillery train, he made a surprise crossing of the snowbound Alps. Ranging ahead went the Chevalier de Bayard, *sans peur et sans reproche*, a living legend among knights who had first marched to Italy with Charles VIII back in 1494 but who had lost none of his elan. Prospero Colonna, the ageing condottiere sent to hold the Alpine passes, scoffed at the French advance. 'Have they wings?' he is meant to have asked. He would hold Bayard like 'a pigeon in a cage'. But Bayard was already riding hard into hostile territory. One evening, as Prospero Colonna dined in the little town of Villafranca, he found, to his horror, that the legendary chevalier was already upon him, inside the gates. There was nothing for it but to surrender. 'Such is the fortune of war,' Bayard consoled him; 'sometimes you lose and sometimes you win.'

Colonna's capture left Milan's Italian allies in disarray, but the French still had to face the dreaded Swiss pikes. At Marignano, the two armies met. The outnumbered Swiss charged in with their usual murderous courage, while François's cannons raked bloodily through their lines. For hours, long into the night, the battle hung in the balance. The Swiss pushed forward towards the French artillery, but each time they were stopped by François's German mercenaries, the Black Legion, while Bayard and the king led their heavy lancers in a series of desperate charges against the Swiss flank. The next morning, Venetian reinforcements arrived at last to support the French, and the Swiss were pushed back, with a loss of some ten thousand lives.

For all the fine chivalry on display, the battle itself had been a blood-soaked chaos, a massacre by the rather tame standards of Italian Renaissance warfare. And the massacre could easily have gone the other way, but for the diligent leadership of the king's cousin Charles, duke of Bourbon, the Constable of France.

Bourbon was the greatest lord in France after the king himself, in both land and lineage. His ancestors had bled for France at Crécy and Agincourt. His father had died holding Naples for King Charles VIII. His mother was a Gonzaga, sister of Francesco, marquis of Mantua, the lover of Lucrezia Borgia.

From these distinguished antecedents, the duke had inherited a certain long-faced melancholy and a deep sense of aristocratic pride. Still, he got on with his cousin François well enough, and the king, recognizing his indispensability, had appointed him Constable of France, supreme commander of the royal army. At Marignano, Bourbon had led the vanguard, bravely holding out against the Swiss assault until reinforcements arrived.

But the age of the indispensable magnate was coming to an end. Henry VIII of England was impressed by Charles de Bourbon when they met at the Field of the Cloth of Gold in 1520, but he saw perfectly clearly the threat that such a man might pose. 'If that noble were a subject of mine,' he remarked, 'his head would not remain long upon his shoulders.'

Bourbon had served his king loyally and at great cost, leaving a younger brother dead on the field at Marignano, but in the years that followed, the king seemed determined to insult him, treating him coolly, appointing lesser men to higher offices. In 1521, the same year as the Diet of Worms, Bourbon's wife died, and the lands he held through her were suddenly vulnerable. The king seized the opportunity. On the one hand, he threatened a lawsuit to strip Bourbon of the contested estates. At the same time, the king's mother Louise, forty-five years old, offered her hand in marriage. Had he led her on? Had she been driven mad with love for the much younger duke, as later accounts would have it? Either way, as far as Bourbon's land was concerned, the lover and the lawsuit came to much the same thing.

Once, the story goes, François had wondered aloud to the duke of Bourbon what sort of bribe would tempt him to rebel against the crown. 'Sire,' Bourbon is supposed to have replied, 'the offer of three kingdoms such as yours would not be enough. But an affront would be sufficient.'

That affront had now been delivered. Bourbon rejected the queen mother's proposal in a fury. 'I, who have been married to the best woman in all France, am counselled now to marry the worst woman in the world?' The words, as Queen Louise herself promised when she heard them, would cost him dear.

Throughout 1522 Bourbon's position worsened. The lawsuit, with the king as his opponent, would hardly go his way, whatever the merits of the case. And Bourbon feared that the king, having taken his lands, might make an attempt on his liberty, or even his life.

But François was not the only monarch now taking an interest in the duke of Bourbon. That summer, messengers from Spain and England began to arrive at Bourbon's ducal palaces. His imperial majesty, Charles V, was prepared to take full advantage of the division between François and his most powerful vassal. The queen mother might have been an unacceptable match, but would Bourbon consent to marry the sister of an emperor? An emperor, moreover, who was willing to set the rebel duke on the throne of France.

By 1523, the plan was well advanced. Henry VIII of England would invade France from the north, supported by footmen from the Netherlands. Charles V would bring landsknechts from Germany and heavy cavalry from Spain. At the same time, the duke of Bourbon would lead an uprising with his own vassals and retainers. He expected half the nobility of France to join his cause.

But Bourbon put too much faith in his noble friends. François was soon well aware of what Bourbon was plotting. In August 1523 the two men were still professing friendship to one another, but both knew the game was up. With no sign of English or Spanish armies rushing to the rescue, and loyal French regiments marching to arrest him, Bourbon fled into the mountains with a handful of companions to throw himself on the mercy of the Holy Roman Emperor.

Six weeks later, the travel-worn duke of Bourbon arrived in Mantua. His relatives, the Gonzagas, led by the redoubtable widow, Isabella d'Este, welcomed him warmly. Politics aligned neatly with family feeling: Italy had once again become a battlefield.

The French had suffered a major defeat in Lombardy in 1522 (at the aged hands of Prospero Colonna) and Milan was now under imperial control. Bourbon threw himself into the fight, now on the imperial side. By the River Sesia, in April 1524, Bourbon and the imperialists destroyed an invading French army. Here, the duke came face-to-face with his old comrade the Chevalier de Bayard, who had taken an arquebus stone to the spine while rallying the French rearguard. Bourbon did what he could for the old knight, but there was no saving him.

There was no time to mourn. Bourbon and the imperialists pushed on into France, easily capturing the smaller towns and cities of Provence. At Marseilles, however, facing determined French defenders, Bourbon's imperial coalition fell apart. The Germans wavered in the breach; the Spaniards gave way behind them, and suddenly the whole army was in retreat, heading back to Italy again.

Their trials were just beginning. As Bourbon retreated from France, François launched another great expedition to recapture Milan, re-enacting his bold Alpine crossing of ten years before. By the time Bourbon reached Lombardy, François and his famous lancers were already there.

Now, though, at the moment of opportunity, the French delayed. François was so confident in his position that he neglected to chase down the ragged remains of the imperial army. Instead, he divided his forces: a strong detachment was sent down south to press Naples, while François himself laid a leisurely siege to the city of Pavia in the north.

It was a crucial respite, and the duke of Bourbon did not waste it. That winter, he headed north alone. When he returned, he brought with him the greatest soldier in Germany: the lord of Mindelheim, Georg von Frundsberg.

Frundsberg's military career was as long and distinguished as the Chevalier de Bayard's had been. But while Bayard had dedicated himself to the old-fashioned arts of knightly combat, Frundsberg had learned his trade as a foot soldier, in hard, unsentimental warfare against the Swiss. From them, he had learned to appreciate the power of the pike, how deadly a cheap length of pole with a steel tip could be, even against the grandest paladin.

Over the decades, Frundsberg had fostered the development of a new sort of German infantry. These were the landsknechts, an unruly mob, hard to control, famous for their boastful violence and the extravagance of their slashed and ribboned costumes, plumes and striped hose and giant codpieces.

But they were fearfully effective. François of France had seen it for himself, when the mercenary landsknechts of the Black Legion held the guns against the Swiss at Marignano. Now, under the dauntless Frundsberg, they came to fight for their emperor.

The armies met outside the walls of Pavia on 24 February 1525. The imperialists had now managed to gather around 23,000 men, of whom 6,000 were landsknechts, but the French remained confident. Numbers were still on their side. They had Swiss mercenaries, their famous artillery, King François and his lancers.

But though King François charged in with his usual dash, he soon found the battle turning against him. The advancing French got in the way of their own artillery. The gendarmes, the finest cavalry in the world, were hedged in by landsknecht pikes, their shining plate useless against the Spanish arquebusiers firing from every ditch and copse. As the arquebus stones poured in, the French courage failed. Retreating, they crashed through their own infantry, and now the rout spread. François, his lance broken, pressed forward, sword in hand. But his army was crumbling. He was wounded in the face and the hand. His horse was killed under him, and now he was on his knees, in a thicket of mercenary pikes.

But François was too valuable a prize to be allowed the luxury of a glorious death. That evening, the king of France dined as a prisoner of the emperor. He had come to Italy after the fugitive Bourbon, and Bourbon had brought him low. 'All is lost', François wrote to his mother, 'save honour and my skin.'

* * *

The French defeat at Pavia sent waves of alarm through Italy. Many of the Italian princes had aligned themselves with François; among them, the pope in Rome.

Pope Leo X, a Medici, had died in 1521. His successor, Adrian of Utrecht, was a trusted associate of the emperor, but his Flemish austerity and zeal for church reform made him unpopular in Rome. Worn out and dejected, the pious Pope Adrian died in 1523, to universal rejoicing.

From 1523 to the Battle of Pavia, the papal throne had been occupied by another Medici, Leo's brother, who ruled as Pope Clement VII. A lifetime in his brother's shadow had given Clement a cautious character, prone to indecision. He acquired a reputation for avarice, a charge that was unjust but quite inescapable. There was no money to spend. His profligate brother Leo had left the papal coffers bare.

The news of the disaster at Pavia sent the pope into a tortured dither of despair. He had tried to maintain a pose of neutrality during the conflict, but there was no doubt where his true sympathies had lain. The Medici were traditionally francophile. Giovanni de' Medici, the best soldier in Italy, had been fighting openly on the French side, and there was little doubt that it was papal gold that had kept his soldiers fed.

Just five days after Pavia the first aftershocks of the battle reached Rome, as the pro-imperial Colonna launched an assault against their ancient rivals the Orsini, who had supported France. Fighting between the factions spilled across the heart of the city, as partisans of the two great families played out yet again their centuries-old feud in Rome's streets.

'I shall go into Italy and revenge myself on those who have injured me,' the emperor had promised, 'especially on that poltroon the pope. Some day, perhaps, Martin Luther will become a man of weight.'

But in practice, Charles found, there were limits to how far his vengeance could be pressed. He might have dreamed of using Luther against the pope, but in fact, the Lutheran enthusiasm gripping Germany was a problem for the emperor more than anyone. All across his German territories, poor labourers and farmers sensed the cracks that were spreading through the vast structures of authority that oppressed them. In 1525, they rose in revolt, insurgent bands joining together to form huge peasant armies marching against their feudal overlords.

Georg Frundsberg, the hero of Pavia, had been a supporter of Martin Luther at the Diet of Worms. Many of his men, his beloved landsknechts, had Lutheran sympathies. Now, as the peasants muddled their way to war, Frundsberg and Luther worked together to teach them the error of their rebellion: from Luther they had stern lessons in theology; from Frundsberg they learned how helpless a mere farmer was in battle against a professional man of war.

The Peasants' War became a massacre. The peasant leader Thomas Müntzer, a preacher and old admirer of Luther's, was tortured and killed. Still, the whole thing had been a distraction for the imperialists. Bourbon too was preoccupied: his dreams of conquering France had failed. His promised bride, the emperor's sister, was now being married off to King François as part of the post-Pavia peace deal. Mustering his wounded dignity, he set off for Spain, hoping at least to be rewarded with the duchy of Milan.

Meanwhile, the pay due to the imperial troops in Italy was by now 600,000 ducats in arrears, an absurd sum, far more than even the imperial treasury could easily raise. Without funds, the conquest of Italy would have to wait. Charles would have to be content with peace, and whatever money he could extort from Rome and Milan.

But as time passed, and the hammer of imperial retribution failed to fall, the mood in the Vatican began to curdle from fear to resentment. In January 1526 François bought his freedom, leaving Charles with oaths and hostages and protestations of eternal peace. But the terms that had been demanded of him were impossibly harsh, and François had no intention of sticking to them, hostages or no. The pope was happy to absolve him of promises. In June the College of Cardinals ratified a new league against the emperor, uniting the Swiss, the French, Venice, Florence, Milan and Rome for the defence of Italy.

This was a bold idea, still novel, though not entirely new. Niccolo

Machiavelli had caught the mood early, writing of an Italy longing 'to see her liberator appear. Nor can one express the love with which he would be received in all those provinces which have suffered so much from these foreign scourings.'

Petrarch, who, over the preceding decades, had provided Italy with a unifying vernacular of love, was pressed into service again, now as a patriot. 'Virtue will take up arms,' Machiavelli quoted from the poem *Mia Italia*, 'and put madness to flight.'

> *Virtu contro al Furore*
> *Prendera l'arme, e fia il combatter corto:*
> *Che l'antico valore*
> *Negli italici cuor non e ancor morto.**

There was much high talk of this sort in the optimistic summer of 1526. And so, wearily, as winter set in, Georg von Frundsberg once again summoned his landsknechts. The Alpine crossing was bitter, but Frundsberg and his men set their faces to the freezing wind. Their mission was holy, their destination clear. Where their grandfathers had gone as pilgrims, they now would go as cleansing angels: *nach Rom.*

The avatar of the *antico valore* burning in Italian hearts was the pope's young relative Giovanni de' Medici, better known as Giovanni dalle Bande Nere. He was a son of Caterina Sforza, the virago of Forli, the only one of her children to inherit any of her fighting spirit. Now, in the winter of 1526, the young Medici, last of the great condottieri, prepared to defend Italy as best he could.

Medici's crack troops, the Black Bands, as history would remember them, were among the best fighters Italy could muster: well-trained infantry; light cavalry who could fire arquebuses from the saddle. When Frundsberg and his landsknechts arrived among the marshes of Lombardy, they encountered a stiffer resistance than they had expected from mere Italians. Cold and wet, exhausted by their Alpine

---

* 'Virtue will take up arms and put madness to flight, if the bravery of old is not yet dead in Italian hearts.'

crossing and cut off from the duke of Bourbon, the German situation grew more desperate every day as Medici's men sniped and harried.

But though men like Machiavelli might dream, even such a leader as Giovanni of the Black Bands could not unite the feuding statelets of Italy. Already, the Colonna had launched a devastating surprise attack on Rome, sacking the Borgo – stripping Raphael's tapestries from the Sistine Chapel – and forcing the pope to spend precious resources guarding his southern flank. Meanwhile, on the northern front, it was clear that Frundsberg was being resupplied in secret by the Gonzagas of Mantua who were, after all, related to Charles de Bourbon.

Worse yet, although the landsknechts had crossed the Alps without cannon, the men of the Black Bands now started taking fire from deadly accurate falconets, supplied by that famous artillery nerd Alfonso d'Este, husband of the late Lucrezia Borgia. In a skirmish outside the fortress of Governelo, a cannon ball struck Medici above the right knee. A few days later, he died of his wounds.

So much for Italy. Frundsberg and his landsknechts safely crossed the great barrier that was the River Po. The remaining Italian forces were led by a nephew of Pope Julius II, Francesco Maria della Rovere, a man determined to avoid battle at any cost. Most of the Swiss mercenaries had deserted. Of French, let alone English, reinforcements there was no sign.

And then, as 1526 came to its bitter close, Bourbon and his Spaniards set out from Milan.

It had not been easy for Bourbon to get his army moving. As a renegade Frenchman, he had trouble asserting his authority over the emperor's Spanish captains. His exact authority had been left frustratingly unclear. Worst of all, his men had still not been paid.

Only by threatening the Milanese with a full-scale sack was Bourbon able to scrape together enough ducats to persuade his troops to march. The threat was hardly an idle one. It was all Bourbon could do to prevent his Spaniards putting the city to the sword, and the landsknechts, who lacked not only pay but even food and fresh clothes, might happily have come to join in. As things were there was widespread looting, even of monasteries and churches.

But the necessary sum was raised. On 2 January 1526 the imperial army set off towards Ferrara, the last friendly city before papal territory began. There, the combined force of Spaniards and landsknechts paused to resupply. The duke, Alfonso d'Este, provided food, medicine and heavy cannon.

His bankers provided cash. Charles V had unleashed a huge army on Italy, but he himself remained in Spain, and sent no word to his desperate generals on how these thousands of mercenaries were supposed to be paid. For the moment, Bourbon and his officers took out personal loans to the enormous sum of 27,000 ducats.

It was not enough. First the Spaniards mutinied, ransacking Bourbon's quarters. They smashed the general's bed and all his furniture, but found hardly any money. The man who had been the richest noble in France was now worth little more than the men he led.

The landsknechts, fearing the Spaniards would get a better deal, then turned on Frundsberg. These were his companions in arms, his 'beloved sons'. Now they dared to turn their pikes against their own captain. It was an unbearable blow for the old man. As he pleaded with them, he suffered an apoplexy and collapsed on to a military drum. He could march no further. When the imperial army left him behind, they left behind the only man who could control those deadly Germans.

Just at this worst possible juncture, bad news arrived from the south. The imperial viceroy in Naples, pressed by papal troops, had signed a truce with the pope. An envoy arrived in camp bearing 60,000 ducats extorted from the Vatican, on receipt of which Bourbon and his men were to pack up their pikes and march back north again.

This messenger was almost torn to pieces by the furious mercenaries. Sixty thousand ducats was a fortune, but not once it was divided between more than twenty thousand hungry men. It would take more than that, Bourbon told the pope, to stop his army now.

As the imperial troops plundered and burned their way across the Apennines, new offers from Florence and Rome were outstripped by Bourbon's demands. They promised 60,000 ducats, he wanted 90,000 more. They offered 150,000. He asked for 240,000. By April, 300,000 ducats was the price. The Spanish 'were in a state of mortal sin', their captains mockingly explained, 'and wanted to go to Rome to gain absolution'.

All spring the weather had been foul. Snow and rain had turned the roads to swamps. The gaudy costumes of the landsknechts were reduced to muddy rags, hanging off gaunt frames. Most of the *tross-frauen*, the women of the baggage train, had been sent away – each company was allowed to retain the services of just three prostitutes – but still there were as many mouths to feed as in a decent-sized city, just with the men alone. The country had been stripped bare of food. From time to time, the Germans found stashes of strong Italian wine, which made them first dangerous and then very sick.

In their weakened state, it was easy for them to drink themselves to death. They were surviving by this time on little more than grass and donkey meat. But desperation drove them on. Della Rovere and the Venetians were not far behind. Starvation was never far away. But ahead, they knew, waited the bottomless riches of papal Rome.

Having abandoned their women and even their precious artillery, the mercenaries, now joined by every bandit and masterless soldier in central Italy, were covering twenty miles a day. They forded swollen rivers clinging to horses' tails; no time for bridge-building. Down the pilgrim route they came, the old Via Cassia, destroying any town that dared to stand in their way.

At the beginning of May, the vast and starving rabble that once had been the imperial army arrived in the Roman Campagna. They paused at Isola Farnese, on the ruins of the long forgotten city of Veii, sacked by the Romans some two millennia before. It meant nothing to the desperate landsknechts. They knew only that Rome was now less than a day's march away: that, after all they had suffered, the long-awaited judgement was now close at hand.

* * *

'They come to overthrow the Church', wrote one papal advisor, 'and the faith of Christ.' It was said that Frundsberg had brought with him a golden rope for the pope's neck. His now leaderless men could hardly be expected to show any mercy to the papal Antichrist.

In the streets people whispered about evil portents. The violent interruption of the Holy Week festivities by the naked prophet on top of the statue, a Sienese mystic known as Brandano, had set everyone to counting omens: the Tiber had flooded; a statue mysteriously collapsed; a bolt of lightning had struck the Vatican; a mule gave birth in the Palazzo della Cancelleria. The landsknechts might have been oblivious to the significance of Veii, but the Romans could perceive all too clearly the poetic workings of an unkind fate. Out on the river, boatmen did a brisk trade ferrying frightened citizens down to Ostia and the sea.

But there was much complacency too. Many of the poor expected to live no worse under an emperor than under a pope. Of the eighty thousand or so people in the city, many were immigrants, from Italy or further afield. A Venetian painter, a Flemish banker, a Greek prostitute, none had much reason to regard the pope's battle as their own. Many Romans, both poor and noble, felt protected by their German or Spanish blood, or by longstanding imperial connections. There were people in Rome like Isabella d'Este, whose own son Ferrante Gonzaga was a captain in the invading army and whose brother-in-law was its commander, Charles de Bourbon.

As the imperialists advanced through the Campagna, a meeting of leading citizens was called in the church of Santa Maria in Aracoeli up on the Capitoline. It had been a favourite church of Cola di Rienzo; the Capitoline hill was the symbolic heart of communal power in Rome. But when the pope's representative begged for funds to raise more troops, the wealthy burghers gave him little more than pocket change.

The papal forces were badly outnumbered. The commander, a rather plodding veteran named Renzo da Ceri, could rely on the professionalism of the Swiss Guard, formed by Pope Julius II some twenty years earlier. There also remained in Rome some veterans of

Giovanni de' Medici's Black Bands. But the pope had disbanded most of his troops and there was no money to hire any more.

Out went the drummers to summon the militia of Rome's thirteen *rioni*. But only six of the thirteen sent any men, and far fewer than they might have mustered. Most of the fighting men in the city had already been hired as guards for the mansions of the rich. Renzo da Ceri was forced to enrol whoever he could find: he took any country bandit who could hold a sword; he took the servants and stableboys from the great *palazzi*; goldsmiths and sculptors would man the guns; he would hold off the landsknechts with cooks and kitchen knives.

On 5 May 1527 Charles de Bourbon – penniless, a traitor to his king – led his army of bandits and mutineers down the slope of Monte Mario towards Rome. He might have had as many as thirty thousand men under his command – twenty thousand veteran landsknechts and Spaniards, plus every deserter and highwayman in Italy, drawn in by the scent of plunder.

On the Janiculum, at the monastery of Sant'Onofrio, Bourbon made his headquarters. The vast papal capital spread out before him: to the right, the filthy alleys of Trastevere; to the left, the walled outcrop around St Peter's, known as the Borgo; rising in the dark, the vast round shadow of the Castel Sant'Angelo. Bourbon had the overwhelming advantage in terms of numbers, but still, that night, the future seemed desperate. The men were ragged, exhausted, faint with hunger. An enemy army was following close behind. Ahead were the walls of Rome, ancient and much patched against decay but still imposing in their vast circuit.

There was nothing for it, one officer wrote, but to 'take fortune by the forelock'. But the way ahead was hardly straightforward. The imperialists had long ago abandoned their cannon. The night of 5 May was spent knotting crude ladders out of rope and trellises from the local vineyards – and if those ladders failed and the city could hold out for a few days more, the imperialists would starve.

At four in the morning, Bourbon rode out before his assembled companies, a pale phantom in his white surcoat, lonely against the cold of the early dawn. There was not much he could say. There was money and safety within the walls and only death without. The Spanish led the way, advancing in silence, ready to win or die. The Germans followed behind, a shuffling forest of pikes in the dark. The only sound was the frantic ringing of Rome's bells.

The imperialist assault was directed at three points on the walls of the Borgo, with a diversionary attack to the north, at the Milvian Bridge. Bourbon had hopes of forcing the Porta San Spirito, by the old pilgrim hospital where the walls were especially low.

At first, however, the defenders kept up a deadly arquebus fire, driving the landsknechts back from the walls. From behind the papal lines came a thunder of heavy guns, firing from the parapet of the Castel Sant'Angelo. This fortress was vital to Rome's defence, just as it had been for Belisarius and his Greeks a thousand years before, and its deadly reach, augmented by gunpowder, scratched bloody streaks through the German lines even beyond the walls.

The attackers were in disarray. But now, as one witness put it, 'God manifested himself for them.' All around the walls, a fog rose up from the Tiber mud, 'a thick mist which covered and protected them so that the papalists could not see from where the attack was coming'. The guns on Sant'Angelo fell silent. The arquebusiers on the walls were shooting blind, reduced to hurling insults: 'Jews, infidels… Lutherans!'

And while the attackers came on with steady purpose and inexhaustible numbers, the defenders were few and disorganized. Much later, the brilliant goldsmith (and braggart and murderer) Benvenuto Cellini would tell how he had arrived at the walls with a couple of friends to find a chaotic scene. 'The battle raged there desperately,' he claimed, 'and there was the densest fog imaginable.' Young men lay dying all around. Cellini and his friends, like many of Rome's amateur defenders, immediately decided to go home again.

Before abandoning their posts, however, the three discharged their arquebuses into the landsknecht crowd. 'When we had fired two rounds apiece I crept cautiously up to the wall and observing among the enemy a most extraordinary confusion, I discovered that one of our shots had killed the Constable of Bourbon.'

It was just like Cellini to claim the death of Bourbon for himself. Even if his tall story was true, there was little glory in it. Bourbon, like Bayard before him, was brought down by a humble arquebus ball that struck him in the groin. 'Notre dame, je suis mort!' he exclaimed. But later, as he was bleeding out in the fog, his wits abandoned him and he imagined himself back on that miserable march through Italy, repeating the words, over and over, 'to Rome, to Rome'.

Bourbon's death also sealed the fate of the city. As news spread, jubilant defenders came down off the walls to boast of the great victory they had won. But out in the mist, the landsknechts and Spaniards were still massing. They had nowhere else to go, so they continued the assault.

When the fog began to clear, between six and seven o'clock, the imperialists had just managed to break into the city. By San Spirito they got in by crawling through an old window that had been opened in the wall for a private house. By the Belvedere, at the Vatican Palace, the landsknechts dug their way through with a pick. The breach was only big enough for one man to pass through at a time, but it was enough. At the first sight of imperialists within the walls, most of the defenders immediately fled.

Only the bravest stayed to die. Only one man in ten survived of the regional militia of Parione. A goldsmith, Bernardino Passeri, rejected Cellini's pragmatic example and staged a last stand by the church of San Spirito, where he did heroic murder before at last he was cut down. Not a single boy was left alive among the students of the Collegio Capranica.

The professionals, the men of the Black Bands and the Swiss Guard, had always detested each other. Now they died together, annihilated under the shadow of St Peter's. The last of the Swiss made their stand by the obelisk that stood in Nero's Circus, staining the ground where the blood of Rome's first martyrs once had flowed. Their captain, Röist, was carried home, mortally wounded, to die in his wife's arms. He lingered too long for a peaceful death, however; imperialist soldiers broke down the door and butchered him.

Pope Clement, all this while, had been saying Masses in the Vatican. In the nick of time, he was bundled out of the palace along the raised walkway that led to the Castel Sant'Angelo, while Spanish arquebusiers took pot shots at him from below. The fortress was already crammed with refugees, mostly men, and they pressed so thick at the gates that when the castellan dropped the portcullis it crushed people standing beneath. One cardinal, spotted in the crowd after the gate had been closed, had to be dragged up the walls by rope in a vegetable basket.

Cellini, the goldsmith, had made sure to get inside in time, and attached himself to an artillery crew. The bombardier was a man named Giuliano Fiorentino:

> Leaning there against the battlements, the unhappy man could see his house being sacked, and his wife and children outraged. Fearing to strike his own folk, he dared not discharge the cannon, and flinging the burning fuse upon the ground, he wept as though his heart would break, and tore his cheeks with both his hands.

Cellini took over, unrestrained by sentimental worries about friendly fire. And perhaps he was right. There were four or five thousand Roman citizens packed into the space under the castle, but it made little difference if they died now under their own cannon. The walls had fallen. Smoke from burning palaces was darkening the sky. The battle was over, and now the real massacre began.

Some awful madness had gripped the landsknechts and the Spaniards. Everyone they met, they killed. They killed women in the streets and priests in their churches. They killed the orphans at La Pieta. The invalids at the Hospital of San Spirito were thrown out of the windows into the Tiber to drown.

The guns of Sant'Angelo pushed the attackers away from the Borgo, for the time being. Trastevere had no such protection. At the convent of Santa Rufina, the nuns tried to defend themselves with boiling water and kitchen skewers. They did not survive long. At the Ponte Sisto, a group of nobles led by Pier Paolo Tebaldi and three Orsini brothers had gathered to hold the bridge like Horatius against the Etruscans. At the same time, a deputation of citizens led by Giacomo Frangipane was attempting cross the bridge to negotiate a peace deal. But antique names were no defence against the furious landsknechts. From the windows of their palaces, lords and ladies saw the peace envoys scattered and Rome's last defenders swept away. The river was full of drowning refugees; the streets were charnel houses. 'Hell itself was a more beautiful sight to behold.'

The landsknechts made for the Campo dei Fiori; the Spaniards for the Piazza Navona, still in their various companies. They feared a counter-attack, or the arrival of reinforcements from beyond the walls. But as evening fell, fear was overcome by lust and greed. The Spaniards, soon followed by the landsknechts, spread out through the city, and where they went, the cries of women began to heard above the sound of falling roofs and burning houses. Some were raped and then murdered. Others raped and raped again. Some were raped and forced to watch their daughters raped. Some killed themselves, before or afterwards. Some girls were killed to save their honour, by their fathers.

As well as women, the soldiers wanted ransoms. This was the payday for which they had waited so long, and they were determined to extract every copper from the conquered Romans. There would be no more random slaughter. Now that the first frenzy of victory had worn off, they understood that a scared Roman was more valuable than a dead one, that they could sell the lives they held in their hands rather than throwing them pointlessly away. A crust of vile method now formed around their madness: the helpless citizens were sized up, assessed, as if by tax collectors, their ransoms set according to their station.

Clerks and lawyers, notaries, jewellers, artists, scholars, all were worth squeezing. Desperate letters started going out to friends and relatives around Italy. 'Help me!' a Venetian in Rome wrote to his brother: *Aiutame per l'amor de Dio! Aiutame per l'amor de la Nostra*

Donna. Spaniards had dislocated his arms with rope; they had held his feet over the fire. Every scrap of paper in the house was spent on begging letters, for, if he could not raise an impossible 1,000 ducats in twenty-six days, they would cut him to pieces. 'I have lost everything,' he wrote, 'but care nothing for that. Only I do not wish to die so young!'

The richest prizes waited in the palaces of the rich. Here, behind barricaded doors, with those hired mercenaries that the defence of the walls had so much missed, Rome's nobles had hoped to hold out against the marauders. But they had underestimated the force of the attackers' greed. Near the Pantheon a certain Signora Lomellini had seventy men to defend her property. They fought and died for her, as promised, but the attackers were relentless. Lomellini tried to escape down a rope, fell, broke a leg and was gunned down in her own courtyard.

Resistance was fatal. The only hope for the inhabitants of the besieged *palazzi* was to allow one of the Spanish or German companies to send their assessors in; to pay whatever outrageous price was asked in order to be left alone. No one was exempt. Isabella d'Este, whose son and nephew were commanders in the imperial army, had offered protection to some three thousand refugees. But when her son arrived to see her he was accompanied by a rapacious little Spaniard who explained that Isabella and her household would have to be ransomed like the rest. There was nothing for it. The rumour in the city was that two million ducats were stashed within her *palazzo*. She could buy protection, or she could fend for herself among the mercenaries.

Four pro-imperial cardinals had remained in their palaces, trusting in the emperor's favour to keep them safe. They too were forced to buy protection from Spanish soldiers, paying ransoms of up to 45,000 ducats each. But no agreement could be trusted in that hellish city. Once the Spaniards had been paid off, they left the cardinals to the mercies of the landsknechts, who now demanded an even greater sum.

*

Not even cardinals could pay such fortunes twice over, so the palaces were sacked and the inhabitants beaten or killed. Cardinal Cajetan, one of the first to men to defend the church against Martin Luther, was among several princes of the church to be dragged through the streets and tortured.

Pope Clement, before the city fell, had entertained an optimistic dream: that God, having assembled so many enemies of the true religion in one place, intended, in his mysterious way, 'to make a notable example of them by having them all cut to pieces'.

The truth had been precisely otherwise. Now, finding themselves masters of the papal Babylon, the landsknechts passed the time with ever more inventive blasphemies. One priest was murdered for refusing to give holy communion to a donkey. A cardinal was carried through the streets in a coffin while the Lutherans sang mocking obsequies, then buried alive until he promised a large enough ransom.

Nunneries were violated, the nuns bought and sold in the street. St Peter's Basilica was used as a cavalry stable. The high altar became a butcher's block, to which hundreds of men were brought for slaughter. At San Giovanni in Laterano, the landsknechts forced their way into that great treasury of relics, the Sancta Sanctorum. The Holy Lance that had pierced Jesus's side was paraded through the streets on a German pike. The head of St Andrew was used as a football. All over Rome, shrivelled bits of saint were dug out of their jewelled reliquaries, exposed to the sun again after centuries of gloomy veneration. Arquebusiers practised their aim on holy bones.

There were fewer and fewer places left to plunder, but it was well known that Rome was rich, its inhabitants fat with the gold they had swindled from pious Germans. The Romans might protest that they had nothing left, that they had already paid, but the landsknechts knew there was always something hidden in reserve. They hung people by their arms or by their genitals; dangled them by their feet from the tops of towers; they beat them and buried them and burned them with hot irons; they cut off ears and noses; they fed men their own balls. The Spaniards were the most expert torturers, it was agreed, efficient and unsentimental. They tied a Venetian to a tree and pulled out his fingernails, one a day until he died of pain.

No discipline remained among the conquerors. Drunken mercenaries paraded through the streets in plundered satin. Gambling debts were paid in gold and jewels. There was less and less food. It cost less to buy a girl than to buy an egg.

Outbreaks of violence between roving bands of plunderers became more common. A group of Spaniards, defending a trove, were barricaded into a house and burned alive. The coins were sifted from the ashes and found to be only coppers. There were rumours now of hoards concealed in sewers and cesspits. Roman families were forced to muck out their own latrines, to spread the filth for inspection on their floors.

As summer advanced, the smell became unbearable. There were corpses everywhere, one Spaniard recorded, rotting in houses or gnawed at by dogs in the street: 'No one has troubled to bury them and they are beyond counting. The stink of their putrefaction makes it impossible to enter the city, and those who are in Rome get a mouthful.'

'In Rome, the chief city of Christendom, no bells ring, no churches are open. No Masses are said.' The landsknechts were damned just as surely as their victims. Some had already managed to drink themselves to death. Others had been murdered by the Spaniards. Now, the survivors of that invincible infantry were taken off by cholera and malaria, and by the inevitable outbreak of the plague.

No army had ridden to the rescue of the Romans. The pope, in the Castel Sant'Angelo, had been forced to surrender in June when his supplies ran out. That summer he remained a captive, imprisoned in his own fortress in the stifling city while his bankers struggled to raise a ransom. He was allowed to send an emissary to the emperor: Alessandro Farnese, the petticoat cardinal, brother of that Giulia who had been mistress to Alexander Borgia. But as soon as Farnese was clear of Rome, he fled to Mantua, abandoning his mission. The pope was alone.

The imperialists were still in command of the city in September. The more sober of the landsknechts had taken themselves off to the *campagna* to sack the surrounding towns. Now they returned, to see what last dregs could be extracted from the wreck of Rome. Not until February 1528 did the last of the imperialist army trickle out of the city. Of the 22,000 who had marched with Charles de Bourbon, only some 12,000 remained.

The Romans had suffered worse. The pre-war population of around ninety thousand had been reduced by perhaps two-thirds. No one could count how many had been killed, how many had fled, how many starved or died of the plague. Later, they would tell stories about those final days of occupation, of secret revenges taken in the dark as fugitives emerged from caves and catacombs to slit landsknecht throats. They invented fairytale victories: the cunning wife who pushes three Germans down a well; the boy who drowns his captors by leaving them in an oarless boat; the baker who tricks landsknechts into his oven. Fortified by small fantasies, they began to rebuild their shattered lives and homes.

* * *

'Now I recognize the justice of God,' one Spaniard wrote, 'who forgets not, even if his coming tarries.' The Emperor Charles, who had once tried to suppress Luther's ideas, found that he had become 'Luther's captain'. His army had been the instrument of Protestant indignation against the corruption and idolatry of Rome.

In Germany meanwhile, Lutheranism flourished unimpeded by any papal interference. At the Diet of Augsburg, three years after the sack, the Augsburg Confession was presented to the emperor, twenty-eight articles that became the founding document of the new Lutheran church.

Meanwhile, the emperor's allies were telling everyone who would listen that the sack had been an inevitable and condign punishment for the pope's misdeeds, and that anyway the emperor had had nothing to do with it. But Europe was horrified by the scale of the atrocity. 'What unheard of barbarity!' wrote Desiderus Erasmus. The emperor's troops had behaved worse than the Goths or the Vandals. Rome was 'the common mother of all peoples', and Rome's catastrophe 'was the catastrophe of all the nations... Assuredly this was more truly the destruction of the world than of a city'.

Rome had been hollowed out. The shops stood looted and empty. Hundreds of years' worth of accumulated treasure had been stolen or smashed or burned. Every orchard was stripped bare; every vineyard trampled. The sheep and goats and pigs had all been slaughtered. The city and surrounding countryside would not fully recover for decades.

The intellectual life that had made Rome a centre of the Italian Renaissance was ruined and dispersed. Those writers and scholars who had survived the torture and the plague left the city, never to return. The landsknechts had been great enthusiasts for burning books, destroying any documents or records they could get their hands on. Priceless libraries had been destroyed. Augusto Valdo, a professor at the University of La Sapienza, saw his life's work, his book on Pliny, torn up for kitchen fires.

Art suffered too. Statues were smashed. Lutheran graffiti was carved into frescoed walls. The artists of the school of Raphael had all fled, and ended up scattered across Italy and Europe, where they spread the techniques, the *maniera*, that Raphael and Michelangelo had pioneered.

Michelangelo himself had been in Florence during the sack. In 1533, he was summoned back to Rome for the first post-sack commission of papal art. A few weeks before Clement's death in 1534, Michelangelo returned to the Sistine Chapel, where, on the great end wall, he began to paint his *Last Judgement*. Where the Sistine ceiling was an ascent towards the sublime, the *Last Judgement* is a vortex, a great swirl of naked flesh reaching both up towards the heavens and down to the torments of hell.

Renaissance Rome was finished. The wealth was gone: people guessed that as many as twelve million ducats had been looted from the city. The extravagant parties were a memory. The great age of the courtesans was over. The idea of the papal principality – of independent popes ruling as lords in the Patrimony of St Peter – had crumbled like the fraudulent Donation of Constantine on which it was based. There would be no room for little statelets in the new Europe that was emerging, a continent of unified nations and great powers. As Italians tried to understand the lessons of the sack, they came back more and more to the idea of a national and independent Italy.

But though a Roman era had ended, the city itself, as always, would live on. Not for the first time, Rome raised itself from the ruins in a new form, harder and stronger than before. In 1547 the ageing Michelangelo was commissioned to revive the works on the unfinished dome of the new Basilica of St Peter. Despite all Luther's fulminations, a great stretched hemisphere of stone began to rise above the depopulated city. The Protestant Reformation had torn the church in half, but Catholicism was not finished yet. Under the dome, these words are carved: 'Thou art Peter, and upon this rock I shall build my church.'

18

THE IMPRESARIO

Bernini in the wilderness

———

1644–1648

FEBRUARY 1628. A shining piece of God floats in the Vatican. In the Pauline Chapel, to be precise, where a fragment of Christ's body hangs above the altar – the Blessed Sacrament, displayed in a heavy monstrance of glass and gold. Once it was bread. Now it is changed, in ways that surpass mere human understanding. 'This is my body, which is given for you.'

It is important to insist on this point. Away to the north, Germans and Swiss and English and Scots deny this eucharistic miracle, this 'transubstantiation' of bread into flesh. Outside, in the Roman streets, it is carnival time, the last week of merriment before Lent, and the Romans have other things on their mind than theology. But in here, at least, it is important to insist on the fine points of doctrine, here in the Pauline Chapel, by the Basilica of St Peter, the rock of the church.

And it is easy to believe in the miracle today. The Pauline Chapel has been transformed for the *quarantore*, forty hours of solemn adoration, competing with the carnival pleasures outside. No one with eyes and a heart could resist the spectacle that has been laid on for the occasion. The host, suspended in mid-air, glows translucent in its frame, shooting out rays of sculpted gold. Around it hangs a great apparatus of stucco and painted wood, representing the glory of heaven, shining with such splendour that it dazzles the faithful in the chapel below.

The light seems to come from everywhere, beaming from on high as if heaven truly had opened up in this chapel, at this moment – as if real angels were flying among these puffy painted clouds. Only by coming very close to the altar is the trick revealed: 2,000 hidden lamps are burning behind the scenes, invisible among carefully placed mirrors. Science, not spirit, is behind this miracle. This light is not from God. It is the work of a more worldly magician: the Cavaliere, Gian Lorenzo Bernini.

* * *

Much blood had been spilt over the Eucharist. Ever since Luther had nailed his theses to the church's door, the cracks in Christendom had been widening and deepening. Protestants, as they now called themselves, had split from Rome over the question of salvation: could it be achieved by pious deeds (or bought indulgences), or was it to be had by faith alone?

Once free of papal control, however, the Protestant reformers found that they had less in common than they had supposed. In Switzerland, the warlike Huldrych Zwingli preached a sterner doctrine than Luther's. The two men could not agree on the theology of the Eucharist: was God really present at his supper, or was the sharing of bread and wine a mere commemoration, as Zwingli taught? Luther rejoiced when Zwingli was spitted on a Catholic pike in 1531.

Any lingering hopes of a united Protestantism were quickly dashed. In 1534, radical anabaptists staged an uprising in Munster, rejecting the comfortable accommodation that Lutherans had come to with the secular state. Their holy 'king', John of Leiden, established an apocalyptic regime of polygamy and carnival. When imperial forces finally regained control of the city, they tore his body apart with red-hot tongs.

Meanwhile, in Geneva a young theologian named John Calvin was working out his own vision for a Reformed Protestant church. He had his own ideas about eucharistic theology, different from Zwingli's and as far from Luther, more or less, as Luther was from Rome.

Where German was spoken, Lutheranism usually won out. In

France and the Netherlands, the Reformed church as envisioned by Calvin made the greatest advances, entangling itself in the dynastic competition between the houses of Bourbon, Valois and Guise. In England, Henry VIII had broken with Roman Catholicism without much clear idea of what might take its place. Bohemians remained faithful to their old teacher Jan Hus, burned at the stake over a century before. The currents of Luther's Reformation were now divided between a dozen local theologians and preachers, not just Luther and Calvin but also Laski and Cranmer, Bucer, Melanchthon and Knox, or the Spaniard Michael Servetus, so heterodox that Calvin had him burned.

All across Europe, dukes and bishops and petty princes found themselves unmoored, buffeted by the competing demands of faith and politics, snatched up in sudden eddies of pent-up fervour. In Lyon, Orleans, Le Mans, Rouen and Caen, armed French Huguenots rose up to impose their own particular brand of Reformed Protestantism.

Pamphlets and printed books fed the popular enthusiasm, spreading radical ideas, vernacular Bibles giving Europe's burghers access to holy scripture – God, speaking to them at last in a language they could understand. A mass-produced edition of biblical psalms was a Huguenot bestseller – the songs of King David translated into French verse with tunes to match. A tune could be a secret signal, wherever Protestants lived under cover. And where they held power they could join their voices in triumphant song. Psalm 68: 'Let God arise, let his enemies be scattered.' Psalm 124: 'Our soul is escaped as a bird out of the snare.' Or, always popular, Psalm 115: 'Their idols are silver and gold, the work of men's hands. They have mouths, but they speak not: eyes have they, but they see not: they have ears, but they hear not.'

Here was a pleasure widely shared among the many varieties of Protestantism: to come like Moses from the mountain against the cathedrals and monasteries of the false religion, to smash their painted windows and cast down the false idols and grind their precious images, their statues and their icons, into dust.

Rome had experienced Protestant fury at first hand. Still, it was not obvious, in the years after the sack, that the rift in Christendom could not be healed. The Protestant reformers, after all, were inheritors of a tradition with deep roots in the Catholic Church. The Protestants criticized Catholic luxury, corruption in the church, simony, the sale of indulgences, extravagance, decadence, impious bishops, crude, ill-educated priests – but all those abuses had been condemned by Catholics themselves. Many clerics accepted the need for reform of morals and practice. It did not follow that reform must lead to schism.

In 1534, the papal tiara passed from the demoralized Clement VII to the so-called petticoat cardinal, Alessandro Farnese. Farnese, now Pope Paul III, set up a commission of cardinals to investigate the failings of the church. Their report, *De emendanda ecclesia*, was so damning that Luther published his own German edition.

The reformists in the Curia became known as the *spirituali*. There was a Venetian, Cardinal Contarini, and the exiled Englishman, Cardinal Pole. Lay supporters included the poet Vittoria Colonna and her friend, the ever more irascible Michelangelo. There were things to be learned from Protestantism, the *spirituali* believed. And much sense to Luther's theology. Pole and Colonna and the rest were not unsympathetic to the idea of justification by faith alone, and they shared with Luther an evangelical enthusiasm for the authority of scripture over the messy old traditions of the church.

Protestant preachers had tapped a deep well of popular enthusiasm. Catholics had to find an answer to this, an activist passion that could work with, rather than against, the Roman church. Spain, where contact with Moors and Jews had produced a rich tradition of mysticism, was the perfect terrain for a new Catholic outpouring.

In 1521, a French cannonball ended the military career of a young Spaniard named Ignatius Loyola. A painful recovery awakened something in his soul. After a miraculous vision at the shrine of the Black Madonna of Montserrat, he put aside his sword and pledged his service to God.

Loyola soon acquired followers. The Jesuits, as they came to be called, arrived in Rome in the late 1530s, where they were warmly received by Vittoria Colonna and the *spirituali*. War with the Ottomans had thwarted their planned pilgrimage to Jerusalem. A mission to convert Rome's prostitutes was undermined by public mockery. But Loyola and his fellows were devoted soldiers in Christ, unshakeable in their willingness to fight for the souls of unbelievers. The Society of Jesus would become one of the most influential organizations of the Catholic Church.

But new Catholic orders were springing up left and right: Capuchins, Ursulines, Oratorians, Theatines, Barnabites. In Spain, the Jesuits supported a levitating nun known as Teresa of Ávila, whose followers, the Discalced Carmelites, were distinguished from their Carmelite brethren by their symbolic refusal to wear proper shoes.

The *spirituali* welcomed the new religious enthusiasm, but free-thinking cardinals like Contarini and Pole did not represent the only tendency within the Catholic Church. In 1541, a Catholic–Protestant dialogue at the imperial Diet of Regensburg ended in failure. Contarini had longed to find a theological middle ground. On the crucial question of transubstantiation, however, neither he nor the Protestant representatives would give an inch. There would be no agreement. The *spirituali* were discredited. Some of their leading thinkers fled north, condemned as heretics; Contarini died under house arrest. A new movement now ruled in Rome: the *zelanti*, led by the zealot-in-chief, Cardinal Gian Pietro Carafa.

The petticoat pope was browbeaten into setting up a Roman inquisition, with Carafa as an inquisitor general. 'Even if my own father were a heretic,' Carafa swore, 'I would gather the wood to burn him.' Meanwhile, divisions were hardening within the Holy Roman Empire. In 1546 the Protestant princes of the Schmalkaldic League rose up against Charles V; theological battles now played out as open war.

The pope had called an ecumenical council of the church at Trent in 1545, and the bellicose climate did not encourage compromise. The need for change was clear, but that change would not be in a Protestant direction. At Trent, through months of argument and discussion, the variations and wrinkles within Catholic belief were carefully ironed flat. Proper doctrine on hitherto ambiguous technicalities was carefully specified. No crypto-Lutheran *spirituali* were to find shelter in the bosom of Carafa's new church.

In 1555, Carafa finally managed to get himself elected pope. Now the inquisition was given free rein at last. Remaining *spirituali* were arrested. Suspect books were banned and publicly burned. The church's index of forbidden books would expand, by the end of the century, to include the works of Erasmus, Machiavelli and even Petrarch. Jews in Rome and the Papal States were forced into ghettos for the first time, and made to wear special yellow hats. Vittoria Colonna had died in 1547, and Michelangelo, approaching his eightieth year, was protected by his reputation – but Carafa found the perfect way to strike at the old man. Michelangelo's art was degenerate, the pope decreed. The heroic nudes spreading themselves around the Sistine Chapel would have to be censored, their shame concealed by newly painted figleaves.

This was a dangerous time for the Jesuits too. Ignatius Loyola died in 1556, and Carafa moved quickly to curb the order's independence of spirit. By the time the final session of the Council of Trent came to a close in 1563, nearly twenty years after it was convened, the focus of Jesuit energies had shifted north. They now understood that their true mission was to defend Europe from the Protestant heresy, to win over wavering hearts.

The order's mother church in Rome was built as the physical expression of the Jesuit commitment to exemplary Catholicism. They were sensitive to northern accusations of extravagance and decadence. The Gesù, as the church was called, started off as a grand but simple space, a space of harmonious lines and perfect geometry.

But Catholicism and Protestantism had been set on different paths. And among those qualities that set Catholicism apart, the Jesuits learned, was one that might be a powerful weapon in the great battle to come. The Protestants tended towards iconoclasm, towards puritan austerity. Churches like the Gesù, on the other hand, would become showcases for a wild and gaudy splendour of new religious art.

* * *

A benevolent God, wishing to adorn his church, could not have created a better tool for the job than Gian Lorenzo Bernini. *Un mostro d'ingenio*, they called him – a 'monster of genius'.

Bernini was eight years old when he came to Rome. His father, a successful Florentine sculptor, had won a commission from the pope. In 1606, Bernini senior brought his young family to a new life in the crowded alleyways of the Ripetta, where the Tiber wound its way through the heart of Rome.

Even then, the child's abilities were apparent. He had an ordinary education, but was bright and precocious, and not held back by modesty. His intellect, he would tell his son, had, even then, been 'both universal and profound'. Very soon, the young prodigy came to the attention of the pope, Paul V, a great enthusiast for works of art. Bernini's drawing of the head of St Paul, done on the spot, was confident and masterful. 'This child', Pope Paul exclaimed, 'will be the Michelangelo of his age.'

Papal favour was a valuable prize for a young artist. Above all, it allowed the boy Bernini to learn as Michelangelo had done, by copying surviving examples of ancient art. If Bernini's father wondered where he was, the answer was always the same: he was roaming the corridors of the Vatican, communing with his 'girlfriends', as he called them – the ancient statues in the papal collection.

Over and over again he drew his favourites, the Apollo Belvedere, the Antinous, the Laocoön. One of Bernini's earliest jobs as a professional sculptor was in fact the restoration of an ancient find: workmen digging foundations for a new church of the Discalced Carmelites unearthed an extraordinary classical statue of a sleeping woman. The viewer is delighted, drawn in – and then they see the penis nested between the figure's milk-white thighs. Surprise and delight, a lesson Bernini learned well.

But Bernini would not quite be a new Michelangelo. Michelangelo, in his mid-twenties, had done a David, the famous statue that still stands in Florence today. Bernini did one too, when he was about the same age. Michelangelo's David is a graceful nude, still and poised, a creature of perfect beauty. Bernini's is very different. His body is bent and twisted. His arm is wound up to swing. His thighs are wrapped in a whirl of flying fabric, and his face – his face is Bernini's, the face of the artist himself, screwed up into a grimace of concentration, as if to say, 'let the giant-killing begin'.

This was the great age of *magnificenza* – the culture of splendid display. Rome's recovery had been slow, after the catastrophe of 1527. The loss of great swathes of northern Europe to Protestantism had hardly helped. But by the end of the 1580s, a reorganized papal administration had managed, through the efficient taxation of the Papal States, to refill Rome's coffers.

The great architect of this renewal was Pope Sixtus V, an insomniac old tyrant who, from 1585 to 1590, managed to impose his own order on the city. New piazzas and avenues were cut through the medieval tangle, creating a new geography of Catholic order, nice straight lines connecting Rome's old pilgrim basilicas. Whatever did not fit Sixtus's vision was ruthlessly demolished. Fortunately, he died before he could entirely dismantle the baths of Diocletian, or the arch of Janus Quadrifrons, or turn the Colosseum into a wool factory, but the Septizodium of Septimius Severus, fourteen centuries old, was completely dismantled, along with the remains of the old papal palace at the Lateran.

Above all, Sixtus loved restoring obelisks. All over the city, these ancient pillars of plundered Egyptian granite were dug up, cleared of mud and weeds and thrust into the sky. He was lucky to have the help of a genius architect and engineer, Domenico Fontana. In a feat unequalled since ancient times, Fontana moved Rome's only unbroken obelisk, a 327-ton behemoth, from its old position in Nero's Circus to stand in front of St Peter's Basilica. There it still stands, shouting Rome's retumescence to the world.

The new bureaucracy that funded all this display was run by cardinals who, unabashed by Protestant reproaches, used their position to become extremely rich. Richest and most powerful of all was the 'cardinal nephew', a title that had, through the generations of papal nepotism, acquired something close to official status in Rome.

One such cardinal nephew was Bernini's first great patron. Scipione Borghese, known as 'the delight of Rome', was the nephew of Paul V, raised to the cardinalate when Paul became pope in 1605. It was he who had arranged that first papal meeting for the young prodigy, when Bernini first was called a new Michelangelo.

Scipione was a notorious epicure and pederast, but whatever dark rumours might cling to him, he outshone with displays of personal magnificence on a scale that had hardly been seen in Rome since the coming of the Goths. His brand-new villa, set in beautiful, classically inspired parkland on the Pincian hill, was a palace of wonders – a palace that, notably, had not a single bedroom, being intended solely for entertaining and showing off. Of all the treasures on show, the finest were the early works of Gian Lorenzo Bernini, executed in a burst of brilliant creativity between 1621 and 1625. The subjects were drawn from ancient myth: pious Aeneas escaping Troy with his father and son; Proserpina, crying out in fear as Pluto sinks his fingers into her thigh; Daphne, fleeing Apollo, frozen in Bernini's vision at the very moment when her skin turns into bark.

A talent like Bernini's was never going to be allowed to spend itself on profane subjects for long. In 1623, another grand patron of Bernini's, Cardinal Maffeo Barberini, was elected pope, taking the name Urban VIII.

As Pope Julius II had had his Michelangelo, so, Urban was determined, would he have his Gian Lorenzo Bernini. The sculptor was still young, only halfway through his twenties when Urban took the papal throne, but the esteem in which the pope held him made him by far the most sought-after artist in Rome. Even to be allowed to commission him in those days was a mark of very special papal favour.

He was a sculptor above all, but neither Urban nor Bernini himself recognized any limits to his genius. Urban wanted his own set of frescoes to match the Sistine ceiling and was forever badgering Bernini to do more painting. It is probably thanks to Urban that we have Bernini's self-portrait, painted at around this time. It shows a man of around twenty-five, handsome, with dark hair, full lips, black eyes. His gaze is piercing, hyper-attentive, the way an antelope might look at a passing lion.

Urban also set Bernini to architecture. In 1629, the young man was appointed chief architect of St Peter's, set in charge of what was by then the most expensive and longest-running building project in Europe. Work on the new basilica had begun under Julius II over a century before, proceeding in fits and starts ever since. The list of chief architects read like a roll call of Renaissance talent: Sangallo and Bramante had laid the first groundwork, marked out a graceful, symmetrical plan; Michelangelo, in his old age, had raised the dome, a huge half-ovoid of brick and lead; Carlo Maderno, from 1602, oversaw the final destruction of the ancient Constantinian basilica. The ground on which it had stood was enclosed by an enormous new nave, thrusting, squat and massive, towards Rome.

This was the largest cathedral in the world, enclosing a cavernous space, a wonder of clean lines and precise Renaissance geometry.* It was exactly what the church had needed after the Council of Trent: pure, grand, impeccable in its abstraction, a defiant statement of mightier than thou piety in the face of the Protestant insurrection. In the evolving artistic climate of the seventeenth century, however, in a world of *magnificenza* and princely display, the echoing interior seemed rather bare. It was here that Bernini would make his mark.

Pope Urban's plan, which he set in motion as soon as he gained the papacy, was to create a new structure to fill the basilica's perfect emptiness. The result, inaugurated at the feast of Saints Peter and Paul in 1633, was the famous baldacchino of St Peter's – an ornate canopy, raised on four pillars, 29 metres above the basilica's high altar, framing the space in which priests would perform the sacred drama of the Eucharist. The basic form comes from simpler sacred enclosures in

* To convey an idea of the building's size, Mark Twain retold a story he had heard of ten thousand soldiers who came to St Peter's to hear mass. Their commanding officer came to the basilica and was surprised not to find them. But there they were, all ten thousand, sitting quietly in one of the transepts.

other churches, but also recalls the fabric canopies that shaded popes and princes during state processions. Bernini takes the visual language of a passing display and freezes it for eternity.

The baldacchino weighs more than 6 tons. To find so much bronze, the pope was forced to strip the ancient beams from the portico of the Pantheon. '*Quod non fecerunt barbari, fecerunt Barberini,*' said Rome's wags, punning on the pope's family name: 'What the barbarians didn't do, the Barberini did.'

But for all its weight, Bernini would not allow his metal canopy to sit still. Within the great stillness of the basilica, Bernini's four bronze columns are not straight, but twisted into four spirals of black and gold – four tornados, spinning forever over Peter's tomb.

The spiral pillars that frame the altar are themselves enclosed by the four huge piers that support the dome above, and these piers were an integral part of Bernini's vision. As architect of St Peter's, Bernini led a team of other architects and sculptors whom he set to work on the backdrop for his bronze extravaganza, elaborating the piers with niches and statues and ornate balconies.

This sort of collaboration was perfectly normal for Bernini. The only way he could keep up the prodigious output that was demanded of him was by outsourcing in this way. Indeed, his ability to run a team was a vital part of his talent: Bernini was always a great impresario, the visionary director, strutting among his players.

Of course there was friction. One of Bernini's collaborators on the baldacchino was the underappreciated Francesco Borromini – a more radical and innovative architect, but not blessed with Bernini's courtly charm. Borromini's hatred of Bernini, learned at St Peter's, lasted for the next thirty years.

Another sculptor, Francesco Mochi, was criticized for the clingy, wind-blown robe he had carved on a figure of St Veronica. If there was any defect, he was sorry, Mochi is said to have replied, but the flapping was no fault of his. Rather, Bernini should blame the gale that came howling through the cracks that his overambitious works had made in Michelangelo's dome.

*

The cracks in the dome were not, in fact, Bernini's fault – but the accusation that he had dangerously weakened the supporting piers would dog him for the rest of his life. Some time around 1635, anxious and overworked, he fell seriously ill. The pope, distraught, sent him a medicinal draught of julep with crushed gemstones.

To cheer himself up, Bernini took to staging comedies. The princely courts of the seventeenth century loved theatre, which was, after all, a wonderful opportunity for showing off. Italy was leading the development of a new dramatic form, the opera. Monteverdi's *Orfeo*, the first great example of the genre, was made for the Gonzaga descendants of Isabella d'Este in Mantua in 1607.

As usual, Bernini's polymath talent knew no limits. The English diarist John Evelyn, visiting Rome, heard of a 'publiq Opera (for so they call shews of that kind) wherein he painted the scenes, cut the statues, invented the engines, compos'd the musiq, writ the comedy, and built the theatre'.

This was an exaggeration, but not by much. Bernini controlled every aspect of his shows, which he put on regularly at his own home each carnival season. The players were drawn from his own large household but under Bernini's direction they all performed like veterans, we are told. In rehearsal, Bernini acted out all the parts himself to show how it should be done.

The scripts were witty: sometimes bawdy, with the flavour of the then wildly popular *commedia dell'arte*; sometimes, within limits, they are even political. Bernini was compared to Plautus himself by some critics, and the pope liked to make him repeat his jokes at court after performances, 'giving unconcealed signs of pleasure over them'.

But above all Bernini was known for his brilliant special effects. At one show, the *Inundation of the Tiber*, in 1638, a flood of water came rushing down the stage and threatened to swamp the audience before, at the last second, being drained away through a concealed trapdoor. At another, a stagehand set the scenery on fire, as if by accident. The spectators, knowing how common and how deadly theatre fires could be, rushed for the exits. But then, a miracle: the scene was transformed by hidden mechanisms from a blazing inferno to a well-watered garden. The delighted crowd, records Bernini's son, were full of praise for this 'clever deception'.

There was no special effect, however, no theatrical prestidigitation that would make those troublesome cracks in the dome disappear. And indeed, the matter of the dome was only the first chapter in what would become a very damaging narrative. Bernini, as architect of St Peter's, had started work on a pair of bell towers to lend height and grandeur to the basilica's rather stumpy western end. But as construction continued through the early 1640s, the weight of the monumental bell towers caused a new set of cracks, now spreading dangerously across the main façade.

Again, Bernini might plausibly have pleaded that the fault lay with previous architects, not with his own designs. But Bernini's enemies smelled blood. This was an embarrassment to the church, the cracks a blemish on the face of Christendom.

In 1644, Pope Urban VIII died. At the worst possible moment, Bernini had lost his most powerful defender.

Bernini and Urban had been famously close. The pope used to have Bernini eat at his table. Sometimes, when the pope retired to bed, Bernini would come and close his shutters for him. Bernini, in a jealous rage, once sent a servant to cut the face of a woman he loved. The pope absolved him by letter, declaring him 'an exceptional human being, a sublime genius, born by directive of Divine Providence...'

People had been quite willing to see something sinister in this extraordinary intimacy. When illness delayed Pope Urban's coronation, he made a ceremonial appearance at his window to reassure the crowds that he was not dead. But even seeing him in the flesh, they were full of doubt: this was not the real pope, they began to shout, but some theatrical trick, dreamed up by his illusionist in chief, the Cavaliere Bernini.

In 1644, Urban VIII was replaced by Innocent X, formerly known as Giovanni Pamphili. The Pamphili had suffered under Urban and his Barberini clan. Now, the old Barberini regime would be swept aside. Bernini, the Barberini favourite, was banished from the Vatican.

His bell towers on St Peter's were condemned. In 1647, his enemies finally got their way: the offending towers, so carefully built, were dismantled, vanishing along with Bernini's reputation.

* * *

These had been testing years for the broader Catholic Church – a church that had been, for nearly a century now, locked into an amplifying cycle of religious violence.

The first serious blood had been shed in France, where lines of sectarian tension ran alongside dynastic strife. In 1572, after the wedding of Princess Marguerite de Valois to Henry, the Protestant Bourbon king of Navarre, a leading Protestant nobleman was shot at in the street by a Catholic assassin. To pre-empt Protestant retaliation, the fanatical Catholics of Paris took to arms. On the eve of the feast of St Bartholomew, some two or three thousand Huguenots were slaughtered in Paris. As news of the purge spread through the country, thousands more were murdered in their homes.

As Protestants were being killed by Catholics, Catholics were facing a major military challenge from the Ottoman Turks. In 1565, the crusading order of Knights Hospitaller, also known as the Knights of St John, had barely managed to hold their base at Malta against a huge Ottoman fleet.* In 1570 the Ottomans launched a massive invasion of Cyprus, another crusader outpost, then controlled by the Venetians. The last Venetian stronghold at Famagusta fell in 1571 after a heroic resistance. The Venetian commander, Marco Antonio Bragadin, was mutilated and flayed alive, his stuffed skin hung from a galley mast.

Ottoman supremacy at sea was a huge threat to the Catholic powers of the Mediterranean. In Spain, King Philip II commanded the wealth of Potosí, the flood of silver grubbed from the holy mountain by armies of Andean slaves.† But though he brooded in his sombre

---

* The capital of Malta, Valletta, is named after the Grand Master of the Knights of St John, who led the defence: Jean Parisot de La Vallette.
† The *Cerro Rico* at Potosí, in what is now Bolivia, had been a holy mountain

palace, the inquisitor-haunted Escorial, shaped like St Lawrence's gridiron, his resources were needed in the north, to crush the revolt of the Protestant cities of Holland.

For a moment, it seemed as though no one could defend Italy from the raiding Ottoman fleets. But the papacy, in the hour of its need, was saved by the loyal Jesuits, the soldiers of God. The superior general of the Order at the time was Francisco de Borja, grandson of Juan Gandia and therefore great-grandson of Roderigo Borgia himself, the church's most notorious pope. But Borja was as indefatigable in defence of the church as his ancestors had been in plundering it. By energetic transnational diplomacy, Borja and the Jesuits assembled a coalition under Don John of Austria which destroyed a huge Ottoman fleet at Lepanto, not far from Cape Actium. The Ottoman threat to the western Mediterranean was finished for good.

Victory over the Ottomans was a mighty feather in the Catholic cap. The papal commander at the battle, one Marc' Antonio Colonna, was received in Rome with a triumph worthy of an ancient general. In Germany and the north, Protestant nobles stared at the ground when their Catholic rivals taunted them: where were you when we fought at Lepanto?

This was ten years after the end of the Council of Trent, and Catholic reformers understood that God had sent them a clear sign of his favour. Protestants had rejected what they saw as the quasi-pagan cult of Mary and all the saints. Now the Roman church moved in the opposite direction. The victory at Lepanto had been won by intercession of Our Lady, the pope declared: Mary of the Immaculate Conception, free of original sin; the Great Mother in Heaven; the

---

for the Inca, associated with Pachamama, Mother Earth. In Catholic art of the sixteenth and seventeenth centuries, the mountain occasionally appears with the face and hands of the Virgin Mary. The volume of silver mined from the mountain was indeed prodigious, but so was the cost in human lives – the number of deaths in the Potosí mines has been estimated in the millions.

Woman of the Apocalypse, who tramples the devil and has the sun and the moon under her shoe. Jesuits took up the theme, spreading the use of rosaries as an aid to lay devotion throughout Europe.

Marian devotion was part of a strong Catholic response to the Protestant challenge. It would not be so easy to defeat the Antichrist as many Lutherans and Calvinists had supposed. But by 1618 they were ready to have another try. A hundred years had passed since Luther had posted his ninety-five theses. Halley's comet was burning balefully in the sky. Whipped up by fervid preachers and apocalyptic visions, the Protestant princes of Germany prepared themselves for war.

The struggle was initiated by the Defenestration of Prague, when a crowd of Czech Hussites threw the regents of the Catholic Holy Roman Emperor from a window of Prague Castle. They survived, either because they were caught by the Virgin Mary or because they landed in a dung heap – but the emperor could hardly tolerate such rebellion from his heretical subjects. At the Battle of White Mountain in 1620, an imperial army put the Hussites to flight.

The kingdom of Bohemia was forcibly re-Catholicized. One Jesuit, a certain Father Firmus, was famous for trampling the heresy out of the Czechs with a pair of special spiked clogs. The remaining Hussites were scattered to the winds.

Once again, the Virgin had intervened on the side of her Catholic faithful. In Rome, a church belonging to the Discalced Carmelites was renamed in honour of the battle: Santa Maria della Vittoria.

It was in this church that Bernini began work on what would become the masterpiece of his years in the wilderness. Unwelcome at Pope Innocent X's Vatican, where the remains of his rejected bell towers were being cleared from St Peter's, Bernini now had the leisure to accept private clients. In 1647 an aristocratic Venetian family by the name of Cornaro commissioned a chapel to be built inside the church of Santa Maria della Vittoria in honour of the founder of the Discalced Carmelites, Teresa of Ávila.

Teresa, the levitating Spanish nun so favoured by the early Jesuits, was remembered as one of the leading lights of the sixteenth-century Catholic revival. In 1622 she was declared a saint, canonized alongside the Jesuit Ignatius Loyola at a magnificent ceremony at St Peter's. The image of the nun, famously austere in life, was paraded through the streets of Rome to the sound of trumpets and fireworks and hymns specially written for the occasion.

Her saintly speciality had been mystic prayer. She had had visions, and wrote about them in poetic and passionate terms. One episode became known as her transverberation – her 'striking through and through'. She had been, she said, visited by an angel, 'very beautiful'. He held:

> A long golden spear, and at the end of the iron tip I seemed to see a point of fire. With this he seemed to pierce my heart several times so that it penetrated to my entrails. When he drew it out… he left me completely afire with a great love for God.

There was pain in this vision, 'so sharp that it made me utter several moans'; but 'so excessive was the sweetness caused me by this intense pain that one can never wish to lose it'. This was a spiritual pain, Teresa insisted, 'though the body has a share in it – indeed, a great share.'

This was the moment Bernini meant to recreate. It would require the full breadth of his talent. Above all, he drew on his skills as an impresario.

He would set his marble actors on a stage worthy of the occasion: an oval niche, framed by the outline of a classical temple whose pillars and curving architrave give the illusion of massive scale, as if viewed through a fisheye lens.

To each side the chapel is panelled in precious marbles, swirling-patterned alabaster. Above, at the apex of the chapel vault, the dove of the Holy Spirit spreads its wings before a painted sun. Clouds spill downwards into the chapel, and as they fall the plaster on which they are painted starts to swell into three dimensions, obscuring the walls as if heaven itself were breaking in through the chapel ceiling.

Twenty years before, in 1628, Bernini had used light to dazzling effect for the eucharistic devotion of the *quarantore*. Now he deployed all his optical wizardry again: daylight, coming through the chapel window, streamed down on to St Teresa in her niche, through a hidden skylight behind that curving architrave. Coloured glass stained it gold. Concealed mirrors, now lost, reflected the real light on to a fan of gilded rays, to illuminate the angel and saint below.

Standing erect, the angel – a Cupid, escaped from ancient Rome – draws back his burning shaft, ready to strike again. His left hand plucks at her habit, and, though she is covered head to foot, the swirling folds of the fabric reveal the turmoil beneath. She has half-fallen back, supported by a cloud. Her arm hangs limp. And from the hem of her robe, her left foot peeps, tender and delicate.

But above all, you see her face. The middle-aged St Teresa has been given the features of a young woman. Her lips are parted, head thrown back, marble cheeks glowing in the light. Her eyelids are half-shut, but if you look closely, you can see that her eyes have rolled back in their sockets. This is the face of ecstasy.

Michelangelo, in his sculptures, had obsessed over finding the right block of marble – the perfect block in which he might discover the perfect form within.

Bernini was no Michelangelo. He happily carved his figures from multiple pieces of stone, figures which anyway were not perfect but human, naturalistic in their imperfection, dynamic in their movements, figures swept by passion, instinct, appetite.

And Bernini's works did not end with his statues. In the Cornaro Chapel, the spotlit figures on their podium are only the focus of a wider scene, a multimedia spectacular of gold and fresco and stucco and polychromatic stone. And light above all – light that, according to the science of the Jesuits, was an emanation of Spirit, the visible proof of God, working in his world.

Bernini made the stage and made the actors. He even made an audience. On each wall are sculpted figures of the commissioning family, illustrious Cornaros both living and dead. They sit at carved

rails that recall theatre boxes or perhaps *palchi*, the fabric-hung balconies from which Roman grandees in *palazzi* watched devotional
performances in the streets. And below, outlined in coloured marble
on the floor, are skeletons watching the drama in attitudes of rapt
prayer.

Bernini judged the Cornaro Chapel to be 'the least bad work
I have ever done'. But although later art historians have tended to
agree with him, the response at the time was somewhat muted, or
at least less enthusiastic than the responses to which he had become
accustomed as a papal favourite. Some viewers even thought that his
depiction of Teresa's ecstasy had strayed rather from the path of strict
decorum. Bernini had dragged St Teresa 'into the dirt', one critic
wrote, 'to make a Venus not only prostrate but prostituted'. 'If that
is Divine Love,' a French visitor is supposed to have said, 'why then,
I know it well!'

But Bernini had not made Teresa look so sensuous by accident, nor
had he slipped some sort of obscene subtext past the Roman inquisition. The erotic charge of his marble figures comes straight from the
writings of St Teresa herself. And St Teresa was writing in a tradition
that went back to the Bible. 'Let him kiss me with the kisses of his
mouth,' says the Song of Solomon, 'for thy love is better than wine.'

The joining of man and woman was understood to be analogous
to the longing of the soul for God. And why not? Christ himself had
been made flesh. At the Last Supper he gave up his body, a body
that was miraculously and physically present wherever Catholics
celebrated the Eucharist. Christ's death had been profoundly carnal:
Catholics were encouraged to meditate on the gory particularities of
the Passion, thorns and whips and nails; to follow Doubting Thomas
and probe Christ's bleeding wounds.

There was no reason to expect that the flesh should be indifferent
to the yearnings of the spirit. Teresa's was a sublime and spiritual
ecstasy of which crude earthly passion was merely the shadow. The
soul moved with the body, and under Bernini's hand, Teresa's body
revealed the presence of the divine.

*

The emphasis of Catholic reform had shifted since the Council of Trent, away from reform of the institution and towards reform of the soul. Teresa of Ávila, the new favourite of the church establishment, had been a perfect exponent of this trend: in her writings, she guided Catholics on a journey through an *Interior Castle*, a castle whose doors were unlocked by prayer.

In the Cornaro Chapel, Bernini staged the conclusion of Teresa's journey, her ecstatic encounter with the Godhead – a dissolution of self that resembled the lesser dissolutions of sex and death, even as it surpassed them. If Bernini brought sex into the church of Santa Maria della Vittoria, it was in order to draw people higher, to draw them towards their own encounters with God.

This was very much in line with wider Catholic thinking. To celebrate the canonization of Ignatius Loyola in 1622, the students at the Jesuit College in Rome had put on a spectacular theatrical show, with singing and ballet, prancing devils, Wisdom speaking from a throne of clouds.

The 1622 extravaganza was not a one-off. At hundreds of Jesuit schools across Catholic Europe, theatre had become a vital part of the curriculum. For those students who became priests, acting was training for their mission. Ignatius is said to have encouraged young Jesuits to practise public speaking among the ruins of ancient Rome, that the example of the ancient orators might inspire them in their preaching among heretics and heathens.

And Jesuit theatre could have a very salutary effect on its audiences too. In the rustic villages of Italy, where superstition still lurked, Jesuit missionaries were welcomed like rock stars. Protestant preachers, in their bare northern churches, could sometimes be rather dry, academic theologians blasting biblical exegesis at the stiff-collared burghers shivering in the pews. Jesuit preaching was a carnival of plays and processions: local worthies wearing chains as 'slaves of the Virgin'; penitents wailing and licking the ground; everywhere, the defiant forty-hour adoration of the Eucharistic Host, the glorious *quarantore* whose imagery Bernini had done so much to advance.

These European spectacles could also be put to great effect in the wider world. 'Nothing has attracted the poetry-loving Indians more effectively than our plays,' one missionary wrote from the New World. Christian dramas from Rome travelled thousands of miles of ocean to become 'Kirishitan monogatari' in Edo-period Japan. Jesuits preached in China and Goa, in South America and in the forests of Canada. And when, as sometimes happened, they became unwelcome to the local regime, they met martyrdom with open arms – after lifetimes of drama, at last, the ultimate star turn.

With the Jesuits as his foot soldiers in the *propaganda fide*, the pope spread his spiritual dominion around the globe. But though the faith was successfully propagated in Cathay or Kongo, Catholicism could not reclaim the lost territories of the Protestant north.

Back in the 1620s, when Bernini was the darling of Rome, Catholic forces had been gaining ground after their victory at the White Mountain. By the 1640s, however, when Bernini was banished from St Peter's to work at Santa Maria della Vittoria, things had changed. The Catholic armies of the Holy Roman Empire had subdued the Czechs, but over the course of what came to be known as the Thirty Years War, they were challenged by Danes, Swedes, Dutch, Scots, English and at last, most dangerously, the French who, though Catholic themselves, had been funding the Protestant war against the Habsburg emperor all along.

Over the course of those three decades, perhaps eight million people were killed by plague or famine or violence. A century of escalating religious conflict found its apogee in acts of extraordinary barbarism: the routine murder of peasants; the Catholic sack of Magdeburg, where almost the entire population of the city was slaughtered; a renewed enthusiasm for witch trials – hundreds of men, women and children tortured, then burned alive. More Germans perished, as a percentage of the population, than during the whole period from 1914 to 1944.

At last, in 1648, an army of Lutheran Swedes battled its way to Prague to bring the fighting to an exhausted end. The goodwill of Our Lady of Victory had proved finite at last. For a hundred years and more

Catholics had dreamed of reuniting the churches of Europe under Rome, by Jesuit spectacle, inquisitorial zeal, or finally by force of arms. At the Peace of Westphalia that dream died at last. The princedoms of Germany won the freedom to choose their own religion, Catholic, Lutheran or even Calvinist. The authority of the Holy Roman Empire over its German territories, already weak, was reduced even further. Claims to universal authority, whether of popes or emperors, gave way to a new European landscape of individual sovereign states.

* * *

In Rome, Pope Innocent X was horrified by the peace. The concessions granted to 'the heretics and their successors' were, he declared, 'null, void, invalid, iniquitous, unjust, condemnable, reprobate, inane, and without legal force or effect'.

To make his feelings even clearer, if that were possible, Innocent would use the unrivalled expressive power of Roman art. His Pamphili clan had a palace on the Piazza Navona, the long open space that had once been the Stadium of Domitian. This piazza, Pope Innocent would transform into a monumental space, an elaborate setting for an extravagant display of personal and papal grandeur.

The great concern in 1648 was that the piazza should have its own obelisk. Innocent had already found one, a smallish specimen that had been manufactured for the Emperor Domitian back in the first century AD. Later it had decorated the *spina* of the Circus of Maxentius, that lonely chariot course out among the weeds of the Appian Way. There, for centuries, the fallen obelisk had mouldered.

Now, Innocent would restore the obelisk to its former glory. The hieroglyphs on the obelisk's flank were to be translated by no less a scholar than the Jesuit Athanasius Kircher, a man who, incidentally, was at the forefront of research into the possibilities of projecting images via magic lanterns. The obelisk was to be raised above a public fountain – the provision of water was still, as it always had been, the most convincing way to demonstrate beneficence in Rome. Water would be diverted from the Acqua Vergine at the expense of the Trevi fountain, which was in the territory of the Barberini.

One problem remained: who could build a sufficiently glorious fountain? Under Pope Urban, Bernini would have had the job – but Bernini, like all the Barberini hangers-on, was out of favour. So Pope Innocent held a competition, soliciting designs from all the leading artists in the city. Best of them all was Borromini, the morose genius who had helped Bernini with his baldacchino. He proposed a fountain representing the four great rivers of the world.

But Bernini was not the sort to allow himself to be upstaged for long. His path to redemption lay in an unexpected quarter. Rome's great dramaturge would return to papal favour with the help of a character from low comedy: La Pimpaccia, they called her, meaning something like 'wicked Mrs Punch'. But for all the insults, Donna Olimpia Maidalchini was the most powerful woman in Rome.

Maidalchini was Pope Innocent's sister-in-law, and had once been his lover, or so the gossips whispered. By 1650, she was a middle-aged widow, a plump basilisk in a peaked hood, known by all to be the real power behind the papal throne. 'It was simply a disgrace', one furious cardinal screamed at her, 'that the governance of Rome was in the hands of a whore.'

But if La Pimpaccia was fierce, she was also greedy, and Bernini, the celebrity artist, had cash to burn. He had already tried to buy her support in the matter of the bell towers, for a bribe of 1,000 doubloons. Now, hearing of the papal competition for the new fountain, he turned to her again, doubtless with more money in his hand.

A plan was hatched. One evening, the pope was attending dinner at Donna Olimpia's residence on the Piazza Navona. On his way out after the meal, his eye was drawn by the flash of polished silver: there, placed strategically in his line of vision, was a scale model of a fountain, bearing an obelisk and representing the four great rivers of the world.

The pope's reaction was everything that Bernini could have hoped for. For half an hour, the story goes, Pope Innocent gazed at the model, in 'a state of near ecstasy'. He knew exactly the trick that had been played. 'This design', he told Donna Olimpia, 'could have come from no one else but Bernini.' There was now 'no choice but to employ

Bernini', the pope admitted, because 'anyone who does not want to use Bernini's designs must simply keep from setting eyes on them.'

Bernini was restored to papal favour. His fountain, unveiled in 1651 at the Pamphili end of the Piazza Navona, was a triumph. Four river-gods lounged magnificent, each with his identifying symbol: the River Plate hoards coins, the wealth of South America; the Nile, source unknown, covers his head; the navigable Ganges holds an oar; the Danube, representing Europe, reaches out towards the papal coat of arms. In the background are figures of extraordinary naturalism and vitality: a prowling lion; a palm bending in the wind. What could the Protestants boast, when every continent bent to the papal will?

At the centre, Bernini had raised the pope's obelisk – and here he had wrought another of his showman's miracles: the obelisk was supported not on a solid plinth but rather raised on a rock arch, with clear air beneath. It seemed impossible that the thing could stand, but there it was, a levitating finger of Aswan granite.

There were some mutterings of discontent. You could tell by the murmuring of Rome's talking statues, Pasquino and Marforio, the latter an ancient river god, the former a mutilated old torso of Menelaus, set up in a little square on its own. What humans dared not say, the statues might, by way of little notes, attached to them by Roman wits.

And the wits were dismayed by Bernini's fountain. Rome at that time was recovering from a major famine, and yet the popes spent all their money on useless stone. 'We don't want obelisks, we want food!' the statues protested. 'Command that these rocks be made bread!' they joked, quoting the Gospel. Verily, man shall not live by bread alone, but bread surely helped. What magic was it that held the obelisk aloft? Why! It was the hungry labour of Rome's poor.

But the project would not be stopped. The whole of Rome was being transformed, reworked in that extravagant style that would, in time, become known as baroque, with Bernini as its prime exemplar. All over the city, church fronts of brick and fresco and mosaic, masterpieces of medieval art, were covered over with façades of rippling marble, keplerian ovals and sweeping curves. Everywhere was movement and distortion, a city as if seen in a fairground mirror.

One of the greatest examples of this baroque architecture was rising over the Piazza Navona at that very moment: the church of Sant'Agnese in Agone, in memory of St Agnes, the young girl martyred by Diocletian thirteen centuries before. The architect was Borromini. His brilliant touch was evident in the oval concavity of the façade, the graceful flow of the entrance steps. He was still furious with Bernini, of course, for the usurpation of the fountain project, and the hostility was returned. People used to joke that Bernini's figure of the River Plate, on the fountain of the four rivers, was shielding his eyes from the horror of Borromini's architecture.

Worse insult was to follow. Work on Sant'Agnese dragged. Borromini lost faith in his patrons and resigned. But then, when the Pamphili renewed their interest in the church in 1666, they appointed Bernini, not Borromini, to design a pediment to cap off the façade. Borromini could take no more. In 1667, sick and depressed, he propped his sword against his bed and threw himself upon it like a Roman general.

Even here misfortune pursued him. He had meant to go out in true antique style, but he missed his aim. It was many hours before he died of his wound at last.

Bernini left an indelible mark on Rome. He is everywhere in the city. His trace: the swirl of sculpted drapery; passion, frozen in marble; the tenderness of lip and hand. Above all, where Bernini has been, there is drama, the sense of a grand stage.

No visitor to Rome can miss it, for almost every visitor experiences the impact of Bernini's last great gift to the church: his renovation of the Piazza San Pietro. There, around Pope Sixtus's giant obelisk, Bernini designed a vast elliptical colonnade of white Tuscan columns, reaching out from the basilica façade – two encircling arms to embrace the faithful, the arms of a church that still, after all the fighting, believed it could enfold all the people of the world, Catholic, heretic and infidel.

When the faithful gathered in that square, for papal blessings, they stood, as all Romans always really stood, as both audience and actors in that great arena – witnesses to, and participants in, the symbolic enactment of Catholic devotion and Catholic unity. All faces turned towards the basilica, jostling for a view. No one wanted to be blocked behind the obelisk, and the result was – and is – that, viewed from above, the obelisk seemed to cast a shadow in the piazza, drawing lines through the crowd where it blocked the line of sight.

That line in the crowd leads forward – forward towards the pope on his balcony, but further too. Follow that vector, those implied geometries, and you come inside the basilica itself, up that titanic nave to the space under the dome, to the twisting columns of Bernini's baldacchino. Straight on, past the high altar, the line continues, into the apse, the eastern end, towards the rising sun. There is preserved the throne of St Peter himself – or, what is supposed to be his throne – Rome's first bishop's see, the seat on which is built the Catholic Church.

And here too, it is immediately obvious, Bernini has been. Here are the curves and ovals, the twisting figures, the flowing cloth. Here are the gilded rays, the stucco clouds, the stained glass. And in the centre, at the eastern point of the basilica, a magician's trick: a window glowing with the glory of celestial light.

19

THE MINE OF CONTEMPLATION

Romantics in Rome

———

1816–1821

A ROMAN NIGHT, February 1787. The air is clear. The full moon casts a frigid pallor over the city, striking an answering glow from the church domes that rise above the sleeping streets: the Gesù, Sant'Andrea della Valle, St Peter's, enormous in the distance.

It is late, and the city sleeps – labourers, shopkeepers, prostitutes behind their shuttered windows. Only towards the disabitato, Rome's empty quarter, does any movement disturb the *darkness*. Out there, away from the medieval alleys and the Renaissance palaces, a curious party of travellers can be made out, picking their way across a broad patch of open space that stretches, desolate in the moonlight, out from the further slope of the Capitoline.

The *campo vaccino*, the Romans call it – the cow field, sometimes used for markets, a broad sweep of pasture, rutted with cart tracks, crossed by a double line of scrubby elms. The travellers step carefully in the dark, between heaps of mule droppings and cow dung that sticks to their boots. But here and there a moon-bleached outline breaks clear of the mud: to the left, the half-buried arch of Septimius Severus, a shelter for wandering goats; to the right, three columns of the Temple of Castor and Pollux – three white widows, supporting a corpse of mutilated architrave. Interred beneath this field, sunk in the black earth, are the remnants of the Roman Forum.

The travellers pass on, under the broken apse of Maxentius's basilica, past the Arch of Titus where it sits embedded in a Frangipane wall. And now they pause. Here is the Colosseum, broken but still magnificent, its half-shattered ring of arcades rising mountainous over the wreck-strewn moonscape below.

It is quiet, but the ruin is not deserted. There is a hermit who lives under the arches, bothering the old bricks with his prayers. And some beggars too have found shelter among the vaults. They have built a fire of damp wood against the chill and, as the travellers watch, a breeze blows the smoke into the arena, seeping through holes and crannies, filling the bowl of the amphitheatre, heavy as sea mist. The beggars and their fire, the hermit and his prayers, all vanish into the cloud. All signs of life are extinguished, muffled in formless white. Only far above, the Colosseum still lofts its bulk, vast masses of light and shadow against the starry sky.

And the travellers, the tourists, are delighted. This is exactly the sort of thing they came to see.

* * *

Rome had always attracted travellers – pilgrims, lawyers, diplomats, churchmen, artists. But towards the end of the seventeenth century, a new idea began to take hold among the gentry of northern Europe: that a trip to Italy, and Rome especially, was an indispensable part of a noble education.

From Germany and France and Holland, and above all from prosperous Britain, a stream of young men – and a few women – handsomely equipped, heads stuffed with classical learning and apt quotations, set off southward on what came to be called the Grand Tour.

The journey was, one English clergyman wrote, like the 'journey of life'. The pleasures of France were childish, of a 'gay fluttering kind'. By degrees, as the tourist approached Italy, the experience became more solid and manly, culminating at Rome. After Rome, other destinations could only disappoint. The thrill of the tour declined until the traveller returned home at last with the habit of an old man: 'being tiresome to his friends, by a perpetual repetition of past adventures'.

The Grand Tour certainly could be adventurous. The crossing of the Alps was a major undertaking on its own: the long ride upwards by precipitous roads; narrow bridges spanning torrents that crashed foaming into the abyssal depths; the bitter cold of the high passes. Then the descent, white-knuckled tourists wobbling in sedan chairs, or hurtling down by sled with their hired mountaineers whooping behind.

Italy brought its own hardships: hours rattling along in public coaches, on paving that might have seen two thousand years of continuous use. It was wise to travel armed in case of highwaymen, with a sword and a brace of pistols. Prudent travellers brought special iron contraptions to block their bedroom doors against cutthroats at the dubious roadside inns.

And what inns! 'No words can express the wretchedness', one tourist remembered: damp sheets, straw beds, 'infinite numbers of gnats, bugs, fleas and lice'. The food was miserable beyond imagining: soup with bits of liver, a dish of brains, the carcass of some roadside fowl, 'boiled to rags' and served on filthy pewter.

The Campagna outside Rome made a similarly unfavourable impression on travelling British squires. What had once been some of the richest countryside in Europe was now a bandit-ridden desert, scarred by centuries of despotism and war. Letters home to England are full of regretful musings on what might be achieved with such land by the application of good Protestant labour and modern agronomy.

Englishmen arriving in Rome were always struck by the backwardness of the place: Edward Gibbon, arriving in the city in 1764, remarked that the population, not more than 170,000, was 'far below the measure of the great capitals of Europe'.* The construction boom of the

---

* The French scholar Charles de Brosses remarked of Rome that 'of the

extravagant seventeenth century had depleted papal resources. Smoke and grime had blackened those gleaming counter-Reformation façades. Anyway, for Gibbon and his ilk, all that recent splendour only served to recall 'the abuses of the government': Rome's palaces were 'costly monuments of elegance and servitude', of the corruption of fat cardinals and papal *nepoti*. The arts of architecture, sculpture and painting, all the expensive tools of baroque display, were judged to have been 'prostituted in their service'.

Away from those palaces, the desperate condition of ordinary Romans assaulted the senses of northern visitors: crowds of monks and beggars, thin children, dingy houses, the ever-present smell of dung and 'garlick'. Nor was the travellers' mood improved by contact with Rome's larcenous customs officers, headquartered in an old temple of Hadrian near the Piazza Colonna. Thither the English were conducted in their carriages, red-faced with helpless fury as their luggage was subjected to the special diligence of unbribed officialdom.

At last, after two or three hours of such treatment, the unlucky tourist might be allowed to retreat to his lodgings. There were rooms to be had around the Piazza di Spagna – the English ghetto, as it was jokingly called. Foreign artists had long haunted the area, picking up life-drawing models who touted for business on the Spanish Steps, the ornamental staircase that connected the piazza to the church of Trinità dei Monti. Now the tourists moved in: cafes on the square were loud with English voices, the clink of glasses, the clack of billiard balls. A whole expatriate society could be found there, from humble artists and architects to the most exalted aristocracy. The Old Pretender, King James III of England, as he styled himself, could occasionally be glimpsed – or, after James's death, his son Charles, 'Bonnie Prince Charlie', defeated but still insisting on the obsolete Stuart claim.

A little of Rome's vitality now revealed itself. The energy of the city could be felt among the hawkers and mountebanks of the piazza,

---

population, a quarter are priests, a quarter are statues, a quarter are people who do nothing'.

the beggars, the street performers, the puppeteers. For many young tourists, Rome's famous prostitutes were a major diversion. James Boswell, on Ash Wednesday 1765, resolved to have a new girl every day while he was in the city. Inspired by the ancient love poets of Rome, he 'sallied forth of an evening like an imperious lion' to take the women of the city in his jaws.

Ash Wednesday was just after the Roman carnival, which might explain why Boswell was so overheated. To educated tourists, the antique Saturnalian spirit that animated the carnival was perfectly clear. The Romans took their carnival liberties with a confidence born of centuries of unbroken tradition. Grandees dressed up as beggars. Men dressed as young women mingled saucily with the crowd. Young women appeared at the opera dressed as military officers, flaunting their epaulettes. Priapic pulcinellas waggled their horns at Roman matrons, or fought mock battles with their rivals the *quaccheri*, whose costume imitated the severity of Quaker dress. Boys blew shells like horns. Lovers pelted each other with sugared almonds. Girls defended themselves with bunches of reed blossoms, gathered into a broom.

The streets were filled with outlandish costumes: theatrical, mythical, satirical. One man was got up as an obelisk. Another as a crooked lawyer. Another as a conjuror. Another as a ghost, draped in a bedsheet. A particularly good joke was to adopt tourist dress: a flapping frock coat and giant artist's pencil; an affected grimace worn under a pompous northern hat.

This was all very droll. But it was not what had drawn the tourists to Rome. 'A new race of pilgrims', as Gibbon put it, 'from the remote, and once savage countries of the north', had descended on the city, not to sample its present delights but rather to tread 'the footsteps of heroes', to see 'the relics, not of superstition, but of empire'.

'I can neither forget nor express,' wrote Gibbon:

> The strong emotions which agitated my mind as I first approached and entered the *eternal* city. After a sleepless night, I trod with a lofty step the ruins of the Forum: each memorable spot where

Romulus *stood*, or Tully [Cicero] spoke, or Caesar fell, was at once present to my eye.

Here was a new wonder for the Romans to lampoon: tourists, rooted to the ground, staring in rapture at some filthy patch of muddy earth, some pile of weed-covered brick. Educated tourists, steeped since early youth in Livy and Virgil and Cicero, could travel to a city that was invisible to many of its own inhabitants – a lost Rome springing up before their eyes from the tumbled rocks.

Just as the tourist city was invisible to the native Romans, so the present-day reality of Rome sometimes faded from tourist sight. Gibbon describes, in a famous passage, the moment when he decided to write his *Decline and Fall of the Roman Empire*, 'musing amidst the ruins of the Capitol, while the barefoot friars were singing vespers in the Temple of Jupiter'. But there were no ruins visible on the Capitol in 1764, when Gibbon saw it. On the contrary, the piazza on top of the hill was a very fine architectural space, designed by Michelangelo himself and surrounded by palazzi. The church of the Aracoeli, in which the friars were singing, might have had a pleasingly melancholy aspect but it certainly was not, nor ever had been, a Temple of Jupiter. No matter. For the tourist, what Rome was could never be allowed to obstruct the view of what Rome was supposed to have been.

The great visionary of this way of seeing Rome was a Venetian architect and printmaker, Giambattista Piranesi. Prints of his *Views of Rome* became the indispensable souvenirs of the Grand Tour – etchings that picked out in perfect detail the ancient ruins hiding amid the jumbled fabric of the modern city while also managing to infuse the dead stones with some of their antique vigour. His shadows were always darker. His skies, even in black and white, still glowed. And where time's ravages had shrunk and worn the ancient buildings, Piranesi was perfectly happy to restore their lost ornament, or stretch perspective to give them back their proper grandeur of scale. Piranesi, wrote the architect Robert Adam, was the only Italian artist who might truly be said 'to breathe the ancient air'.

For Piranesi, and the many British architects who followed

his example, Rome's ruins were a mine of inspiration. Each day they rode out into the great green sweep of Rome's *disabitato*, the sparsely populated area of pasture and vineyard that took up a good portion of the space within the vast circuit of the Aurelian walls. There, where no modern buildings obscured the remains of the vanished city, the tourists went prospecting with their sketch pads for treasures in the mud: acanthus scrolls wreathing an ancient capital; marble cornices with their deep-drilled patterns of egg and dart. Here and there grotesque figures peeped between the weeds: fauns, satyrs, tritons, nymphs, blank-eyed survivors of Rome's wreck, now rescued by northern pencils to live again, carved into the walls and furnishings of rain-sodden stately homes. Estates belonging to aristocratic tourists were suddenly full of Corinthian columns and classical rotundas – the English countryside breaking out into a rash of knock-off Pantheons.

Piranesi's great rival was a German, Johann Joachim Winckelmann, a Brandenburg cobbler's son who had contrived, by sheer force of desire coupled with native brilliance, to get himself to Rome in 1755 to join the household of one Cardinal Albani, then Rome's leading collector of antiquities.

Rome, Winckelmann wrote, 'is the school for the whole world'. He had been 'purged and tested here', he believed, his aesthetic spirit challenged and refined by exposure to the masterworks of ancient art. Like Piranesi, he drew from the city a profound sense of inspiration, albeit with less room for imaginative license: 'the only way for us to become great... is by imitating the ancients', he sternly enjoined.

Winckelmann's *History of the Art of Antiquity*, published in 1764, was a landmark in the development of what the Germans called *Altertumswissenschaft*, the scientific study of the ancient world. After thousands of hours among Rome's remaining ancient statues, Winckelmann had developed a complete theory of the stylistic evolution and later degeneration of ancient art, dividing 'antiquity' into different periods arranged around the zenith, as he saw it: the pure, refined art of classical Greece during the fifth century BC.

Art was a pursuit of ideal beauty, Winckelmann believed, a beauty the Greeks had found – as Michelangelo later did – in the human form. Now Winckelmann applied a scholar's precision to the examination of Rome's greatest sculpture, the Apollo Belvedere, a degenerate Roman copy to be sure but still partaking in the perfect harmony of Greek art. He measured the line of chin and nose, the flare of the nostrils, the arch of the chest – even the drape of the testicles: the left ought always to be larger than the right, Winckelmann determined.

Tourists could only dream of attaining Winckelmann's level of understanding, but dream they did. With hired guides called *ciceroni* – and Winckelmann himself was sometimes available, to the right sort of party – the tourists raced dutiful circuits of Rome's various collections, together holding some 10,000 surviving specimens of antique art. The hopeless agitation of new arrivals in the galleries reminded Johann Wolfgang von Goethe, at Rome in 1787, of wasps batting themselves against a window to bounce off and go buzzing stupidly off along the walls of the endless rooms.

Exposure to all this art was meant to be an education in taste. Goethe, already a literary celebrity when he arrived in Rome, was humbled by the experience: 'No one who has not been here can have any conception of what an education Rome is,' he wrote. 'One is, so to speak, reborn and one's former ideas seem like a child's swaddling clothes.' Only after months in the city did Goethe begin to feel he was getting towards the truth contained in all that unyielding marble: 'the splendour of the objects by which I am surrounded makes me forget myself,' he wrote home, 'and carries me as far and as high as my innermost being permits. My eye is becoming better trained than I would have believed possible... Here I feel like a fish in the water.'

All very well for Goethe. For those with less exalted sensibilities, the constant quest for discernment could be a burden. The painter Joshua Reynolds, studying in Rome around 1750, saw tourists so busy taking notes from their hired *ciceroni* that 'they scarcely ever looked at the paintings the whole time'.

Tourist society was neurotically obsessed with artistic hierarchies:

what were the five finest statues in Rome? How to choose between the Farnese Hercules and the Dying Gladiator? Between the grace of the Apollo Belvedere and the agony of Laocoön? Who, in order, were the finest painters? One French scholar went so far as to assign to each painter a set of scores for their various abilities in composition, design, colouring and expression, as if playing at Top Trumps. Michelangelo was comfortably outscored by Correggio, Domenichino and the cousins Carracci – artists rarely mentioned in the same breath as the great master today.

Tourists carefully mouthed the accepted judgements of the moment. Raphael, the prince of artists, was praised for his special 'grace'. Michelangelo was admired for his grasp of the sublime, though considered rather 'savage' in his expression. His *Last Judgement* was preferred to the neglected Sistine ceiling, although the ceiling at least did better in tourist estimation than the fifteenth-century frescoes decorating the walls.

Meanwhile, Bernini and Caravaggio and the other artists of the baroque were neglected. The tourists were engaged on a Platonic search for perfect truth and beauty, and the theatricality of Bernini's work disturbed them – his insistence on the heat of the moment, as compared to ancient statues' cool eternity. They hated his David, scowling and biting his lip. His fleshy sculpted figures, Winckelmann said, looked as if they all had dropsy. And his St Teresa in the Cornaro Chapel was found to be scandalous, a debased product of Catholic superstition which was shown to be little more than antique paganism in disguise.

Rome's Catholic spectacle left Protestant tourists entirely unmoved. Goethe saw the pope celebrate High Mass with the entire Roman clergy in St Peter's Basilica on Christmas Day but, though he conceded the service had a certain magnificence, he found in the end that the splendour on display was off-putting. 'Do not come between me and the sun of sublime art,' he wanted to exclaim. 'I am too old for anything but truth. Rites, operas, processions, ballets, they all run off me like water off a duck's back.'

Romans, impoverished and undereducated though they might be, had always felt a certain pride in being residents of St Peter's city. Though they might lack bread, they could bask at least in the reflected dignity of all those fine-robed cardinals and feast their eyes on the glory of marble façades and soaring domes.

But the Protestant tourists of the eighteenth century came to Rome with an attitude that was, in a sense, just as threatening to Roman values as the violence of the Lutheran landsknechts had been two hundred years before. The things the Romans prized were brought low, Rome's gilded relics were dismissed as baubles, her rites as the barbarous fopperies of a degenerate people; her processions were idolatry, her saints were false gods, her inhabitants were squatters, profaning the sacred soil on which they trod. Goethe, at a Candlemas service in the Sistine Chapel, could only think of how the candles being blessed were the same candles that had blackened the Sistine ceiling. One day, having bribed his way into the chapel to gaze at the frescoes, he took a noonday nap on the pope's sacred chair.

Rome's religious treasures were rubbished by the tourists. At the same time, Rome's rubbish was treasured. Tourists astonished the Romans by their veneration of marble lumps that might, not many generations before, have been fed straight into the nearest lime kiln to make cement. There was a brown statue of Minerva in Rome whose hand was supposed to have been polished white by the kisses of the *milordi Inglesi*. More baffling still, Piranesi had encouraged in the tourists an enthusiasm for the great sewer, the Cloaca Maxima, whose outlet, built, supposedly, by Tarquin the Proud, could still be seen opening into the Tiber. English gentlemen went trooping by the dozen to see the hole, like so many tiny proctologists peering solemnly into the gaping dark.

Still, if the tourists were so interested in Roman detritus, the Romans would play along. Landowners started selling excavation rights to their fields, and Roman entrepreneurs picked over the ground again and again in the hope of finding some precious fragment that might attract a scholarly German or deep-pocketed Englishman. Goethe himself was delighted to buy a shard of painted terracotta which his Roman wig-maker found in a pile of rubble above the Piazza di Spagna. Many of his fellow tourists would have happily seen the whole of modern Rome blown up and cleared away for the chance to get at the ancient substrata beneath.

It was Goethe who recorded, on 2 January 1787, the great pleasure he had found in a moonlit view of the smoke-filled Colosseum the night before. Tourists were turning their back on the living city; turning away from the monks and the beggars and prostitutes and the carnival buffoons, preferring the company of the illustrious ghosts who haunted the *disabitato*.

The physical Rome of the present was neglected in favour of vaporous ideal cities: the Romes of the glorious past, and the as yet unrealized Romes of the enlightened European future. 'The observation that all greatness is transitory,' Goethe wrote, 'should not make us despair; on the contrary, the realization that the past was great should stimulate us to create something of consequence ourselves.'

In an Ovidian love elegy, written in Rome, Goethe allows the god Amor, Love, (or, backwards, Roma), to give him a lesson: 'I, your teacher, am always young… Live happily and the past will live in you.'

'How I have been reborn!' Goethe was moved to exclaim. 'How renewed and fulfilled I feel!' But such optimism was sometimes hard to sustain. 'The more I see of this city,' Goethe wrote at the time of his moonlight walk, 'the more I feel myself getting into deep waters.'

And when, on his final night in Rome, he passed by the moonlit Colosseum again, he turned away from the ruin with a shudder. Now it was not Ovid's love poetry that he remembered, but rather the poetry of Ovid's exile: *Tristia*, Book One, Poem Three, in which Ovid, weeping in the moonlight, leaves Rome for the last time. 'I could not get him out of my head,' Goethe recalled. 'I tried to recite his poem to myself, and part of it came back word for word, but the only effect of this was to confuse and frustrate my own composition, and when, later, I tried to take it up again, I could get nowhere with it.'

* * *

Goethe left Rome in 1787. Two years later, on 14 July 1789, a Paris mob stormed the Bastille, a great royal fortress, signalling the end of absolute monarchy in France. Here was a moment to create 'something of consequence', as Goethe had put it. The grip of primitive feudalism was weakened. No longer were men bound by superstitious fear of church and king. It was time, the revolutionaries hoped, to clear away the weeds of ignorance, to let the light of civilization shine at last.

Karl Marx, writing in 1851, reflected that 'all great world-historic facts... appear, so to speak, twice... The tradition of all dead generations weighs like a nightmare on the brains of the living.' In 'epochs of revolutionary crisis they anxiously conjure up the spirits of the past to their service, borrowing from them names, battle slogans, and costumes in order to present this new scene in world history in time-honoured disguise.' The French Revolution, following this pattern, had 'draped itself', he said, 'in the guise of the Roman Republic.'

Certainly, ancient precedent was alive in the minds of revolutionaries. 'We were raised in the schools of Rome and Athens,' wrote one leading Jacobin, 'and in the pride of the Republic... It was a foolish government which thought we could exult in the fathers of the *patria*, of the capitol, without being horrified by the eaters of men at Versailles.'

Now the lawyers and doctors and journalists who filled the new National Convention told out in Ciceronian tones the spirit of Roman liberty; the mob, the *sans-culottes*, wore bonnets derived from Roman freedmen's caps, and they marched down streets renamed after Brutus and the Gracchus brothers. The symbols of the ancient Roman commonwealth were deployed with new enthusiasm: the toga, the curule chair, the *fasces* – the bundled axe and sticks that had been the badges of lawful Roman authority. The great painter of the Revolution, Jacques-Louis David, had studied for years in Rome alongside the grand tourists. When he depicted the revolutionary Tennis Court Oath of 1789, he drew the men of the Estates General with right arms outstretched, palms down, saluting stiffly in what he thought was the ancient Roman style.

*

All across Europe, forward-thinking youths thrilled to the news of the French Revolution. Many Englishmen travelled to Paris in those early years to witness the new epoch dawning there. The Declaration of the Rights of Man and of the Citizen, issued by France's National Assembly in 1789, was a triumph of international liberalism. Thomas Jefferson helped in the drafting of it. Another American revolutionary, the Norfolk-born Thomas Paine, even got himself elected to France's National Convention.

But the liberals who flocked to the standard of the new *res publica* soon learned at first hand the truth that Marx would later recognize: that when history repeats itself, it does so first as tragedy and then as farce. It had taken nearly five centuries for the Roman republic to unravel. The French republic failed in just ten years, racing through the stages of decline: class conflict, mob violence, factionalism. By 1793 revolutionary ideals had produced a full-blown Reign of Terror – an outbreak of deadly political score-settling such as had hardly been seen since the days of Sulla's proscriptions.

The government that followed the Terror was increasingly venal and corrupt. And, just as Rome's decadence had produced a Caesar, so too in France. The old monarchies of Europe were all conspiring against the republic, and among the generals sent out in its defence was one who showed some of that same Caesarian boldness of ambition. Sent against the Habsburg territory in Italy, this young Corsican, Napoleon Bonaparte, baffled the Austrians and their Italian allies with his decisiveness, his speed of march and countermarch. With an outnumbered, underfed, half-equipped army, he captured the strategic city of Mantua and defeated the combined forces of Piedmont, Tuscany and the Papal States.

In 1799, having shown himself to be the finest general in France, Napoleon launched a full takeover of the republic. At one point, Napoleon found himself like Caesar on the ides of March, surrounded by furious legislators intent on violence. But Napoleon had what Caesar had lacked: the support of a party of veteran grenadiers. At the first prick of the bayonet, republican opposition to Bonaparte rapidly deflated.

Like Augustus long before, Napoleon preserved the appearance of republican government. There was a senate, a tribunate and three consuls, of whom Napoleon was the first 'consul for life', from 1802. *Dictator perpetuus*.

Onwards he raced through Roman history. It had taken a generation at least for the Caesars to fully acknowledge their imperial status. Napoleon had himself crowned emperor – by the pope, no less – in 1804.

Out through Europe Napoleon's regiments marched, carrying eagle standards like the Roman legions. They took Spain and Italy, crossed the Rhine, pushed deep into Germany, then Poland. At Moscow the new empire reached its zenith. And then, re-enacting decades in a single year, the empire collapsed. The legions were hunted through a Russian winter by wild cossacks; the eagle standards lost in the snow. Fall. Exile. Elba. Brief resurgence, a hundred extraordinary days in 1815. Then Waterloo, Ney's charge, battalion squares, Blucher, *la garde recule, sauve qui peut*.

* * *

After twenty-six years of more or less constant fighting, peace was restored in Europe. At last, the Grand Tour could resume. A new generation of northern visitors began trickling into Italy – young tourists who, for most of their lifetimes, had known Rome only as an inaccessible dream.

Among them was George Gordon, the notorious Lord Byron, whose scandalous life had made him a literary celebrity. Banished from polite English society, Byron wandered Europe with his fictional avatar, Childe Harold, attached to him like a shadow. *Childe Harold's Pilgrimage*, a narrative poem, of which three long cantos had so far been published, had been a huge hit, a *succès de scandale*. Harold himself, a dark, attractive figure, full of melancholy fire, was the mouthpiece of a new spirit, a new sensibility. The Romantic era had begun.

For Gibbon and Goethe and Winckelmann and the great eighteenth-century tourists of the Enlightenment, the ruins of Rome had been a source not just of memory but of hope. In the ruins they sought patterns that might show Europe how to live anew.

But the Napoleonic catastrophe had cast a dark cloud over the scene. 'France got drunk with blood to vomit crime,' says Childe Harold, 'And fatal have her Saturnalia been / To Freedom's cause.'

It had been possible, in 1789, to believe in the imminent dawning of a new political age – one in which ancient Liberty might triumph over the feeble monarchies of Europe. But those hopes had died with the Terror. Liberty had led to the guillotine. Napoleon had drenched Europe in a tide of blood. The old dynasties, recovering from their narrow escape, had renewed their sclerotic grip on power – were now recruiting busy armies of secret police to weed out any trace of republican sentiment that might remain among their downtrodden people.

So, where tourists of the eighteenth century had found inspiration, Byron took a bleaker lesson from the remains of ancient Rome. On the Palatine hill, where the imperial palaces lay buried in owl-haunted desolation, he saw a universal destiny:

> *There is the moral of all human tales;*
> *'Tis but the same rehearsal of the past,*
> *First Freedom, and then Glory – when that fails,*
> *Wealth, vice, corruption, – barbarism at last.*

*

'History, with all her volumes vast, / Hath but *one* page,' Childe Harold declares. The template of decline that France had followed had been laid out in Rome, the inevitable fall towards 'barbarism at last' written for all to read in every broken arch, each pile of mouldering brick. 'Temples, baths or halls? Pronounce who can,' Childe Harold murmurs over the ruins, 'for all that learning reap'd / From her research hath been that these are walls.'

'Tully was not more eloquent than thou,' says Harold, warming to the theme, 'Thou nameless column with the buried base.'

But here Byron has taken a certain liberty. The column to which Childe Harold addresses himself is the Column of Phocas, a late-antique monument to an undistinguished emperor, erected in the Roman Forum to stand over what had been left of the city by Belisarius and the Ostrogoths.

Certainly the column, when Byron saw it in 1817, presented a pleasingly mournful aspect, standing lonely in the wreck of the Forum. But it was by no means nameless, nor was its base buried. In fact, the base had been excavated by archaeologists working for the Napoleonic regime some four years earlier, revealing a carved inscription with the name of the column's dedicatee.

Napoleon's attitude to Rome had been very much in line with the tradition of Enlightenment tourists. The city, which he or his allies controlled more or less continuously from 1799, was a pattern and inspiration. Napoleonic administrators did their best to clear the major ruins of their centuries of accreted clutter. The goatherds were driven from the arch of Septimius Severus; the fishmongers banned from the portico of the Pantheon. Whole battalions of Roman poor were marched into the Forum to earn their keep by shifting the mud that had been brought in over the years by the flooding of the Tiber, digging down towards the level of the original paving stones.

The excavated treasures of the ancient city were precious relics sanctifying Napoleon's new empire. Anything that could be moved was carted off to France – priceless collections of ancient art installed at the Louvre for the edification of the Paris bourgeoisie. What could not be moved was copied: the Arch of Titus became the Arc de Triomphe; Napoleon's victory at Austerlitz was celebrated with a bronze replica of Trajan's Column.

This sort of learned imitation was despised by the English Romantics. Napoleon – wasting away under the eye of his British guards on St Helena – was a 'bastard Caesar', following 'at apish distance' and 'with steps unequal' the lofty example of antiquity. The whole effort of scientific enquiry, of finding the patterns, as Winckelmann had tried to do, the project of *Altertumswissenschaft*, all these were rejected. Byron was as steeped in classical learning as any tourist, but he remembered the 'drill'd dull lessons' of his schooldays only with displeasure. In the face of the great night that had fallen on Rome, the visitor, Byron thought, could only feel his way blindly:

But Rome is as the desert, where we steer
Stumbling o'er recollections; now we clap
Our hands, and cry 'Eureka!' it is clear
When but some false mirage of ruin rises near.

Rome was dead and gone, Byron insisted, and to probe it as the archaeologists had done was both pointless and profane. 'The very sepulchres lie tenantless,' says Childe Harold. There could be no fit successors to Rome's greatness, and there was nothing left for anyone to resurrect:

The Niobe of nations! there she stands,
Childless and crownless, in her voiceless woe;
An empty urn within her wither'd hands,
Whose holy dust was scatter'd long ago.

*

Out on the Via Appia, Byron did feel the pull of the old tourist fantasy. Standing beside the enormous drum-like tomb of Caecilia Metella, he was swept up in the thrill of his own cultivated ignorance: what was she like, this Metella? Old? Young? Faithless? True? Fair? Stern? 'I know not why – but standing thus by thee / It seems as if I had thy inmate known,' says Childe Harold to the tomb. And now, 'other days come back on me / With recollected music.' This was the beginning of an old-fashioned touristic reverie:

Yet could I seat me by this ivied stone
Till I had bodied forth the heated mind,
Forms from the floating wreck which Ruin leaves behind.

Childe Harold feels the temptation of Enlightenment optimism. Perhaps, he thinks, from the planks of the 'floating wreck' of Rome, he might be able to construct 'a little bark of hope, once more / To battle with the ocean.' Can he create a figment strong enough to withstand the 'ceaseless roar / Which rushes on the solitary shore / Where all lies foundered that was ever dear'?

But here he recollects himself – remembers the times in which he lives. Having built his little boat, in this turbulent metaphor, where would he steer? There is 'no home, nor hope, nor life, save what is here'.

'Then let the winds howl on!' Harold cries. 'Their harmony shall henceforth be my music.' Like the tourists, Harold – Byron – loves Rome. But where the tourists found hope, Harold finds an answering despair: a sadness that engulfs and subsumes his own. 'Oh Rome! my country! city of the soul! / The orphans of the heart must turn to thee.'

* * *

Three weeks was all the time Byron needed for his Roman visit. Not for him the hours with sketchpad and trowel, the plodding round after some learned guide. He came, he saw, he departed – off back to his base at Venice to resume his life of pleasure and dissolution.

It was there, in the summer of the following year, that another young English poet found him. Percy Bysshe Shelley was another exile – chased from home by hostile opinion and impatient creditors. The whiff of atheism and political radicalism that clung to him was too strong for post-Napoleonic England, and the danger of his ideas was proved, in society's eyes, by his disastrous family life. In 1814, Shelley had run away to Switzerland with a brilliant sixteen-year-old named Mary Godwin, leaving his pregnant wife Harriet behind him. Two years later, Harriet drowned herself in the Serpentine.

In 1816, Percy and Mary Shelley – as she would soon be – made another trip to Switzerland, this time at the urging of Mary's step-sister, Claire Clairmont, who had fallen in love with Lord Byron. When Byron arrived at Lake Geneva that summer, he found Claire, the 'foolish girl', lying in wait, determined, as he put it, 'to unphilos-ophize him'.

This, to some extent, she succeeded in doing, but the affair never really took off. Between Byron and Shelley, however, the sympathy was immediate. Both were romantic outcasts, aristocratic rebels against the stifling conservatism of home. Both were haunted by scandal: Shelley's misdeeds were as nothing beside the lurid deviancies of which Byron was accused, in particular the suspicion of incest with his half-sister Augusta Leigh.

For two months, Claire, Byron and the Shelleys made a happy enough little party, four banished souls, swapping ghost stories under the dark shoulders of the Swiss Alps. Shelley and Byron went boating together; they talked philosophy and politics; they made little local pilgrimages to beauty spots immortalized by Jean Jacques Rousseau and to the house where Gibbon had written his *Decline and Fall.*

Above all, in Byron, Shelley recognized a supremely talented poet. He was 'mad as the winds', Shelley conceded, and 'slave to the vilest and most vulgar prejudices', but *Childe Harold's Pilgrimage* proved Byron's powers. When Shelley returned to England in the autumn of 1816, he bore the newly completed manuscript of the poem's Canto III – a canto in which, Shelley thought, Byron's genius had soared to the most exalted heights.

Byron had soared among the mountains, but when Shelley saw him again at Venice in the summer of 1818, he found him wallowing in baser pleasures. He was looking older – paunchy and somehow despondent, despite his assortment of hired company. His palazzo, near the Grand Canal, was part harem and part menagerie, infested with tame monkeys and large birds.

It was an awkward scene in which to discuss delicate business: Claire Clairmont, the unphilosophizer, had given birth to a daughter, and it was the question of the child's future that had occasioned Shelley's visit.

Escaping from the palazzo, the two men took a gondola ride across the lagoon. Having settled the matter of the daughter, they moved on to poetry. Shelley was waiting eagerly for the fourth and final canto of *Childe Harold's Pilgrimage*, and Byron read him a few verses. More and more, though, Shelley found Byron's thoughts turning to the wrongs he had suffered and his own injured feelings. 'He is heartily and deeply discontented with himself,' Shelley reported to a friend. His thoughts had become 'a distorted mirror' in which nothing could be seen but 'objects of contempt and despair'.

And this depression had found its outlet in debauchery. 'The Italian women with whom he associates,' wrote Shelley:

Are perhaps the most contemptible of all who exist under the moon – the most ignorant, the most disgusting, the most bigoted; * * * * an ordinary Englishman cannot approach them. Well, L.B. is familiar with the lowest sort of these women, the people his gondolieri pick up in the streets.

Canto IV of *Childe Harold's Pilgrimage*, which Shelley had been so much looking forward to, now proved a bitter disappointment. 'The spirit in which it is written is, if insane, the most wicked and mischievous insanity that ever was given forth,' Shelley declared. 'It is a kind of obstinate and self-willed folly.'

Shelley found the bleakness of Canto IV profoundly disturbing and misguided. The high sentiments to which his friend had aspired in Switzerland had somehow been corrupted in Italy, curdled into a sort of grandiloquent despair.

For Shelley was an optimist at heart. He was one of the few whose faith in the possible betterment of human society had survived the upheavals of the preceding decades. And he would convince Lord Byron yet. In November 1818, as he and Mary read Canto IV together, they approached the appointed battleground. The Shelleys were going to Rome.

'Behold me in the capital of the vanished world!' Shelley wrote to a friend. Not even the city's famous customs men could dim his ardour. As they rifled through his luggage, all he could think of was the grandeur of the ancient columns that adorned the dogana headquarters; the wonder of the carved marble cornice, reminding him of 'masses of wave-worn precipice, which overhang you, far, far on high... The impression of [the city] exceeds anything I have ever experienced in my travels.' Rome contained – and here he stole a phrase from Childe Harolde – 'mines of inexhaustible contemplation'.

Like Byron, Shelley was much taken with the 'sublime desolation of the scene'. Each day of that first visit in 1818, he and Mary descended to the Forum, 'a kind of desert full of heaps of stones and pits' (the remains of the Napoleonic excavations). Setting forth 'in the purple and golden light of an Italian evening', he watched the moon rise soft above the wreck, shivered at the shattered arches of Maxentius's basilica, saw Orion twinkling between the pillars of the Temple of Concord.

And Shelley surpassed Byron in his disregard for the modern inhabitants of the city. 'In the first enthusiasm of your recognition of ancient times,' he wrote, 'you see nothing of the Italians.' Rome was 'a city, as it were, of the dead, or rather of those who cannot die, and who survive the puny generations which inhabit and pass over the spot which they have made sacred to eternity'.

St Peter's, in all its glory, was judged to exhibit 'littleness on a large scale', though Shelley did approve of Bernini's colonnade. Both Percy and Mary Shelley were interested in Catholic ritual, perhaps because it seemed so extravagantly pagan in character. But Shelley's atheism rings loud in his description of the Arch of Constantine, 'exquisitely beautiful and perfect' to be sure, but dedicated to a 'Christian reptile', a 'stupid and wicked monster' whose pet religion had corrupted the very arts that adorned his monument.

Shelley had started reading Winckelmann's *History of Ancient Art*, but was really no more keen than Byron to engage in scholarly *Altertumswissenschaft*. 'I have said what I feel without entering into any critical discussion of the ruins of Rome,' he wrote to a friend. Let the guidebooks occupy themselves with such 'shew-knowledge'. Shelley dreaded sounding like a common tourist, reciting facts that were already so well known. Like Byron, Shelley felt that Rome was best appreciated under a veil of romantic moonlight, rather than the glare of Enlightenment scholarship.

But for all they had in common, Shelley and Byron's impressions of the city soon began to diverge. Among the ruins, where Byron had seen a tale of inevitable decline, Shelley found an unexpected beauty. The weeds that choked the Caesars' palaces had been, for Byron, tokens of decay; for Shelley, they were agents of a wondrous transformation:

The Coliseum is unlike any work of human hands I ever saw before... the arches built of massy stones are piled on one another, and jut into the blue air, shattered into the forms of overhanging rocks. It has been changed by time into the image of an amphitheatre of rocky hills overgrown by the wild olive, the myrtle, and the fig-tree... the copsewood overshadows you as you wander through its labyrinths, and the wild weeds of this climate of flowers bloom under your feet.

Nature, which Shelley revered over any god, had wrought a miracle in the ancient amphitheatre. 'I can scarcely believe that when encrusted with Dorian marble and ornamented by columns of Egyptian granite, its effect could have been so sublime.'

> *Rome is fallen, ye see it lying,*
> *Heaped in undistinguished ruin:*
> *Nature is alone undying.*

The Colosseum was 'a nursling of man's art, abandoned by his care, and transformed by the enchantment of Nature into a likeness of her own creations, and destined to partake their immortality'.

At the end of 1818, the Shelleys went on to visit Naples and pay homage to the infernal fires of Mount Vesuvius. They returned to Rome in the spring of 1819, and now Shelley discovered a new wonder. While exploring the vast ruins of the baths of Caracalla, the poet found an ancient staircase winding up through the centre of one of the piles to emerge high above the city, where the giant vaults of the baths hung like concrete hills, floating in the sky.

Here too, nature had been at work. The ancient structure had, over the centuries, been completely overgrown. Shelley found himself in a tangled wilderness of myrtle and bay and blossoming laurustinus and wild fig, untouched thickets sinking their roots into the antique brickwork. Secret paths wound their way through the blooming copsewood, leading past great chasms where the building had split apart into peaks and lofty precipices.

Shelley plunged into this landscape with the thrill of a mountaineer, drinking in the flower-scented air. At last, overcome with delight, he came upon a sort of glade of moss within the labyrinth. Flinging himself among the anemones and violets, he felt 'sensations of voluptuous faintness, like the combinations of sweet music'. Up there, on the ruins of the ancient city, Shelley had found a paradise.

This was an ecstasy undreamed of by the melancholy Byron. Back in 1816, by Lake Geneva, Shelley had read to Byron the myth of Prometheus, the titan who stole fire from the gods, and who taught humanity the arts of civilization. It was a cautionary tale. Prometheus, who had dared too much on behalf of his mortal protégés, was was chained by Zeus to a rock in the Caucasus where an eagle made a daily buffet of his immortal liver.

Byron saw something of himself in the story: a noble spirit, condemned by fate to suffer unjust agonies. More broadly, Prometheus could be a figure for all humankind, enslaved and helpless, with almighty Zeus standing in for the reactionary forces of church and crown. In Prometheus's story, man might foresee 'his own funereal destiny', Byron wrote, 'his wretchedness and his resistance'. The only salvation lay in pride – a pride like that of Milton's Satan, hopeless but yet somehow glorious in its mad defiance of overwhelming authority, its joyful embrace of suffering. 'Triumphant where it dares defy, / And making Death a Victory.'

Byron's Childe Harold, striding the ruins of Rome, embodied that Promethean defiance – a defiance that reaches its thunderous climax when he finds himself amid the dark wildernesses of the Colosseum. Not for him the Shelleyan raptures over flowers and fig trees. Byron felt, in a way that Shelley did not, the ancient darkness of the place: 'Here, where Murder breathed her bloody steam', where 'man was slaughter'd by his fellow man… for the imperial pleasure.'

There was a presence in the ruins, Byron felt, wandering the empty passageways in the dark. His voice was too loud; his footsteps seemed to disturb the dead whose dust lay heavy in the starlit arena. In a passage that became famous, Childe Harold seems to see in ghostly outline the form of a gladiator, lying before him:

He leans upon his hand – his manly brow
Consents to death, but conquers agony,
And his droop'd head sinks gradually low –
And through his side the last drops, ebbing slow
From the red gash, fall heavy, one by one,
Like the first of a thunder-shower; and now
The arena swims around him – he is gone,
Ere ceased the inhuman shout which hail'd the wretch who won.

The Colosseum had been an arena, then a fortress, then a quarry, then a dumping ground, then, latterly, a Christian shrine, dedicated to the thousands of supposed martyrs who had perished there. It had become, to the tourists of the previous generation, a sign of human greatness, of the possibilities of human achievement.

But Byron found the grimness of the spot, the cruelty of lives cut short, of young men 'butchered to make a Roman holiday'.

'Then in this magic circle raise the dead!' Harold cries into the gloom. Here, where the gladiators suffered, he will bare his own suffering. He too has been wounded, he, like a new Prometheus, 'chain'd and tortured':

Have I not suffered things to be forgiven?
Have I not had my brain sear'd, my heart riven,
Hopes sapp'd, name blighted, Life's life lied away?
[...]
From mighty wrongs to petty perfidy
Have I not seen what human things could do?

Childe Harold has tasted the rot at the heart of humanity. Now, in the great arena, on ground hallowed by gladiator blood, Harold summons a dread power to bring him justice: Nemesis, to whom the gladiators used to pray. 'In this thy former realm, I call thee from the dust!'

Like Prometheus, Childe Harold has not shrunk from suffering. He has, as he says, iron in his soul. But if he suffers, 'shall they not mourn?' – they, the petty detractors, the turners of cold shoulders, the arbiters of decency, all those who cast Byron into exile and cut him off from love.

In this page a record will I seek.
Not in the air shall these my words disperse,
Though I be ashes; a far hour shall wreak
The deep prophetic fulness of this verse,
And pile on human heads the mountain of my curse!

*

There, in the darkest heart of vanished Rome, Byron gained, through Childe Harold, what he regarded as a brilliant poetic victory. With furious grandeur, Byron cursed his enemies with what he described, rather unconvincingly, as 'forgiveness'. Let them suffer, he decreed, the 'late remorse of love'.

This was all far too vengeful for Shelley's liking. Up in his perch atop the baths of Caracalla, inspired by the bright blue sky of Rome and the awakening spring, Shelley was creating an answering masterpiece to stand against Childe Harold and Byronic pessimism. Byron had set himself up as a sort of Promethean figure, ennobled by suffering. Shelley now produced his *Prometheus Unbound*, a verse drama about the tortured titan's final victory, his liberation from his eternal bonds.

Childe Harold, in his suffering, cursed his oppressors. Likewise, Shelley's Prometheus has uttered a terrible curse against Zeus, king of the gods. But where Childe Harold sees his curse as a victory, inflicting upon his enemies the 'late remorse of love', Shelley's Prometheus comes to understand that the curse he has uttered entraps not only Zeus, the intended victim, but also himself. Communing from his crag with the spirits of mountains and waters, with the serenest air and the whirlwinds over the abyss, Prometheus lifts his curse entirely. He wishes no living thing to suffer pain.

And in that moment, with the entry of compassion into his tortured heart, his bonds begin to break. The titan, representing human thought and reason, will be united with divine Nature, and set free. Humanity will be transformed by love. The symbols of the old order, 'sceptres, tiaras, swords, and chains, and tomes of reasoned wrong', will be rendered void – the emblems of oppression now as empty of meaning as the untranslatable hieroglyphs that decorate Roman obelisks, an orphaned language from a vanished world.

* * *

Prometheus Unbound was finished in Rome at the beginning of April 1819. It was a bold declaration of hope: that there existed, within humanity, the possibility of redemption through love – that humans might escape the long oppression of tyranny, of Byron's prophecy 'wealth, vice, corruption, barbarism at last'.

But Shelley's spirit was about to be tested. On 26 April, Mary Shelley wrote to a friend of 'the effects of the Roman air, producing colds, depression and even fever to the feeblest of our party'. Percy Shelley might have been inspired by the blue skies of the Roman spring, but his physical health was stubbornly poor. There was talk of leaving the city earlier than had been planned, to get away from the bad air, take refuge in some more salubrious climate where everyone might gather their strength.

Rome would not let go of them so easily. Shelley had always been very taken with the charm of Rome's cemetery for non-Catholics. 'The English burying place is a green slope near the walls,' he wrote:

> The most beautiful and solemn cemetery I ever beheld. To see the sun shining on its bright grass, fresh, when we first visited it, with the autumnal dews, and hear the whispering of the wind among the leaves of the trees which have overgrown the tomb of Cestius, and the soil which is stirring in the sun-warm earth… one might, if one were to die, desire the sleep they seem to sleep.

Shelley imagined lying in the cemetery himself, but there was a crueller fate in store: on 2 June, the Shelleys' four-year-old son William, whom they called Willmouse, fell seriously ill. He was their dearest and only living child, and had been the delight of that Roman spring, with his babyish sketches and lisping Italian. Somewhere he had learned the phrase 'O dio che bella!' and would pipe up proudly whenever he saw something he liked. Now he was stricken, and Shelley was desperate.

He refused to leave the boy's bedside. But there was nothing anyone could do. By the fourth, Willmouse was suffering convulsions. On the seventh, very quietly, he died, and went to join the sleepers under the green slope of the English burying place.

The Shelleys left Rome three days later, never to return. Only in verse did Percy Shelley revisit the Eternal City. 'Go thou to Rome', he wrote, in his *Adonais*, in 1821.

> *Go thou to Rome – at once the Paradise,*
> *The grave, the city, and the wilderness;*
> *And where its wrecks like shattered mountains rise,*
> *And flowering weeds, and fragrant copses dress*
> *The bones of Desolation's nakedness,*
> *Pass, till the Spirit of the spot shall lead*
> *Thy footsteps to a slope of green access*
> *Where, like an infant's smile, over the dead*
> *A light of laughing flowers along the grass is spread.*

The previous year, in November 1820, a third Romantic poet had arrived in Italy. John Keats was a little-known but serious-minded poet whose talent had been noticed by Shelley years before in England, though he regarded him as having a long way yet to come. Reading Keats's *Endymion* in 1819, Shelley's first response was that 'much praise is due to me for having read [it], the Author's intention appearing to be that no person should possibly get to the end of it. Yet,' he conceded, 'it is full of some of the highest and the finest gleams of poetry.'

Perhaps Keats might have carried on that poetic dispute that Byron and Shelley had been conducting across Rome's ruins. He might have carried their battling verses even higher, found yet deeper truths buried in Rome's inexhaustible mine.

Instead it was Rome itself that would have the final word. Keats, suffering from the terminal stages of consumption, had come to Italy in hopes of recovering his health, but the chill of the Roman winter only accelerated his decline. His coach, filled with wildflowers gathered by his loyal friend and nurse, Joseph Severn, rolled past the

Colosseum, but Keats was too sick to care. By the time he arrived at his rented lodgings on the Piazza di Spagna, he had coughed up the last dregs of his poetry and could only lie in his narrow cot, half-mad with pain, listening to the tinkling of the Barcaccia and the tourists mouthing platitudes on the Spanish Steps.

It was to be a bad death. His lungs tortured him all night, and most of the days. His physician refused him laudanum, and put him on a starvation diet in hope of curing his 'digestion', allowing him each day a piece of bread and a single anchovy. Keats longed to die – regarded himself as being dead already – but it was two months before he finally expired, two months during which he begged for food and laudanum, cursed Severn in his delirium, then wept piteously in his remorse. He suffered, wrote Severn, 'despair in every shape. His imagination and memory present every image in horror, so strong that morning and night I tremble for his Intellect... How he can be Keats again from all this I have little hope.'

Shelley had been delighted to hear that Keats was coming to Italy. He and Mary had established themselves in Pisa, where they had found a certain contentment. Mary was taking Greek lessons from an attractive Phanariot Prince, Alexander Mavrocordato. Percy, meanwhile, had bought himself a little dinghy to go boating with his friend Edward Williams. On their maiden voyage the pair capsized in a canal, and Shelley, who could not swim, was only barely rescued. But the drenching put him in high spirits. Only when he returned to Pisa was his mood dampened by the news that Keats had died at last.

On 23 February, around four in the morning, 'the first approaches of death came on', Severn recorded. 'The phlegm seemed boiling in his throat, and increased until 11, when he gradually sunk into death – so quiet that I still thought he slept.'

Off they took him to the English burying place, the *cimitero acattolico*, to lie by little Willmouse and the rest of the Protestant dead. On his tombstone, Keats had requested his now-famous epitaph: 'Here lies one whose name was writ in water.'

So it had seemed to Keats as he gasped his final breaths. During his lifetime, his poetry had attracted little notice, except for the occasional hostile review. He died a failure, more or less unknown. 'The many troubles, persecutions, and may I say cruelties he has borne now weigh heavy on him,' Severn had written. 'If he dies I am witness that he dies of a broken heart and spirit.'

Shelley was convinced that one cruelty in particular had done the damage: 'Young Keats', Shelley wrote to Byron, 'died lately at Rome from the consequences of breaking a blood-vessel, in paroxysms of despair at the contemptuous attack on his book in the "Quarterly Review".' This conservative periodical had been an implacable critic of Shelley's too, and all Shelley's pent-up sense of injury could now find its outlet in righteous indignation on Keats's behalf. 'I have dipped my pen in consuming fire for his destroyers,' Shelley promised. *Adonais* was the result: a funeral elegy for Keats in which Shelley deploys his fullest powers of high sentiment and classical erudition to pronounce upon the anonymous critic a terrible and solemn curse:

> *Live thou, whose infamy is not thy fame!*
> *Live! fear no heavier chastisement from me,*
> *Thou noteless blot on a remembered name!*
> *But be thyself, and know thyself to be!*
> *And ever at thy season be thou free*
> *To spill the venom when thy fangs o'erflow:*
> *Remorse and Self-contempt shall cling to thee;*
> *Hot Shame shall burn upon thy secret brow,*
> *And like a beaten hound tremble thou shalt – as now.*

The verse is arranged in Spenserian stanzas. It is the same form, very distinctive, that Byron used in *Childe Harolde*.

And indeed, the Shelley of *Adonais* is hardly to be recognized as the same hopeful spirit who created *Prometheus Unbound*. He inserts himself into his own poem as a 'stranger' mourning at Keats's tomb, with 'branded and ensanguined brow'.

'Go thou to Rome!' he tells his reader. Go to the English burying place and pause a while among the silent dead. Pause among the mournful graves, and know this:

Too surely shalt thou find
Thine own well full, if thou returnest home,
With tears and gall.

Tears and gall, Shelley had found indeed. What then to do?

From the world's bitter wind,
Seek shelter in the shadow of the tomb.

*

'Roll on, thou deep and dark blue Ocean – roll!' cries Childe Harold at the end of his pilgrimage. 'Man marks the earth with ruin.' Only in trackless Ocean is there peace, where no shadow of man's presence can be felt, no monument to man's vanity erected. The only shadow a man may cast there is his own, Byron says:

When, for a moment, like a drop of rain,
He sinks into thy depths with bubbling groan,
Without a grave, unknell'd, uncoffin'd, and unknown.

On the last day of April 1822 Shelley arrived at the ocean's edge. The Shelleys had decided to settle for the summer at the Casa Magni in Liguria, a large but dilapidated house set in beautiful isolation on the shore, where a line of impassable hills plunged darkly into the wild sea. The journey in was by boat, their luggage piled in crates upon the sand.

With them came the Williamses: Shelley's sailing companion Edward Williams and his pretty wife Jane, with whom Shelley was increasingly besotted. Claire Clairmont, Mary's wild stepsister, came too. Her daughter by Lord Byron, the five-year-old Allegra, had died of typhus two weeks earlier, in the convent to which her father had consigned her. Claire was half-mad with grief and fury, and the strain told on everyone. Walking on the terrace under the moonlight one evening, Shelley froze and caught Williams's arm, staring at the pale line of surf and crying aloud: 'There it is again! – there!' He saw, as he later explained, a naked child rising from the sea to clap its hands and smile at him.

On 12 May, a new boat Shelley had ordered came sailing round the headland – a two-masted schooner, fast and beautiful. She 'sailed like a witch', Williams recorded, keel cutting through waves that were purpled by the floating sails of portuguese men o' war, driven inland by electric summer storms. This was a joy to Shelley. Out on the water with the Williamses, Jane playing to him on her guitar, he found a new happiness. Mary, however, was pregnant and felt trapped on that desolate shore. She was troubled and ill. Then, on 16 June, she suffered a miscarriage and nearly died: Shelley sat her in an ice bath, which seems to have stopped the haemorrhage, but she was slow to recover. Shelley had more visions: Edward and Jane covered in blood, the sea flooding the house, the whole Casa Magni crumbling down into the waves.

July came with blast of heat. Shelley and Williams sailed to Livorno, 50 miles through the heavy air, to see Byron about a new magazine, *The Liberal*, which Shelley and some friends had been planning. The first night in harbour they slept on deck on cushions borrowed from Byron's ship, the *Bolivar*.

On 8 July, after five days of largely fruitless discussion, Shelley and Williams left for home, setting off around two in the afternoon. The haze over the sea was thickening as their sails disappeared into the distance. There were clouds sitting heavy on the horizon and, as the sun dipped, the weather came in fast, driving the Italian fishing boats into harbour. One captain, sailing drenched into Livorno, said he had passed the Englishmen in their boat, labouring against the swell. He had begged them to abandon ship and come aboard his larger vessel – or at least to reef their sails and try to ride out the squall. But when Williams (it was believed) made as if to do so, Shelley is supposed to have seized his arm angrily. The sound of a shrill 'No!' carried distinctly over the waves. And then the boat, still at full sail, disappeared into the storm.

Shelley's body washed ashore ten days later, along with those of Edward Williams and Charles Vivian, their teenage boatboy. They recognized him by his trousers and by the volume of Keats's poetry stuffed into his jacket pocket. The flesh of his face and arms had been eaten away – erased by the sea, the mouth that spoke, the hand that held the pen.

In accordance with Italian quarantine laws, his body was burned on the beach where it came in, with Byron and a few others in attendance. The ashes were eventually brought to Rome, to lie near the bones of Keats and of Shelley's own young son.

In England, the news of Shelley's death was greeted in some quarters with scornful pleasure. 'Shelley, the writer of some infidel poetry, has been drowned,' reported the *Courier*. 'Now he knows whether there is a God or no.'

The liberal cause was struggling in England. And even Shelley, once the most fiery of radicals, had, towards the end of his life, begun to despair of the world of men, tending more and more towards Platonic abstraction. 'He hath awakened from the dream of life,' Shelley said of Keats, in *Adonais*. The living are in fact 'lost in stormy visions', fighting phantom enemies.

> *Fear and grief*
> *Convulse us and consume us day by day,*
> *And cold hopes swarm like worms within our living clay.*

In similar vein, Byron's Childe Harold, in the Colosseum, had reflected on the emptiness of human life:

> *What matters where we fall to fill the maws*
> *Of worms – on battle-plains or listed spot?*
> *Both are but theatres where the chief actors rot.*

But there had always been, for all Byron's dark pronouncements, a latent seam of idealism under his melancholy. As he watched the flames of Shelley's funeral pyre, an answering fire was smouldering within his bulky frame. Things were stirring again in Europe: freedom's banner streaming 'like the thunder-storm against the wind'. Through his latest mistress, Teresa Guiccioli, he had become involved with the intrigues of the Carbonari, Italians conspiring in secret against their Habsburg overlords. And for a while, for Shelley's sake, he lent his support to *The Liberal*, a little voice of radical politics shouting shrilly against the reactionary gale.

But soon, a greater opportunity would present itself for action. Greece, birthplace of art, cradle of philosophy, was in revolt against the Ottomans. Mary Shelley's old friend Prince Mavrocordato had raised an army. From all over Europe, earnest young philhellenes had gathered to his flag. Here, after years of bitterness and dissolution, of flagging vigour and greying hair, was something worthy of Lord Byron.

In July 1823, one year after Shelley's death, Byron set sail in the *Bolivar*, heading for Greece. And in the end, it did not matter that his crusade was a failure, that after a few months of ineffectual soldiering he succumbed ingloriously to a fever at Missolonghi in 1824. He had died for a cause, and Shelley would have been proud of him.

* * *

The Romantic moment was drawing to a close. With peace and rapid industrialization came the railway, bringing a new generation of tourists south through Europe. They were less grand this time, and more numerous: lawyers and brokers and manufacturers, shuffling round the sights, clutching tight their Murray Guides and their plump children.

By repetition in these guidebooks, the verses Shelley and Byron had pronounced over the city became commonplaces. The novelist Nathaniel Hawthorne described in his *Marble Faun* the parties of English or American tourists paying 'the inevitable visit by moonlight' to the Colosseum, 'exalting themselves with raptures that were Byron's, not their own'. It is a mark of the foolishness of Henry James's Daisy Miller that she dies of so sentimental an affliction as a Roman fever. Mark Twain, meanwhile, congratulates himself on being the only man in decades to have described the arena without once having used Byron's old phrase 'butchered to make a Roman Holiday'.*

---

* Not only had Byron's dying gladiator become a cliché, but the very basis for the Byronic passage had been fatally undermined. Childe Harold's

Such mockery was far from the worst of it. The Colosseum had been, for the Romantics, a moonlit wilderness. 'It will not bear the brightness of the day,' Byron had warned. But the mood of the times was changing. The spirit of *Altertumswissenschaft*, of science, of archaeology, was in the ascendant once again. In 1870, the antiquarians would gain control of the Colosseum and of Shelley's paradise above the baths of Caracalla. With painstaking rigour, urged on by nationalist enthusiasm, the new curators stripped the ruins bare, down to the last plant. There were new ideologies abroad in Europe that had no time for shady thickets and mossy glades. Once again, the ancient buildings had work to do.

---

vision is clearly derived from a famous ancient statue, known at the time as the Dying Gladiator. However, the scholarship of later generations would show, conclusively, that the gladiator was not a gladiator at all, but rather a dying Gaul.

20

BLOOD OF ITALY

Garibaldi and the defence of Rome

1849

.

NOVEMBER 1848. THE Council of Deputies gathers at the Palazzo della Cancelleria for the opening of a new session. An elected council allowed to meet in the pope's own city? These are not ordinary times.

The mood is tense, volatile. Popular passion is running high. The streets around the Cancelleria, and the piazza in front, are full. There is no ceremony planned, no spectacle to witness, but these days any political event draws a crowd, restless and watchful, like birds feeling the crackle of a distant thunderstorm.

There is a strong military presence around the palace, but this too is nothing much out of the ordinary. A battalion of the civic guard has been deployed to the piazza, eyed somewhat warily by a detachment of papal police. There are uniforms in the crowd as well, ragged and mismatched kit worn by hangdog soldiers with nowhere to go and nothing to do.

A sudden hubbub, a turning of heads. A carriage has entered the square and pulls up, to howls of derision from the assembled spectators. Out climbs the chief minister of the papal government, Count Pellegrino Rossi. With firm step and disdainful smile he strides towards the Cancelleria, a desperate undersecretary flapping in his wake. There have been threats made, ominous warnings given. But there are always threats, and Count Rossi is not a man to be daunted by a plebeian mob.

But his patrician hauteur endangers more than his own life. The assassins, when they strike, move with practised speed. From one side, a man wrapped in a cloak strikes the count with an umbrella. As he turns his head, another man slides a stiletto downwards through the base of his neck – not much blood but no need for a second blow. And as Rossi falls, his government falls too. The pope has lost control of Rome.

* * *

It took a single blade to kill Pellegrino Rossi, but more than fifty years of Italian history put their force into that fatal thrust: the great strands of cause and consequence fusing together at the stiletto point.

Indeed, the blade that killed Pellegrino Rossi was, in a sense, a distant cousin of the guillotine. When the armies of revolutionary France invaded Italy under General Bonaparte in 1796, they brought with them the spirit of the Jacobins, the Paris radicals who had claimed the head of King Louis XVI three years before. Soon, almost all the duchies and petty kingdoms of the Italian peninsula had tasted French-style revolutionary government: democratic, anti-clerical and republican.

Jacobinism gained its footing in the cities. The countryside, however, generally remained loyal to the old authorities, bishop, duke or king. In 1799, with Austrian support, armies of peasants and bandits overthrew most of the Jacobin governments.

Napoleon Bonaparte toppled the French republic and installed himself as emperor. Marching south, he imposed a new settlement on the troublesome Italians. Rome, Tuscany and the northwest were annexed to the French empire. Naples and the south were given to Napoleon's brother to rule as a client state. In the northeast, from the rich territories of Venice and Milan, Napoleon made himself another little puppet state, the kingdom of Italy.

Napoleon lost control of Italy in 1814, and the Battle of Waterloo in 1815 put a permanent end to his ambitions. At the Congress of

Vienna, the victorious powers – Britain, Russia, Prussia and Habsburg Austria – restored Europe's old regimes. French expansionism would in future be carefully contained. To maintain the balance of power, much of Italy was put under the armed protection of the Habsburg empire.

The chancellor of the Habsburg empire at the time was Prince Klemens von Metternich. It was Metternich, above all, who had shaped the post-war European order. He was determined not to allow any further outbreaks of revolution.

From Vienna, Metternich sent out his agents to eradicate any lingering traces of Jacobinism. There were to be no more constitutions or representative assemblies, no free press, no political associations. And the memory of the Bonapartist kingdom of Italy was to be thoroughly stamped out. Italy, Metternich famously declared, was nothing but a 'geographical expression'.

The kingdom of Italy had been dominated by France, ruled directly by Napoleon himself, and had covered less than half of the Italian peninsula. Nevertheless, the brief existence of a state called Italy had caused an old idea to stir once again in Italian minds.

For centuries, the peninsula had been divided. Internal quarrels had left the Italians unable to resist foreign domination. The country had been impoverished by endless wars, serving as a battleground for Europe's great powers.

And ancient rivalries always simmered. Loyalties were local, above all, owed to village or neighbourhood more than to any nation.* Ordinary Italians in the fields and in the towns spoke dialects that were sometimes mutually incomprehensible – to a Lombard farmer, for example, the speech of a Sicilian would have sounded as foreign as French or Portuguese.

But despite all this division, there had long been a dream of Italy. Petrarch, back in the fourteenth century, had urged Cola di Rienzo

---

* Italy was and is the land of *campanilismo*, pride in one's own district, as marked out by the local church with its bell tower, or *campanile*.

to unite Italy. Machiavelli, two hundred years later, had wept for the Italians, 'more enslaved than the Hebrews', and urged unity against the Habsburgs and the Valois. Literature helped smooth over linguistic divisions. Petrarch's popularity helped make his native Tuscan dialect a preferred form of the language among educated Italians. Although Tuscan was not widely spoken among the poor, it was at least quite commonly understood.

An idea had slowly taken hold: Italy might not be a state, but the Italians did at least constitute a single nation – one people with shared virtues and shared vices, bound by a common culture and heritage, heirs to a richer civilization than that of the barbarians beyond the Alps.

Then had come Napoleon, erasing, by a wave of his hand, the old borders that divided Italy. There had been advantages to his rule: new roads, a middle-class bureaucracy, an end to some of the stifling feudal privilege of clerics and aristocrats. Young men, even of quite modest means, had been allowed to serve as officers in the Grande Armée, Italians winning victories on foreign soil.

After Napoleon's fall, Italy was once again divided into petty despotisms. Many found their prospects cut off, their horizons suddenly narrowed. But even as Metternich's secret police shut down the clubs and the printing presses, young men and women still wondered: what might be achieved if Italy could be united again?

Northern tourists, arriving after the end of the Napoleonic wars, brought with them a romantic idea of Italy as the country of dissolution and decline. '*O patria mia*,' lamented the greatest of the Italian Romantics, Count Giacomo Leopardi, in 1818:

> *O patria mia, vedo le mura e gli archi*
> *E le colonne e i simulacri e l'erme*
> *Torri degli avi nostri,*
> *Ma la gloria non vedo,*
> *Non vedo il lauro e il ferro ond'eran carchi*
> *I nostri padri antichi.*

My native land, I do the walls behold,
The arches, columns, statues and deserted
Towers by our forebears builded,
But not the glory, not
The laurel and the weapons that of old
Our fathers bore.

Political activity was closed off, so young Italians turned to art, encoding their hopes and resentments in novels, poems and plays. The use of historical settings provided some cover from the censors. There was new enthusiasm for tales of the medieval Lombard League, Italian cities banding together against Frederick Barbarossa, a teutonic tyrant whose modern equivalent was perfectly clear. Italy's oppressors appeared in fiction as Huns or Visigoths; the Italians as rebel Scots or Hebrew slaves.

This period saw the great flowering of Italian romantic opera. In the eighteenth century, opera had been dominated by *castrati*, plump singing eunuchs whose performances privileged vocal virtuosity over intensity of feeling. The Jacobin revolutions had brought a new seriousness to proceedings: republican librettists chose stories from ancient history; their heroes, plucked from the pages of Plutarch or Livy, abandoned the flighty upper reaches of the vocal range, preferring to sing in tenor or manly baritone.

When Napoleon was banished, the tenors and baritones remained, singing out romantic defiance from the stages of Milan, Naples and Rome. 'Let the trumpet sound', goes a typical line from Bellini's *I Puritani*; 'intrepid I will fight like a strong man. It is a fine thing to face death crying "Freedom!"'

Increasingly, these leading men were joined by great massed choruses, whose hymns could rouse audiences to a frenzy. '*O mia patria,*' sing the Hebrew slaves of Verdi's *Nabucco*, '*si bella e perduta*': 'so beautiful and lost!' For an Italian audience, such lines could hardly fail to strike home.

Melodies from hit operas formed a new musical vocabulary of patriotism, spilling out of the theatres to be recapitulated in churches, at grand salons, even on the streets, cranked out by wandering organ grinders. The whole peninsula resounded with choruses and arias, as if Italy herself were calling her children to arms. 'Where are thy sons?' Leopardi exclaims.

> *Nessun pugna per te? non ti difende*
> *Nessun de' tuoi? L'armi, qua l'armi: io solo*
> *Combatterò, procomberò sol io.*
> *Dammi, o ciel, che sia foco*
> *Agl'italici petti il sangue mio.*

> *Will no one fight for thee? None of thine own*
> *Defend thee? – Arms, bring arms! Alone will I*
> *Do battle, lone on stricken field expire.*
> *Grant heaven my blood may then*
> *In all Italian bosoms burn like fire.*

*

In this heightened atmosphere, many young men felt the need to move from words to action, chafing against the 'cemetery-like peace' that Metternich and his Austrians had imposed.

In the early days of the post-Napoleonic restoration, the main opportunities for active opposition lay with the secret societies. There were dozens of these organizations in Italy, with wildly different practices and aspirations, from radical masonic lodges to revolutionary cults: the Adelfi, the Federati, the Republican Brother Protectors, the Perfect Sublime Masters, the Society of the Black Pin. Most popular of all was the order of the Carbonari, the 'Charcoal Burners'.

The origins of the Carboneria were mysterious. Carbonari, the 'good cousins' as they called themselves, might variously trace the roots of their society back to Scotland, medieval France, Philip of Macedon or the Bavarian illuminati. Only masters of the order were allowed to know the secret truth: that the first Carbonaro had been none other than Jesus Christ, the Grand Master of the Universe himself.

Initiation into the Carboneria had all the trappings a young man could wish for: passwords, mystic rites, secret handshakes. But, despite all the fun and games, the secret societies were capable of acts of un-impeachable gravity. In December 1820, setting off through Ravenna to meet his latest mistress, Lord Byron was interrupted by the sound of gunshots. There in the street lay the city's military commandant, two bullets in his stomach and one in his chest, bleeding out on the pavement. The assassin was long gone, his sawn-off gun abandoned in the road, but still only the English lord dared do anything to help the dying man. With Carbonari everywhere, it was unwise to look too sympathetic to the oppressors.

In 1820 and 1821, the Carbonari played a leading role in two very serious insurrections: an uprising in the Bourbon kingdom of the Two Sicilies and an attempted military coup in Piedmont, the vital north-Italian buffer state on the French border. For an instant, Metternich's careful order seemed to shake. The Bourbon king in Naples was forced to grant a liberal constitution. In Piedmont, the rebels took over the capital, Turin. The regimes Metternich had set up as the building blocks of his post-Napoleonic order proved, under pressure, to be alarmingly fragile.

In the end, Austrian troops were called in to quell the uprisings. The secret societies were sternly repressed. But the revolts of 1820–1 had caused a terrible loss of face for Italy's local autocrats, whose reliance on Austrian arms was made embarrassingly clear. Now Italy's myriad factions of radicals and liberals had a foreign foe against whom they could unite. 'They despise you, young men of Italy,' one defeated rebel leader wrote about the Austrians. 'They hope that a soft and lazy life will have unnerved you. They think that your courage is of words not deeds.'

* * *

In April 1821, a boy named Giuseppe Mazzini saw a man begging in the streets of Genoa. He was immensely struck, he later recalled, by the man's face, energetic and severe, by the 'fiery glance' he cast about him, the blackness of his beard. He held out a white handkerchief: 'For the refugees of Italy.'

The survivors of the Piedmontese uprising had trickled into Genoa one by one over the preceding days. The city was sympathetic to their cause, but there was no hope of defending it against the Austrians. All that remained was to scrape enough money to pay their way across the sea. They drifted through the streets in their out-of-town clothes, some with a warlike air, others deep in silent sorrow.

Mazzini never forgot them. He saw, in a flash of understanding, the road that lay ahead, the struggle for Italian liberty, 'and the thought that I too must bear my part'. By night, he dreamed of the silent refugees. Boyishly, he longed to follow them into their heroic exile. Grieving for his country, he took to wearing only mourning black.

At school, he stumbled upon the work of the exiled Romantic Ugo Foscolo. Foscolo's great work, *The Last Letter of Jacopo Ortis*, is an entire epistolary novel about despair and suicide, and the teenage Mazzini read it so many times he had it practically by heart. His poor mother was desperate. Her son seemed ready at any moment to follow Ortis's example.

'We young men were all Romantics,' Mazzini remembered. The young rebelled against both eighteenth-century decadence and the sober neoclassicism that had succeeded it. Romanticism was wild where classicism was contained; was guided by love more than duty, by nature more than learning, by inspiration more than precedent. The path was a dark and melancholy one, but for young men adrift in a hostile world it offered at least the hope of meaning, the possibility of change.

Mazzini was troubled, however, by a certain emptiness behind all that tempestuous feeling. A literature unmoored from anything but individual fancy could never be true art, he believed. There had to be some guiding principle, some objective greater than the self. And so Mazzini put aside any notion of a literary career. Not for him, the 'courage of words not deeds'. In 1827 Giuseppe Mazzini was inducted into the order of the Carbonari.

The association was neither a long nor a happy one. The vigilance of the Piedmontese authorities was making life difficult for the Carbonari. Real revolutionary activity was almost impossible, and the leaders of

The pyramid of Cestius, built into the Aurelian walls, as seen by Piranesi. By the pyramid, below the walls, is the Cimitero Acattolico where Keats and Shelley are buried.

Shelley was captivated by the beauty of the cemetery with its melancholy tombs. 'One might,' he wrote, 'if one were to die, desire the sleep they seem to sleep.'

The Coliseum at Rome by Moonlight, Frederick Lee Bridell, 1859.
The work of Byron and other romantics established the night-time
visit to the Colosseum as a staple of the Victorian itinerary.

The view over the Forum, the *Campo Vaccino*,
painted by William Turner in 1839.

Giuseppe Garibaldi, photographed in 1860. That year, Garibaldi and his thousand red shirts landed in Sicily, initiating the final conflict that led to the unification of Italy.

The commanding view over the rooftops of Rome from the summit of the Janiculum. The 'Altar of the Fatherland' can be seen in the distance, recognisable by its brash white marble.

The Charge of the Lancers, 1915, by Umberto Boccioni, regarded as the best of the Futurist painters.

Mussolini as he liked to be seen, in his characteristic attitude:
the posing hero of Italy, thrusting out his manly jaw.

Margherita Sarfatti in the 1920s. After the march on Rome in
1922, her influence over Mussolini began to decline.

A column of US troops crosses the Piazza del Popolo
after the liberation of Rome in June 1944.

Aïché Nana, nude on the floor of the Rugantino restaurant in Trastevere:
the striptease scandalized Rome, and was an inspiration for *La Dolce Vita*.

Marcello Mastroianni and Anita Ekberg in the iconic Trevi fountain
scene from *La Dolce Vita*. Ekberg was impervious to the cold water.
Mastroianni was permitted to wear waders for close-ups.

the order filled the time with bogus ritual and petty infighting.

But in the summer of 1830 there was news of a successful liberal uprising in Paris. Hope sprang again in the hearts of the Italian Carbonari. Revolutionary plans were dusted off. Young gentlemen set themselves to casting bullets and preparing for war. Amid all this, Mazzini was sent to a hotel to meet a certain Major Cottin, to initiate him into the second rank of the Carboneria.

The major was halfway through his oath when a little window opened in the wall by the bed. A nose and pair of beady eyes appeared at the gap, gave Mazzini a hard stare, then disappeared.

Cottin had turned informer. A few days later, Mazzini was picked up by the Piedmontese police as he was leaving his house. He had just enough time to dispose of his most incriminating possessions: a sword stick, a coded letter, the text of the Carbonari oath and a pocketful of home-made rifle ammunition.

As weapons against Metternich's order, these props were absurd. But the penalties for sedition were real enough. Mazzini spent months in solitary confinement in the Piedmontese royal fortress at Savona with only Tacitus, Byron and the Bible for company.* He still had hopes of revolution and sent a stream of coded messages from his cell: the first letter of every second word spelled out his real message to the Carbonari – and, to further confound the guards, the message was all in Latin.

It became clear, however, that no outside force would end his captivity. There were revolutions in 1830–1 in Parma, Modena and the Papal States, but these were soon crushed, with Austrian help. Only Mazzini's personal insignificance saved him in the end: without a witness willing to swear to his guilt, the Piedmontese authorities decided he wasn't worth keeping, and let him go.

*

* Mazzini's father asked what crime his son had committed. The authorities replied that Mazzini was 'a young man of talent, very fond of solitary walks by night, and habitually silent as to the subject of [his] meditations, and that the government was not fond of young men of talent, the subject of whose musings was unknown to it.'

Bitterly disappointed, Mazzini set off into exile. At this critical moment in Italy's struggle, the Carbonari had proved themselves worthless. The leaders of the revolts had failed to grasp the need for unity, for Italians to rise as one against the occupying power. And the rebels had been too tame, too optimistic about the chance of finding a compromise, too willing to confine their revolutionary efforts to the borders of their own *piccola patria*. While the various rebel governments tried to negotiate individually, the Austrians could eliminate pockets of resistance one by one.

The Carbonari had no vision, Mazzini concluded, no true sense of purpose. Their revolutions had been corrupted by pragmatism, by the caution of petty materialists who reckoned strength in cannon and shot and marching boots.

Mazzini would waste no more time trying to galvanize the Carboneria's corpse. During his months in prison he dreamed of a new organization, one that would be powered by faith and will and purity of spirit. Mazzini's *Giovine Italia* – Young Italy – would win liberty by appealing to the 'true instincts and tendencies of the Italian heart'.

Mazzini's programme was clear and uncompromising. Italy should have liberty – that is, rights, democracy, a republican constitution; it should be united, gathering in all the territories of the Italian peoples; and it should be independent, beholden to no power but itself.

But Mazzini's vision transcended mere politics. Like most educated Italians, he was not oblivious to the impression his country made on foreigners. Italy was treated as a sort of memorial garden, a reminder that even the greatest civilizations sicken and die. The surviving Italians were 'as indolent as orientals in their daily lives', one traveller wrote. 'Life is nothing more than a dream-filled sleep under a beautiful sky.'

This long slumber of the Italian spirit was a commonplace of patriotic writing. Anaesthetized by tyranny, Italians had become indolent, devotees of *dolce far niente*. They had lost their thrust, become effeminate in their idleness, undisciplined, frivolous, a nation of *castrati* and lady's men.

For Italy to become a true nation-state, Mazzini believed, it would first be necessary to awaken the Italians. This national awakening would be a renewal of Italy's manhood, a regeneration of Italian will, almost a religious redemption. A redemption – literally, a buying back. And the price would be high. 'Liberty is bought with blood and sacrifice,' Mazzini wrote. His new Italians would prove their worth to the doubting foreigners, showing their 'blood flowing as the price of peace'.

There was something Shelleyan in Mazzini's approach, in his faith in the perfectibility of man. But Shelley had been a pacifist. Mazzini believed that the regeneration of Italy would come through war. 'After many centuries of slavery, a nation can only be regenerated through virtue, or through death.' This was a version of the Christian story: only through death could Italy achieve its resurrection – what later generations would learn to call its resurgence, its *risorgimento*.

* * *

'What does he do, the pope?' asked the poet Giuseppe Belli in 1835.

> *Cosa fa er Papa? Eh ttrinca, fa la nanna,*
> *taffia, pijja er caffè, sta a la finestra,*
> *se svaria, se scrapiccia, se scapestra,*
> *e ttiè Rroma pe ccammera-locanna.*

> *What does he do, the Pope? He fools around,*
> *Has sleepy-poos, drinks coffee, stuffs his face,*
> *Waves from the window, slobs around the place,*
> *takes Rome to be his private stomping ground.*

Such was the view from the streets, expressed in the pungent Roman dialect of Belli's verse. The pope is the big boss, the man who gets the last bowl of soup.

> *Lui l'aria, l'acqua, er zole, er vino, er pane,*
> *li crede robba sua: È tutto mio;*
> *come a sto monno nun ce fussi un cane.*

The air, the water, sun, the bread and wine
He thinks he owns the lot – it's mine, all mine!
As if he were the last shit in the universe.

Much less rosy was the view from the Vatican. The revolutionary upheavals at the end of the eighteenth century had given the popes a major scare. Jacobinism had turned resolutely anti-clerical. Churches in France were converted to 'Temples of Reason'. Monks and nuns were turned out of their monasteries, bishops sent to the guillotine.

And the excesses of the 1790s had been the culmination of alarming long-term trends. Enlightenment ideas had eaten away at the authority of the church; European rulers were more ready than ever to challenge the papacy and its agents. In 1773, Pope Clement IX was even forced to dissolve the Jesuit Order. The stormtroopers of the counter-Reformation – men whose reach had extended from Brazil to Japan, whose schools had educated half the noblemen in Europe – were disarmed and abandoned, swamped by the rising tides of pantheism, materialism and natural science.

When Metternich restored the old regimes in 1814, the church was determined to fight back against modernity. The Jesuits were restored to their former authority. Ecclesiastical courts were reopened. The Jewish ghettos, abolished by Napoleon, were once again enclosed. The *zelanti* were back in force, with their inquisitions and their *Index of Banned Books*. Dissenters and liberals found themselves entombed in the Castel Sant'Angelo, or chained to a bench in the papal galleys.

In the clandestine fight against the Carbonari, the restoration popes had weapons of their own. In the anti-Jacobin struggles of 1799, Italy's devout peasants had made impressive demonstrations of their willingness to do violence on behalf of their Holy Mother Church. After the rebellions of 1820–1, Pope Pius VII had excommunicated the Carbonari en masse, condemning their 'vain and wicked philosophy'. Now the peasant soldiers of the Holy Faith, the *Sanfedisti*, faced the bourgeois radicals of the secret societies in a twilight war, bludgeons and daggers wielded in the service of God or Liberty.

*

'Depravity exults,' Pope Gregory XVI warned in 1832. 'Science is impudent; liberty, dissolute... The torches of treason are being lit everywhere.'

So indeed they were. Membership of Mazzini's *Giovine Italia* was climbing into the thousands; his writings were passed from hand to hand through universities and regimental messes, his ideas whispered through fencing clubs and boarding schools.

Again and again, young Mazzinians hurled themselves against the unyielding edifices of restoration tyranny. Attempted uprisings in 1833 and 1834 ended in disaster. But Mazzini bore the execution of his agents in good heart: 'Ideas ripen quickly when they are nourished by the blood of martyrs.'

Through the 1830s and into the 1840s, Mazzini kept the faith. In 1844 two young Venetians, the Bandiera brothers, earned themselves an eternal place in the annals of liberty with a foolhardy attempt to stir up a revolt in Calabria. The authorities were well aware of their plans, and the locals proved entirely indifferent, but the Bandiera brothers went to the firing squad as bravely as anyone could wish, with the tune of an operatic chorus on their lips: 'Whoever dies for their country has truly lived.'

With the help of Mazzini's indefatigable pen, the Bandiera brothers became heroes of the revolution. Their deaths would set the fires of liberty blazing in more hearts. Their blood would pay for the redemption of Italy.

But while Mazzini was spinning his stories, the currents of patriotic opinion were moving in a more moderate and pragmatic direction. Many of those who opposed the old regimes were equally alarmed by the Mazzinian eagerness for revolution. Not everyone shared Mazzini's confidence in the essential good nature of the people, once released from the constraints imposed by church and king.

How then should Italy be freed from foreign domination? One idea was to unite behind the king of Piedmont, Carlo Alberto. Piedmont was the only Italian state that could muster a meaningful military force, and one of the few not to be directly ruled by a member of the house of Habsburg. With Piedmont in the lead, a coalition of Italian states might just be strong enough to expel the Austrians.

As for the question of Italy – although true national unity was not necessarily the goal, the moderates of the gentlemen's clubs and stock exchanges were always keen to see customs barriers removed, marshes drained, railway lines extended. Theirs would be a state brought together by mutual interest, not airy ideals.

The second major school of thought recommended an Italian federation ruled by the pope from Rome. There were obvious difficulties with this notion. The pope's position in Italy was an anomalous one: he was the spiritual father of almost the entire population of the peninsula, but also the temporal lord of one of its competing territories – a territory that stretched the width of Italy from sea to sea, standing quite literally in the way of Italian unification. Meanwhile his court, the papal Curia, was full of senior ecclesiastics with links not just to Italy but to dioceses across Europe.

But popes had been negotiating these complexities for a thousand years. It was not absurd, therefore, to imagine that the right pope might be able to add Saviour of Italy to his roles. Something along these lines had taken place in the twelfth century, when the 'Guelph' cities of Italy formed the Lombard League against the Holy Roman Emperor Frederick Barbarossa. The so-called 'neo-Guelphs' hoped that this miracle might be repeated in the nineteenth.

In 1846, the hopes of the neo-Guelphs were raised by the death of of the arch-conservative Gregory XVI. His replacement, Pius IX, known as Pio Nono, was believed to be a liberal, and his early actions seemed to confirm it. An amnesty for political prisoners, granted in July 1846, was in keeping with old papal tradition, but was greeted as the dawning of a new age.

The worst excesses of the papal secret police were curbed and the grip of the clergy on government very slightly relaxed. There was talk of progress and reform, of telegraphs and gas lighting. The pope was willing to build a railway line, one of those arteries of modernity that Pope Gregory had punningly dismissed as *chemins d'enfer*. Most worryingly of all, from an Austrian perspective, the pope agreed to a customs union with Tuscany and Piedmont. The federalist ideas of the neo-Guelphs seemed every day to be gaining momentum.

The people of Rome had been slow to pick up the new nationalist enthusiasm. They were conscious of their special status as inhabitants of the papal capital and, though they mocked their popes, there was a sort of loyalty behind the laughter, as if with children ribbing an eccentric uncle. After all:

> *Quer trerregno che ppoi pare un zuppriso*
> *vô ddí cche llui commanna e sse ne frega,*
> *ar monno, in purgatorio e in paradiso.*

> *That triple crown that looks like a rice ball*
> *Means he's the boss, and don't have to make nice*
> *Down here, in purgatory, nor in Paradise.*

Now that the pope was a liberal, however, popular enthusiasm for reform could grow unchecked. The church in Rome was built on popular participation, in ceremonies, Masses, blessings, sermons, theatricals. These assemblies became occasions for further reformist demands, presented as declarations of loyalty to the beloved Pio Nono.

The rulers of Italy were losing control of the situation. By April 1847 the far-sighted Prince von Metternich was deeply worried about 'the possible diffusion of these erroneous ideas of nationality. Such ideas are being dangerously exploited by elements of disorder who are pitting themselves against the hard reality of political fact.'

In order to reacquaint the Italians with the most pertinent 'political facts', the Austrians moved to take over the papal city of Ravenna. This only made the situation worse. Pio Nono had little choice but to complain, and the sight of the pope resisting the foreign oppressor stirred up a volatile combination of patriotism and offended religious feeling. That December, the opera season in Rome opened with a performance of Verdi's *Attila*, a bombastic drama of brave Roman soldiers and their saintly pope defending Italy against the pagan Huns. It was received with wild displays of emotion. 'I stand ready for every conflict,' sings a Roman general in resounding baritone. 'If I must fall, I shall fall as a brave man... and over the last Roman all Italy will weep.'

By this time, however, a certain froideur had crept into the pope's dealings with the Roman people. On New Year's Day 1848, Pio Nono at first refused to grant his subjects the traditional blessing at the Quirinal Palace. He relented in the end, but the mood that night at the opera was highly charged. In the stalls, the crowd chanted the name of a popular leader. The boxes, on the other hand, were occupied by a larger than usual number of men wearing the uniform of the papal guard.

Whatever plans the pope had made, he was soon to be overtaken by events. A virulent potato blight in 1845 and the failure of wheat and rye crops in 1846 caused starvation across the countryside of Europe (most devastatingly in Ireland). Food riots in the cities led to broader manifestations of unrest. All through 1847 the old regimes struggled to contain the violence, but in 1848 things started to unravel. In January, an uprising in Palermo expelled the Bourbon authorities and installed a liberal constitution. In February, the barricades went up in Paris. The king, Louis Philippe, was forced to abdicate, and a Second French Republic was declared.

Then, in March, there was an uprising in Vienna itself. On 13 March Prince Klemens von Metternich, the architect of the European order, was forced into exile, banished from the great Austrian empire he had done so much to create.

The news crackled down the telegraph lines and off the printing presses of Europe. Metternich, the reactionary-in-chief, had been defeated. In Berlin, Zagreb, Prague, Krakow, Budapest and Stockholm, people took to the streets demanding an end to autocracy. There were successful democratic uprisings in Venice and in Milan, where ordinary citizens pushed out the Austrian garrison in five days, the famous *Cinque Giornate*, of hard street fighting.

Regimes that wanted to survive were forced to adapt. The grand duke of Tuscany and the king of Piedmont were forced to grant liberal constitutions. In Rome, the pope did the same, allowing an elected body, the Council of Deputies, to take part in government. The Roman people had not had so much power since the Middle Ages. As news of Metternich's fall spread across the city, the church bells rang in celebration; the arms of Austria were burned in the streets, while a carabinieri band played a mock funeral march.

Italy's moment seemed to have come. King Carlo Alberto of Piedmont, sensing opportunity, declared war on Austria. Tuscany, Naples and the Papal States rallied in support. The moderates were to be vindicated. An Italian coalition, with king and pope at its head, marched against the Austrians. Field Marshal Radetzky, the commander of Habsburg forces in Italy, was in retreat.

And then, very quickly, the moderate dream fell apart. King Carlo Alberto of Piedmont had too clear an eye for his own advantage and soon alienated the other Italian leaders. On 29 April a nervous Pio Nono withdrew from the war effort, repudiating the 'treacherous advice... of those who would have the Roman Pontiff to be the head and to preside over the formation of some sort of novel republic of the whole Italian people.'

So much for the neo-Guelph solution. Then in July, abandoned by its allies, the vaunted Piedmontese army was defeated by Radetzky and his Austrians. King Carlo Alberto retreated to his own borders, abandoning the Milanese and the Venetians to their fate.

The pope was becoming increasingly desperate. His abandonment of the Italian cause had infuriated the nationalists; the liberals were pressing for greater and greater reform, chipping away at the foundations of papal autocracy. Hardline reactionaries thought he had already gone too far by issuing a constitution back in March, while on the other hand the radicals refused to recognize his right to issue any sort of constitution at all.

In September, hoping to restore some sort of order, Pius appointed the moderate Count Pellegrino Rossi as his chief minister. Rossi was highly competent, proud but dedicated. He might even have succeeded in saving the pope's authority, given time. But Rossi's highhanded moderation had the effect of alienating all factions at once.

The Cancelleria, where the deputies met, was built with stone plundered from the Theatre of Pompey – from the monumental complex, in other words, where Julius Caesar had been murdered, nineteen centuries before. The radicals who murdered Rossi on 15 November 1848 orchestrated their attempt to bring that ancient precedent to mind: the grand arrival at the legislature, the same jostling crowd, the same weapons. A stiletto on the steps of the Cancelleria to echo the dagger of Brutus the Liberator.

For the murder of Rossi was no isolated killing but rather the signal for a revolution. The radicals were determined to end the temporal power of the papacy once and for all. Besieged in the Quirinal Palace, taking fire from a hostile crowd, Pius saw that all was lost. On 24 November, disguised as a humble priest, the pope fled Rome.

* * *

Giuseppe Mazzini had never been an advocate of political assassination and always condemned the murder of Rossi. But here was a moment of opportunity. The king was defeated. The pope was gone. The moderates, the pragmatists, the materialists, all were thoroughly discredited. 'The royal war is over,' he declared after the defeat of the Piedmontese army. 'The war of the people begins.'

The murder of Pellegrino Rossi had whipped Rome into a frenzy of revolutionary excitement. It was by no means certain what direction things would take. Most ordinary Romans were ambivalent at best about the loss of their Holy Father. Among the revolutionary leaders, some only hoped to remove the pope's temporal power while others dreamed of dismantling the entire Roman church.

Opinions also differed widely on the national question. Many revolutionaries were interested in Rome's freedom only. There were problems enough within the city walls without worrying about the liberty of Italy.

But the agents of Mazzini's *Giovine Italia* were hard at work in Rome, and patriotic feeling ran high. The opera season was starting again. Giuseppe Verdi had created a new historical epic for the occasion, *The Battle of Legnano*, celebrating a famous victory of the

Lombard League over Frederick Barbarossa. With the papal censors gone, there was no need for restraint. The tenor joins the Knights of Death, swears to die before he will surrender, leaps from a castle tower crying 'long live Italy'. All this was received, in Rome's Teatro Argentina, with wild enthusiasm, the crowd demanding encores until the singers could hardly croak.

By February, the revolutionary state was beginning to set itself in order. On the fifth, a newly elected constituent assembly met for the first time. It had become clear that the pope would not compromise: 'abominable, monstrous, illegal, impious, absurd, sacrilegious and outrageous to every law, human and divine' was how he described the proceedings.

This at least had the effect of simplifying matters. At two in the morning on 8 February 1849, the constituent assembly, having debated through the night, declared by a large majority that the temporal power of the papacy was henceforth at an end, and that Rome would be a republic.

One of the first acts of the new Roman republic was to grant citizenship to Giuseppe Mazzini. 'I entered the city one evening early in March', Mazzini remembered, 'with a deep sense of awe, almost of worship. Rome was to me... the temple of Humanity.'

Mazzini had been deeply dismayed by the failures of 1848, but 'as I passed through the Porta del Popolo, I felt an electric thrill run through me – a spring of new life'.

He had long dreamed of the coming of the Third Rome, as he called it. That evening he addressed the constituent assembly:

> After the Rome of conquering soldiers, after the Rome of the triumphant Word... there shall come the Rome of virtue and example; after the city of the Emperors, after that of the Popes, shall come that of the People. But the Rome of the People has arisen; it is here.

Mazzini saw a city that could lead Italy and Europe towards freedom. And Europe's embattled autocrats feared the same. The word 'republic', with its echoes of the French Revolution, struck fear into the hearts of kings.

But the reactionaries and despots had not given up hope. Indeed, the revolutionary wave that had swept across Europe in 1848 was receding by 1849. Urban radicals found that their ideas had little purchase out in the countryside, where the vast majority of Europe's people still lived. Revolutionary governments proved factious and inefficient; mob violence alienated elite opinion, driving moderates back towards the secure authority of church and king.

In Austria the Habsburg regime had survived the upheavals of the previous year and was now re-establishing itself by force, one rebel city at a time. In the kingdom of the Two Sicilies, Ferdinand II added the nickname 'Bomba' to his titles by the indiscriminate shelling of the city of Messina, which had already surrendered to him. In Tuscany, a republic declared in February collapsed in mid-April, and the grand duke returned.

Even in republican France there had been a counter-revolution. History repeats itself, Marx said, first as tragedy, then as farce. France's Second Republic fell to a second Bonaparte, Louis-Napoleon, a nephew of Napoleon I. In 1852, he would declare himself emperor, just as his uncle had done.

The new Roman republic found itself encircled by hostile powers. No help would come from Italy. Milan had fallen to the Austrians. Venice was besieged and starving. Piedmont had attempted a second attack on Austria in March but had once again been soundly beaten.

Now, the conservative powers all turned towards Rome. The pope, safe in Neapolitan territory, was clamouring to be restored to his throne, and all the Catholic monarchs were eager to oblige.

But if the reactionaries had men and guns and money on their side, Mazzini at least had faith and the fiery conviction of the rightness of his cause. More than that, he had command of the stage. In the Eternal City, on ground hallowed by the footsteps of Brutus, the Gracchi and Cicero, Mazzini would make his stand before the world.

*

With the news of the second Piedmontese defeat, in 1849, the Roman assembly began preparing for war. In times of crisis, the ancient republic had appointed a dictator, and the assembly now tried to do the same, offering the role to the brave but not at all warlike Giuseppe Mazzini.

Mazzini turned them down. He was willing, at most, to form part of a triumvirate (though he was not above specifying who the other two members of the body ought to be). It was vital, he understood, to avoid the appearance of a populist tyranny. 'Here in Rome,' he told the assembly, 'we may not be moral mediocrities.' If Rome was to awaken Europe, there must be no stain on the honour of the republic.

Revolutionary regimes across Europe had often tended to violence. Internal disorder and ideological competition, combined with genuine external threats, frequently produced purges and terrors, just as in the days of Marat and Robespierre. But Mazzini, with his saintly charisma, his glowing purity of vision, cast an extraordinary spell over the city. The British poet Arthur Hugh Clough recorded his impression of those days, in perfect Virgilian hexameter:

It is most curious to see what a power a few calm words (in
Merely a brief proclamation) appear to possess on the people.
Order is perfect, and peace; the city is utterly tranquil;
[...]
Oh, could they but be allowed this chance of redemption! – but clearly
That is not likely to be. Meantime, notwithstanding all journals,
Honour for once to the tongue and the pen of the eloquent writer!
Honour to speech! and all honour to thee, thou noble Mazzini!

Mazzini was waging a war of ideas. 'Great revolutions,' he wrote, 'are the work rather of principles than of bayonets.' Victory required that those principles be widely known. Even in Rome's moment of crisis, Mazzini made a point of staying in touch with sympathetic foreign writers in the city. The American journalist Margaret Fuller was paid a visit just two days after Mazzini's arrival in the city: 'He looks more divine than ever,' she recorded. 'If anyone can save Italy from her foes, inward and outward, it will be he.'

The absence of the pope was a nagging problem. Mazzini was a deist rather than a Christian but he made sure to attend Easter Sunday Mass. There would be no Jacobin Temples of Reason. At the same time, he tried to shift the focus of Rome's ceremonial life away from the now headless church. In April, as the republic's enemies closed in, he organized a patriotic festival by the ancient Roman Forum, the ruins of the Colosseum lit up in revolutionary green, white and red.

Mazzini had dressed the set. It was time for the appearance of his leading actor.

Years before, way back in the early 1830s, Mazzini's writings had won the admiration and loyalty of a young sailor named Giuseppe Garibaldi. After the failed rebellions of 1833–4, Garibaldi, like many other members of the *Giovine Italia*, was forced to flee Italy.

But instead of retreating to France, or to England as Mazzini did, Garibaldi took ship for South America, where wars of independence were being fought in Brazil and Uruguay.

Through the late 1830s and early 1840s, as the fortunes of the *Giovine Italia* ebbed, word started to come to Italy of a rebel general leading an 'Italian Legion' in the defence of Montevideo. These Italian exiles had performed great deeds among the gauchos on the Uruguay River, it was said – had proved Italian valour against the perfidious Argentines.

The legend of the warrior Garibaldi was eagerly fed by Mazzini himself. Successful radicals, having forbidden the worship of saints and princes, liked to raise up revolutionary heroes in their stead. During the French Revolution, these heroes had been in the classical mould: handsome, clean-shaven, sober and restrained, full of stoical Roman virtue. In Garibaldi, however, Mazzini recognized a hero of a different breed. Garibaldi, the long-haired guerilla, was a perfect Romantic figure, passionate and buccaneering, driven by honour and love. Women at home in Italy read of his first meeting with his warrior wife Anita, a fiery horsewoman from southern Brazil: how he had first spied her from his ship through a telescope; how he rowed to shore to find her, hunted through the town for her; how their eyes finally met; how they gazed at each other as if remembering a forgotten love; how Garibaldi addressed her, his first words, '*tu devi esser mia*' – 'You must be mine!'

The uprisings of 1848 drew Garibaldi home to Italy. He arrived on a ship called *Speranza* – 'Hope' – and great hopes indeed were attached to his coming. Fed by Mazzini's propaganda, his legend had grown out of all proportion. What could one man, with just sixty-three companions and a single ship, do against the might of Austria?

When Garibaldi came ashore in Italy, he was welcomed like a hero stepping out of a fairy tale, as if King Arthur and all his knights had come sailing back from Avalon. His legionaries were veteran fighters and had spent the whole voyage singing patriotic hymns and doing gymnastics – but though they might be the very flower of Italian manhood, they hardly fitted into the well-drilled army of Piedmont. When Garibaldi offered his sword to Carlo Alberto, the king turned him down.

Mazzini had been disappointed by Garibaldi's willingness to work with the crown. Garibaldi was a man of action, willing to fight for whoever promised a united Italy. Mazzini, the idealist, believed victory could come only if the battle itself were pure.

But Mazzini recognized, as Carlo Alberto did not, the value of the so-called Garibaldini. After the Piedmontese defeat in Lombardy, through the bleak winter of 1848, Mazzini had noted Garibaldi's refusal to give up the fight, the indefatigable energy with which he kept on marching and raiding and recruiting, always looking for the next opportunity to strike a blow. When Mazzini was made triumvir of Rome in March 1849 he did not, despite his reservations, scorn the services of Garibaldi and the Italian Legion.

* * *

On 27 April, as Rome's enemies closed in, the Garibaldini came marching down the Corso. They now numbered over a thousand, a motley band, from veterans of Uruguay to impetuous boys barely into their teens, swept up in the fever-dream of liberty. They wore any uniform or none. They rode in no sort of order, booted or bare legged, burned brown by the sun, black ostrich feathers nodding from their tall puritan hats. They carried rifles or muskets, or long-bladed lances. Their faces, streaked with sweat and dust under their beards, gave them the look of brigands, rather than a proper military force.

The officers were as colourful as their men. There was Ugo Bassi, the rebel Barnabite friar who served as the legion's chaplain; Goffredo Mameli, just twenty-one, a Genoese poet; Andrea Masina, of Bologna, who rode with a squadron of lancers he had raised himself, resplendent in blue coats and red fezzes. Most striking of all, to the Romans, was Andrea Aguyar, a freed slave who had followed Garibaldi from Montevideo. The 'ebony Hercules', as one witness called him, cut a formidable figure on the battlefield on his jet-black horse, his dark cloak flowing about him as he swung his spear with its bright-red pennant. Aguyar was also said to be proficient in the use of the lasso, which he used to great effect against enemy cavalrymen.

A few days later, the Garibaldini were reinforced by a regiment of Lombard volunteers under their young Milanese commander Luciano Manara. The Lombards wore the uniform of the Piedmontese *bersaglieri*, a mobile light infantry force whose elite reputation they would do much to cement, and they regarded the undisciplined legionaries as little better than a 'tribe of Indians'.

The patriarch of this hodgepodge tribe was Garibaldi himself, looking like a gaucho in his distinctive white poncho and loose-fitting red shirt. As well as the eccentric costume, descriptions from the time emphasize his stillness, or the remarkable quality of his eyes, which appeared at times almost to change colour, as if in response to some inner squall of passion. His hair and beard were long and fair, framing an open, freckled face. In battle, he looked like a roused lion, shaking his shaggy mane.

Many of those who met him found his appeal almost overwhelming. A young Italian artist remembered going to see him 'out of curiosity':

Oh! I shall never forget that day when I first saw him on his beautiful white horse in the market-place, with his noble aspect, his calm kind face, his high smooth forehead, his light hair and beard – everyone said the same. He reminded us of nothing so much as of our Saviour's head in the galleries. I could not resist him. I left my studio. I went after him; thousands did likewise. He had only to show himself. We all worshipped him; we could not help it.

*

Garibaldi needed all the followers he could get. For as the Italian Legion entered Rome from one side, an army of perhaps ten thousand Frenchmen was approaching from the other direction.

Louis-Napoleon, the soon-to-be Emperor Napoleon III, intended to win the race to restore the pope to the city of St Peter. The rural Catholics who had helped him to power would be pleased; let the democrats in Paris moan all they liked at the immorality of making war on a fellow republic.

General Oudinot, the leader of the expeditionary force, was expecting a swift, if not bloodless, victory. After all, as one haughty officer put it, 'Italians do not fight' – *les Italiens ne se battent pas.*

Rome had not yet distinguished itself in the battle for Italian freedom. The serious-minded radicals of Lombardy thought the city was corrupt and superstitious. 'The Italian people had almost lost their Religion of Rome', Mazzini wrote; 'they too' – like British Romantics, he means – 'had begun to look upon her as a sepulchre, and such she seemed.'

But Mazzini felt 'the immortality stirring beneath those ruins' – felt 'the pulsations of the immense eternal life of Rome through the artificial crust with which priests and courtiers had covered the great sleeper as with a shroud. I had faith in her.' The Romans would fight and, if victory proved impossible, they would offer up to Italy their *morituri te salutant* from the Eternal City's walls.

Garibaldi and his legionaries were posted to the centre of the Roman defence, guarding the Porta San Pancrazio and the Janiculum. The walls of this section were in comparatively good repair, built by Bernini's patron, Pope Urban VIII, to defend the old weakness that had been exploited a century before by the landsknechts and the Constable de Bourbon. But though the walls were strong, they would not stand long against modern siege artillery. Not far beyond the gates was a complex of grand country villas on the high ground, from which a properly sited battery could easily smash a path through to the Janiculum. These villas were the key to Rome's defence, for an enemy who controlled the Janiculum could, if he chose, bombard Rome to dust.

It was from these villas, therefore, on 30 April 1849, that Garibaldi spied the French army approaching. In their confidence, the French had hardly even bothered to reconnoitre. They were advancing against a gate that, although it looked vulnerable on their maps, had in fact been walled up years before.

Thwarted by the unexpected blockage, the French battalions spread out left and right, looking for a place to force their way in. But the fire from the defenders on the walls, a mixture of former papal regulars and civil guards, was consistent and determined. Half the artists in Rome had gone to the defences. The students had all volunteered. Patrician ladies had taken to the streets, digging ditches and erecting barricades, or setting up field hospitals.

At every point, the advancing French battalions found themselves rebuffed. The walls were being held with fine republican enthusiasm. And then, from the strategic villas, high on the French right flank, came the attack of the Garibaldini.

Arthur Hugh Clough had gone that morning to the Caffè Nuovo off the Corso:

Caffe-latte! I call to the waiter, – and Non c'e latte,
This is the answer he makes me, and this is the sign of a battle.

He wanders through the empty streets, under windows hung with Italian tricolors. Rome's tourists have gathered on the Pincian hill: Englishmen, Germans, some Dutch, and even some French – these last protected by a particular decree of Mazzini – trying to make out the progress of the battle on the Janiculum.

So we stand and stare, and see, to the left of St Peter's,
Smoke, from the cannon, white, – but that is at intervals only, –
Black, from a burning house, we suppose, by the Cavalleggieri;
And we believe we discern some lines of men descending
Down through the vineyard-slopes, and catch a bayonet gleaming.
Every ten minutes, however, – in this there is no misconception, –
Comes a great white puff from behind Michel Angelo's dome, and
After a space the report of a real big gun, – not the Frenchman's! –
That must be doing some work. And so we watch and conjecture.

The approach of dinner time brought Clough – or, more accurately, his poetic avatar Claude – back down to street level. Everyone expected the French to break into the city. Women and children had gathered in a particular house for safety, and Clough was full of morbid imaginings: would it be necessary to fight for the women's safety? Did honour demand that he die for them?

But then the first stragglers started coming back from the Janiculum, and there was 'talk, though you don't believe it, of guns and prisoners taken'. By hard fighting through the gardens and the vineyards, at point of bayonet and sabre's edge, Garibaldi and his legionaries had pushed the French off the hill, driving them back up the road in disarray. Contrary to every expectation – except, perhaps, Garibaldi's own – the Roman republic had won a famous victory.

* * *

Garibaldi wanted to chase the French army back into the sea, but Mazzini wouldn't let him. Rome was to be the sacred battleground. Anyway, despite Garibaldi's confidence, it was far from certain that the Italians could defeat the French in open battle.

Also, Mazzini understood that in the long run the Roman republic had little hope of success unless the French republic stood at its side. He still had allies in Paris, fellow democrats, who might change the mind of Louis-Napoleon or, failing that, effect his overthrow. Accordingly, the French prisoners taken by Garibaldi on 30 April were released unconditionally.* The French wounded were carefully nursed back to health.

And Mazzini's hopes were not wholly unjustified. Finding Rome so stoutly defended, the French commander, General Oudinot, called off his assault and settled to await further instructions.

Garibaldi and his men were sent southwards. A Neapolitan army, advancing against Rome, had penetrated as far as the Alban hills, and the Italian Legion was sent to push them back again, along with the other regiments of volunteers: the students, a regiment of *emigranti*, even a few hundred customs officers, the *finanzieri*. Best of all, he had the formidable Lombard *bersaglieri*, with whose commanding officer, Luciano Manara, Garibaldi soon became close friends.

This was the sort of fighting Garibaldi enjoyed. Out in the open countryside, he could return to the guerilla style of war he had practised in South America. Gustav von Hoffstetter, a Swiss major of the *bersaglieri*, was struck by the disorderly way in which the Garibaldini made their camp, throwing themselves down to sleep wherever they stopped, heads resting on their American-style saddles, while the carcass of some rustled sheep or ox roasted slowly over the cookfires. Garibaldi himself lay at his ease under a makeshift parasol, reclining on an old tigerskin.

In battle, however, Garibaldi was 'a devil, a panther', and the mad onrush of his 'troop of brigands' was more than the Neapolitans could resist. Before long, the army of 'King Bomba' was sent scurrying back towards the the Neapolitan border.

Meanwhile, back in Rome, an envoy had arrived from Louis-Napoleon to discuss terms. Ferdinand de Lesseps was much impressed with Mazzini, who was living a life of monastic simplicity in the smallest available apartment in the Quirinal Palace. All day the triumvir was available to his people. In the evenings, he dined

---

* A British captain in Rome witnessed French prisoners being cheered in the streets as fellow republicans. The Romans gave them food and, as an afterthought, took some of them round St Peter's and to see the other sights, before sending on their way.

modestly at a two-franc restaurant before retiring to his room, when circumstances allowed, to sing and play the guitar.

At the end of May, the Garibaldini were recalled to Rome. France agreed to a truce. Indeed, de Lesseps promised, the French would defend the Roman republic against its enemies. Garibaldi and his legionaries looked forward to a few days' rest before being sent off against the Austrians who were advancing past Bologna.

But while Louis-Napoleon had sent de Lesseps to make peace, he had sent a quite different set of instructions to General Oudinot: 'Our military honour is at stake, I will not suffer it to be compromised. You may rely on being reinforced.'

Those reinforcements had now arrived. Oudinot's original army of 10,000 or so had grown to 20,000, with more on the way, plus six artillery batteries with heavy siege guns. On 1 June, one day after the agreement between Mazzini and de Lesseps was signed, Oudinot announced that the treaty was void. He would allow three days for any French citizens to leave Rome. On 4 June, a new assault would begin.

The fourth of June, Oudinot had specified. It was a surprise, therefore, when, on the night of 2 June the defenders of the strategically vital villa complex outside the Porta San Pancrazio were woken by the sound of French engineers blowing a breach in their perimeter wall. They were four hundred men against thousands, taken unaware. There was nothing for it but to retreat towards the walls of Rome.

Around three in the morning, news of Oudinot's treachery reached Garibaldi.* He and Masina, the commander of the red-hatted Bolognese lancers, rode at top speed for the Piazza San Pietro, where the rest of the Italian Legion was mustering. By now, the bells of the city were ringing their alarms into the night. Orderlies were rushing to and fro through the dark streets, summoning sleeping officers to

---

* Oudinot had promised to defer '*l'attaque de la place*' until 4 June. His casuistical justification for the surprise attack on the second was that '*la place*' referred only to the area within Rome's walls.

their posts. Still, it was half past five by the time the Garibaldini had climbed the steep and narrow stairway that ran from the slums of Trastevere to the top of the Janiculum.

There, in the first faint light of the morning, Garibaldi saw the battlefield laid out before him. Running north and south across his front was the Janiculum wall, its massive bastions projecting westwards towards the open country on the other side. Directly ahead was the Porta San Pancrazio. Four hundred metres beyond that, a hill rose opposite the gate, and there, looming in the dark, was the bulk of the Villa Corsini, where the French cannons had already established themselves. If Garibaldi could not recapture this villa, the city would surely fall.

He poured his legionaries into the attack. Off they went, the young romantics, full of courage, glowing with the idea of Italy. But the path ahead was a terrible one. There was only one way to the Villa Corsini – a straight road, right down the throat of the French guns. The villa's grounds were defended by a high boundary wall with a single gate. Through this narrow opening, all attacking forces had to pass.

On the far side of this gateway the ground sloped gently upward, a landscape built for pleasure but now a perfect killing field. Attackers would be funnelled between box hedges as they charged up towards the house. French sharpshooters were positioned behind marble statues and under the cover of a row of ornamental orange trees.

Beyond the orange trees was the villa. It was four storeys high, but the lower two were blank and windowless. A pair of grand external staircases zigzagged up to a balcony and only from there was it possible to get into the house itself.

The Romans watched from the Janiculum as company after company of Garibaldini hurled themselves down the road, through that deadly garden and up the stairs to the balcony, where they could just make out the glint of waiting guns. There were great cheers each time a group of legionaries set off through the Porta San Pancrazio. Morale was high. A band was playing the *Marseillaise*, a reproachful taunt against the French, who should have been their fellow revolutionaries.

But the mood grew bleaker and bleaker as the spectators saw how few of Garibaldi's men came back again. Garibaldi's chief of staff, Daverio, was killed in an early assault. The lancer, Masina, took a bullet to the arm, though he refused to go to the field hospital until Garibaldi expressly ordered him to. Another captain, the Genoese patriot Nino Bixio, was carried off the hill with what looked like a mortal wound. On the way down he met the Lombard *bersaglieri* coming up, and just about managed to gasp out a cheery greeting.

Arriving at the Porta San Pancrazio, the *bersaglieri* found the Italian Legion in desperate condition. Garibaldi was labouring to hold them together, riding back and forth where the fire was thickest, himself miraculously unharmed though his white poncho was perforated with bullet holes.

Undaunted, the *bersaglieri* rushed in force towards the Villa Corsini, the black plumes on their hats nodding in the sun. They were the best soldiers in Rome, eager to prove themselves, disciplined and not afraid to die. But climbing up through the villa gardens was like advancing through a hailstorm. Thirty paces from the steps the assault slowed, then faltered. They could not go forward, but they refused to go back. Instead, they knelt down where they were and opened fire on the French soldiers above.

It was a suicidal contest. Exposed on the slope, they were easy targets. Still, it was ten minutes before their colonel, Manara, sounded the retreat. As the surviving *bersaglieri* ran back towards the narrow garden gate, the slaughter intensified. To the Swiss major, Hoffstetter, it seemed as though his men were stumbling on some hidden root or uneven ground. He could not imagine, otherwise, why so many were falling. But those who fell did not get up again, and any man who stopped to reach out a helping hand would fall himself. Some who had reached cover turned back to save their friends, but only ended up lying beside them.

Garibaldi kept sending men up the lane. Emilio Dandolo, nineteen years old, was still at the Porta San Pancrazio when he heard that his brother Enrico was among the dead. 'A sort of careless fatalism had made us feel as if it were impossible for one of two beings so closely attached to be left without the other.' Yet it was so. For the first time, Dandolo felt 'the real nature of cold-blooded war' but, not wanting to upset his men by a display of emotion, all he could do was pace up and down and chew on his pistol barrel.

Then came the call: an officer and twenty men, needed for 'a difficult undertaking'. With twenty of his bravest men, Dandolo set off towards the Villa Corsini. 'Spare your ammunition', Garibaldi had instructed. 'To the bayonet at once.' But by the time Dandolo arrived at the entrance to the villa only twelve of his twenty men remained. What could he do? His men unloaded their guns in the direction of the French, then retreated at a run. Only six made it back alive.

Now at last Garibaldi gave the order to do what should have been done earlier: the Roman battery on the bastion by the Porta San Pancrazio turned its guns against the Villa Corsini. By the late afternoon, the whole façade of the building had been smashed to rubble. The interior of the villa was exposed as if it were an open doll's house. French soldiers could be seen clinging on by their fingers as sections of floor gave way.

As the fire from the defenders slackened, Garibaldi once again gave the order to attack. It was the cavalryman, Masina, who led the charge this time, his wounded arm bound up in a sling. He and his lancers crossed the ground at a gallop, up through the gardens to clatter up the ruined steps and into the villa itself. With a great roar, the Roman infantry followed behind, the survivors of the Legion and the *bersaglieri*; the students' battalion, the artists, the civic guard. At last, they had occupied the Villa Corsini in real force.

And there, they discovered what the bravest of their comrades had discovered before them: that although the Villa Corsini was a fortress from one direction, it was wide open from the other. From the loggia on the villa's western side they saw the gardens open out into a broad field, shaded by umbrella pines. And under the pines, regiment after regiment of fresh Frenchmen.

* * *

There was no defending the Villa Corsini. The Italians fought on for as long as they could. At one point, to make cover, they piled bodies up like sandbags, fighting from behind a wall of their own dead. Mazzini had reckoned strength in faith and courage, not boots and bayonets. But no amount of courage would hold the villa, and no amount of courage, in the end, would hold Rome.

All through June, Rome's defenders were steadily pushed back. Garibaldi's losses were terrible. Masina died during the final retreat from the Villa Corsini. His body, in its gaudy red fez, lay rotting for a month out in no-man's-land. Garibaldi's loyal friend Aguyar, the 'ebony Hercules', was blown up by a shell near the church of Santa Maria in Trastevere. Mameli, the boy poet, was shot in the knee. He was 'radiant', Garibaldi recalled, in a letter to the boy's mother, 'his face shining because he had shed his blood for his country'. He died a month later, of creeping gangrene. Last of the officers to die was Luciano Manara, the colonel of the Lombard *bersaglieri*, shot dead in the final French assault.

For nearly a month, the Romans had endured the French bombardment from the ruins of the Villa Corsini, as the assault trenches crept ever closer to the walls. At midday on 30 June, as Manara lay dying, Garibaldi was summoned to the Capitoline hill, where Mazzini and the Roman assembly were debating whether or not to continue the defence. Covered in dust and blood and sweat, he told them that the battle was lost. He and any who wished to follow him would leave the city, to carry on the fight as best they could. *'Dovunque saremo, colà sarà Roma'* – 'Wherever we are, there will be Rome.'

In the Piazza San Pietro Garibaldi gathered the survivors: 'I offer neither pay, nor quarters, nor provisions', he told them; 'I offer hunger, thirst, forced marches, battles and death. Let him who loves his country in his heart and not with his lips only, follow me.'*

---

* Winston Churchill adapted Garibaldi's words for the House of Commons in May 1940: 'I have nothing to offer but blood, toil, tears and sweat. We have before us an ordeal of the most grievous kind. We have before us many, many long months of struggle and of suffering.'

As the French entered Rome from the west, Garibaldi and his followers rode out in the other direction, past the Lateran Basilica and into a countryside swarming with hostile troops. The American journalist Margaret Fuller watched them go:

> I longed for Walter Scott to be on earth again, and see them; all are light, athletic, resolute figures, many of the forms of the finest manly beauty of the South, all sparkling with its genius and ennobled by the resolute spirit, ready to dare, to do, to die… Never have I seen a sight so beautiful, so romantic and so sad.

They were a melancholy crew indeed, and their insurgency was not destined to last long. Still, they made a memorable scene, riding off into the pages of legend. Garibaldi had managed, at last, to procure a uniform for the Italian legion: they all wore dyed red shirts.

Rome fell. Mazzini fled into exile. Garibaldi's men gradually trickled away. Many of his surviving companions, including the faithful friar, Ugo Bassi, were caught by the Austrians and sent to the firing squad.

Garibaldi's beloved Anita, pregnant with his child, had come to join him in Rome, and had insisted on joining his retreat. During the journey she sickened, and in the marshes near Venice, she died. Only now, after so much struggle and suffering, did Garibaldi finally break down. His friends could hardly tear him away from her body, but there was nothing for it. They were being hunted by Austrian soldiers, and their pursuers were never far behind. They left Anita in a shallow grave and carried on.

By great good luck, and by the courage of the patriots who hid him and helped him on his way, Garibaldi managed to escape capture. On 2 September 1849, after two months on the run, he boarded a boat for the island of Elba and the relative safety of Piedmontese territory. He was heartbroken and alone. The great uprisings of 1848 had ended in utter defeat and failure. The old regimes, supported by Austria, were stronger than ever before.

On the Janiculum, Garibaldi and Mazzini had poured out the blood of some three or four thousand young men, a libation to the spirit of Italy. And to what effect? Was it by such futile slaughters that Italy was to be redeemed?

As it turned out, the defeat of 1849 was prelude to the final victory. Mazzini had set the Roman republic up as a demonstration of true Italian virtue, the national spirit in which he had always believed, just and democratic, mild in government and fierce in war. And the demonstration had the desired effect. In the USA and Britain, public opinion turned firmly in Italy's favour.*

In France, too, there was a regretful sense of not having been on the side of justice. In 1859, following some expert diplomacy by the Piedmontese prime minister, Camillo Benso, count of Cavour, Napoleon III was persuaded to join forces with the kingdom of Piedmont to defeat the Austrians at the Battle of Solferino.† Lombardy was added to the territories of the Piedmontese crown, soon followed by the remaining states of northern and central Italy.

Meanwhile Garibaldi, coming out of exile with a thousand new red-shirted legionaries, landed in Sicily under the protective eye of a British warship. The Bourbon army outnumbered the Legion by more than a hundred to one, but they crumbled in the face of the red-shirts' enthusiasm. In Sicilian villages, Garibaldi was greeted as a living saint.

In October 1860 the victorious Legion encountered the Piedmontese army south of Rome. Garibaldi controlled the whole of southern Italy. Cavour, a moderate royalist, feared a resurgence of Mazzinian republicanism. But in the interests of Italian unity, Garibaldi was willing to compromise: he freely ceded his territory to King Vittorio Emanuele II, formerly king of Piedmont, now king of Italy.

---

* The British public had been broadly sympathetic to Mazzini from the start, though not unanimously so. Firmly in General Oudinot's camp were the *Times* and the paper that killed Keats, the *Quarterly Review*.
† The battle of Solferino was the last major battle in which the opposing armies were led in person by their respective monarchs. It was, however, a very modern slaughter. It was seeing the carnage of Solferino that prompted the Swiss businessman Henri Dunant to found the International Red Cross.

It was not a perfect victory. Mazzini's vision of an awakened Italy remained unfulfilled. To the south, Sicily was in a state of deep unrest, which soon broke out into a bloody civil war. To the north, the Austrians still held Venice, and most of the old Venetian territory around the Adriatic coast.

And in Rome, the papal despotism of Pio Nono still held out. The pope had become a figure of almost exaggerated conservatism. In his famous *Syllabus of Errors*, issued in 1864, Pius laid out eighty falsehoods condemned by the church. The last of the eighty errors was the idea that 'the Roman Pontiff can, and ought to, reconcile himself, and come to terms with, progress, liberalism and modern civilization.'

In 1866 Italy occupied Venice (though not the whole of Venice's old territory). In 1870, Garibaldi's old comrade Nino Bixio, who had survived the wound he took on 3 June 1849, led a division of the Italian army to capture papal Rome.

Italy's great resurgence, her *risorgimento*, was complete, or so everyone wanted to believe. On the Janiculum, the royal authorities set up busts of the Garibaldini, looking out over the landscape in which so many of them had fought and died, the martyrs of the Third Rome.*

But the tensions left unresolved by Garibaldi's compromise continued to rankle: the missing territory, the impoverished south, the incomplete democracy, the anomalous role of the entrenched and intransigent pope, sulking in the Vatican. The problems of the *risorgimento* have not been completely resolved even today.

---

* A notable omission from these marble ranks is Andrea Aguyar, the Roman republic's only black man.

21

THE GHETTO

Margherita Sarfatti and Benito Mussolini

———

1922–1944

A N OCTOBER MORNING. Romans are on their way to work. The river slides dull and yellow under the plane trees of Lungotevere de' Cenci, past the windows of the Great Synagogue of Rome.

Inside the synagogue sits Rosina Sorani, assistant to the president of Rome's Jewish community, doing her best to look calm. The synagogue has had an unexpected visitor this morning: he is a scholar, he says. An expert in paleography and Semitic philology. He has come to the Roman ghetto in search of books.

And his hopes have in every way been satisfied. The Great Synagogue holds two of the most important libraries in Rome. There are manuscripts from Portugal, Spain and Sicily, from Salonica and Constantinople. There are rare works of philosophy, medicine and mathematics, of the most rigorous Talmudic exegesis and the most esoteric mysticism; pages written in forgotten alphabets and vanished dialects, the treasures of Jewish civilization, gathered by a community that has survived in this city for two thousand years.

With delicate hands, the visitor turns the pages of codices and incunabula, of papyri and palimpsests. He savours the softness of ancient vellum, the rich leather bindings. He is meticulous and gentle, his eyes widening in scholarly appreciation. He knows exactly what all this is worth.

Satisfied, he returns to Rosina Sorani, drawing himself up in his uniform. The libraries are under sequestration, he tells her. He has noted everything. Soon, the books will be taken away for further study. If any go missing, she, Rosina Sorani, will be shot.

It is said quite casually. He turns to go, summoning his SS guards. She hears his footsteps echoing down the stairs and out into the cold light of 1943.

* * *

The Jews first came to Rome in the days of Julius Caesar. It was Pompey the Great who, in 63 BC, laid siege to Jerusalem and brought the first captives weeping from Israel to the banks of the Tiber.

In Rome, amid the babble of a thousand conquered nations, the Jews survived. They made their homes in the slums of the Transtiberim, earning livings, raising families, holding on to the memory of their distant God.

A century later, the grandchildren of the captives felt the first ripples of schism washing in from Jerusalem, rumours of a Messiah who included gentiles as well as Jews in his promise of salvation. And when Rome burned, under Nero, they saw the fury of the emperor directed against the followers of this Christ.

Nero was overthrown by Titus and Vespasian, two grim soldiers, father and son, who built their reputations by laying waste to rebellious Judea. From the parade floats of Titus's triumphal procession, Rome's Jews learned the fate of a homeland they had never seen: rich tableaux showed the ground awash with blood, temples burning, 'rivers flowing, not over a cultivated land, nor supplying drink to man and beast, but across a country still on every side in flames'.

Thousands of new Jewish captives came with Titus, women and children with the shock of war still fresh in their eyes, and the dust of Israel still on their feet. Rome had room for them all. In the monumental heart of the city, the Arch of Titus preserved the memory of Judea's humiliation, the looted menorah of the Temple painted like a brand of shame on its marble flank.

But on the outskirts, in crude shacks and dark tenements, Jewish life went on. The poet Juvenal saw Jews living out along the Via Appia, sleeping on straw, their possessions in baskets on their backs. Romans had noticed the particular strangeness of their cult. 'They reckon pork no less vile than human flesh,' the poet wrote. 'They worship only the clouds, and the spirit of the sky… and whatever Moses set down in his arcane tome.'

An air of oriental mystique allowed some Jews to make a living as fortune tellers, but a Jewish priestess, be she the faithful emissary of the very highest heavens, could never fill her palm so well as the fat priests of Isis and Osiris. Poor Jewish women 'will read your dreams any way you like for a handful of coppers'.

For three hundred years, Judaism in Rome was one cult among many – scorned, taxed, but tolerated. Then came Constantine and the vision at the Milvian Bridge; Christ reigned victorious over the empire. Isis, Mithras, Sol, almighty Jupiter, Mars, Vesta with her sacred flame, all would be banished from the new Christian Rome.

Christians and Jews had long regarded one another with suspicion, if not outright hostility. Jesus had, of course, been a Jew, but this was a fact neither side was keen to emphasize. The first Christians had been oppressed by the Jewish authorities in Jerusalem and, in turn, in their Gospels, painted the Jews in a distinctly unfriendly light. Much was made of the role of the Jews in Jesus' crucifixion: 'I am innocent of the blood of this just person,' says Pontius Pilate, the Roman, washing his hands. 'His blood be on us, and on our children,' the Jews reply.

It was easy to regard Titus's destruction of Jerusalem in AD 70 as the judgement of God. The Jews had, inexplicably, failed to recognize the Messiah whose coming was foretold in their own sacred scriptures. No wonder their kingdom had been put to fire and the sword.

The Jews, meanwhile, had reacted to the disasters that afflicted them by drawing into themselves, circumscribing more carefully than ever the proper boundaries of their one true religion. Let there be no more heretical 'messiahs' to practise sorcery upon the superstitious mob. God's chosen people would go forth bravely upon the face of the waters, and wait for the deluge to pass.

When Christianity became an imperial religion, the Jews had reason to fear the worst. But although the Christians were uncompromising in their dealings with pagans and heretics, they felt a certain ambivalence towards the Jews, whose religion, though it had been superseded, was nonetheless the forefather of their own. St Augustine condemned the 'impious brutality' of the Jews, who had put Christ to death, and who, in their 'perversity and malice', refused to believe in him. They were justly scattered, with the mark of Cain upon them.

But the mark of Cain, in Genesis, is both a curse and a protection. 'Whosoever slayeth Cain, vengeance shall be taken on him sevenfold', God decrees. Likewise, says St Augustine, 'not by bodily death shall the ungodly race of carnal Jews perish'. Rather, 'the continued preservation of the Jews will be proof to believing Christians of the subjection merited by those who, in the pride of their kingdom, put the Lord to death.'

The Jews were to be God's unwilling witnesses, messengers of the scriptural prophecies whose fulfillment they had seen but did not believe, doomed to wander in exile until, by their final conversion, they should usher in the second coming and the end of the world.

The popes of the Middle Ages mostly kept to the spirit of St Augustine's pronouncements. Jews were condemned but protected, kept separate and subordinate to Christians, but preserved from the worst excesses of Christian zealotry. There were to be no beatings, no forced conversions, no kidnappings of children, no burnings of synagogues – though the fact that these prohibitions had so often to be repeated reveals their helplessness against the prejudice of ordinary Europeans.

During the First Crusade, wandering armies of fanatics often turned their anger against the infidels they found nearest at hand. Perhaps a quarter of the Jews in northern France and Germany died in the resulting pogroms. A hundred years later, rumours began to spread of Jews using the blood of Christian children in their Passover ceremonies; a libel first deployed by Romans against Christians was now turned by Christians against the persecuted Jews, to evil effect.

The pattern was repeated during the Black Death of the fourteenth century. Jews were accused of poisoning the wells, of attracting the wrath of God by their mere presence. But the Jews were spared in one place at least: the papal city of Avignon. Pope Gregory the Great, centuries before, had offered the Jews 'the shield of our protection', and that tradition held. In Rome, the descendants of Titus's Jewish captives were kept comparatively safe, there in the very bosom of the Christian church.

There was a price for this protection. Gold, of course – the Jews had been specially taxed since the days of the Caesars – but, more importantly, they bought their continued survival by ritual humiliation. When a new pope went in procession through Rome, the city's Jews would meet him on the way to the Lateran, lined up in their ceremonial finery to acclaim him. There, as the city mob howled and jeered around them, the elders of the people would fall to their knees and offer up their holy scripture. Each pope, taking the richly decorated tome, would pronounce some variation on an ancient formula: 'We confirm the Law, but condemn the Jewish people and their interpretation.' Then he would drop the book into the mud.

The Jews served a vital role in Rome's ritual economy: to be publicly and ceremonially wrong. The Jews were living proof that the forces of error were defanged, subjected to the rightful dominion of God's holy church. They served as a sort of internalized Other, against which Christians might safely define themselves.

So life went on over the centuries, with each new pope bringing a new relaxation or strengthening of anti-Jewish laws, according to his temperament. In 1468 it was decreed that the Jews should join the Roman carnival for a special running race along the Corso, an innovation that proved a great hit. Participation was mandatory; the course, a gauntlet of Christian hostility and scorn. And new twists were always being added. Sometimes the 'carnal' Jews were fed a great rich meal before the race, that as they ran they might sick it up again. By the 1600s they were running dressed in nothing but loincloths, and their spot in the day's billing was between the races of the donkeys and buffaloes.

It became traditional for the Jews to decorate part of the processional route for the accession of a new pope. The Jews had special responsibility for the section around the Arch of Titus: they decked their conqueror's monument with flowers, and polished the marble on which were carved the captured menorah and the weeping Hebrew slaves.

But, in-between these ordeals, there was space for Rome's Jews to survive, and even to prosper. Many professions were forbidden them, but among the permitted few were moneylending and medicine, in which roles some Jews attained high importance at the courts of sympathetic popes. It was a Jewish physician, for example, who tended to the syphilitic bodies of Julius II and Alexander VI, Roderigo Borgia.

Under Roderigo Borgia Rome's Jewish population was swelled by the arrival of Sephardic refugees from Spain. Wherever there was religious conflict, the Jews were the first victims. With the final annexation of Muslim Granada by Ferdinand and Isabella, the Jews had to choose between exile and conversion at the point of a sword.

This pattern of threat and repression played out in full following the Protestant Reformation. Luther was no friend to Jews – his seven-point plan for solving 'the Jewish problem' included levelling all synagogues, burning Jewish books and setting the Jews themselves to hard labour – but the Roman church, powerless against the Lutherans, turned its fear and anger against easier victims. In 1555 Pope Paul IV, champion of the church's *zelanti*, issued his landmark bull *Cum nimis absurdum*: 'It is absurd and improper', he declared, 'that the Jews who have fallen into eternal servitude by their own guilt should presume… to make so bold as to live intermingled with Christians.'

Jews were forbidden to practise all trades and handicrafts. Jewish physicians could no longer treat Christians. No Jew could employ Christian servants. The tribute they had to pay was steeply increased. In public, all Jews had to wear a special yellow hat. Most burdensome of all, the Jews, for the first time in Rome's history, were confined to a ghetto, surrounded by a wall and gates that were locked, at night, with iron chains.

*

For the next three centuries Rome's three thousand or so Jews lived in a space that should have housed perhaps a quarter of that number – a narrow strip of land running along the bank of the Tiber between the Vicolo Cenci and the old fishmarket, where the church of Sant'Angelo in Pescheria rose above the ancient Porticus of Octavia and the Fabrician Bridge. Overcrowding led to disease: the alleys of the ghetto were breeding grounds for cholera and plague. The overstuffed apartment blocks, mongrel constructions forever growing up and out, closed overhead like a jungle canopy. Against the outer walls of the buildings lapped the yellow waves of the Tiber, choppy and foul, always threatening to rise up and overwhelm the low-lying streets. The Jews would cling together during these inundations, huddling for shelter in stairwells and attics while the flood of filth oozed through the rooms below.

It was possible to escape the ghetto. All it took was to renounce one's ancient faith, and there were some who did. Europe had not yet fully taken to heart the racist idea of Jewish 'blood'. Jewish bodies stank, a Jesuit wrote in 1662, but upon baptism their godless stench was miraculously washed away. One of medieval Rome's great families, the Pierleoni, came from converted Jewish stock, and converts were zealous in their efforts to pass the message on. One convert had a verse from Isaiah painted on a church opposite the ghetto: 'I have spread out my hands all the day unto a rebellious people, that walk in a way that is not good.' Successive popes added to the conversionist pressure, forcing the Jews to listen to Christian sermons on set days each year.

Nevertheless, the Jews continued to maintain their traditions, and eke out their livelihoods. Forbidden from all trades, they made their livings off rags and old iron, *stracci ferracci*. The Jewish peddler was a familiar figure in the streets, yellow-hatted, calling 'Hep! Hep! Hep!'

The historian Ferdinand Gregorovius was struck by the Jews when he stayed in Rome during the 1850s, their poverty and pride. Entering the ghetto, he found 'Israel before its booths, buried in restless toil and distress'. The Jews sat in their doorways, framed against the darkness of dismal rooms, surrounded by rags and scraps. 'Pieces of junk of every kind and colour are heaped high before the doors'; a history of Rome in scraps and tatters.

> For they are as much researchers in Roman antiquity as are those in Rome who grovel through rubble in order to bring to the light of day the stump of a column, a fragment of a relief… or similar plunder. The Hebrew Winckelmann in the ghetto exposes his rags for sale with a certain pride like that of the dealer in marble fragments. The latter swaggers with a piece of *giallo antico*, and the Jew can rival him with an excellent scrap of yellow satin; porphyry? – here is an excellently patterned scrap of crimson damask; *verde antico*? – here is a beautiful green velvet patch of exquisite antiquity.

Their poverty was extreme, but Gregorovius did not wish to leave his reader with that overriding impression. 'I prefer to say that the Jews of Rome are rich in humanity to one another, that the prosperous cheerfully help the poor, that the self-sacrificing solidarity of the family… can nowhere show itself so strong and beneficent as here.'

Jewish life in Rome seemed timeless, but even the high walls of the ghetto could not muffle the shocks that were shaking the world outside. The Enlightenment had rattled the foundations of Catholic authority: to modern rationalists, nothing seemed so backward as the church's long repression of the Jews.

When Napoleon's victorious armies brought the values of the French Revolution to Rome in 1798, the gates of the ghetto were thrown open. When Napoleon fell in 1814, Metternich's restoration slammed them shut again. Pius IX, flirting with liberalism in the 1840s, relaxed Rome's anti-Jewish laws. But after the rebellion of 1848, he made his city an outpost of reactionary thinking. In 1860, Garibaldi and Cavour united Italy. Only Rome held out. By 1870, when Piedmontese *bersaglieri* finally broke their way in through the Porta Pia, Rome's was the only ghetto being enforced in the whole of Europe.

The age of emancipation was at hand. In Italy, as across Europe, the walls of the ghettos were torn down. The Jews were free. No longer were they defined by their religion. Under a new identity they could participate in public life as fully as anyone: Rome's Jews were now Italians.

Rome is often understood as a palimpsest, a vast text on which new meanings are constantly overwritten. Now once again the architects were set to work like busy scribes, erasing here, adding there, changing lines, imparting new contexts and significances. The Rome of the Caesars had passed, and now the Rome of the popes was beginning to fade. A new Italian Rome was being constructed: a young nation's proud capital.

Rewriting the city was not easy to do, as many of Rome's previous masters had discovered. No city in Europe was so rich in the symbols of vanished power. Still, the agents of the new Italian monarchy did their best. In 1885, work began on a vast monument to dominate the city from the Capitoline hill, towering over the ancient Forum on one side and the churches of the medieval centre on the other. Pompous, brutal, grandiloquent, a vulgar behemoth of imported marble, horribly destructive of the historic district over which it was built, the Altar of the Fatherland, dedicated to King Vittorio Emanuele II of Italy, is, in a way, perfectly in keeping with the longstanding spirit of Roman architecture.

At the same time, a less prominent but no less profound transformation was taking place in the old Jewish ghetto. The Tiberside slum in which the Jews had been confined had become an embarrassment to modern and liberal Rome. City planners spoke of a 'risanamento'. The pestilential alleyways and ramshackle houses were levelled to make way for a fresh new urban district, built on the best principles of order and civic hygiene.

To crown this new district, the Jewish community embarked upon the construction of a Great Synagogue, in the latest style. The old synagogues of the ghetto had been modest affairs, designed to escape notice. The new synagogue rose proudly above the Tiber bank. Its square cupola declared itself different, but equal in standing, to the domes of the city churches all around.

Addressing an audience of government ministers at the

inauguration of the new synagogue in 1904, the president of Rome's Jewish community declared the victory of 'liberty, equality and love'.

> Here today, as free citizens, we have been free to build this Temple... between the monument to Vittorio Emanuele II and the monument to Garibaldi, the two great makers of our Italy – this Temple stands today, majestically free and surrounded by the free and pure sun.

* * *

With the end of the ghetto, Rome's Jews were able to disperse into wider Italian society. And this dispersal was not just physical but also ideological. These were, as the old curse has it, interesting times.

There was, quite naturally, a great deal of enthusiasm among the Jews for various forms of Italian nationalism. The invention of Italy had released them from centuries of papal despotism, and although the new nation was still extremely fragile, politically unstable and divided between an industrial north and an impoverished and embittered south, there were still many who believed either in the Piedmontese monarchy or in some Mazzinian vision of an Italian republic.

Italy's Jews were better integrated than any Jewish population in Europe. Nevertheless, there were some who doubted their ability ever to be truly recognized as Italians. Further north, European nationalism had turned increasingly inhospitable. A prejudice that had always been a matter of religion now expressed itself in the language of science. 'You cannot resign from your race,' warned an Austrian nationalist. The 'Jewish question' was one of 'race, morals and culture', wrote a German philosopher – a question that would have a 'world-historical answer'. In the face of such hostility, many Jews came to agree with the principles of Zionism, the idea that Jews should have a national homeland of their own.

And then there were many Jews who, like others of the educated middle class, went further, beyond all talk of nations and races. The only human divisions that mattered were economic ones: aristocracy, proletariat and bourgeoisie. The nationalist revolutions of the nineteenth century had replaced feudalism with bourgeois capitalism. But surely the bourgeois nationalists would now be superseded in their turn by the triumph of the proletariat and the new dawn of socialism.

The leaders of the Italian socialist party gathered in Milan, and Jews were prominent among them. Claudio Treves, editor of the socialist newspaper *Avanti!*, was a Jew. The founder of the party, Filippo Turati, was the lover and partner of an exiled Russian anarchist named Anna Kuliscioff, née Rosenstein. Her salon, at the opening of the twentieth century, was the most important centre of socialist thought in Italy.

And then, sometime around 1902, Kuliscioff acquired a rival. In Venice, where she grew up, they called her the Red Virgin: a Jewish heiress, beautiful, cultivated and above all, ambitious. Her name was Margherita Sarfatti.

Kuliscioff was the acknowledged doyenne of Italian socialism. Her partnership with Turati gave her unparalleled authority in party circles; he served as a willing male mouthpiece, a man who could win for her ideas the recognition they deserved. Sarfatti, presiding over a rival and lesser salon, was restless in the older woman's shadow. Her husband Cesare, a Zionist lawyer, was loyal, rich and amiable, but not the man to carry her to greatness.

It was with some interest, therefore, that Sarfatti read her husband's letter from the Socialist National Congress of 1912. A young journalist from Forlì had dazzled the socialist delegates with his fiery eloquence, displaying a passionate commitment to the revolutionary socialist cause, in opposition to lukewarm reformists like Kuliscioff and Turati. 'Be sure to note his name, because this young man is the man of the future.'

Certainly, this Benito Mussolini was a rough type. He came from humble stock, a family of rural socialists from the Romagna. At school, he was bright but volatile. He was expelled from one institution for stabbing a fellow pupil in the hand. As a youth, he had tramped the roads of Switzerland, working as a labourer, attending socialist meetings in the evenings. He had taken many lovers, dossing down in their rented rooms, learning what he could before moving on.

Anna Kuliscioff thought Mussolini was a cheap poetaster who had read too much Nietzsche. But Sarfatti didn't altogether mind if the young man got up her rival's nose. His table manners, she recalled later, were terrifying. She and Cesare were astonished by 'the incredibly creative gyrations he engaged in when using a knife and fork'.

His performance at the National Convention had won him the editorship of *Avanti!*, the official party newspaper, based in Milan. There he soon became interested in Sarfatti, who was the paper's art critic – the first woman ever to hold such a position in Italy. 'I noticed his big black eyes flecked with yellow,' she remembered. 'They darted so quickly from side to side in their sockets as he spoke. I watched his hard and cruel-looking mouth. I felt the animal energy that he exuded.' He liked to quote Nietzsche at her, provocatively: 'Are you going to women? Do not forget the whip!'

His manners were crude, and his origins low. But he had charisma, boldness and ambition. And he was, Sarfatti noted, 'a quick study'. She liked to take credit for his transformation. She taught him the right shape for his shirt collars, and the correct way to knot a tie. Once, she dared to recommend a particular brand of toothpaste. He understood her insinuation, and never forgot the insult. Years later, out of nowhere, he brought it up.

Still, he bought the toothpaste. Here was a man who could perhaps be moulded into someone remarkable, a new leader for a new age.

War was coming to Europe. Everyone could feel it, and some actively desired it. This was a chance for Italy to prove her mettle, many nationalists hoped, establishing herself among the great powers. Romantic ideas about war, in the spirit of Mazzini and Garibaldi, were as alive as ever in the hearts of Italy's young men. Success on the battlefield might allow Italy to reclaim those northern patches of territory still held by the Austrians, completing at last the unfinished work of the Risorgimento.

In Milan, meanwhile, the loudest pro-war voices belonged to the Futurists, a group of artists and writers well known to Margherita

Sarfatti.* War was the 'only hygiene of the world', wrote the Futurist leader Filippo Marinetti, the only force that could cleanse Italy of her dead traditions, her morbid obsession with the past, her 'putrid gangrene of professors, archaeologists, tour-guides and antiquarians, the countless museums that cover her like so many cemeteries'. Through the transformative power of violence, Marinetti foresaw that a new and superior breed of Italian could emerge: the Futurist *uomo moltiplicato*, a creature of flesh, oil, metal and blood, symbiotically fused with his own machine gun.

To the socialists, however, only one war was acceptable: the international revolutionary struggle of the proletariat. The wars of nation against nation were only of interest to the bourgeoisie, hoping to profit off blood that, inevitably, was shed by the working class.

Mussolini, the young socialist firebrand, had always been a proud defender of this orthodoxy. It was his determined opposition to the colonial invasion of Libya by Italy in 1911 that had made his reputation.† When Archduke Franz Ferdinand of Austria was assassinated in Sarajevo in 1914 by a Serb nationalist, Mussolini stuck to the party line: not one man, not one penny should be spent in the service of bourgeois imperialism, even as the other nations of Europe rushed to war.

When the fighting began, the socialist parties of Europe found it increasingly hard to maintain their commitment to internationalism. It was not easy to proclaim solidarity with the German proletariat when that same proletariat, heavily armed, was advancing across the French and Belgian border.

In France, Belgium, Germany and Austria, the socialist parties quickly discovered patriotism. Even in neutral Italy, many began to waver. At *Avanti!*, the editorials maintained an anti-interventionist stance, but behind the scenes there were signs that Mussolini's position

---

* The best of the Futurist artists, Umberto Boccioni, had been a lover of Sarfatti's.
† The fighting in Libya saw history's first recorded aerial bombing raid. Marinetti, who was a war correspondent on the scene, called the battles in Libya the most beautiful aesthetic spectacles of his life.

was evolving. He spoke of the barbarity of pan-Germanic imperial-ism, the fate of poor ravaged Belgium, the plight of those Italians who still languished under imperial Austrian rule. His sympathies, like those of many Italian leftists, were firmly on the Franco-British side, against the autocratic Central Powers.

In October 1914, Mussolini published a long article in *Avanti!* calling upon the socialist party to move from absolute neutrality to what he called 'engaged neutrality'. 'We have the privilege of living at the most tragic hour in world history,' he wrote. 'Do we – as men and as socialists – want to be inert spectators of this huge drama? Or do we want to be, in some way and some sense, the protagonists?'

Mussolini's friends and colleagues, including his former lover Angelica Balabanoff, were horrified. He was forced to resign as editor of *Avanti!*, and a month later he was expelled from the socialist party altogether. 'You hate me because you still love me,' he shouted at the assembled deputies.

Mussolini was expelled, but not undone. Many other socialists were quietly leaning towards intervention, including the Sarfattis. In December 1914 Margherita wrote in *Avanti!* that although she favoured neutrality, it was not a vice to love one's country. Mussolini had somehow acquired the funds to start his own newspaper, *Il Popolo d'Italia*, and his enemies (correctly, as it turned out) suspected the involvement of a foreign power. But the man appointed to investigate the matter was none other than Cesare Sarfatti, who had himself already made a substantial secret contribution to Mussolini's budget. The funding of *Il Popolo d'Italia* was declared entirely above board.

While the majority of Italians were still reluctant to fight, the inter-ventionist minority was gathering support. Mussolini was pushing for the formation of a new movement, the revolutionary action groups, or *fasci d'azione rivoluzionaria*, as they called themselves. Allied with eccentrics like the Futurists, as well as nationalists of various sorts, this new movement did its best to push Italy into the war.

Events were picking up speed. The grandsons of Giuseppe Garibaldi were already fighting on the front line at the head of a new

Italian Legion in France. At the end of 1914, young Bruno Garibaldi was killed charging a German position; some 300,000 people came to see his funeral procession in Rome.

In Milan, the Futurists tore an Austrian flag to shreds on stage at the opera. In Rome, Mussolini and Marinetti were arrested when a pro-war demonstration was broken up by truncheon-wielding police-men. At an event to celebrate the anniversary of Garibaldi's Sicilian expedition of 1860, the leader of the Italian volunteers in France, Peppino Garibaldi, was received with passionate enthusiasm. 'Blessed are those young men who hunger and thirst for glory, for they shall be filled,' promised the priapic celebrity and poet Gabriele d'Annunzio.

In May 1915, d'Annunzio appeared on the Capitoline hill in Rome, where he reached for even more delirious heights of patriotic rhetoric:

> No we are not and do not want to be just a museum, a hotel, a vacation resort, a Prussian-blue horizon where foreigners come for their honeymoons, a market where things are bought and sold. Our genius demands that we should put our stamp on the molten metal of the new world... This war, though it may seem destructive, will be the most fruitful means of creating beauty and virtue that has appeared on the earth.

*

The interventionists of 1915 had been anxious to get Italy into the war as soon as possible, fearing that the fighting would be over before they could join in. But the war lasted years. By the time the Central Powers surrendered in 1918, it had cost 650,000 Italian lives.

Had there been beauty, as d'Annunzio had foretold? Few thought so. The Italian trenches had a squalor that matched anything on the Western Front. Still, even as his Futurist friends died around him, Filippo Marinetti at least did thrill to the music of the artillery, delighting in the hyper-kinetic dance of metal and flesh.

What of the glory that d'Annunzio had promised Italy's young men? It was in short supply. For years the front hardly moved, pushing back and forth along the northern shore of the Adriatic, thousands of lives spent for each few acres of rocky ground. Then, in 1917, the

Austrians successfully broke the Italian line at Caporetto. Hundreds of thousands of demoralized Italian soldiers surrendered. The rest were driven in a humiliating retreat back towards Italy.

But at the Piave River, not far from Venice, the Italians held. The bravest Italian soldiers had been drafted into special units known as *arditi* – the daring ones – and the exploits of these black-uniformed assault troops became legendary. At night they would swim like crocodiles across the Piave, with daggers in their teeth, to murder Austrian sentries on the far bank.

At last, with Germany starving under British blockade and the United States pouring its inexhaustible resources into the war, the Italians managed to push the Austrians back. Here was a victory of sorts. But Italy had proved nothing. In the context of the wider war, the campaign had been little more than a sideshow.

Mussolini had served at the front as a corporal in the *bersaglieri*. He didn't see much action: in February 1917 he was injured when a mortar barrel exploded during a training exercise, and spent the rest of his war in a military hospital. Much was later made of the courage with which he faced the surgeon's knife, though it is not quite clear, even today, what injuries exactly the surgeon was treating. His supposed shrapnel wounds may really have been the gummas of tertiary syphilis.

A far greater commitment to the war was made by Margherita Sarfatti, who lost her son. Roberto Sarfatti, like young Jewish men all over Europe, rushed to die for his country. He was seventeen, brave and clumsy in his uniform, when he led a platoon of *arditi* in a suicidal bayonet charge against an Austrian position on the Col d'Echelle in 1918. A machine-gun bullet hit him in the forehead and made a pulp of his fragile courage. His mother, wearing black, collected a gold medal for bravery on her son's behalf and a lock of his bloodstained hair. Mussolini wrote a glowing obituary for *Il Popolo d'Italia*.

The blow brought Sarfatti closer to Mussolini. They had long ago become lovers – she was a liberated woman, and he had an insatiable sexual appetite – but the relationship now acquired a new emotional depth. He, perhaps, could give some meaning to her loss. 'We draw tight around you, Mussolini,' she wrote, soon after her son's death. 'Make sure, you who can, that so much sacrifice bears its precious fruit.'

Many thousands of Italian mothers were in the same position. Half a million Italian soldiers had died in the war; the same number again were so-called *mutilati*, the permanently injured. And for what? A little territory in the Alps and on the Adriatic coast. When it came to the post-war settlement, Italy remained very clearly the least of the victorious powers.

The warnings of the anti-war socialists had largely been justified: the war had been a great expenditure for very little gain. Now, with the state severely weakened, some socialists hoped to emulate the Bolshevik uprising that had toppled the tsar in 1917. Each new strike looked as if it might be the start of the proletarian revolution.

On the other hand, many veterans, especially the *arditi*, felt lost and leaderless. Their courage and their sacrifice had been betrayed, they felt, by politicians who had made a victory feel like a defeat. Italy should have been united in triumph. Instead, the treacherous socialists, the defeatists, the German-sympathizing internationalists, were tearing it apart.

Mussolini was alert to every opportunity. He still controlled his newspaper, *Il Popolo d'Italia*, now a leading voice for Italy's millions of demobilized soldiers. His interventionist movement, the *fasci d'azione*, provided a model for a new association, the ex-servicemens' leagues, or *fasci di combattimento*. Many unemployed veterans joined the new *fasci*. They adopted the manner and symbols of the *arditi*: the bold swagger, the anthem and war cry, the daggers and the black shirts, the swift resort to violence.

Often at Mussolini's side was Margherita Sarfatti, deep in heroic mourning. She had made her son an icon of *arditismo*, and lent her intellectual and cultural weight to the young 'fascist' movement. She had great hopes for Mussolini and his *fasci*. These men who had been purified and tested in war might redeem Italy, she believed, sweeping away the tired and corrupt parliamentary system to replace it with government by an elite. Fascists should be young, strong, united, undaunted as her son had been, proud inheritors of the classical tradition, forging a sublime order out of the chaotic violence of the Great War.

In 1919, Mussolini stood in the parliamentary elections alongside a list of candidates including the Futurist Marinetti, the conductor Arturo Toscanini, and an assortment of other fascists and fascist sympathizers. His programme was a confused mixture of revolutionary leftism and hard nationalism, and the attempt was not a success. The election was dominated by the socialists, who marched a coffin under the window of Mussolini's apartment to taunt him for his failure. Mussolini missed this grim parade – he was at the offices of *Il Popolo d'Italia* with Sarfatti at the time – but it caused great alarm to his neglected and long-suffering wife Rachele, who spent that morning crouched behind the locked door with her children, clutching a pair of stolen hand grenades.

The socialists had triumphed at the elections, but there were more ways to power than through the Chamber of Deputies. One of the first actions of the newly formed *fasci di combattimento* had been a raid on the offices of the socialist newspaper *Avanti!*, led by Marinetti with a handful of Futurists and *arditi*. After the electoral humiliation of 1919, the paramilitary Blackshirts, as everyone called them, embarked on a campaign of terror and violence. Fascist squads would raid provincial towns, torching the local socialist party offices, smashing the presses of socialist newspapers and administering rough justice to any 'traitors' they found within.

There was brutality on both sides – revolutionary socialists had a long tradition of violence of their own – but fascists combined military organization with a diabolical creativity. The trademark fascist assault involved forcing a victim to drink a large dose of laxative castor oil. Sarfatti justified this violence as the product of youthful high spirits:

> It was like a practical joke or an adventure story, played out with no sense of menace, with the lads' faces uncovered for all to see, in an open-hearted crusade against petty local tyrants who'd

be 'kidnapped and put in prison' briefly, as a prank, or made to drink a glass of castor oil.

In fact, these 'pranks' amounted to the most sadistic and humiliating torture. In high doses, the laxative produced cramps and convulsions, and was sometimes fatal. Victims were sometimes force-fed through a tube. Sometimes it was mixed with paraffin or iodine. Victims were dragged from their homes in the middle of the night, forced to drink the oil in front of their families, or in the streets, or left with their trousers tied so that they couldn't be removed. When the effects wore off at last, the victim would totter home in their foul soiled clothes.

The membership of the fascist squads was growing and changing. Many local fascist chiefs were little more than gangsters, using the black shirt as a convenient cover for racketeering and violence. Through 1920 and 1921 the fascist raids grew ever bolder. The police, many of whom were themselves war veterans, were slow to enforce the law against Blackshirt thugs. Many sections of the establishment saw the fascists as ugly but useful tools in the struggle that really mattered, against Lenin's Communist International.

By 1922 Sarfatti was urging her lover to send the Blackshirts against Rome. The movement was not popular in the capital; the fascist national conference, held at Rome in 1921, had seen rural fascists fighting running battles with locals in the streets of Trastevere.

But Sarfatti had invested a great deal of effort, money and feeling into the fascist project. Her commitment was total. 'I vowed myself to you,' she wrote, addressing Mussolini in 1922, 'my lord and husband, my chief, my lover. With the unwavering faith and loyalty of a firm follower of the cause, as an Italian woman.' And the moment was right. A huge socialist general strike in August 1922 had once again raised the spectre of revolution. The fascists had broken the strike with truncheons and castor oil, with the tacit approval of the authorities. But as the threat of socialism receded, the fascist paramilitaries would not be tolerated for long.

At the end of October, the Blackshirts prepared for action. There was no disguising what was afoot: the question was how the authorities would respond. Mussolini, the former radical socialist, had prepared the ground well, making conciliatory speeches about the national importance of church and king.

Mussolini was nervous, but as plans gathered pace, he and Sarfatti presented a front of perfect sangfroid. On the final crucial evenings, as his paramilitaries mustered to march on Rome, Mussolini appeared at the theatre in Milan, either with his wife or, according to other reports, with Sarfatti. On the night of 27 October, the fascist columns were halted on the march by heavy rain, and blocked by army units. The black-shirted rabble faced regular soldiers in uneasy silence, both sides desperate to avoid an all-out confrontation. In Sarfatti's telling of it, Mussolini now had a crisis of confidence, even considered fleeing to Switzerland. She gave him a firm look, and restored his courage. Together, they returned to her box, to watch the third act.

The next day, a telegram came from Rome. The government had asked the king to declare martial law. At the last moment the king, doubting the loyalty of his army, had refused to do so. Now Mussolini was being invited to Rome to form a new government. The rough peasant boy from the Romagna, having cast aside most of his political principles and almost all his friends, would become Italy's youngest ever prime minister.

On 31 October 1922 the Blackshirts marched in triumph through Rome's empty streets. Sarfatti imagined it as the dawn of a new order, inheriting the ancient legacy of Italy. She loved the antique names under which the Blackshirts were organized:

> The legions, the squadrons, the maniples and chief maniples, centurions and consuls; the division into *princeps* and *triarii*; the rapid ordered marches, three abreast. How different from the old slow rambling and disordered processions – like those of the socialists – which proved resistant to all attempts to give them an order and design.

This was empty talk. The Blackshirts were a rabble. If the army had offered even a hint of resistance, they would have evaporated.

Mussolini's power was insubstantial: crude bombast backed by the petty violence of a schoolyard bully. Swaggering in the Chamber of Deputies, chin thrust out in that bluffer's pose the world would soon come to know so well, he threatened the assembled politicians: he had 300,000 young men at his command; they would follow him to the death; 'I could have made this dingy and gloomy hall into a bivouac for my legions.' It was a giant lie, from the leader of a few thousand rebellious thugs. But Italy bought it.

* * *

Many years later, in bitter exile, Margherita Sarfatti remembered the exhilaration of those first days after the march on Rome, the moonlit nights she and Mussolini spent together. He would serenade her on the violin as she gazed into the velvet blue of the Roman sky, musing on how far they had come, and the glories that still lay ahead.

She remembered a spring morning in April 1923, riding on horseback along the Appian Way:

> The air was infused with that balmy golden light so special to Lazio. Around us stood tall cypresses, the ruined marble slabs and statues of ancient tombs, the arches of aqueducts dating back thousands of years, all shining in the sun. They spoke of eternity.

At her side, awkward in the saddle, rode her lover, her hero, 'the man whom every Italian looked to as the possible builder of a new Italian history'. They shared a dream, Sarfatti believed – a dream of an Italy that was truly united, an Italy of justice and peace, an Italy whose perfection might justify the price that had been paid in the war.

Sarfatti was working hard for the cause. She was running a new magazine, *Gerarchia*, intended to be the leading voice in the formation of fascist culture. She was fighting for Italy on the battlefield of ideas. Art had gone astray after the Renaissance. She deplored the baroque artifices of the 1600s, the *seicento*.

Sarfatti assembled her own cohort of Italian painters. She called her new movement the *novecento Italiano*, the definitive art of the

Italian 1900s. The artists of the *novecento* would be modern, she decreed, building a new edifice in the space that the anarchic Futurists had cleared. At the same time, they would be distinguished by a certain *clasicità*: not the dusty neoclassicism of foreign antiquarians but a lived inheritance – a native artistic genius, passed down in the blood from ancient Rome.

She was still living in Milan. Mussolini used to call her by telephone, sometimes three times a day. She liked it when he called in the middle of dinner parties. 'The Duce is calling', she would tell her guests. 'How lovely he is to me! He always wishes me well!' Every few weeks she would come to Rome on the train. He was living in the Grand Hotel, in those early days, near the baths of Diocletian. Sarfatti would creep in by way of the service stairs.

Mussolini's new duties kept him busy. He prided himself on being a hard worker and an obsessive for detail. As a leader he was aloof and arrogant, with few trusted subordinates. He liked to run the most important ministries himself, adding their portfolios to his own. When he was not working, there were women, Sarfatti knew, an endless number, lining up to be loved by their great Duce.

Still, Sarfatti and Mussolini enjoyed what time they could. The king gave Mussolini the use of a private beach at Castelporziano near the ancient port of Ostia. Here Mussolini would spend happy afternoons reading and practising his front crawl, a skill which he, a country boy, had acquired late, and of which he was very proud.

These were happy memories too: intimate lunches on the beach under the pines; joyrides in the motor boat, tearing about over the dark water where the Tiber meets the sea. Or just sunbathing – she reading, he strutting in his swimming costume, going on about his future, his plans, his big ideas. There was a darkness to him sometimes, she recognized. She remembered an autumn day when she caught him staring at his arm under his woollen vest: 'See this?' he said. 'I mean this fuzzy little hair on my left arm. Well it happens to be more dear to me than the rest of all humanity.'

'I suddenly felt very frightened,' Sarfatti remembered. 'No doubt he was just making a joke, nothing more.'

But Mussolini was happy at the seaside. Sarfatti was still able to interest him sexually. Later, she started coming with her daughter, Fiammetta, in her teens, bold and quite beautiful, though her mother had not seen fit to burden her with much education. Sarfatti could hardly fail to follow Mussolini's peering eyes – but then she had always called herself a liberated woman.

Mussolini used his position to secure for himself a limitless supply of sexual partners. A French journalist, Madeleine Coraboeuf, left an account of one of his rote seductions. She goes to interview him in his grand office, the Sala del Mappamondo in the Palazzo Venezia. It is a long walk to his desk. There is the Duce, hurriedly taking off his reading glasses, the dome of his bald head misted with cologne. His bulging eyes still have their old intensity. He keeps his voice soft and low. He paces about. He has only a few minutes, but before she goes, he puts his hands on her shoulders, fixes her with his gaze.

When she comes back the next day, he picks up where he left off, hands on shoulders. Then, in French, delivers his line: 'Have you thought of me a little?' He grows bolder. Leans in. 'I think you are beautiful. You please me!' Her mouth brushes against his.

The third appointment, in his private apartments:

> Catlike, as if about to grasp a prey, Benito has returned, and he comes towards me... He has embraced me again, growing very tender... Then a sort of frenzy sweeps him, he becomes brutal and he says: 'You have known Il Duce – now you shall know the man!'

He leaps at her. Before she has time to gasp, she is caught up in his arms.

This was more attention than most of his women got. At the Palazzo Venezia, he had a special secretarial office to vet his fan mail, selecting likely candidates to be led into the Sala del Mappamondo. New conquests, if the account of his valet is to be believed, were taken to one of the padded window seats. For second-timers, the carpet under his desk would do perfectly well. Sometimes Mussolini didn't even bother to take his boots off.

*

There was no controlling Mussolini's sexual appetite. The best Sarfatti could hope to do, as his longest-standing mistress, was maintain some measure of control over his domestic scene. It was she who found Mussolini his first Roman apartment on the Via Rasella, complete with a housekeeper she had chosen specially: a peasant woman named Cesira Carocci, stern and reliable, and without even a shred of sex appeal.

On the Via Rasella, in 1924, they rode out Mussolini's first real crisis. Some fascist thugs had been seen bundling a socialist deputy, Giacomo Matteotti, into a car in Rome. A few weeks later, Matteotti's remains were found buried outside the city. There was widespread outrage. With his enemies calling for his resignation, Mussolini took to his bed, crippled with stomach pains, vomiting blood as Sarfatti or the loyal Cesira mopped his brow, his breath stinking in the darkened room.

For months it looked as though Mussolini's government would fall. The Blackshirts were growing unruly. Mussolini was sick and desperate. Sarfatti reassured him by telephone, urged him to stay calm, to keep his temper: 'You'll see, everything will work out.'

And then, one day in January 1925, he appeared in the Chamber of Deputies, as bold as ever, striking that old defiant pose, chest puffed, chin thrust forward.

> I, and I alone, assume the political, moral and historical respon-
> sibility for everything that has happened... Italy, my friends,
> demands peace, tranquility and constructive calm. We will give
> it these things, if possible with love, but if necessary with force.

The socialist and communist deputies had removed themselves from parliament the previous June, in what they called a new Aventine Secession, imitating the plebs of the ancient Roman republic. The only effect was to leave to field clear for Mussolini. From 1925, he ruled Italy not as a prime minister but as a dictator in all but name.

Happy days returned at the Via Rasella. Someone gave Mussolini a lion cub, which he loved. He called it Italia, and let it live inside the apartment, much to Cesira's dismay. He was busier than ever. Sarfatti was working on a biography, *Dux*, an extraordinarily successful work of propaganda that became an international bestseller. The Duce was 'an archetype of the Italian,' she wrote. He was 'Roman from top to toe and to the marrow of his bones... the resurrection of the pure Italic type, which after many centuries flourishes once again.' Her attention to Mussolini's heritage is remarkable. Had she forgotten, for a moment, that this was a heritage she did not share?

Even as Sarfatti shaped Mussolini's legend, she had less and less access to the man himself. He once kept her waiting five hours to see him, sitting in an antechamber enduring the stares of the generals and ministers passing by.

She had suffered some bruising misfortunes. Her husband Cesare died in 1924. They had loved each other, despite their separate lives; had been faithful companions as they followed Mussolini on the journey to fascism. In the same year she broke her leg, an injury that never properly healed. She travelled to Berlin for corrective surgery. Mussolini was delighted with the specialist's name, Katzenstein. 'It's a Jewish name so it means he is a very good surgeon. I can rest assured.' He telephoned her in Germany to play her *Clair de Lune* on the violin.

'The popes were wise to always choose Jews as their physicians,' Mussolini used to say. He did his best to make sure that Jews were in charge of his family's health. A Jew fixed his teeth, and dealt with his halitosis. Another Jew was the family gynaecologist.

Rachele Mussolini and the children had stayed in Milan after the march on Rome. Only in 1929 did they finally come to join him. The Duce had set up house at the Villa Torlonia, and here he played at paterfamilias, coming home everyday for lunch: milk, a little spaghetti, fruit for his constipation.

Sarfatti hated Mussolini's crude wife and his dull, lumpy children. It was she who had arranged the new family set-up, and she knew it was a sham; she was not the only mistress coming and going freely by back entrances. But she understood that this was the way things had to be. In her youth she had been a committed feminist, and early fascism had borne traces of her and Mussolini's radical origins. Women's suffrage was part of the 1919 fascist manifesto. But over the years, fascism had moved rightwards, and Sarfatti had followed, uncomplaining.

Feminist periodicals were shut down, or relaunched as fashion magazines. Women's suffrage was out of the question. Mussolini became obsessed with the nation's birthrate. There were incentives for large families. Women were urged to return to the countryside; to take up their traditional roles as mothers and wives. Sarfatti accepted that in fascist Italy women could hope only to be mothers of heroes, as she was. They were fit only for breeding, as one fascist scientist put it, and their place would be the home – though Sarfatti assumed an exception would be made for members of the cultural elite, such as herself.

It was becoming clear, however, that Mussolini's interest in Sarfatti's 'fascist culture' was shallow at best. The signs had been there for years. Back in 1923, he had opened the inaugural exhibition of Sarfatti's beloved *novecento Italiano* with an improvised speech composed of the rankest banalities, causing her some embarrassment among her cultivated Milanese set.

After this unpromising start, her art movement had not prospered. The greater artists were repelled by her proximity to the regime; lesser artists, on the other hand, were drawn to her notional status as Mussolini's muse, diluting Sarfatti's vision. She came under attack from rival thinkers: the old Futurist F. T. Marinetti, the philosopher Giovanni Gentile, the critic Giuseppe Bottai, the brutish provincial Blackshirt Roberto Farinacci. Even one of her own novecento stars, Mario Sironi, turned against her, accusing her of promoting 'Jewish art'.

Sarfatti might have expected her lover, Mussolini, to weigh in on her side. Surely she could persuade him of the rightness of her vision, the power of her unique synthesis of classical and modern art. She was to be disappointed. It wasn't that Mussolini preferred someone else's ideas. The truth she had failed to recognize was that, underneath all his grand talk, his intellectual affectations, Mussolini was nothing but a chancer, a tactician, a man who really had no deep ideas at all. The synthesis of fascist theory, one farseeing Blackshirt had once said, is the fist.

By 1931, Sarfatti's physical relationship with Mussolini was over. It was her daughter, now, who was satisfying the Duce, if police reports are to be believed. Sarfatti was older than Mussolini, and had become rather stout. Rachele, the jealous wife, had already made Mussolini fire his old housekeeper, Cesira. Now she asked Mussolini to ban Sarfatti from the Villa Torlonia. He raised little objection.

Sarfatti had lost her allure, but she still hoped Mussolini might value her counsel. She had been at his side for nearly twenty years, was his most loyal friend. But Mussolini resented her presumptions; he hated the way she had inserted herself into his biography, the intimacy she had claimed. It diminished him, he felt, to be so closely associated with this portly Jewess. 'In the fascist regime,' he liked to boast, 'women don't count.'

In 1935, Sarfatti made a final attempt to remind Mussolini of her place in fascist history by commissioning one of her favourite architects to build a monument to her son Roberto, in the hills where he gave his life for Italy. It rained at the unveiling. The Duce was nowhere to be seen.

The Duce had found a woman who would be less threatening to his dignity. Mussolini caught sight of Claretta Petacci while out in his sports car in 1933. He was fifty and she was twenty-one, pretty, with heavy make-up and thick curly hair – not an intellectual, though formidable enough in her own way. She had been a teenage fan of his, had papered her walls with his photographs, had sent him poetry. She would now be permitted to know the Duce in the flesh.

In her diary, she recorded the details of their lovemaking and pillow talk: 'Look at your giant, your big naughty boy. Go on, touch him, look at his big hairy chest.' Women, like nations, he believed, always loved a brute. 'You should be scared of my lovemaking,' he once told her, 'it's like a cyclone, it uproots everything in its path.

You should tremble. If I could have done, today I'd have entered you on a horse.'

Claretta was a jealous lover. It gave her some satisfaction at least to note down the unflattering things Mussolini said about other women. He remembered 'Mercedes, who was so ugly you wanted to throw up', or Cornelia Tanzi, daughter of a brothel-madame, slender and long legged, 'frigid beyond belief'. Tanzi had failed to show sufficient enthusiasm for his caresses. 'Afterwards, I felt nothing but disgust. I wanted to beat her up, throw her on the floor.'

Mussolini maintained a relationship with an old mistress, Alice Pallottelli. But it was nothing to worry about, he told Claretta Petacci. 'There's nothing to attract me there, she's flabby, faded... It's just keeping possession of something which is mine.' Another old flame, Camilla Brambilla, was 'an old slack cow – you could fit several... well, you get my meaning... She's an old whore, a filthy bitch. Women like her or Sarfatti, once they get to a certain age, will go with their drivers, their menservants, the porter – and they'll pay them for the pleasure.' This was an idea that men had been mouthing since the days of ancient Rome: that though men might sleep around, it was women, in the end, who had the lewdest and most shameful appetites.

Sarfatti, as the lover with the most history, came in for the worst invective. 'She was an unpleasant woman,' said Mussolini. 'I put up with her, she bored me.' He boasted that he had had sex with other women right in front of her, in the open. 'I kept going with her' – she, the loyal companion of his most perilous years – 'only because it suited me.'

He remembered the first time he and Sarfatti had slept together, back in Milan when he was nobody. He had been unable to perform, he claimed, because Sarfatti was a Jew. 'I just couldn't do it, because of this terrible smell they have. Perhaps it's to do with their diet.' From somewhere in his mind, Mussolini had dredged up the old Jesuit idea of a special Jewish stink.

'Antisemitism does not exist in Italy,' said Mussolini in 1932. 'Italians of Jewish birth have shown themselves good citizens and they fought bravely in the war.' This was the year before Adolf Hitler was appointed chancellor of Germany. German antisemitism was becoming a major political force: an engine of hatred driving a National Socialist movement that was, in many ways, inspired by Mussolini's fascism.

At first Mussolini was publicly scornful of his Nazi imitators, and their obsession with the Jews. 'Thirty centuries of history allow us to regard with supreme pity certain doctrines from beyond the Alps.'

But Mussolini was perfectly willing to traffic in the commonplaces of anti-Jewish rhetoric. He had, in 1929, scored a major diplomatic victory with the signing of the Lateran Treaty, ending the long dispute between the kingdom of Italy and the Vatican. Having embraced Catholicism, the Duce soon adopted the anti-Judaic language of the church: 'They're a cursed race,' he told Petacci once. 'They killed God.'

Sarfatti had encouraged Mussolini's *rapprochement* with the pope, and converted to Catholicism herself in 1928. This was enough to render her perfectly respectable in the eyes of the church. She had hardly engaged with Judaism as a religion since her embrace of socialism, some three decades earlier.

But the new antisemitism growing in Germany was a matter of race, not faith. Semitic ancestry was not something to be washed away in the baptismal font. And similar racist ideas had long been dormant in Mussolini, ready to be called forth whenever the occasion arose. Way back when he first met Sarfatti he had commented on her 'stinginess', her 'cunning', her 'sly and greedy' nature. 'Of course,' he said, 'that one is a Jew.'

And in 1919, he had held forth in *Il Popolo d'Italia* about the menace of international Jewry, both the plutocrats of London and Paris and the Bolsheviks of Moscow. 'Is not Bolshevism, by chance, the revenge of Judaism on Christianity? This argument demands thought... Race does not betray race.' Fascism had elevated above all the idea of the nation – a nation that was coming to be defined more and more in terms of heritage and blood. In such a nation, it was becoming clear, the Jews did not belong.

*

This idea of the nation gathered importance as the 1930s progressed. 'In fascist doctrine,' Mussolini wrote, 'empire is not only a territorial, military or commercial expression, but also a spiritual and moral one.' Empire was an expression of national virility. As Mussolini conquered women, so Italy would take territory, brutishly, forcefully, needing no justification but its own strength.

The chosen target was Ethiopia, the only territory in Africa not already occupied by a European power. Italy had already attempted to annex Ethiopia back in 1896, an attempt than ended in humiliating defeat. Now that embarrassment would be paid for. Through 1935 and 1936 Italians deployed the full technology of war against the Ethiopians. When riflemen and tanks failed, Mussolini turned to long-range artillery and mustard gas, flattening villages and hospitals. He ordered his generals by telegram 'to carry out [a] systematic campaign of terror and extermination against rebel natives'. The Duce's sons were there flying bombing missions. A group of horsemen splattered by explosives reminded Vittorio Mussolini of a rose in bloom. It was 'magnificent sport', he reported. 'Exceptionally good fun.'

The conquest of Ethiopia brought a new sort of racial consciousness into Italian culture. Mussolini was determined that there should be no mingling of conquerors and natives, that the Italians should realize the superiority of the white race over the black. A system of segregation was imposed on Addis Ababa. Sexual intercourse between Italians and Ethiopians was forbidden; three Italian women who slept with Ethiopians were beaten and sent to labour camps to serve as an example.

The war also pushed Mussolini into the arms of the one European power that had refused to condemn it. Let others complain as they liked, there would be no pearl-clutching from Adolf Hitler. The only thing Hitler wanted was for Mussolini to attend to the problem of the Italian Jews. There was celebration in Germany when, in June 1938, the *Giornale d'Italia* published Mussolini's *Manifesto on Race*. Italians were true Aryans, the manifesto declared. Jews were neither Aryan nor Italian. In November that year, Mussolini issued a set of German-style anti-Jewish laws.

A few days earlier, Claretta Petacci attended an anniversary celebration for the end of the First World War. Amid the pomp and the banners, the cheering crowds on the Piazza Venezia, she noticed the forlorn figure of Margherita Sarfatti. 'I didn't care,' she wrote down in her diary, 'but the thought troubled me that that old ruin had once been his lover.'

It was the last time they would see each other. Petacci would die with Mussolini in 1945, executed by anti-fascist partisans. Their bodies were put on display, hung upside-down in front of a Milanese petrol station.

But by that time Sarfatti was already far away. On 14 November 1938, she had crossed the border to Switzerland and exile. She had given everything to fascism, and fascism had cast her out. There was nothing more she could do.

* * *

On 13 October 1943, two freight cars with German markings rolled down the tram tracks on the Lungotevere de' Cenci, stopping outside the Great Synagogue in Rome. They had come, as promised, for the books.

The assistant, Rosina Sorani, delayed the looting of the libraries for as long as she could. On the following morning a German officer arrived to supervise proceedings, and the loading began. Hundreds of priceless books were stacked in careful layers in the freight cars, padded with corrugated paper. The operation was methodical, and yet also somehow chaotic. The Italian porters, animated by some rebellious spirit, amused themselves by throwing manuscripts out of the window.

Ugo Foà, president of Rome's Jewish community, was deeply dismayed by the loss. And yet, he reassured people, there was no need to panic. For five years Mussolini had been going on about the 'Jewish problem', but in practice his antisemitic measures had never amounted to as much as the Nazis hoped. Italians, even committed fascists, showed a surprising lack of appetite for pogroms. Antisemitic laws, where possible, were quietly ignored. Between 1938 and

1943, not a single Italian Jew was deported to Hitler's 'labour camps'.

But circumstances had recently changed. Italy's entry into the Second World War had been a humiliating disaster. For all Mussolini's priapic imperialism, the Italian armed forces had wilted rapidly when asked to do anything harder than bombing Ethiopians from the air. On 24 July 1943, with Allied troops spreading across Sicily, Mussolini's government collapsed. On 3 September a secret armistice was signed. Soon Italy would rejoin the war on the Allied side.

German troops rescued Mussolini and installed him as a puppet of the Führer. Rome was taken by a German garrison. And now, for the first time, the Nazis were free to behave as they liked. The SS commandant in the city, Obersturmbannführer Herbert Kappler, had already made good use of this new freedom by extorting money from Rome's Jews: 50 kilograms of gold, the price for their continued existence. Woe to the conquered.

But the Jews had paid. As news spread of Kappler's demand, hundreds of people had come to the synagogue, clutching little treasures: necklaces, earrings, watches. Among them had been some Catholics, shyly entering the unfamiliar temple to help as best they could. Even priests had come, with contributions of church gold.

And in this familiar extortion the Jews found a degree of comfort. They had suffered such things before. They had been victimized in this way for hundreds of years. And yet they had always survived in the Eternal City.

But on the sabbath, 16 October 1943, an hour before dawn, SS soldiers took up positions around the Roman ghetto. All across the city, covered trucks were crawling through the rain, German drivers slow in unfamiliar streets. Each team had a list of names and addresses. Everything had been expertly organized.

Some Jewish families had moved to respectable middle-class areas, following the emancipation of 1870. These received no warning. Only a knock upon the door. Then the cold fright of peering from bedroom windows to see German uniforms. A pulling on of clothes. A stiffening of lips. The soldiers gave out instructions, printed neatly on cards.

All Jews were to be transferred. They would have twenty minutes to pack. They should bring food and valuables.

In the old ghetto, meanwhile, the whole neighbourhood was in a state of loud alarm. Voices cried out from the streets, some in the old giudeo-romanesco dialect, others in harsh German. It was believed that the Nazis were looking for labourers. Some men fled across the rooftops, never dreaming that the SS would take their wives and children.

But then they saw their families driven weeping from their houses – wives and children, the old and the sick, herded into those covered army trucks. Some were calm. Others were pleading, crying for help, clinging to each other for reassurance. Everyone hoped for the best. There had been rumours, from the east, but no one in that moment could believe them.

All morning long, the Germans kept up their work. The captives were brought to the Collegio Militare, not far from the blank windows of the Vatican. Some drivers had detoured past St Peter's to have a look. Papal territory was officially neutral. A few paces away, between the encircling arms of Bernini's colonnade, the Piazza san Pietro was beyond the legal reach of the German Reich.

It might have been possible to make a run for it. But few had any interest in escaping on their own. The raid of 16 October caught over a thousand Jews: households, clans, whole neighbourhoods. One Jewish man, distributing food among the captives, opened a side door to find an unguarded exit to the street. He went off to find a tobacconist, stocked up on cigarettes, then returned to the Collegio Militare, to rejoin his family and friends. They spent that night huddled together in the bare classrooms of the military school.

In fact, on the morning after the German raid, the number of captured Jews was found to have grown by one: a pregnant woman had given birth to a baby in the night, condemned as soon as it was born.

The Jews waited, and talked, and worried, and helped each other as well as they could. And on the other side of the city, down the railway tracks from the north, a long train of cattle cars came rolling in.

*

All around Europe, the fate of the Jewish communities under Nazi rule rested, to a great extent, in the hands of the gentiles among whom they lived. In Rome, the situation was a comparatively lucky one. Pope Pius XII never publicly protested as the city's Jews were abducted, but he did offer sanctuary to as many as he could. Some five thousand Roman Jews were hidden on church land to await the end of the war.

Ordinary Romans helped too, most of the time. The SS report on the events of 16 October described the behaviour of the Italian people as 'outright passive resistance which in many individual cases amounted to active resistance'. Thousands more Jews were hidden around the city, taken in by communists, socialists, conservatives and Catholics. Thanks to this help, most of Rome's Jews were able to survive.

Some at least appreciated what the Jews had always meant to the city. An underground newspaper gave voice to Roman disgust:

> The Germans during the night and all day long went around Rome seizing Italians for their furnace in the north. The Germans would like us to believe that these people are in some way alien to us, that they are of another race. But we feel them as part of our flesh and blood. They have always lived, fought, and suffered with us.

This was a fine sentiment. And that newspaper was still circulating a week later when a thousand of the most Roman Romans, whose roots in the city were two millennia deep, arrived at Auschwitz Birkenau. There, they were stripped and shaved – the men, the women and the children – and driven into the gas chamber where, over the course of several minutes, they succumbed to the effects of hydrogen cyanide. Their bodies were burned in a furnace, and their bones were ground to dust.

22

THE PARADE

Federico Fellini and La Dolce Vita

1958

A BACCHANAL AT the baths of Caracalla. The sound of rock and roll bouncing off the brickwork. Whoops of laughter. The stamp of dancing feet. Twisting figures casting long shadows, nymphs and satyrs, dancing in the dark.

The stars of Rome are here. An American, drunk and belligerent, slumps in his seat. Another, still wearing the goatish make-up of a costume drama, capers wildly. But all eyes are on the beauty who leads the dance. Sylvia, she's called. A platinum bombshell. A hybrid miracle of nature and corsetry, a body spilling from a dress like fruit from a cornucopia, bounty from the gods.

She is merry, wild, always ready to conduct the revels. Her whole existence is built on being the very life of the party – she must perform or die. So she dances, Diana of the wood, casting right and left for a scent, for a trail she can follow. And now she catches something, and is off. 'Come on everybody!' – her English is faintly accented – and they come, pell mell in wild parade, to the sound of rock and roll, off the stage where they were dancing and out into the shadows of the ruin, the satyrs and the nymphs, the actors and the actresses.

And then someone calls cut, and lights go on, and the music stops. And everyone files back to their place for another take. And Sylvia is not Sylvia, and the baths are not the baths, and the city is nothing but an illusion of cinema. And all eyes turn now to the man in command of this cardboard carnival: the director, Federico Fellini.

* * *

Federico Fellini arrived in Rome in the early spring of 1939, a young provincial fresh off the train. The moment, like many other important moments in his life, would eventually make its way into one of his films: a slim young man in a white suit steps on to the platform at Termini station in a cloud of steam; the camera close behind him, plunges into the crowd, blue-jacketed porters and hotel doormen in peaked hats, nuns in their habits, priests, soldiers in uniform, Wehrmacht men and gleaming Italian cuirassiers. The young man, smiling, peers around at the costumes, delighted with the drama around him.

Fascism had marked the city. Mussolini's architects had torn their way through the urban undergrowth, demolishing whole neighbourhoods. Tangled streets, the growth of centuries, surrendered helplessly before the bulldozer blades of modernity. Broad new avenues proclaimed the Duce's triumph over the city: one, the Via dei Fori Imperiali, crashed its way through the archaeological zone between the Palazzo Venezia and the Colosseum; another, Via della Conciliazione, cut a path to the Vatican, celebrating a new entente between the pope and the fascist regime.

From the periphery, new fascist monuments shouted new answers to the giant old ruins of the city's heart. They spoke the old architectural language but with harsh and strident accents: an obelisk that was stepped like a skyscraper, 300 tons of blinding carrara marble, jabbing at the sky; a stadium full of nude statues, thrusting and heavy-jawed; even a sort of modernist colosseum, with the same piled arcades as the original but this time arranged into an orderly square.

But Rome had absorbed this sort of bombast before. Kings, popes, emperors and despots of every kind had been trying to bend the city to their will for three thousand years. And yet the city remained what it had always been: a stubborn chaos of humanity and decay.

Into this rebellious city, Fellini enthusiastically cast himself. He had a good eye for faces, and soon found he could make a little money sketching portraits of people at cafe tables. He quickly caught on to the spirit of the place. Punters hoping for a flattering likeness would often find that the young man had rendered them in leering caricature.

Fellini was discovering a gift for comedy. He had set his heart on journalism, and he soon managed to get a job at a satirical magazine called *Marc'Aurelio*, contributing funny stories and punchlines for cartoons. Before long, he was one of *Marc'Aurelio*'s most popular writers. He was well paid, though he never seemed to have any money. He was living fast and free. He loved variety shows, and was a familiar figure backstage, a youthful devotee of an old and dying art.

For all shows in Rome were dwindling then, shrinking in the shadow of the biggest show of all, Rome's most important industry after church and state: the cinema.

In 1896, the Lumiere brothers brought their newly invented 'cinématographe' to Italy. At first moving pictures were a circus novelty, a sideshow, competing with jugglers and acrobats. But Italians soon saw the potential of the new medium. In 1905, Filoteo Alberini produced Italy's first true work of cinema, *La Presa di Roma*, a ten-minute film celebrating the capture of the city by Italian forces in 1870. It was projected on a giant screen outside the Porta Pia, on the very spot where the events the film was describing had actually taken place.

From 1905 to 1915 Italy saw an extraordinary boom in cinematic production. The most successful films were fantasies or historical epics, each outdoing the last in scale and ambition. The culminating masterpiece came in 1914, from a director named Giovanni Pastrone. His *Cabiria*, with title cards written by the notorious Gabriele d'Annunzio, told the story of a Roman girl in Carthage during the Second Punic War. It was an extraordinary spectacle: real elephants crossing the Alps; thousands of extras, lavishly costumed; enormous sets that looked as if they had been assembled by giants. The film produced one of Italian cinema's first real movie stars – a strongman, Bartolomeo Pagano, whose character, the herculean Maciste, appeared in some twenty-six sequels produced over the following ten years.

This new medium, which could fix even a humble strongman so firmly in the national consciousness, was of great interest to Benito Mussolini. Cinema is the strongest weapon, a fascist slogan declared, *l'arma piu forte*.

The film industry declined after the end of the First World War. Mussolini, as he consolidated his hold on power through the twenties and thirties, was determined to reverse the slide, and the fascist government poured money into a new state-of-the-art studio complex to be built on the outskirts of Rome. On 21 April 1937, the anniversary of Rome's foundation, Mussolini presided at the grand inauguration of a new 'cinema city' – Cinecittà.

Somehow, the Duce managed not to choke the industry with fascist propaganda. Mussolini's son Vittorio was a film buff, who gathered around himself some directors and screenwriters of genuine quality. Among them was Federico Fellini, whose jokes, resolutely apolitical, had begun to make their way on to the silver screen.

Still, even if his film-makers were not all slavish propagandists, Mussolini was pleased with his investment in cinema. He enjoyed a triumphant visit to the set of one new historical epic he had funded, *Scipio l'Africano*, a tale of the Punic Wars, starring the inaptly named Annibale Ninchi. An Italian army division supplied the legions of extras. Dressed in Roman costume, in a new Roman Forum built of plywood and papier-mâché, they threw out stiff armed salutes in the bogus 'antique' style, and cheered him to the skies: Duce! Duce!

That was in 1936. By 1942, when Fellini's screenwriting career was taking off, Mussolini's imperial fantasies had been blown away. In the Sahara Desert the Duce's extras had experienced real war, and had been found terribly wanting. Fellini travelled to Libya at the end of that year to help shoot a film he had scripted, but he and his crew only barely made it home again. Fellini was on one of the last transports out of Tripoli before the arrival of the British Eighth Army, his plane skimming the waves to avoid the Spitfires marauding overhead.

In 1943, Mussolini was ousted by the Fascist Grand Council. Italy surrendered to the Allies but was held and occupied by the Germans. Rome came under direct Nazi control. Now there was no more time for cinema; it was all Fellini could do to avoid the draft. Caught up in a German sweep, he avoided the labour camps by pretending to recognize an officer who happened to be walking by, embracing him with loud cries of 'Fritz! Fritz!' By the time the officer recovered from this friendly assault, the other soldiers had moved on.

Allied forces arrived in Rome on 5 June 1944. The Germans had left without a fight; American tanks rolled into the city in triumph, cheered by the Roman crowds. But times were hard. To survive, Fellini opened a store on the Via Nazionale, the Funny Face Shop, where he drew souvenir cartoons for passing soldiers – your portrait done in ten minutes, only three dollars. The GIs had money to spare, and occasionally even a bar of military-issue chocolate, or a carton of American cigarettes.

And then, one afternoon not long after the liberation, Roberto Rossellini walked in. Rossellini had been the best Italian director of the early 1940s, one of Vittorio Mussolini's protégés. But Mussolini was gone, and Rossellini had a new film in mind, a film that would provide the world with the defining image of the Roman experience during the Second World War.

* * *

Rome: Open City, began shooting early in 1945, with German troops still on Italian soil. The film dealt with very recent history. It was a story of Rome under the German occupation, of the martyrdoms of two men, a Catholic priest and a communist partisan, natural opponents united in patriotic resistance.

Italy in the last year of the war had been a country deeply divided. In the south, Allied armies advancing up the peninsula had, for the moment, preserved the monarchy of King Vittorio Emmanuele III, with the support of the landowning aristocracy and the Catholic Church. Meanwhile the great industrial cities of the north were held by the Wehrmacht. Mussolini, deposed in 1943, had been reinstalled by the Germans as a puppet dictator, and his remaining battalions of loyal fascists joined with the SS in a brutal campaign against the Italian resistance.

The anti-fascist resistance movement drew recruits from across Italian society, but the most substantial contribution to the struggle was made by the so-called Garibaldi brigades, affiliated with the Italian Communist Party. And here, Allied commanders forsaw a problem. For now, the resistance was making a vital contribution to the war effort. It was by no means clear, however, when the war ended, that these victorious partisans would tolerate the restoration of any sort of capitalist status quo.

But there could be no successful socialist revolution in Italy while American and British forces stood ready to interpose their armed veto. To avoid the sort of post-war bloodshed that occurred in Greece, for example, the Italian Communist Party settled on a strategy of delay. They would hand over their guns and submit to the old structures of class and capital, at least for the time being.

Peace demanded certain compromises, and those compromises could only be rendered tolerable by a rapid reshaping of Italy's historical imagination. The country's imperial adventures under fascism, the years as an Axis power, the violence perpetrated on Italians by other Italians – all these uncomfortable histories were subordinated to the great story of resistance and liberation.

No one could deny that Italy had paid a heavy price for its liberation. Of the 100,000 Italians estimated to have fought with the resistance, more than half were killed or seriously wounded. Thousands more civilians were murdered in German reprisals. Of these, 335 were killed on a single day in Rome itself, political prisoners and Jews, led in groups of five into the tunnels of an old pozzolana quarry by the Via Ardeatina, to kneel by the corpses of those who had gone before them, adding their own bodies to the pile as they fell.

And though those murdered men and women had been animated by contradictory ideas and ideologies, their differences were obscured by their shared sacrifice. When, in 1946, the discredited Italian monarchy was replaced by a constitutional republic, that republic took the heroism of the anti-fascist resistance for its founding myth.

Communists and capitalists, atheists and Catholics, peasants from the hills of the Mezzogiorno and workers from the factories of Milan and Turin – all had bled for Italy, and their blood had redeemed the country's honour. It was not felt necessary to dwell on the number of Italians who had remained loyal to Mussolini, nor on the fact that the post-war bureaucratic apparatus of the new republic was inherited more or less unchanged from the defeated fascist state.

Rome: Open City was to be perhaps the greatest dramatic expression of Italy's wartime sacrifice. Fellini's role in the production was a small but important one: Rossellini was casting the role of Don Pietro, the heroic priest who dies for the resistance. Fellini, a great lover of variety shows, had struck up a useful friendship with one of the stars of the Roman theatre, Aldo Finzi, who, Rosselini had decided, was just the man for the part. Finzi agreed to play the priest, and Fellini came with him to help write some of his dialogue.

No one was being properly paid. There was no film stock to be bought – the cameraman made do with whatever celluloid he could scavenge on the black market. Half the rolls were out of date. Meanwhile the studios at Cinecittà were all out of commision: the complex had been damaged by Allied bombing raids, and the ruins were now full of starving refugees, sheltering amid the abandoned sets and rotting costumes.

But Rossellini's story was the story of the city itself. Rome, bomb-scorched and desperate, would be his set, and there, in the real city, his actors would portray a reality through which they themselves had just lately lived. Anna Magnani, the volcanic talent who played the female lead in the film, was a true Roman from the streets, a child of the city's slums. The fates of the various characters in the drama were taken from real life. When, in one iconic scene, Magnani's pregnant heroine Pina was shot down in the street by the SS, it was more a re-enactment than a fiction. A pregnant Roman woman, Teresa Gullace, had been killed in exactly the same way only the year before.

And if, amid all this tragedy, there was the odd whimsical moment here or there, that was Fellini's fault. In the scene for which Fellini was most directly responsible, the saintly priest Don Pietro prevents a dotty old man from blowing his cover by bopping him on the head with a frying pan.

Rome: Open City was an international success – a success that signalled the start of a new era of Italian cinema. Contemporary critics, looking for an organizing principle around which the masterpieces of the post-war years could be arranged, would settle upon the term 'neorealism'. Neorealist films were to be recognized by their lack of cinematic artifice. They would, where possible, use non-professional actors, and rely on actual locations rather than constructed sets. Above all, they shared a high sense of social purpose. Cinema should abandon the fantasies that had sustained it in the old days before the war. The new age demanded something real.

A neorealist director – to the extent that any were willing to accept that label – needed only to direct his camera at the reality of the world around him. Giuseppe de Santis, a former resistance fighter, dramatized the plight of itinerant rice pickers. Luchino Visconti, a Marxist aristocrat, shot a film with Sicilian fishermen essentially playing themselves. Vittorio de Sica, who had been a matinée idol before the war, now worked behind the camera, making films about shoeshine boys and bicycle thieves. A young Michelangelo Antonioni made a short film about the lives of Roman street sweepers.

These films revealed an Italy of poverty, hunger and desperation. In the background, often, was a sort of Marxist idea that film-makers might dispel the 'false consciousness' that clung to the Italian proletariat. Surely, if Italians could be induced to see the real state of the country, the day of the long-awaited socialist revolution would then be near at hand!

Neorealist films did well, critically at least, if not always commercially. Italy remained desperately poor. Rossellini, at least, could hope for funding from the US, where *Rome: Open City* had been a major hit. His next post-war film addressed the American presence in Italy directly. Each narrative episode of Rossellini's *Paisà* told the story of an encounter between conquered Italy and American military power: GIs trying to communicate with Sicilian villagers; army chaplains meeting Catholic monks; a black military policeman led through the ruins of Naples by an orphaned boy.

Working with Rossellini on *Paisà*, Fellini began to appreciate the true value of the director's craft. He admired the 'loving eyes' through which Rossellini observed the world around him. It was possible, Fellini saw, to make a film 'without deceits, without presumptions'.

But although *Paisà* would eventually be recognized as a classic, it endured a tepid early reception in both Italy and America. The Italian film market was flooded with American imports, slick dramas that provided Italian audiences with just the sort of bourgeois escapism that the advocates of neorealism deplored. American films had bigger budgets and more famous stars; for a while, it was not clear that the Italian film industry would survive at all. Anna Magnani led a rally of film-makers in the Piazza del Popolo in 1949. Addressing the crowd, she appeared almost overcome with emotion. Years of suffering, she said, had been devoted to the post-war resurrection of Italian cinema: 'To prevent that effort from having been in vain, help us!' – *Aiutateci, aiutateci, aiutateci!*

As it turned out, Italian cinema would not just survive, but prosper. In 1948, the United States government had voted in favour of the vast post-war aid package known as the Marshall Plan. Billions of dollars were devoted to the rebuilding of Europe, and Italy, with its threateningly lively communist party, was among the foremost recipients. Only a rapid increase in Italian living standards, it was believed, would counter communism's dangerous allure.

In an effort to renew the country's stocks of capital, a law was passed that prohibited American studios from taking profits out of Italy. The money American films made in Italian theatres was left marooned in Italian banks. There was nothing in Italy to spend the money on – until, that is, some bright executive had the idea of making American films at Cinecittà.

In 1951, Metro-Goldwyn-Mayer released *Quo Vadis*, a sword-and-sandals epic shot entirely in Rome in dazzling Technicolor. Peter Ustinov played Nero, a bravura performance that would have made the long-dead emperor proud. Deborah Kerr was the comely Christian, rescued miraculously from the arena.

And with that, Hollywood on the Tiber was born. *Quo Vadis* was a hit, and now more studios came to follow Metro-Goldwyn-Mayer's example. Italian labour was cheap, and the facilities were excellent. Cinecittà became a hub of creative activity: of costumiers and carpenters, stuntmen and film technicians. Above all, the set designers were at work again, building colosseums and chariots, palaces and forums, an unreal city of simulacra, of scattered Roman fragments waiting to be brought to life by the camera's organizing eye.

In-between filming, American cast and crew members spent their money in Rome. Five years after the end of the war, the city was beginning to recover a little of its old energy. There were tourists again, picking their way through the ruins of the Forum, guidebooks in hand, or peering up at Keats's old rooms by the Spanish Steps. Vespas and Fiat Topolinos, fresh from the production lines in Turin, rattled along cobbled streets, gleaming heralds of a new consumer age.

And on one shady street winding north from the Piazza Barberini to the Aurelian walls, new sounds began to disturb the evening quiet: laughter rising from cafe tables, the muffled notes of jazz and mambo out of basement bars, the occasional hush that marked the arrival of a foreign movie star. Rome was beginning to have a nightlife. Before long this street, the Via Veneto, would be the most glamorous – and notorious – nightspot in the world.

* * *

With all the Hollywood money flowing into Cinecittà, new possibilities began to open up for Italian film-makers. In 1951, even the inexperienced Federico Fellini was allowed to take a turn behind the camera, his first solo directing job: *Lo Sceicco Bianco* – the White Sheik.

The first day on set was a disaster, or so Fellini liked to remember. It was a story he repeated with, as his biographer put it, 'theme and variations'. As he set off to the shoot, his heart was racing 'like someone about to take an exam'. He stopped into a church on the way to calm his nerves, and found the place laid out for a funeral. It felt like a bad omen. He made some vague promises about changing his ways, then drove off, only to discover that one of his tyres was flat.

His actors and crew were waiting for him on a beach near Fiumicino: his star, Alberto Sordi; the cameramen and lighting technicians, the cinematographer, the head stagehand, a little army waiting on his orders. There was even a camel, borrowed from the zoo.

When Fellini arrived at last, he was gripped with panic. The scene was a failed seduction on a sailing dinghy – and he had no idea how to shoot it. He did his best to look as though he was deep in artistic contemplation. Really, he was stumped by the basic technical challenge: how to keep his camera pointed the right way while bobbing around on the open sea.

By sunset, everyone just felt sorry for him. That evening, he was summoned to see the producer, who complimented him on his suntan, the solitary achievement of the day. What would he do tomorrow? With a boldness he did not feel, he replied that he would fake it: the sea scene would be filmed with the boat just sitting on the beach. Impossible, said the production director. "'I think it's doable..."' I responded. I wasn't sure at all, but it didn't break my foolish calm.'

The next day, miraculously, the plan worked.

And so I gained control over my film, and from that moment, without knowing anything about camera lenses or technique, without knowing anything about anything, I became a despotic director who wants what he wants, demanding, stubborn and capricious, with all of the defects and all of the qualities I'd always loathed and envied in real directors.

*

Only three years had passed since the release of Vittorio de Sica's famous *Bicycle Thieves* – a classic statement of neorealism. Fellini had learned his craft from Rossellini himself. But the final cut of *Lo Sceicco Bianco* showed that the young director had his own ideas about what cinema was, and what it ought to be.

The film's protagonist, Wanda, arrives in Rome on her honeymoon, an innocent from the provinces. Her husband thinks they are there to get a blessing from the pope, but she has something better in mind: she will find the hero of her favourite *fotoromanzo*, a man known as the White Sheik.

Fotoromanzi were popular magazines whose wild stories were illustrated with elaborately staged photographs. Wanda's star-struck enthusiasm draws her into this fictive world. Hunting for her White Sheik, she happens to fall in with the cast of the *fotoromanzo*, in full Bedouin costume, on the way to the seaside to do their next shoot. Delighted, Wanda joins them.

The parallel between *fotoromanzi* and cinema is clear. But what Wanda finds in Rome is not the sort of truth-telling drama to which neorealists might aspire. The world of the White Sheik is as unreal as the sheik himself. Her hero is nothing but a cheap seducer; the Arabian desert of which she dreams is just a stretch of ordinary beach, near Rome.

Wanda's foray into the world beyond the camera leads to disaster. In the end, abandoned and despairing, she tries to kill herself, leaping into the Tiber in the manner of a dramatic heroine – but she picks a spot where the river runs only a foot deep. All she manages is to get a bit wet.

Neorealist cinema was supposed to lead Italians towards truth and virtue. The images Fellini was interested in drew people in the opposite direction.

Lo Sceicco Bianco was not a great success. Fellini's next film did better. *I Vitelloni*, released in 1953, drew on his memories of provincial youth in Rimini before the war, and was judged to show a lot of promise.

But it was his third full-length feature film that really announced Fellini as a major directorial talent. *La Strada* starred Anthony Quinn alongside Fellini's wife, Giulietta Masina. The film follows a circus strongman named Zampanò and his assistant, the innocent Gelsomina, wandering the roads of rural Italy.

Much about this film was in the neorealist tradition. It was shot on location, in the impoverished Italian countryside. An entire village of peasants appeared as extras – Fellini recruited them by persuading a priest to celebrate the feast of the local patron saint a few days early.

But when the film premiered in 1954, the champions of neorealism greeted it with dismay and disdain. It was not a badly acted film, conceded the great Marxist film critic Guido Aristarco, nor badly directed. But 'we have declared, and do declare, that it is *wrong*; its perspective is wrong'.

At the end of the war, though the communists had laid down their arms, they certainly had not abandoned the struggle for Italy's soul. But the Italian Communist Party faced a formidable opponent. To counter the communist appeal to the working class, conservatives and Catholics had created a new mass movement: Christian Democracy, for the defence of church and family against godless Stalinism.

Parish priests across Italy urged their flocks to vote for the Christian Democrats. American diplomats let it be known that a vote for the Communist Party would lead to the immediate cessation of aid from the Marshall Plan. Propaganda posters portrayed communists as wolves or snakes, threatening Italian virtue with the poison of 'free love'.* In 1948, Christian Democracy scored a major electoral victory, relegating the Communist Party to a state of permanent opposition.

By the 1950s communists and Christian Democrats were engaged in a desperate culture war, and cinema occupied a vital position on the front lines. By 1954, the year *La Strada* came out, the pro-Christian Democrat church organization Catholic Action was running a network of over 4,000 cinemas, at which the working classes could enjoy a careful selection of the latest Hollywood hits. In the same year, the first televisions arrived in Italian homes. Much airtime was given over to educational Catholic programming. A daily half-hour slot called *Carosello* was permitted to vary the programme, mixing advertisements with engaging little stories and cartoons to introduce a generation of Italian children to the safe pleasures of consumerism.

---

* In one poster, Stalin crushes the monument to Victor Emmanuel II in Rome under his boot. This, evidently, was supposed to be a bad thing.

While Christian Democracy had a commanding grip on mass entertainment, the communists retained a strong position within Italian high culture. Most serious Italian critics and directors in those days were at least broadly in sympathy with the Communist Party. Luchino Visconti, who had a film competing at the Venice Film Festival in the same year as *La Strada*, had been an active member of the communist resistance.

The prize ceremony that year was a fractious affair. Tempers ran high. Fellini and Visconti's respective assistant directors almost came to blows in the auditorium. Fellini's error was simple. In that volatile political climate, he had made a film that was oblivious to its own historical moment. *La Strada* was 'the poetry of the solitary man'.

Neorealist films tended to understand character as a function of socioeconomic circumstance. The protagonist of Vittorio de Sica's *Bicycle Thieves*, say, is completely defined by his economic situation, by the getting, and losing, of a bicycle. He stands for a certain type of person at a particular place and time. Gelsomina and Zampanò in *La Strada*, on the other hand, spring not from any particular social reality but from Federico Fellini's own private dreams. They are human archetypes, creatures of myth, of fairy tale.

'Where was Zampanò when the partisan war was being fought?' one heckler demanded. 'There are more Zampanòs in the world than bicycle thieves,' Fellini would say, 'and the story of a man who discovers his neighbour is just as important and as real as the story of a strike.'

In America the quality of the film Fellini had made was more quickly recognized. In 1957 *La Strada* was the first winner of the newly established Oscar for best foreign language film. Fellini was swamped with offers of work, though not of the sort he wanted. Producers, then as now, were only interested in sequels. They wanted him

> to make Gelsomina on a Bicycle, or anything with Gelsomina in the title… They all wanted Gelsomina. I could have earned a fortune selling her name to doll manufacturers, to sweet firms;

even Walt Disney wanted to make an animated cartoon about her. I could have lived on Gelsomina for twenty years!

The popularity of the character owed a great deal to Giulietta Masina's extraordinary performance: poetic and delicate, with a clown-like pathos that made people call her the female Charlie Chaplin. Her greatest role, however, was yet to come: in Fellini's 1957 *Notti di Cabiria*, Masina played Maria 'Cabiria' Ceccarelli, a Roman prostitute searching for love.

Masina's Cabiria, named after the famous silent film of 1914, was an extraordinary character, a prostitute with the innocence of a little girl, simultaneously suspicious and naïve, tough and fragile, capable of swinging in a moment from despair to joy. She longs for love and marriage, an escape from 'the life', as people called it. She has dreams. And she will, inevitably, be disappointed.

Masina gave everything to the part. As a director, her husband was harder on her than anyone: he took her imperfections personally, as if she were an extension of himself. They recorded some thirty takes of the final betrayal scene, Cabiria throwing herself to the ground, over and over again. Masina ended the shoot limping. The film that resulted is a masterpiece.

Like Fellini's other early films, *Notti di Cabiria* has roots in neo-realism. Much more than *La Strada*, it deals with the hard reality of Italian life. The film reveals a Rome blighted by poverty, a city whose famous urban centre was ringed by a desolate periphery of modern slums, whose proud monuments were the night-time haunts of thieves, pimps and prostitutes.

Fellini's guide to this Roman underworld was a writer named Pier Paolo Pasolini, later one of the great figures of Italian cinema in his own right. Pasolini was a man of somewhat scandalous reputation – he had been expelled from the Communist Party following a scandal involving three teenage boys – but he was an acute and passionate observer of Roman street life. He saw, with a poet's eyes, the beauty and desperation of the Roman poor: a young chestnut seller from Trastevere, dark skinned, hunched over his stove; boys swimming in the Tiber; a hustler selling rotten dogfish from a market stall by Monte Testaccio.

Pasolini knew poverty first hand. He lived himself in one of the so-called *borgate*, the bleak suburban neighbourhoods that had grown up around the outskirts of Rome. Some *borgate* had been built before the war to house poor Romans whose homes in the city centre had fallen foul of fascist town planners. But there were never enough apartments to go around. By the time Fellini was shooting *Notti di Cabiria* Rome's population had reached two million, almost twice its pre-war level. After the war ended, thousands of new immigrants had flooded into the capital from the devastated countryside. They arrived hungry, illiterate, sometimes barely even speaking Italian. Whole families would occupy a single room, crowded into grim apartment blocks that rose, inhuman in their monotony and scale, from the rubbish-strewn wasteland at the city's edge.

There was no meaningful regulation, no space left for shops or parks. This was the age of the *bustarella*, the 'little envelope', which, filled with cash and directed into the correct pocket, allowed property speculators to operate with a completely free hand. By the end of the building boom, in 1970, some 400,000 Romans lived in buildings that did not officially exist, that were ugly, unsafe, unsanitary. Just as in the days of ancient Rome, so in the modern city the poor were always in danger of being crushed by a collapsing apartment block.

Worse even than the *borgate* were the shanty towns. Pasolini left a vivid account of one, *il Mandrione*, not far from Cinecittà, built along a railway line under the arches of a ruined aqueduct:

> These are not human habitations lined up in the mud; they are animal dens, kennels. They are built out of a few rotten boards, peeling walls, scrap metal, and wax paper. In the place of a door, there is often a filthy curtain. Through the tiny windows, one can see the interiors, the two boards on which five or six people sleep, a chair, a few boxes… A little door opens, a prostitute pours out the water from her chamber pot among the little children playing in the street, and a customer emerges. Old ladies

call out like barking dogs. And then, all of a sudden, they begin
to cackle as they see a cripple dragging himself out of his lair,
carved into the wall of the aqueduct.

Such was the world Fellini set himself to recreate. Cabiria's 'house',
of which she is very proud, is a single room set in a patch of waste
ground, walls made of piled breeze blocks.* Even this primitive shack
has been hard earned. 'Oh, if you knew what I endured to get this
money,' says Cabiria in the film. She has been a prostitute for as long
as she can remember. For many women and children during the hard
years after the war, the only alternative to prostitution was to starve.
They embarked upon the life that so many Roman girls had lived
before.

But although the suffering in the shanty towns was all too real,
Fellini could not be kept on the neorealist straight and narrow. His
stories seem to resist gravity, rising above reality like balloons escaping
their string. The real woman on whom the story of Cabiria was based
was found beheaded beside a lake in the Castelli Romani. Cabiria
ends up overlooking the same lake, led to the edge of a precipice by
her treacherous lover. But, when the moment of Cabiria's downfall
arrives, Fellini refuses to give her the final fatal push. Instead, the
despairing prostitute is allowed to step away from the brink, to climb
up through the trees towards the road. There, she encounters one of
Fellini's parades – a troop of young people, bacchantes returning after
a revel, walking along to the sound of a guitar. Almost unconsciously,
Cabiria joins them. They dance about her. And she, ruined and des-
titute, turns her face towards the camera and smiles.

* * *

* Fellini had spotted just such a ramshackle house while filming on location
for *Il Bidone* the year before. Fascinated that anyone could live in such a
hovel, he went over, pushed open the door, and stuck his head inside. To
his surprise, he saw that the interior of the shack was impeccably neat and
tidy, someone's well-loved little home. He only had a second to take in the
scene. The woman who lived there took him for a bailiff, and chased him
back to his car, pelting him with insults and melon rinds.

In one scene, early in the film, Cabiria leaves her usual post on the Passeggiata Archaeologica to try her luck at the most desirable spot in Rome, the Via Veneto. Here, just a short drive from the teeming desolation of the *borgate*, the city was booming.

Likewise Fellini's career. *Notti di Cabiria* was showered with prizes: a best actress award for Giulietta Masina at Cannes, and a second consecutive best foreign language film Oscar for Fellini. They needed a special room at their house for all the trophies. Fellini called it the sanctuary of divine love.

Stars were queuing up to work with the great director. The next project he had in mind was a film with Sophia Loren, a famous beauty – one of the sort the Italians called *maggiorate*, for their 'advantaged' physiques. Italian cinema had moved on since the days of the fiery but unconventional-looking Anna Magnani. The new generation of stars, women like Loren or Gina Lollobrigida, began their careers by winning beauty pageants before bringing their talents to the silver screen.

The atmosphere on the Via Veneto was heating up. The intellectuals and literati who had colonized the Caffe Rosati on one side of the street were outnumbered by the movie stars who gathered at the Strega-Zeppa Caffe on the other, arriving in the small hours after the evening shows with their publicists and flatterers and assorted hangers-on to drink away the hours until dawn.

One of Fellini's scriptwriters, Ennio Flaiano, was a regular at the Caffe Rosati, and watched with dismay the takeover of the street. He described a society 'that frolics between eroticism, alienation, boredom and sudden affluence', an atmosphere that was aggressive, almost subtropical. The Via Veneto was 'no longer a street, but a beach... Even the conversations are seaside resort: baroque and jocular; and they are concerned with an exclusively gastro-sexual reality'. In this city, he wrote, 'scandals explode with all the violence of summer storms'.

In the summer of 1958, the year after the release of *Notti di Cabiria*, just such a scandal burst over Rome. It happened in Trastevere, at a restaurant where an ambitious socialite was having a party. Some of the most glamorous figures in Rome had been persuaded to come, aristocrats and movie stars. Nicolò Pignatelli Aragona Cortes, a prince of the Holy Roman Empire, was there. So was Anna Maria Mussolini, the Duce's youngest daughter, who had managed to carve a career for herself in radio, working under a pseudonym.

More importantly, Anita Ekberg had made an appearance. The Swedish actress was, by common consensus, the most desirable woman then in Rome, a *maggiorata* above all others, an explosion of curves and charisma and bright blonde hair. She, ever the performer, was doing her best to create a little buzz. She had kicked off her shoes, was dancing the mambo.

But Ekberg was about to be upstaged by another woman. Nobody knew the girl's name – some young hopeful dreaming of stardom – but suddenly, there she was, taking off her clothes.

It wasn't that anyone minded. On the contrary, it was a diverting spectacle at an otherwise rather dull party. Young aristocrats spread out their jackets on the floor, providing the girl with a sort of carpet on which to dance. But they, and she, had forgotten about the cameras. The audience that evening extended far beyond the walls of the Trastevere restaurant. The whole world would see the striptease, as captured by the prying lens of Rome's most successful celebrity photographer, Tazio Secchiaroli.

Secchiaroli's photographs caused an uproar. Rome was still, at heart, a conservative city – the pope's city. The Vatican expressed its strongest disapproval. The behaviour of the naked girl – Aïché Nana, her name turned out to be – was bad enough; she was eventually punished for her immodesty with a two-month prison term. Much worse, however, was that she had been surrounded by members of the highest papal aristocracy, whose imagined misdeeds filled the Roman middle classes with horrified titillation. 'This is How the Upper Crust Undress', declared one headline.

A scandal of such magnitude could hardly fail to attract the attention of Federico Fellini. It was the photographers, above all, who interested him. That autumn, he invited a few of Rome's best 'action photographers' to dinner, to quiz them on their adventures. The photographer at the striptease, Tazio Secchiaroli, sat in the place of honour beside him, pleased to have the opportunity to show off his much-maligned art.

Secchiaroli and his colleagues were the wolves of the Via Veneto. Wherever the stars went, the photographers would hunt them out, each night finding the plumpest celebrity target. Everyone who was anyone passed through Rome in those days: Ava Gardner, Audrey Hepburn, Ingrid Bergman, Gary Cooper, Rock Hudson, Cary Grant, a roll-call of Hollywood royalty. But getting the right shot was hard. There were no easily portable zoom lenses. Photographers had to get right up into their target's face, half-blinding them with the flashbulb.

This photographic assault could be infuriating for its victims. Anita Ekberg would one day chase a pack of photographers away from her house by shooting at them with a bow and arrow. Generally, though, angry stars just made for better photographs. One of Secchiaroli's best pictures was a shot of King Farouk of Egypt, an exile in Rome since his overthrow by Colonel Nasser in 1952. The deposed monarch stares up at the photographer's lens, frozen in the moment of his dawning fury. In the next instant, his bulky frame will be lurching up towards Secchiaroli, quivering with violent intent, a brief moment of righteous anger breaking the sad trajectory of his slow decline.

Fellini absorbed every detail. As the evening went on, the stories grew wilder and wilder. 'They thought up all kinds of tall stories for my benefit', Fellini recalled. 'In the end, Secchiaroli said "stop inventing, you idiots, you're talking to an old hand at the game".'

The project Fellini had been planning with Sophia Loren had fallen through. Now he had in mind a sequel to *I Vitelloni*, based on his memories of arriving in Rome as a young man. The more he thought about Secchiaroli's adventures, however, and the more time he spent watching the photographers at work on the Via Veneto, the less interested he became in dimly remembered history. The film he really wanted to make now was a film about the present moment, the scandalous summer of 1958, this age of gossip journalism and camera flashes. He would call it The Sweet Life – *La Dolce Vita*.

Fellini began collecting stories. There was Aïché Nana's striptease, of course, and another incident that Secchiaroli had witnessed: an outbreak of pious hysteria in the countryside, when two local children claimed to have seen the Virgin Mary. A rival photographer, Pierluigi Praturlon, had some tales of his own: he had once seen Anita Ekberg bathing her sore feet in the Trevi fountain in front of a pair of awe-struck carabinieri.

Other stories Fellini read about, or heard about from friends. He liked to kidnap his favoured consultants – Pasolini, once again, was a vital source of inspiration – and drive with them through the outskirts of the city, round and round for hours like a dynamo, as if drawing energy directly from the streets. A few incidents in particular caught his attention: a writer's suicide in 1950; a grotesque and unidentifiable fish that washed up on the shore near Rimini in 1934; a scandal from 1958, when a young British actress named Belinda Lee, the mistress of Prince Filippo Orsini, took an overdose of sleeping pills.

At the same time, Fellini was collecting people. The central character he had in mind was to be a celebrity journalist, one of those men who, in documenting the scene around themselves, come also to participate in it. The role needed an actor who was supremely pliable – someone who would not impose too strong a character of his own on the action around him. Fellini's backers hoped for an American star (Paul Newman was briefly considered for the part) but Fellini had already decided on his leading man: Marcello Mastroianni, an actor mostly known, at that time, for playing cab drivers. He had a very 'ordinary face', as Fellini approvingly told him when he went to discuss the job. Mastroianni asked to see a script. The scriptwriter, Ennio Flaiano, went off and returned with a pile of papers, but every page was blank, except for one. There Mastroianni found one of Fellini's cartoons: a man, swimming in the sea; his grotesquely elon-gated penis dangling down to the sea floor, surrounded by dancing mermaids. Mastroianni blushed, went silent. But what could he say? At last: 'Oh, sure: it seems very interesting. Where do I sign?' The part was his, and the character was named Marcello, after him.

There was no script for Mastroianni, and there was not much of a plot. 'Let's not worry for now about the logic or the narrative', Fellini told his screenwriters. 'We have to make a statue, break it, and recompose the pieces.'

And slowly, the pieces were falling into place. Pasolini was helping with the casting. Fellini had persuaded some international talent to come on board: the Romanian actress Nadia Grey; from France, Anouk Aimée and Alain Cuny. To play the part of Marcello's father, Fellini recruited none other than Annibale Ninchi, the man who had starred in the epic production of *Scipio l'Africano* that had given so much cheer to Mussolini back in 1936. Ninchi played Marcello's father because he bore an extraordinary resemblance to Fellini's own.

Alongside the professionals, Fellini was gathering interesting people for cameo roles. Adriano Celentano, a pioneer of Italian rock and roll, sang in the nightclub scene at the baths of Caracalla; Nico, the German model and singer who would later win fame with the Velvet Underground, appeared as the girlfriend of a Roman aristocrat; Iris Tree, a poet and fashion icon of the 1920s, recited one of her works at the salon of Fellini's doomed intellectual, Steiner. Best of all, perhaps, from Fellini's point of view, the film featured a performance from Ferdinand Guillaume, better known as Polidor, a man who, fifty years before, had been Italian silent cinema's most celebrated clown. When Marcello takes his father to a nightclub, Polidor appears like a miracle, playing his trumpet with perfect melancholy, and leading a flock of magically animated balloons.

The greatest coup really, though, was the casting of the irresistible Anita Ekberg as a glamorous foreign movie star. Fellini was so overwhelmed when he met her that he could hardly speak: 'You are my imagination come to life', he said. She, in her bewitching Swedish accent, replied: 'I do not go to bed with you.'

Everywhere in the background of *La Dolce Vita*, figures from Roman high-life can be made out, aristocrats and celebrities more or less playing themselves. In a sense this was something like the old neorealist method. Fellini took true stories from Roman life; he recruited performers whose real lives matched the lives of the characters they portrayed; he promised an accurate and faithful portrait of life on the Via Veneto, just as neorealist films had shown life in fishing villages and urban slums.

But the 'realness' for which neorealist films were praised had, of course, always meant something more than mere verisimilitude. For the defenders of neorealism, working-class lives were real in a way that the celebrity world of the Via Veneto was not. The Via Veneto was a dream, or perhaps a nightmare, a moonlit world of carnival inversion where the day began at midnight and ended at dawn, a world populated by the phantoms of Cinecittà – men and women whose very livelihoods consisted in the spinning of illusions, who gathered after dark to put on another show for Secchiaroli and his pack of prowling photographers.

In this film about performers, the cameramen too had a prominent role. As he moves through the Via Veneto, Marcello is often accompanied by a photographer named Paparazzo – a name that came to be used to describe Tazio Secchioroli and all his kind. In Italian, the word Paparazzo is suggestive of a buzzing mosquito. Late on in the film, attracted by the whiff of tragedy, Paparazzo and his colleagues gather like flies to torment a woman who, although she does not yet know it, has suffered a terrible loss. 'You must have mistaken me for someone else,' she cries, in confusion. 'I'm not famous.' Paparazzo is relentless. It is an extraordinarily damning portrait of the character in the film whose role most closely approximate the role of Fellini himself.

For those whose lives were illuminated by the flashbulbs of the paparazzi, Rome was just one more elaborate set. They were on a stage, a stage that had been trodden for nearly three thousand years. And Fellini, making *La Dolce Vita*, layered artifice upon artifice. Nearly every scene that appears to be shot in the city, including the action on the Via Veneto itself, was in fact shot on specially constructed sets at Cinecittà. 'In my film I invented a non-existent Via Veneto, enlarging and altering it with poetic licence, until it took on the dimensions of a large allegorical fresco.' Filming on this artificial Via Veneto was much easier, and produced much better results.* In the end, Fellini almost felt that the Via Veneto in Rome was the fake, and his version, on sound stage five at Cinecittà, was the real thing.

* * *

La Dolce Vita was released in 1960 to a storm of controversy. Conservatives were horrified by Fellini's unflattering portrait of decadent aristocracy, and the church objected strongly to his (quite tame) recreation of the notorious Trastevere striptease. One Jesuit who dared defend the film in print was not only banned from reviewing films, but from watching them altogether.

On the other hand, left-wing critics who had hated the fairytale poetry of *La Strada* now rallied in support of a film they saw as a devastating satire on the Roman upper classes. Complete strangers would now call out to Fellini in the streets: 'Bravo! Keep it up!' 'Keep *what* up?' he wondered.

At least his old friend Pasolini understood things right. Fellini had revealed a world of 'mortifying characters, cynics, wretches, but somehow full of life'. The secret of the film, Pasolini saw, was Fellini's inexhaustible capacity for love.

The frenzy of publicity around the film, both good and bad, resulted in unprecedented public interest. Cinemas were overrun. Tickets were sold and resold for ten times their proper price. Critically and at the box office, the film was an extraordinary success; Fellini was established as a directorial superstar.

What was this Dolce Vita that everyone so wanted to see? The conventional account of the film's structure gives it seven parts, episodes from the life of Marcello Rubini, a Roman gossip journalist: Marcello accompanies an heiress, Maddalena, to the home of a prostitute in a

---

* One attempt to shoot a vehicular sequence live on the real Via Veneto was ruined by a strange man with a beret who had occupied a strategic position outside the Excelsior hotel. Each time Fellini's car went by, the man with the beret would 'shout an absolutely unrepeatable oath at me in Roman dialect'.

flooded apartment block, where they have sex; Marcello is dazzled by Sylvia, a foreign movie star; Marcello meets a friend, the intellectual, Steiner, who will later kill himself, along with both his children; Marcello and his suicidal fiancée, Emma, drive out of town to report on a bogus miracle; Marcello's father comes to town, and they go to an unfashionable nightclub to watch a show; Marcello goes to a party at an aristocratic villa where they commune with the spirits of the dead; Marcello drinks too much at an 'orgy', at which a divorcée performs a striptease.

Framing these jumbled episodes are two symbolic moments that serve as a prologue and an epilogue. The beginning of the film finds Marcello in a helicopter, following a large stone statue of Jesus being delivered by air to the Vatican. At the end of the film, he finds the corpse of a monstrous sea creature, stranded on the beach at dawn. A little way away stands Paola, a young girl who looks like an angel from an Umbrian church. She calls out to him – words he cannot quite hear.

The moment that made the greatest impression on audiences was a rare sequence that Fellini shot entirely on location: when Marcello follows the dazzling Sylvia into the Trevi fountain after the rock and roll dancing at the baths of Caracalla. The scene was shot in March. The water was freezing cold, but Ekberg plunged into the fountain without hesitation, rather to the annoyance of Mastroianni, who resorted to vodka in order to keep up. For the close-up shots, to his relief, he was allowed to put on a pair of fishermans' waders.

Meanwhile, around the famous square, a crowd had gathered. Even before its release, the film had gained a certain notoriety. Here was an opportunity to see Via Veneto glamour at work, a chance to see another page being written in Rome's long history.

The crowd that gathered that night, and the millions who have watched the scene since, must be forgiven if they have sometimes had the wrong idea about what Fellini's vision means. *La Dolce Vita*, as epitomized by that scene in particular, has become a byword for romance, for a particular Roman atmosphere to which tourists can aspire.

But the Rome of the Dolce Vita, of the Via Veneto, was a fleeting and unreal thing, an overheated vapour that disappeared almost as soon as Fellini pointed his camera at it. And that scene in the Trevi fountain, iconic as it became, is the story of a failure. Sylvia, effulgent as a goddess, invites Marcello to join her in the purifying spring. He, the bourgeois hack, pauses to take off his shoes. And at the moment when he hoped for a transforming kiss, a kiss that might have released him from the burden of himself, he feels, suddenly, the echoing distance between them. She, benevolent but mocking, can only offer him a charade: she reaches down, and scoops up a handful of holy water to drizzle on his head. And then the night is over, and the dream is over, and Marcello stands, cold and bedraggled, in the dawn.

Over and over again through *La Dolce Vita* Marcello tries to find meaning – some higher truth or purpose to which he can cling, some little measure of salvation. Over and over again he falls short, and the world falls short, Rome falls short. He ends up sitting on the beach beside the stranded sea creature, Leviathan, staring into its dead, empty eyes.

And what has it all amounted to, all his effort? What have we just seen? With its endless cameos, its episodic structure, its capering progress of characters with nowhere to go, the film has the feeling of one of Fellini's beloved parades. *La Dolce Vita* is the story of a man's descent into hell, of Marcello's complete undoing. But the film, somehow, does not follow Marcello down into despair. The camera, the instrument of Fellini's capacity to love, stays and endures. It watches the film's characters as they troop off towards the abyss, watches them without pity and without condemnation, watches them forever, so that they are always going but never gone. Marcello was always trying to escape, to find a meaning beyond the tawdry prison of his immediate surroundings. But the camera stays where it is, and sees what it sees. Everything that there is, it seems to say – all the meaning that there is – is here.

EPILOGUE

I FIRST SAW Rome when I was eighteen, just at the beginning of the twenty-first century. We came by cargo ship from Valencia, had no money at all, no idea of anything. That was before smartphones and data roaming, so we just wandered, three shambling boys in too-big jeans; got lost; ended up sharing two cellophane-wrapped panini on a grass verge by a traffic intersection somewhere near the Baths of Caracalla.

Some seven million tourists might visit Rome on a normal year, and many more on a jubilee. Mostly they can afford a guidebook. With itineraries and online reviews and all the torrents of data a phone can download, they gather in top-rated places, perch in flocks around the Trevi fountain and up and down the Spanish Steps, queue to go round the weedkiller-bleached wreckage of the Colosseum, the Forum with its unidentifiable outcroppings of antique brick. Under Michelangelo's ceiling tourists gather like souls in limbo, peering upward for salvation while the papal security guards intone their hopeless litany: silence please; no photo; no photo.

Everyone seems to enjoy it. I certainly have done. But I'm not sure that the tourist crowds are any less lost than we were, that first time, eating our lunch in the exhaust fumes. Which of us had found the real Rome?

It has become conventional to refer to Rome as a palimpsest: a text endlessly written and wiped clean and rewritten. But the metaphor is a good one. For nearly three thousand years, Rome's rulers have been rewriting the city to their own purposes. Nero built a Golden House; Titus obliterated it with his Colosseum. Constantine built a basilica over the burial ground of his defeated enemies. Colonna barons quarried ancient monuments for their fortified towers. Sixteenth-century popes hid medieval churches behind baroque façades. Nineteenth-century nationalists raised their great Altar of the Fatherland on the ancient and sacred ground of the Capitoline Hill.

But no monument, however grandiose, is ever powerful enough to erase the traces of what has gone before. The result is the city as it strikes the tourist today: a baffling cacophony of rival messages, rival claims to glory, accumulated over three millennia and still competing for the world's attention.

How then is anyone to read the Eternal City? The problem is almost as old as the city itself. Indeed, if Rome deserves to be called 'eternal' at all, it is not for the mere duration of its existence, long though this has been, but for the infinite variety of its possible meanings. Is it a city of human pleasures, of love and good pizza? A city of silver-screened romance? A city of god? A city of sin? A city of power? A city of decay? It has had all these aspects and a thousand more.

And though many, over the years, have claimed to find the true essence and meaning of the city, each reader of the city distorts that meaning around themselves. For centuries people have thrilled themselves with the discovery that, by a miracle, all Rome's countless aspects converge on their own position; that Rome's boundless answers are all aimed at their own particular questions; that Rome's whole past has led inexorably to their present, and that from their present all Rome's futures spring. Everyone thinks they live at time's hinge. And everyone ends up a dusty detail in someone else's history book.

In a way, the plight of the modern tourist amid Rome's baffling profusion is not so different from the challenge that has faced Romans all through time. The city has always had too much symbolic power, too much history. It demands of each of us that we read and write it at the same time, that we create from its chaos our own meanings.

This book is my attempt to give Rome meaning. It also records the attempts of those who have gone before: desperate attempts by poor, weak, inadequate humans to give meaning to the city, and its history; attempts to locate themselves within a story, at the heart of a story, to create a narrative to live in. This book is, in a sense, the history of an imagined city, from the myth of Romulus to the fantastical world of Fellini's cinema, where the truth-telling camera is an instrument of deception and where painted sets and scenery are more real than the city's real streets.

Attempts to shape Rome's history have ended in failure, delusion, humiliation: Cola di Rienzo, fat and old, stabbed to death on the Capitoline; Elagabalus, the dancing emperor, thrown into the sewer. I'm haunted by soldiers, giving their lives in Rome for lost causes, to achieve objectives whose significance would vanish within a generation, objectives that hardly register against the great dark sweep of Rome's three thousand years.

That, in the end, is what this book is about: humans trying, and often failing, to live in history. And although it is a book full of failure and death, it is not, I hope, too pessimistic. The whole beauty of humanity, after all, lies in the attempt.

SOURCES FOR
QUOTED MATERIAL

69   Plutarch, *The Life of Tiberius Gracchus*, ch. 9.

113   Virgil, *Aeneid* VIII, 689ff, trans. Noonie Minogue.

118   Ovid, *Amores* I.1, trans. Noonie Minogue.

120   Ovid, *Amores* III.2, trans. Noonie Minogue.

121   Ovid, *Amores* I.5, trans. Noonie Minogue.

124   Ovid, *Amores* II.17, trans. Noonie Minogue.

131–2   Ovid, *Metamorphoses* XV.871ff, trans. Noonie Minogue.

158–9   Juvenal, *Satires* 3.243ff, trans. Ferdinand Addis.

167   Juvenal, *Satires* 3.153ff, trans. Ferdinand Addis.

169   Juvenal, *Satires* 6.247ff, trans. Ferdinand Addis.

172   Juvenal, *Satires* 6.103ff, trans. Ferdinand Addis.

209   Acts 17.22-24

234   Orientius of Auch, *Commonitorium*, in *Poetae Christianae Minores*, ed. R. Ellis.

236–7   Cassiodorus, *Variae* III.30.

245   Procopius, *History of the Wars* VI.iii.18–19.

265   Liudprand of Cremona, *Retribution* III.44, trans. Paolo Squatriti.

311–2   Petrarch, Canzoniere 335.1–4

323–4   Revelation, 21.2,22–24.

330   Revelation, 19.11–16.

331   Petrarch, *Variae* XL.

338   *Cronica dell'Anonimo Romano*, XXVII.2.

393   Michelangelo, *Complete Poems*, 5, trans. David Bevan.

447   St Teresa, *Life* XIX.

471   Lord Byron, *Childe Harold's Pilgrimage*, IV.108.

473   Lord Byron, *Childe Harold's Pilgrimage*, IV.81.

473   Lord Byron, *Childe Harold's Pilgrimage*, IV.79.

473   Lord Byron, *Childe Harold's Pilgrimage*, IV.104.

480   Lord Byron, *Childe Harold's Pilgrimage*, IV.140.

481   Lord Byron, *Childe Harold's Pilgrimage*, IV.135.

483   Percy Bysshe Shelley, *Adonais* 49.

485   Percy Bysshe Shelley, *Adonais* 37.

486   Percy Bysshe Shelley, *Adonais* 51.

486   Lord Byron, *Childe Harold's Pilgrimage* IV.179.

488   Percy Bysshe Shelley, *Adonais* 39.

488   Lord Byron, *Childe Harold's Pilgrimage* IV.139.

494–5 From Giacomo Leopardi, *Canti I, All'Italia*.

495   From Giacomo Leopardi, *Canti I, All'Italia*.

501   Giuseppe Belli, *Sonetti Romaneschi*, trans. Mike Stocks.

501–2 Giuseppe Belli, *Sonetti Romaneschi*, trans. Mike Stocks.

505   Giuseppe Belli, *Sonetti Romaneschi*, trans. Mike Stocks.

511   Arthur Hugh Clough, *Amours de Voyage* II.9.

517   Arthur Hugh Clough, *Amours de Voyage* II.5.

534   From Ferdinand Gregorovius, *The Ghetto and the Jews of Rome* (1966).

BIBLIOGRAPHY

PRIMARY SOURCES

Appian, *The Civil Wars* (tr. John Carter), Penguin Classics, 2005.

Cassiodorus, *Variae*, (tr. S. J. B. Barnish), Liverpool University Press, 1992.

Cato and Varro, *On Agriculture*, (tr. W. D. Hooper; Harrison Boyd Ash), Loeb Classical Library, 1934.

Catullus. Tibullus. Pervigilium Veneris, (tr. F. W. Cornish; J. P. Postgate; J. W. Mackail), Loeb Classical Library, 1913.

Cicero, *In Catilinam 1–4. Pro Murena. Pro Sulla. Pro Flacco,* (tr. C. MacDonald), Loeb Classical Library, 1976.

Eusebius, *The Church History*, (tr. Paul L. Maier), Kregel Academic, 2007.

Horace, *Odes and Epodes*, (tr. Niall Rudd), Loeb Classical Library, 2004.

In Praise of Later Roman Emperors: The Panegyrici Latini, (tr. C. E. V. Nixon, Barbara Saylor Rodgers), University of California Press, 1994.

Juvenal, *The Sixteen Satires*, (tr. Peter Green), Penguin Books, 1998.

Lactantius, *De Mortibus Persecutorum*, (tr. J.L. Creed), Clarendon Press, 1984.

Livy, *The Early History of Rome: Books I–V of The History of Rome From its Foundations,* (tr. Aubrey de Selincourt), Penguin Classics, 2002.

Martial, *Epigrams*, (tr. James Michie), Random House, 2011.

Martial, *Liber Spectaculorum, edited with Introduction, Translation and Commentary by Kathleen M. Coleman*, Oxford University Press, 2006.

Ovid, *Art of Love. Cosmetics. Remedies for Love. Ibis. Walnut-tree. Sea Fishing. Consolation,* (tr. J. H. Mozley), Loeb Classical Library, 1929.

Ovid, *Fasti,* (tr. James G. Frazer), Loeb Classical Library, 1931.

Ovid, *Heroides. Amores.* (tr. Grant Showerman), Loeb Classical Library, 1914.

Ovid, *Metamorphoses, Vol. 2: Books 9–15,* (tr. Frank Justus Miller), Loeb Classical Library 1916.

Ovid, *Metamorphoses, Vol. I: Books 1–8,* (tr. Frank Justus Miller), Loeb Classical Library 1916.

Ovid, *Tristia. Ex Ponto,* (tr. A. L. Wheeler), Loeb Classical Library, 1924.

Petronius, *The Satyricon,* (tr. J.P. Sullivan), Penguin Books, 2011.

Plautus, *Amphitryon. The Comedy of Asses. The Pot of Gold. The Two Bacchises. The Captives,* (tr. Wolfgang de Melo), Loeb Classical Library, 2011.

Plautus, *Casina. The Casket Comedy. Curculio. Epidicus. The Two Menaechmuses,* (tr. Wolfgang de Melo), Loeb Classical Library, 2011.

Plautus, *Rome and the mysterious Orient : three plays by Plautus.* (tr. and ed. Amy Richlin), University of California Press, 2005.

Plautus, *The Little Carthaginian. Pseudolus. The Rope,* (tr. Wolfgang de Melo), Loeb Classical Library, 2012.

Plutarch, *Roman lives: A Selection of Eight Roman Lives,* (tr. Robin Waterfield) Oxford University Press, 2008.

Polybius, *The Histories, Volume III: Books 5–8,* (tr. W.R. Paton), Loeb Classical Library, 2001.

Procopius, *The Wars of Justinian,* (tr. H.B. Dewing), Hackett, 2014.

Seneca, *Dialogues and Essays,* (tr. John Davie), Oxford University Press, 2007.

St Augustine, *City of God,* (tr. Henry Bettenson), 2003.

Suetonius, *The Twelve Caesars,* (tr. Robert Graves) Penguin Classics, 2007.

Tacitus, *The Annals of Imperial Rome,* (tr. Michael Grant), Penguin Classics, 1973.

The Bible: Authorized King James Version with Apocrypha, (ed. Robert Carroll), Oxford University Press, 2008.

The Last Poets of Imperial Rome, (tr. Harold Isbell), Penguin Books, 1983.

Virgil, *Aeneid: Books 7–12. Appendix Vergiliana,* (tr. H. Rushton Fairclough), Loeb Classical Library, 2001.

Virgil, *Eclogues. Georgics. Aeneid: Books 1–6,* (tr. H. Rushton Fairclough), Loeb Classical Library, 1999.

- - - - - -

Anonimo Romano, *Vita di Cola di Rienzo,* (tr. John W. Wright), Pontifical Institute of Medieval Studies, 1975.

Belli, Giuseppe Gioachino, *Sonnets,* (tr. Mike Stocks), Oneworld Classics, 2007.

Bernini, Domenico, *The Life of Gian Lorenzo Bernini* (tr. and ed. Franco Mormando), Pennsylvania State University Press, 2011.

Burchard, Johann, *At the Court of the Borgia: Being an Account of the Reign of Alexander VI*, (tr. George Parker), Folio Society, 1963.

Byron, Lord *The Major Works,* (ed. Jerome J. McGann), Oxford University Press, 2008.

Cellini, Benvenuto, *My Life,* (tr. Julia Conaway Bondanella, Peter Bondanella), Oxford University Press, 2009.

Clough, Arthur Hugh, *Selected Poems,* (ed. Shirley Chew), Fyfield, 1987.

Fellini, Federico, *Making a Film*, (tr. Christopher Burton White), Contra Mundum Press, 2015.

Gibbon, Edward, *The History of the Decline and Fall of the Roman Empire: three vols*, (ed. David Womersley), Penguin Classics, 1996.

Goethe, *Italian Journey,* (tr. Robert R. Heitner), Princeton University Press, 1994.

Leopardi, Giacomo. *Poems*, (ed. and tr. John Heath Stubbs), J, Lehman, 1946.

Mazzini, Joseph. *Life and Writings vols 1-6*, Smith, Elder and Co., 1890–91.

Michelangelo: Life, Letters and Poetry, (tr. George Bull, Peter Porter), Oxford University Press, 2008.

Milanesi ed., *Il sacco di Roma del mdxxvii : narrazioni di contemporanei*, Firenze: G. Barbèra, 1867.

Nichols, Francis Morgan ed., *The Marvels of Rome: Mirabilia Urbis Romae*, Italica Press, 1986.

Pasolini, Pier Paolo, *Stories from the City of God*, (ed. Walter Siti, tr. Marina Harss), Handsel Books, 2003.

Petrarch, *The Revolution of Cola di Rienzo*, (tr. Mario Cosenza), Italica Press, 1996.

Petrarch's Africa I–IV: a translation and commentary, (tr. Erik Z.D. Ellis), Baylor University, 2007.

Petrarch's Lyric Poems, (tr. and ed. Robert M. Durling), Harvard University Press, 1976.

Sarfatti, Margherita, *My Fault: Mussolini As I knew Him,* (ed. Brian Sullivan), Enigma Books, 2014.

Severn, Joseph, *Letters and Memoirs,* (ed. Grant F. Scott), Routledge, 2016.

Shelley, Percy Bysshe, *Essays, Letters from Abroad, Translations and Fragments,* two vols, Wentworth Press 2016.

Shelley, Percy Bysshe, *Selected Poems and Prose,* (ed. Jack Donovan, Cian Duffy), Penguin Classics, 2016.

Squatriti, Paolo, *The Complete Works of Liudprand of Cremona*, Catholic University of America Press, 2008.

Vasari, Giorgio. *Lives of the Artists*, (tr. George Bull), Penguin Classics, 2003.

SECONDARY SOURCES

General

Beard, Mary, John North, and S. R. F. Price. *Religions of Rome, vols 1 and 2*. Cambridge: Cambridge University Press, 1998.

Beard, Mary, *SPQR: A History of Ancient Rome*. London: Profile Books, 2015.

Boardman, Jonathan, *Rome: A Cultural History*. Northampton, MA: Interlink Books, 2008.

Bosworth, R. J. B. *Whispering city: Modern Rome and its Histories*. New Haven, CT: Yale University Press, 2011.

Claridge, Amanda, and Claire Holleran, *A Companion to the City of Rome*. Oxford: Wiley-Blackwell, 2012.

Claridge, Amanda, Judith Toms, and Tony Cubberley, *Rome: An Oxford Archaeological Guide to Rome*. Oxford: Oxford University Press, 1998.

Duffy, Eamon, *Saints and Sinners: A History of the Popes*. New Haven, CT: Yale University Press, 2014.

Erdkamp, Paul, *The Cambridge Companion to Ancient Rome*. Cambridge: Cambridge University Press, 2013.

Gilmour, David, *The Pursuit of Italy: A History of a Land, its Regions, and Their Peoples*. New York: Farrar, Straus and Giroux, 2011.

Grant, Michael, *History of Rome*. Englewood Cliffs, NJ: Prentice Hall, 1978.

Gregorovius, Ferdinand, *History of the City of Rome in the Middle Ages*, 8 vols. Translated from the 4th German edition. London: George Bell, 1900.

Hibbert, Christopher, *Rome: The Biography of a City*. London: Penguin, 2001.

Hughes, Robert, *Rome: A Cultural, Visual, and Personal History*. New York: Alfred A. Knopf, 2011.

Knapp, Robert C., *Invisible Romans: Prostitutes, Outlaws, Slaves, Gladiators, Ordinary Men and Women – the Romans That History Forgot*. London: Profile Books, 2011.

Mali, Joseph, *Mythistory: The Making of a Modern Historiography*. Chicago: The University of Chicago Press, 2003.

Richardson, Lawrence. *A New Topographical Dictionary of Ancient Rome.* Baltimore: Johns Hopkins University Press, 1992.

CHAPTER SPECIFIC BIBLIOGRAPHY

The Wolf Children

Cornell, Tim, *The Beginnings of Rome: Italy and Rome from the Bronze Age to the Punic Wars (c.1000–264 BC)*, London: Routledge, 2012.

Vout, Caroline, *The Hills of Rome: Signature of an Eternal City.* Cambridge: Cambridge University Press, 2012.

Wiseman, T. P., *Remus: A Roman Myth.* Cambridge: Cambridge University Press, 1995.

Wiseman, T. P., *The Myths of Rome.* Exeter: University of Exeter Press, 2004.

Barbarians

Bridgman, Timothy P, 'The "Gallic Disaster": Did Dionysius I of Syracuse Order It?', in *Proceedings of the Harvard Celtic Colloquium*, vol. 23, 40–51. Department of Celtic Languages & Literatures, Harvard University, 2003.

Cunliffe, Barry W., *The Ancient Celts.* Oxford: Oxford University Press, 1997.

Rosenberger, Veit. 'The Gallic Disaster', *The Classical World* 96, no. 4 (2003): 365–73.

Sabin, Philip, 'The face of Roman battle', *The Journal of Roman Studies* 90 (2000): 1–17.

The Little Carthaginian

Daly, Gregory, *Cannae:The Experience of Battle in the Second Punic War.* London: Routledge, 2005.

Leigh, Matthew, *Comedy and the Rise of Rome.* Oxford: Oxford University Press, 2004.

Manuwald, Gesine, *Roman Republican Theatre.* Cambridge: Cambridge University Press, 2011.

Marshall, C.W., *The Stagecraft and Performance of Roman Comedy.* Cambridge: Cambridge University Press, 2006.

Moore, Timothy J., 'Palliata Togata: Plautus, Curculio 462–86', in *The American Journal of Philology* 112, no. 3 (1991): 343–62.

Moore, Timothy J., *The Theatre of Plautus: Playing to the Audience*. Austin: University of Texas Press, 2010.

Segal, Erich, *Roman Laughter: the Comedy of Plautus*. Cambridge, MA: Harvard University Press, 1968.

Slater, Niall W., 'Plautine Negotiations: the Poenulus Prologue Unpacked', in *Yale Classical Studies* 29 (1992): 131–46.

Wiseman, T. P., *Roman drama and Roman history*. Exeter: University of Exeter Press, 1998.

Concord

Astin, A. E., *Scipio Aemilianus*. Oxford: Clarendon Press, 1967.

Patterson, John R., *Political Life in the City of Rome*. London: Bristol Classical, 2000.

Richardson, Keith, *Daggers in the Forum: The Revolutionary Lives and Violent Deaths of the Gracchus Brothers*. London: Cassell, 1976.

Stockton, D. L., *The Gracchi*. Oxford: Oxford University Press, 1979.

The Ides of March

Goldsworthy, Adrian K., *Caesar: The Life of a Colossus*. London: Weidenfeld & Nicolson, 2006.

Griffin, Miriam, *A Companion to Julius Caesar*. Oxford: Wiley-Blackwell, 2015.

Tempest, Kathryn, *Cicero: Politics and Persuasion in Ancient Rome*. London: Continuum, 2011.

The Art of Love

Favro, Diane G., *The Urban Image of Augustan Rome*. Cambridge: Cambridge University Press, 1996.

Griffin, Jasper, *Latin Poets and Roman Life*. London: Bristol Classical Press, 1994.

Hardie, Philip R., *The Cambridge Companion to Ovid*. Cambridge: Cambridge University Press, 2002.

Levick, Barbara, *Augustus: Image and Substance*. London: Taylor and Francis, 2014.

Volk, Katharina, *Ovid*. Oxford: Wiley-Blackwell, 2010.

The Emperor's Show

Buckley, Emma, and Martin Dinter, *A Companion to the Neronian Age*. Oxford: Wiley-Blackwell, 2013.

Engberg, Jakob, *Impulsore Chresto: Opposition to Christianity in the Roman Empire c. 50–250 AD*. Frankfurt am Main: P. Lang, 2007.

Griffin, Miriam T., *Nero: The End of a Dynasty*. London: Taylor & Francis, 1987.

Lampe, Peter, and Marshall D. Johnson D. Johnson, *From Paul to Valentinus: Christians at Rome in the First Two Centuries*. London: T & T Clark, 2003.

Lössl, Josef, *The Early Church: History and Memory*. London: T & T Clark, 2010.

Gladiators

Carter, Michael J., 'Gladiatorial combat: the rules of engagement', *The Classical Journal* (2006): 97–114.

Corbeill, Anthony, 'Thumbs in Ancient Rome; Pollex as Index', *Memoirs of the American Academy in Rome* 42 (1997): 1–21.

Dunkle, Roger, *Gladiators: Violence and Spectacle in Ancient Rome*. London: Taylor and Francis, 2013.

Hopkins, Keith, and Beard, Mary, *The Colosseum*. London: Profile Books, 2011.

Junkelmann, M., '4. Roman Gladiatorial Combat: Technical and Practical Aspects', in Proc. Int. Symposium of Ancient Mediterranean World, vol. 13, no. 14, 45–50. 2003.

Shadrake, Susanna, *The World of the Gladiator*. Stroud: Tempus, 2005.

A God Dances

Ando, Clifford, *Imperial Rome AD 193 to 284: The Critical Century*. Edinburgh: Edinburgh University Press, 2012.

Bruun, Christer, 'The Antonine Plague in Rome and Ostia', in *Journal of Roman Archaeology* 16 (2003): 426–34.

Grant, Michael, *The Severans: The Changed Roman Empire*. London: Routledge, 1996.

Icks, Martijn, *The Crimes of Elagabalus: the Life and Legacy of Rome's Decadent Boy Emperor*. London: I.B. Tauris, 2011.

Israelowich, Ido, 'The rain miracle of Marcus Aurelius: (re-) construction of consensus', in *Greece & Rome* 55, no. 1 (2008): 83–102.

Levick, Barbara, *Julia Domna, Syrian Empress*. London: Routledge, 2007.

Conquer by This!

Alföldi, Andrew, and Marvin C. Ross, 'Cornuti: A Teutonic Contingent in the Service of Constantine the Great and Its Decisive Role in the Battle at the Milvian Bridge. With a Discussion of Bronze Statuettes of Constantine the Great', in *Dumbarton Oaks Papers* 13 (1959): 169–183.

Barnes, Timothy D., *Constantine: Dynasty, Religion and Power in the Later Roman Empire*. Oxford: Wiley-Blackwell, 2014.

Holloway, R. R., *Constantine & Rome*. New Haven, CT: Yale University Press, 2004.

Pohlsander, Hans A., *Helena: Empress and Saint*. Chicago, IL: Ares Publishers, 1995.

Potter, D. S., *Constantine the Emperor*. Oxford: Oxford University Press, 2013.

Speidel, Michael P., 'Maxentius and His Equites Singulares in the Battle at the Milvian Bridge' in *Classical Antiquity* 5, no. 2 (1986): 253–62.

Stephenson, I. P. *Romano-Byzantine Infantry Equipment*. Stroud: Tempus, 2006.

Van Dam, Raymond. *Remembering Constantine at the Milvian Bridge*. Cambridge: Cambridge University Press, 2011.

Under Siege

Dodge, H., ' "Greater than the Pyramids": the water supply of ancient Rome', in *Oxford University School Of Archaeology Monograph* 54 (2000): 166–209.

Fagan, Garrett G., *Bathing in Public in the Roman world*. Ann Arbor, MI: University of Michigan Press, 2002.

Goldsworthy, Adrian, *The Fall of the West: The Death of the Roman Superpower*. London: Orion, 2009.

Llewellyn, Peter, *Rome in the Dark Ages*. London: Constable, 1996.

Moore, Frank Gardner, 'On urbs aeterna and urbs sacra', in *Transactions of the American Philological Association (1869–1896)* 25 (1894): 34–60.

Perkins, Bryan, *The Fall of Rome: And the End of Civilization*. Oxford: OUP Oxford, 2005.

Schiavone, Aldo, *The End of the Past: Ancient Rome and the Modern West*. Cambridge, MA: Harvard University Press, 2000.

Wilson, Andrew, 'The water-mills on the Janiculum' in *Memoirs of the American Academy in Rome* 45 (2000): 219–46.

The Clan

Heather, Peter, *The Restoration of Rome: Barbarian Popes & Imperial Pretenders*. London: Pan Macmillan, 2013.

Hetherington, Paul, *Medieval Rome: A Portrait of the City and its Life*. Oakville, Ontario: Rubicon Press, 1994.

Krautheimer, Richard, *Rome: Profile of a City, 312–1308*. Princeton, NJ: Princeton University Press, 2000.

Miller, Maureen C., *Clothing the Clergy: Virtue and Power in Medieval Europe, c. 800–1200*. Ithaca, NY: Cornell University Press, 2014.

Skinner, Patricia, *Women in Medieval Italian society 500–1200*. Harlow: Pearson Education, 2001.

Wickham, Chris, *Medieval Rome: Stability and Crisis of a City, 900–1150*. Oxford: Oxford University Press, 2015.

Rome-seekers

Birch, Debra J., *Pilgrimage to Rome in the Middle Ages: Continuity and Change*. Woodbridge: Boydell Press, 1998.

Kessler, Herbert L. and Johanna Zacharias, *Rome 1300: On the Path of the Pilgrim*. New Haven, CT: Yale University Press, 2000.

Kinney, Dale, 'Rome in the Twelfth Century: Urbs fracta and renovatio', in *Gesta* 45, no. 2 (2006): 199–220.

Magoun, Jr, Francis P., 'The Rome of Two Northern Pilgrims: Archbishop Sigeric of Canterbury and Abbot Nikolás of Munkathverá', in *Harvard Theological Review* 33, no. 4 (1940): 267–89.

Magoun, Jr, Francis P., 'The Pilgrim-Diary of Nikulas Munkathvera: The Road to Rome', *Mediaeval Studies* 6 (1944): 314–54.

Twyman, Susan, *Papal Ceremonial at Rome in the Twelfth Century*. Woodbridge: Boydell Press, 2010.

Warland, Rainer. 'Arch of S. Maria Maggiore in Rome', *Acta ad Archaeologiam et Artium Historiam Pertinentia* 17 (2003): 127–41.

The Laureate

Bishop, Morris, *Petrarch and His World*. Port Washington, NY: Kennikat Press, 1973.

Collins, Amanda, *Greater than Emperor: Cola di Rienzo (ca. 1313–54) and the World of Fourteenth-century Rome*. Ann Arbor, MI: University of Michigan Press, 2002.

Kirkham, Victoria and Armando Maggi, *Petrarch: A Critical Guide to the Complete Works*. Chicago, IL: University of Chicago Press, 2009.

Mela, Pomponius and Frank E. Romer, *Pomponius Mela's Description of the World*. Ann Arbor, MI: University of Michigan Press, 1998.

Musto, Ronald G., *Apocalypse in Rome: Cola di Rienzo and the Politics of the New Age*. Berkeley, CA: University of California Press, 2003.

Wilkins, Ernest H., 'The coronation of Petrarch', in *Speculum* 18, no. 2 (1943): 155–97.

Wilkins, Ernest H., *Studies in the Life and Work of Petrarch*, Mediaeval Academy of America, 1955.

My Debt to Nature

Arrizabalaga, Jon, John Henderson, and R. K. French, *The Great Pox: The French Disease in Renaissance Europe*. New Haven, CT: Yale University Press, 1997.

Bradford, Sarah, *Lucrezia Borgia: Life, Love and Death in Renaissance Italy*. London: Penguin, 2005.

Cohen, Elizabeth S., 'Honor and gender in the streets of early modern Rome', in *The Journal of Interdisciplinary History* 22, no. 4 (1992): 597–625.

Cohen, Elizabeth S., 'Seen and Known: Prostitutes in the Cityscape of Late-sixteenth-century Rome', in *Renaissance Studies* 12, no. 3 (1998): 392–409.

Gregorovius, Ferdinand, *Lucretia Borgia: According to Original Documents and Correspondence of her Day*. (tr. John Leslie Garner.) London: John Murray, 1904

The Vault of Heaven

Burke, Peter, *The Italian Renaissance: Culture and Society in Italy*. Princeton, NJ: Princeton University Press, 2014.

De Tolnay, Charles, *The Sistine Chapel Ceiling*, Princeton, NJ: Princeton University Press, 1943

De Tolnay, Charles, *The Youth of Michelangelo*, Princeton, NJ: Princeton University Press, 1943

Forcellino, Antonio, *Michelangelo: A Tormented Life*. Cambridge, UK: Polity, 2009.

Hirst, Michael, *Michelangelo: The Achievement of Fame, 1475–1534, Vol. 1.* New Haven, CT: Yale University Press, 2011.

King, Ross, *Michelangelo & the Pope's Ceiling.* New York: Walker & Co, 2003.

Seymour, Charles (ed.), *Michelangelo, The Sistine Chapel Ceiling: illustrations, introductory essays, backgrounds and sources, critical essays. Vol. 1.* New York: WW Norton & Company, 1972.

Wind, Edgar and Elizabeth Sears, *The Religious Symbolism of Michelangelo: The Sistine Ceiling.* Oxford: Oxford University Press, 2000.

Judgement

Chamberlin, E. R. *The Sack of Rome.* London: B.T. Batsford, 1979.

Chastel, André, *The Sack of Rome, 1527.* Princeton, N.J: Princeton University Press, 1983.

Hook, Judith, *The Sack of Rome : 1527.* London: Palgrave Macmillan, 2004.

M. Whitford, David, 'The Papal Antichrist: Martin Luther and the Underappreciated Influence of Lorenzo Valla', *Renaissance Quarterly* 61, no. 1 (2008): 26–52.

The Impresario

Fehrenbach, Frank, 'Bernini's light' in *Art history* 28, no. 1 (2005): 1–42.

MacCulloch, Diarmaid, *Reformation: Europe's House Divided, 1490–1700.* London: Penguin, 2004.

Mormando, Franco, *Bernini: His Life and His Rome.* Chicago IL: University of Chicago Press, 2011.

Warwick, Genevieve, *Bernini: Art as Theatre.* New Haven CT: Yale University Press, 2012.

The Mine of Contemplation

Hibbert, Christopher, *The Grand Tour.* London: Methuen, 1987.

Holmes, Richard, *Shelley: The Pursuit.* London: Harper Perennial, 2005.

Robinson, Charles E. (ed.), *Shelley and Byron: The Snake and Eagle Wreathed in Fight.* Baltimore MD: Johns Hopkins University Press, 1976.

Saunders, Timothy, Charles Martindale, Ralph Pite, and Mathilde Skoie (eds), *Romans and Romantics.* Oxford: Oxford University Press, 2012.

Blood of Italy

Gossett, Philip, 'Becoming a Citizen: The Chorus in Risorgimento Opera', *Cambridge Opera Journal* 2, no. 1 (1990): 41–64.

Gossett, Philip, 'Giuseppe Verdi and the Italian Risorgimento', *Studia Musicologica* 52, no. 1–4 (2011): 241–57.

Ipson, Douglas L., 'Attila Takes Rome: The Reception of Verdi's Opera on the Eve of Revolution', in *Cambridge Opera Journal* 21, no. 3 (2009): 249–56.

Mack-Smith, Denis (ed.), *The Making of Italy: 1796–1870*. London: Walker, 1968.

Patriarca, Silvana and Lucy Riall (eds), *The Risorgimento Revisited: Nationalism and Culture in Nineteenth-century Italy*. London: Palgrave Macmillan, 2012.

Patriarca, Silvana, 'Indolence and Regeneration: Tropes and Tensions of Risorgimento patriotism', in *The American Historical Review* 110, no. 2 (2005): 380–408.

Rath, R. John, 'The Carbonari: Their Origins, Initiation Rites, and Aims', in *The American Historical Review* 69, no. 2 (1964): 353–70.

Riall, Lucy, *Garibaldi: Invention of a Hero*. New Haven CT: Yale University Press, 2008.

Riall, LucyH *The Italian Risorgimento: State, Society and National Unification*. London: Routledge, 2002.

Trevelyan, George Macaulay, *Garibaldi's Defence of the Roman Republic*. London: Longmans, Green, and Company, 1914.

The Ghetto

Berghaus, Günter, 'Violence, War, Revolution: Marinetti's Concept of a Futurist Cleanser for the World', in *Annali d'Italianistica* 27 (2009): 23–71.

Bosworth, Richard JB., *Mussolini*. London: Bloomsbury Publishing, 2014.

Cannistraro, Philip V., and Brian R. Sullivan., *Il Duce's Other Woman*. New York: William Morrow & Co, 1993.

De Grand, Alexander, 'Women under Italian fascism', in *The Historical Journal* 19, no. 4 (1976): 947–68.

Gregorovius, Ferdinand, *The Ghetto and the Jews of Rome*. New York: Schocken Books, 1966.

Katz, Robert, *Black Sabbath: A Journey Through a Crime Against Humanity*. London: Macmillan, 1969.

Michaelis, Meir, *Mussolini and the Jews: German-Italian Relations and the Jewish Question in Italy, 1922–45*. Oxford: Oxford University Press, 1978.

Olla, Roberto, *Il Duce and His Women: Mussolini's Rise to Power*. Richmond: Alma, 2012.

Pugliese, Stanislao G., 'Bloodless torture: The Books of the Roman Ghetto under the Nazi occupation', in *Libraries & Culture* (1999): 241–53.

The Parade

Bondanella, Peter, *A History of Italian Cinema*. London: A&C Black, 2009.

Bondanella, Peter E., *The Cinema of Federico Fellini*. Princeton, NJ: Princeton University Press, 1992.

Gundle, Stephen, *Death and the Dolce Vita: The Dark Side of Rome in the 1950s*. London: Canongate Books, 2011.

Kezich, Tullio, 'Federico Fellini and the Making of La Dolce Vita', in *Cineaste* 31, no. 1 (2005): 8–14.

Kezich, Tullio, *Federico Fellini: His Life and Work*. London: I.B. Tauris, 2007.

Levy, Shawn, *Dolce Vita Confidential: Fellini, Loren, Pucci, Paparazzi, and the Swinging High Life of 1950s Rome*. London: Weidenfeld & Nicolson, 2017.

ACKNOWLEDGEMENTS

This book would not have been possible without the support of a great many people. It was a characteristically bold move of Anthony Cheetham to conceive and back a project like this, and he proved superhumanly patient as successive deadlines came and went. Many thanks are due to all at Head of Zeus. My editor Neil Belton was a well of knowledge and inspiration, encouraging me in the right directions, even as he tamed the worst excesses of my prose. Georgina Blackwell expertly shepherded the text through the final processes of publication, and her creative vision was indispensable in the composition of the plate sections. Jamie Whyte made the excellent maps of ancient and modern Rome.

Staff at the London Library and at the libraries of The Warburg Institute and Roman Society provided the vital space for research. Dr Josephine Quinn offered wise advice on book writing. Noonie Minogue and David Bevan were perfect companions on my trips to Rome, each bringing their own deep knowledge to bear on the Eternal City. They also provided elegant translations of Latin and Italian texts: Noonie of Ovid and Virgil; David of a poem by Michelangelo.

Jon Elek, my agent, has been a genial and fortifying presence behind the scenes. Ian Thompson read through the final manuscript with an expert eye, and saved me from more than one embarrassing slip.

Writing can be lonely and maddening. For years, my generous family have put up with my moaning and listened patiently to my fears. They have read early drafts, shared good wisdom, kept me cheerful. Above all, I am grateful to Laura, who has had to live with me all this time. With infinite patience, she helped coax each chapter into existence. She has been the first reader and first editor of this book, and if it has any value at all, it is thanks to her.

IMAGE CREDITS

INDEX